## ALSO BY DORIS LESSING

*The Grass Is Singing*
*This Was the Old Chief's Country* (stories)
*The Habit of Loving* (stories)
*In Pursuit of the English*
*Going Home*
*Fourteen Poems*
*The Golden Notebook*
*A Man and Two Women* (stories)
*Particularly Cats*
*Briefing for a Descent into Hell*
*The Temptation of Jack Orkney and Other Stories*
*The Summer Before the Dark*
*A Small Personal Voice*
*The Memoirs of a Survivor*
*African Stories*
*Stories*
*The Diary of a Good Neighbour* (under the pseudonym Jane Somers)*
*If the Old Could . . .* (under the pseudonym Jane Somers)*
*The Good Terrorist*
*Prisons We Choose to Live Inside*
*The Wind Blows Away Our Words*
*The Fifth Child*

### CHILDREN OF VIOLENCE

*Martha Quest*
*A Proper Marriage*
*A Ripple from the Storm*
*Landlocked*
*The Four-Gated City*

### CANOPUS IN ARGOS: ARCHIVES

*Re: Colonised Planet 5, Shikasta*
*The Marriages Between Zones Three, Four, and Five*
*The Sirian Experiments*
*The Making of the Representative for Planet 8*
*Documents Relating to the Sentimental Agents in the Volyen Empire*

*Published together as *The Diaries of Jane Somers*

# THE
# *Doris Lessing*
# READER

# THE

# *Doris Lessing*

# READER

*Alfred A. Knopf*

NEW YORK 1988

THIS IS A BORZOI BOOK
PUBLISHED BY ALFRED A. KNOPF, INC.


*Published in the United States by Alfred A. Knopf, Inc., New York.*
*Distributed by Random House, Inc., New York.*

*Owing to limitations of space, all acknowledgments for permission to reprint previously published material can be found on page 637.*

*Library of Congress Cataloging-in-Publication Data*
*Lessing, Doris May.*
*The Doris Lessing reader / Doris Lessing.*
*p. cm.*
ISBN 0-394-57307-2
*I. Title.*
PR6023.E833A6 *1988* *823'.914—dc19* *88-12689* CIP

*Manufactured in the United States of America*
*First Edition*

*For darling Chloe, with my love*

With my warmest thank-yous for Robert Gottlieb,

who has been my friend and the best of all possible editors

for twenty-five years.

# *Contents*

STORIES

## FROM THE NOVELS

## NON-FICTION

# STORIES

# *The Old Chief Mshlanga*

They were good, the years of ranging the bush over her father's farm which, like every white farm, was largely unused, broken only occasionally by small patches of cultivation. In between, nothing but trees, the long sparse grass, thorn and cactus and gully, grass and outcrop and thorn. And a jutting piece of rock which had been thrust up from the warm soil of Africa unimaginable eras of time ago, washed into hollows and whorls by sun and wind that had traveled so many thousands of miles of space and bush, would hold the weight of a small girl whose eyes were sightless for anything but a pale willowed river, a pale gleaming castle—a small girl singing: "Out flew the web and floated wide, the mirror cracked from side to side . . ."

Pushing her way through the green aisles of the mealie stalks, the leaves arching like cathedrals veined with sunlight far overhead, with the packed red earth underfoot, a fine lace of red starred witchweed would summon up a black bent figure croaking premonitions: the Northern witch, bred of cold Northern forests, would stand before her among the mealie fields, and it was the mealie fields that faded and fled, leaving her among the gnarled roots of an oak, snow falling thick and soft and white, the woodcutter's fire glowing red welcome through crowding tree trunks.

A white child, opening its eyes curiously on a sun-suffused landscape, a gaunt and violent landscape, might be supposed to accept it as her own, to take the msasa trees and the thorn trees as familiars, to feel her blood running free and responsive to the swing of the seasons.

This child could not see a msasa tree, or the thorn, for what they were. Her books held tales of alien fairies, her rivers ran slow and peaceful, and she knew the shape of the leaves of an ash or an oak, the names of the little creatures that lived in English streams, when the words "the veld" meant strangeness, though she could remember nothing else.

Because of this, for many years, it was the veld that seemed unreal; the sun was a foreign sun, and the wind spoke a strange language.

The black people on the farm were as remote as the trees and the rocks. They were an amorphous black mass, mingling and thinning and massing like tadpoles, faceless, who existed merely to serve, to say "Yes, Baas," take their money, and go. They changed season by season, moving from one farm to the next, according to their outlandish needs, which one did not have to understand, coming from perhaps hundreds of miles north or east, passing on after a few months—where? Perhaps even as far away as the fabled gold mines of Johannesburg, where the pay was so much better than the few shillings a month and the double handful of mealie meal twice a day which they earned in that part of Africa.

The child was taught to take them for granted: the servants in the house would come running a hundred yards to pick up a book if she dropped it. She was called "Nkosikaas"—Chieftainess, even by the black children her own age.

Later, when the farm grew too small to hold her curiosity, she carried a gun in the crook of her arm and wandered miles a day, from vlei to vlei, from kopje to kopje, accompanied by two dogs: the dogs and the gun were an armor against fear. Because of them she never felt fear.

If a native came into sight along the kaffir paths half a mile away, the dogs would flush him up a tree as if he were a bird. If he expostulated (in his uncouth language which was by itself ridiculous) that was cheek. If one was in a good mood, it could be a matter for laughter. Otherwise one passed on, hardly glancing at the angry man in the tree.

On the rare occasions when white children met together they could amuse themselves by hailing a passing native in order to make a buffoon of him; they could set the dogs on him and watch him run; they could tease a small black child as if he were a puppy—save that they would not throw stones and sticks at a dog without a sense of guilt.

Later still, certain questions presented themselves in the child's mind; and because the answers were not easy to accept, they were silenced by an even greater arrogance of manner.

It was even impossible to think of the black people who worked about the house as friends, for if she talked to one of them, her mother would come running anxiously: "Come away; you mustn't talk to natives."

It was this instilled consciousness of danger, of something unpleasant, that made it easy to laugh out loud, crudely, if a servant made a mistake in his English or if he failed to understand an order—there is a certain kind of laughter that is fear, afraid of itself.

One evening, when I was about fourteen, I was walking down the side of a mealie field that had been newly plowed, so that the great red clods showed fresh and tumbling to the vlei beyond, like a choppy red sea; it was that hushed and listening hour, when the birds send long sad calls from tree to tree, and all the colors of earth and sky and leaf are deep and golden. I had my rifle in the curve of my arm, and the dogs were at my heels.

In front of me, perhaps a couple of hundred yards away, a group of three Africans came into sight around the side of a big ant-heap. I whistled the dogs close in to my skirts and let the gun swing in my hand, and advanced, waiting for them to move aside, off the path, in respect for my passing. But they came on steadily, and the dogs looked up at me for the command to chase. I was angry. It was "cheek" for a native not to stand off a path, the moment he caught sight of you.

In front walked an old man, stooping his weight on to a stick, his hair grizzled white, a dark red blanket slung over his shoulders like a cloak. Behind him came two young men, carrying bundles of pots, assegais, hatchets.

The group was not a usual one. They were not natives seeking work. These had an air of dignity, of quietly following their own purpose. It was the dignity that checked my tongue. I walked quietly on, talking softly to the growling dogs, till I was ten paces away. Then the old man stopped, drawing his blanket close.

"Morning, Nkosikaas," he said, using the customary greeting for any time of the day.

"Good morning," I said. "Where are you going?" My voice was a little truculent.

The old man spoke in his own language, then one of the young men stepped forward politely and said in careful English: "My Chief travels to see his brothers beyond the river."

A Chief! I thought, understanding the pride that made the old man stand before me like an equal—more than an equal, for he showed courtesy, and I showed none.

The old man spoke again, wearing dignity like an inherited garment, still standing ten paces off, flanked by his entourage, not looking at me (that would have been rude) but directing his eyes somewhere over my head at the trees.

"You are the little Nkosikaas from the farm of Baas Jordan?"

"That's right," I said.

"Perhaps your father does not remember," said the intrepreter for the old man, "but there was an affair with some goats. I remember seeing you when you were . . ." The young man held his hand at knee level and smiled.

We all smiled.

"What is your name?" I asked.

"This is Chief Mshlanga," said the young man.

"I will tell my father that I met you," I said.

The old man said: "My greetings to your father, little Nkosikaas."

"Good morning," I said politely, finding the politeness difficult, from lack of use.

"Morning, little Nkosikaas," said the old man, and stood aside to let me pass.

I went by, my gun hanging awkwardly, the dogs sniffing and growling, cheated of their favorite game of chasing natives like animals.

Not long afterwards I read in an old explorer's book the phrase: "Chief Mshlanga's country." It went like this: "Our destination was Chief Mshlanga's country, to the north of the river; and it was our desire to ask his permission to prospect for gold in his territory."

The phrase "ask his permission" was so extraordinary to a white child, brought up to consider all natives as things to use, that it revived those questions, which could not be suppressed: they fermented slowly in my mind.

On another occasion one of those old prospectors who still move over Africa looking for neglected reefs, with their hammers and tents, and pans for sifting gold from crushed rock, came to the farm and, in talking of the old days, used that phrase again: "This was the Old Chief's country," he said. "It stretched from those mountains over there way back to the river, hundreds of miles of country." That was his name for our district: "The Old Chief's Country"; he did not use our name for it—a new phrase which held no implication of usurped ownership.

As I read more books about the time when this part of Africa was opened up, not much more than fifty years before, I found Old Chief Mshlanga had been a famous man, known to all the explorers and prospectors. But then he had been young; or maybe it was his father or uncle they spoke of—I never found out.

During that year I met him several times in the part of the farm that was traversed by natives moving over the country. I learned that the path up the side of the big red field where the birds sang was the recognized highway for migrants. Perhaps I even haunted it in the hope of meeting him: being greeted by him, the exchange of courtesies, seemed to answer the questions that troubled me.

Soon I carried a gun in a different spirit; I used it for shooting food and not to give me confidence. And now the dogs learned better manners. When I saw a native approaching, we offered and took greetings; and slowly that other landscape in my mind faded, and my feet struck directly on the African soil, and I saw the shapes of tree and hill clearly, and the black people moved back, as it were, out of my life: it was as if I stood aside to watch a slow intimate dance of landscape and men, a very old dance, whose steps I could not learn.

But I thought: this is my heritage, too; I was bred here; it is my country as well as the black man's country; and there is plenty of room for all of us, without elbowing each other off the pavements and roads.

It seemed it was only necessary to let free that respect I felt when I was talking with old Chief Mshlanga, to let both black and white people meet gently, with tolerance for each other's differences: it seemed quite easy.

Then, one day, something new happened. Working in our house as servants were always three natives: cook, houseboy, garden boy. They used to change as the farm natives changed: staying for a few months, then moving on to a new job, or back home to their kraals. They were thought of as "good" or "bad" natives; which meant: how did they behave as servants? Were they lazy, efficient, obedient, or disrespectful? If the family felt good-humored, the phrase was: "What can you expect from raw black savages?" If we were angry, we said: "These damned niggers, we would be much better off without them."

One day, a white policeman was on his rounds of the district, and he said laughingly: "Did you know you have an important man in your kitchen?"

"What!" exclaimed my mother sharply. "What do you mean?"

"A Chief's son." The policeman seemed amused. "He'll boss the tribe when the old man dies."

"He'd better not put on a Chief's son act with me," said my mother.

When the policeman left, we looked with different eyes at our cook: he was a good worker, but he drank too much at weekends—that was how we knew him.

He was a tall youth, with very black skin, like black polished metal, his tightly growing black hair parted white man's fashion at one side, with a metal comb from the store stuck into it; very polite, very distant, very quick to obey an order. Now that it had been pointed out, we said: "Of course, you can see. Blood always tells."

My mother became strict with him now she knew about his birth and prospects. Sometimes, when she lost her temper, she would say: "You aren't the Chief yet, you know." And he would answer her very quietly, his eyes on the ground: "Yes, Nkosikaas."

One afternoon he asked for a whole day off, instead of the customary half-day, to go home next Sunday.

"How can you go home in one day?"

"It will take me half an hour on my bicycle," he explained.

I watched the direction he took; and the next day I went off to look for this kraal; I understood he must be Chief Mshlanga's successor: there was no other kraal near enough our farm.

Beyond our boundaries on that side the country was new to me. I followed unfamiliar paths past kopjes that till now had been part of the jagged horizon, hazed with distance. This was Government land, which had never been cultivated by white men; at first I could not understand why it was that it appeared, in merely crossing the boundary, I had entered a completely fresh type of landscape. It was a wide green valley, where a small river sparkled, and vivid water-birds darted over the rushes. The grass was thick and soft to my calves, the trees stood tall and shapely.

I was used to our farm, whose hundreds of acres of harsh eroded soil bore trees that had been cut for the mine furnaces and had grown thin and twisted, where the cattle had dragged the grass flat, leaving innumerable crisscrossing trails that deepened each season into gullies, under the force of the rains.

This country had been left untouched, save for prospectors whose picks had struck a few sparks from the surface of the rocks as they wandered by; and for migrant natives whose passing had left, perhaps, a charred patch on the trunk of a tree where their evening fire had nestled.

It was very silent: a hot morning with pigeons cooing throatily, the midday shadows lying dense and thick with clear yellow spaces of sunlight between and in all that wide green parklike valley, not a human soul but myself.

I was listening to the quick regular tapping of a woodpecker when slowly a chill feeling seemed to grow up from the small of my back to my shoulders, in a constricting spasm like a shudder, and at the roots of my hair a tingling sensation began and ran down over the surface of my flesh, leaving me goosefleshed and cold, though I was damp with sweat. Fever? I thought; then uneasily, turned to look over my shoulder; and realized suddenly that this was fear. It was extraordinary, even humiliating. It was a new fear. For all the years I had walked by myself over this country I had never known a moment's uneasiness; in the beginning because I had been supported by a gun and the dogs, then because I had learned an easy friendliness for the Africans I might encounter.

I had read of this feeling, how the bigness and silence of Africa, under the ancient sun, grows dense and takes shape in the mind, till even the birds seem to call menacingly, and a deadly spirit comes out of the trees and the rocks. You move warily, as if your very passing disturbs something old and evil, something dark and big and angry that might suddenly rear and strike from behind. You look at groves of entwined trees, and picture the animals that might be lurking there; you look at the river running slowly, dropping from level to level through the vlei, spreading into pools where at night the buck come to drink, and the crocodiles rise and drag them by their soft noses into underwater caves. Fear possessed me. I found I was turning round and round, because of that shapeless menace behind me that might reach out and take me; I kept glancing at the files of kopjes which, seen from a different angle, seemed to change with every step so that even known landmarks, like a big mountain that had sentineled my world since I first became conscious of it, showed an unfamiliar sunlit valley among its foothills. I did not know where I was. I was lost. Panic seized me. I found I was spinning round and round, staring anxiously at this tree and that, peering up at the sun which appeared to have moved into an eastern slant, shedding the sad yellow light of sunset. Hours must have passed! I looked at my watch and found that this state of meaningless terror had lasted perhaps ten minutes.

The point was that it was meaningless. I was not ten miles from home: I had only to take my way back along the valley to find myself at the fence; away among the foothills of the kopjes gleamed the roof of a neighbor's house, and a couple of hours' walking would reach it. This was the sort of fear that contracts the flesh of a dog at night and sets him howling at the full moon. It had nothing to do with what I thought or felt; and I was more disturbed by the fact that I could become its victim than of the physical sensation itself: I walked steadily on, quieted, in a divided mind, watching my own pricking nerves and apprehensive glances from side to side with a disgusted amusement. Deliberately I set myself to think of this village I was seeking, and what I should do when I entered it—if I could find it, which was doubtful, since I was walking aimlessly and it might be anywhere in the hundreds of thousands of acres of bush that stretched about me. With my mind on that village, I realized that a new sensation was added to the fear: loneliness. Now such a terror of isolation invaded me that I could hardly walk; and if it were not that I came over the crest of a small rise and saw a village below me, I should have turned and gone home. It was a cluster of thatched huts in a clearing among trees. There were neat patches of mealies and pumpkins and millet, and cattle grazed under some trees at a distance. Fowls scratched among the huts, dogs lay sleeping on the grass, and goats friezed a kopje that jutted up beyond a tributary of the river lying like an enclosing arm round the village.

As I came close I saw the huts were lovingly decorated with patterns of yellow and red and ochre mud on the walls; and the thatch was tied in place with plaits of straw.

This was not at all like our farm compound, a dirty and neglected place, a temporary home for migrants who had no roots in it.

And now I did not know what to do next. I called a small black boy, who was sitting on a log playing a stringed gourd, quite naked except for the strings of blue beads round his neck, and said: "Tell the Chief I am here." The child stuck his thumb in his mouth and stared shyly back at me.

For minutes I shifted my feet on the edge of what seemed a deserted village, till at last the child scuttled off, and then some women came. They were draped in bright cloths, with brass glinting in their ears and on their arms. They also stared, silently; then turned to chatter among themselves.

I said again: "Can I see Chief Mshlanga?" I saw they caught the name; they did not understand what I wanted. I did not understand myself.

At last I walked through them and came past the huts and saw a clearing under a big shady tree, where a dozen old men sat cross-legged on the ground, talking. Chief Mshlanga was leaning back against the tree, holding a gourd in his hand, from which he had been drinking. When he saw me, not a muscle of his face moved, and I could see he was not pleased: perhaps he was afflicted with my own shyness, due to being unable to find the right forms of courtesy for the occasion. To meet me, on our own farm, was one thing; but I should not have come here. What had I expected? I could not join them socially: the thing was unheard of. Bad enough that I, a white girl, should be walking the veld alone as a white man might: and in this part of the bush where only Government officials had the right to move.

Again I stood, smiling foolishly, while behind me stood the groups of brightly clad, chattering women, their faces alert with curiosity and interest, and in front of me sat the old men, with old lined faces, their eyes guarded, aloof. It was a village of ancients and children and women. Even the two young men who kneeled beside the Chief were not those I had seen with him previously: the young men were all away working on the white men's farms and mines, and the Chief must depend on relatives who were temporarily on holiday for his attendants.

"The small white Nkosikaas is far from home," remarked the old man at last.

"Yes," I agreed, "it is far." I wanted to say: "I have come to pay you a friendly visit, Chief Mshlanga." I could not say it. I might now be feeling an urgent helpless desire to get to know these men and women as people, to be accepted by them as a friend, but the truth was I had set out in a spirit of curiosity: I had wanted to see the village that one day our cook, the reserved and obedient young man who got drunk on Sundays, would one day rule over.

"The child of Nkosi Jordan is welcome," said Chief Mshlanga.

"Thank you," I said, and could think of nothing more to say. There was a silence, while the flies rose and began to buzz around my head; and the wind shook a little in the thick green tree that spread its branches over the old men.

"Good morning," I said at last. "I have to return now to my home."

"Morning, little Nkosikaas," said Chief Mshlanga.

I walked away from the indifferent village, over the rise past the staring amber-eyed goats, down through the tall stately trees into the great rich green valley where the river meandered and the pigeons cooed tales of plenty and the woodpecker tapped softly.

The fear had gone; the loneliness had set into stiff-necked stoicism; there was now a queer hostility in the landscape, a cold, hard, sullen indomitability that walked with me, as strong as a wall, as intangible as smoke; it seemed to say to me: you walk here as a destroyer. I went slowly homewards, with an empty heart: I had learned that if one cannot call a country to heel like a dog, neither can one dismiss the past with a smile in an easy gush of feeling, saying: I could not help it, I am also a victim.

I only saw Chief Mshlanga once again.

One night my father's big red land was trampled down by small sharp hooves, and it was discovered that the culprits were goats from Chief Mshlanga's kraal. This had happened once before, years ago.

My father confiscated all the goats. Then he sent a message to the old Chief that if he wanted them he would have to pay for the damage.

He arrived at our house at the time of sunset one evening, looking very old and bent now, walking stiffly under his regally draped blanket, leaning on a big stick. My father sat himself down in his big chair below the steps of the house; the old man squatted carefully on the ground before him, flanked by his two young men.

The palaver was long and painful, because of the bad English of the young man who interpreted, and because my father could not speak dialect, but only kitchen kaffir.

From my father's point of view, at least two hundred pounds' worth of damage had been done to the crop. He knew he could not get the money from the old man. He felt he was entitled to keep the goats. As for the old Chief, he kept repeating angrily: "Twenty goats! My people cannot lose twenty goats! We are not rich, like the Nkosi Jordan, to lose twenty goats at once."

My father did not think of himself as rich, but rather as very poor. He spoke quickly and angrily in return, saying that the damage done meant a great deal to him, and that he was entitled to the goats.

At last it grew so heated that the cook, the Chief's son, was called from the kitchen to be interpreter, and now my father spoke fluently in English, and our cook translated rapidly so that the old man could understand how very angry my father was. The young man spoke without emotion, in a mechanical way, his eyes lowered, but showing how he felt his position by a hostile uncomfortable set of the shoulders.

It was now in the late sunset, the sky a welter of colors, the birds singing their last songs, and the cattle, lowing peacefully, moving past us towards their sheds for the night. It was the hour when Africa is most beautiful; and here was this pathetic, ugly scene, doing no one any good.

At last my father stated finally: "I'm not going to argue about it. I am keeping the goats."

The old Chief flashed back in his own language: "That means that my people will go hungry when the dry season comes."

"Go to the police, then," said my father, and looked triumphant.

There was, of course, no more to be said.

The old man sat silent, his head bent, his hands dangling helplessly over his withered knees. Then he rose, the young men helping him, and he stood facing my father. He spoke once again, very stiffly; and turned away and went home to his village.

"What did he say?" asked my father of the young man, who laughed uncomfortably and would not meet his eyes.

"What did he say?" insisted my father.

Our cook stood straight and silent, his brows knotted together. Then he spoke. "My father says: All this land, this land you call yours, is his land, and belongs to our people."

Having made this statement, he walked off into the bush after his father, and we did not see him again.

Our next cook was a migrant from Nyasaland, with no expectations of greatness.

Next time the policeman came on his rounds he was told this story. He remarked: "That kraal has no right to be there; it should have been moved long ago. I don't know why no one has done anything about it. I'll have a chat with the Native Commissioner next week. I'm going over for tennis on Sunday, anyway."

Sometime later we heard that Chief Mshlanga and his people had been moved two hundred miles east, to a proper Native Reserve; the Government land was going to be opened up for white settlement soon.

I went to see the village again, about a year afterwards. There was nothing there. Mounds of red mud, where the huts had been, had long swathes of rotting thatch over them, veined with the red galleries of the white ants. The pumpkin vines rioted everywhere, over the bushes, up the lower branches of trees so that the great golden balls rolled underfoot and dangled overhead: it was a festival of pumpkins. The bushes were crowding up, the new grass sprang vivid green.

The settler lucky enough to be allotted the lush warm valley (if he chose to cultivate this particular section) would find, suddenly, in the middle of a mealie field, the plants were growing fifteen feet tall, the weight of the cobs dragging at the stalks, and wonder what unsuspected vein of richness he had struck.

# A Sunrise on the Veld

Every night that winter he said aloud into the dark of the pillow: Half past four! Half past four! till he felt his brain had gripped the words and held them fast. Then he fell asleep at once, as if a shutter had fallen; and lay with his face turned to the clock so that he could see it first thing when he woke.

It was half past four to the minute, every morning. Triumphantly pressing down the alarm-knob of the clock, which the dark half of his mind had outwitted, remaining vigilant all night and counting the hours as he lay relaxed in sleep, he huddled down for a last warm moment under the clothes, playing with the idea of lying abed for this once only. But he played with it for the fun of knowing that it was a weakness he could defeat without effort; just as he set the alarm each night for the delight of the moment when he woke and stretched his limbs, feeling the muscles tighten, and thought: Even my brain—even that! I can control every part of myself.

Luxury of warm rested body, with the arms and legs and fingers waiting like soldiers for a word of command! Joy of knowing that the precious hours were given to sleep voluntarily!—for he had once stayed awake three nights running, to prove that he could, and then worked all day, refusing even to admit that he was tired; and now sleep seemed to him a servant to be commanded and refused.

The boy stretched his frame full-length, touching the wall at his head with his hands, and the bedfoot with his toes; then he sprang out, like a fish leaping from water. And it was cold, cold.

He always dressed rapidly, so as to try and conserve his night-warmth till the sun rose two hours later; but by the time he had on his clothes his hands were numbed and he could scarcely hold his shoes.

These he could not put on for fear of waking his parents, who never came to know how early he rose.

As soon as he stepped over the lintel, the flesh of his soles contracted on the chilled earth, and his legs began to ache with cold. It was night: the stars were glittering, the trees standing black and still. He looked for signs of day, for the greying of the edge of a stone, or a lightening in the sky where the sun would rise, but there was nothing yet. Alert as an animal, he crept past the dangerous window, standing poised with his hand on the sill for one proudly fastidious moment, looking in at the stuffy blackness of the room where his parents lay.

Feeling for the grass-edge of the path with his toes, he reached inside another window farther along the wall, where his gun had been set in readiness the night before. The steel was icy, and numbed fingers slipped along it, so that he had to hold it in the crook of his arm for safety. Then he tiptoed to the room where the dogs slept, and was fearful that they might have been tempted to go before him; but they were waiting, their haunches crouched in reluctance at the cold, but ears and swinging tails greeting the gun ecstatically. His warning undertone kept them secret and silent till the house was a hundred yards back: then they bolted off into the bush, yelping excitedly. The boy imagined his parents turning in their beds and muttering: Those dogs again! before they were dragged back in sleep; and he smiled scornfully. He always looked back over his shoulder at the house before he passed a wall of trees that shut it from sight. It looked so low and small, crouching there under a tall and brilliant sky. Then he turned his back on it, and on the frowsting sleepers, and forgot them.

He would have to hurry. Before the light grew strong he must be four miles away; and already a tint of green stood in the hollow of a leaf, and the air smelled of morning and the stars were dimming.

He slung the shoes over his shoulder, veldskoen that were crinkled and hard with the dews of a hundred mornings. They would be necessary when the ground became too hot to bear. Now he felt the chilled dust push up between his toes, and he let the muscles of his feet spread and settle into the shapes of the earth; and he thought: I could walk a hundred miles on feet like these! I could walk all day, and never tire!

He was walking swiftly through the dark tunnel of foliage that in daytime was a road. The dogs were invisibly ranging the lower travelways of the bush, and he heard them panting. Sometimes he felt a cold muzzle on his leg before they were off again, scouting for a trail to follow. They were not trained, but free-running companions of the hunt, who often tired of the long stalk before the final shots, and went off on their own pleasure. Soon he could see them, small and wild-looking in a wild strange light, now that the bush stood trembling on the verge of color, waiting for the sun to paint earth and grass afresh.

The grass stood to his shoulders; and the trees were showering a faint silvery rain. He was soaked; his whole body was clenched in a steady shiver.

Once he bent to the road that was newly scored with animal trails, and regretfully straightened, reminding himself that the pleasure of tracking must wait till another day.

He began to run along the edge of a field, noting jerkily how it was filmed over with fresh spiderweb, so that the long reaches of great black clods seemed netted in glistening grey. He was using the steady lope he had learned by watching the natives, the run that is a dropping of the weight of the body from one foot to the next in a slow balancing movement that never tires, nor shortens the breath; and he felt the blood pulsing down his legs and along his arms, and the exultation and pride of body mounted in him till he was shutting his teeth hard against a violent desire to shout his triumph.

Soon he had left the cultivated part of the farm. Behind him the bush was low and black. In front was a long vlei, acres of long pale grass that sent back a hollowing gleam of light to a satiny sky. Near him thick swathes of grass were bent with the weight of water, and diamond drops sparkled on each frond.

The first bird woke at his feet and at once a flock of them sprang into the air calling shrilly that day had come; and suddenly, behind him, the bush woke into song, and he could hear the guinea fowl calling far ahead of him. That meant they would now be sailing down from their trees into thick grass, and it was for them he had come: he was too late. But he did not mind. He forgot he had come to shoot. He set his legs wide, and balanced from foot to foot, and swung his gun up and down in both hands horizontally, in a kind of improvised exercise, and let his head sink back till it was pillowed in his neck muscles, and watched how above him small rosy clouds floated in a lake of gold.

Suddenly it all rose in him: it was unbearable. He leaped up into the air, shouting and yelling, wild, unrecognizable noises. Then he began to run, not carefully, as he had before, but madly, like a wild thing. He was clean crazy, yelling mad with the joy of living and a superfluity of youth. He rushed down the vlei under a tumult of crimson and gold, while all the birds of the world sang about him. He ran in great leaping strides, and shouted as he ran, feeling his body rise into the crisp rushing air and fall back surely on to sure feet; and thought briefly, not believing that such a thing could happen to him, that he could break his ankle any moment, in this thick tangled grass. He cleared bushes like a duiker, leaped over rocks; and finally came to a dead stop at a place where the ground fell abruptly away below him to the river. It had been a two-mile-long dash through waist-high growth, and he was breathing hoarsely and could no longer sing. But he poised on a rock and looked down at stretches of water that gleamed through stooping trees, and thought suddenly, I am fifteen! Fifteen! The words came new to him; so that he kept repeating them wonderingly, with swelling excitement; and he felt the years of his life with his hands, as if he were counting marbles, each one hard and separate and compact, each one a wonderful shining thing. That was what he was: fifteen years of this rich soil, and this slow-moving water, and air that smelled like a challenge whether it was warm and sultry at noon, or as brisk as cold water, like it was now.

There was nothing he couldn't do, nothing! A vision came to him, as he stood there, like when a child hears the word "eternity" and tries to understand it, and time takes possession of the mind. He felt his life ahead of him as a great and wonderful thing, something that was his; and he said aloud, with the blood rising to his head: all the great men of the world have been as I am now, and there is nothing I can't become, nothing I can't do; there is no country in the world I cannot make part of myself, if I choose. I contain the world. I can make of it what I want. If I choose, I can change everything that is going to happen: it depends on me, and what I decide now.

The urgency, and the truth and the courage of what his voice was saying, exulted him so that he began to sing again, at the top of his voice, and the sound went echoing down the river gorge. He stopped for the echo, and sang again: stopped and shouted. That was what he was!—he sang, if he chose; and the world had to answer him.

And for minutes he stood there, shouting and singing and waiting for the lovely eddying sound of the echo; so that his own new strong thoughts came back and washed round his head, as if someone were answering him and encouraging him; till the gorge was full of soft voices clashing back and forth from rock to rock over the river. And then it seemed as if there was a new voice. He listened, puzzled, for it was not his own. Soon he was leaning forward, all his nerves alert, quite still: somewhere close to him there was a noise that was no joyful bird, nor tinkle of falling water, nor ponderous movement of cattle.

There it was again. In the deep morning hush that held his future and his past was a sound of pain, and repeated over and over: it was a kind of shortened scream, as if someone, something, had no breath to scream. He came to himself, looked about him, and called for the dogs. They did not appear: they had gone off on their own business, and he was alone. Now he was clean sober, all the madness gone. His heart beating fast, because of that frightened screaming, he stepped carefully off the rock and went towards a belt of trees. He was moving cautiously, for not so long ago he had seen a leopard in just this spot.

At the edge of the trees he stopped and peered, holding his gun ready; he advanced, looking steadily about him, his eyes narrowed. Then, all at once, in the middle of a step, he faltered, and his face was puzzled. He shook his head impatiently, as if he doubted his own sight.

There, between two trees, against a background of gaunt black rocks, was a figure from a dream, a strange beast that was horned and drunken-legged, but like something he had never even imagined. It seemed to be ragged. It looked like a small buck that had black ragged tufts of fur standing up irregularly all over it, with patches of raw flesh beneath . . . but the patches of rawness were disappearing under moving black and came again elsewhere; and all the time the creature screamed, in small gasping screams, and leaped drunkenly from side to side, as if it were blind.

Then the boy understood: it *was* a buck. He ran closer, and again stood still, stopped by a new fear. Around him the grass was whispering and alive. He looked wildly about, and then down. The ground was black with ants, great energetic ants that took no notice of him, but hurried and scurried towards the fighting shape, like glistening black water flowing through the grass.

And, as he drew in his breath and pity and terror seized him, the beast fell and the screaming stopped. Now he could hear nothing but one bird singing, and the sound of the rustling, whispering ants.

He peered over at the writhing blackness that jerked convulsively with the jerking nerves. It grew quieter. There were small twitches from the mass that still looked vaguely like the shape of a small animal.

It came into his mind that he should shoot it and end its pain; and he raised the gun. Then he lowered it again. The buck could no longer feel; its fighting was a mechanical protest of the nerves. But it was not that which made him put down the gun. It was a swelling feeling of rage and misery and protest that expressed itself in the thought: if I had not come it would have died like this: so why should I interfere? All over the bush things like this happen; they happen all the time; this is how life goes on, by living things dying in anguish. He gripped the gun between his knees and felt in his own limbs the myriad swarming pain of the twitching animal that could no longer feel, and set his teeth, and said over and over again under his breath: I can't stop it. I can't stop it. There is nothing I can do.

He was glad that the buck was unconscious and had gone past suffering so that he did not have to make a decision to kill it even when he was feeling with his whole body: this is what happens, this is how things work.

*It was right*—that was what he was feeling. *It was right and nothing could alter it.*

The knowledge of fatality, of what has to be, had gripped him and for the first time in his life; and he was left unable to make any movement of brain or body, except to say: "Yes, yes. That is what living is." It had entered his flesh and his bones and grown into the furthest corners of his brain and would never leave him. And at that moment he could not have performed the smallest action of mercy, knowing as he did, having lived on it all his life, the vast unalterable, cruel veld, where at any moment one might stumble over a skull or crush the skeleton of some small creature.

Suffering, sick, and angry, but also grimly satisfied with his new stoicism, he stood there leaning on his rifle, and watched the seething black mound grow smaller. At his feet, now, were ants trickling back with pink fragments in their mouths, and there was a fresh acid smell in his nostrils. He sternly controlled the uselessly convulsing muscles of his empty stomach, and reminded himself: the ants must eat too! At the same time he found that the tears were streaming down his face, and his clothes were soaked with the sweat of that other creature's pain.

The shape had grown small. Now it looked like nothing recognizable. He did not know how long it was before he saw the blackness thin, and bits of white showed through, shining in the sun—yes, there was the sun, just up, glowing over the rocks. Why, the whole thing could not have taken longer than a few minutes.

He began to swear, as if the shortness of the time was in itself unbearable, using the words he had heard his father say. He strode forward, crushing ants with each step, and brushing them off his clothes, till he stood above the skeleton, which lay sprawled under a small bush. It was clean-picked. It might have been lying there years, save that on the white bone were pink fragments of gristle. About the bones ants were ebbing away, their pincers full of meat.

The boy looked at them, big black ugly insects. A few were standing and gazing up at him with small glittering eyes.

"Go away!" he said to the ants, very coldly. "I am not for you—not just yet, at any rate. Go away." And he fancied that the ants turned and went away.

He bent over the bones and touched the sockets in the skull; that was where the eyes were, he thought incredulously, remembering the liquid dark eyes of a buck. And then he bent the slim foreleg bone, swinging it horizontally in his palm.

That morning, perhaps an hour ago, this small creature had been stepping proud and free through the bush, feeling the chill on its hide even as he himself had done, exhilarated by it. Proudly stepping the earth, tossing its horns, frisking a pretty white tail, it had sniffed the cold morning air. Walking like kings and conquerors it had moved through this free-held bush, where each blade of grass grew for it alone, and where the river ran pure sparkling water for its slaking.

And then—what had happened? Such a swift surefooted thing could surely not be trapped by a swarm of ants?

The boy bent curiously to the skeleton. Then he saw that the back leg that lay uppermost and strained out in the tension of death was snapped midway in the thigh, so that broken bones jutted over each other uselessly. So that was it! Limping into the ant-masses it could not escape, once it had sensed the danger. Yes, but how had the leg been broken? Had it fallen, perhaps? Impossible, a buck was too light and graceful. Had some jealous rival horned it?

What could possibly have happened? Perhaps some Africans had thrown stones at it, as they do, trying to kill it for meat, and had broken its leg. Yes, that must be it.

Even as he imagined the crowd of running, shouting natives, and the flying stones, and the leaping buck, another picture came into his mind. He saw himself, on any one of these bright ringing mornings, drunk with excitement, taking a snap shot at some half-seen buck. He saw himself with the gun lowered, wondering whether he had missed or not; and thinking at last that it was late, and he wanted his breakfast, and it was not worthwhile to track miles after an animal that would very likely get away from him in any case.

For a moment he would not face it. He was a small boy again, kicking sulkily at the skeleton, hanging his head, refusing to accept the responsibility.

Then he straightened up, and looked down at the bones with an odd expression of dismay, all the anger gone out of him. His mind went quite empty: all around him he could see trickles of ants disappearing into the grass. The whispering noise was faint and dry, like the rustling of a cast snakeskin.

At last he picked up his gun and walked homewards. He was telling himself half defiantly that he wanted his breakfast. He was telling himself that it was getting very hot, much too hot to be out roaming the bush.

Really, he was tired. He walked heavily, not looking where he put his feet. When he came within sight of his home he stopped, knitting his brows. There was something he had to think out. The death of that small animal was a thing that concerned him, and he was by no means finished with it. It lay at the back of his mind uncomfortably.

Soon, the very next morning, he would get clear of everybody and go to the bush and think about it.

# *The Habit of Loving*

In 1947 George wrote again to Myra, saying that now the war was well over she should come home and marry him. She wrote back from Australia, where she had gone with her two children in 1943 because there were relations there, saying she felt they had drifted apart; she was no longer sure she wanted to marry George. He did not allow himself to collapse. He cabled her the air fare and asked her to come over and see him. She came, for two weeks, being unable to leave the children for longer. She said she liked Australia; she liked the climate; she did not like the English climate any longer; she thought England was, very probably, played out; and she had become used to missing London. Also, presumably, to missing George Talbot.

For George this was a very painful fortnight. He believed it was painful for Myra, too. They had met in 1938, had lived together for five years, and had exchanged for four years the letters of lovers separated by fate. Myra was certainly the love of his life. He had believed he was of hers until now. Myra, an attractive woman made beautiful by the suns and beaches of Australia, waved goodbye at the airport, and her eyes were filled with tears.

George's eyes, as he drove away from the airport, were dry. If one person has loved another truly and wholly, then it is more than love that collapses when one side of the indissoluble partnership turns away with a tearful goodbye. George dismissed the taxi early and walked through St. James's Park. Then it seemed too small for him, and he went to the Green Park. Then he walked into Hyde Park and through to Kensington Gardens. When the dark came and they closed the great gates of the park he took a taxi home. He lived in a block of flats near the Marble Arch. For five years Myra had lived with him there, and it was here he had expected to live with her again. Now he moved into a new flat near

Covent Garden. Soon after that he wrote Myra a very painful letter. It occurred to him that he had often received such letters, but had never written one before. It occurred to him that he had entirely underestimated the amount of suffering he must have caused in his life. But Myra wrote him a sensible letter back, and George Talbot told himself that now he must finally stop thinking about Myra.

Therefore he became rather less of a dilettante in his work than he had been recently, and he agreed to produce a new play written by a friend of his. George Talbot was a man of the theatre. He had not acted in it for many years now; but he wrote articles, he sometimes produced a play, he made speeches on important occasions and was known by everyone. When he went into a restaurant people tried to catch his eye, and he often did not know who they were. During the four years since Myra had left, he had had a number of affairs with young women round and about the theatre, for he had been lonely. He had written quite frankly to Myra about these affairs, but she had never mentioned them in her letters. Now he was very busy for some months and was seldom at home; he earned quite a lot of money, and he had a few more affairs with women who were pleased to be seen in public with him. He thought about Myra a great deal, but he did not write to her again, nor she to him, although they had agreed they would always be great friends.

One evening in the foyer of a theatre he saw an old friend of his he had always admired, and he told the young woman he was with that that man had been the most irresistible man of his generation—no woman had been able to resist him. The young woman stared briefly across the foyer and said, "Not really?"

When George Talbot got home that night he was alone, and he looked at himself with honesty in the mirror. He was sixty, but he did not look it. Whatever had attracted women to him in the past had never been his looks, and he was not much changed: a stoutish man, holding himself erect, grey-haired, carefully brushed, well-dressed. He had not paid much attention to his face since those many years ago when he had been an actor; but now he had an uncharacteristic fit of vanity and remembered that Myra had admired his mouth, while his wife had loved his eyes. He took to taking glances at himself in foyers and restaurants where there were mirrors, and he saw himself as unchanged. He was becoming conscious, though, of a discrepancy between that suave exterior and what he felt. Beneath his ribs his heart had become swollen and soft and painful, a monstrous area of sympathy playing enemy to what he had been. When people made jokes he was often unable to laugh; and his manner of talking, which was light and allusive and dry, must have changed, because more than once old friends asked him if he was depressed, and they no longer smiled appreciatively as he told his stories. He gathered he was not being good company. He understood he might be ill, and he went to the doctor. The doctor said there was nothing wrong with his heart, he had thirty years of life in him yet—luckily, he added respectfully, for the British theatre.

George came to understand that the word "heartache" meant that a person could carry a heart that ached around with him day and night for, in his case, months. Nearly a year now. He would wake in the night, because of the pressure of pain in his chest; in the morning he woke under a weight of grief. There seemed to be no end to it; and this thought jolted him into two actions. First, he wrote to Myra a tender, carefully phrased letter, recalling the years of their love. To this he got, in due course, a tender and careful reply. Then he went to see his wife. With her he was, and had been for many years, good friends. They saw each other often, but not so often now the children were grown-up; perhaps once or twice a year, and they never quarreled.

His wife had married again after they divorced, and now she was a widow. Her second husband had been a member of Parliament, and she worked for the Labour Party, and she was on a Hospital Advisory Committee and on the Board of Directors of a progressive school. She was fifty, but did not look it. On this afternoon she was wearing a slim grey suit and grey shoes, and her grey hair had a wave of white across the front which made her look distinguished. She was animated, and very happy to see George; and she talked about some deadhead on her hospital committee who did not see eye to eye with the progressive minority about some reform or other. They had always had their politics in common, a position somewhere left of center in the Labour Party. She had sympathized with his being a pacifist in the First World War—he had been for a time in prison because of it; he had sympathized with her militant feminism. Both had helped the strikers in 1926. In the Thirties, after they were divorced, she had helped with money when he went on tour with a company acting Shakespeare to people on the dole, or hunger-marching.

Myra had not been at all interested in politics, only in her children. And in George, of course.

George asked his first wife to marry him again, and she was so startled that she let the sugar tongs drop and crack a saucer. She asked what had happened to Myra, and George said: "Well, dear, I think Myra forgot about me during those years in Australia. At any rate, she doesn't want me now." When he heard his voice saying this it sounded pathetic, and he was frightened, for he could not remember ever having to appeal to a woman. Except to Myra.

His wife examined him and said briskly: "You're lonely, George. Well, we're none of us getting any younger."

"You don't think you'd be less lonely if you had me around?"

She got up from her chair in order that she could attend to something with her back to him, and she said that she intended to marry again quite soon. She was marrying a man considerably younger than herself, a doctor who was in the progressive minority at her hospital. From her voice George understood that she was both proud and ashamed of this marriage, and that was why she was hiding her face from him. He congratulated her and asked if there wasn't perhaps a chance for him yet? "After all, dear, we were happy together, weren't we? I've never really understood why that marriage ever broke up. It was you who wanted to break it up."

"I don't see any point in raking over that old business," she said, with finality, and returned to her seat opposite him. He envied her very much, looking young with her pink and scarcely lined face under that brave lock of deliberately whitened hair.

"But dear, I wish you'd tell me. It doesn't do any harm now, does it? And I always wondered. . . . I've often thought about it and wondered." He could hear the pathetic note in his voice again, but he did not know how to alter it.

"You wondered," she said, "when you weren't occupied with Myra."

"But I didn't know Myra when we got divorced."

"You knew Phillipa and Georgina and Janet and Lord knows who else."

"But I didn't care about them."

She sat with her competent hands in her lap, and on her face was a look he remembered seeing when she told him she would divorce him. It was bitter and full of hurt. "You didn't care about me either," she said.

"But we were happy. Well, I was happy . . ." he trailed off, being pathetic against all his knowledge of women. For, as he sat there, his old rake's heart was telling him that if only he could find them, there must be the right words, the right tone. But whatever he said came out in this hopeless, old dog's voice, and he knew that this voice could never defeat the gallant and crusading young doctor. "And I did care about you. Sometimes I think you were the only woman in my life."

At this she laughed. "Oh, George, don't get maudlin now, please."

"Well, dear, there was Myra. But when you threw me over there was bound to be Myra, wasn't there? There were two women, you and then Myra. And I've never never understood why you broke it all up when we seemed to be so happy."

"You didn't care for me," she said again. "If you had, you would never have come home from Phillipa, Georgina, Janet, et al., and said calmly, just as if it didn't matter to me in the least, that you had been with them in Brighton or wherever it was."

"But if I had cared about them I would never have told you."

She was regarding him incredulously, and her face was flushed. With what? Anger? George did not know.

"I remember being so proud," he said pathetically, "that we had solved this business of marriage and all that sort of thing. We had such a good marriage that it didn't matter, the little flirtations. And I always thought one should be able to tell the truth. I always told you the truth, didn't I?"

"Very romantic of you, dear George," she said dryly; and soon he got up, kissed her fondly on the cheek, and went away.

He walked for a long time through the parks, hands behind his erect back, and he could feel his heart swollen and painful in his side. When the gates shut, he walked through the lighted streets he had lived in for fifty years of his life, and he was remembering Myra and Molly, as if they were one woman, merging into each other, a shape of warm easy intimacy, a shape of happiness walking beside him. He went into a little restaurant he knew well, and there was a girl sitting there who knew him because she had heard him lecture once on the state of the British theatre. He tried hard to see Myra and Molly in her face, but he failed; and he paid for her coffee and his own and went home by himself. But his flat was unbearably empty, and he left it and walked down by the Embankment for a couple of hours to tire himself, and there must have been a colder wind blowing than he knew, for next day he woke with a pain in his chest which he could not mistake for heartache.

He had flu and a bad cough, and he stayed in bed by himself and did not ring up the doctor until the fourth day, when he was getting lightheaded. The doctor said it must be the hospital at once. But he would not go to the hospital. So the doctor said he must have day and night nurses. This he submitted to until the cheerful friendliness of the nurses saddened him beyond bearing, and he asked the doctor to ring up his wife, who would find someone to look after him who would be sympathetic. He was hoping that Molly would come herself to nurse him, but when she arrived he did not like to mention it, for she was busy with preparations for her new marriage. She promised to find him someone who would not wear a uniform and make jokes. They naturally had many friends in common; and she rang up an old flame of his in the theatre who said she knew of a girl who was looking for a secretary's job to tide her over a patch of not working, but who didn't really mind what she did for a few weeks.

So Bobby Tippett sent away the nurses and made up a bed for herself in his study. On the first day she sat by George's bed sewing. She wore a full dark skirt and a demure printed blouse with short frills at the wrist, and George watched her sewing and already felt much better. She was a small, thin, dark girl, probably Jewish, with sad black eyes. She had a way of letting her sewing lie loose in her lap, her hands limp over it; and her eyes fixed themselves, and a bloom of dark introspection came over them. She sat very still at these moments, like a small china figure of a girl sewing. When she was nursing George, or letting in his many visitors, she put on a manner of cool and even languid charm; it was the extreme good manners of heartlessness, and at first George was chilled: but then he saw through the pose; for whatever world Bobby Tippett had been born into he did not think it was the English class to which these manners belonged. She replied with a "yes," or a "no," to questions about herself; he gathered that her parents were dead, but there was a married sister she saw sometimes; and for the rest she had lived around and about London, mostly by herself, for ten or more years. When he asked her if she had not been lonely, so much by herself, she drawled, "Why, not at all, I don't mind being alone." But he saw her as a small, brave child, a waif against London, and was moved.

He did not want to be the big man of the theatre; he was afraid of evoking the impersonal admiration he was only too accustomed to; but soon he was asking her questions about her career, hoping that this might be the point of her enthusiasm. But she spoke lightly of small parts, odd jobs, scene-painting and understudying, in a jolly good-little-trouper's voice; and he could not see that he had come any closer to her at all. So at last he did what he had tried to avoid and, sitting up against his pillows like a judge or an impresario, he said: "Do something for me, dear. Let me see you." She went next door like an obedient child, and came back in tight black trousers, but still in her demure little blouse, and stood on the carpet before him, and went into a little song-and-dance act. It wasn't bad. He had seen a hundred worse. But he was very moved; he saw her now above all as the little urchin, the gamin, boy-girl and helpless. And utterly touching. "Actually," she said, "this is half of an act. I always have someone else."

There was a big mirror that nearly filled the end wall of the large, dark room. George saw himself in it, an elderly man sitting propped up on pillows watching the small doll-like figure standing before him on the carpet. He saw her turn her head towards her reflection in the darkened mirror, study it, and then she began to dance with her own reflection, dance against it, as it were. There were two small, light figures dancing in George's room; there was something uncanny in it. She began singing, a little broken song in stage cockney, and George felt that she was expecting the other figure in the mirror to sing with her; she was singing at the mirror as if she expected an answer.

"That's very good, dear," he broke in quickly, for he was upset, though he did not know why. "Very good indeed." He was relieved when she broke off and came away from the mirror, so that the uncanny shadow of her went away.

"Would you like me to speak to someone for you, dear? It might help. You know how things are in the theatre," he suggested apologetically.

"I don't maind if I dew," she said in the stage cockney of her act; and for a moment her face flushed into a mocking, reckless, gamin-like charm. "Perhaps I'd better change back into my skirt?" she suggested. "More natural-like for a nurse, ain't it?"

But he said he liked her in her tight black trousers, and now she always wore them, and her neat little shirts; and she moved about the flat as a charming feminine boy, chattering to him about the plays she had had small parts in and about the big actors and actresses and producers she had spoken to, who were, of course, George's friends or, at least, equals. George sat up against his pillows and listened and watched, and his heart ached. He remained in bed longer than there was need, because he did not want her to go. When he transferred himself to a big chair, he said: "You mustn't think you're bound to stay here, dear, if there's somewhere else you'd rather go." To which she replied, with a wide flash of her black eyes, "But I'm resting, darling, resting. I've nothing better to do with myself." And then: "Oh aren't I *awful,* the things wot I sy?"

"But you do like being here? You don't mind being here with me, dear?" he insisted.

There was the briefest pause. She said: "Yes, oddly enough I do like it." The "oddly enough" was accompanied by a quick, half-laughing, almost flirtatious glance; and for the first time in many months the pressure of loneliness eased around George's heart.

Now it was a happiness to him because when the distinguished ladies and gentlemen of the theatre or of letters came to see him, Bobby became a cool, silky little hostess; and the instant they had gone she relapsed into urchin charm. It was a proof of their intimacy. Sometimes he took her out to dinner or to the theatre. When she dressed up she wore bold, fashionable clothes and moved with the insolence of a mannequin; and

George moved beside her, smiling fondly, waiting for the moment when the black, reckless, freebooting eyes would flash up out of the languid stare of the woman presenting herself for admiration, exchanging with him amusement at her posing, amusement at the world; promising him that soon, when they got back to the apartment, by themselves, she would again become the dear little girl or the gallant, charming waif.

Sometimes, sitting in the dim room at night, he would let his hand close over the thin point of her shoulder; sometimes, when they said good night, he bent to kiss her, and she lowered her head, so that his lips encountered her demure, willing forehead.

George told himself that she was unawakened. It was a phrase that had been the prelude to a dozen warm discoveries in the past. He told himself that she knew nothing of what she might be. She had been married, it seemed—she dropped this information once, in the course of an anecdote about the theatre; but George had known women in plenty who after years of marriage had been unawakened. George asked her to marry him; and she lifted her small sleek head with an animal's startled turn and said: "Why do you want to marry me?"

"Because I like being with you, dear. I love being with you."

"Well, I like being with you." It had a questioning sound. She was questioning herself? "Strainge," she said in cockney, laughing. "Strainge but trew."

The wedding was to be a small one, but there was a lot about it in the papers. Recently several men of George's generation had married young women. One of them had fathered a son at the age of seventy. George was flattered by the newspapers, and told Bobby a good deal about his life that had not come up before. He remarked, for instance, that he thought his generation had been altogether more successful about this business of love and sex than the modern generation. He said, "Take my son, for instance. At his age I had had a lot of affairs and knew about women; but there he is, nearly thirty, and when he stayed here once with a girl he was thinking of marrying I know for a fact they shared the same bed for a week and nothing ever happened. She told me so. Very odd it all seems to me. But it didn't seem odd to her. And now he lives with another young man and listens to that long-playing record thing of his, and he's engaged to a girl he takes out twice a week, like a schoolboy. And there's my daughter, she came to me a year after she was married, and she was in an awful mess, really awful. . . . It seems to me your generation are very frightened of it all. I don't know why."

"Why my generation?" she asked, turning her head with that quick listening movement. "It's not my generation."

"But you're nothing but a child," he said fondly.

He could not decipher what lay behind the black, full stare of her sad eyes as she looked at him now; she was sitting cross-legged in her black glossy trousers before the fire, like a small doll. But a spring of alarm had been touched in him and he didn't dare say any more.

"At thirty-five, I'm the youngest child alive," she sang, with a swift sardonic glance at him over her shoulder. But it sounded gay.

He did not talk to her again about the achievements of his generation.

After the wedding he took her to a village in Normandy where he had been once, many years ago, with a girl called Eve. He did not tell her he had been there before.

It was spring, and the cherry trees were in flower. The first evening he walked with her in the last sunlight under the white-flowering branches, his arm around her thin waist, and it seemed to him that he was about to walk back through the gates of a lost happiness.

They had a large comfortable room with windows which overlooked the cherry trees and there was a double bed. Madame Cruchot, the farmer's wife, showed them the room with shrewd, non-commenting eyes, said she was always happy to shelter honeymoon couples, and wished them a good night.

George made love to Bobby, and she shut her eyes, and he found she was not at all awkward. When they had finished, he gathered her in his arms, and it was then that he returned simply, with an incredulous awed easing of the heart, to a happiness which—and now it seemed to him fantastically ungrateful that he could have done—he had taken for granted for so many years of his life. It was not possible, he thought, holding her compliant body in his arms, that he could have been by himself, alone, for so long. It had been intolerable. He held her silent breathing body, and he stroked her back and thighs, and his hands remembered the emotions of nearly fifty years of loving. He could feel the memoried emotions of his life flooding through his body, and his heart swelled with a joy it seemed to him he had never known, for it was a compound of a dozen loves.

He was about to take final possession of his memories when she turned sharply away, sat up, and said: "I want a fag. How about yew?"

"Why, yes, dear, if you want."

They smoked. The cigarettes finished, she lay down on her back, arms folded across her chest, and said, "I'm sleepy." She closed her eyes. When he was sure she was asleep, he lifted himself on his elbow and watched her. The light still burned, and the curve of her cheek was full and soft, like a child's. He touched it with the side of his palm, and she shrank away in her sleep, but clenched up, like a fist; and her hand, which was white and unformed, like a child's hand, was clenched in a fist on the pillow before her face.

George tried to gather her in his arms, and she turned away from him to the extreme edge of the bed. She was deeply asleep, and her sleep was unsharable. George could not endure it. He got out of bed and stood by the window in the cold spring night air, and saw the white cherry trees standing under the white moon, and thought of the cold girl asleep in her bed. He was there in the chill moonlight until the dawn came; in the morning he had a very bad cough and could not get up. Bobby was charming, devoted, and gay. "Just like old times, me nursing you," she commented, with a deliberate roll of her black eyes. She asked Madame Cruchot for another bed, which she placed in the corner of the room, and George thought it was quite reasonable she should not want to catch his cold; for he did not allow himself to remember the times in his past when quite serious illness had been no obstacle to the sharing of the dark; he decided to forget the sensualities of tiredness, or of fever, or of the extremes of sleeplessness. He was even beginning to feel ashamed.

For a fortnight the Frenchwoman brought up magnificent meals, twice a day, and George and Bobby drank a great deal of red wine and of calvados and made jokes with Madame Cruchot about getting ill on honeymoons. They returned from Normandy rather earlier than had been arranged. It would be better for George, Bobby said, at home, where his friends could drop in to see him. Besides, it was sad to be shut indoors in springtime, and they were both eating too much.

On the first night back in the flat, George waited to see if she would go into the study to sleep, but she came to the big bed in her pajamas, and for the second time he held her in his arms for the space of the act, and then she smoked, sitting up in bed and looking rather tired and small and, George thought, terribly young and pathetic. He did not sleep that night. He did not dare move out of bed for fear of disturbing her, and he was afraid to drop off to sleep for fear his limbs remembered the habits of a lifetime and searched for hers. In the morning she woke smiling, and he put his arms around her, but she kissed him with small gentle kisses and jumped out of bed.

That day she said she must go and see her sister. She saw her sister often during the next few weeks and kept suggesting that George should have his friends around more than he did. George asked why didn't the sister come to see her here, in the flat? So one afternoon she came to tea. George had seen her briefly at the wedding and disliked her, but now for the first time he had a spell of revulsion against the marriage itself. The sister was awful—a commonplace, middle-aged female from some suburb. She had a sharp, dark face that poked itself inquisitively into the corners of the flat, pricing the furniture, and a thin acquisitive nose bent to one side. She sat, on her best behavior, for two hours over the teacups, in a mannish navy blue suit, a severe black hat, her brogued feet set firmly side by side before her; and her thin nose seemed to be carrying on a silent, satirical conversation with her sister about George. Bobby was being cool and well-mannered, as it were, deliberately tired of life, as she always was when guests were there, but George was sure this was simply on his account. When the sister had gone, George was rather querulous about her; but Bobby said, laughing, that of course she had known George wouldn't like Rosa; she *was* rather ghastly; but then who had suggested inviting her? So Rosa came no more, and Bobby went out to meet her for a visit to the pictures, or for shopping. Meanwhile, George sat alone and thought uneasily about Bobby, or visited his old friends. A few months after they returned from Normandy, someone suggested to George that perhaps he was ill. This made George think about it, and he realized he was not far from being ill. It was because he could not sleep. Night after night he lay beside Bobby, after her cheerfully affectionate submission to him; and he saw the soft curve of her cheek on the pillow, the long dark lashes lying close and flat. Never had anything in his life moved him so deeply as that childish cheek, the shadow of those lashes. A small crease in one cheek seemed to him the signature of emotion; and the lock of black glossy hair falling across her forehead filled his throat with tears. His nights were long vigils of locked tenderness.

Then one night she woke and saw him watching her.

"What's the matter?" she asked, startled. "Can't you sleep?"

"I'm only watching you, dear," he said hopelessly.

She lay curled up beside him, her fist beside her on the pillow, between him and her. "Why aren't you happy?" she asked suddenly; and as George laughed with a sudden bitter irony, she sat up, arms around her knees, prepared to consider this problem practically.

"This isn't marriage; this isn't love," he announced. He sat up beside her. He did not know that he had never used that tone to her before. A portly man, his elderly face flushed with sorrow, he had forgotten her for the moment, and he was speaking across her from his past, resurrected in her, to his past. He was dignified with responsible experience and the warmth of a lifetime's responses. His eyes were heavy, satirical, and condemning. She rolled herself up against him and said with a small smile, "Then show me, George."

"Show you?" he said, almost stammering. "Show you?" But he held her, the obedient child, his cheek against hers, until she slept; then a too close pressure of his shoulder on hers caused her to shrink and recoil from him away to the edge of the bed.

In the morning she looked at him oddly, with an odd sad little respect, and said, "You know what, George? You've just got into the habit of loving."

"What do you mean, dear?"

She rolled out of bed and stood beside it, a waif in her white pajamas, her black hair ruffled. She slid her eyes at him and smiled. "You just want something in your arms, that's all. What do you do when you're alone? Wrap yourself around a pillow?"

He said nothing; he was cut to the heart.

"My husband was the same," she remarked gaily. "Funny thing is, he didn't care anything about me." She stood considering him, smiling mockingly. "Strainge, ain't it?" she commented and went off to the bathroom. That was the second time she had mentioned her husband.

That phrase, "the habit of loving," made a revolution in George. It was true, he thought. He was shocked out of himself, out of the instinctive response to the movement of skin against his, the pressure of a breast. It seemed to him that he was seeing Bobby quite newly. He had not really known her before. The delightful little girl had vanished, and he saw a young woman toughened and wary because of defeats and failures he had never stopped to think of. He saw that the sadness that lay behind the black eyes was not at all impersonal; he saw the first sheen of grey lying on her smooth hair; he saw that the full curve of her cheek was the beginning of the softening into middle age. He was appalled at his egotism. Now, he thought, he would really know her, and she would begin to love him in response to it.

Suddenly, George discovered in himself a boy whose existence he had totally forgotten. He had been returned to his adolescence. The accidental touch of her hand delighted him; the swing of her skirt could make him shut his eyes with happiness. He looked at her through the jealous eyes of a boy and began questioning her about her past, feeling that he was slowly taking possession of her. He waited for a hint of emotion in the drop of her voice, or a confession in the wrinkling of the skin by the full, dark, comradely eyes. At night, a boy again, reverence shut him into ineptitude. The body of George's sensuality had been killed stone dead. A month ago he had been a man vigorous with the skilled harboring of memory; the long use of his body. Now he lay awake beside this woman, longing—not for the past, for that past had dropped away from him, but dreaming of the future. And when he questioned her, like a jealous boy, and she evaded him, he could see it only as the locked virginity of the girl who would wake in answer to the worshiping boy he had become.

But still she slept in a citadel, one fist before her face.

Then one night she woke again, roused by some movement of his. "What's the matter *now,* George?" she asked, exasperated.

In the silence that followed, the resurrected boy in George died painfully.

"Nothing," he said. "Nothing at all." He turned away from her, defeated.

It was he who moved out of the big bed into the narrow bed in the study. She said with a sharp, sad smile, "Fed up with me, George? Well, I can't help it, you know. I didn't ever like sleeping beside someone very much."

George, who had dropped out of his work lately, undertook to produce another play, and was very busy again; and he became drama critic for one of the big papers and was in the swim and at all the first nights. Sometimes Bobby was with him, in her startling, smart clothes, being amused with him at the whole business of being fashionable. Sometimes she stayed at home. She had the capacity of being by herself for hours, apparently doing nothing. George would come home from some crowd of people, some party, and find her sitting cross-legged before the fire in her tight trousers, chin in hand, gone off by herself into some place where he was now afraid to try and follow. He could not bear it again, putting himself in a position where he might hear the cold, sharp words that showed she had never had an inkling of what he felt, because it was not in her nature to feel it. He would come in late, and she would make them both some tea; and they would sit hand in hand before the fire, his flesh and memories quiet. Dead, he thought. But his heart ached. He had become so used to the heavy load of loneliness in his chest that when, briefly, talking to an old friend, he became the George Talbot who had never known Bobby, and his heart lightened and his oppression went, he would look about him, startled, as if he had lost something. He felt almost lightheaded without the pain of loneliness.

He asked Bobby if she weren't bored, with so little to do, month after month after month, while he was so busy. She said no, she was quite happy doing nothing. She wouldn't like to take up her old work again?

"I wasn't ever much good, was I?" she said.

"If you'd enjoy it, dear, I could speak to someone for you."

She frowned at the fire but said nothing. Later he suggested it again, and she sparked up with a grin and: "Well, I don't maind if I dew. . . ."

So he spoke to an old friend, and Bobby returned to the theatre, to a small act in a little intimate revue. She had found somebody, she said, to be the other half of her act. George was very busy with a production of *Romeo and Juliet,* and did not have time to see her at rehearsal, but he was there on the night *The Offbeat Revue* opened. He was rather late and stood at the back of the gimcrack little theatre, packed tight with fragile little chairs. Everything was so small that the well-dressed audience looked too big, like oversize people crammed in a box. The tiny stage was left bare, with a few black-and-white posters stuck here and there, and there was one piano. The pianist was good, a young man with black hair falling limp over his face, playing as if he were bored with the whole thing. But he played very well. George, the man of the theatre, listened to the first number, so as to catch the mood, and thought, Oh Lord, not again. It was one of the songs from the First World War, and he could not stand the flood of easy emotion it aroused. He refused to feel. Then he realized that the emotion was, in any case, blocked; the piano was mocking the song; "There's a Long, Long Trail" was being played like a five-finger exercise; and "Keep the Home Fires Burning" and "Tipperary" followed, in the same style, as if the piano were bored. People were beginning to chuckle, they had caught the mood. A young blond man with a mustache and wearing the uniform of 1914 came in and sang fragments of the songs, like a corpse singing; and then George understood he was supposed to be one of the dead of that war singing. George felt all his responses blocked, first because he could not allow himself to feel any emotion from that time at all—it was too painful; and then because of the five-finger exercise style, which contradicted everything, all pain or protest, leaving nothing, an emptiness. The show went on; through the Twenties, with bits of popular songs from that time, a number about the General Strike, which reduced the whole thing to the scale of marionettes without passion, and then on to the Thirties. George saw it was a sort of potted history, as it were—Noël Coward's falsely heroic view of his time parodied. But it wasn't even that. There was no emotion, nothing. George did not know what he was supposed to feel. He looked curiously at the faces of the people around him and saw that the older people looked puzzled, affronted, as if the show were an insult to them. But the younger people were in the mood of the thing. But what mood? It was the parody of a parody. When the Second World War was evoked by "Run Rabbit Run," played like *Lohengrin,* while the soldiers in the uniforms of the time mocked their own understated heroism from the other side of death, then George could not stand it. He did not look at the stage at all. He was waiting for Bobby to come on, so he could say that he had seen her. Meanwhile he smoked and watched the face of a very young man near him; it was a pale, heavy, flaccid face, but it was responding, it seemed from a habit of rancor, to everything that went on on the stage. Suddenly, the young face lit into sarcastic delight, and George looked at the stage. On it were two urchins, identical, it seemed, in tight black glossy trousers, tight crisp white shirts. Both had short black hair, neat little feet placed side by side. They were standing together, hands crossed loosely before them at the waist, waiting for the music to start. The man at the piano, who had a cigarette in the corner of his mouth, began playing something very sentimental. He broke off and looked with sardonic inquiry at the urchins. They had not moved. They shrugged and rolled their eyes at him. He played a marching song, very loud and pompous. The urchins twisted a little and stayed still. Then the piano broke fast and sudden into a rage of jazz. The two puppets on the stage began a furious movement, their limbs clashing with each other and with the music, until they fell into poses of helpless despair while the music grew louder and more desperate. They tried again, whirling themselves into a frenzied attempt to keep up with the music. Then, two waifs, they turned their two small white sad faces at each other, and, with a formal nod, each took a phrase of music from the fast flood of sound that had already swept by them, held it, and began to sing. Bobby sang her bad stage-cockney phrases, meaningless, jumbled up, flat, hopeless; the other urchin sang drawling languid phrases from the upper-class jargon of the moment. They looked at each other, offering the phrases, as it were, to see if they would be accepted. Meanwhile, the hard, cruel, hurtful music went on. Again the two went limp and helpless, unwanted, unaccepted. George, outraged and hurt, asked himself again: What am I feeling? What am I supposed to be feeling? For that insane nihilistic music demanded some opposition, some statement of affirmation, but the two urchins, half-boy, half-girl, as alike as twins (George had to watch Bobby carefully so as not to confuse her with "the other half of her act"), were not even trying to resist the music. Then, after a long, sad immobility, they changed roles. Bobby took the languid jaw-writhing part of a limp young man, and the other waif sang false-cockney phrases in a cruel copy of a woman's voice. It was the parody of a parody. George stood tense, waiting for a resolution. His nature demanded that now, and quickly, for the limp sadness of the turn was unbearable, the two false urchins should flash out in some sort of rebellion. But there was nothing. The jazz went on like hammers; the whole room shook—stage walls, ceiling—and it seemed the people in the room jigged lightly and helplessly. The two children on the stage twisted their limbs into the willful mockery of a stage convention, and finally stood side by side, hands hanging limp, heads lowered meekly, twitching a little while the music rose into a final crashing discord and the lights went out. George could not applaud. He saw that the damp-faced young man next to him was clapping wildly, while his lank hair fell all over his face. George saw that the older people were all, like himself, bewildered and insulted.

When the show was over, George went backstage to fetch Bobby. She was with "the other half of the act," a rather good-looking boy of about twenty, who was being deferential to the impressive husband of Bobby. George said to her: "You were very good, dear, very good indeed." She looked smilingly at him, half mocking, but he did not know what it was she was mocking now. And she had been good. But he never wanted to see it again.

The revue was a success and ran for some months before it was moved to a bigger theatre. George finished his production of *Romeo and Juliet,* which, so the critics said, was the best London had seen for many years, and refused other offers of work. He did not need the money for the time being, and besides, he had not seen very much of Bobby lately.

But of course now she was working. She was at rehearsals several times a week, and away from the flat every evening. But George never went to her theatre. He did not want to see the sad, unresisting children twitching to the cruel music.

It seemed Bobby was happy. The various little parts she had played with him—the urchin, the cool hostess, the dear child—had all been absorbed into the hard-working female who cooked him his meals, looked after him, and went out to her theatre giving him a friendly kiss on the cheek. Their relationship was most pleasant and amiable. George lived beside this good friend, his wife Bobby, who was doing him so much credit in every way, and ached permanently with loneliness.

One day he was walking down the Charing Cross Road, looking into the windows of bookshops, when he saw Bobby strolling up the other side with Jackie, the other half of her act. She looked as he had never seen her: her dark face was alive with animation, and Jackie was looking into her face and laughing. George thought the boy very handsome. He had a warm gloss of youth on his hair and in his eyes; he had the lithe, quick look of a young animal.

George was not jealous at all. When Bobby came in at night, gay and vivacious, he knew he owed this to Jackie and did not mind. He was even grateful to him. The warmth Bobby had for "the other half of the act" overflowed towards him; and for some months Myra and his wife were present in his mind, he saw and felt them, two loving presences, young women who loved George, brought into being by the feeling between Jackie and Bobby. Whatever that feeling was.

*The Offbeat Revue* ran for nearly a year, and then it was coming off, and Bobby and Jackie were working out another act. George did not know what it was. He thought Bobby needed a rest, but he did not like to say so. She had been tired recently, and when she came in at night there was strain beneath her gaiety. Once, at night, he woke to see her beside his bed. "Hold me for a little, George," she asked. He opened his arms and she came into them. He lay holding her, quite still. He had opened his arms to the sad waif, but it was an unhappy woman lying in his arms. He could feel the movement of her lashes on his shoulder, and the wetness of tears.

He had not lain beside her for a long time—years, it seemed. She did not come to him again.

"You don't think you're working too hard, dear?" he asked once, looking at her strained face; but she said briskly, "No, I've got to have something to do, can't stand doing nothing."

One night it was raining hard, and Bobby had been feeling sick that day, and she did not come home at her usual time. George became worried and took a taxi to the theatre and asked the doorman if she was still there. It seemed she had left some time before. "She didn't look too well to me, sir," volunteered the doorman, and George sat for a time in the taxi, trying not to worry. Then he gave the driver Jackie's address; he meant to ask him if he knew where Bobby was. He sat limp in the back of the taxi, feeling the heaviness of his limbs, thinking of Bobby ill.

The place was in a mews, and he left the taxi and walked over rough cobbles to a door which had been the door of stables. He rang, and a young man he didn't know let him in, saying yes, Jackie Dickson was in. George climbed narrow, steep, wooden stairs slowly, feeling the weight of his body, while his heart pounded. He stood at the top of the stairs to get his breath, in a dark which smelled of canvas and oil and turpentine. There was a streak of light under a door; he went towards it, knocked, heard no answer, and opened it. The scene was a high, bare, studio sort of place, badly lighted, full of pictures, frames, junk of various kinds. Jackie, the dark, glistening youth, was seated cross-legged before the fire, grinning as he lifted his face to say something to Bobby, who sat in a chair, looking down at him. She was wearing a formal dark dress and jewelry, and her arms and neck were bare and white. She looked beautiful, George thought, glancing once, briefly, at her face, and then away; for he could see on it an emotion he did not want to recognize. The scene held for a moment before they realized he was there and turned their heads, with the same lithe movement of disturbed animals, to see him standing there in the doorway. Both faces froze. Bobby looked quickly at the young man, and it was in some kind of fear. Jackie looked sulky and angry.

"I've come to look for you, dear," said George to his wife. "It was raining and the doorman said you seemed ill."

"It's very sweet of you," she said and rose from the chair, giving her hand formally to Jackie, who nodded with bad grace at George.

The taxi stood in the dark, gleaming rain, and George and Bobby got into it and sat side by side, while it splashed off into the street.

"Was that the wrong thing to do, dear?" asked George, when she said nothing.

"No," she said.

"I really did think you might be ill."

She laughed. "Perhaps I am."

"What's the matter, my darling? What is it? He was angry, wasn't he? Because I came?"

"He thinks you're jealous," she said shortly.

"Well, perhaps I am rather," said George.

She did not speak.

"I'm sorry, dear, I really am. I didn't mean to spoil anything for you."

"Well, that's certainly *that,*" she remarked, and she sounded impersonally angry.

"Why? But why should it be?"

"He doesn't like—having things asked of him," she said, and he remained silent while they drove home.

Up in the warmed, comfortable old flat, she stood before the fire, while he brought her a drink. She smoked fast and angrily, looking into the fire.

"Please forgive me, dear," he said at last. "What is it? Do you love him? Do you want to leave me? If you do, of course you must. Young people should be together."

She turned and stared at him, a black strange stare he knew well.

"George," she said, "I'm nearly forty."

"But darling, you're a child still. At least, to me."

"And he," she went on, "will be twenty-two next month. I'm old enough to be his mother." She laughed, painfully. "Very painful, maternal love . . . or so it seems . . . but then how should I know?" She held out her bare arm and looked at it. Then, with the fingers of one hand she creased down the skin of that bare arm toward the wrist, so that the aging skin lay in creases and folds. Then, setting down her glass, her cigarette held between tight, amused, angry lips, she wriggled her shoulders out of her dress, so that it slipped to her waist, and she looked down at her two small, limp, unused breasts. "Very painful, dear

George," she said, and shrugged her dress up quickly, becoming again the formal woman dressed for the world. "He does not love me. He does not love me at all. Why should he?" She began singing:

*"He does not love me*
*With a love that is trew. . . ."*

Then she said, in stage cockney, "Repeat; I could 'ave bin 'is muvver, see?" And with the old rolling derisive black flash of her eyes she smiled at George.

George was thinking only that this girl, his darling, was suffering now what he had suffered, and he could not stand it. She had been going through this for how long now? But she had been working with that boy for nearly two years. She had been living beside him, George, and he had had no idea at all of her unhappiness. He went over to her, put his old arms around her, and she stood with her head on his shoulder and wept. For the first time, George thought, they were together. They sat by the fire a long time that night, drinking, smoking, and her head was on his knee and he stroked it, and thought that now, at last, she had been admitted into the world of emotion and they would learn to be really together. He could feel his strength stirring along his limbs for her. He was still a man, after all.

Next day she said she would not go on with the new show. She would tell Jackie he must get another partner. And besides, the new act wasn't really any good. "I've had one little act all my life," she said, laughing. "And sometimes it's fitted in, and sometimes it hasn't."

"What was the new act? What's it about?" he asked her.

She did not look at him. "Oh, nothing very much. It was Jackie's idea, really. . . ." Then she laughed. "It's quite good really, I suppose. . . ."

"But what is it?"

"Well, you see. . . ." Again he had the impression she did not want to look at him. "It's a pair of lovers. We make fun . . . it's hard to explain, without doing it."

"You make fun of love?" he asked.

"Well, you know, all the attitudes . . . the things people say. It's a man and a woman—with music, of course. All the music you'd expect, played offbeat. We wear the same costume as for the other act. And then we go through all the motions. . . . It's rather funny, really . . ." she trailed off, breathless, seeing George's face. "Well," she said, suddenly very savage, "if it isn't all bloody funny, what is it?" She turned away to take a cigarette.

"Perhaps you'd like to go on with it after all?" he asked ironically.

"No. I can't. I really can't stand it. I can't stand it any longer, George," she said, and from her voice he understood she had nothing to learn from him of pain.

He suggested they both needed a holiday, so they went to Italy. They traveled from place to place, never stopping anywhere longer than a day, for George knew she was running away from any place around which emotion could gather. At night he made love to her, but she closed her eyes and thought of the other half of the act; and George knew it and did not care. But what he was feeling was too powerful for his old body; he could feel a lifetime's emotions beating through his limbs, making his brain throb.

Again they curtailed their holiday, to return to the comfortable old flat in London.

On the first morning after their return, she said: "George, you know you're getting too old for this sort of thing—it's not good for you; you look ghastly."

"But, darling, why? What else am I still alive for?"

"People'll say I'm killing you," she said, with a sharp, half-angry, half-amused, black glance.

"But, my darling, believe me . . ."

He could see them both in the mirror; he, an old pursy man, head lowered in sullen obstinacy; she . . . but he could not read her face.

"And perhaps *I'm* getting too old?" she remarked suddenly.

For a few days she was gay, mocking, then suddenly tender. She was provocative, teasing him with her eyes; then she would deliberately yawn and say, "I'm going to sleep. Goodnight, George."

"Well of course, my darling, if you're tired."

One morning she announced she was going to have a birthday party; it would be her fortieth birthday soon. The way she said it made George feel uneasy.

On the morning of her birthday she came into his study where he had been sleeping, carrying his breakfast tray. He raised himself on his elbow and gazed at her, appalled. For a moment he had imagined it must be another woman. She had put on a severe navy blue suit, cut like a man's; heavy black-laced shoes; and she had taken the wisps of black hair back off her face and pinned them into a sort of clumsy knot. She was suddenly a middle-aged woman.

"But, my darling," he said, "my darling, what have you done to yourself?"

"I'm forty," she said. "Time to grow up."

"But, my darling, I do so love you in your nice clothes. I do so love you being beautiful in your lovely clothes."

She laughed, and left the breakfast tray beside his bed, and went clumping out on her heavy shoes.

That morning she stood in the kitchen beside a very large cake, on which she was carefully placing forty small pink candles. But it seemed only the sister had been asked to the party, for that afternoon the three of them sat around the cake and looked at one another. George looked at Rosa, the sister, in her ugly, straight, thick suit, and at his darling Bobby, all her grace and charm submerged into heavy tweed, her hair dragged back, without makeup. They were two middle-aged women, talking about food and buying.

George said nothing. His whole body throbbed with loss.

The dreadful Rosa was looking with her sharp eyes around the expensive flat, and then at George and then at her sister.

"You've let yourself go, haven't you, Bobby?" she commented at last. She sounded pleased about it.

Bobby glanced defiantly at George. "I haven't got time for all this nonsense any more," she said. "I simply haven't got time. We're all getting on now, aren't we?"

George saw the two women looking at him. He thought they had the same black, hard, inquisitive stare over sharp-bladed noses. He could not speak. His tongue was thick. The blood was beating through his body. His heart seemed to be swelling and filling his whole body, an enormous soft growth of pain. He could not hear for the tolling of the blood through his ears. The blood was beating up into his eyes, but he shut them so as not to see the two women.

# *The Eye of God in Paradise*

O—— in the Bavarian Alps is a charming little village. It is no more charming, however, than ten thousand others; although it is known to an astonishing number of people, some of whom have actually been there, while others have savored its attractions in imagination only. Pleasure resorts are like film stars and royalty who—or so one hopes—must be embarrassed by the figures they cut in the fantasies of people who have never met them. The history of O—— is fascinating; for this is true of every village. Its location has every advantage, not least that of being so near to the frontier that when finally located on the map it seems to the exuberant holiday-making fancy that one might toss a stone from it into Austria. This is, of course, not the case, since a high wall of mountains forms a natural barrier to any such adventure, besides making it essential that all supplies for O—— and the ten or a dozen villages in the valley above it must come from Germany. This wall of mountains is in fact the reason why O—— is German, and has always been German; although its inhabitants, or so it would seem from the songs and stories they offer the summer and winter visitors on every possible occasion, take comfort from the belief that Austria is at least their spiritual home. And so those holiday-makers who travel there in the hope of finding the attractions of two countries combined are not so far wrong. And there are those who go there because of the name, which is a homely, simple, gentle name, with none of the associations of, let us say, Berchtesgaden, a place in which one may also take one's ease, if one feels so inclined. O—— has never been famous; never has the spotlight of history touched it. It has not been one of those places that no one ever heard of until woken into painful memory, like Seoul, or Bikini, or, for that matter, this same Berchtesgaden, although that is quite close enough for discomfort.

Two holiday-makers who had chosen O—— out of the several hundred winter resorts that clamored for their patronage were standing in one of the upper streets on the evening of their arrival there. The charming little wooden houses weighted with snow, the delightful little streets so narrow and yet so dignified as to make the great glittering cars seem pretentious and out of place, the older inhabitants in their long dark woolen skirts and heavy clogs, even a sleigh drawn by ribboned horses and full of holiday-makers—all this was attractive, and undeniably what they had come for; particularly as slopes suitable for skiing stretched away on every side. Yet there was no denying that something weighed on them; they were uneasy. And what this thing was does not need to be guessed at, since they had not ceased to express it, and very volubly, since their arrival.

This was a pleasure resort; it existed solely for its visitors. In winter, heavy with snow, and ringing with the shouts of swooping skiers; in summer, garlanded with flowers and filled with the sounds of cowbells—it was all the same: summer and winter dress were nothing but masks concealing the fact that this village had no existence apart from its flux of visitors, which it fed and supplied by means of the single rickety little train that came up from the lowlands of Bavaria, and which in turn it drained of money spent freely on wooden shoes, carved and painted wooden bottles, ironwork, embroidered aprons, ski trousers and sweaters, and those slender curved skis themselves that enabled a thousand earth-plodders to wing over the slopes all through the snow months.

The fact is that for real pleasure a pleasure resort should have no one in it but its legitimate inhabitants, oneself, and perhaps one's friends. Everyone knows it, everyone feels it; and this is the insoluble contradiction of tourism; and perhaps the whole edifice will collapse at that moment when there is not one little town, not one village in the whole of Europe that has not been, as the term is, exploited. No longer will it be possible to drive one's car away into the mountains in search of that unspoiled village, that Old World inn by the stream; for when one arrives most certainly a professional host will hasten out, offering professional hospitality. What then? Will everyone stay at home?

But what of poor, war-denuded Europe, whose inhabitants continue to live, a little sullenly perhaps, under the summer and winter eyes of their visitors, eyes that presumably are searching for some quality, some good, that they do not possess themselves, since otherwise why have they traveled so far from themselves in order to examine the lives of other people?

These were the sorts of reflections—which, it must be confessed, could scarcely be more banal—that were being exchanged by our two travelers.

There they stood, outside a little wayside booth, or open shop, that sold not carved bottles or leather aprons but real vegetables and butter and cheese. These goods were being bought by a group of American wives who were stationed here with their husbands as part of the army of occupation. Or, rather, their husbands were part of the machinery which saw to it that American soldiers stationed all over the American zone of occupation could have pleasant holidays in the more attractive parts of Europe.

Between small, green-painted houses, the snow was pitted and rutted in the narrow street, glazed with the newly frozen heat of tramping feet. In places it was stained yellow and mounded with dark horse droppings, and there was a strong smell of urine mingling with the fresh tang of winter cabbage, giving rise to further reflections about the superiority of automobiles over horses—and even, perhaps, of wide streets over narrow ones, for at every moment the two travelers had to step down off the small pavement into the strong-smelling snow to allow happy groups of skiers to pass by; had to stand back again to make room for the cars that were trying to force a passage up to the big hotels where the American soldiers were holidaying with their wives or girls.

There were so many of the great powerful cars, rocking fast and dangerously up over the slippery snow, that it was hard to preserve the illusion of an unspoiled mountain village. And so the two lifted their eyes to the surrounding forests and peaks. The sun had slipped behind the mountains, but had left their snowfields tinted pink and gold, sentineled by pine groves which, now that the light had gone from them, loomed black and rather sinister, inevitably suggesting wolves, witches, and other creatures from a vanished time—a suggestion, however, tinged with bathos, since it was obvious that wolves or witches would have got short shrift from the mighty creators of those powerful machines. The tinted glitter of the smooth slopes and the black stillness of the woods did their best to set the village in a timelessness not disturbed by the gear and machinery of the traveling cages that lifted clear over intervening valleys to the ledge of a mountain where there was yet another hotel, and the amenities of civilization. And perhaps it was a relief, despite all the intrusions of the machinery of domesticity and comfort, to rest one's eyes on those forests, those mountains, whose savagery seemed so innocent. The year was 1951; and while the inhabitants of the village seemed almost feverishly concerned to present a scene of carefree charm, despite all their efforts the fact which must immediately strike everyone was that most of the people in the streets wore the uniform of the war which was six years past, and that the language most often overheard was American. But it was not possible to stand there, continually being edged this way and that on and off the pavement, with one's eyes fixed determinedly on natural beauty, particularly as the light was going fast and now the houses, shops, and hotels were taking their nocturnal shape and spilling the white pallor of electricity from every door and window, promising warmth, promising certain pleasure. The mountains had massed themselves, black against a luminous sky. Life had left them and was concentrating down in the village. Everywhere came groups of skiers hastening home for the night, and everywhere among them those men and women who proclaimed themselves immediately and at first glance as American. Why? Our two stood there, looking into first one face and then the next, trying to define what it was that set them apart. A good-looking lot, these policemen of Europe. And well-fed, well-dressed . . . They were distinguished above all, perhaps, by their assurance! Or was this noisy cheerfulness nothing more than the expression of an inner guilt because the task of policing and preserving order earned such attractive holidays? In which case, it was rather to their credit than not.

But when the four Army wives had finished their bargaining at the vegetable and dairy stall and went up the steep street, walking heavily because of their crammed baskets, they so dominated the scene in their well-cut trousers and their bright jackets that the women selling produce and the locals who had been waiting patiently for the four to conclude their shopping seemed almost unimportant, almost like willing extras in a crowd scene from a film called, perhaps, *Love in the Alps,* or *They Met in the Snow.*

And six years had been enough to still in the hearts of these Germans—for Germans they were, although Austria was no more than a giant's stone-throw away—all the bitterness of defeat? They were quite happy to provide a homely and picturesque background for whatever nationalities might choose to visit them, even if most were American, and many British—as our two conscientiously added, trying not to dissociate themselves from their responsibilities, even though they felt very strongly that the representatives of *their* country were much too naturally modest and tactful to appropriate a scene simply by the fact that they were in it.

It was hard to believe; and the knowledge of the secret angers, or at the very best an ironical patience, that must be burning in the breasts of their hosts, the good people of the village of O——, deepened an uneasiness which was almost (and this was certainly irrational) a guilt which should surely have no place in the emotions of a well-deserved vacation.

Guilt about what? It was absurd.

Yet, from the moment they had arrived on the frontier—the word still came naturally to them both—and had seen the signs in German; had heard the language spoken all around them; had passed through towns whose names were associated with the savage hate and terror of headlines a decade old—from that moment had begun in both the complicated uneasiness of which they were so ashamed. Neither had admitted it to the other; both were regretting they had come. Why—they were both thinking—why submit ourselves, when we are on vacation and won't be able to afford another one for goodness knows how long, to something that must be unpleasant? Why not say simply and be done with it that, for us, Germany is poisoned? We never want to set foot in it again or hear the language spoken or see a sign in German. We simply do not want to think about it; and if we are unjust and lacking in humanity and reason and good sense then—why not? One cannot be expected to be reasonable about everything.

Yet here they were.

The man remarked, after a long silence, "Last time I was here there was nothing of *that.*"

Down the other side of the street, pressed close to the wall to avoid a big car that was going by, came a group of five girls in local peasant costume. All day these girls had been serving behind the counters, or in the restaurants, wearing clothes such as girls anywhere in Europe might wear. Now their individual faces had dwindled behind great white starched headdresses. Their bodies were nothing more than supports for the long-sleeved, long-skirted, extinguishing black dresses. The whole costume had something reminiscent of the prim fantasy of the habits of certain orders of nuns. They were plodding resignedly enough—since, after all, they were being well paid for doing this—down over the snow towards one of the big hotels where they would regale the tourists with folk songs before slipping home to change into their own clothes in time to spend an hour or so with their young men.

"Well, never mind, I suppose one does like to see it?" The woman slipped her arm through his.

"Oh, I suppose so, why not?"

They began to walk down the street, leaning on each other because of the slipperiness of the rutted snow.

It hung in the balance whether one or other of them might have said something like: Suppose we all stopped coming? Suppose there were no tourists at all; perhaps they would simply cease to exist? Like actors who devote so much of themselves to acting they have no emotions left over for their own lives but continue to exist in whatever part they are playing. . . .

But neither of them spoke. They turned into the main street of the village, where there were several large hotels and restaurants.

Very easily one of them might have remarked to the other, with a kind of grumbling good humor: It's all very well, all these things we're saying about tourists, but we are tourists ourselves?

Come, come, the other would have replied. Clearly we are tourists on a much higher level than most!

Then they would have both laughed.

But at the same moment they stopped dead, looking at some queer hopping figure that was coming along the pavement over the badly lighted snow. For a moment it was impossible to make out what this great black jumping object could be that was coming fast towards them along the ground. Then they saw it was a man whose legs had been amputated and who was hopping over the snow like a frog, his body swinging and jerking between his heavy arms like the body of some kind of insect.

The two saw the eyes of this man stare up at them as he went hopping past.

At the station that day, when they arrived, two men hacked and amputated by war almost out of humanity, one without arms, his legs cut off at the knee; one whose face was a great scarred eyeless hollow, were begging from the alighting holiday-makers.

"For God's sake," said the man suddenly, as if this were nothing but a continuation of what they had been saying, "for God's sake, let's get out of here."

"Oh, *yes,*" she agreed instantly. They looked at each other, smiling, acknowledging in that smile all that they had not said that day.

"Let's go back. Let's find somewhere in France."

"We shouldn't have come."

They watched the cripple lever himself up over a deep doorstep, dragging his body up behind his arms, using the stump of his body as a support while he reached up with long arms to ring the bell.

"What about the money?" she asked.

"We'll go home when it runs out."

"Good, we'll go back tomorrow."

Instantly they felt gay; they were leaving tomorrow.

They walked along the street, looking at the menus outside the hotels. He said, "Let's go in here. It's expensive, but it's the last night."

It was a big, brown, solid-looking hotel called the Lion's Head; and on the old-fashioned gilded signboard was a great golden lion snarling down at them.

Inside was a foyer, lined with dark, shining wood; there were dark, straight-backed wooden settles around the walls and heavy arrangements of flowers in massive brass tubs. Glass doors opened into the restaurant proper. This was a long room lined with the same gleaming dark wood, and in each corner stood even larger brass tubs crammed with flowers. The tablecloths were heavy white damask; a profusion of cutlery and glass gleamed and glittered. It was a scene of solid middle-class comfort. A waiter showed them to an empty table at one side. The menu was placed between them. They exchanged a grimace, for the place was far too expensive for them, particularly as now they were committed to spending so much of their money on fares away and out of Germany into France—a country where they would feel no compulsion at all to make disparaging and ironical remarks about tourists or tourism.

They ordered their dinner and, while they waited, sat examining the other diners. The Americans were not here. Their hotels were the big, new, modern ones at the top of the village. The clientele here was solidly German. Again the two British tourists were conscious of a secret, half-ashamed unease. They looked from one face to another, thinking: Six years ago, what were you doing? And you—and you? We were mortal enemies then; now we sit in the same room, eating together. You were the defeated.

This last was addressed as a reminder to themselves, for no people could have looked less defeated than these. A more solid, sound, well-dressed, comfortable crowd could not be imagined; and they were eating with the easy satisfaction of those who cannot imagine ever being short of a meal. Yet six years ago . . .

The waiter brought two plates of soup, very big plates, monogrammed with the sign of the Lion's Head, so full that they asked him to take them away and divide one portion between the two of them. For they had observed that a single portion (served on large metal dishes) of any dish here was enough for two English stomachs. Not that they were not more than willing to do as well as these people around them—the defeated—whose capacity seemed truly incredible. But one day in this country of hearty eaters had not enlarged their stomachs to German capacity; and now that they were leaving, not later than tomorrow, it was too late.

They consumed their half-portions of very strong meat soup, full of vegetables; and pointed out to each other that, even so, their plates held twice as much as they would in England; and continued to dart curious, half-guilty glances at their fellow diners.

Six years ago these people were living amid ruins, in cellars, behind any scrap of masonry that remained standing. They were half starved, and their clothes were rags. An entire generation of young men were dead. Six years. A remarkable nation, surely.

The jugged hare came and was eaten with appreciation.

They had ordered pastries with cream; but alas, before they could eat them, they had to restore themselves with strong cups of coffee.

Back in France, they told themselves and each other, they would find themselves at home, at table as well as spiritually. By this time tomorrow, they would be in France. And now, with the last meal over and the bill to pay, came the moment of general reckoning, soon over, and in fact accomplished hastily on the back of an envelope.

To take a train, third-class, back to the nearest suitable spot in the French Alps would use up half of their available currency; and it would be a choice of staying out their full three weeks and eating one meal a day—and that a very slender meal—or staying a week and then going home.

They did not look at each other as they reached this final depressing conclusion. They were thinking, of course, that they were mad to leave at all. If to come to Germany was the result of some sort of spiritual quixotry, a symptom of moral philanthropy suitable only for liberal idealists whom—they were convinced—they both despised, then to leave again was simply weak-minded. In fact, their present low-spiritedness was probably due to being overtired, for they had spent two successive nights sitting up on hard wooden train seats, sleeping fitfully on each other's shoulders.

They would have to stay. And now that they reached this conclusion, depression settled on them both; and they looked at the rich Germans who surrounded them with a gloomy hatred which in their better moments they would have utterly repudiated.

Just then the waiter came forward, followed by an energetically striding young man apparently fresh from a day's skiing, for his face was flaming scarlet under untidy shags of sandy hair. They did not want him at their table, but the restaurant was now quite full. The waiter left their bill on the tablecloth; and they occupied themselves in finding the right change, under the interested inspection of the young sportsman, who, it seemed, was longing to advise them about money and tips. Resenting his interest, they set themselves to be patient. But the waiter did not return for some time, so busy was he at the surrounding tables; and they watched a party of new arrivals who were settling down at a nearby table that had been reserved for them. There came first a handsome woman in her early middle age, unfastening a shaggy, strong-looking fur coat of the kind worn for winter sports or bad weather outdoors. She flung this open on her chair, making a kind of nest, in which she placed herself, wrapping it closely around her legs. She was wearing a black wool dress, full-skirted and embroidered in bright colors, a dress which flirted with the idea of a peasant naïveté. Having arranged herself, she raised her face to greet the rest of her family with a smile that seemed to mock and chide them for taking so long to follow after her. It was a handsome face: she was a fine-looking woman, with her fair curling hair, and a skin bronzed deep with the sun and oil of many weeks of winter sport. Next came a young lad, obviously her son, a very tall, good-looking, attractive youth, who began teasing her because of her hurry to begin eating. He flashed his white strong teeth at her, and his young blue eyes, until she playfully took his arm and shook him. He protested. Then both, with looks of mock concern because this was a public place, desisted, lowered their voices, and sat laughing while the daughter, a delightfully pretty girl of fifteen or so, and the father, a heavy, good-humored gentleman, took the two empty chairs. The family party was complete. The waiter was attentive for their order, which was for four tall glasses of beer, which they insisted on having that moment, before they could order or even think of food. The waiter hurried off to fetch the beer, while they settled down to study the menus. And one could be sure that there would be no half-portions for this family, either for financial reasons or because they suffered from limitations of appetite.

Watching this family, it came home to the couple from Britain that what they were resenting was very likely their sheer capacity for physical enjoyment. Since, like all British people of their type, they spent a great deal of emotional energy on complaining about the inability of their countrymen to experience joy and well-being, they told themselves that what they felt was both churlish and inconsistent. The woman said to the man, in a conciliating, apologetic, almost resigned voice, "They really are extraordinarily good-looking."

To this he responded with a small ironical grimace; and he returned his attention to the family.

Mother, father, and son were laughing over some joke, while the girl turned a very long tapering glass of beer between thumb and forefinger of a thin, tanned hand so that the frost beads glittered and spun. She was staring out of the family group, momentarily lost to it, a fair, dreaming tendril of a girl with an irregular wedge of a little face. Her eyes wandered over the people at the tables, encountered those of our couple, and lingered in open, bland curiosity. It was a gaze of frank unselfconsciousness, almost innocence; the gaze of a protected child who knew she might commit no folly on her own individual account, since the family stood between her and the results of folly. Yet, just then, she chose to be out of the family group; or at least she gazed out of it as one looks through an open door. Her pale, pretty eyes absorbed what she wanted of the British couple, and, at their leisure, moved on to the other diners; and all the time her fingers moved slowly up and down the slim cold walls of her beer glass. The woman, finding in this girl a poetic quality totally lacking from the stolid burghers who filled this room, indicated her to the man by saying: "She's charming." Again he grimaced, as if to say: Every young girl is poetic. And: She'll be her mother in ten years.

Which was true. Already the family had become aware of the infidelity of this, their youngest member; already the handsome mother was leaning over her daughter, rallying her for her dreamy inattention, claiming her by little half-caressing, peremptory exclamations. The solid, kindly father laid his brown and capable hand on the girl's white-wool-covered forearm and bent towards her with solicitude, as if she were sick. The boy put a large forkful of meat into his mouth and ate it ruminantly, watching his sister with an irreverent grin. Then he said in a low tone some word that was clearly an old trumpet for disagreement between them, for she swung her chin towards him petulantly, with a half-reproachful and half-resentful epithet. The brother went on grinning, protective but derisive; the father and mother smiled tenderly at each other because of the brother-and-sister sparring.

No, clearly, this young girl had no chance of escaping from the warm prison of her family; and in a few years she would be a capable, handsome, sensual woman, married to some manufacturer carefully chosen for her by her father. That is, she would be unless another war or economic cataclysm intervened and plunged all her people into the edge-of-disaster hunger-bitten condition from which they had just emerged. Though they did not look as if they had. . . .

Returned full circle to the point of their complicated and irrational dislike, the man and woman raised ironical eyes at each other, and the man said briefly: "Blond beasts."

These two were of another family of mankind from most of the people in the restaurant.

The man was Scotch, small-built, nervous, energetic, with close-springing black hair, white freckled skin, quick, deep blue eyes. He tended to be sarcastic about the English, among whom, of course, he had spent most of his life. He was busy, hard-working, essentially pragmatic, practical, and humane. Yet above and beyond all these admirably useful qualities was something else, expressed in his characteristic little grimace of ironical bitterness, as if he were saying: Well, yes, and then?

As for her, she was small, dark, and watchful, Jewish in appearance and arguably by inheritance, since there had been a Jewish great-grandmother who had escaped from pogrom-loving Poland in the last century and married an Englishman. More potent than the great-grandmother was the fact that her fiancé, a medical student and refugee from Austria, had been killed in the early days of the war flying over this same country in which they now sat and took their holiday. Mary Parrish was one of those people who had become conscious of their claims to being Jewish only when Hitler drew their attention to the possibility they might have some.

She now sat and contemplated the handsome German family and thought: Ten years ago . . . She was seeing them as executioners.

As for the man, who had taken his name, Hamish, from a string of possible names, some of them English, because of another kind of national pride, he had served in his capacity as a doctor on one of the commissions that, after the war, had tried to rescue the debris of humanity the war had left all over Europe.

It was no accident that he had served on this commission. Early in 1939 he had married a German girl, or, rather, a Jewish girl, studying in Britain. In July of that year she had made a brave and foolhardy attempt to rescue some of her family who had so far escaped the concentration camps, and had never been heard of since. She had simply vanished. For all Hamish knew, she was still alive somewhere. She might very well be in this village of O——. Ever since yesterday morning when they entered Germany, Mary had been watching Hamish's anxious, angry, impatient eyes moving, preoccupied, from the face of one woman to another: old women, young women; women on buses, trains, platforms; women glimpsed at the end of a street; a woman at a window. And she could feel him thinking: Well, and if I did see her, I wouldn't recognize her.

And his eyes would move back to hers; she smiled; and he gave his small, bitter, ironical grimace.

They were both doctors, both hard-working and conscientious, both very tired because, after all, while living in Britain has many compensations, it is hard work, this business of maintaining a decent level of life with enough leisure for the pursuits that make life worthwhile, or at least to cultivated people, which they both were, and determined to remain. They were above all, perhaps, tired people.

They were tired and they needed to rest. This was their holiday. And here they sat, knowing full well that they were pouring away energies into utterly useless, irrelevant and, above all, unfair, emotions.

The word "unfair" was one they both used without irony.

She said, "I think one week in France would be better than three here. Let's go. I really do think we should."

He said, "Let's go into one of the smaller villages higher up the valley. They are probably just ordinary mountain villages, not tarted-up like this place."

"We'll go tomorrow," she agreed with relief.

Here they both became alert to the fact that the young man who had sat down at their table was watching them, at the same time as he heartily chewed a large mouthful of food, and looked for an inlet into their conversation. He was an unpleasant person. Tall, with an uncoordinated, bony look, his blue eyes met the possibilities of their reaction to him with a steady glare of watchful suspicion out of an ugly face whose skin had a peculiar harsh red texture. The eyes of our couple had been, unknown to them, returning again and again to this remarkable scarlet face, and at the back of their minds they had been thinking professionally: A fool to overheat himself in this strong reflected light up here.

Now, at the same moment, the two doctors realized that the surface of his face was a skin graft; that the whole highly colored, shiny, patchy surface, while an extraordinarily skillful reconstruction of a face, was nothing but a mask, and what the face had been before must be guessed at. They saw, too, that he was not a young man, but, like themselves, in early middle age. Instantly pity fought with their instinctive dislike of him; and they reminded themselves that the aggressive glare of the blue eyes was the expression of the pitiful necessity of a wounded creature to defend itself.

He said in stiff but good English, or, rather, American: "I must beg your pardon for interrupting your conversation, and beg leave to introduce myself—Doctor Schröder. I wish to place myself at your service. I know this valley well, and can recommend hotels in the other villages."

He was looking at Hamish, as he had from the time he began speaking, though he gave a small, minimal bow when Mary Parrish introduced herself, and instantly returned his attention to the man.

Both the British couple felt discomfort; but it was hard to say whether this was because of the man's claim on their pity, because of their professional interest in him, which they must disguise, or because of the impolite insistence of his manner.

"That is very kind of you," said Hamish; and Mary murmured that it was very kind. They wondered whether he had heard his "blond beasts." They wondered what other indiscretions they might have committed.

"As it happens," said Doctor Schröder, "I have a very good buddy who runs a guesthouse at the top of the valley. I was up there this morning, and she has a dandy room to let."

Once again they indicated that it was very kind of him.

"If it is not too early for you, I shall be taking the nine-thirty autobus up the valley tomorrow for a day's skiing, and I shall be happy to assist you."

And now it was necessary to take a stand one way or the other. Mary and Hamish glanced at each other inquiringly; and immediately Doctor Schröder said, with a perceptible increase of tension in his manner, "As you know, at this time in the season, it is hard to find accommodation." He paused, seemed to assure himself of their status by a swift inspection of their clothes and general style, and added: "Unless you can afford one of the big hotels—but they are not of the cheapest."

"Actually," said Mary, trying to make of what he must have heard her say before a simple question of caprice, "actually we were wondering whether we might not go back to France? We are both very fond of France."

But Doctor Schröder was not prepared to take this from them. "If it is a question of skiing, then the weather report announced today that the snow is not as good in the French Alps as it is with us. And, of course, France is much more expensive."

They agreed that this was so; and he continued to say that if they took the empty room at his buddy's guest house it would cost them much less than it would at a German pension, let alone a French pension. He examined their clothes again and remarked, "Of course, it must be hard for you to have such unfortunate restrictions with your travel allowance. Yes, it must be annoying. For people of a good salary and position it must be annoying."

For both these two the restrictions of the travel allowance merely confirmed a fact: they could not have afforded more than the allowance in any case. They realized that Doctor Schröder was quite unable to decide whether they were rich and eccentric English people who notoriously prefer old clothes to new clothes, or whether they were rich people deliberately trying to appear poor, or whether they were poor. In the first two cases they would perhaps be eager to do some trade in currency with him? Was that what he wanted?

It seemed it was; for he immediately said that he would be very happy to lend them a modest sum of dough, in return for which he would be glad if they would do the same for him when he visited

London, which he intended to do very soon. He fastened the steady glare of his eyes on their faces—or, rather, on Hamish's face—and said: "Of course, I am prepared to offer every guarantee." And he proceeded to do so. He was a doctor attached to a certain hospital in the town of S—— and his salary was regular. If they wished to make independent inquiries they were welcome to do so.

And now Hamish intervened to make it clear that they could not afford to spend on this vacation one penny more than the travel allowance. For a long moment Doctor Schröder did not believe him. Then he examined their clothes again and openly nodded.

Now, perhaps, the man would go away?

Not at all. He proceeded to deliver a harangue on the subject of his admiration for Britain. His love for the entire British nation, their customs, their good taste, their sportsmanship, their love of fair play; their history, and their art were the ruling passions of his life. He went on like this for some minutes, while the British couple wondered if they ought to confess that their trade was the same as his. But, if they did, presumably it would let them in for even closer intimacy. And by a hundred of the minute signs which suffice for communication between people who knew each other well, they had said that they disliked this man intensely and wished only that he would go away.

But now Doctor Schröder inquired outright what profession his new friend Mr. Anderson pursued; and when he heard that they were both doctors, and attached to hospitals whose names he knew, his expression changed. But subtly. It was not surprise, but rather the look of a prosecutor who has been cross-examining witnesses and at last got what he wants.

And the British couple were beginning to understand what it was Doctor Schröder wanted of them. He was talking with a stiff, brooding passion of resentment about his position and prospects as a doctor in Germany. For professional people, he said, Germany was an unkind country. For the business people—yes. For the artisans—yes. The workers were all millionaires these days, yes sir! Better far to be a plumber or an electrician than a doctor. The ruling dream of his life was to make his way to Britain, and there become an honored and—be it understood—a well-paid member of his profession.

Here Doctors Anderson and Parrish pointed out that foreign doctors were not permitted to practice in Britain. They might lecture; they might study; but they might not practice. Not unless, added Doctor Parrish, possibly reacting to the fact that not once had this man done more than offer her the barest minimum of politeness until he had recognized that she, as well as Hamish, was a doctor and therefore possibly of use to him—not unless they were refugees, and even then they must take the British examinations.

Doctor Schröder did not react to the word "refugee."

He returned to a close cross-examination about their salaries and prospects, dealing first with Mary's, and then, in more detail, with Hamish's. At last, in response to their warning that for him to become a doctor in Britain would be much more difficult than he seemed to think, he replied that in this world everything was a question of pulling strings. In short, he intended they should pull strings for him. It was the most fortunate occurrence of his life that he had happened to meet them that evening, the happiest and the best-timed. . . .

At this, the eyes of the British couple met on a certain suspicion. Ten minutes later in the talk it emerged that he knew the lady who ran the house where they had taken a room, and therefore he probably had heard from her that she had a British doctor as a lodger. Very likely he had arranged with the waiter to be put at their table. For he must know the people of the village well: he had been coming for his winter holidays to O—— since he was a small child—Doctor Schröder held out his hand below table level to show how small. Yes, all those years of winters O—— had known Doctor Schröder, save for the years of war, when he was away serving his country.

There was a small stir in the restaurant. The family were rising, gathering their wraps, and departing. The lady first, her shaggy brown coat slung over her handsome shoulders, her rosy lower lip caught by her white teeth as she searched for her belongings she might have forgotten. Then she extended her smile, so white against the clear brown skin, and waited for her son to take her by the shoulder and propel her, while she laughed, protesting, to the door. There, when it opened, she shivered playfully, although it was only the door to the vestibule. Behind her came the pretty, rather languid girl; then the stout authoritative father, shepherding his family away and out to the snow-cold air. The family vanished, leaving their table a mess of empty glasses, plates, broken bread, cheeses, fruit, wine. The waiter cleared the table with a look as if he found it a privilege.

The British couple also rose and said to Doctor Schröder that they would think over his suggestion and perhaps let him know in the morning. His thin-skinned shiny face tilted up at them, and leveled into an affronted mask as he stood up and said, "But I understood all arrangements were made."

And how had they got themselves into this position, where they could not exercise simple freedom of choice without upsetting this extremely dislikable person? But they knew how. It was because he was a wounded man, a cripple; because they knew that his fixed aggression was part of his laudable determination not to let that shockingly raw face drive him into self-pity and isolation. They were doctors, and they were reacting above all to the personality of a cripple. When they said that they were tired and intended to go to bed early, and he replied instantly, insulted, that he would be happy to accompany them to a certain very pleasant place of entertainment, they knew that they could bring themselves to do no more than say they could not afford it.

They knew he would immediately offer to be their host. He did, and they politely refused as they would refuse an ordinary acquaintance, and were answered by the man who could tolerate no refusal, because if he once accepted a refusal, he would be admitting to himself that his face put him outside simple human intercourse.

Doctor Schröder, who had spent all the winter holidays of his life in this valley, naturally knew the proprietor of the hotel where he proposed to take them; and he guaranteed them a pleasant and relaxing evening while he fixed on them a glare of suspicious hate.

They walked together under the snow-weighted eaves of the houses, over snow rutted by the hundred enormous American cars which had rocked over it that day, to the end of the street where there was a hotel whose exterior they had already inspected earlier that day and rejected on the grounds that anything inside it must necessarily be too expensive for them. Immediately outside, on the seared snow, sat the man without legs they had seen earlier. Or rather he stood, his head level with their hips, looking as if he were buried to hip-level in the snow, holding out a cloth cap to them. His eyes had the same bold, watchful glare as those of Doctor Schröder.

Doctor Schröder said, "It's a disgrace that these people should be allowed to behave like this. It makes a bad impression on our visitors." And he led the British couple past the cripple with a look of angry irritation.

Inside was a long room sheltered by glass on two sides from the snow which could be seen spinning down through the areas of yellow light conquered from the black mass of the darkness by the room and its warmth and its noise and its people. It was extraordinarily pleasant to enter this big room, so busy with pleasure, and to see the snow made visible only during its passage through the beams from the big windows, as if the wildness of the mountain valley had been admitted just so far as would give the delight of contrast to the guests who could see savagery as a backdrop of pretty, spinning white flakes.

There was a small band, consisting of piano, clarinet, and drum, playing the kind of jazz that makes a pleasant throb, like a blood-beat, behind conversation.

The family had moved themselves from the table in the restaurant to a table here and sat as before in a close group. The British couple found an empty table near them, which Doctor Schröder approved; and when the waiter came knew they had been right—the drinks were very expensive and this was not a place where one might lightly sip one drink for a whole evening while richer people drank seriously. One was expected to drink; people were drinking, although a small beer cost nearly ten shillings. They saw, too, that Doctor Schröder's boast that he had special privileges here because he was a friend of the proprietor was untrue. His passport here, as everywhere else, was his raw, shiny face. When the proprietor glanced towards him during his hospitable passage among the tables, he did so with a nod and a smile, but it was a smile that had the overkindness of controlled hostility. And his eyes lingered briefly on the British couple, who, after this inspection, were forced to feel that everyone else in this place was German. The Americans were in their own rich hotels; the impoverished British in the cheap guest-houses; this place was for wealthy Germans. And the British couple wondered at the insistence of Doctor Schröder in bringing them here. Was it possible that he really believed he had a special place in the heart of the proprietor? Yes, it was; he kept smiling and nodding after the turned back of the fat host, as if to say: You see, he knows me; then smiling at them, proud of his achievement. For which he was prepared to pay heavily in actual money. He counted out the price of the drinks with the waiter with a painful care for the small change of currency that they understood very well. What recompense could they possibly give this man; what was he wanting so badly? Was it really only that he wanted to live and work in Britain?

Again Doctor Schröder began to talk, and again of his admiration for their country, leaning across the table, looking into their faces, as if this was a message of incalculable importance to them both.

He was interrupted by the clarinet player who stood up, took a note from the regular ground-throb of the music, and began to develop a theme of his own from it. Couples went on to a small area of shiny floor not occupied by tables, and which was invaded at every moment by the hurrying waiters with their trays of drinks. They were dancing, these people, for the pleasure not of movement, but of contact. A dozen or a score of men and women, seemingly held upright by the pressure of the seated guests around them, idled together, loosely linked, smiling, skeptical, good-natured with the practice of pleasure.

Immediately the dancing was broken up because the group of folk singers had come in at the big glass entrance door, in their demure conventual dress, and now stood by the band waiting.

The woman at the next table gave a large cheerful shrug and said, "This is the fifth time. This is my fifth home-evening." People turned to smile at the words *"heimat-abend,"* indulgent with the handsome woman and her look of spoiled enjoyment. Already one of the folk singers was moving among the tables to collect their fee, which was high; and already the rich Papa was thrusting towards the girl a heap of money, disdaining the change with a shake of his head—change, however, which she did not seem in any urgency to give him. When she reached the table where our couple sat with Doctor Schröder, Hamish paid, and not with good grace. After all, the prices were high enough here without having to pay more for folk songs which one did not necessarily want to listen to at all.

When the girl made her rounds and collected her money, she rejoined the group, which formed itself together near the band and sang, one after another, songs of the valley, in which yodeling figured often and loudly, earning loud applause.

It was clear that Doctor Schröder, who listened to the group with a look of almost yearning nostalgia, did not feel its intrusion as an irritant at all. Folk songs, his expression said, were something he could listen to all night. He clapped often and glanced at his guests, urging them to share his sentimental enjoyment.

At last the group left; the clarinet summoned the dancers to the tiny floor; and Doctor Schröder resumed his hymn of love for Britain. Tragic, he said, having stated and restated the theme of praise—tragic that these two countries had ever had to fight at all. Tragic that natural friends should have been divided by the machinations of interested and sinister groups. The British couple's eyes met ironically over the unspoken phrase "international Jewry," and even with the consciousness of being pedantic, if not unfair. But Doctor Schröder did not believe in the unstated. He said that international Jewry had divided the two natural masters of Europe, Germany and Britain; and it was his passionate belief that in the future these two countries should work together for the good of Europe and thus, obviously, of the whole world. Doctor Schröder had had good friends, friends who were almost brothers, killed on the fronts where British and German troops had been maneuvered into hostility; and he grieved over them even now as one does for sacrificed victims.

Doctor Schröder paused, fixed them with the glare of his eyes, and said: "I wish to tell you that I, too, was wounded: perhaps you have not noticed. I was wounded on the Russian front. My life was despaired of.

But I was saved by the skill of our doctors. My entire face is a witness to the magnificent skill of our German doctors."

The British couple hastened to express their surprise and congratulations. Oddly enough, they felt a lessened obligation towards compassion because of Doctor Schröder's grotesque and touching belief that his face was nearly normal enough to be unnoticed. He said that the surface of his face had burned off when a tank beside him had exploded into pieces, showering him with oil. He had fought for three years with the glorious armies of his country all over the Ukraine. He spoke like a survivor from the Grande Armée to fellow admirers of "The Other," inviting and expecting interested congratulation. "Those Russians," he said, "are savages. Barbarians. No one would believe the atrocities they committed. Unless you had seen it with your own eyes, you would not believe the brutality the Russians are capable of."

The British couple, now depressed into silence, and even past the point where they could allow their eyes to meet in ironical support of each other, sat watching the languidly revolving dancers.

Doctor Schröder said insistently, "Do you know that those Russians would shoot at our soldiers as they walked through the streets of a village? An ordinary Russian peasant, if he got the chance, would slaughter one of our soldiers? And even the women—I can tell you cases of Russian women murdering our soldiers after pretending to be buddies with them."

Mary and Hamish kept their peace and wondered how Doctor Schröder had described to himself the mass executions, the hangings, the atrocities of the German Army in Russia. They did not wonder long, for he said, "We were forced to defend ourselves. Yes, I can tell you that we had to defend ourselves against the savagery of those people. The Russians are monsters."

Mary Parrish roused herself to say, "Not such monsters, perhaps, as the Jews?" And she tried to catch and hold the fanatic eyes of their host with her own. He said, "Ah, yes, we had many enemies." His eyes, moving fast from Hamish's face to Mary's, paused and wavered. It occurred to him perhaps that they were not entirely in accordance with him. For a second his ugly, blistered mouth twisted in what might have been doubt. He said politely, "Of course, our Führer went too far in his zeal against our enemies. But he understood the needs of our country."

"It is the fate of great men," said Hamish, in the quick sarcastic voice that was the nearest he ever got to expressed anger, "to be misunderstood by the small-minded."

Doctor Schröder was now unmistakably in doubt. He was silent, examining their faces with his eyes, into which all the expression of his scarred face was concentrated, while they suffered the inner diminishment and confusion that happen when the assumptions on which one bases one's life are attacked. They were thinking dubiously that this was the voice of madness. They were thinking that they knew no one in Britain who would describe it as anything else. They were thinking that they were both essentially, self-consciously, of that element in their nation dedicated to not being insular, to not falling into the errors of complacency; and they were, at this moment, feeling something of the despair that people like them had felt ten, fifteen years ago, watching the tides of madness rise while the reasonable and the decent averted their eyes. At the same time, they were feeling an extraordinary but undeniable reluctance to face the fact that Doctor Schröder might represent any more than himself. No, they were assuring themselves, this unfortunate man is simply a cripple, scarred mentally as well as physically, a bit of salvage from the last war.

At this moment the music again stopped, and there was an irregular clapping all over the room; clearly there was to be a turn that the people there knew and expected.

Standing beside the piano was a small, smiling man who nodded greetings to the guests. He was dark, quick-eyed, with an agreeable face that the British couple instinctively described as "civilized." He nodded to the pianist, who began to improvise an accompaniment to his act; he was half-singing, half-talking the verse of a song or ballad about a certain general whose name the British couple did not recognize. The accompaniment was a steady, military-sounding thump-thump against which the right hand wove fragments of "Deutschland Uber Alles" and the Horst Wessel song. The refrain was: "And now he sits in Bonn."

The next verse was about an admiral, also now sitting in Bonn.

The British couple understood that the song consisted of the histories of a dozen loyal German militarists who had been overzealous in their devotion to their Führer; had been sentenced by the Allied courts of justice to various terms of imprisonment, or to death; "and now they sat in Bonn."

All that was fair enough. It sounded like a satire on Allied policy in Germany, which—so both these conscientious people knew and deplored—tended to be overgenerous to the ex-murderers of the Nazi regime. What could be more heartening than to find their own view expressed there, in this comfortable resort of the German rich? And what more surprising?

They looked at Doctor Schröder and saw his eyes gleaming with pleasure. They looked back at the urbane, ironical little singer, who was performing with the assurance of one who knows himself to be perfectly at one with his audience, and understood that this was the type of ballad adroitly evolved to meet the needs of an occupied people forced to express themselves under the noses of a conqueror. True that the American Army was not here, in this room, this evening; but even if they had been, what possible exception could they have taken to the words of this song?

It was a long ballad, and when it was ended there was very little applause. Singer and audience exchanged with each other smiles of discreet understanding, and the little man bowed this way and that. He then straightened himself, looked at the British couple, and bowed to them. It was as if the room caught its breath. Only when they looked at Doctor Schröder's face, which showed all the malicious delight of a child who had thumbed his nose behind teacher's back, did they understand what a demonstration of angry defiance that bow had been. And they understood, with a sinking of the heart, the depths of furious revengeful humiliation which made such a very slight gesture so extremely satisfying to these rich burgesses, who merely glanced discreetly, smiling lightly, at these conquerors in their midst—conquerors who were so much shabbier than they were, so much more worn and tired—and turned away, exchanging glances of satisfaction, to their batteries of gleaming glasses filled with wine and with beer.

And now Mary and Hamish felt that this demonstration, which presumably Doctor Schröder had shared in, perhaps even invited, released them from any obligation to him; and they looked at him with open dislike, indicating that they wished to leave.

Besides, the waiter stood beside them, showing an open insolence that was being observed and admired by the handsome matron and her husband and her son; the girl was, as usual, dreaming some dream of her own and not looking at anyone in particular. The waiter bent over them, put his hands on their still half-filled glasses, and asked what they would have.

Hamish and Mary promptly drank what remained of their beer and rose. Doctor Schröder rose with them. His whole knobby, ugly body showed agitation and concern. Surely they weren't going? Surely, when the evening was just beginning, and very soon they would have the privilege of hearing again the talented singer who had just retired, but only for a short interval. Did they realize that he was a famous artist from M——, a man who nightly sang to crammed audiences, who was engaged by the management of this hotel, alas, only for two short weeks of the winter season?

This was either the most accomplished insolence or another manifestation of Doctor Schröder's craziness. For a moment the British couple wondered if they had made a mistake and had misunderstood the singer's meaning. But one glance around the faces of the people at the near tables was enough: each face expressed a discreetly hidden smile of satisfaction at the rout of the enemy—routed by the singer, and by the waiter, their willing servant who was nevertheless at this moment exchanging democratic grins of pleasure with the handsome matron.

Doctor Schröder was mad, and that was all there was to it. He both delighted in the little demonstration of hostility and, in some involved way of his own, wanted them to delight in it—probably out of brotherly love for him. And now he was quite genuinely agitated and hurt because they were going.

The British couple went out, past the smiling band, past the conscious waiter, while Doctor Schröder followed. They went down the iced steps of the hotel and stopped by the legless man, who was still rooted in the snow like a plant, where Hamish gave him all the change he had, which amounted to the price of another round of drinks had they stayed in the big warm room.

Doctor Schröder watched this and said at once, with indignant reproach, "You should not do this. It is not expected. Such people should be locked away." All his suspicion had returned; they must, obviously, be rich, and they had been lying to him.

Mary and Hamish went without speaking down the snow-soft street, through a faint fall of white snow; and Doctor Schröder came striding behind them, breathing heavily. When they reached the door of the little house where they had a room, he ran around them and stood facing them, saying hurriedly, "And so I shall see you tomorrow at the autobus, nine-thirty."

"We will get in touch with you," said Hamish politely, which, since they did not know his address, and had not asked for it, was as good as dismissing him.

Doctor Schröder leaned toward them, examining their faces with his gleaming, suspicious eyes. He said, "I will attend you in the morning," and left them.

They let themselves in and ascended the shallow wooden stairs to their room in silence. The room was low and comfortable, gleaming with well-polished wood. There was an old-fashioned rose-patterned jug and basin on the washstand and an enormous bed laden with thick eiderdowns. A great, shining, blue-tiled stove filled half a wall. Their landlady had left a note pinned to one of the fat pillows, demanding politely that they should leave, in their turn, a note for her outside their door, saying at what hour they wished to receive their breakfast tray.

She was the widow of the pastor. She now lived by letting this room to the summer and winter visitors. She knew this couple were not married because she had had, by regulation, to take down particulars from their passports. She had said nothing of any disapproval she might have felt. The gods of the tourist trade must not be offended by any personal prejudice she might hold; and she must have prejudices, surely, as the widow of a man of God, even against a couple so obviously respectable as this one?

Mary said, "I wish she'd turn us out in a fit of moral indignation. I wish someone would have a fit of moral indignation about something, instead of everything simmering and festering in the background."

To which he replied, with the calm of a practical man, "We will get up extremely early and leave this valley before our friend Doctor Fascist can see us. I don't think I could bear to exchange even one more word with him." He wrote a short note to the widow of the pastor, demanding breakfast for seven o'clock; left it outside the door; and, thus well-organized, invited Mary to come to bed and stop worrying.

They got into bed and lay side by side. This was not a night when their arms could hold any comfort for each other. This was a night when they were not a couple, they were two people. Their dead were in the room with them—if Lise, his wife, could be called dead. For how were they to know? War above all breeds a knowledge of the fantastic, and neither of them heard one of the extraordinary and impossible stories of escape, coincidence, and survival without thinking: Perhaps Lise is alive somewhere after all. And the possible aliveness of Hamish's dead wife had kept alive the image of the very young medical student who, being a medical student, had no right to risk himself in the air at all; but who had in fact taken wing out of his furious misery and anger because of the Nazis and had crashed in flames a year later. These two, the pretty and vivacious Lise and the gallant and crusading airman, stood by the enormous, eiderdown-weighted bed and said softly: You must include us, you must include us.

And so it was a long time before Mary and Hamish slept.

Both awoke again in the night, aware of the snow-sheen on the windowpanes, listening to the soft noises of the big porcelain stove which sounded as if there were a contented animal breathing beside them in the room. Now they thought that they were leaving this valley because, out of some weakness of character apparently inherent in both of them, they had put themselves in a position where, if they took a room higher up the valley, it would have to be a room chosen for them by Doctor Schröder, since they could not bring themselves to be finally rude to him because of that scarred face of his.

No, they preferred to conclude that Doctor Schröder summed up in his personality and being everything they hated in this country, Germany, the great catalyst and mirror of Europe: summed it up and presented it to them direct and unambiguously, in such a way that they must reject or accept it.

Yet how could they do either? For to meet Doctor Schröder at all made it inevitable that these two serious and conscience-driven people must lie awake and think: One nation is not very different from another. . . . (For if one did not take one's stand on this proposition where did one end?) And therefore it followed that they must think: What in Britain corresponds to Doctor Schröder? What unpleasant forces are this moment simmering in the sewers of our national soul that might explode suddenly into shapes like Doctor Schröder? Well, then? And what deplorable depths of complacency there must be in us both that we should feel so superior to Doctor Schröder—that we should wish only that he might be pushed out of sight somewhere, like a corpse in a house full of living people; or masked like a bad smell; or exorcised like an evil spirit?

Were they or were they not on vacation? They were; and therefore exempt by definition from lying awake and thinking about the last war; lying awake and worrying about the possible next war; lying awake and wondering what perverse masochism had brought them here at all.

At the dead and silent hour of four, when not a light glimmered anywhere in the village, they were both awake, lying side by side in the great feather-padded bed, discussing Doctor Schröder in depth. They analyzed him politically, psychologically, and medically—particularly medically—and at such length that when the maid came in with their early breakfast they were extremely reluctant to wake up. But they forced themselves to wake, to eat and to dress, and then went downstairs where their landlady was drinking coffee in her kitchen. They put their problem to her. Yesterday they had agreed to stay with her for a week. Today they wanted to leave. Since it was the height of the season, presumably she would let her room today? If not, of course, they would be delighted to pay what they were morally bound to do.

Frau Stohr dismissed the subject of payment as irrelevant. At this time of the year her bell rang a dozen times a day with inquiries for rooms by people who had arrived at the station and hoped, usually overoptimistically, to find empty rooms in the village. Frau Stohr was upset that her two guests wished to leave. They were not comfortable? They were badly served?

They hastened to assure her that the place was everything they wanted. At the moment they felt it was. Frau Stohr was the most pleasant sight in an early morning after a night of conscience-searching. She was a thin and elderly lady, her white hair drawn back into a tight knot which was stuck through with stiff utilitarian pins almost the size of knitting needles. Her face was severe, but tranquil and kindly. She wore a long, full, black woolen skirt, presumably a practical descendant of the great woolen skirts of the local peasant costume. She wore a long-sleeved striped woolen blouse fastened high at the throat with a gold brooch.

They found it very hard to say that they wanted to leave the valley the day after arriving in it. The rectitude of this admirable old lady made it difficult. So they said they had decided to take a room farther up the valley where the snow slopes organized for skiing would be closer to the villages. For, above all, they did not want to hurt Frau Stohr's national feelings; they intended to slip quietly down to the station and take the first train away from the place, away and out of Germany into France.

Frau Stohr instantly agreed. She had always thought it more suitable for the serious skiers to find homes farther up the valley. But there were people who came to the winter sports not for the sport, but for the atmosphere of the sport. As for herself, she never tired of seeing the young people at their tricks on the snow. Of course, when she had been a girl, it was not a question of tricks at all; skis were simply a means of getting from one place to another quickly . . . but now, of course, all that had changed, and someone like herself who had been almost born on skis, like all the children of the valley, would find it embarrassing to stand on skis again with nothing to show in the way of jumps and turns. Of course, at her age she seldom left the house, and so she did not have to expose her deficiencies. But her two guests, being serious skiers, must be feeling frustrated, knowing that all the long runs and the big ski lifts were at the head of the valley. Luckily she knew of a lady in the last village of the valley who had a free room and would be just the person to look after them.

Here she mentioned the name of the lady recommended by Doctor Schröder the night before, and it was extraordinary how this name, yesterday associated with every kind of unpleasantness, became attractive and reassuring, simply because it came from the lips of Frau Stohr.

Mary and Hamish exchanged looks and came to a decision without speaking. In the sober light of early morning, all the very sound arguments against leaving the valley returned to them. And after all, Doctor Schröder was staying in O—— itself, and not in the village thirty miles up the valley. At worst he might come and visit them.

Frau Stohr offered to telephone Frau Länge, who was a good woman and an unfortunate one. Her husband had been killed in the last war.

Here Frau Stohr smiled at them with the gentle tolerance of the civilized who take it for granted that war between nations need not destroy their common humanity and understanding. Yes, yes, as long as men were so stupid there would be wars and, afterwards, widows like poor Frau Länge, who had lost not only her husband but her two sons, and now lived alone with her daughter, taking in lodgers.

Frau Stohr and the British couple, united on the decent common ground of the international humanitarian conscience, smiled at each other, thinking compassionately of Frau Länge. Then Frau Stohr went to the telephone and engaged the room on behalf of her two guests, for whom she was prepared to vouch personally. Then they settled the bill, thanked each other, and separated—Mary and Hamish with their cases in their hands and their skis over their shoulders towards the bus stop, and Frau Stohr to her knitting and her cup of coffee in her big heated kitchen.

It was a clear morning, the sun sparkling pinkly over the slopes of snow where the pine trees stood up, stiff and dark. The first bus of the day was just leaving, and they found places in it. They sat behind two small, pigtailed blond girls who saw nobody else in the bus, but held each other's hands and sang one folk song after another in small, clear voices. Everyone in the bus turned to smile with affectionate indulgence at them. The bus climbed slowly up and up, along the side of the snow-filled valleys; and as the skiing villages came into sight, one after another, the bus stopped, shedding some passengers and taking on others, but always full; up and up while the two small girls sang, holding hands, looking earnestly into each other's faces, so as to be sure they were keeping time, and never once repeating a song.

The British couple thought it unlikely that they could find, in their own country, two small girls who could sing, without repeating themselves, for two solid hours of a bus journey, even if their British stiff-lippedness would allow them to open their mouths in public in the first place. These two singing children comforted Mary and Hamish quite remarkably. This was the real Germany—rather old-fashioned, a bit sentimental, warm, simple, kindly. Doctor Schröder and what he stood for was an unlucky and not very important phenomenon. Everything they had felt yesterday was the result of being overtired. Now they examined the pleasant villages through which they passed with anticipation, hoping that the one they were committed to would be equally as full of modest wooden chalets and apparently inexpensive restaurants.

It was. At the very head of the valley where the mountain barrier beyond which lay Innsbruck rose tall and impregnable, there was a small village, as charming as all the others. Here, somewhere, was the house of Frau Länge. They made inquiries at a hotel and were directed. A path ran off from the village uphill among the pine woods to a small house about a mile away. The isolation of this house appealed naturally to the instincts of the British couple, who trudged towards it over cushions of glittering snow, feeling grateful to Frau Stohr. The path was narrow, and they had constantly to stand aside while skiers in bright clothes whizzed past them, laughing and waving. The proficiency of the sun-bronzed gods and goddesses of the snowfields discouraged Mary and Hamish, and perhaps half the attraction of that isolated house was that they could make their tame flights over the snow in comparative privacy.

The house was square, small, wooden; built on a low mound of snow in a space surrounded by pine woods. Frau Länge was waiting for them at her front door, smiling. For some reason they had imagined her in the image of Frau Stohr; but she was a good twenty years younger, a robust, straw-headed, red-cheeked woman wearing a tight scarlet sweater and a tight, bright blue skirt. Behind her was a girl, obviously her daughter, a healthy, brown, flaxen-haired girl. Both women occupied themselves with a frank and intensive examination of their new guests for the space of time it took them to cross the snow to the house. The room they were given was at the front of the house, looking away from the village up into a side valley. It was a room like the one they had occupied for the one night at Frau Stohr's: low, large, gleaming with waxed wood, and warmed by an enormous tiled stove. Frau Länge took their passports to write down their particulars, and when she returned them it was with a change of manner which made Mary Parrish and Hamish Anderson know they had been accepted into a freemasonry with their hostess. She said, while her frankly vulgar blue eyes continued a minute examination of them and their belongings, that her dear aunt Frau Stohr, who was not really her aunt, just a second cousin, called Aunt out of respect for her age and position as widow of the pastor, had spoken for them; that she had every confidence in any person recommended from that quarter. And she had heard, too, from dear Doctor Schröder, who was an old friend, a friend of many years, ah—what a brave man. Did they notice his face? Yes, truly? Did they know that for two years he had lain in hospital while a new face was molded for him and covered with skin taken from his thighs? Poor man. Yes, it was the barbarity of those Russians that was responsible for Doctor Schröder's face. Here she gave an exaggerated sigh and a shrug and left them.

They reminded themselves that they had hardly slept for three nights of their precious holiday, and this doubtless accounted for their present lack of enthusiasm for the idea of putting on skis. They went to sleep and slept the day through; that evening they were served a heavy meal in the living room by Frau Länge herself, who stood chatting to them until they asked her to sit down. Which she did, and proceeded to cross-examine them about the affairs of the British royal family. It was impossible to exaggerate the degree of enthusiasm aroused in Frau Länge by the royal family. She followed every move made by any member of it through a dozen illustrated papers. She knew what they all ate, how they liked things cooked, and how served. She knew the type of corset favored by the Queen, the names of the doctors attending her, the methods of upbringing planned for the royal children, the favorite colors of the two royal Elizabeths and the royal Margaret.

The British couple, who were by temperament republicans and who would have described themselves as such had the word not, at that time, been rather *vieux jeu,* acquired an impressive amount of information about "their" royal family, and felt inadequate, for they were unable to answer any of her questions.

To escape from Frau Länge they went back to their room. They discovered that this house was not at all as isolated as it had seemed during the day when the pine trees had concealed from them buildings farther up the little side valley. Lights sparkled in the trees, and it seemed that there were at least two large hotels less than half a mile away. Music streamed towards them across the dark snow.

In the morning they found there were two American hotels; that is, hotels specifically for the recreation of American troops. Frau Länge used the word "American" with a mixture of admiration and hatred. And she took it for granted that they, who were after all partners with the Americans (and the Russians, of course) in this business of policing the defeated country, should share this emotion with her. It was because they shared with her, Frau Länge, the quality of not being rich.

"Ah," she said, with a false and hearty shrug of her shoulders, a false humility in her voice, "it is a terrible thing, the way they come here and behave as if they owned our country." And she stood at the window, while the British couple ate their breakfast, watching the American soldiers and their wives and their girlfriends swooping past down the slopes; and on her face was a bitter envy, an admiring spite, as if she were thinking: Yes? Then wait and see!

Later that day they saw the daughter standing displayed on her doorstep in well-cut ski trousers and sweater, like a girl in a poster, looking at the American soldiers. And they heard her call out, every time a single man went past: "Yank-ee." The soldier would look up and wave, and she waved back shouting: "I love you, Buddy." At last one came over; and the two went off on skis, down to the village.

Frau Länge, who had seen them watching, said, "Ach, these young girls, I was one myself." She waited until they smiled their tolerant complicity—and waited in such a way they felt they could do no less, seeing that their passports proved they had no right to different standards; and said, "Yes, when one is young one is foolish. I remember how I fell in love with every man I saw. Ach, yes, it was so. I was living in Munich when I was a girl. Yes, youth has no discrimination. I was in love with our Führer, yes, it is true. And before that in love with a Communist leader who lived in our street. And now I tell my Lili it is lucky that she falls in love with the American Army, because she is in love with democracy." Frau Länge giggled and sighed.

At all the heavy meals she served them—sausage and sauerkraut and potatoes; sauerkraut, potatoes, and beef stew—she stood by them, talking, or sat modestly at the other end of the polished wood table, one plump forearm resting before her, one hand stroking and arranging her bright yellow hair, and talked and talked. She told them the history of her life while they ate. Her mother died of hunger in the First World War. Her father was a carpenter. Her elder brother was a political; he was a Social Democrat, and so she had been a Social Democrat, too. And then he had been a Communist; and so she voted for the Communists, God forgive her. And then there came the Führer; and her brother told her he was a good man, and so she became a Nazi. Of course, she was very young and foolish in those days. She told them, giggling, how she had stood in those vast crowds while the Führer spoke, shrieking with enthusiasm. "For my brother was in the uniform, yes, and he was so good-looking, you would never believe it."

The British couple remembered listening on the radio to the sound of those fanatic crowds roaring and yelling approval to the dedicated, hysterical, drum-beating voice; they watched Frau Länge and imagined her a young girl, sweating and scarlet-faced, yelling with the thousands, arm in arm with her girlfriend, who was of course in love with the uniformed brother. Then, afterwards cooling her sore throat with beer in a café, she would perhaps have giggled with the girlfriend at the memory of her intoxication. Or perhaps she had not giggled. At any rate, she had married and come here to the mountains and had three children.

And now her man was dead, killed on the front near Stalingrad. And one son had been killed in North Africa, and another at Avranches. And when her Lili leaned out of the window giggling and waving at a passing American soldier she giggled and said, with a glance at the British couple, "Lucky for us we aren't in the Russian zone, because if so Lili would have loved a Russki." And Lili giggled and leaned farther out of the window and waved and called "Buddy, I love you."

Frau Länge, conscious perhaps that the continued politeness of her British guests need not necessarily mean agreement, would sometimes straighten her shoulders into prim self-righteousness, look in front of her with lowered and self-conscious eyelids, and say with murmuring shocked rectitude: "Yes, Lili, say what you like, but we are lucky this time to have English people as guests. They are people like ourselves who have suffered from this terrible war. And they will go back home and tell their friends what we suffer because our country is divided. For it is clear they are shocked. They did not know of the humiliations we have to undergo."

At this Mary Parrish and Hamish Anderson would say nothing at all, but politely passed each other the salt or the dumplings and shortly afterwards excused themselves and went to their room. They were sleeping a good deal, for, after all, they were people kept permanently short of sleep. And they ate heartily if not well. They skied a little and lay often in the sun, acquiring a layer of brown that they would lose within a week of returning to London. They were feeling rested. They were in a lethargy of physical contentment. They listened to Frau Länge, accepted her scolding because of their total ignorance of the manners and habits of the royal families of Europe, watched the daughter go off with this U.S. soldier or that; and when Doctor Schröder arrived one afternoon to take coffee with Frau Länge, they were happy to join the party. Frau Länge had explained to them that it was the dream of Doctor Schröder's life to reach the United States. Unfortunately, every attempt he had made to do this had failed. It was, perhaps, easy for them to arrange a visa for Doctor Schröder from London? No? It was difficult there, too? Ach, if she were a young woman she too would go to the United States; that was the country of the future, was it not? She did not blame Doctor Schröder that he wished so much to go there. And if she were in a position to assist him, they must believe her that she would, for friends should always help each other.

They had decided that it was Frau Länge's plan to marry Lili to the doctor. But it seemed Lili did not share this idea, for although she knew he was coming, she did not appear that evening. And perhaps Frau Länge was not altogether sorry, for while the word "flirtation" could hardly be used of a relationship like this one, it was extremely amiable. Frau Länge sighed a great deal, her silly blue eyes fastened on the terrible shining mask of her friend's face, saying, "*Ach, mein Gott, mein Gott, mein Gott!*" while Doctor Schröder accepted the tribute like a film star bored with flattery, making polite gestures of repudiation with one hand, using the other to eat with. He stayed the night, ostensibly on the old sofa in the kitchen.

In the morning he woke Mary and Hamish at seven to say that unfortunately he was leaving the valley because he was due to take up his duties at the hospital, that he was delighted to have been of service to them, that he hoped they would arrange their return journey so as to pass through the city where his hospital was, and asked for their assurances that they would.

The departure of Doctor Schröder brought it home to them that their own vacation would end in a week and that they were bored, or on the point of becoming bored. They had much better rouse themselves, leave the snow mountains, and go down to one of the cities below, take a cheap room, and make an effort to meet some ordinary people. By this they meant neither the rich industrialists who frequented this valley, nor people like Frau Stohr, who were manifestly something left over from an older and more peaceful time; nor like Frau Länge and her daughter Lili; nor like Doctor Schröder. Saying goodbye to Frau Länge was almost painless for, as she said instantly, a day never passed without at least one person knocking on her door and asking for a room because, as everyone in the village knew, she gave good value for money. This was true: Frau Länge was a natural landlady; she had given them far more than had been contracted for in the way of odd cups of coffee and above all in hours of fraternal conversation. But at last she accepted their plea that they wanted to spend a week in their professional guise, seeing hospitals and making contact with their fellow doctors. "In that case," she said at once, "it is lucky that you know Doctor Schröder, for there could be no better person to show you everything that you need to see." They said that they would look up Doctor Schröder the moment they arrived, if they should happen to pass through his town, and with this the goodbyes were made.

They made the journey by bus down the long winding valley to the mother village, O——, caught the little rickety train, spent another uncomfortable night sitting up side by side on the hard wooden benches, and at last reached the city of Z——, where they found a small room in a cheap hotel. And now they were pledged to contact ordinary people and widen their view of present-day Germany. They took short walks through the streets of the city, surrounded by ordinary people, looked into their faces, as tourists do, made up stories about them, and got into brief conversation from which they made large generalizations. And, like every earnest tourist, they indulged in fantasies of how they would stop some pleasant-faced person in the street and say: We are ordinary people, completely representative of the people of our country. You are obviously an ordinary person, representative of yours. Please divulge and unfold yourself to us, and we will do the same.

Whereupon this pleasant-faced person would let out an exclamation of delight, strike his forehead with his fist and say: But my friends! There is nothing I would like better. With which he would take them to his house, flat, or room; and a deathless friendship would begin, strong enough to outlast any international misunderstandings, accidents, incidents, wars, or other phenomena totally undesired by the ordinary people on both sides.

They did not contact Doctor Schröder, since they had taken good care not to choose the town he was working in. But from time to time they thought how pleasant it would have been if Doctor Schröder had not been such an utterly disgusting person; if he had been a hard-working, devoted, idealistic doctor like themselves, who could initiate them into the medical life of Germany, or at least of one city, without politics entering their intercourse at all.

Thinking wistfully along these lines led them into a course of action foreign to their naturally diffident selves. It so happened that about a year before, Doctor Anderson had got a letter from a certain Doctor Kroll, who was attached to a hospital just outside the city of Z——, congratulating him on a paper he had published recently and enclosing a paper of his own which dealt with a closely related line of research. Hamish remembered reading Doctor Kroll's paper and diagnosing it as typical of the work put out by elderly and established doctors who are no longer capable of plowing original furrows in the field of medicine but, because they do not wish to seem as if they have lost all interest in original research, from time to time put out a small and harmless paper which amounts to an urbane comment on the work of other people. In short, Doctor Anderson had despised the paper sent to him by his colleague in Germany and had done no more than write him a brief letter of thanks. Now he remembered the incident and told Mary Parrish about it, and both wondered if they might telephone Doctor Kroll and introduce themselves. When they decided that they should, it was with a definite feeling that they were confessing a defeat. Now they were going to be professional people, nothing more. The "ordinary people" had totally eluded them. Conversations with three workmen (on buses), two housewives (in cafés), a businessman (on a train), two waiters and two maids (at the hotel) had left them dissatisfied. None of these people had come out with the final, pithy, conclusive statement about modern Germany that they so badly needed. In fact none of them had said more than what their counterparts in Britain would have done. The nearest to a political comment any one of them had made was the complaint by one of the maids that she did not earn enough money and would very likely go to England where, she understood, wages were much higher.

No, contact with that real, sound, old-fashioned, healthy Germany, as symbolized by the two little girls singing on the bus, had failed them. But certainly it must be there. Something which was a combination of the rather weary irony of the refugees both had known, the bitter affirmation of the songs of Bertolt Brecht, the fighting passion of a Dimitrov (though of course Dimitrov was not a German), the innocence of the little girls, the crashing chords of Beethoven's Fifth. These qualities were fused in their minds into the image of a tired, skeptical, sardonic, but tough personage, a sort of civilized philosopher prepared at any moment to pick up a rifle and fight for the good and the right and the true. But they had not met anyone remotely like this. As for the two weeks up in the valley, they had simply wiped them out. After all, was it likely that a valley given up wholly to the pursuit of pleasure, and all the year round at that, could be representative of anything but itself?

They would simply accept the fact that they had failed, and ring up Doctor Kroll, and spend the remaining days of their vacation acquiring information about medicine. They rang up Doctor Kroll, who, rather to their surprise, remembered the interesting correspondence he had had with Doctor Anderson and invited them to spend the next morning with him. He sounded not at all like the busy head of a hospital, but more like a host. Having made this arrangement, Doctors Parrish and Anderson were on the point of going out to find some cheap restaurant—for their reserve of money was now very small indeed—when Doctor Schröder was announced to them. He had traveled that afternoon all the way from S—— especially to greet them, having heard from his buddy Frau Länge that they were here. In other words, he must have telephoned or wired Frau Länge, who knew their address since she was forwarding letters for them; his need for them was so great that he had also traveled all the way from S——, an expensive business, as he did not hesitate to point out.

The British couple, once again faced with the scarred face and bitter eyes of Doctor Schröder, once again felt a mixture of loathing and compassion and limply made excuses because they had chosen to stop in this town and not in S——. They said they could not possibly afford to spend the evening, as he wanted to do, in one of the expensive restaurants; refused to go as his guests, since he had already spent so much money on coming to meet them; and compromised on an agreement to drink beer with him. This they did in various beer cellars where the cohorts of the Führer used to gather in the old days. Doctor Schröder told them this in a way that could be taken either as if he were pointing out a tourist attraction or as if he were offering them the opportunity to mourn a lost glory with him. His manner towards them now fluctuated between hostility and a self-abasing politeness. They, for their part, maintained their own politeness, drank their beer, occasionally caught each other's eye, and suffered through an evening which, had it not been for Doctor Schröder, might have been a very pleasant one. From time to time he brought the conversation around to the possibilities of his working in Britain; and they repeated their warnings, until at last, although he had not mentioned the United States, they explained that getting visas to live in that part of the world would be no easier in Britain than it was here. Doctor Schröder was not at all discomposed when they showed that they were aware of his real objective. Not at all; he behaved as if he had told them from the start that the United States was his ideal country. Just as if he had never sung songs of praise to Britain, he now disparaged Britain as part of Europe, which was dead and finished, a parasite on the healthy body of America. Quite obviously all people of foresight would make their way to America—he assumed that they, too, had seen this obvious truth, and had possibly already made their plans? Of course he did not blame anyone for looking after himself first, that was a rule of nature; but friends should help each other. And who knew but that once they were all in America Doctor Schröder might be in a position to help Doctors Anderson and Parrish? The wheel of chance might very well bring such a thing to pass. Yes, it was always advisable in this world to plan well ahead. As for himself, he was not ashamed to admit that it was his first principle; that was why he was sitting this evening in the city of Z——, at their service. That was why he had arranged a day's leave from his own hospital—not the easiest thing to do, this, since he had just returned from a fortnight's holiday—in order to be their guide around the hospitals of Z——.

Mary and Hamish, after a long stunned silence, said that this kindness to them was overwhelming. But unfortunately they had arranged to spend tomorrow with Doctor Kroll of such-and-such a hospital.

The eyes of Doctor Schröder showed a sudden violent animation. The shiny stretched mask of his face deepened its scarlet and, after a wild angry flickering of blue light at the name of Kroll, the eyes settled into a steady, almost anguished glare of inquiry.

It appeared that at last they had hit upon, quite by chance, the way to silence Doctor Schröder.

"Doctor Kroll," he said, with the sigh of a man who, after long searching, finds the key. "Doctor Kroll. I see. Yes."

At last he had placed them. It seemed that Doctor Kroll's status was so high, and therefore, presumably, their status also, that he could not possibly aspire to any equality with them. Perfectly understandable that they did not need to emigrate to America, being the close friends of Doctor Kroll. His manner became bitter, brooding, and respectful, and at the most suggested that they might have said, nearly three weeks ago on that first evening in O——, that they were intimates of Doctor Kroll, thereby saving him all this anguish and trouble and expense.

Doctor Kroll, it emerged, was a man loaded with honors and prestige, at the very height of his profession. Of course, it was unfortunate that such a man should be afflicted in the way he was. . . .

And how was Doctor Kroll afflicted?

Why, didn't they know? Surely, they must! Doctor Kroll was for six months in every year a voluntary patient in his own hospital—yes, that was something to admire, was it not?—that a man of such brilliance should, at a certain point in every year, hand over his keys to his subordinates and submit to seeing a door locked upon himself, just as, for the other six months, he locked doors on other people. It was very sad, yes. But of course they must know all this quite well, since they had the privilege of Doctor Kroll's friendship.

Mary and Hamish did not like to admit that they had not known it was a mental hospital that Doctor Kroll administered. If they did, they would lose the advantage of their immunity from Doctor Schröder, who had, obviously, already relinquished them entirely to a higher sphere. Meanwhile, since his evening was already wasted, and there was time to fill in, he was prepared to talk.

By the time the evening had drawn to a close in a beer cellar where one drank surrounded by great wooden barrels from which the beer was drawn off direct into giant-sized mugs—the apotheosis of all beer cellars—they had formed an image of Doctor Kroll as a very old, Lear-like man, proud and bitter in the dignified acceptance of his affliction; and although neither of them had any direct interest in the problems of the mentally sick, since Mary Parrish specialized in small children and Hamish Anderson in geriatrics, they were sympathetically looking forward to meeting this courageous old man.

The evening ended without any unpleasantness because of the invisible presence of Doctor Kroll. Doctor Schröder returned them to the door of their hotel, shook their hands, and wished them a happy conclusion to their vacation. The violent disharmony of his personality had been swallowed entirely by the self-abasing humility into which he had retreated, with which he was consoling himself. He said that he would look them up when he came to London, but it was merely conventional. He wished them a pleasant reunion with Doctor Kroll and strode off through the black, cold, blowing night towards the railway station, springing on his long lean legs like a black-mantled grasshopper—a hooded, bitter, energetic shape whirled about by flurries of fine white snow that glittered in the streetlights like blown salt or sand.

Next morning it was still snowing. The British couple left their hotel early to find the right bus stop, which was at the other end of the city in a poor suburb. The snow fell listlessly from a low grey sky, and fine shreds of dingy snow lay sparse on the dark earth. The bombs of the recent war had laid the streets here flat for miles around. The streets were etched in broken outlines, and the newly laid railway lines ran clean and shining through them. The station had been bombed, and there was a wooden shed doing temporary duty until another could be built. A dark-wrapped, dogged crowd stood bunched around the bus stop. Nearby a mass of workmen were busy on a new building that rose fine and clean and white out of the miles of damaged houses. They looked like black and energetic insects at work against the stark white of the walls. The British couple stood hunching their cold shoulders and shifting their cold feet with the German crowd, and watched the builders. They thought that it was the bombs of their country which had created this havoc; thought of the havoc created in their country by the bombs of the people they now stood shoulder to shoulder with, and sank back slowly into a mood of listless depression. The bus was a long time coming. It seemed to grow colder. From time to time people drifted past to the station shed or added themselves to the end of the bus queues, or a woman went past with a shopping basket. Behind the ruined buildings rose the shapes and outlines of the city that had been destroyed and the outlines of the city that would be rebuilt. It was as if they stood solid among the ruins and ghosts of dead cities and cities not yet born. And Hamish's eyes were at work again on the faces of the people about them, fixed on the face of an old shawled woman who was passing; and it seemed as if the crowd, like the streets, became transparent and fluid, for beside them, behind them, among them stood the dead. The dead of two wars peopled the ruined square and jostled the living, a silent snowbound multitude.

The silence locked the air. There was a low, deep thudding that seemed to come from under the earth. It was from a machine at work on the building site. The machine, low in the dirty snow, lifted black grappling arms like a wrestler or like someone in prayer; and the sound of its laboring traveled like a sensation of movement through the cold earth, as if the soil were hoarsely breathing. And the workmen swarmed and worked around the machine and over the steep sides of the new building. They were like children playing with bricks. Half an hour before a giant of a man in black jackboots had strode past their block building and carelessly kicked it down. Now the children were building it again, under the legs of a striding race of great black-booted giants. At any moment another pair of trampling black legs might come straddling over the building and down it would go, down into ruin, to the accompaniment of crashing thunder and bolts of lightning. All over the soil of patient Europe, soil soaked again and again by blood, soil broken again and again by angry metal, the small figures were at work, building their bright new houses among the shells and the ruins of war; and in their eyes was the shadow from the great marching jackbooted feet, and beside each of them, beside every one of them, their dead, the invisible, swarming, memoried dead.

The crowd continued to wait. The machine kept up its hoarse breathing. From time to time a shabby bus came up, a few people climbed in, the bus went off, and more people came dark-clothed through the thinly falling snow to join the crowd, which was very similar to a British crowd in its stolid disciplined quality of patience.

At last a bus with the number they had been told to look for drew up, and they got into it with a few other people. The bus was half empty. Almost at once it left the city behind. Doctor Kroll's hospital, like so many of the similar hospitals in Britain, was built well outside the city boundaries so that the lives of healthy people might not be disturbed by thoughts of those who had to retreat behind the shelter of high walls. The way was straight on a good narrow road, recently rebuilt over flat black plains streaked and spotted with snow. The quiet, windless air was full of fine particles of snow that fell so slowly it seemed that the sky was falling, as if the slow weight of the snow dragged the grey covering over the black flat plains down to the earth. They traveled forward in a world without color.

Doctor Kroll's hospital made itself visible a long way off over the plain. It consisted of a dozen or more dark, straight buildings set at regular angles to each other, like the arrangements of the sheds in the concentration camps of the war. Indeed, at a distance, the resemblance to the mechanical order of a concentration camp was very great; but as the bus drew nearer the buildings grew and spread into their real size and surrounded themselves with a regular pattern of lawns and shrubs.

The bus set them down outside a heavy iron gate; and at the entrance of the main building, which was high and square, they were welcomed by a doctor whose enthusiasm was expressly delegated from Doctor Kroll, who was impatiently waiting for them upstairs. They went up several staircases and along many corridors, and thought that whatever bleak impression this place might give from the outside, great care had been given to banishing bleakness from within. The walls were all covered by bright pictures, which there was no time to examine now, as they hurried after their busy guide; flowers stood on high pedestals at every turning of the corridor, and the walls and ceiling and woodwork were painted in clean white and blue. They were thinking sympathetically of the storm-driven Lear whom they were so soon to meet, as they passed through these human and pleasant corridors; they were even thinking that perhaps it was an advantage to have as director of a mental hospital a man who knew what it was like to spend time inside it as a victim. But their guide remarked, "This is, of course, the administrative block and the doctors' quarters. Doctor Kroll will be happy to show you the hospital itself later."

With this he shook them by the hand, nodded a goodbye and went, leaving them outside the half-open door of what looked like a middle-class living room.

A hearty voice called out that they must come in; and they went into a suite of two rooms, half divided by sheets of sliding glass, brightly lighted, pleasantly furnished, and with nothing in it reminiscent of an office but a single small desk in the farther of the two rooms. Behind the desk sat a handsome man of late middle age who was rising to greet them. It occurred to them, much too late, that this must be Doctor Kroll; and so their greetings, because they were shocked, were much less enthusiastic than his. His greetings were in any case much more like a host's than a colleague's. He was apparently delighted to see them and pressed them to sit down while he ordered some coffee. This he did by going to the house telephone on the desk in the room beyond the pane of glass; and the two looked at each other, exchanging surprise, and then, finally, pleasure.

Doctor Kroll was, to begin with, extremely distinguished, and they remembered something Doctor Schröder had said the night before, to the effect that he came from an old and respected family; that he was, in short, an aristocrat. They had to accept the word when looking at Doctor Kroll himself, even though they could not conceivably take it from Doctor Schröder. Doctor Kroll was rather tall and managed to combine heaviness and leanness in a remarkable way, for while he was a man of whom one instinctively wondered how much he must weigh when he stood on a scale, he was not fat, or even plump. But he was heavy; and his face, which had strong and prominent bones, carried a weight of large-pored flesh. Yet one would have said, because of the prominent dome of pale forehead and because of the large, commanding nose, and because of the deep dark lively eyes, that it was a lean face. And his movements were not those of a heavy man; he had quick impatient gestures and his large, handsome hands were in constant movement. He returned, smiling, from giving orders about the coffee, sat down in an easy chair opposite the two British doctors, and proceeded to entertain them in the most urbane and pleasant way in the world. He spoke admirable English, he knew a good deal about Britain, and he now discussed the present state of affairs in Britain with assurance.

His admiration for Britain was immense. And this time the British couple were flattered. This was something very different from hearing praise from that appalling Doctor Schröder. Until the coffee came, and while they were drinking it, and for half an hour afterwards, they discussed Britain and its institutions. The British couple listened to a view of Britain that they disagreed with profoundly, but without irritation, since it was natural that a man like this should hold conservative ideas. Doctor Kroll believed that a limited monarchy was the best guarantee against disorder and was, in fact, the reason for the well-known British tolerance, which was a quality he admired more than any other. Speaking as a German, and therefore peculiarly equipped to discuss the dangers of anarchy, he would say that the best thing the Allied Armies could have done would have been to impose upon Germany a royal family, created, if necessary, from the shreds and fragments of the unfortunately dwindling royal families of Europe. Further, he believed that this should have been done at the end of the First World War, at the Treaty of Versailles. When Britain, usually so perspicacious in matters of this kind, had left Germany without a royal safeguard, they had made the worst mistake of their history. For a royal family would have imposed good conduct and respect for institutions and made an upstart like Hitler impossible.

At this point the eyes of the British pair met again, though briefly. There was no doubt that to hear Hitler described as an upstart revived some of the sensations they felt when listening to Doctor Schröder or Frau Länge. A few seconds later they heard him being referred to as a mongrel upstart, and unease definitely set in, beneath the well-being induced by the good coffee and their liking for their host.

Doctor Kroll developed his theme for some time, darting his lively and intelligent glances at them, offering them more coffee, offering them cigarettes, and demanded from them an account of how the Health Service worked in Britain. He took it for granted that neither would approve of a scheme which gave people something for nothing, and he commiserated with them for their subjection to state tyranny. They ventured to point out to him certain advantages they felt it had; and at last he nodded and admitted that a country as stable and well-ordered as their own might very well be able to afford extravagant experiments that would wreck other countries—his own, for instance. But he did feel disturbed when he saw their country, which he regarded as the bulwark of decency against socialism in Europe, giving in to the mob.

Here they suggested that they did not want to take up more of his time than was necessary; he must be very busy. For surely the director of such a large hospital could not possibly afford to devote so much time to every foreign doctor who wished to see over it? Or could it be his devotion to Britain that made him so ready to devote his time to them?

At any rate, he seemed disappointed at being reminded of what they had come for. He even sighed and sat silent a little, so that Doctor Anderson, out of politeness, mentioned the paper he had received from him so that they might, if Doctor Kroll wished it, discuss the subject of their research. But Doctor Kroll merely sighed again and said that these days he had very little time for original work; such was the penalty one must pay for accepting the burdens of administration. He rose, all his animation gone, and invited them to step into the other room beyond the glass panel where he would collect his keys. So the three of them went into the inner drawing room, which was an office because of the desk and the telephone; and there Mary Parrish's attention was drawn to a picture on the wall above the desk. At a distance of six or eight feet it was a gay fresh picture of a cornfield painted from root-vision, or field-mouse view. The sheaves of corn rose startlingly up, bright and strong, mingled with cornflowers and red poppies, as if one were crouching in the very center of a field. But as one walked toward the picture it vanished, it became a confusion of bright paint. It was fingerpainted. The surface of the canvas was as rough as a plowed field. Mary Parrish walked up to it, into the bright paint, took a few steps back, and back again; and, behold, the picture re-created itself, the cornfield strong and innocent, with something of the sensual innocence of Renoir's pictures. She was so absorbed that she started when Doctor Kroll dropped a heavy hand on her shoulder and demanded, Was she fond of painting? Instantly both she and Hamish assured him that they were enthusiastically fond of pictures.

Doctor Kroll dropped back on the surface of his very neat desk—so neat one could not help wondering how much it was used—the very large black bunch of keys he had removed from it; and he stood in front of the cornfield picture, his hand on Mary's shoulder.

"This," he said, "is what I am really interested in. Yes, yes; this, you must agree, is more interesting than medicine."

They agreed, since they had just understood that this was the artist in person. Doctor Kroll proceeded to take out from a large cupboard set into the wall a thick stack of pictures, all fingerpainted, all with the rough staring surface of thick paint, all of which created themselves at ten paces into highly organized and original pictures.

Soon both rooms were full of pictures that leaned against chairs, tables, walls, and along the sliding glass panels. Doctor Kroll, his fine hands knotted together in anxiety because of their possible reception of his work, followed them around as they gazed at one picture after another. It became evident that the pictures separated themselves into two categories. There were those, like the cornfield, done in bright clear colors, very fresh and lyrical. Then there were those which, close up, showed grim rutted surfaces of dirty black, grey, white, a sullen green, and—recurring again and again—a characteristic sullen shade of red, a dark, lightless, rusty red like old blood. These pictures were all extraordinary and macabre, of graveyards and skulls and corpses, of war scenes and bombed buildings and screaming women and houses on fire with people falling from burning windows like ants into flames. It was quite extraordinary how, in the space of a few seconds, these two conventional and pretty rooms had been transformed by these pictures into an exhibition of ghoulishness, particularly as the scenes of the pictures were continually vanishing altogether into areas of thick paint that had been smeared, rubbed, piled, worked all over the canvas an inch or so thick by the handsome fingers of Doctor Kroll. Standing at six feet from one picture, the proper distance to view the work of Doctor Kroll, the picture they had been examining five moments before, and which they had now moved away from, lost its meaning and disintegrated into a surface of jumbled and crusted color. They were continually stepping forward or stepping back from chaos into moments of brief, clear, startling illumination. And they could not help wondering if Doctor Kroll was gifted with a peculiar vision of his own, a vision perhaps of his fingertips, which enabled him to *see* his work as he stood up against it, rubbing and plastering the thick paint onto the canvas; they even imagined him as a monster with arms six feet long, standing back from his canvas as he worked on it like a clambering spider. The quality of these pictures was such that, as they examined them, they could not help picturing the artist as a monster, a maniac, or kind of gifted insect. Yet, turning to look at Doctor Kroll, there he stood, a handsome man who was the very essence of everything that was conservative, correct, and urbane.

Mary, at least, was feeling a little giddy. She sought out the battling blue eyes of her partner, Hamish, and understood that he felt the same. For this was an exact repetition of their encounter with Doctor Schröder with his scarred face that demanded compassion. In saying what they thought of his work to Doctor Kroll, they must remember that they were speaking to a man who gallantly and bravely volunteered to hand the keys of sanity over to a subordinate and retired into madness for six months of the year, when, presumably, he painted these horrible pictures, whose very surfaces looked like the oozing, shredding substance of decomposing flesh.

Meanwhile, there he stood beside them, searching their faces anxiously.

They said, in response to his appeal, that this was obviously a real and strong talent. They said that his work was striking and original. They said they were deeply impressed.

He stood silent, not quite smiling, but with a quizzical look behind the fine eyes. He was judging them. He knew what they were feeling and was condemning them, in the same way as the initiated make allowances for the innocent.

Doctor Anderson remarked that it must be admitted that the pictures were rather strong? Not to everybody's taste, perhaps? Perhaps rather savage?

Doctor Kroll, smiling urbanely, replied that life tended sometimes to be savage. Yes, that was his experience. He deepened his smile and indicated the cornfield on the wall behind his desk and said that he could see Doctor Anderson preferred pictures like that one?

Doctor Anderson took his stand, and very stubbornly, on the fact that he preferred that picture to any of the others he had seen.

Mary Parrish moved to stand beside Doctor Anderson and joined him in asserting that to her mind this picture was entirely superior to all the others; she preferred the few bright pictures, all of which seemed to her to be loaded with a quality of sheer joy, a sensuous joy, to the others which seemed to her—if he didn't mind her saying so—simply horrible.

Doctor Kroll turned his ironical, dark gaze from one face to the other and remarked: "So." And again, accepting their bad taste: "So."

He remarked, "I am subject to fits of depression. When I am depressed, naturally enough, I paint these pictures." He indicated the lightless pictures of his madness. "And when I am happy again, and when I have time—for, as I have said, I am extremely busy—I paint pictures such as these. . . ." His gesture towards the cornfield was impatient, almost contemptuous. It was clear that he had hung the joyous cornfield on the wall of his reception room because he expected all his guests or visiting colleagues to have the bad taste to prefer it.

"So," he said again, smiling dryly.

At which, Mary Parrish—since he was conveying a feeling of total isolation—said quickly, "But we are very interested. We would love to see some more, if you have time."

It seemed that he needed very much to hear her say this. For the ironical condemnation left his face and was succeeded by the pathetic anxiety of the amateur artist to be loved for his work. He said that he had had two exhibitions of his paintings, that he had been misunderstood by the critics, who had praised the paintings he did not care for, so that he would never again expose himself publicly to the stupidity of critics. He was dependent for sympathy on the understanding minority, some of them chance visitors to his hospital; some of them even—if they did not mind his saying so—inmates of it. He would, for two such delightful guests as his visitors from England, be happy to show more of his work.

With this he invited them to step into a passage behind his office. Its walls were covered from floor to ceiling with pictures. Also the walls of the passage beyond it.

It was terrifying to think of the energy this man must have when he was "depressed." Corridor after corridor opened up, the walls all covered with canvases loaded with thick, crusted paint. Some of the corridors were narrow, and it was impossible to stand far enough back for the pictures to compose themselves. But it seemed that Doctor Kroll was able to see what his hands had done even when he was close against the canvas. He would lean into a big area of thick, dry paint from which emerged fragmentarily a jerky branch that looked like a bombed tree, or a bit of cracked bone, or a tormented mouth, and say: "I call this picture 'Love.' " Or Victory, or Death; for he liked this kind of title. "See? See that house there? See how I've put the church?" And the two guests gazed blankly at the smears of paint and wondered if perhaps this canvas represented the apotheosis of his madness and had no form in it at all. But if they stepped back against the opposite wall as far as they could, and leaned their heads back to gain an extra inch of distance, they could see that there was a house or a church. The house was also a skull; and the dead grey walls of the church oozed rusty blood, or spilled a gout of blood over the sills of its windows, or its door ejected blood like a person's mouth coughing blood.

Depression again weighed on the pair, who, following after the dignified back of Doctor Kroll as he led them into yet another picture-filled corridor, instinctively reached for each other's hands, reached for the warm contact of healthy flesh.

Soon their host led them back into the office, where he offered them more coffee. They refused politely but asked to see his hospital. Doctor Kroll carelessly agreed. It was not, his manner suggested, that he did not take his hospital seriously, but that he would much rather, now he had been given the privilege of a visit from these rarely sympathetic people, share with them his much higher interests: his love for their country, his art. But he would nevertheless escort them around the hospital.

Again he took up the great bundle of black keys and went before them down the corridor they had first entered by. Now they saw that the pictures they had noticed then were all by him; these were the pictures he despised and hung for public view. But as they passed through a back door into a courtyard he paused, held up his keys, smiling, and indicated a small picture by the door. The picture was of the keys. From a scramble of whitey-grey paint came out, very black and hard and shining, a great jangling bunch of keys that also looked like bells, and, from certain angles, like staring eyes. Doctor Kroll shared a smile with them as if to say: An interesting subject?

The three doctors went across a courtyard into the first block, which consisted of two parallel very long wards, each filled with small, tidy, white beds that had a chair and a locker beside them. On the beds sat, or leaned, or lay, the patients. Apart from the fact that they tended to be listless and staring, there was nothing to distinguish this ward from the ward of any public hospital. Doctor Kroll exchanged brisk greetings with certain of his patients; discouraged an old man who grasped his arm as he passed and said that he had a momentous piece of news to tell him which he had heard that moment over his private wireless station, and which affected the whole course of history; and passed on smiling through this building into the next. There was nothing new here. This block, like the last, had achieved the ultimate in reducing several hundred human beings into complete identity with each other. Doctor Kroll said, almost impatiently, that if you had seen one of these wards you had seen them all, and took off at a tangent across a courtyard to another of these regular blocklike buildings which was full of women. It occurred to the British pair that the two buildings on the other side of the court had men in them only; and they asked Doctor Kroll if he kept the men in the line of buildings on one side of the court, and the women on the other—for there was a high wire fence down the court, with a door in it that he opened and locked behind him. "Why, that is so," said Doctor Kroll indifferently.

"Do the men and the women meet—in the evenings, perhaps?"

"Meet? No."

"Not at social evenings? At dances perhaps? At some meals during the week?"

Here Doctor Kroll turned and gave his guests a tolerant smile. "My friends," he said, "sex is a force destructive enough even when kept locked up. Do you suggest that we should mix the sexes in a place like this, where it is hard enough to keep people quiet and unexcited?"

Doctor Anderson remarked that in progressive mental hospitals in Britain it was a policy to allow men and women to mix together as much as was possible. For what crime were these poor people being punished, he inquired hotly, that they were treated as if they had taken perpetual vows of celibacy?

Doctor Parrish noted that the word "progressive" fell very flat in this atmosphere. Such was the power of Doctor Kroll's conservative personality that it sounded almost eccentric.

"So?" commented Doctor Kroll. "So the administrators of your English hospitals are prepared to give themselves so much unnecessary trouble?"

"Do the men and women never meet?" insisted Doctor Parrish.

Doctor Kroll said tolerantly that at night they behaved like naughty schoolchildren and passed each other notes through the wire.

The British couple fell back on their invincible politeness and felt their depression inside them like a fog. It was still snowing lightly through the heavy grey air.

Having seen three buildings all full of women of all ages, lying and sitting about in the listlessness of complete idleness, they agreed with Doctor Kroll it was enough; they were prepared to end their tour of inspection. He said that they must return with him for another cup of coffee, but first he had to make a short visit, and perhaps they would be kind enough to accompany him. He led the way to another building set rather apart from others, whose main door he opened with an enormous key from his bunch of keys. As soon as they were inside it became evident that this was the children's building. Doctor Kroll was striding down the main passage, calling aloud for some attendant, who appeared to take instructions.

Meanwhile, Mary Parrish, doctor who specialized in small children, finding herself at the open door of a ward, looked in, and invited Doctor Anderson to do the same. It was a very large room, very clean, very fresh, with barred windows. It was full of cots and small beds. In the center of the room a five-year-old child stood upright against the bars of a cot. His arms were confined by a straitjacket, and because he could not prevent himself from falling, he was tied upright against the bars with a cord. He was glaring around the room, glaring and grinding his teeth. Never had Mary seen such a desperate, wild, suffering little creature as this one. Immediately opposite the child sat a very large tow-headed woman, dressed in heavy striped grey material, like a prison dress, knitting as comfortably as if she were in her kitchen.

Mary was speechless with horror at the sight. She could feel Hamish stiff and angry beside her.

Doctor Kroll came back down the passage, saw them, and said amiably: "You are interested? So? Of course, Doctor Parrish, you said children are your field. Come in, come in." He led the way into the room, and the fat woman stood up respectfully as he entered. He glanced at the straitjacketed child and moved past it to the opposite wall, where there was a line of small beds, placed head to foot. He pulled back the coverings one after another, showing a dozen children aged between a year and six years—armless children, limbless children, children with enormous misshapen heads, children with tiny heads and monstrous bodies. He pulled the coverings off, one after another, replacing them as soon as Mary Parrish and Hamish Anderson had seen what he was showing them, and remarked: "Modern drugs are a terrible thing. Now these horrors are kept alive. Before, they died of pneumonia."

Hamish said, "The theory is, I believe, that medical science advances so fast that we should keep even the most apparently hopeless people alive in case we find something that can save them?"

Doctor Kroll gave them the ironical smile they had seen before, and said, "Yes, yes, yes. That is the theory. But for my part . . . "

Mary Parrish was watching the imprisoned little boy, who glared from a flushed wild face, straining his small limbs inside the thick stuff of the straitjacket. She said, "In Britain straitjackets are hardly ever used. Certainly not for children."

"So?" commented Doctor Kroll. "So? But sometimes it is for the patient's own good."

He advanced towards the boy and stood before the bars of the cot, looking at him. The child glared back like a wild animal into the eyes of the big doctor. "This one bites if you go too near him," commented Doctor Kroll; and with a nod of his head invited them to follow him out.

"Yes, yes," he remarked, unlocking the big door and locking it behind them, "there are things we cannot say in public, but we may agree in private that there are many people in this hospital who would be no worse for a quick and painless death."

Again he asked that they would excuse him, and he strode off to have a word with another doctor, who was crossing the court in his white coat, with another big bunch of black keys in his hand.

Hamish said, "This man told us that he has directed this hospital for thirty years."

"Yes, I believe he did."

"So he was here under Hitler."

"The mongrel upstart, yes."

"And he would not have kept his job unless he had agreed to sterilize

Jews, serious mental defectives, and communists. Did you remember?"

"No, I'd forgotten."

"So had I."

They were silent a moment, thinking of how much they had liked, how much they still liked, Doctor Kroll.

"Any Jew or mental defective or communist unlucky enough to fall into Doctor Kroll's hands would have been forcibly sterilized. And the very ill would have been killed outright."

"Not necessarily," she objected feebly. "After all, perhaps he refused. Perhaps he was strong enough to refuse."

"Perhaps."

"After all, even under the worst governments there are always people in high places who use their influence to protect weak people."

"Perhaps."

"And he might have been one."

"We should keep an open mind?" he inquired, quick and sarcastic. They stood very close together under the cold snow in a corner of the grey courtyard. Twenty paces away, behind walls and locked doors, a small boy, naked save for a straitjacket and tied to bars like an animal, was grinding his teeth and glaring at the fat knitting wardress.

Mary Parrish said miserably, "We don't know, after all. We shouldn't condemn anyone without knowing. For all we know he might have saved the lives of hundreds of people."

At this point Doctor Kroll came back, swinging his keys.

Hamish inquired blandly, "It would interest us very much to know if Hitler's regime made any difference to you professionally?"

Doctor Kroll considered this question as he strolled along beside them. "Life was easy for no one during that time," he said.

"But as regards medical policy?"

Doctor Kroll gave this question his serious thought, and said, "No, they did not interfere very much. Of course, on certain questions, the gentlemen of the Nazi regime had sensible ideas."

"Such as? For instance?"

"Oh, questions of hygiene? Yes, one could call them questions of social hygiene." He had led them to the door of the main building, and now he said: "You will, I hope, join me in a cup of coffee before you leave? Unless I can persuade you to stay and have a meal with us?"

"I think we should catch our bus back to town," said Hamish, speaking firmly for both of them. Doctor Kroll consulted his watch. "Your bus will not be passing for another twenty minutes." They accompanied him back through the picture-hung corridors to his office.

"And I would like so much to give you a memento of your visit," he said, smiling at them both. "Yes, I would like that. No, wait for one minute; I want to show you something."

He went to the wall cupboard and took out a flat object wrapped in a piece of red silk. He unwrapped the silk and brought forth another picture. He set this picture against the side of the desk and invited them to stand back and look at it. They did so, already prepared to admire it, for it was a product of one of the times when he was not depressed. It was a very large picture, done in clear blues and greens, the picture of a forest—an imaginary forest with clear streams running through it, a forest where impossibly brilliant birds flew, and full of plants and trees created in Doctor Kroll's mind. It was beautiful, full of joy and tranquillity and light. But in the center of the sky glared a large black eye. It was an eye remote from the rest of the picture; and obviously what had happened was that Doctor Kroll had painted his fantasy forest, and then afterwards, looking at it during some fit of misery, had painted in that black, condemnatory, judging eye.

Mary Parrish stared back at the eye and said, "It's lovely; it's a picture of paradise." She felt uncomfortable at using the word "paradise" in the presence of Hamish, who by temperament was critical of words like these.

But Doctor Kroll smiled with pleasure, and laid his heavy hand on her shoulder, and said: "You understand. Yes, you understand. That picture is called *The Eye of God in Paradise*. You like it?"

"Very much," she said, afraid that he was about to present that picture to her. For how could they possibly transport such a big picture all the way back to Britain and what would she do with it when she got there? For it would be dishonest to paint out the black, wrathful eye: one respected, naturally, an artist's conception even if one disagreed with it. And she could not endure to live with that eye, no matter how much she liked the rest of the picture.

But it seemed that Doctor Kroll had no intention of parting with the picture itself, which he wrapped up again in its red silk and hid in the cupboard. He took from a drawer a photograph of the picture and offered it to her, saying, "If you really like my picture—and I can see that you do, for you have a real feeling, a real understanding—then kindly take this as a souvenir of a happy occasion."

She thanked him, and both she and Hamish looked with polite gratitude at the photograph. Of course it gave no idea at all of the original. The subtle blues and greens had gone, were not hinted at; and even the softly waving grasses, trees, plants, foliage were obliterated. Nothing remained but a reproduction of crude crusts of paint, smeared thick by the fingers of Doctor Kroll, from which emerged the hint of a branch, the suggestion of a flower. Nothing remained except the black, glaring eye, the eye of a wrathful and punishing God. It was the photograph of a roughly scrawled eye, as a child might have drawn it—as, so Mary could not help thinking, that unfortunate straitjacketed little boy might have drawn the eye of God, or of Doctor Kroll, had he been allowed to get his arms free and use them.

The thought of that little boy hurt her; it was still hurting Hamish, who stood politely beside her. She knew that the moment they could leave this place and get on to the open road where the bus passed would be the happiest of her life.

They thanked Doctor Kroll profoundly for his kindness, insisted they were afraid they might miss their bus, said goodbye, and promised letters and an exchange of medical papers of interest to them all—promised, in short, eternal friendship.

Then they left the big building and Doctor Kroll and emerged into the cold February air. Soon the bus came and picked them up, and they traveled back over the flat black plain to the city terminus.

The terminus was exactly as it had been four or five hours before. Under the low grey sky lay the black chilled earth, the ruins of streets, the already softening shapes of bomb craters, the big new shining white building covered with the energetic shapes of the workers. The bus queue still waited patiently, huddled into dark, thick clothes, while a thin bitter snow drifted down, down, hardly moving, as if the sky itself were slowly falling.

Mary Parrish took out the photograph and held it in her chilly gloved hand.

The black angry eye glared up at them.

"Tear it up," he said.

"No," she said.

"Why not? What's the use of keeping the beastly thing?"

"It wouldn't be fair," she said seriously, returning it to her handbag.

"Oh, *fair,*" he said bitterly, with an impatient shrug.

They moved off side by side to the bus stop where they would catch a bus back to their hotel. Their feet crunched sharply on the hard earth. The stillness, save for the small shouts of the men at work on the half-finished building, save for the breathing noise of the machine, was absolute. And this queue of people waited like the other across the square, waited eternally, huddled up, silent, patient, under the snow; listening to the silence, under which seemed to throb from the depths of the earth the memory of the sound of marching feet, of heavy, black-booted marching feet.

# *How I Finally Lost My Heart*

It would be easy to say that I picked up a knife, slit open my side, took my heart out, and threw it away; but unfortunately it wasn't as easy as that. Not that I, like everyone else, had not often wanted to do it. No, it happened differently, and not as I expected.

It was just after I had had a lunch and a tea with two different men. My lunch partner I had lived with for (more or less) four and seven-twelfths years. When he left me for new pastures, I spent two years, or was it three, half dead, and my heart was a stone, impossible to carry about, considering all the other things weighing on one. Then I slowly, and with difficulty, got free, because my heart cherished a thousand adhesions to my first love—though from another point of view he could be legitimately described as either my second *real* love (my father being the first) or my third (my brother intervening).

As the folk song has it:

> *I have loved but three men in my life,*
> *My father, my brother, and the man that took my life.*

But if one were going to look at the thing from outside, without insight, he could be seen as (perhaps, I forget) the thirteenth, but to do that means disregarding the inner emotional truth. For we all know that those affairs or entanglements one has between *serious* loves, though they may number dozens and stretch over years, *don't really count.*

This way of looking at things creates a number of unhappy people, for it is well known that what doesn't really count for me might very well count for you. But there is no way of getting over this difficulty, for a *serious* love is the most important business in life, or nearly so. At any rate, most of us are engaged in looking for it. Even when we are in fact being very serious indeed with one person we still have an eighth of an eye cocked in case some stranger unexpectedly encountered might turn out to be even more serious. We are all entirely in agreement that we are in the right to taste, test, sip, and sample a thousand people on our way to the *real* one. It is not too much to say that in our circles tasting and sampling is probably the second most important activity, the first being earning money. Or to put it another way, if you are serious about this thing, you go on laying everybody that offers until something clicks and you're all set to go.

I have digressed from an earlier point: that I regarded this man I had lunch with (we call him A) as my first love; and still do, despite the Freudians, who insist on seeing my father as A and possibly my brother as B, making my (real) first love C. And despite, also, those who might ask: What about your two husbands and all those affairs?

What about them? I did not *really* love them, the way I loved A.

I had lunch with him. Then, quite by chance, I had tea with B. When I say B, here, I mean my *second* serious love, not my brother, or the little boys I was in love with between the ages of five and fifteen, if we are going to take fifteen (arbitrarily) as the point of no return . . . which last phrase is in itself a pretty brave defiance of the secular arbiters.

In between A and B (my count) there were a good many affairs, or samples, but they didn't score. B and I *clicked,* we went off like a bomb, though not quite as simply as A and I had clicked, because my heart was bruised, sullen, and suspicious because of A's throwing me over. Also there were all those ligaments and adhesions binding me to A still to be loosened, one by one. However, for a time B and I got on like a house on fire, and then we came to grief. My heart was again a ton weight in my side.

*If this were a stone in my side, a stone,*
*I could pluck it out and be free. . . .*

Having lunch with A, then tea with B, two men who between them had consumed a decade of my precious years (I am not counting the test or trial affairs in between) and, it is fair to say, had balanced all the delight (plenty and intense) with misery (oh Lord, Lord)—moving from one to the other, in the course of an afternoon, conversing amiably about this and that, with meanwhile my heart giving no more than slight reminiscent tugs, the fish of memory at the end of a long slack line . . .

To sum up, it was salutary.

Particularly as that evening I was expecting to meet C, or someone who might very well turn out to be C; though I don't want to give too much emphasis to C, the truth is I can hardly remember what he looked like, but one can't be expected to remember the unimportant ones one has sipped or tasted in between. But after all, he might have turned out to be C, we might have *clicked,* and I was in that state of mind (in which we all so often are) of thinking: He might turn out to be the one. (I use a woman's magazine phrase deliberately here, instead of saying, as I might: *Perhaps it will be serious.*)

So there I was (I want to get the details and atmosphere right) standing at a window looking into a street (Great Portland Street, as a matter of fact) and thinking that while I would not dream of regretting my affairs, or experiences, with A and B (it is better to have loved and lost than never to have loved at all), my anticipation of the heart because of spending an evening with a possible C had a certain unreality, because there was no doubt that both A and B had caused me unbelievable pain. Why, therefore, was I looking forward to C? I should rather be running away as fast as I could.

It suddenly occurred to me that I was looking at the whole phenomenon quite inaccurately. My (or perhaps I am permitted to say our?) way of looking at it is that one must search for an A, or a B, or a C or a D with a certain combination of desirable or sympathetic qualities so that one may click, or spontaneously combust: or to put it differently, one needs a person who, like a saucer of water, allows one to float off on him/her, like a transfer. But this wasn't so at all. Actually one carries with one a sort of burning spear stuck in one's side, that one waits for someone else to pull out; it is something painful, like a sore or a wound, that one cannot wait to share with someone else.

I saw myself quite plainly in a moment of truth: I was standing at a window (on the third floor) with A and B (to mention only the mountain peaks of my emotional experience) behind me, a rather attractive woman, if I may say so, with a mellowness that I would be the first to admit is the sad harbinger of age, but is attractive by definition, because it is a testament to the amount of sampling and sipping (I nearly wrote "simpling" and "sapping") I have done in my time. . . . There I stood, brushed, dressed, red-lipped, kohl-eyed, all waiting for an evening with a possible C. And at another window overlooking (I think I am right in saying) Margaret Street, stood C, brushed, washed, shaved, smiling: an attractive man (I think) and *he* was thinking: Perhaps she will turn out to be D (or A or 3 or ? or %, or whatever symbol he used). We stood, separated by space, certainly, in identical conditions of pleasant uncertainty and anticipation, and we both held our hearts in our hands, all pink and palpitating and ready for pleasure and pain, and we were about to throw these hearts in each other's face like snowballs, or cricket balls (How's that?) or, more accurately, like great bleeding wounds: "Take my wound." Because the last thing one ever thinks at such moments is that he (or she) will say: Take *my* wound, please remove the spear from *my* side. No, not at all; one simply expects to get rid of one's own.

I decided I must go to the telephone and say, C!—You know that joke about the joke-makers who don't trouble to tell each other jokes, but simply say Joke 1 or Joke 2, and everyone roars with laughter, or snickers, or giggles appropriately. . . . Actually one could reverse the game by guessing whether it was Joke C(b) or Joke A(d) according to what sort of laughter a person made to match the silent thought. . . . Well, C (I imagined myself saying), the analogy is for our instruction: Let's take the whole thing as read or said. Let's not lick each other's sores; let's keep our hearts to ourselves. Because just consider it, C, how utterly absurd—here we stand at our respective windows with our palpitating hearts in our hands. . . .

At this moment, dear reader, I was forced simply to put down the telephone with an apology. For I felt the fingers of my left hand push outwards around something rather large, light, and slippery—hard to describe this sensation, really. My hand is not large, and my heart was in a state of inflation afer having had lunch with A, tea with B, and then looking forward to C. . . . Anyway, my fingers were stretching out rather desperately to encompass an unknown, largish, lightish object, and I said: Excuse me a minute, to C, looked down, and there was my heart, in my hand.

I had to end the conversation there.

For one thing, to find that one has achieved something so often longed for, so easily, is upsetting. It's not as if I had been trying. To get something one wants simply by accident—no, there's no pleasure in it, no feeling of achievement. So to find myself heart-whole, or, more accurately, heart-less, or at any rate, rid of the damned thing, and at such an awkward moment, in the middle of an imaginary telephone call with a man who might possibly turn out to be C—well, it was irritating rather than not.

For another thing, a heart, raw and bleeding and fresh from one's side, is not the prettiest sight. I'm not going into that at all. I was appalled, and indeed embarrassed that *that* was what had been loving and beating away all those years, because if I'd had any idea at all—well, enough of that.

My problem was how to get rid of it.

Simple, you'll say, drop it into the waste bucket.

Well, let me tell you, that's what I tried to do. I took a good look at this object, nearly died with embarrassment, and walked over to the rubbish can, where I tried to let it roll off my fingers. It wouldn't. It was stuck. There was my heart, a large red pulsing bleeding repulsive object, stuck to my fingers. What was I going to do? I sat down, lit a cigarette (with one hand, holding the matchbox between my knees), held my hand with the heart stuck on it over the side of the chair so that it could drip into a bucket, and considered.

*If this were a stone in my hand, a stone,*
*I could throw it over a tree. . . .*

When I had finished the cigarette, I carefully unwrapped some tin foil of the kind used to wrap food in when cooking, and I fitted a sort of cover around my heart. This was absolutely and urgently necessary. First, it was smarting badly. After all, it had spent some forty years protected by flesh and ribs, and the air was too much for it. Secondly, I couldn't have any Tom, Dick, and Harry walking in and looking at it. Thirdly, I could not look at it for too long myself, it filled me with shame. The tin foil was effective, and indeed rather striking. It is quite pliable and now it seemed as if there were a stylized heart balanced on my palm, like a globe, in glittering, silvery substance. I almost felt I needed a scepter in the other hand to balance it. . . . But the thing was, there is no other word for it, in bad taste. I then wrapped a scarf around hand and tin-foiled heart, and felt safer. Now it was a question of pretending to have hurt my hand until I could think of a way of getting rid of my heart altogether, short of amputating my hand.

Meanwhile I telephoned (really, not in imagination) C, who now would never be C. I could feel my heart, which was stuck so close to my fingers that I could feel every beat or tremor, give a gulp of resigned grief at the idea of this beautiful experience now never to be. I told him some idiotic lie about having flu. Well, he was all stiff and indignant, but concealing it urbanely, as I would have done, making a joke but allowing a tiny barb of sarcasm to rankle in the last well-chosen phrase. Then I sat down again to think out my whole situation.

There I sat.

What was I going to do?

There I sat.

I am going to have to skip about four days here, vital enough in all conscience, because I simply cannot go heartbeat by heartbeat through my memories. A pity, since I suppose this is what this story is about; but in brief: I drew the curtains, I took the telephone off the hook, I turned on the lights, I took the scarf off the glittering shape, then the tin foil; then I examined the heart. There were two-fifths of a century's experience to work through, and before I had even got through the first night, I was in a state hard to describe. . . .

*Or if I could pull the nerves from my skin*
*A quick red net to drag through a sea for fish. . . .*

By the end of the fourth day I was worn out. By no act of will, or intention, or desire, could I move that heart by a fraction—on the contrary, it was not only stuck to my fingers, like a sucked boiled sweet, but was actually growing to the flesh of my fingers and my palm.

I wrapped it up again in tin foil and scarf, and turned out the lights and pulled up the blinds and opened the curtains. It was about ten in the morning, an ordinary London day, neither hot nor cold nor clear nor clouded nor wet nor fine. And while the street is interesting, it is not exactly beautiful, so I wasn't looking at it so much as waiting for something to catch my attention while thinking of something else.

Suddenly I heard a tap-tap-tapping that got louder, sharp and clear, and I knew before I saw her that this was the sound of high heels on a pavement though it might just as well have been a hammer against stone. She walked fast opposite my window and her heels hit the pavement so hard that all the noises of the street seemed absorbed into that single tap-tap-clang-clang. As she reached the corner at Great Portland Street two London pigeons swooped diagonally from the sky very fast, as if they were bullets aimed to kill her; and then as they saw her they swooped up and off at an angle. Meanwhile she had turned the corner. All this has taken time to write down, but the thing happening took a couple of seconds: the woman's body hitting the pavement bang-bang through her heels then sharply turning the corner in a right angle; and the pigeons making another acute angle across hers and intersecting it in a fast swoop of displaced air. Nothing to all that, of course, nothing—she had gone off down the street, her heels tip-tapping, and the pigeons landed on my windowsill and began cooing. All gone, all vanished, the marvelous exact coordination of sound and movement, but it had happened, it had made me happy and exhilarated, I had no problems in this world, and I realized that the heart stuck to my fingers was quite loose. I couldn't get it off altogether, though I was tugging at it under the scarf and the tin foil, but almost.

I understood that sitting and analyzing each movement or pulse or beat of my heart through forty years was a mistake. I was on the wrong track altogether: this was the way to attach my red, bitter, delighted heart to my flesh for ever and ever. . . .

*Ha! So you think I'm done! You think. . . .*
*Watch, I'll roll my heart in a mesh of rage*
*And bounce it like a handball off*
*Walls, faces, railings, umbrellas, and pigeons' backs. . . .*

No, all that was no good at all; it just made things worse. What I must do is to take myself by surprise, as it were, the way I was taken by surprise over the woman and the pigeons and the sharp sounds of heels and silk wings.

I put on my coat, held my lumpy scarfed arm across my chest, so that if anyone said: What have you done with your hand? I could say: I've banged my finger in the door. Then I walked down into the street.

It wasn't easy to go among so many people, when I was worried that they were thinking: What has that woman done to her hand? because that made it hard to forget myself. And all the time it tingled and throbbed against my fingers, reminding me.

Now I was out, I didn't know what to do. Should I go and have lunch with someone? Or wander in the park? Or buy myself a dress? I decided to go to the Round Pond, and walk around it by myself. I was tired after four days and nights without sleep. I went down into the underground at Oxford Circus. Midday. Crowds of people. I felt self-conscious, but of course need not have worried. I swear you could walk naked down the street in London and no one would even turn round.

So I went down the escalator and looked at the faces coming up past me on the other side, as I always do; and wondered, as I always do, how strange it is that those people and I should meet by chance in such a way, and how odd that we would never see each other again, or, if we did, we wouldn't know it. And I went onto the crowded platform and looked at the faces as I always do, and got into the train, which was very full, and found a seat. It wasn't as bad as at rush hour, but all the seats were filled. I leaned back and closed my eyes, deciding to sleep a little, being so tired. I was just beginning to doze off when I heard a woman's voice muttering, or rather declaiming:

> *"A gold cigarette case, well, that's a nice thing, isn't it, I must say,*
> *a gold case, yes. . . ."*

There was something about this voice which made me open my eyes: on the other side of the compartment, about eight persons away, sat a youngish woman, wearing a cheap green cloth coat, gloveless hands, flat brown shoes, and lisle stockings. She must be rather poor—a woman dressed like this is a rare sight, these days. But it was her posture that struck me. She was sitting half-twisted in her seat, so that her head was turned over her left shoulder, and she was looking straight at the stomach of an elderly man next to her. But it was clear she was not seeing it: her young staring eyes were sightless, she was looking inwards.

She was so clearly alone, in the crowded compartment, that it was not as embarrassing as it might have been. I looked around, and people were smiling, or exchanging glances, or winking, or ignoring her, according to their natures, but she was oblivious of us all.

She suddenly aroused herself, turned so that she sat straight in her seat, and directed her voice and her gaze to the opposite seat:

> "*Well so that's what you think, you think that, you think that do you, well, you think I'm just going to wait at home for you, but you gave her a gold case and . . .*"

And with a clockwork movement of her whole thin person, she turned her narrow pale-haired head sideways over her left shoulder, and resumed her stiff empty stare at the man's stomach. He was grinning uncomfortably. I leaned forward to look along the line of people in the row of seats I sat in, and the man opposite her, a young man, had exactly the same look of discomfort which he was determined to keep amused. So we all looked at her, the young, thin, pale woman in her private drama of misery, who was so completely unconscious of us that she spoke and thought out loud. And again, without particular warning or reason, in between stops, so it wasn't that she was disturbed from her dream by the train stopping at Bond Street, and then jumping forward again, she twisted her body frontways, and addressed the seat opposite her (the young man had got off, and a smart grey-curled matron had got in):

> "*Well I know about it now, don't I, and if you come in all smiling and pleased well then I know, don't I, you don't have to tell me, I know, and I've said to her, I've said, I know he gave you a gold cigarette case. . . .*"

At which point, with the same clockwork impulse, she stopped, or was checked, or simply ran out, and turned herself half-around to stare at the stomach—the same stomach, for the middle-aged man was still there. But we stopped at Marble Arch and he got out, giving the compartment, rather than the people in it, a tolerant half-smile which said: I am sure I can trust you to realize that this unfortunate woman is stark staring mad. . . .

His seat remained empty. No people got in at Marble Arch, and the two people standing waiting for seats did not want to sit by her to receive her stare.

We all sat, looking gently in front of us, pretending to ourselves and to each other that we didn't know the poor woman was mad and that in fact we ought to be doing something about it. I even wondered what I should say: Madam, you're mad—shall I escort you to your home? Or:

Poor thing, don't go on like that, it doesn't do any good, you know—just leave him, that'll bring him to his senses. . . .

And behold, after the interval that was regulated by her inner mechanism had elapsed, she turned back and said to the smart matron who received this statement of accusation with perfect self-command:

> *"Yes, I know! Oh yes! And what about my shoes, what about them, a golden cigarette case is what she got, the filthy bitch, a golden case. . . ."*

Stop. Twist. Stare. At the empty seat by her.

Extraordinary. Because it was a frozen misery, how shall I put it? A passionless passion—we were seeing unhappiness embodied; we were looking at the essence of some private tragedy—rather, Tragedy. There was no emotion in it. She was like an actress doing Accusation, or Betrayed Love, or Infidelity, when she has only just learned her lines and is not bothering to do more than get them right.

And whether she sat in her half-twisted position, her unblinking eyes staring at the greenish, furry, ugly covering of the train seat, or sat straight, directing her accusation to the smart woman opposite, there was a frightening immobility about her—yes, that was why she frightened us. For it was clear that she might very well (if the inner machine ran down) stay silent, forever, in either twisted or straight position, or at any point between them—yes, we could all imagine her, frozen perpetually in some arbitrary pose. It was as if we watched the shell of some woman going through certain predetermined motions.

For *she* was simply not there. *What* was there, who she was, it was impossible to tell, though it was easy to imagine her thin, gentle little face breaking into a smile in total forgetfulness of what she was enacting now. She did not know she was in a train between Marble Arch and Queensway, nor that she was publicly accusing her husband or lover, nor that we were looking at her.

And we, looking at her, felt an embarrassment and shame that was not on her account at all. . . .

Suddenly I felt, under the scarf and the tin foil, a lightening of my fingers, as my heart rolled loose.

I hastily took it off my palm, in case it decided to adhere there again, and I removed the scarf, leaving balanced on my knees a perfect stylized heart, like a silver heart on a Valentine card, though of course it was three-dimensional. This heart was not so much harmless, no that isn't the word, as artistic, but in very bad taste, as I said. I could see that the people in the train, now looking at me and the heart, and not at the poor madwoman, were pleased with it.

I got up, took the four or so paces to where she was, and laid the tin-foiled heart down on the seat so that it received her stare.

For a moment she did not react, then with a groan or a mutter of relieved and entirely theatrical grief, she leaned forward, picked up the glittering heart, and clutched it in her arms, hugging it and rocking it back and forth, even laying her cheek against it, while staring over its top at her husband as if to say: Look what I've got, I don't care about you and your cigarette case, I've got a silver heart.

I got up, since we were at Notting Hill Gate, and, followed by the pleased congratulatory nods and smiles of the people left behind, I went out onto the platform, up the escalators, into the street, and along to the park.

No heart. No heart at all. What bliss. What freedom . . .

*Hear that sound? That's laughter, yes.*
*That's me laughing, yes, that's me.*

# England versus England

"I think I'll be off," said Charlie. "My things are packed." He had made sure of getting his holdall ready so that his mother wouldn't. "But it's early," she protested. Yet she was already knocking red hands together to rid them of water while she turned to say goodbye: she knew her son was leaving early to avoid the father. But the back door now opened and Mr. Thornton came in. Charlie and his father were alike: tall, over-thin, big-boned. The old miner stooped, his hair had gone into grey wisps, and his hollow cheeks were coal-pitted. The young man was still fresh, with jaunty fair hair and alert eyes. But there were scoops of strain under his eyes.

"You're alone," said Charlie involuntarily, pleased, ready to sit down again. The old man was not alone. Three men came into view behind him in the light that fell into the yard from the door, and Charlie said quickly: "I'm off, Dad, it's goodbye till Christmas." They all came crowding into the little kitchen, bringing with them the spirit of facetiousness that seemed to Charlie his personal spiteful enemy, like a poltergeist always standing in wait somewhere behind his right shoulder. "So you're back to the dreaming spires," said one man, nodding goodbye. "Off to t'palaces of learning," said another. Both were smiling. There was no hostility in it, or even envy, but it shut Charlie out of his family, away from his people. The third man, adding his tribute to this, the most brilliant son of the village, said: "You'll be coming back to a right Christmas with us, then, or will you be frolicking with t'lords and t'earls you're the equal of now?"

"He'll be home for Christmas," said the mother sharply. She turned her back on them, and dropped potatoes one by one from a paper bag into a bowl.

"For a day or so, any road," said Charlie, in obedience to the prompting spirit. "That's time enough to spend with t'hewers of wood and t'drawers of water." The third man nodded, as if to say: That's right! and put back his head to let out a relieved bellow. The father and the other two men guffawed with him. Young Lennie pushed and shoved Charlie encouragingly and Charlie jostled back, while the mother nodded and smiled because of the saving horseplay. All the same, he had not been home for nearly a year, and when they stopped laughing and stood waiting for him to go, their grave eyes said they were remembering this fact.

"Sorry I've not had more time with you, son," said Mr. Thornton, "but you know how 'tis."

The old miner had been union secretary, was now chairman, and had spent his working life as miners' representative in a dozen capacities. When he walked through the village, men at a back door, or a woman in an apron, called: "Just a minute, Bill," and came after him. Every evening Mr. Thornton sat in the kitchen, or in the parlor when the television was claimed by the children, giving advice about pensions, claims, work rules, allowances; filling in forms; listening to tales of trouble. Ever since Charlie could remember, Mr. Thornton had been less his father than the father of the village. Now the three miners went into the parlor, and Mr. Thornton laid his hand on his son's shoulder, and said: "It's been good seeing you," nodded, and followed them. As he shut the door he said to his wife: "Make us a cup of tea, will you, lass?"

"There's time for a cup, Charlie," said the mother, meaning there was no need for him to rush off now, when it was unlikely any more neighbors would come in. Charlie did not hear. He was watching her slosh dirty potatoes about under the running tap while with her free hand she reached for the kettle. He went to fetch his raincoat and his holdall, listening to the nagging inner voice which he hated, but which he felt as his only protection against the spiteful enemy outside: "I can't stand it when my father apologizes to me—he was apologizing to me for not seeing more of me. If he wasn't as he is, better than anyone else in the village, and our home the only house with real books in it, I wouldn't be at Oxford. I wouldn't have done well at school, so it cuts both ways." The words "cuts both ways" echoed uncannily in his inner ear, and he felt queasy, as if the earth he stood on was shaking. His eyes cleared on the sight of his mother, standing in front of him, her shrewd, non-judging gaze on his face. "Eh, lad," she said, "you don't look any too good to me." "I'm all right," he said hastily, and kissed her, adding: "Say my piece to the girls when they come in." He went out, with Lennie behind him.

The two youths walked in silence past fifty crammed lively brightly lit kitchens whose doors kept opening as the miners came in from the pit for their tea. They walked in silence along the fronts of fifty more houses. The fronts were all dark. The life of the village, even now, was in the kitchens where great fires roared all day on the cheap coal. The village had been built in the Thirties by the company, now nationalized. There were two thousand houses, exactly alike, with identical patches of carefully tended front garden, and busy backyards. Nearly every house had a television aerial. From every chimney poured black smoke.

At the bus stop Charlie turned to look back at the village, now a low hollow of black, streaked and spattered with sullen wet lights. He tried to isolate the gleam from his own home, while he thought how he loved his home and how he hated the village. Everything about it offended him, yet as soon as he stepped inside his kitchen he was received into warmth. That morning he had stood on the front step and looked out on lines of grey stucco houses on either side of grey tarmac; on grey ugly lampposts and greyish hedges, and beyond to the grey minetip and the neat black diagram of the minehead.

He had looked, listening while the painful inner voice lectured: "There's nothing in sight, not one object or building anywhere, that is beautiful. Everything is so ugly and mean and graceless that it should be bulldozed into the earth and out of the memory of man." There was not even a cinema. There was a post office, and attached to it a library that had romances and war stories. There were two miners' clubs for drinking. And there was television. These were the amenities for two thousand families.

When Mr. Thornton stood on his front step and looked forth he smiled with pride and called his children to say: "You've never seen what a miners' town can be like. You couldn't even imagine the conditions. Slums, that's what they used to be. Well, we've put an end to all that. . . . Yes, off you go to Doncaster, I suppose, dancing and the pictures—that's all you can think about. And you take it all for granted. Now, in our time . . ."

And so when Charlie visited his home he was careful that none of his bitter criticisms reached words, for above all, he could not bear to hurt his father.

A group of young miners came along for the bus. They wore smartly shouldered suits, their caps set at angles, and scarves flung back over their shoulders. They greeted Lennie, looked to see who the stranger was, and when Lennie said: "This is my brother," they nodded and turned quickly to board the bus. They went upstairs, and Lennie and Charlie went to the front downstairs. Lennie looked like them, with a strong cloth cap and a jaunty scarf. He was short, stocky, strong—"built for t'pit," Mr. Thornton said. But Lennie was in a foundry in Doncaster. No pit for him, he said. He had heard his father coughing through all the nights of his childhood, and the pit wasn't for him. But he had never said this to his father.

Lennie was twenty. He earned seventeen pounds a week, and wanted to marry a girl he had been courting for three years now. But he could not marry until the big brother was through college. The father was still on the coal face, when by rights of age he should have been on the surface, because he earned four pounds a week more on the face. The sister in the office had wanted to be a schoolteacher, but at the moment of decision all the extra money of the family had been needed for Charlie. It cost them two hundred pounds a year for his extras at Oxford. The only members of the family not making sacrifices for Charlie were the schoolgirl and the mother.

It was half an hour on the bus, and Charlie's muscles were set hard in readiness for what Lennie might say, which must be resisted. Yet he had come home thinking: Well, at least I can talk it out with Lennie, I can be honest with him.

Now Lennie said facetiously, but with an anxious loving inspection of his brother's face: "And what for do we owe the pleasure of your company, Charlie boy? You could have knocked us all down with a feather when you said you were coming this weekend."

Charlie said angrily: "I got fed with t'earls and t'dukes."

"Eh," said Lennie quickly, "but you didn't need to mind *them,* they didn't mean to rile you."

"I know they didn't."

"Mum's right," said Lennie, with another anxious but carefully brief glance, "you're not looking too good. What's up?"

"What if I don't pass t'examinations," said Charlie in a rush.

"Eh, but what is this, then? You were always first in school. You were the best of everyone. Why shouldn't you pass, then?"

"Sometimes I think I won't," said Charlie lamely, but glad he had let the moment pass.

Lennie examined him again, this time frankly, and gave a movement like a shrug. But it was a hunching of the shoulders against a possible defeat. He sat hunched, his big hands on his knees. On his face was a small critical grin. Not critical of Charlie, not at all, but of life.

His heart beating painfully with guilt, Charlie said: "It's not as bad as that, I'll pass." The inner enemy remarked softly: "I'll pass, then I'll get a nice pansy job in a publisher's office with the other wet-nosed little boys, or I'll be a sort of clerk. Or I'll be a teacher—I've no talent for teaching, but what's that matter? Or I'll be on the management side of industry, pushing people like Lennie around. And the joke is, Lennie's earning more than I shall for years." The enemy behind his right shoulder began satirically tolling a bell and intoned: "Charlie Thornton, in his third year at Oxford, was found dead in a gas-filled bed-sitting-room this morning. He had been overworking. Death from natural causes." The enemy added a loud rude raspberry and fell silent. But he was waiting: Charlie could feel him there waiting.

Lennie said: "Seen a doctor, Charlie boy?"

"Yes. He said I should take it easy. That's why I came home."

"No point killing yourself working."

"No, it's not serious, he just said I must take it easy."

Lennie's face remained grave. Charlie knew that when he got home he would say to the mother: "I think Charlie's got summat on his mind." And his mother would say (while she stood shaking chips of potato into boiling fat): "I expect sometimes he wonders is the grind worth it. And he sees you earning, when he isn't." She would say, after a silence during which they exchanged careful looks: "It must be hard for him, coming here, everything different, then off he goes, everything different again."

"Shouldn't worry, Mum."

"I'm not worrying. Charlie's all right."

The inner voice inquired anxiously: "If she's on the spot about the rest, I suppose she's right about the last bit too—*I suppose I am all right?*"

But the enemy behind his right shoulder said: "A man's best friend is his mother, she never lets a thing pass."

Last year he had brought Jenny down for a weekend, to satisfy the family's curiosity about the posh people he knew these days. Jenny was a poor clergyman's daughter, bookish, a bit of a prig, but a nice girl. She had easily navigated the complicated currents of the weekend, while the family waited for her to put on "side." Afterwards Mrs. Thornton had said, putting her finger on the sore spot: "That's a right nice girl. She's a proper mother to you, and that's a fact." The last was not a criticism of the girl, but of Charlie. Now Charlie looked with envy at Lennie's responsible profile and said to himself: Yes, he's a man. He has been for years, since he left school. Me, I'm a proper baby, and I've got two years over him.

For above everything else, Charlie was made to feel, every time he came home, that these people, his people, were serious; while he and the people with whom he would now spend his life (if he passed the examination) were not serious. He did not believe this. The inner didactic voice made short work of any such idea. The outer enemy could, and did, parody it in a hundred ways. His family did not believe it, they were proud of him. Yet Charlie felt it in everything they said and did. They protected him. They sheltered him. And above all, they still paid for him. At his age, his father had been working in the pit for eight years.

Lennie would be married next year. He already talked of a family. He, Charlie (if he passed the examination), would be running around licking people's arses to get a job, Bachelor of Arts, Oxford, and a drug on the market.

They had reached Doncaster. It was raining. Soon they would pass where Doreen, Lennie's girl, worked. "You'd better get off here," Charlie said. "You'll have all that drag back through the wet." "No, s'all right, I'll come with you to the station."

There were another five minutes to go. "I don't think it's right, the way you get at Mum," Lennie said, at last coming to the point.

"But I haven't said a bloody word," said Charlie, switching without having intended it into his other voice, the middle-class voice which he was careful never to use with his family except in joke. Lennie gave him a glance of surprise and reproach and said: "All the same. She feels it."

"But it's bloody ridiculous." Charlie's voice was rising. "She stands in that kitchen all day, pandering to our every whim, when she's not doing housework or making a hundred trips a day with that bloody coal. . . ." In the Christmas holidays, when Charlie had visited home last, he had fixed up a bucket on the frame of an old pram to ease his mother's work. This morning he had seen the contrivance collapsed and full of rainwater in the backyard. After breakfast Lennie and Charlie had sat at the table in their shirt-sleeves watching their mother. The door was open into the backyard. Mrs. Thornton carried a shovel whose blade was nine inches by ten, and was walking back and forth from the coalhole in the yard, through the kitchen, into the parlor. On each inward journey, a small clump of coal balanced on the shovel. Charlie counted that his mother walked from the coalhole to the kitchen fire and the parlor fire thirty-six times. She walked steadily, the shovel in front, held like a spear in both hands, and her face frowned with purpose. Charlie had dropped his head onto his arms and laughed soundlessly until he felt Lennie's warning gaze and stopped the heave of his shoulders. After a moment he had sat up, straight-faced. Lennie said: "Why do you get at Mum, then?" Charlie said: "But I haven't said owt." "No, but she's getting riled. You always show what you think, Charlie boy." As Charlie did not respond to this appeal—for far more than present charity—Lennie went on: "You can't teach an old dog new tricks." "Old! She's not fifty!"

Now Charlie said, continuing the early conversation: "She goes on as if she were an old woman. She wears herself out with nothing—she could get through all the work she has in a couple of hours if she organized herself. Or if just for once she told us where to get off."

"What'd she do with herself then?"

"Do? Well, she could do something for herself. Read. Or see friends. Or something."

"She feels it. Last time you went off she cried."

"She *what?*" Charlie's guilt almost overpowered him, but the inner didactic voice switched on in time and he spoke through it: "What right have we to treat her like a bloody servant? Betty likes her food this way and that way, and Dad won't eat this and that, and she stands there and humors the lot of us—like a servant."

"And who was it last night said he wouldn't have fat on his meat and changed it for hers?" said Lennie smiling, but full of reproach.

"Oh, I'm just as bad as the rest of you," said Charlie, sounding false. "It makes me wild to see it," he said, sounding sincere. Didactically he said: "All the women in the village—they take it for granted. If someone organized them so they had half a day to themselves sometimes, they'd think they were being insulted—they can't stop working. Just look at Mum, then. She comes into Doncaster to wrap sweets two or three times a week—well, she actually loses money on it, by the time she's paid bus fares. I said to her, 'You're actually losing money on it,' and she said: 'I like to get out and see a bit of life.' A bit of life! Wrapping sweets in a bloody factory. Why can't she just come into town of an evening and have a bit of fun without feeling she has to pay for it by wrapping sweets, sweated bloody labor? And she actually loses on it. It doesn't make sense. They're human beings, aren't they? Not just . . ."

"Not just what?" asked Lennie angrily. He had listened to Charlie's tirade, his mouth setting harder, his eyes narrowing. "Here's the station," he said in relief. They waited for the young miners to clatter down and off before going forward themselves. "I'll come with you to your stop," said Charlie; and they crossed the dark, shiny, grimy street to the opposite stop for the bus which would take Lennie back to Doreen.

"It's no good thinking we're going to change, Charlie boy."

"Who said change?" said Charlie excitedly; but the bus had come, and Lennie was already swinging onto the back. "If you're in trouble just write and say," said Lennie, and the bell pinged and his face vanished as the lit bus was absorbed by the light-streaked drizzling darkness.

There was half an hour before the London train. Charlie stood with the rain on his shoulders, his hands in his pockets, wondering whether to go after his brother and explain—what? He bolted across the street to the pub near the station. It was run by an Irishman who knew him and Lennie. The place was still empty, being just after opening time.

"It's you, then," said Mike, drawing him a pint of bitter without asking. "Yes, it's me," said Charlie, swinging himself up onto a stool.

"And what's in the great world of learning?"

"Oh Jesus, *no!*" said Charlie. The Irishman blinked, and Charlie said quickly: "What have you gone and tarted this place up for?"

The pub had been paneled in dark wood. It was ugly and comforting. Now it had half a dozen bright wallpapers and areas of shining paint, and Charlie's stomach moved again, light filled his eyes, and he set his elbows hard down for support, and put his chin on his two fists.

"The youngsters like it," said the Irishman. "But we've left the bar next door as it was for the old ones."

"You should have a sign up: Age This Way," said Charlie. "I'd have known where to go." He carefully lifted his head off his fists, narrowing his eyes to exclude the battling colors of the wallpapers, the shine of the paint.

"You look bad," said the Irishman. He was a small, round, alcoholically cheerful man who, like Charlie, had two voices. For the enemy—that is, all the English whom he did not regard as a friend, which meant people who were not regulars—he put on an exaggerated brogue which was bound, if he persisted, to lead to the political arguments he delighted in. For friends like Charlie he didn't trouble himself. He now said: "All work and no play."

"That's right," said Charlie. "I went to the doctor. He gave me a tonic and said I am fundamentally sound in wind and limb. 'You are sound in wind and limb,' he said," said Charlie, parodying an upper-class English voice for the Irishman's pleasure.

Mike winked, acknowledging the jest, while his professionally humorous face remained serious. "You can't burn the candle at both ends," he said in earnest warning.

Charlie laughed out. "That's what the doctor said. 'You can't burn the candle at both ends,' he said."

This time, when the stool he sat on, and the floor beneath the stool, moved away from him, and the glittering ceiling dipped and swung, his eyes went dark and stayed dark. He shut them and gripped the counter tight. With his eyes still shut, he said facetiously: "It's the clash of cultures, that's what it is. It makes me lightheaded." He opened his eyes and saw from the Irishman's face that he had not said these words aloud.

He said aloud: "Actually the doctor was all right, he meant well. But Mike, I'm not going to make it, I'm going to fail."

"Well, it won't be the end of the world."

"*Jesus.* That's what I like about you, Mike, you take a broad view of life."

"I'll be back," said Mike, going to serve a customer.

A week ago Charlie had gone to the doctor with a cyclostyled leaflet in his hand. It was called "A Report Into the Increased Incidence of Breakdown Among Undergraduates." He had underlined the words: "Young men from working-class and lower-middle-class families on scholarships are particularly vulnerable. For them, the gaining of a degree is obviously crucial. In addition they are under the continuous strain of adapting themselves to middle-class mores that are foreign to them. They are victims of a clash of standards, a clash of cultures, divided loyalties."

The doctor, a young man of about thirty, provided by the college authorities as a sort of father figure to advise on work problems, personal problems, and (as the satirical alter ego took pleasure in pointing out) on clash-of-culture problems, glanced once at the pamphlet and handed it back. He had written it. As, of course, Charlie had known. "When are your examinations?" he asked. *Getting to the root of the matter, just like Mum,* remarked the malevolent voice from behind Charlie's shoulder.

"I've got five months, doctor, and I can't work and I can't sleep."

"For how long?"

"It's been coming on gradually." *Ever since I was born,* said the enemy.

"I can give you sedatives and sleeping pills, of course, but that's not going to touch what's really wrong."

*Which is all this unnatural mixing of the classes. Doesn't do, you know. People should know their place and stick to it.* "I'd like some sleep pills, all the same."

"Have you got a girl?"

"Two."

The doctor paid out an allowance of man-of-the-world sympathy, then shut off his smile and said: "Perhaps you'd be better with one?"

*Which, my mum figure or my lovely bit of sex?* "Perhaps I would, at that."

"I could arrange for you to have talks with a psychiatrist—well, not if you don't want," he said hastily, for the alter ego had exploded through Charlie's lips in a horse laugh and: "What can the trick cyclist tell me I don't know?" He roared with laughter, flinging his legs up; and an ashtray went circling around the room on its rim. Charlie laughed, watched the ashtray, and thought: There, I knew all the time it was a poltergeist sitting there behind my shoulder. I swear I never touched that damned ashtray.

The doctor waited until it circled near him, stopped it with his foot, picked it up, laid it back on the desk. "It's no point your going to him if you feel like that."

*All avenues explored, all roads charted.*

"Well now, let's see, have you been to see your family recently?"

"Last Christmas. No, doctor, it's not because I don't want to, it's because I can't work there." *You try working in an atmosphere of trade union meetings and the telly and the pictures in Doncaster. You try it, doc. And besides all my energies go into not upsetting them. Because I do upset them. My dear doc, when we scholarship boys jump our class, it's not we who suffer, it's our families. We are an expense, doc. And besides—write a thesis, I'd like to read it. . . . Call it: Long-term effects on working-class or lower-middle-class family of a scholarship child whose existence is a perpetual reminder that they are nothing but ignorant non-cultured clods. How's that for a thesis, doc? Why, I do believe I could write it myself.*

"If I were you, I'd go home for a few days. Don't try to work at all. Go to the pictures. Sleep and eat and let them fuss over you. Get this prescription made up and come and see me when you get back."

"Thanks, doc, I will." *You mean well.*

The Irishman came back to find Charlie spinning a penny, so intent on this game that he did not see him. First he spun it with his right hand, anticlockwise, then with his left, clockwise. The right hand represented his jeering alter ago. The left hand was the didactic and rational voice. The left hand was able to keep the coin in a glittering spin for much longer than the right.

"You ambidextrous?"

"Yes, always was."

The Irishman watched the boy's frowning, teeth-clenched concentration for a while, then removed the untouched beer and poured him a double whisky. "You drink that and get on the train and sleep."

"Thanks, Mike. Thanks."

"That was a nice girl you had with you last time."

"I've quarreled with her. Or rather, she's given me the boot. And quite right too."

After the visit to the doctor Charlie had gone straight to Jenny. He had guyed the interview while she sat, gravely listening. Then he had given her his favorite lecture on the crass and unalterable insensibility of anybody anywhere born middle-class. No one but Jenny ever heard this lecture. She said at last: "You *should* go and see a psychiatrist. No, don't you see, it's not fair."

"Who to, me?"

"No, me. What's the use of shouting at me all the time? You should be saying these things to him."

*"What?"*

"Well, surely you can see that. You spend all your time lecturing me. You make use of me, Charles." (She always called him Charles.)

What she was really saying was: You should be making love to me, not lecturing me. Charlie did not really like making love to Jenny. He forced himself when her increasingly tart and accusing manner reminded him that he ought to. He had another girl, whom he disliked, a tall crisp middle-class girl called Sally. She called him, mocking: Charlie boy. When he had slammed out of Jenny's room, he had gone to Sally and fought his way into her bed. Every act of sex with Sally was a slow, cold subjugation of her by him. That night he had said, when she lay at last, submissive, beneath him: "Horny-handed son of toil wins by his unquenched virility beautiful daughter of the moneyed classes. And doesn't she love it."

"Oh yes I do, Charlie boy."

"I'm nothing but a bloody sex symbol."

"Well," she murmured, already self-possessed, freeing herself, "that's all I am to you." She added defiantly, showing that she did care, and that it was Charlie's fault: "And I couldn't care less."

"Dear Sally, what I like about you is your beautiful honesty."

"Is that what you like about me? I thought it was the thrill of beating me down."

Charlie said to the Irishman: "I've quarreled with everyone I know in the last weeks."

"Quarreled with your family, too?"

*"No,"* he said, appalled, while the room again swung around him. "Good Lord no," he said in a different tone—grateful. He added savagely: "How could I? I can never say anything to them I really think." He looked at Mike to see if he had actually said these words aloud. He had, because now Mike said: "So you know how I feel. I've lived thirty years in this mucking country, and if you arrogant sods knew what I'm thinking half the time."

"Liar. You say whatever you think, from Cromwell to the Black and Tans and Casement. You never let up. But it's not hurting yourself to say it."

"Yourself, is it?"

"Yes. But it's all insane. Do you realize how insane it all is, Mike? There's my father. Pillar of the working class. Labour Party, trade union, the lot. But I've been watching my tongue not to say I spent last term campaigning about—he takes it for granted even *now* that the British should push the wogs around."

"You're a great nation," said the Irishman. "But it's not your personal fault, so drink up and have another."

Charlie drank his first Scotch, and drew the second glass towards him. "Don't you see what I mean?" he said, his voice rising excitedly. "Don't you see that it's all *insane?* There's my mother, her sister is ill and it looks as if she'll die. There are two kids, and my mother'll take them both. They're nippers, three and four, it's like starting a family all over again. She thinks nothing of it. If someone's in trouble, she's the mug, every time. But there she sits and stays: 'Those juvenile offenders ought to be flogged until they are senseless.' She read it in the papers and so she says it. She said it to me and I kept my mouth shut. And they're all alike."

"Yes, but you're not going to change it, Charlie, so drink up."

A man standing a few feet down the bar had a paper sticking out of his pocket. Mike said to him: "Mind if I borrow your paper for the winners, sir?"

"Help yourself."

Mike turned the paper over to the back page. "I had five quid on today," he said. "Lost it. Lovely bit of horseflesh, but I lost it."

"Wait," said Charlie excitedly, straightening the paper so he could see the front page. WARDROBE MURDERER GETS SECOND CHANCE, it said. "See that?" said Charlie. "The Home Secretary says he can have another chance; they can review the case, he says."

The Irishman read, cold-faced. "So he does," he said.

"Well, I mean to say, there's some decency left, then. I mean if the case can be reviewed it shows they do *care* about something at least."

"I don't see it your way at all. It's England versus England, that's all. Fair play all round, but they'll hang the poor sod on the day appointed as usual." He turned the newspaper and studied the race news.

Charlie waited for his eyes to clear, held himself steady with one hand flat on the counter, and drank his second double. He pushed over a pound note, remembering it had to last three days, and that now he had quarreled with Jenny there was no place for him to stay in London.

"No, it's on me," said Mike. "I asked you. It's been a pleasure seeing you, Charlie. And don't take the sins of the world on your personal shoulders, lad, because that doesn't do anyone any good, does it, now?"

"See you at Christmas, Mike, and thanks."

He walked carefully out into the rain. There was no solitude to be had on the train that night, so he chose a compartment with one person in it, and settled himself in a corner before looking to see who it was he had with him. It was a girl. He saw then that she was pretty, and then that she was upper-class. Another Sally, he thought, sensing danger, seeing the cool, self-sufficient little face. Hey, there, Charlie, he said to himself, keep yourself in order, or you've had it. He carefully located himself: *he,* Charlie, was now a warm, whisky-comforted belly, already a little sick. Close above it, like a silent loudspeaker, was the source of the hectoring voice. Behind his shoulder waited his grinning familiar. *He must keep them all apart.* He tested the didactic voice: "It's not her fault, poor bitch, victim of the class system, she can't help she sees everyone under her like dirt. . . ." But the alcohol was working strongly and meanwhile his familiar was calculating: "She's had a good look, but can't make me out. My clothes are right, my haircut's on the line, but there's something that makes her wonder. She's waiting for me to speak, then she'll make up her mind. Well, first I'll get her, and then I'll speak."

He caught her eyes and signaled an invitation, but it was an aggressive invitation, to make it as hard for her as he could. After a bit, she smiled at him. Then he roughened his speech to the point of unintelligibility and said: " 'Appen you'd like t'window up? What wi' t'rain and t'wind and all."

"What?" she said sharply, her face lengthening into such a comical frankness of shock that he laughed out, and afterwards inquired impeccably: "Actually it is rather cold, isn't it? Wouldn't you like to have the window up?" She picked up a magazine and shut him out, while he watched, grinning, the blood creep up from her neat suit collar to her hairline.

The door slid back; two people came in. They were a man and his wife, both small, crumpled in face and flesh, and dressed in their best for London. There was a fuss and a heaving of suitcases and murmured apologies because of the two superior young people. Then the woman, having settled herself in a corner, looked steadily at Charlie, while he thought: Deep calls to deep, *she* knows who I am all right; she's not foxed by the trimmings. He was right, because soon she said familiarly: "Would you put the window up for me, lad? It's a rare cold night and no mistake."

Charlie put up the window, not looking at the girl, who was hiding behind the magazine. Now the woman smiled, and the man smiled too, because of her ease with the youth.

"You comfortable like that, Father?" she asked.

"Fair enough," said the husband on the stoical note of the confirmed grumbler.

"Put your feet up beside me, any road."

"But I'm all right, lass," he said bravely. Then, making a favor of it, he loosened his laces, eased his feet inside too new shoes, and set them on the seat beside his wife.

She, for her part, was removing her hat. It was of shapeless grey felt, with a pink rose at the front. Charlie's mother owned just such a badge of respectability, renewed every year or so at the sales. Hers was always bluish felt, with a bit of ribbon or coarse net, and she would rather be seen dead than without it in public.

The woman sat fingering her hair, which was thin and greying. For some reason, the sight of her clean pinkish scalp shining through the grey wisps made Charlie wild with anger. He was taken by surprise, and again summoned himself to himself, making the didactic voice lecture: "The working woman of these islands enjoys a position in the family superior to that of the middle-class woman, et cetera, et cetera, et cetera." This was an article he had read recently, and he continued to recite from it, until he realized the voice had become an open sneer, and was saying: "Not only is she the emotional bulwark of the family, but she is frequently the breadwinner as well, such as wrapping sweets at night, sweated labor for pleasure, anything to get out of the happy home for a few hours."

The fusion of the two voices, the nagging inside voice and the jeer from the dangerous force outside, terrified Charlie, and he told himself hastily: You're drunk, that's all; now keep your mouth shut, for God's sake.

The woman was asking him: "Are you feeling all right?"

"Yes, I'm all right," he said carefully.

"Going all the way to London?"

"Yes, I'm going all the way to London."

"It's a long drag."

"Yes, it's a long drag."

At this echoing dialogue, the girl lowered her magazine to give him a sharp contemptuous look, up and down. Her face was now smoothly pink, and her small pink mouth was judging.

"You have a mouth like a rosebud," said Charlie, listening horrified to these words emerging from him.

The girl jerked up the magazine. The man looked sharply at Charlie, to see if he had heard aright, and then at his wife, for guidance. The wife looked doubtfully at Charlie, who offered her a slow desperate wink.

She accepted it, and nodded at her husband: boys will be boys. They both glanced warily at the shining face of the magazine.

"We're on our way to London too," said the woman.

"So you're on your way to London."

Stop it, he told himself. He felt a foolish slack grin on his face, and his tongue was thickening in his mouth. He shut his eyes, trying to summon Charlie to his aid, but his stomach was rolling, warm and sick. He lit a cigarette for support, watching his hands at work. "Lily-handed son of learning wants a manicure badly," commented a soft voice in his ears; and he saw the cigarette poised in a parody of a cad's gesture between displayed nicotined fingers. Charlie, smoking with poise, sat preserving a polite, sarcastic smile.

He was in the grip of terror. He was afraid he might slide off the seat. He could no longer help himself.

"London's a big place, for strangers," said the woman.

"But it makes a nice change," said Charlie, trying hard.

The woman, delighted that a real conversation was at last under way, settled her shabby old head against a leather bulge, and said: "Yes, it does make a nice change." The shine on the leather confused Charlie's eyes; he glanced over at the magazine, but its glitter, too, seemed to invade his pupils. He looked at the dirty floor for comfort and said: "It's good for people to get a change now and then."

"Yes, that's what I tell my husband, don't I, Father? It's good for us to get away now and then. We have a married daughter in Streatham."

"It's a great thing, family ties."

"Yes, but it's a drag," said the man. "Say what you like, but it is. After all, I mean, when all is said and done." He paused, his head on one side, with a debating look, waiting for Charlie to take it up.

Charlie said: "There's no denying it, say what you like, I mean, there's no doubt about *that.*" And he looked interestedly at the man for his reply.

The woman said: "Yes, but the way I look at it, you've got to get *out* of yourself sometimes, look at it that way."

"It's all very well," said the husband, on a satisfied but grumbling note, "but if you're going to do that, well, for a start-off, it's an expense."

"If you don't throw a good penny after a bad one," said Charlie judiciously. "I mean, what's the point?"

"Yes, that's it," said the woman excitedly, her old face animated. "That's what I say to Father, what's the point if you don't sometimes let yourself go?"

"I mean, life's bad enough as it is," said Charlie, watching the magazine slowly lower itself. It was laid precisely on the seat. The girl now sat, two small brown-gloved hands in a ginger-tweeded lap, staring him out. Her blue eyes glinted into his, and he looked quickly away.

"Well, I can see that right enough," said the man, "but there again, you've got to know where to stop."

"That's right," said Charlie, "you're dead right."

"I know it's all right for some," said the man, "I know that, but if you're going to do that, you've got to consider. That's what I think."

"But Father, you know you enjoy it, once you're there and Joyce has settled you in your corner with your own chair and your cup to yourself."

"Ah," said the man, nodding heavily, "but it's not as easy as that, now, is it? Well, I mean, that stands to reason."

"Ah," said Charlie, shaking his head, feeling it roll heavily in the socket of his neck, "but if you're going to consider at all, then what's the point? I mean, what I think is, for a start-off, there's no doubt about it."

The woman hesitated, started to say something, but let her small bright eyes falter away. She was beginning to color.

Charlie went on compulsively, his head turning like a clockwork man's: "It's what you're used to, that's what I say, well I mean. *Well,* and there's another thing, when all is said and done, and after all, if you're going to take one thing with another . . ."

"Stop it," said the girl, in a sharp high voice.

"It's a question of principle," said Charlie, but his head had stopped rolling and his eyes had focused.

"If you don't stop I'm going to call the guard and have you put in another compartment," said the girl. To the old people she said in a righteous scandalized voice: "Can't you see he's laughing at you? Can't you see?" She lifted the magazine again.

The old people looked suspiciously at Charlie, dubiously at each other. The woman's face was very pink and her eyes bright and hot.

"I think I am going to get forty winks," said the man, with general hostility. He settled his feet, put his head back, and closed his eyes.

Charlie said: "Excuse me," and scrambled his way to the corridor over the legs of the man, then the legs of the woman, muttering: "Excuse me, excuse me, I'm sorry."

He stood in the corridor, his back jolting slightly against the shifting wood of the compartment's sides. His eyes were shut, his tears running. Words, no longer articulate, muttered and jumbled somewhere inside him, a stream of frightened protesting phrases.

Wood slid against wood close to his ear, and he heard the softness of clothed flesh on wood.

"If it's that bloody little bint I'll kill her," said a voice, small and quiet, from his diaphragm.

He opened his murderous eyes on the woman. She looked concerned.

"I'm sorry," he said, stiff and sullen, "I'm sorry, I didn't mean . . ."

"It's all right," she said, and laid her two red hands on his crossed quivering forearms. She took his two wrists, and laid his arms gently down by his sides. "Don't take on," she said, "it's all right, it's all right, son."

The tense rejection of his flesh caused her to take a step back from him. But there she stood her ground and said: "Now look, son, there's no point taking on like that, well, is there? I mean to say, you've got to take the rough with the smooth, and there's no other way of looking at it."

She waited, facing him, troubled but sure of herself.

After a while Charlie said: "Yes, I suppose you're right."

She nodded and smiled, and went back into the compartment. After a moment, Charlie followed her.

# *Outside the Ministry*

As Big Ben struck ten, a young man arrived outside the portals of the Ministry, and looked sternly up and down the street. He brought his wrist up to eye level and frowned at it, the very picture of a man kept waiting, a man who had expected no less. His arms dropped, elbow flexed stiff, hand at mid-thigh level, palm downwards, fingers splayed. There the hand made a light movement, balanced from the wrist, as if sketching an arpeggio, or saying goodbye to the pavement—or greeting it? An elegant little gesture, full of charm, given out of an abundant sense of style to the watching world. Now he changed his stance, and became a man kept waiting, but maintaining his dignity. He was well-dressed in a dark suit which, with a white shirt and a small grey silk bow tie that seemed positively to wish to fly away altogether, because of the energy imparted to it by his person, made a conventional enough pattern of color—dark grey, light grey, white. But his black glossy skin, setting off this soberness, made him sparkle, a dandy—he might just as well have been wearing a rainbow.

Before he could frown up and down the street again, another young African crossed the road to join him. They greeted each other, laying their palms together, then shaking hands; but there was a conscious restraint in this which the first seemed to relish, out of his innate sense of drama, but made the second uneasy.

"Good morning, Mr. Chikwe."

"Mr. Mafente! Good morning!"

Mr. Mafente was a large smooth young man, well dressed too, but his clothes on him were conventional European clothes, suit, striped shirt, tie; and his gestures had none of the inbuilt delighting self-parody of the other man's. He was suave, he was dignified, he was calm; and this in spite of a situation which Mr. Chikwe's attitude (magisterial, accusing) said clearly was fraught with the possibilities of evil.

Yet these two had known each other for many years; had worked side by side, as the political situation shifted, in various phases of the Nationalist movement; had served prison sentences together; had only recently become enemies. They now (Mr. Chikwe dropped the accusation from his manner for this purpose) exchanged news from home, gossip, information. Then Mr. Chikwe marked the end of the truce by a change of pose, and said, soft and threatening: "And where is your great leader? Surely he is very late?"

"Five minutes only," said the other, smiling.

"Surely when at last we have achieved this great honor, an interview with Her Majesty's Minister, the least we can expect is punctuality from the great man?"

"I agree, but it is more than likely that Her Majesty's Minister will at the last moment be too occupied to see us, as has happened before."

The faces of both men blazed with shared anger for a moment: Mr. Chikwe even showed a snarl of white teeth.

They recovered themselves together and Mr. Mafente said: "And where is your leader? Surely what applies to mine applies to yours also?"

"Perhaps the reasons for their being late are different? Mine is finishing his breakfast just over the road there and yours is—I hear that the night before last your Dr. Devuli was observed very drunk in the home of our hospitable Mrs. James?"

"Possibly, I was not there."

"I hear that the night before that he passed out in the hotel before some unsympathetic journalists and had to be excused."

"It is possible, I was not there."

Mr. Chikwe kept the full force of his frowning stare on Mr. Mafente's bland face as he said softly: "Mr. Mafente!"

"Mr. Chikwe?"

"Is it not a shame and a disgrace that your movement, which, though it is not mine, nevertheless represents several thousand people (not millions, I am afraid, as your publicity men claim)—is it not a pity that this movement is led by a man who is never sober?"

Mr. Mafente smiled, applauding this short speech which had been delivered with a grace and an attack wasted, surely, on a pavement full of London office workers and some fat pigeons. He then observed, merely: "Yet it is Mr. Devuli who is recognized by Her Britannic Majesty's Minister?"

Mr. Chikwe frowned.

"And it is Mr. Devuli who is recognized by those honorable British philanthropic movements—the Anti-Imperialist Society, the Movement for Pan-African Freedom, and Freedom for British Colonies?"

Here Mr. Chikwe bowed, slightly, acknowledging the truth of what he said, but suggesting at the same time its irrelevance.

"I hear, for instance," went on Mr. Mafente, "that the Honorable Member of Parliament for Sutton North-West refused to have your leader on his platform on the grounds that he was a dangerous agitator with left-wing persuasions?"

Here both men exchanged a delighted irrepressible smile—that smile due to political absurdity. (It is not too much to say that it is for the sake of this smile that a good many people stay in politics.) Mr. Chikwe even lifted a shining face to the grey sky, shut his eyes, and while offering his smile to the wet heavens lifted both shoulders in a shrug of scorn.

Then he lowered his eyes, his body sprang into a shape of accusation and he said: "Yet you have to agree with me, Mr. Mafente—it is unfortunate that such a man as Mr. Devuli should be so widely accepted as a national representative, while the virtues of Mr. Kwenzi go unacknowledged."

"We all know the virtues of Mr. Kwenzi," said Mr. Mafente, and his accent on the word "we," accompanied by a deliberately cool glance into the eyes of his old friend, made Mr. Chikwe stand silent a moment, thinking. Then he said softly, testing it: "Yes, yes, yes. And—*well,* Mr. Mafente?"

Mr. Mafente looked into Mr. Chikwe's face, with intent, while he continued the other conversation: "Nevertheless, Mr. Chikwe, the situation is as I've said."

Mr. Chikwe, responding to the look, not the words, came closer and said: "Yet situations do not have to remain unchanged?" They looked deeply into each other's face as Mr. Mafente inquired, almost mechanically: "Is that a threat, perhaps?"

"It is a political observation . . . Mr. Mafente?"

"Mr. Chikwe?"

"This particular situation could be changed very easily."

"Is that so?"

"You know it is so."

The two men were standing with their faces a few inches from each other, frowning with the concentration necessary for the swift mental balancing of a dozen factors: so absorbed were they that clerks and typists glanced uneasily at them, and then, not wishing to be made uneasy, looked away again.

But here they felt approaching a third, and Mr. Mafente repeated quickly: "Is that a threat, perhaps?" in a loud voice, and both young men turned to greet Devuli, a man ten or more years older than they, large, authoritative, impressive. Yet even at this early hour he had a look of dissipation, for his eyes were red and wandering, and he stood upright only with difficulty.

Mr. Mafente now fell back a step to take his place half a pace behind his leader's right elbow; and Mr. Chikwe faced them both, unsmiling.

"Good morning to you, Mr. Chikwe," said Mr. Devuli.

"Good morning to you, Mr. Devuli. Mr. Kwenzi is just finishing his breakfast, and will join us in good time. Mr. Kwenzi was working all through the night on the proposals for the new constitution."

As Mr. Devuli did not answer this challenge, but stood, vague, almost swaying, his red eyes blinking at the passersby, Mr. Mafente said for him: "We all admire the conscientiousness of Mr. Kwenzi." The "we" was definitely emphasized, the two young men exchanged a look like a nod, while Mr. Mafente tactfully held out his right forearm to receive the hand of Mr. Devuli. After a moment the leader steadied himself, and said in a theatening way that managed also to sound like a grumble: "I, too, know all the implications of the proposed constitution, Mr. Chikwe."

"I am surprised to hear it, Mr. Devuli, for Mr. Kwenzi, who has been locked up in his hotel room for the last week, studying it, says that seven men working for seventy-seven years couldn't make sense of the constitution proposed by Her Majesty's Honourable Minister."

Now they all three laughed together, relishing absurdity, until Mr. Chikwe reimposed a frown and said: "And since these proposals are so complicated, and since Mr. Kwenzi understands them as well as any man with mere human powers could, it is our contention that it is Mr. Kwenzi who should speak for our people before the Minister."

Mr. Devuli held himself upright with five fingers splayed out on the forearm of his lieutenant. His red eyes moved somberly over the ugly façade of the Ministry, over the faces of passing people, then, with an effort, came to rest on the face of Mr. Chikwe. "But I am the leader, I am the leader acknowledged by all, and therefore I shall speak for our country."

"You are not feeling well, Mr. Devuli?"

"No, I am not feeling well, Mr. Chikwe."

"It would perhaps be better to have a man in full possession of himself speaking for our people to the Minister?" (Mr. Devuli remained silent, preserving a fixed smile of general benevolence.) "Unless, of course, you expect to feel more in command of yourself by the time of"—he brought his wrist smartly up to his eyes, frowned, dropped his wrist—"ten-thirty a.m., which hour is nearly upon us?"

"No, Mr. Chikwe, I do not expect to feel better by then. Did you not know, I have severe stomach trouble?"

"You have stomach trouble, Mr. Devuli?"

"You did not hear of the attempt made upon my life when I was lying helpless with malaria in the Lady Wilberforce Hospital in Nkalolele?"

"Really, Mr. Devuli, is that so?"

"Yes, it is so, Mr. Chiwke. Some person bribed by my enemies introduced poison into my food while I was lying helpless in hospital. I nearly died that time, and my stomach is still unrecovered."

"I am extremely sorry to hear it."

"I hope that you are. For it is a terrible thing that political rivalry can lower men to such methods."

Mr. Chikwe stood slightly turned away, apparently delighting in the flight of some pigeons. He smiled, and inquired: "Perhaps not so much political rivalry as the sincerest patriotism, Mr. Devuli? It is possible that some misguided people thought the country would be better off without you."

"It must be a matter of opinion, Mr. Chikwe."

The three men stood silent: Mr. Devuli supported himself unobtrusively on Mr. Mafente's arm; Mr. Mafente stood waiting; Mr. Chikwe smiled at pigeons.

"Mr. Devuli?"

"Mr. Chikwe?"

"You are of course aware that if you agree to the Minister's proposals for this constitution civil war may follow?"

"My agreement to this constitution is because I wish to avert bloodshed."

"Yet when it was announced that you intended to agree, serious rioting started in twelve different places in our unfortunate country."

"Misguided people—misguided by your party, Mr. Chikwe."

"I remember, not twelve months ago, that when you were accused by the newspapers of inciting to riot, your reply was that the people had minds of their own. But of course that was when you refused to consider the constitution."

"The situation has changed, perhaps?"

The strain of this dialogue was telling on Mr. Devuli: there were great beads of crystal sweat falling off his broad face, and he mopped it with the hand not steadying him, while he shifted his weight from foot to foot.

"It is your attitude that has changed, Mr. Devuli. You stood for one man, one vote. Then overnight you became a supporter of the weighted vote. That cannot be described as a situation changing, but as a political leader changing—*selling out.*" Mr. Chikwe whipped about like an adder and spat these two last words at the befogged man.

Mr. Mafente, seeing that his leader stood silent, blinking, remarked quietly for him: "Mr. Devuli is not accustomed to replying to vulgar abuse, he prefers to remain silent." The two young men's eyes consulted; and Mr. Chikwe said, his face not four inches from Mr. Devuli's: "It is not the first time a leader of our people has taken the pay of the whites and has been disowned by our people."

Mr. Devuli looked to his lieutenant, who said: "Yet it is Mr. Devuli who has been summoned by the Minister, and you should be careful, Mr. Chikwe—as a barrister you should know the law: a difference of political opinion is one thing, slander is another."

"As, for instance, an accusation of poisoning?"

Here they all turned, a fourth figure had joined them. Mr. Kwenzi, a tall, rather stooped, remote man, stood a few paces off, smiling. Mr. Chikwe took his place a foot behind him, and there were two couples, facing each other.

"Good morning, Mr. Devuli."

"Good morning, Mr. Kwenzi."

"It must be nearly time for us to go in to the Minister," said Mr. Kwenzi.

"I do not think that Mr. Devuli is in any condition to represent us to the Minister," said Mr. Chikwe, hot and threatening. Mr. Kwenzi nodded. He had rather small direct eyes, deeply inset under his brows, which gave him an earnest focused gaze which he was now directing at the sweat-beaded brow of his rival.

Mr. Devuli blurted, his voice rising: "And who is responsible? Who? The whole world knows of the saintly Mr. Kwenzi, the hard-working Mr. Kwenzi, but who is responsible for my state of health?"

Mr. Chikwe cut in: "No one is responsible for your state of health but yourself, Mr. Devuli. If you drink two bottles of hard liquor a day, then you can expect your health to suffer for it."

"The present health of Mr. Devuli," said Mr. Mafente, since his chief was silent, biting his lip, his eyes red with tears as well as with liquor, "is due to the poison which nearly killed him some weeks ago in the Lady Wilberforce Hospital in Nkalolele."

"I am sorry to hear that," said Mr. Kwenzi mildly. "I trust the worst is over?"

Mr. Devuli was beside himself, his face knitting with emotion, sweat drops starting everywhere, his eyes roving, his fists clenching and unclenching.

"I hope," said Mr. Kwenzi, "that you are not suggesting I or my party had anything to do with it?"

"Suggest!" said Mr. Devuli. "*Suggest?* What shall I tell the Minister? That my political opponents are not ashamed to poison a helpless man in hospital? Shall I tell him that I have to have my food tasted, like an Eastern potentate? No, I cannot tell him such things—I am helpless there too, for he would say, 'Black savages, stooping to poison, what else can you expect?' "

"I doubt whether he would say that," remarked Mr. Kwenzi. "His own ancestors considered poison an acceptable political weapon, and not so very long ago either."

But Mr. Devuli was not listening. His chest was heaving, and he sobbed out loud. Mr. Mafente let his ignored forearm drop by his side, and stood away a couple of paces, gazing somberly at his leader. After this sorrowful inspection, which Mr. Kwenzi and Mr. Chikwe did nothing to shorten, he looked long at Mr. Chikwe, and then at Mr. Kwenzi. During this three-sided silent conversation, Mr. Devuli, like a dethroned king in Shakespeare, stood to one side, his chest heaving, tears flowing, his head bent to receive the rods and lashes of betrayal.

Mr. Chikwe at last remarked: "Perhaps you should tell the Minister that you have ordered a bulletproof vest like an American gangster? It would impress him no doubt with your standing among our people?" Mr. Devuli sobbed again, and Mr. Chikwe continued: "Not that I do not agree with you—the vest is advisable, yes. The food tasters are not enough. I have heard our young hotheads talking among themselves and you would be wise to take every possible precaution."

Mr. Kwenzi, frowning, now raised his hand to check his lieutenant: "I think you are going too far, Mr. Chikwe, there is surely no need . . ."

At which Mr. Devuli let out a great groan of bitter laughter, uncrowned king reeling under the wet London sky, and said: "Listen to the good man, he knows nothing, no—he remains upright while his seconds do his dirty work, listen to the saint!"

Swaying, he looked for Mr. Mafente's forearm, but it was not there. He stood by himself, facing three men.

Mr. Kwenzi said: "It is a very simple matter, my friends. Who is going to speak for our people to the Minister? That is all we have to decide now. I must tell you that I have made a very detailed study of the proposed constitution and I am quite sure that no honest leader of our people could accept it. Mr. Devuli, I am sure you must agree with me—it is a very complicated set of proposals, and it is more than possible there may be implications you have overlooked?"

Mr. Devuli laughed bitterly: "Yes, it is possible."

"Then we are agreed?"

Mr. Devuli was silent.

"I think we are all agreed," said Mr. Chikwe, smiling, looking at Mr. Mafente, who after a moment gave a small nod, and then turned to face his leader's look of bitter accusation.

"It is nearly half past ten," said Mr. Chikwe. "In a few minutes we must present ourselves to Her Majesty's Minister."

The two lieutenants, one threatening, one sorrowful, looked at Mr. Devuli, who still hesitated, grieving, on the pavement's edge. Mr. Kwenzi remained aloof, smiling gently.

Mr. Kwenzi at last said: "After all, Mr. Devuli, you will certainly be elected, certainly we can expect that, and with your long experience the country will need you as Minister. A minister's salary, even for our poor country, will be enough to recompense you for your generous agreement to stand down now."

Mr. Devuli laughed—bitter, resentful, scornful.

He walked away.

Mr. Mafente said: "But Mr. Devuli, Mr. Devuli, where are you going?"

Mr. Devuli threw back over his shoulder: "Mr. Kwenzi will speak to the Minister."

Mr. Mafente nodded at the other two, and ran after his former leader, grabbed his arm, turned him around. "Mr. Devuli, you must come in with us, it is quite essential to preserve a united front before the Minister."

"I bow to superior force, gentlemen," said Mr. Devuli, with a short sarcastic bow, which, however, he was forced to curtail: his stagger was checked by Mr. Mafente's tactful arm.

"Shall we go in?" said Mr. Chikwe.

Without looking again at Mr. Devuli, Mr. Kwenzi walked aloofly into the Ministry, followed by Mr. Devuli, whose left hand lay on Mr. Mafente's arm. Mr. Chikwe came last, smiling, springing off the balls of his feet, watching Mr. Devuli.

"And it is just half past ten," he observed, as a flunkey came forward to intercept them. "Half past ten to the second. I think I can hear Big Ben itself. Punctuality, as we all know, gentlemen, is the cornerstone of that efficiency without which it is impossible to govern a modern state. Is it not so, Mr. Kwenzi? Is it not so, Mr. Mafente? Is it not so, Mr. Devuli?"

# *One off the Short List*

When he had first seen Barbara Coles, some years before, he only noticed her because someone said: "That's Johnson's new girl." He certainly had not used of her the private erotic formula: *Yes, that one.* He even wondered what Johnson saw in her. She won't last long, he remembered thinking as he watched Johnson, a handsome man, but rather flushed with drink, flirting with some unknown girl while Barbara stood by a wall looking on. He thought she had a sullen expression.

She was a pale girl, not slim, for her frame was generous, but her figure could pass as good. Her straight yellow hair was parted on one side in a way that struck him as gauche. He did not notice what she wore. But her eyes were all right, he remembered: large, and solidly green, square-looking because of some trick of the flesh at their corners. Emerald-like eyes in the face of a schoolgirl, or young schoolmistress who was watching her lover flirt and would later sulk about it.

Her name sometimes cropped up in the papers. She was a stage decorator, a designer, something on those lines.

Then a Sunday newspaper had a competition for stage design and she won it. Barbara Coles was one of the "names" in the theatre, and her photograph was seen about. It was always serious. He remembered having thought her sullen.

One night he saw her across the room at a party. She was talking with a well-known actor. Her yellow hair was still done on one side, but now it looked sophisticated. She wore an emerald ring on her right hand that seemed deliberately to invite comparison with her eyes. He walked over and said: "We have met before, Graham Spence." He noted, with discomfort, that he sounded abrupt. "I'm sorry, I don't remember, but how do you do?" she said, smiling. And continued her conversation.

He hung around a bit, but soon she went off with a group of people she was inviting to her home for a drink. She did not invite Graham. There was about her an assurance, a carelessness, that he recognized as the signature of success. It was then, watching her laugh as she went off with her friends, that he used the formula: *Yes, that one.* And he went home to his wife with enjoyable expectation, as if his date with Barbara Coles were already arranged.

His marriage was twenty years old. At first it had been stormy, painful, tragic—full of partings, betrayals, and sweet reconciliations. It had taken him at least a decade to realize that there was nothing remarkable about this marriage that he had lived through with such surprise of the mind and the senses. On the contrary, the marriages of most of the people he knew, whether they were first, second, or third attempts, were just the same. His had run true to form even to the serious love affair with the young girl for whose sake he had *almost* divorced his wife—yet at the last moment had changed his mind, letting the girl down so that he must have her for always (not unpleasurably) on his conscience. It was with humiliation that he had understood that this drama was not at all the unique thing he had imagined. It was nothing more than the experience of everyone in his circle. And presumably in everybody else's circle too?

Anyway, round about the tenth year of his marriage he had seen a good many things clearly, a certain kind of emotional adventure went from his life, and the marriage itself changed.

His wife had married a poor youth with a great future as a writer. Sacrifices had been made, chiefly by her, for that future. He was neither unaware of them nor ungrateful; in fact he felt permanently guilty about it. He at last published a decently successful book, then a second, which now, thank God, no one remembered. He had drifted into radio, television, book reviewing.

He understood he was not going to make it; that he had become—not a hack, no one could call him that—but a member of that army of people who live by their wits on the fringes of the arts. The moment of realization was when he was in a pub one lunchtime near the BBC where he often dropped in to meet others like himself: he understood that was why he went there—they *were* like him. Just as that melodramatic marriage had turned out to be like everyone else's—except that it had been shared with one woman instead of with two or three—so it had turned out that his unique talent, his struggles as a writer had led him here, to this pub and the half-dozen pubs like it, where all the men in sight had the same history. They all had their novel, their play, their book of poems, a moment of fame, to their credit. Yet here they were, running television programs about which they were cynical (to each other or to their wives) or writing reviews about other people's books. Yes, that's what he had become, an impresario of other people's talent. These two moments of clarity, about his marriage and about his talent, had roughly coincided; and (perhaps not by chance) had coincided with his wife's decision to leave him for a man younger than himself who had a future, she said, as a playwright. Well, he had talked her out of it. For her part, she had to understand he was not going to be the T. S. Eliot or Graham Greene of our time—but after all, how many were? She must finally understand this, for he could no longer bear her awful bitterness. For his part, he must stop coming home drunk at five in the morning, and starting a new romantic affair every six months which he took so seriously that he made her miserable because of her implied deficiencies. In short he was to be a good husband. (He had always been a dutiful father.) And she a good wife. And so it was: the marriage became stable, as they say.

The formula: *Yes, that one* no longer implied a necessarily sexual relationship. In its more mature form, it was far from being something he was ashamed of. On the contrary, it expressed a humorous respect for what he was, for his real talents and flair, which had turned out to be not artistic after all, but to do with emotional life, hard-earned experience. It expressed an ironical dignity, a proving to himself not only: I can be honest about myself, but also: I have earned the best in *that* field whenever I want it.

He watched the field for the women who were well known in the arts, or in politics; looked out for photographs, listened for bits of gossip. He made a point of going to see them act, or dance, or orate. He built up a not unshrewd picture of them. He would either quietly pull strings to meet a woman or—more often, for there was a gambler's pleasure in waiting—bide his time until he met her in the natural course of events, which was bound to happen sooner or later. He would be seen out with her a few times in public, which was in order, since his work meant he had to entertain well-known people, male and female. His wife always knew, he told her. He might have a brief affair with this woman, but more often than not it was the appearance of an affair. Not that he didn't get pleasure from other people envying him—he would make a point, for instance, of taking this woman into the pubs where his male colleagues went. It was that his real pleasure came when he saw her surprise at how well she was understood by him. He enjoyed the atmosphere he was able to set up between an intelligent woman and himself: a humorous complicity which had in it much that was unspoken, and which almost made sex irrelevant.

Onto the list of women with whom he planned to have this

relationship went Barbara Coles. There was no hurry. Next week, next month, next year, they would meet at a party. The world of well-known people in London is a small one. Big and little fishes, they drift around, nose each other, flirt their fins, wriggle off again. When he bumped into Barbara Coles, it would be time to decide whether or not to sleep with her.

Meanwhile he listened. But he didn't discover much. She had a husband and children, but the husband seemed to be in the background. The children were charming and well brought up, like everyone else's children. She had affairs, they said; but while several men he met sounded familiar with her, it was hard to determine whether they had slept with her, because none directly boasted of her. She was spoken of in terms of her friends, her work, her house, a party she had given, a job she had found someone. She was liked, she was respected, and Graham Spence's self-esteem was flattered because he had chosen her. He looked forward to saying in just the same tone: "Barbara Coles asked me what I thought about the set and I told her quite frankly. . . ."

Then by chance he met a young man who did boast about Barbara Coles; he claimed to have had the great love affair with her, and recently at that; and he spoke of it as something generally known. Graham realized how much he had already become involved with her in his imagination because of how perturbed he was now, on account of the character of this youth, Jack Kennaway. He had recently become successful as a magazine editor—one of those young men who, not as rare as one might suppose in the big cities, are successful from sheer impertinence, effrontery. Without much talent or taste, yet he had the charm of his effrontery. "Yes, I'm going to succeed, because I've decided to; yes, I may be stupid, but not so stupid that I don't know my deficiencies. Yes, I'm going to be successful because you people with integrity, et cetera, et cetera, simply don't believe in the possibility of people like me. You are too cowardly to stop me. Yes, I've taken your measure and I'm going to succeed because I've got the courage not only to be unscrupulous but to be quite frank about it. And besides, you admire me; you must, or otherwise you'd stop me. . . ." Well, that was young Jack Kennaway, and he shocked Graham. He was a tall, languishing young man, handsome in a dark melting way, and, it was quite clear, he was either asexual or homosexual. And this youth boasted of the favors of Barbara Coles; boasted, indeed, of her love. Either she was a raving neurotic with a taste for neurotics; or Jack Kennaway was a most accomplished liar; or she slept with anyone. Graham was intrigued. He took Jack Kennaway out to dinner in order to hear him talk about Barbara Coles. There was no doubt the two were pretty close—all those dinners, theatres, weekends in the country—Graham Spence felt he had put his finger on the secret pulse of Barbara Coles; and it was intolerable that he must wait to meet her; he decided to arrange it.

It became unnecessary. She was in the news again, with a run of luck. She had done a successful historical play, and immediately afterwards a modern play, and then a hit musical. In all three, the sets were remarked on. Graham saw some interviews in newspapers and on television. These all centered around the theme of her being able to deal easily with so many different styles of theatre; but the real point was, of course, that she was a woman, which naturally added piquancy to the thing. And now Graham Spence was asked to do a half-hour radio interview with her. He planned the questions he would ask her with care, drawing on what people had said of her, but above all on his instinct and experience with women. The interview was to be at nine-thirty at night; he was to pick her up at six from the theatre where she was currently at work, so that there would be time, as the letter from the BBC had put it, "for you and Miss Coles to get to know each other."

At six he was at the stage door, but a message from Miss Coles said she was not quite ready, could he wait a little. He hung about, then went to the pub opposite for a quick one, but still no Miss Coles. So he made his way backstage, directed by voices, hammering, laughter. It was badly lit, and the group of people at work did not see him. The director, James Poynter, had his arm around Barbara's shoulders. He was newly well known, a carelessly good-looking young man reputed to be intelligent. Barbara Coles wore a dark blue overall, and her flat hair fell over her face so that she kept pushing it back with the hand that had the emerald on it. These two stood close, side by side. Three young men, stagehands, were on the other side of a trestle which had sketches and drawings on it. They were studying some sketches. Barbara said, in a voice warm with energy: "Well, so I thought if we did *this*—do you see, James? What do you think, Steven?" "Well, love," said the young man she called Steven, "I see your idea, but I wonder if . . ." "I think you're right, Babs," said the director. "Look," said Barbara, holding one of the sketches towards Steven, "look, let me show you." They all leaned forward, the five of them, absorbed in the business.

Suddenly Graham couldn't stand it. He understood he was shaken to his depths. He went offstage, and stood with his back against a wall in the dingy passage that led to the dressing rooms. His eyes were filled with tears. He was seeing what a long way he had come from the crude, uncompromising, admirable young egomaniac he had been when he was twenty. That group of people there—working, joking, arguing, yes, that's what he hadn't known for years. What bound them was the democracy of respect for each other's work, a confidence in themselves and in each other. They looked like people banded together against a world which they—no, not despised, but which they measured, understood, would fight to the death, out of respect for what *they* stood for, for what *it* stood for. It was a long time since he felt part of that balance. And he understood that he had seen Barbara Coles when she was most herself, at ease with a group of people she worked with. It was then, with the tears drying on his eyelids, which felt old and ironic, that he decided he would sleep with Barbara Coles. It was a necessity for him. He went back through the door onto the stage, burning with this single determination.

The five were still together. Barbara had a length of blue gleaming stuff which she was draping over the shoulder of Steven, the stagehand. He was showing it off, and the others watched. "What do you think, James?" she asked the director. "We've got that sort of dirty green, and I thought . . ." "Well," said James, not sure at all, "well, Babs, well . . ."

Now Graham went forward so that he stood beside Barbara, and said: "I'm Graham Spence, we've met before." For the second time she smiled socially and said: "Oh, I'm sorry, I don't remember." Graham nodded at James, whom he had known, or at least had met off and on, for years. But it was obvious James didn't remember him either.

"From the BBC," said Graham to Barbara, again sounding abrupt, against his will. "Oh I'm sorry, I'm so sorry, I forgot all about it. I've got to be interviewed," she said to the group. "Mr. Spence is a journalist." Graham allowed himself a small smile ironical of the word "journalist," but she was not looking at him. She was going on with her work. "We should decide tonight," she said. "Steven's right." "Yes, I am right," said the stagehand. "She's right, James, we need that blue with that sludge-green everywhere." "James," said Barbara, "James, what's wrong with it? You haven't said." She moved forward to James, passing Graham. Remembering him again, she became contrite. "I'm sorry," she said, "we can none of us agree. Well, look"—she turned to Graham—"you advise us, we've got so involved with it that . . ." At which James laughed, and so did the stagehands. "No, Babs," said James, "of course Mr. Spence can't advise. He's just this moment come in. We've got to decide. Well I'll give you till tomorrow morning. Time to go home, it must be six by now."

"It's nearly seven," said Graham, taking command.

"It isn't!" said Barbara, dramatic. "My God, how terrible, how appalling, how could I have done such a thing. . . ." She was laughing at herself. "Well, you'll have to forgive me, Mr. Spence, because you haven't got any alternative."

They began laughing again: this was clearly a group joke. And now Graham took his chance. He said firmly, as if he were her director, in fact copying James Poynter's manner with her: "No, Miss Coles, I won't forgive you, I've been kicking my heels for nearly an hour." She grimaced, then laughed and accepted it. James said: "There, Babs, that's how you ought to be treated. We spoil you." He kissed her on the cheek, she kissed him on both his, the stagehands moved off. "Have a good evening, Babs," said James, going, and nodding to Graham. Who stood concealing his pleasure with difficulty. He knew, because he had had the courage to be firm, indeed, peremptory, with Barbara, that he had saved himself hours of maneuvering. Several drinks, a dinner—perhaps two or three evenings of drinks and dinners—had been saved because he was now on this footing with Barbara Coles, a man who could say: No, I won't forgive you, you've kept me waiting.

She said: "I've just got to . . ." and went ahead of him. In the passage she hung her overall on a peg. She was thinking, it seemed, of something else, but seeing him watching her, she smiled at him, companionably: he realized with triumph it was the sort of smile she would offer one of the stagehands, or even James. She said again: "Just one second . . ." and went to the stage-door office. She and the stage doorman conferred. There was some problem. Graham said, taking another chance: "What's the trouble, can I help?"—as if he could help, as if he expected to be able to. "Well . . ." she said, frowning. Then, to the man: "No, it'll be all right. Good night." She came to Graham. "We've got ourselves into a bit of a fuss because half the set's in Liverpool and half's here and—but it will sort itself out." She stood, at ease, chatting to him, one colleague to another. All this was admirable, he felt; but there would be a bad moment when they emerged from the special atmosphere of the theatre into the street. He took another decision, grasped her arm firmly, and said: "We're going to have a drink before we do anything at all, it's a terrible evening out." Her arm felt resistant, but remained within his. It was raining outside, luckily. He directed her, authoritative: "No, not that pub, there's a nicer one around the corner." "Oh, but I like this pub," said Barbara, "we always use it."

Of course you do, he said to himself. But in that pub there would be the stagehands, and probably James, and he'd lose contact with her. He'd become a *journalist* again. He took her firmly out of danger around two corners, into a pub he picked at random. A quick look around—no, they weren't there. At least, if there were people from the theatre, she showed no sign. She asked for a beer. He ordered her a double Scotch, which she accepted. Then, having won a dozen preliminary rounds already, he took time to think. Something was bothering him—what? Yes, it was what he had observed backstage, Barbara and James Poynter. Was she having an affair with him? Because if so, it would all be much more difficult. He made himself see the two of them together, and thought with a jealousy surprisingly strong: *Yes, that's it.* Meantime he sat looking at her, seeing himself look at her, *a man gazing in calm appreciation at a woman:* waiting for her to feel it and respond. She was examining the pub. Her white woolen suit was belted, and had a not unprovocative suggestion of being a uniform. Her flat yellow hair, hastily pushed back after work, was untidy. Her clear white skin, without any color, made her look tired. Not very exciting, at the moment, thought Graham, but maintaining his appreciative pose for when she would turn and see it. He knew what she would see: he was relying not only on the "warm, kindly" beam of his gaze, for this was merely a reinforcement of the impression he knew he made. He had black hair, a little greyed. His clothes were loose and bulky—masculine. His eyes were humorous and appreciative. He was not, never had been, concerned to lessen the impression of being settled, dependable: the husband and father. On the contrary, he knew women found it reassuring.

When she at last turned, she said, almost apologetic: "Would you mind if we sat down? I've been lugging great things around all day." She had spotted two empty chairs in a corner. So had he, but rejected them, because there were other people at the table. "But my dear, of course!" They took the chairs, and then Barbara said: "If you'll excuse me a moment." She had remembered she needed makeup. He watched her go off, annoyed with himself. She was tired; and he could have understood, protected, sheltered. He realized that in the other pub, with the people she had worked with all day, she would not have thought: I must make myself up, I must be on show. That was for outsiders. She had not, until now, considered Graham an outsider, because of his taking his chance to seem one of the working group in the theatre; but now he had thrown this opportunity away. She returned armored. Her hair was sleek, no longer defenseless. And she had made up her eyes. Her eyebrows were untouched, pale gold streaks above the brilliant green eyes whose lashes were blackened. Rather good, he thought, the contrast. Yes, but the moment had gone when he could say: Did you know you had a smudge on your cheek? Or—my dear girl—pushing her hair back with the edge of a brotherly hand. In fact, unless he was careful, he'd be back at starting point.

He remarked: "That emerald is very cunning," smiling into her eyes.

She smiled politely, and said: "It's not cunning, it's an accident; it was my grandmother's." She flirted her hand lightly by her face, though, smiling. But that was something she had done before, to a compliment she had had before, and often. It was all social, she had become social entirely. She remarked: "Didn't you say it was half past nine we had to record?"

"My dear Barbara, we've got two hours. We'll have another drink or two, then I'll ask you a couple of questions, then we'll drop down to the studio and get it over, and then we'll have a comfortable supper."

"I'd rather eat now, if you don't mind. I had no lunch, and I'm really hungry."

"But my dear, of course." He was angry. Just as he had been surprised by his real jealousy over James, so now he was thrown off balance by his anger: he had been counting on the long quiet dinner afterwards to establish intimacy. "Finish your drink and I'll take you to Nott's." Nott's was expensive. He glanced at her assessingly as he mentioned it. She said: "I wonder if you know Butler's? It's good and it's rather close." Butler's was good, and it was cheap, and he gave her a good mark for liking it. But Nott's it was going to be. "My dear, we'll get into a taxi and be at Nott's in a moment, don't worry."

She obediently got to her feet: the way she did it made him understand how badly he had slipped. She was saying to herself: Very well, he's like that, then all right, I'll do what he wants and get it over with. . . .

Swallowing his own drink, he followed her, and took her arm in the pub doorway. It was polite within his. Outside it drizzled. No taxi. He was having bad luck now. They walked in silence to the end of the street. There Barbara glanced into a side street where a sign said: BUTLER'S. Not to remind him of it, on the contrary, she concealed the glance. And here she was, entirely at his disposal; they might never have shared the comradely moment in the theatre.

They walked half a mile to Nott's. No taxis. She made conversation: this was, he saw, to cover any embarrassment he might feel because of a half-mile walk through rain when she was tired. She was talking about some theory to do with the theatre, with designs for theatre building. He heard himself saying, and repeatedly: "Yes, yes, yes." He thought about Nott's, how to get things right when they reached Nott's. There he took the headwaiter aside, gave him a pound, and instructions. They were put in a corner. Large Scotches appeared. The menus were spread. "And now, my dear," he said, "I apologize for dragging you here, but I hope you'll think it's worth it."

"Oh, it's charming, I've always liked it. It's just that . . ." She stopped herself saying: It's such a long way. She smiled at him, raising her glass, and said: "It's one of my very favorite places, and I'm glad you dragged me here." Her voice was flat with tiredness. All this was appalling; he knew it; and he sat thinking how to retrieve his position. Meanwhile she fingered the menu. The headwaiter took the order, but Graham made a gesture which said: Wait a moment. He wanted the Scotch to take effect before she ate. But she saw his silent order; and, without annoyance or reproach, leaned forward to say, sounding patient: "Graham, please, I've got to eat; you don't want me drunk when you interview me, do you?"

"They are bringing it as fast as they can," he said, making it sound as if she were greedy. He looked neither at the headwaiter nor at Barbara. He noted in himself, as he slipped further and further away from contact with her, a cold determination growing in him—one apart from, apparently, any conscious act of will—that come what may, if it took all night, he'd be in her bed before morning. And now, seeing the small pale face, with the enormous green eyes, it was for the first time that he imagined her in his arms. Although he had said: *Yes, that one,* weeks ago, it was only now that he imagined her as a sensual experience. Now he did, so strongly that he could only glance at her, and then away towards the waiters who were bringing food.

"Thank the Lord," said Barbara, and all at once her voice was gay and intimate. "Thank heavens. Thank every power that is. . . ." She was making fun of her own exaggeration; and, as he saw, because she wanted to put him at his ease after his boorishness over delaying the food. (She hadn't been taken in, he saw, humiliated, disliking her.) "Thank all the gods of Nott's," she went on, "because if I hadn't eaten inside five minutes I'd have died, I tell you." With which she picked up her knife and fork and began on her steak. He poured wine, smiling with her, thinking that *this* moment of closeness he would not throw away. He watched her frank hunger as she ate, and thought: Sensual—it's strange I hadn't wondered whether she would be or not.

"Now," she said, sitting back, having taken the edge off her hunger, "let's get to work."

He said: "I've thought it over very carefully—how to present you. The first thing seems to me, we must get away from that old chestnut: Miss Coles, how extraordinary for a woman to be so versatile in her work. . . . I hope you agree?" This was his trump card. He had noted, when he had seen her on television, her polite smile when this note was struck. (The smile he had seen so often tonight.) This smile said: All right, if you *have* to be stupid, what can I do?

Now she laughed and said: "What a relief. I was afraid you were going to do the same thing."

"Good, now you eat and I'll talk."

In his carefully prepared monologue he spoke of the different styles of theatre she had shown herself mistress of, but not directly: he was flattering her on the breadth of her experience; the complexity of her character, as shown in her work. She ate, steadily, her face showing nothing. At last she asked: "And how did you plan to introduce this?"

He had meant to spring that on her as a surprise, something like: Miss Coles, a surprisingly young woman for what she has accomplished (she was thirty? thirty-two?) and a very attractive one. . . . Perhaps I can give you an idea of what she's like if I say she could be taken for the film star Marie Carletta. . . . The Carletta was a strong earthy blonde, known to be intellectual. He now saw he could not possibly say this: he could imagine her cool look if he did. She said: "Do you mind if we get away from all that—my manifold talents, et cetera. . . ." He felt himself stiffen with annoyance, particularly because this was not an accusation; he saw she did not think him worth one. She had assessed him: This is the kind of man who uses this kind of flattery and therefore . . . It made him angrier that she did not even trouble to say: Why did you do exactly what you promised you wouldn't? She was being invincibly polite, trying to conceal her patience with his stupidity.

"After all," she was saying, "it is a stage designer's job to design what comes up. Would anyone take, let's say, Johnnie Cranmore" (another stage designer) "onto the air or television and say: 'How very versatile you are because you did that musical about Java last month and a modern play about Irish laborers this'?"

He battened down his anger. "My dear Barbara, I'm sorry. I didn't realize that what I said would sound just like the mixture as before. So what shall we talk about?"

"What I was saying as we walked to the restaurant: can we get away from the personal stuff?"

Now he almost panicked. Then, thank God, he laughed from nervousness, for she laughed and said: "You didn't hear one word I said."

"No, I didn't. I was frightened you were going to be furious because I made you walk so far when you were tired."

They laughed together, back to where they had been in the theatre. He leaned over, took her hand, kissed it. He said: "Tell me again." He thought: Damn, now she's going to be earnest and intellectual.

But he understood he had been stupid. He had forgotten himself at twenty—or, for that matter, at thirty; forgotten one could live inside an idea, a set of ideas, with enthusiasm. For in talking about her ideas (also the ideas of the people she worked with) for a new theatre, a new style of theatre, she was as she had been with her colleagues over the sketches or the blue material. She was easy, informal, almost chattering. This was how, he remembered, one talked about ideas that were a breath of life. The ideas, he thought, were intelligent enough; and he would agree with them, with her, if he believed it mattered a damn one way or another, if any of these enthusiasms mattered a damn. But at least he now had the key; he knew what to do. At the end of not more than half an hour, they were again two professionals, talking about ideas they shared, for he remembered caring about all this himself once. *When? How many years ago was it that he had been able to care?*

At last he said: "My dear Barbara, do you realize the impossible position you're putting me in? Margaret Ruyen who runs this program is determined to do you personally; the poor woman hasn't got a serious thought in her head."

Barbara frowned. He put his hand on hers, teasing her for the frown: "No, wait, trust me, we'll circumvent her." She smiled. In fact Margaret Ruyen had left it all to him, had said nothing about Miss Coles.

"They aren't very bright—the brass," he said. "Well, never mind: we'll work out what we want, do it, and it'll be a *fait accompli.*"

"Thank you, what a relief. How lucky I was to be given you to interview me." She was relaxed now, because of the whisky, the food, the wine, above all because of this new complicity against Margaret Ruyen. It would all be easy. They worked out five or six questions, over coffee, and took a taxi through rain to the studios. He noted that the cold necessity to have her, to make her, to beat her down, had left him. He was even seeing himself, as the evening ended, kissing her on the cheek and going home to his wife. This comradeship was extraordinarily pleasant. It was balm to the wound he had not known he carried until that evening, when he had had to accept the justice of the word "journalist." He felt he could talk forever about the state of the theatre, its finances, the stupidity of the government, the philistinism of . . .

At the studios he was careful to make a joke so that they walked in on the laugh. He was careful that the interview began at once, without conversation with Margaret Ruyen; and that from the moment the green light went on, his voice lost its easy familiarity. He made sure that not one personal note was struck during the interview. Afterwards, Margaret Ruyen, who was pleased, came forward to say so; but he took her aside to say that Miss Coles was tired and needed to be taken home at once: for he knew this must look to Barbara as if he were squaring a producer who had been expecting a different interview. He led Barbara off, her hand held tight in his against his side. "Well," he said, "we've done it, and I don't think she knows what hit her."

"Thank you," she said, "it really was pleasant to talk about something sensible for once."

He kissed her lightly on the mouth. She returned it, smiling. By now he felt sure that the mood need not slip again, he could hold it.

"There are two things we can do," he said. "You can come to my club and have a drink. Or I can drive you home and you can give me a drink. I have to go past you."

"Where do you live?"

"Wimbledon." He lived, in fact, at Highgate; but she lived in Fulham. He was taking another chance, but by the time she found out, they would be in a position to laugh over his ruse.

"Good," she said. "You can drop me home then. I have to get up early." He made no comment. In the taxi he took her hand; it was heavy in his, and he asked: "Does James slave-drive you?"

"I didn't realize you knew him—no, he doesn't."

"Well I don't know him intimately. What's he like to work with?"

"Wonderful," she said at once. "There's no one I enjoy working with more."

Jealousy spurted in him. He could not help himself: "Are you having an affair with him?"

She looked: What's it to do with you? but said: "No, I'm not."

"He's very attractive," he said, with a chuckle of worldly complicity. She said nothing, and he insisted: "If I were a woman I'd have an affair with James."

It seemed she might very well say nothing. But she remarked: "He's married."

His spirits rose in a swoop. It was the first stupid remark she had made. It was a remark of such staggering stupidity that . . . he let out a humoring snort of laughter, put his arm around her, kissed her, said: "My dear little Babs."

She said: "Why Babs?"

"Is that the prerogative of James. And of the stagehands?" he could not prevent himself adding.

"I'm only called that at work." She was stiff inside his arm.

"My dear Barbara, then . . ." He waited for her to enlighten and explain, but she said nothing. Soon she moved out of his arm, on the pretext of lighting a cigarette. He lit it for her. He noted that his determination to lay her, and at all costs, had come back. They were outside her house. He said quickly: "And now, Barbara, you can make me a cup of coffee and give me a brandy." She hesitated; but he was out of the taxi, paying, opening the door for her. The house had no lights on, he noted. He said: "We'll be very quiet so as not to wake the children."

She turned her head slowly to look at him. She said, flat, replying to his real question: "My husband is away. As for the children, they are visiting friends tonight." She now went ahead of him to the door of the house. It was a small house, in a terrace of small and not very pretty houses. Inside a little, bright, intimate hall, she said: "I'll go and make some coffee. Then, my friend, you must go home because I'm very tired."

The "my friend" struck him deep, because he had become vulnerable during their comradeship. He said, gabbling: "You're annoyed with me—oh, please don't, I'm sorry."

She smiled, from a cool distance. He saw, in the small light from the ceiling, her extraordinary eyes. "Green" eyes are hazel, are brown with green flecks, are even blue. Eyes are checkered, flawed, changing. Hers were solid green, but really, he had never seen anything like them before. They were like very deep water. They were like—well, emeralds; or the absolute clarity of green in the depths of a tree in summer. And now, as she smiled almost perpendicularly up at him, he saw a darkness come over them. Darkness swallowed the clear green. She said: "I'm not in the least annoyed." It was as if she had yawned with boredom. "And now I'll get the things . . . in there." She nodded at a white door and left him. He went into a long, very tidy white room that had a narrow bed in one corner, a table covered with drawings, sketches, pencils. Tacked to the walls with drawing pins were swatches of colored stuffs. Two small chairs stood near a low round table: an area of comfort in the working room. He was thinking: I wouldn't like it if my wife had a room like this. I wonder what Barbara's husband . . . ? He had not thought of her till now in relation to her husband, or to her children. Hard to imagine her with a frying pan in her hand, or for that matter, cozy in the double bed.

A noise outside: he hastily arranged himself, leaning with one arm on the mantelpiece. She came in with a small tray that had cups, glasses, brandy, coffeepot. She looked abstracted. Graham was on the whole flattered by this: it probably meant she was at ease in his presence. He realized he was a little tight and rather tired. Of course, she was tired too; that was why she was vague. He remembered that earlier that evening he had lost a chance by not using her tiredness. Well now, if he were intelligent . . . She was about to pour coffee. He firmly took the coffeepot out of her hand, and nodded at a chair. Smiling, she obeyed him. "That's better," he said. He poured coffee, poured brandy, and pulled the table towards her. She watched him. Then he took her hand, kissed it, patted it, laid it down gently. Yes, he thought, I did that well.

Now, a problem. He wanted to be closer to her, but she was fitted into a damned silly little chair that had arms. If he were to sit by her on the floor . . . ? But no, for him, the big bulky reassuring man, there could be no casual gestures, no informal postures. Suppose I scoop her out of the chair onto the bed? He drank his coffee as he plotted. Yes, he'd carry her to the bed, but not yet.

"Graham," she said, setting down her cup. She was, he saw with annoyance, looking tolerant. "Graham, in about half an hour I want to be in bed and asleep."

As she said this, she offered him a smile of amusement at this situation—man and woman maneuvering, the great comic situation. And with part of himself he could have shared it. Almost, he smiled with her, laughed. (Not till days later he exclaimed to himself: Lord what a mistake I made, not to share the joke with her then: that was where I went seriously wrong.) But he could not smile. His face was frozen, with a stiff pride. Not because she had been watching him plot—the amusement she now offered him took the sting out of that—but because of his revived determination that he was going to have his own way, he was going to have her. He was not going home. But he felt that he held a bunch of keys, and did not know which one to choose.

He lifted the second small chair opposite to Barbara, moving aside the coffee table for this purpose. He sat in this chair, leaned forward, took her two hands, and said: "My dear, don't make me go home yet, don't, I beg you." The trouble was, nothing had happened all evening that could be felt to lead up to these words and his tone—simple, dignified, human being pleading with human being for surcease. He saw himself leaning forward, his big hands swallowing her small ones; he saw his face, warm with the appeal. And he realized he had meant the words he used. They were nothing more than what he felt. He wanted to stay with her because she wanted him to, because he was her colleague, a fellow worker in the arts. He needed this desperately. But she was examining him, curious rather than surprised, and from a critical distance. He heard himself saying: "If James were here, I wonder what you'd do?" His voice was aggrieved; he saw the sudden dark descend over her eyes, and she said: "Graham, would you like some more coffee before you go?"

He said: "I've been wanting to meet you for years. I know a good many people who know you."

She leaned forward, poured herself a little more brandy, sat back, holding the glass between her two palms on her chest. An odd gesture: Graham felt that this vessel she was cherishing between her hands was herself. A patient, long-suffering gesture. He thought of various men who had mentioned her. He thought of Jack Kennaway, wavered, panicked, said: "For instance, Jack Kennaway."

And now, at the name, an emotion lit her eyes—what was it? He went on, deliberately testing this emotion, adding to it: "I had dinner with him last week—oh, quite by chance!—and he was talking about you."

"Was he?"

He remembered he had thought her sullen, all those years ago. Now she seemed defensive, and she frowned. He said: "In fact he spent most of the evening talking about you."

She said in short, breathless sentences, which he realized were due to anger: "I can very well imagine what he says. But surely you can't think I enjoy being reminded that . . ." She broke off, resenting him, he saw, because he forced her down onto a level she despised. But it was not his level either: it was all her fault, all hers! He couldn't remember not being in control of a situation with a woman for years. Again he felt like a man teetering on a tightrope. He said, trying to make good use of Jack Kennaway, even at this late hour: "Of course, he's a charming boy, but not a man at all."

She looked at him, silent, guarding her brandy glass against her breasts.

"Unless appearances are totally deceptive, of course." He could not resist probing, even though he knew it was fatal.

She said nothing.

"Do you know you are supposed to have had the great affair with Jack Kennaway?" he exclaimed, making this an amused expostulation against the fools who could believe it.

"So I am told." She set down her glass. "And now," she said, standing up, dismissing him. He lost his head, took a step forward, grabbed her in his arms, and groaned: "Barbara!"

She turned her face this way and that under his kisses. He snatched a diagnostic look at her expression—it was still patient. He placed his lips against her neck, groaned "Barbara" again, and waited. She would have to do something. Fight free, respond, something. She did nothing at all. At last she said: "For the Lord's sake, Graham!" She sounded amused: he was again being offered amusement. But if he shared it with her, it would be the end of this chance to have her. He clamped his mouth over hers, silencing her. She did not fight him off so much as blow him off. Her mouth treated his attacking mouth as a woman blows and laughs in water, puffing off waves or spray with a laugh, turning aside her head. It was a gesture half annoyance, half humor. He continued to kiss her while she moved her head and face about under the kisses as if they were small attacking waves.

And so began what, when he looked back on it afterwards, was the most embarrassing experience of his life. Even at the time he hated her for his ineptitude. For he held her there for what must have been nearly half an hour. She was much shorter than he, he had to bend, and his neck ached. He held her rigid, his thighs on either side of hers, her arms clamped to her side in a bear's hug. She was unable to move, except for her head. When his mouth ground hers open and his tongue moved and writhed inside it, she still remained passive. And he could not stop himself. While with his intelligence he watched this ridiculous scene, he was determined to go on, because sooner or later her body must soften in wanting his. And he could not stop because he could not face the horror of the moment when he set her free and she looked at him. And he hated her more, every moment. Catching glimpses of her great green eyes, open and dismal beneath his, he knew he had never disliked anything more than those "jeweled" eyes. They were repulsive to him. It occurred to him at last that even if by now she wanted him, he wouldn't know it, because she was not able to move at all. He cautiously loosened his hold so that she had an inch or so leeway. She remained quite passive. As if, he thought derisively, she had read or been told that the way to incite men maddened by lust was to fight them. He found he was thinking: Stupid cow, so you imagine I find you attractive, do you? You've got the conceit to think that!

The sheer, raving insanity of this thought hit him, opened his arms, his thighs, and lifted his tongue out of her mouth. She stepped back, wiping her mouth with the back of her hand, and stood dazed with incredulity. The embarrassment that lay in wait for him nearly engulfed him, but he let anger postpone it. She said positively apologetic, even, at this moment, humorous: "You're crazy, Graham. What's the matter, are you drunk? You don't seem drunk. You don't even find me attractive."

The blood of hatred went to his head and he gripped her again. Now she had got her face firmly twisted away so that he could not reach her mouth, and she repeated steadily as he kissed the parts of her cheeks and neck that were available to him: "Graham, let me go, do let me go, Graham." She went on saying this; he went on squeezing, grinding, kissing, and licking. It might go on all night: it was a sheer contest of wills, nothing else. He thought: It's only a really masculine woman who wouldn't have given in by now out of sheer decency of the flesh! One thing he knew, however: that she would be in that bed, in his arms, and very soon. He let her go, but said: "I'm going to sleep with you tonight, you know that, don't you?"

She leaned with hand on the mantelpiece to steady herself. Her face was colorless, since he had licked all the makeup off. She seemed quite different: small and defenseless with her large mouth pale now, her smudged green eyes fringed with gold. And now, for the first time, he felt what it might have been supposed (certainly by her) he felt hours ago. Seeing the small damp flesh of her face, he felt kinship, intimacy with her, he felt intimacy of the flesh, the affection and good humor of sensuality. He felt she was flesh of his flesh, his sister in the flesh. He felt desire for her, instead of the will to have her; and because of this, was ashamed of the farce he had been playing. Now he desired simply to take her into bed in the affection of his senses.

She said: "What on earth am I supposed to do? Telephone for the police, or what?" He was hurt that she still addressed the man who had ground her into sulky apathy; she was not addressing *him* at all.

She said: "Or scream for the neighbors, is that what you want?"

The gold-fringed eyes were almost black, because of the depth of the shadow of boredom over them. She was bored and weary to the point of falling to the floor, he could see that.

He said: "I'm going to sleep with you."

"But how can you possibly want to?"—a reasonable, a civilized demand addressed to a man who (he could see) she believed would respond to it. She said: "You know I don't want to, and I know you don't really give a damn one way or the other."

He was stung back into being the boor because she had not the intelligence to see that the boor no longer existed; because she could not see that this was a man who wanted her in a way which she must respond to.

There she stood, supporting herself with one hand, looking small and white and exhausted, and utterly incredulous. She was going to turn and walk off out of simple incredulity, he could see that. "Do you think I don't mean it?" he demanded, grinding this out between his teeth. She made a movement—she was on the point of going away. His hand shot out on its own volition and grasped her wrist. She frowned. His other hand grasped her other wrist. His body hove up against hers to start the pressure of a new embrace. Before it could, she said: "Oh Lord, no, I'm not going through all that again. Right, then."

"What do you mean—right, then?" he demanded.

She said: "You're going to sleep with me. O.K. Anything rather than go through that again. Shall we get it over with?"

He grinned, saying in silence: "No darling, oh no you don't, I don't care what words you use, I'm going to have you now and that's all there is to it."

She shrugged. The contempt, the weariness of it, had no effect on him, because he was now again hating her so much that wanting her was like needing to kill something or someone.

She took her clothes off, as if she were going to bed by herself: her jacket, skirt, petticoat. She stood in white bra and panties, a rather solid girl, brown-skinned still from the summer. He felt a flash of affection for the brown girl with her loose yellow hair as she stood naked. She got into bed and lay there, while the green eyes looked at him in civilized appeal: Are you really going through with this? Do you have to? Yes, his eyes said back: I do have to. She shifted her gaze aside, to the wall, saying silently: Well, if you want to take me without any desire at all on my part, then go ahead, if you're not ashamed. He was not ashamed, because he was maintaining the flame of hate for her which he knew quite well was all that stood between him and shame. He took off his clothes, and got into bed beside her. As he did so, knowing he was putting himself in the position of raping a woman who was making it elaborately clear he bored her, his flesh subsided completely, sad, and full of reproach because a few moments ago it was reaching out for his sister whom he could have made happy. He lay on his side by her, secretly at work on himself, while he supported himself across her body on his elbow, using the free hand to manipulate her breasts. He saw that she gritted her teeth against his touch. At least she could not know that after all this fuss he was not potent.

In order to incite himself, he clasped her again. She felt his smallness, writhed free of him, sat up and said: "Lie down."

While she had been lying there, she had been thinking: The only way to get this over with is to make him big again, otherwise I've got to put up with him all night. His hatred of her was giving him a clairvoyance: he knew very well what went on through her mind. She had switched on, with the determination to *get it all over with,* a sensual good humor, a patience. He lay down. She squatted beside him, the light from the ceiling blooming on her brown shoulders, her flat fair hair falling over her face. But she would not look at his face. Like a bored, skilled wife, she was; or like a prostitute. She administered to him, she was setting herself to please him. Yes, he thought, she's sensual, or she could be. Meanwhile she was succeeding in defeating the reluctance of his flesh, which was the tender token of a possible desire for her, by using a cold skill that was the result of her contempt for him. Just as he decided: Right, it's enough, now I shall have her properly, she made him come. It was not a trick, to hurry or cheat him; what defeated him was her transparent thought: Yes, that's what he's worth.

Then, having succeeded, and waited for a moment or two, she stood up, naked, the fringes of gold at her loins and in her armpits speaking to him a language quite different from that of her green, bored eyes. She looked at him and thought, showing it plainly: What sort of man is it who . . . He watched the slight movement of her shoulders: a just-checked shrug. She went out of the room: then the sound of running water. Soon she came back in a white dressing gown, carrying a yellow towel. She handed him the towel, looking away in politeness as he used it. "Are you going now?'" she inquired hopefully, at this point.

"No, I'm not." He believed that now he would have to start fighting her again, but she lay down beside him, not touching him (he could feel the distaste of her flesh for his) and he thought: Very well, my dear, but there's a lot of the night left yet. He said aloud: "I'm going to have you properly tonight." She said nothing, lay silent, yawned. Then she remarked consolingly, and he could have laughed outright from sheer surprise: "Those were hardly conducive circumstances for making love." She was *consoling* him. He hated her for it. A proper little slut: I force her into bed, she doesn't want me, but she still has to make me feel good, like a prostitute. But even while he hated her he responded in kind, from the habit of sexual generosity. "It's because of my admiration for you, because . . . after all, I was holding in my arms one of the thousand women."

A pause. "The thousand?" she inquired, carefully.

"The thousand especial women."

"In Britain or in the world? You choose them for their brains, their beauty—what?"

"Whatever it is that makes them outstanding," he said, offering her a compliment.

"Well," she remarked at last, inciting him to be amused again, "I hope that at least there's a short list you can say I am on, for politeness' sake."

He did not reply for he understood he was sleepy. He was still telling himself that he must stay awake when he was slowly waking and it was morning. It was about eight. Barbara was not there. He thought: My God! What on earth shall I tell my wife? Where was Barbara? He remembered the ridiculous scenes of last night and nearly succumbed to shame. Then he thought, reviving anger: If she didn't sleep beside me here I'll never forgive her. . . . He sat up, quietly, determined to go through the house until he found her and, having found her, to possess her, when the door opened and she came in. She was fully dressed in a green suit, her hair done, her eyes made up. She carried a tray of coffee, which she set down beside the bed. He was conscious of his big loose hairy body, half uncovered. He said to himself that he was not going to lie in bed, naked, while she was dressed. He said: "Have you got a gown of some kind?" She handed him, without speaking, a towel, and said: "The bathroom's second on the left." She went out. He followed, the towel around him. Everything in this house was gay, intimate—not at all like her efficient working room. He wanted to find out where she had slept, and opened the first door. It was the kitchen, and she was in it, putting a brown earthenware dish into the oven. "The next door," said Barbara. He went hastily past the second door, and opened (he hoped quietly) the third. It was a cupboard full of linen. "This door," said Barbara, behind him.

"So all right then, where did you sleep?"

"What's it to do with you? Upstairs, in my own bed. Now, if you have everything, I'll say goodbye. I want to get to the theatre."

"I'll take you," he said at once.

He saw again the movement of her eyes, the dark swallowing the light in deadly boredom. "I'll take you," he insisted.

"I'd prefer to go by myself," she remarked. Then she smiled: "However, you'll take me. Then you'll make a point of coming right in, so that James and everyone can see—that's what you want to take me for, isn't it?"

He hated her, finally, and quite simply, for her intelligence; that not once had he got away with anything, that she had been watching, since they had met yesterday, every movement of his campaign for her. However, some fate or inner urge over which he had no control made him say sentimentally: "My dear, you must see that I'd like at least to take you to your work."

"Not at all, have it on me," she said, giving him the lie direct. She went past him to the room he had slept in. "I shall be leaving in ten minutes," she said.

He took a shower, fast. When he returned, the workroom was already tidied, the bed made, all signs of the night gone. Also, there were no signs of the coffee she had brought in for him. He did not like to ask for it, for fear of an outright refusal. Besides, she was ready, her coat on, her handbag under her arm. He went, without a word, to the front door, and she came after him, silent.

He could see that every fiber of her body signaled a simple message: Oh God, for the moment when I can be rid of this boor! She was nothing but a slut, he thought.

A taxi came. In it she sat as far away from him as she could. He thought of what he should say to his wife.

Outside the theatre she remarked: "You could drop me here, if you like." It was not a plea, she was too proud for that. "I'll take you in," he said, and saw her thinking: Very well, I'll go through with it to shame him. He was determined to take her in and hand her over to her colleagues, he was afraid she would give him the slip. But far from playing it down, she seemed determined to play it his way. At the stage door, she said to the doorman: "This is Mr. Spence, Tom—do you remember, Mr. Spence from last night?" "Good morning, Babs," said the man, examining Graham, politely, as he had been ordered to do.

Barbara went to the door to the stage, opened it, held it open for him. He went in first, then held it open for her. Together they walked into the cavernous, littered, badly lit place and she called out: "James, James!" A man's voice called out from the front of the house: "Here, Babs, why are you so late?"

The auditorium opened before them, darkish, silent, save for an early-morning busyness of charwomen. A vacuum cleaner roared, smally, somewhere close. A couple of stagehands stood looking up at a drop which had a design of blue-and-green spirals. James stood with his back to the auditorium, smoking. "You're late, Babs," he said again. He saw Graham behind her, and nodded. Barbara and James kissed. Barbara said, giving allowance to every syllable: "You remember Mr. Spence from last night?" James nodded: How do you do? Barbara stood beside him, and they looked together up at the blue-and-green backdrop. Then Barbara looked again at Graham, asking silently: All right now, isn't that enough? He could see her eyes, sullen with boredom.

He said: "Bye, Babs. Bye, James. I'll ring you, Babs." No response, she ignored him. He walked off slowly, listening for what might be said. For instance: Babs, for God's sake, what are you doing with him? Or she might say: Are you wondering about Graham Spence? Let me explain.

Graham passed the stagehands, who, he could have sworn, didn't recognize him. Then at last he heard James's voice to Barbara: "It's no good, Babs, I know you're enamored of that particular shade of blue, but do have another look at it, there's a good girl. . . ." Graham left the stage, went past the office where the stage doorman sat reading a newspaper. He looked up, nodded, went back to his paper. Graham went to find a taxi, thinking: I'd better think up something convincing, then I'll telephone my wife.

Luckily he had an excuse not to be at home that day, for this evening he had to interview a young man (for television) about his new novel.

# *Homage for Isaac Babel*

The day I had promised to take Catherine down to visit my young friend Philip at his school in the country, we were to leave at eleven, but she arrived at nine. Her blue dress was new, and so were her fashionable shoes. Her hair had just been done. She looked more than ever like a pink-and-gold Renoir girl who expects everything from life.

Catherine lives in a white house overlooking the sweeping brown tides of the river. She helped me clean up my flat with a devotion which said that she felt small flats were altogether more romantic than large houses. We drank tea, and talked mainly about Philip, who, being fifteen, has pure stern tastes in everything from food to music. Catherine looked at the books lying around his room, and asked if she might borrow the stories of Isaac Babel to read on the train. Catherine is thirteen. I suggested she might find them difficult, but said: "Philip reads them, doesn't he?"

During the journey I read newspapers and watched her pretty frowning face as she turned the pages of Babel, for she was determined to let nothing get between her and her ambition to be worthy of Philip.

At the school, which is charming, civilized, and expensive, the two children walked together across green fields, and I followed, seeing how the sun gilded their bright friendly heads turned towards each other as they talked. In Catherine's left hand she carried the stories of Isaac Babel.

After lunch we went to the pictures. Philip allowed it to be seen that he thought going to the pictures just for the fun of it was not worthy of intelligent people, but he made the concession, for our sakes. For his sake we chose the more serious of the two films that were showing in the little town. It was about a good priest who helped criminals in New

York. His goodness, however, was not enough to prevent one of them from being sent to the gas chamber; and Philip and I waited with Catherine in the dark until she had stopped crying and could face the light of a golden evening.

At the entrance of the cinema the doorman was lying in wait for anyone who had red eyes. Grasping Catherine by her suffering arm, he said bitterly: "Yes, why are you crying? He had to be punished for his crime, didn't he?" Catherine stared at him, incredulous. Philip rescued her by saying with disdain: "Some people don't know right from wrong even when it's *demonstrated* to them." The doorman turned his attention to the next red-eyed emerger from the dark; and we went on together to the station, the children silent because of the cruelty of the world.

Finally Catherine said, her eyes wet again: "I think it's all absolutely beastly, and I can't bear to think about it." And Philip said: "But we've got to think about it, don't you see, because if we don't it'll just go on and *on,* don't you see?"

In the train going back to London I sat beside Catherine. She had the stories open in front of her, but she said: "Philip's awfully lucky. I wish I went to that school. Did you notice that girl who said hullo to him in the garden? They must be great friends. I wish my mother would let me have a dress like that, it's *not* fair."

"I thought it was too old for her."

"Oh, *did* you?"

Soon she bent her head again over the book, but almost at once lifted it to say: "Is he a very famous writer?"

"He's a marvelous writer, brilliant, one of the very best."

"Why?"

"Well, for one thing he's so simple. Look how few words he uses, and how strong his stories are."

"I see. Do you know him? Does he live in London?"

"Oh no, he's dead."

"Oh. Then why did you—I thought he was alive, the way you talked."

"I'm sorry, I suppose I wasn't thinking of him as dead."

"When did he die?"

"He was murdered. About twenty years ago, I suppose."

*"Twenty years."* Her hands began the movement of pushing the book over to me, but then relaxed. "I'll be fourteen in November," she stated, sounding threatened, while her eyes challenged me.

I found it hard to express my need to apologize, but before I could speak, she said, patiently attentive again: "You said he was murdered?"

"Yes."

"I expect the person who murdered him felt sorry when he discovered he had murdered a famous writer."

"Yes, I expect so."

"Was he old when he was murdered?"

"No, quite young really."

"Well, that was bad luck, wasn't it?"

"Yes, I suppose it was bad luck."

"Which do you think is the very best story here? I mean, in your honest opinion, the very very best one."

I chose the story about killing the goose. She read it slowly, while I sat waiting, wishing to take it from her, wishing to protect this charming little person from Isaac Babel.

When she had finished, she said: "Well, some of it I don't understand. He's got a funny way of looking at things. Why should a man's legs in boots look like *girls?*" She finally pushed the book over at me, and said: "I think it's all morbid."

"But you have to understand the kind of life he had. First, he was a Jew in Russia. That was bad enough. Then his experience was all revolution and civil war and . . ."

But I could see these words bouncing off the clear glass of her fiercely denying gaze; and I said: "Look, Catherine, why don't you try again when you're older? Perhaps you'll like him better then?"

She said gratefully: "Yes, perhaps that would be best. After all, Philip is two years older than me, isn't he?"

A week later I got a letter from Catherine.

> *Thank you very much for being kind enough to take me to visit Philip at his school. It was the most lovely day in my whole life. I am extremely grateful to you for taking me. I have been thinking about the Hoodlum Priest. That was a film which demonstrated to me beyond any shadow of doubt that Capital Punishment is a Wicked Thing, and I shall never forget what I learned that afternoon, and the lessons of it will be with me all my life. I have been meditating about what you said about Isaac Babel, the famed Russian short story writer, and I now see that the conscious simplicity of his style is what makes him, beyond the shadow of a doubt, the great writer that he is, and now in my school compositions I am endeavoring to emulate him so as to learn a conscious simplicity which is the only basis for a really*

*brilliant writing style. Love, Catherine. P.S. Has Philip said anything about my party? I wrote but he hasn't answered. Please find out if he is coming or if he just forgot to answer my letter. I hope he comes because sometimes I feel I shall die if he doesn't. P.P.S. Please don't tell him I said anything, because I should die if he knew. Love, Catherine.*

# Between Men

The chair facing the door was covered in coffee-brown satin. Maureen Jeffries wore dark brown silk tights and a white ruffled shirt. She would look a delectable morsel in the great winged chair. No sooner was she arranged in it, however, than she got out again (with a pathetic smile of which she was certainly unconscious) and sat less dramatically in the corner of a yellow settee. Here she remained some minutes, thinking that after all, her letter of invitation had said, jocularly (she was aware the phrase had an arch quality she did not altogether like): "Come and meet the new me!"

What was new was her hairstyle, that she was a stone lighter in weight, that she had been dowered afresh by nature (a word she was fond of) with delicacy of complexion. There was no doubt all this would be better displayed in the big brown chair: she made the change back again.

The second time she removed herself to the yellow settee was out of decency, a genuine calculation of kindness. To ask Peggy Bayley to visit her at all *was* brave of her, she had needed to swallow pride. But Peggy would not be able to compete with the ruffled lace shirt and all that it set off, and while this would be so precisely because of her advantages—that she was married, comfortably, to Professor Bayley (whose mistress she, Maureen, had been for four years)—nevertheless there was no need to rub in her, Maureen's, renewed and indeed incredible attractiveness, even though it had been announced by the words: "the new me."

Besides, her attractiveness was all that she, Maureen, had to face the world with again, and why not display it to the wife of Professor Bayley, who had not married herself, but had married Peggy instead? Though (she whispered it to herself, fierce and bitter) if she had tricked Tom

Bayley into it, put pressure on him, as Peggy had, no doubt she would be Mrs. Bayley. . . . She would go back to the brown chair.

But if *she* had tricked Tom into it, then it would have served her right, as it certainly served Peggy right, if from the start of this marriage Tom Bayley had insisted on a second bachelor flat into which she, Maureen, was never allowed to go, just as Peggy was not. She, Maureen, would have refused marriage on such terms, she must give herself credit for that; in fact, her insistence on fidelity from Tom, a natural philanderer, was doubtless the reason for his leaving her for Peggy. So on the whole she did not really envy Peggy, who had achieved marriage when she was already nearly forty with the eminent and attractive professor at the price of knowing from the start she would not be the only woman in his life; and knowing, moreover, she had achieved marriage by the oldest trick in the world. . . .

At this point Maureen left the brown chair for the third time, found the yellow settee obvious, and sat on the floor, in the grip of self-disgust. She was viewing the deterioration of her character, even while she was unable to stop the flow of her bitter thoughts about Peggy. Viewing herself clear-sightedly had, in fact, been as much her occupation for the last six months of semi-retreat as losing a stone and regaining her beauty.

Which she had: she was thirty-nine and she had never been more attractive. The tomboy who had left home in Iowa for the freedoms of New York had been lovely, as every fairly endowed young girl is lovely, but what she was now was the product of twenty years of work on herself. And other people's work too. . . . She was a small, round, white-skinned, big-brown-eyed black-haired beauty, but her sympathy, her softness, her magnetism were the creation of the loves of a dozen intelligent men. No, she did not envy her eighteen-year-old self at all. But she did envy, envied every day more bitterly, that young girl's genuine independence, largeness, scope, and courage.

It had been six months ago when her most recent—and, she had hoped, her final—lover, Jack Boles, had left her, and left her in pieces, that it had occurred to her that twenty—indeed, only ten—years ago *she* had discarded lovers, *she* had been the one to say, as Jack had said—embarrassed and guilty, but not more than he could easily come to terms with—"I'm sorry, forgive me, I'm off." And—and this was the point—she had never calculated the consequences to herself, had taken money from no man, save what she considered she had earned, had remained herself always. (In her time with Jack she had expressed opinions not her own to please him: he was a man who disliked women disagreeing with him.) Above all, she had never given a moment's thought to what people might say. But when Jack threw her over, after an affair which was publicized through the newspapers for months ("Famous film director shares flat in Cannes with the painter Maureen Jeffries"), she had thought first of all: I'll be a laughingstock. She had told everyone, with reason, that he would marry her. Then she thought: But he stayed with me less than a year; no one has got tired of me before so quickly. Then: The woman he has thrown me over for is not a patch on me, and she can't even cook. Then back again to the beginning: People must be laughing at me.

Self-contempt poisoned her, particularly as she was unable to let Jack go, but pursued him with telephone calls, letters, reproaches, reminders that he had promised marriage. She spoke of what she had given him, did everything in fact that she despised most in women. Above all, she had not left this flat whose rent he had recently paid for five years. What it amounted to was, he was buying her off with the lease of this flat.

And instead of walking right out of it with her clothes (she was surely entitled to those?) she was still here, making herself beautiful and fighting down terror.

At eighteen, leaving her father's house (he was a post-office clerk), she had had her sex and her courage. Not beauty. For like many other professional beauties, women who spend their lives with men, she was not beautiful at all. What she had was a focused sex, her whole being aware and sharpened by sex, that made her seem beautiful. Now, twenty years later, after being the mistress of eleven men, all of them eminent or at least potentially eminent, she had her sex, and her courage. *But*—since she had never put her own talent, painting, first, but always the career of whichever man she was living with, and out of an instinct of generosity which was probably the best thing in her—she now could not earn a living. At least, not in the style she had been used to.

Since she had left home, she had devoted her talents, her warmth, her imagination to an art teacher (her first lover), two actors (then unknown, now world-famous), a choreographer, a writer, another writer; then, crossing the Atlantic to Europe, a film director (Italy), an actor (France), a writer (London), Professor Tom Bayley (London), Jack Boles, film director (London). Who could say how much of her offered self, her continually poured-forth devotion to their work, was responsible for their success? (As she demanded of herself fiercely, weeping, in the dark hours.)

She now had left her sympathy, her charm, her talents for dress and décor, a minor talent for painting (which did not mean she was not a discriminating critic of other people's work), the fact she was a perfect cook, and her abilities in bed, which she knew were outstanding.

And the moment she stepped out of this flat, she would step out, also, of the world of international money and prestige. To what? Her father, now living in a rooming house in Chicago? No, her only hope was to find another man as eminent and lustrous as the others, for she could no longer afford the unknown geniuses, the potential artists. This was what she was waiting for, and why she remained in the luxurious flat, which must serve as a base; and why she despised herself so painfully; and why she had invited Peggy Bayley to visit her. One: she needed to bolster herself up by seeing this woman, whose career (as the mistress of well-known men) had been similar to hers, and who was now well married. Second: she was going to ask her help. She had gone carefully through the list of her ex-lovers, written to three, and drawn three friendly but unhelpful letters. She had remained, officially, a "friend" of Tom Bayley; but she knew better than to offend his wife by approaching him except with her approval. She would ask Peggy to ask Tom to use his influence to get her a job of the kind that would enable her to meet the right sort of man.

When the doorbell rang, and she had answered it, she went hastily to the big brown chair, this time out of bravado, even honesty. She was appealing to the wife of a man whose very publicized mistress she had been; and she did not wish to soften the difficulties of it by looking less attractive than she could; even though Peggy would enter with nothing left of her own beauty; for three years of marriage with Professor Bayley had turned her into a sensible, good-looking woman, the sleek feline quality gone that had led *her* from Cape Town to Europe as a minor actress, which career she had given up, quite rightly, for the one she was born for.

But Peggy Bayley entered, as it were, four years back: if Maureen was small, delicate, luscious, then Peggy's mode was to be a siren: Maureen jerked herself up, saw Peggy push pale hair off a brown cheek with a white ringed hand and slide her a green-eyed mocking smile. She involuntarily exclaimed: "Tom's ditched you!"

Peggy laughed—her voice, like Maureen's, was the husky voice of the sex-woman—and said: "How did you guess!" At which she turned, her hips angled in a mannequin's pose, letting her gold hair fall over her face, showing off a straight green linen dress that owed everything to a newly provocative body. Not a trace left of the sensible healthy housewife of the last three years: she, like Maureen, was once again focused behind her sexuality, poised on it, vibrating with it.

She said: "We both of us *look* very much the better for being ditched!"

Now, with every consciousness of how she looked, she appropriated the yellow settee in a coil of femininity, and said: "Give me a drink and don't look so surprised. After all, I suppose I could have seen it coming?" This was a query addressed to—a fellow conspirator? No. Victim? No. Fellow artisan—yes. Maureen realized that the only-just-under-the-surface hostility that had characterized their meetings when Peggy was with Tom Bayley had vanished entirely. But she was not altogether happy yet about this flow of comradeship. Frowning, she got out of the brown satin chair, a cigarette clumsy between her lips. She remembered that the frown and the dangling cigarette belonged to the condition of *a woman sure of a man;* her instincts were, then, to lie to Peggy, and precisely because she did not like to admit, even now, long after the fact, just how badly she was alone? She poured large brandies, and asked: "Who did he leave you for?"

Peggy said: "I left him," and kept her green eyes steady on Maureen's face to make her accept it, despite the incredulity she saw there.

"No, really, it's true—of course, there were women all the time, that's why he insisted on the hidey-hole in Chelsea. . . ." Maureen definitely smiled now, to remind her of how often she had *not* acknowledged the reason for the hidey-hole. It had been "Bill's study, where he can get away from dreary domesticity." Peggy accepted the reminder with a small honest smile that nevertheless had impatience: Well of course I told lies and played little games, don't we all?—that's what the smile said; and Maureen's dislike of herself made her say aloud, so as to put an end to her silent rancorous criticism of Peggy: "Well, all right, then. But you did force him to marry you." She had taken three large gulps of brandy. Whereas she had drunk far too much in the months after Jack had left her, during the last weeks her diet had forbidden her alcohol, and she was out of practice. She felt herself already getting tight, and she said: "If I'm going to get tight, then you've got to, too."

"I was drunk every day and night for two months," said Peggy, again with the level green look. "But you can't drink if you want to keep pretty."

Maureen went back to the brown chair, looked at Peggy through coiling blue smoke, and said: "I was drunk all the time for—it was ages. It was disgusting. I couldn't stop."

Peggy said: "Well all right, we've finished with that. But the point was, not the other women—we discussed his character thoroughly when we married and . . ." Here she stopped to acknowledge Maureen's rather sour smile, and said: "It's part of our role, isn't it, to thoroughly discuss their characters?" At this, both women's eyes filled with tears, which both blinked away. Another barrier had gone down.

Peggy said: "I came here to show myself off, because of your boasting little letter—I've been watching you patronize me since I married Tom, being dull and ordinary—I wanted *you* to see the new me! . . . God knows why one loses one's sex when one's settled with a man."

They both giggled suddenly, rolling over, Peggy on her yellow linen, Maureen on her glossy brown. Then at the same moment, they had to fight back tears.

"No," said Maureen, sitting up, "I'm not going to cry, oh no! I've stopped crying, there's not the slightest point."

"Then let's have some more to drink," and Peggy handed over her glass.

They were both tight, already; since both were in any case on the edge of themselves with fasting.

Maureen half filled both glasses with brandy, and asked: "Did you really leave him?"

"Yes."

"Then you've got better reason to like yourself than I have. I fought, and I made scenes, and when I think of it now . . ." She took a brandy gulp, looked around the expensive room, and said: "And I'm still living on him now and that's what's so horrible."

"Well, don't cry, dear," said Peggy. The brandy was slurring her, making her indolent. The "dear" made Maureen shrink. It was the meaningless word of the theatre and film people, which was all right, even enjoyable, with the theatre and film people, but it was only one step from . . .

*"Don't,"* said Maureen, sharp. Peggy widened her long green eyes in a "charming" way, then let them narrow into the honesty of her real nature, and laughed.

"I see your point," she said. "Well, we'd better face it, hadn't we? We're not so far off, are we?"

*"Yes,"* said Maureen. "I've been thinking it out. If we had married them, that marriage certificate, you know, well then, we'd have felt quite all right to take money, in return for everything, everything, everything!" She put her face down and sobbed.

"Shut up," said Peggy. But it sounded because of her tightness like "Shhrrrp."

"No," said Maureen, sitting up and sniffing. "It's true. I've never taken money—I mean I've never taken anything more than housekeeping money and presents of clothes—have you?" Peggy was not looking at her, so she went on: "All right, but I'll take a guess that Tom Bayley's the first man you've taken a settlement from, or alimony—isn't that so? And that's because you were married to him."

"I suppose so. I told myself I wouldn't, but I have."

"And you don't really feel bad about it, just because of that marriage certificate?"

Peggy turned her glass round and round between long soft fingers and at length nodded: I suppose so.

"Yes. Of course. And all the fun we've both made about that marriage certificate in our time. But the point is, taking money when you're married doesn't make you *feel* like a tart. With all the men I've been with, I've always had to argue with myself; I've said, Well, how much would he have to pay for what I do for him—cooking and the housekeeping and the interior decoration and the advice? A fortune! So there's no need for me to feel badly about living in his flat and taking clothes. But I did feel bad, always. But if Jack had married me, living in this bloody flat of his wouldn't make me feel like a bloody tart." She burst into savage angry tears, stopped herself, breathed deeply, and sat silent, breathing deep. Then she got up, refilled her glass and Peggy's, and sat down. The two women sat in silence, until at last Maureen said: "Why did you leave him?"

"When he married me we both thought I was pregnant. . . . No, it's true. I know what you and everyone else said, but it was true. I had no periods for three months, and then I was very ill; they said it was a miscarriage."

"He wants children?"

"Didn't he with you?"

"No."

"Then he's changed. He wants them badly."

"Jack wouldn't hear of children, wouldn't hear of them, but that little bitch he's ditched me for . . . I hear you're great friends with them?" She meant Jack and the girl for whom she was thrown over.

Peggy said: "Jack is a great friend of Tom's." This was very dry, and Maureen said: "Yes. Yes! All Jack's friends—I cooked for them, I entertained them, but do you know not one of them has even rung me up since he left me? They were *his* friends, not mine."

"Exactly. Since I left Tom I haven't seen either Jack or his new girl. They visit Tom."

"I suppose one of Tom's girls got pregnant?"

"Yes. He came to me and told me. I knew what I was supposed to do, and did it. I said: Right, you can have your divorce."

"Then you've got your self-respect, at least."

Peggy turned her glass round, looking into it; it slopped over onto the yellow linen. Both women watched the orange stain spread, without moving, in an aesthetic interest.

"No, I haven't," said Peggy. "Because I said: 'You can have your divorce, but you've got to give me so much money, or else I'll sue you for infidelity—I've got the evidence a thousand times over.' "

"How much?"

Peggy colored, took a gulp of brandy and said: "I'm going to get forty pounds a month alimony. It's a lot for him—he's a professor, not a film director."

"He can't afford it?"

"No. He told me he must give up his hidey-hole. I said: 'Too bad.' "

"What's she like?"

"Twenty-seven. An art student. She's pretty and sweet and dumb."

"But she's pregnant."

"Yes."

"You've never had a baby?"

"No. But I've had several abortions and miscarriages."

The two women looked frankly at each other, their faces bitter.

"Yes," said Maureen. "I've had five abortions and one of them was by one of those old women. I don't even use anything, and I don't get pregnant. . . . How did you like Jack's new girl?"

"I liked her," said Peggy, apologetically.

"She's an intellectual," said Maureen: it sounded like "intelleshual."

"Yes."

"Ever so bright and well-informed." Maureen battled a while with her better self, won the battle, and said: "But *why?* She's attractive, but she's such a schoolgirl; she's a nice bright clever little schoolgirl with nice bright little clothes."

Peggy said: "Stop it. Stop it at once."

"Yes," said Maureen. But she added, out of her agonized depths: "And she can't even cook!"

And now Peggy laughed, flinging herself back and spilling more brandy from her drunken hand. After a while, Maureen laughed too.

Peggy said: "I was thinking, how many times have wives and mistresses said about us: Peggy's such a bore, Maureen's so obvious."

"I can hear them: Of course, they're very pretty, and of course they can dress well, and they're marvelous cooks, and I suppose they're good in bed, but what have they *got?*"

"Stop it," said Peggy.

Both women were now drunk. It was getting late. The room was full of shadow, its white walls fading into blue heights, the glossy chairs, tables, rugs, sending out deep gleams of light.

"Shall I turn on the light?"

"Not yet." Peggy now got up herself to refill her glass. She said: "I hope she has the sense not to throw up her job."

"Who, Jack's redheaded bitch?"

"Who else? Tom's girl is all right, she's actually pregnant."

"You're right. But I bet she does, I bet Jack's trying to make her give it up."

"I know he is. Just before I left Tom—before he threw me over—your Jack and she were over to dinner. Jack was getting at her for her column, he was sniping at her all evening—he said it was a left-wing society hostess's view of politics. A left-wing bird's-eye view, he said."

"He hated me painting," said Maureen. "Every time I said I wanted a morning to paint, he made gibes about Sunday painters. I'd serve him his breakfast, and go up to the studio—well, it's the spare room, really. First he'd shout up funny cracks, then he'd come up and say he was hungry. He'd start being hungry at eleven in the morning. Then if I didn't come down and cook, he'd make love. Then we'd talk about his work. We'd talk about his bloody films all day and half the night. . . ." Maureen's voice broke into a wail: "It's all so unfair, so unfair, so unfair . . . they were all like that. I'm not saying I'd have been a great painter, but I might have been something. Something of my own. . . . Not one of those men did anything but make fun, or patronize me . . . all of them, in one way or another. And of course, one always gives in, because one cares more for . . ."

Peggy who had been half asleep, drooping over her settee, sat up and said: "Stop it, Maureen. What's the good of it?"

"But it's true. I've spent twenty years of my life, eighteen hours a day, bolstering up some man's ambition. Well, isn't it true?"

"It's true, but stop it. We chose it."

"Yes. And if that silly red-haired bitch gives up her job, she'll get what she deserves."

"She'll be where we are."

"But Jack says he's going to marry her."

"Tom married me."

"He was intrigued by that clever little redheaded mind of hers. All those bright remarks about politics. But now he's doing everything he can to stop her column. Not that it would be any loss to the nation, but she'd better watch out, oh yes, she had. . . ." Maureen wove her brandy glass back and forth in front of hypnotized eyes.

"Which is the other reason I came to see you."

"You didn't come to see the new me?"

"It's the same thing."

"Well?"

"How much money have you got?"

"Nothing."

"How long is the lease for this flat?" Maureen held up the fingers of one hand. "Five years? Then sell the lease."

"Oh I couldn't."

"Oh yes you could. It would bring you in about two thousand, I reckon. We could take a flat somewhere less expensive."

"*We* could?"

"And I've got forty pounds a month. Well, then."

"Well then what?" Maureen was lying practically flat in the big chair, her white lace shirt ruffled up around her breasts, so that a slim brown waist and diaphragm showed above the tight brown trousers. She held her brandy glass in front of her eyes and moved it back and forth, watching the amber liquid slopping in the glass. From time to time the brandy fell on her brown stomach flesh and she giggled.

Peggy said: "If we don't do something, I've got to go back to my parents in Outshoorn—they're ostrich farmers. I was the bright girl that escaped. Well, I'll never make an actress. So I'll be back living out my life among the sugar-bushes and the ostriches. And where will you be?"

"Ditto, ditto." Maureen now wriggled her soft brown head sideways and let brandy drip into her mouth.

"We're going to open a dress shop. If there's one thing we both really understand, it's how to dress."

"Good idea."

"What city would you fancy?"

"I fancy Paris."

"We couldn't compete in Paris."

"No, can't compete in . . . How about Rome? I've got three ex-lovers in Rome."

"They're not much good when it comes to trouble."

"No good at all."

"Better stay in London."

"Better stay in London. Like another drink?"

"Yes. Yesssh."

"I'lll get-get-itit."

"Next time, we mustn't go to bed without the marriage shertificate."

"A likely shtory."

"But it's against my prinshiples, bargaining."

"Oh I know, I know."

"Yesh."

"Perhaps we'd better be leshbians, what do you think?"

Peggy got up, with difficulty, came to Maureen, and put her hand on Maureen's bare diaphragm. "Doesh that do anything for you?"

"Not a thing."

"I fanshy men myself," said Peggy, returning to her settee, where she sat with a bump, spilling liquor.

"Me too, and a fat lot of good it duz ush."

"Next time, we don't give up our jobs, we stick with the dress shop."

"Yessh. . . ."

A pause. Then Peggy sat up, and focused. She was pervaded by an immense earnestness. "Listen," she said. "No, damn it, lishen, that's what I mean to shay all the time, I really mean it."

"I do too."

"No. No giving it up the firsht time a m-m-man appearsh. Damn it, I'm drunk, but I mean it. . . . No, Maureen, I'm not going to shtart a dresh shop unless that's undershtood from the shtart. We musht, we *musht* agree to that, work firsht, or elshe, or *else* you know where we're going to end up." Peggy brought out the last in a rush, and lay back, satisfied.

Maureen now sat up, earnest, trying to control her tongue: "But . . . what . . . we are both *good* at, itsh, it's bolshtering up some damned genus, genius."

"Not any more. Oh no. You're got to *promish* me, Maureen, promish me, or *elshe* . . ."

"All right, I promish."

"Good."

"Have another drink?"

"Lovely brandy, lovely lovely lovely blandy."

"Lovely brandy . . ."

# *To Room 19*

This is a story, I suppose, about a failure in intelligence: the Rawlings' marriage was grounded in intelligence.

They were older when they married than most of their married friends: in their well-seasoned late twenties. Both had had a number of affairs, sweet rather than bitter; and when they fell in love—for they did fall in love—had known each other for some time. They joked that they had saved each other "for the real thing." That they had waited so long (but not too long) for this real thing was to them a proof of their sensible discrimination. A good many of their friends had married young, and now (they felt) probably regretted lost opportunities; while others, still unmarried, seemed to them arid, self-doubting, and likely to make desperate or romantic marriages.

Not only they, but others, felt they were well-matched: their friends' delight was an additional proof of their happiness. They had played the same roles, male and female, in this group or set, if such a wide, loosely connected, constantly changing constellation of people could be called a set. They had both become, by virtue of their moderation, their humor, and their abstinence from painful experience, people to whom others came for advice. They could be, and were, relied on. It was one of those cases of a man and a woman linking themselves whom no one else had ever thought of linking, probably because of their similarities. But then everyone exclaimed: Of course! How right! How was it we never thought of it before!

And so they married amid general rejoicing, and because of their foresight and their sense for what was probable, nothing was a surprise to them.

Both had well-paid jobs. Matthew was a subeditor on a large London newspaper, and Susan worked in an advertising firm. He was not the stuff of which editors or publicized journalists are made, but he was much more than "a subeditor," being one of the essential background people who in fact steady, inspire, and make possible the people in the limelight. He was content with this position. Susan had a talent for commercial drawing. She was humorous about the advertisements she was responsible for, but she did not feel strongly about them one way or the other.

Both, before they married, had had pleasant flats, but they felt it unwise to base a marriage on either flat, because it might seem like a submission of personality on the part of the one whose flat it was not. They moved into a new flat in South Kensington on the clear understanding that when their marriage had settled down (a process they knew would not take long, and was in fact more a humorous concession to popular wisdom than what was due to themselves) they would buy a house and start a family.

And this is what happened. They lived in their charming flat for two years, giving parties and going to them, being a popular young married couple, and then Susan became pregnant, she gave up her job, and they bought a house in Richmond. It was typical of this couple that they had a son first, then a daughter, then twins, son and daughter. Everything right, appropriate, and what everyone would wish for, if they could choose. But people did feel these two had chosen; this balanced and sensible family was no more than what was due to them because of their infallible sense for *choosing* right.

And so they lived with their four children in their gardened house in Richmond and were happy. They had everything they had wanted and had planned for.

*And yet . . .*

Well, even this was expected, that there must be a certain flatness. . . .

Yes, yes, of course, it was natural they sometimes felt like this. Like what?

Their life seemed to be like a snake biting its tail. Matthew's job for the sake of Susan, children, house, and garden—which caravanserai needed a well-paid job to maintain it. And Susan's practical intelligence for the sake of Matthew, the children, the house, and the garden—which unit would have collapsed in a week without her.

But there was no point about which either could say: "For the sake of *this* is all the rest." Children? But children can't be a center of life and a reason for being. They can be a thousand things that are delightful, interesting, satisfying, but they can't be a wellspring to live from. Or they shouldn't be. Susan and Matthew knew that well enough.

Matthew's job? Ridiculous. It was an interesting job, but scarcely a reason for living. Matthew took pride in doing it well, but he could hardly be expected to be proud of the newspaper; the newspaper he read, *his* newspaper, was not the one he worked for.

Their love for each other? Well, that was nearest it. If this wasn't a center, what was? Yes, it was around this point, their love, that the whole extraordinary structure revolved. For extraordinary it certainly was. Both Susan and Matthew had moments of thinking so, of looking in secret disbelief at this thing they had created: marriage, four children, big house, garden, charwomen, friends, cars . . . and this *thing,* this entity, all of it had come into existence, been blown into being out of nowhere, because Susan loved Matthew and Matthew loved Susan. Extraordinary. So that was the central point, the wellspring.

And if one felt that it simply was not strong enough, important enough, to support it all, well whose fault was that? Certainly neither Susan's nor Matthew's. It was in the nature of things. And they sensibly blamed neither themselves nor each other.

On the contrary, they used their intelligence to preserve what they had created from a painful and explosive world: they looked around them, and took lessons. All around them, marriages collapsing, or breaking, or rubbing along (even worse, they felt). They must not make the same mistakes, they must not.

They had avoided the pitfall so many of their friends had fallen into—of buying a house in the country *for the sake of the children,* so that the husband became a weekend husband, a weekend father, and the wife always careful not to ask what went on in the town flat which they called (in joke) a bachelor flat. No, Matthew was a full-time husband, a full-time father, and at night, in the big married bed in the big married bedroom (which had an attractive view of the river), they lay beside each other talking and he told her about his day, and what he had done, and whom he had met; and she told him about her day (not as interesting, but that was not her fault), for both knew of the hidden resentments and deprivations of the woman who has lived her own life—and above all, has earned her own living—and is now dependent on a husband for outside interests and money.

Nor did Susan make the mistake of taking a job for the sake of her independence, which she might very well have done, since her old firm, missing her qualities of humor, balance, and sense, invited her often to go back. Children needed their mother to a certain age, that both parents knew and agreed on; and when these four healthy, wisely brought up children were of the right age, Susan would work again, because she knew, and so did he, what happened to women of fifty at the height of their energy and ability, with grown-up children who no longer needed their full devotion.

So here was this couple, testing their marriage, looking after it, treating it like a small boat full of helpless people in a very stormy sea. Well, of course, so it was. . . . The storms of the world were bad, but not too close—which is not to say they were selfishly felt: Susan and Matthew were both well-informed and responsible people. And the inner storms and quicksands were understood and charted. So everything was all right. Everything was in order. Yes, things were under control.

So what did it matter if they felt dry, flat? People like themselves, fed on a hundred books (psychological, anthropological, sociological), could scarcely be unprepared for the dry, controlled wistfulness which is the distinguishing mark of the intelligent marriage. Two people, endowed with education, with discrimination, with judgment, linked together voluntarily from their will to be happy together and to be of use to others—one sees them everywhere, one knows them, one even is that thing oneself: sadness because so much is after all so little. These two, unsurprised, turned towards each other with even more courtesy and gentle love: this was life, that two people, no matter how carefully chosen, could not be everything to each other. In fact, even to say so, to think in such a way, was banal; they were ashamed to do it.

It was banal, too, when one night Matthew came home late and confessed he had been to a party, taken a girl home and slept with her. Susan forgave him, of course. Except that forgiveness is hardly the word. Understanding, yes. But if you understand something, you don't forgive it, you are the thing itself: forgiveness is for what you *don't* understand. Nor had he *confessed*—what sort of word is that?

The whole thing was not important. After all, years ago they had joked: Of course I'm not going to be faithful to you, no one can be faithful to one other person for a whole lifetime. (And there was the word "faithful"—stupid, all these words, stupid, belonging to a savage old world.) But the incident left both of them irritable. Strange, but they were both bad-tempered, annoyed. There was something unassimilable about it.

Making love splendidly after he had come home that night, both had felt that the idea that Myra Jenkins, a pretty girl met at a party, could be even relevant was ridiculous. They had loved each other for over a decade, would love each other for years more. Who, then, was Myra Jenkins?

Except, thought Susan, unaccountably bad-tempered, she was (is?) the first. In ten years. So either the ten years' fidelity was not important, or she isn't. (No, no, there is something wrong with this way of thinking, there must be.) But if she isn't important, presumably it wasn't important either when Matthew and I first went to bed with each other that afternoon whose delight even now (like a very long shadow at sundown) lays a long, wandlike finger over us. (Why did I say sundown?) Well, if what we felt that afternoon was not important, nothing is important, because if it hadn't been for what we felt, we wouldn't be Mr. and Mrs. Rawlings with four children, et cetera, et cetera. The whole thing is *absurd*—for him to have come home and told me was absurd. For him not to have told me was absurd. For me to care or, for that matter, not to care, is absurd . . . and who is Myra Jenkins? Why, no one at all.

There was only one thing to do, and of course these sensible people did it; they put the thing behind them, and consciously, knowing what they were doing, moved forward into a different phase of their marriage, giving thanks for past good fortune as they did so.

For it was inevitable that the handsome, blond, attractive, manly man, Matthew Rawlings, should be at times tempted (oh, what a word!) by the attractive girls at parties she could not attend because of the four children; and that sometimes he would succumb (a word even more repulsive, if possible) and that she, a good-looking woman in the big well-tended garden at Richmond, would sometimes be pierced as by an arrow from the sky with bitterness. Except that bitterness was not in order, it was out of court. Did the casual girls touch the marriage? They did not. Rather it was they who knew defeat because of the handsome Matthew Rawlings' marriage body and soul to Susan Rawlings.

In that case why did Susan feel (though luckily not for longer than a few seconds at a time) as if life had become a desert, and that nothing mattered, and that her children were not her own?

Meanwhile her intelligence continued to assert that all was well. What if her Matthew did have an occasional sweet afternoon, the odd affair? For she knew quite well, except in her moments of aridity, that they were very happy, that the affairs were not important.

Perhaps that was the trouble? It was in the nature of things that the adventures and delights could no longer be hers, because of the four children and the big house that needed so much attention. But perhaps she was secretly wishing, and even knowing that she did, that the wildness and the beauty could be his. But he was married to her. She was married to him. They were married inextricably. And therefore the gods could not strike him with the real magic, not really. Well, was it Susan's fault that after he came home from an adventure he looked harassed rather than fulfilled? (In fact, that was how she knew he had been *unfaithful,* because of his sullen air, and his glances at her, similar to hers at him: What is it that I share with this person that shields all delight from me?) But none of it by anybody's fault. (But what did they feel ought to be somebody's fault?) Nobody's fault, nothing to be at fault, no one to blame, no one to offer or to take it . . . and nothing wrong, either, except that Matthew never was really struck, as he wanted to be, by joy; and that Susan was more and more often threatened by emptiness. (It was usually in the garden that she was invaded by this feeling: she was coming to avoid the garden, unless the children or Matthew were with her.) There was no need to use the dramatic words "unfaithful," "forgive," and the rest: intelligence forbade them. Intelligence barred, too, quarreling, sulking, anger, silences of withdrawal, accusations and tears. Above all, intelligence forbids tears.

A high price has to be paid for the happy marriage with the four healthy children in the large white gardened house.

And they were paying it, willingly, knowing what they were doing. When they lay side by side or breast to breast in the big civilized bedroom overlooking the wild sullied river, they laughed, often, for no particular reason; but they knew it was really because of these two small people, Susan and Matthew, supporting such an edifice on their intelligent love. The laugh comforted them; it saved them both, though from what, they did not know.

They were now both fortyish. The older children, boy and girl, were ten and eight, at school. The twins, six, were still at home. Susan did not have nurses or girls to help her: childhood is short; and she did not regret the hard work. Often enough she was bored, since small children can be boring; she was often very tired; but she regretted nothing. In another decade, she would turn herself back into being a woman with a life of her own.

Soon the twins would go to school, and they would be away from home from nine until four. These hours, so Susan saw it, would be the preparation for her own slow emancipation away from the role of hub-of-the-family into woman-with-her-own-life. She was already planning for the hours of freedom when all the children would be "off her hands." That was the phrase used by Matthew and by Susan and by their friends, for the moment when the youngest child went off to school. "They'll be off your hands, darling Susan, and you'll have time to yourself." So said Matthew, the intelligent husband, who had often enough commended and consoled Susan, standing by her in spirit during the years when her soul was not her own, as she said, but her children's.

What it amounted to was that Susan saw herself as she had been at twenty-eight, unmarried; and then again somewhere about fifty, blossoming from the root of what she had been twenty years before. As if the essential Susan were in abeyance, as if she were in cold storage. Matthew said something like this to Susan one night: and she agreed that it was true—she did feel something like that. What, then, was this essential Susan? She did not know. Put like that it sounded ridiculous, and she did not really feel it. Anyway, they had a long discussion about the whole thing before going off to sleep in each other's arms.

So the twins went off to their school, two bright affectionate children who had no problems about it, since their older brother and sister had trodden this path so successfully before them. And now Susan was going to be alone in the big house, every day of the school term, except for the daily woman who came in to clean.

It was now, for the first time in this marriage, that something happened which neither of them had foreseen.

This is what happened. She returned, at nine-thirty, from taking the twins to the school by car, looking forward to seven blissful hours of freedom. On the first morning she was simply restless, worrying about the twins "naturally enough" since this was their first day away at school. She was hardly able to contain herself until they came back. Which they did happily, excited by the world of school, looking forward to the next day. And the next day Susan took them, dropped them, came back, and found herself reluctant to enter her big and beautiful home because it was as if something was waiting for her there that she did not wish to confront. Sensibly, however, she parked the car in the garage, entered the house, spoke to Mrs. Parkes, the daily woman, about her duties, and went up to her bedroom. She was possessed by a fever which drove her out again, downstairs, into the kitchen, where Mrs. Parkes was making cake and did not need her, and into the garden. There she sat on a bench and tried to calm herself looking at trees, at a brown glimpse of the river. But she was filled with tension, like a panic: as if an enemy was in the garden with her. She spoke to herself severely, thus: All this is quite natural. First, I spent twelve years of my adult life working, *living my own life*. Then I married, and from the moment I became pregnant for the first time I signed myself over, so to speak, to other people. To the children. Not for one moment in twelve years have I been alone, had time to myself. So now I have to learn to be myself again. That's all.

And she went indoors to help Mrs. Parkes cook and clean, and found some sewing to do for the children. She kept herself occupied every day. At the end of the first term she understood she felt two contrary emotions. First: secret astonishment and dismay that during those weeks when the house was empty of children she had in fact been more occupied (had been careful to keep herself occupied) than ever she had been when the children were around her needing her continual attention. Second: that now she knew the house would be full of them, and for five weeks, she resented the fact she would never be alone. She was already looking back at those hours of sewing, cooking (but by herself) as at a lost freedom which would not be hers for five long weeks. And the two months of term which would succeed the five weeks stretched alluringly open to her—freedom. But what freedom—when in fact she had been so careful *not* to be free of small duties during the last weeks? She looked at herself, Susan Rawlings, sitting in a big chair by the window in the bedroom, sewing shirts or dresses, which she might just as well have bought. She saw herself making cakes for hours at a time in the big family kitchen: yet usually she bought cakes. What she saw was a woman alone, that was true, but she had not felt alone. For instance, Mrs. Parkes was always somewhere in the house. And she did not like being in the garden at all, because of the closeness there of the enemy—irritation, restlessness, emptiness, whatever it was—which keeping her hands occupied made less dangerous for some reason.

Susan did not tell Matthew of these thoughts. They were not sensible. She did not recognize herself in them. What should she say to her dear friend and husband, Matthew? "When I go into the garden, that is, if the children are not there, I feel as if there is an enemy there waiting to invade me." "What enemy, Susan darling?" "Well I don't know, really. . . ." "Perhaps you should see a doctor?"

No, clearly this conversation should not take place. The holidays began and Susan welcomed them. Four children, lively, energetic, intelligent, demanding: she was never, not for a moment of her day, alone. If she was in a room, they would be in the next room, or waiting for her to do something for them; or it would soon be time for lunch or tea, or to take one of them to the dentist. Something to do: five weeks of it, thank goodness.

On the fourth day of these so welcome holidays, she found she was storming with anger at the twins: two shrinking beautiful children who (and this is what checked her) stood hand in hand looking at her with sheer dismayed disbelief. This was their calm mother, shouting at them. And for what? They had come to her with some game, some bit of nonsense. They looked at each other, moved closer for support, and went off hand in hand, leaving Susan holding on to the windowsill of the living room, breathing deep, feeling sick. She went to lie down, telling the older children she had a headache. She heard the boy Harry telling the little ones: "It's all right, Mother's got a headache." She heard that *It's all right* with pain.

That night she said to her husband: "Today I shouted at the twins, quite unfairly." She sounded miserable, and he said gently: "Well, what of it?"

"It's more of an adjustment than I thought, their going to school."

"But Susie, Susie darling . . ." For she was crouched weeping on the bed. He comforted her: "Susan, what is all this about? You shouted at them? What of it? If you shouted at them fifty times a day it wouldn't be more than the little devils deserve." But she wouldn't laugh. She wept. Soon he comforted her with his body. She became calm. Calm, she wondered what was wrong with her, and why she should mind so much that she might, just once, have behaved unjustly with the children. What did it matter? They had forgotten it all long ago: Mother had a headache and everything was all right.

It was a long time later that Susan understood that that night, when she had wept and Matthew had driven the misery out of her with his big solid body, was the last time, ever in their married life, that they had been—to use their mutual language—with each other. And even that was a lie, because she had not told him of her real fears at all.

The five weeks passed, and Susan was in control of herself, and good and kind, and she looked forward to the holidays with a mixture of fear and longing. She did not know what to expect. She took the twins off to school (the elder children took themselves to school) and she returned to the house determined to face the enemy wherever he was, in the house, or the garden or—where?

She was again restless, she was possessed by restlessness. She cooked and sewed and worked as before, day after day, while Mrs. Parkes remonstrated: "Mrs. Rawlings, what's the need for it? I can do that, it's what you pay me for."

And it was so irrational that she checked herself. She would put the car into the garage, go up to her bedroom, and sit, hands in her lap, forcing herself to be quiet. She listened to Mrs. Parkes moving around the house. She looked out into the garden and saw the branches shake the trees. She sat defeating the enemy, restlessness. Emptiness. She ought to be thinking about her life, about herself. But she did not. Or perhaps she could not. As soon as she forced her mind to think about Susan (for what else did she want to be alone for?), it skipped off to thoughts of butter or school clothes. Or it thought of Mrs. Parkes. She realized that she sat listening for the movements of the cleaning woman, following her every turn, bend, thought. She followed her in her mind from kitchen to bathroom, from table to oven, and it was as if the duster, the cleaning cloth, the saucepan, were in her own hand. She would hear herself saying: No, not like that, don't put that there. . . . Yet she did not give a damn what Mrs. Parkes did, or if she did it at all. Yet she could not prevent herself from being conscious of her, every minute. Yes, this was what was wrong with her: she needed, when she was alone, to be really alone, with no one near. She could not endure the knowledge that in ten minutes or in half an hour Mrs. Parkes would call up the stairs: "Mrs. Rawlings, there's no silver polish. Madam, we're out of flour."

So she left the house and went to sit in the garden where she was screened from the house by trees. She waited for the demon to appear and claim her, but he did not.

She was keeping him off, because she had not, after all, come to an end of arranging herself.

She was planning how to be somewhere where Mrs. Parkes would not come after her with a cup of tea, or a demand to be allowed to telephone (always irritating, since Susan did not care who she telephoned or how often), or just a nice talk about something. Yes, she needed a place, or a state of affairs, where it would not be necessary to keep reminding herself: In ten minutes I must telephone Matthew about . . . and at half past three I must leave early for the children because the car needs cleaning. And at ten o'clock tomorrow I must remember. . . . She was possessed with resentment that the seven hours of freedom in every day (during weekdays in the school term) were not free, that never, not for one second, ever, was she free from the pressure of time, from having to remember this or that. She could never forget herself; never really let herself go into forgetfulness.

Resentment. It was poisoning her. (She looked at this emotion and thought it was absurd. Yet she felt it.) She was a prisoner. (She looked at this thought too, and it was no good telling herself it was a ridiculous one.) She must tell Matthew—but what? She was filled with emotions that were utterly ridiculous, that she despised, yet that nevertheless she was feeling so strongly she could not shake them off.

The school holidays came round, and this time they were for nearly two months, and she behaved with a conscious controlled decency that nearly drove her crazy. She would lock herself in the bathroom, and sit on the edge of the bath, breathing deep, trying to let go into some kind of calm. Or she went up into the spare room, usually empty, where no one would expect her to be. She heard the children calling "Mother, Mother," and kept silent, feeling guilty. Or she went to the very end of the garden, by herself, and looked at the slow-moving brown river; she looked at the river and closed her eyes and breathed slow and deep, taking it into her being, into her veins.

Then she returned to the family, wife and mother, smiling and responsible, feeling as if the pressure of these people—four lively children and her husband—were a painful pressure on the surface of her skin, a hand pressing on her brain. She did not once break down into irritation during these holidays, but it was like living out a prison sentence, and when the children went back to school, she sat on a white stone near the flowing river, and she thought: It is not even a year since the twins went to school, since *they were off my hands* (What on earth did I think I meant when I used that stupid phrase?), and yet I'm a different person. I'm simply not myself. I don't understand it.

Yet she had to understand it. For she knew that this structure—big white house, on which the mortgage still cost four hundred a year, a husband, so good and kind and insightful; four children, all doing so nicely; and the garden where she sat; and Mrs. Parkes, the cleaning woman—all this depended on her, and yet she could not understand why, or even what it was she contributed to it.

She said to Matthew in their bedroom: "I think there must be something wrong with me."

And he said: "Surely not, Susan? You look marvelous—you're as lovely as ever."

She looked at the handsome blond man, with his clear, intelligent, blue-eyed face, and thought: Why is it I can't tell him? Why not? And she said: "I need to be alone more than I am."

At which he swung his slow blue gaze at her, and she saw what she had been dreading: Incredulity. Disbelief. And fear. An incredulous blue stare from a stranger who was her husband, as close to her as her own breath.

He said: "But the children are at school and off your hands."

She said to herself: I've got to force myself to say: Yes, but do you realize that I never feel free? There's never a moment I can say to myself: There's nothing I have to remind myself about, nothing I have to do in half an hour, or an hour, or two hours. . . .

But she said: "I don't feel well."

He said: "Perhaps you need a holiday."

She said, appalled: "But not without you, surely?" For she could not imagine herself going off without him. Yet that was what he meant. Seeing her face, he laughed, and opened his arms, and she went into them, thinking: Yes, yes, but why can't I say it? And what is it I have to say?

She tried to tell him, about never being free. And he listened and said: "But Susan, what sort of freedom can you possibly want—short of being dead! Am I ever free? I go to the office, and I have to be there at ten—all right, half past ten, sometimes. And I have to do this or that, don't I? Then I've got to come home at a certain time—I don't mean it, you know I don't—but if I'm not going to be back home at six I telephone you. When can I ever say to myself: I have nothing to be responsible for in the next six hours?"

Susan, hearing this, was remorseful. Because it was true. The good marriage, the house, the children, depended just as much on his voluntary bondage as it did on hers. But why did he not feel bound? Why didn't he chafe and become restless? No, there was something really wrong with her and this proved it.

And that word "bondage"—why had she used it? She had never felt marriage, or the children, as bondage. Neither had he, or surely they wouldn't be together lying in each other's arms content after twelve years of marriage.

No, her state (whatever it was) was irrelevant, nothing to do with her real good life with her family. She had to accept the fact that, after all, she was an irrational person and to live with it. Some people had to live with crippled arms, or stammers, or being deaf. She would have to live knowing she was subject to a state of mind she could not own.

Nevertheless, as a result of this conversation with her husband, there was a new regime next holidays.

The spare room at the top of the house now had a cardboard sign saying: PRIVATE! DO NOT DISTURB! on it. (This sign had been drawn in colored chalks by the children, after a discussion between the parents in which it was decided this was psychologically the right thing.) The family and Mrs. Parkes knew this was "Mother's Room" and that she was entitled to her privacy. Many serious conversations took place between Matthew and the children about not taking Mother for granted. Susan overheard the first, between father and Harry, the older boy, and was surprised at her irritation over it. Surely she could have a room somewhere in that big house and retire into it without such a fuss being made? Without it being so solemnly discussed? Why couldn't she simply have announced: "I'm going to fit out the little top room for myself, and when I'm in it I'm not to be disturbed for anything short of fire"? Just that, and finished; instead of long earnest discussions. When she heard Harry and Matthew explaining it to the twins with Mrs. Parkes coming in—"Yes, well, a family sometimes gets on top of a woman"—she had to go right away to the bottom of the garden until the devils of exasperation had finished their dance in her blood.

But now there was a room, and she could go there when she liked, she used it seldom: she felt even more caged there than in her bedroom. One day she had gone up there after a lunch for ten children she had cooked and served because Mrs. Parkes was not there, and had sat alone for a while looking into the garden. She saw the children stream out from the kitchen and stand looking up at the window where she sat behind the curtains. They were all—her children and their friends—discussing Mother's Room. A few minutes later, the chase of children in some game came pounding up the stairs, but ended as abruptly as if they had fallen over a ravine, so sudden was the silence. They had remembered she was there, and had gone silent in a great gale of "Hush! Shhhhhh! Quiet, you'll disturb her. . . ." And they went tiptoeing downstairs like criminal conspirators. When she came down to make tea for them, they all apologized. The twins put their arms around her, from front and back, making a human cage of loving limbs, and promised it would never occur again. "We forgot, Mummy, we forgot all about it!"

What it amounted to was that Mother's Room, and her need for privacy, had become a valuable lesson in respect for other people's rights. Quite soon Susan was going up to the room only because it was a lesson it was a pity to drop. Then she took sewing up there, and the children and Mrs. Parkes came in and out: it had become another family room.

She sighed, and smiled, and resigned herself—she made jokes at her own expense with Matthew over the room. That is, she did from the self she liked, she respected. But at the same time, something inside her howled with impatience, with rage. . . . And she was frightened. One day she found herself kneeling by her bed and praying: "Dear God, keep it away from me, keep him away from me." She meant the devil, for she now thought of it, not caring if she was irrational, as some sort of demon. She imagined him, or it, as a youngish man, or perhaps a middle-aged man pretending to be young. Or a man young-looking from immaturity? At any rate, she saw the young-looking face which, when she drew closer, had dry lines about mouth and eyes. He was thinnish, meager in build. And he had a reddish complexion, and ginger hair. That was he—a gingery, energetic man, and he wore a reddish hairy jacket, unpleasant to the touch.

Well, one day she saw him. She was standing at the bottom of the garden, watching the river ebb past, when she raised her eyes and saw this person, or being, sitting on the white stone bench. He was looking at her, and grinning. In his hand was a long crooked stick, which he had picked off the ground, or broken off the tree above him. He was absentmindedly, out of an absentminded or freakish impulse of spite, using the stick to stir around in the coils of a blindworm or a grass snake (or some kind of snakelike creature: it was whitish and unhealthy to look at, unpleasant). The snake was twisting about, flinging its coils from side to side in a kind of dance of protest against the teasing prodding stick.

Susan looked at him, thinking: Who is the stranger? What is he doing in our garden? Then she recognized the man around whom her terrors had crystallized. As she did so, he vanished. She made herself walk over to the bench. A shadow from a branch lay across thin emerald grass, moving jerkily over its roughness, and she could see why she had taken it for a snake, lashing and twisting. She went back to the house thinking: Right, then, so I've seen him with my own eyes, so I'm not crazy after all—there *is* a danger because I've seen him. He is lurking in the garden and sometimes even in the house, and he wants to *get into me and to take me over.*

She dreamed of having a room or a place, anywhere, where she could go and sit, by herself, no one knowing where she was.

Once, near Victoria, she found herself outside a news agent that had Rooms to Let advertised. She decided to rent a room, telling no one. Sometimes she could take the train in to Richmond and sit alone in it for an hour or two. Yet how could she? A room would cost three or four pounds a week, and she earned no money, and how could she explain to Matthew that she needed such a sum? What for? It did not occur to her that she was taking it for granted she wasn't going to tell him about the room.

Well, it was out of the question, having a room; yet she knew she must.

One day, when a school term was well established, and none of the children had measles or other ailments, and everything seemed in order, she did the shopping early, explained to Mrs. Parkes she was meeting an old school friend, took the train to Victoria, searched until she found a small quiet hotel, and asked for a room for the day. They did not let rooms by the day, the manageress said, looking doubtful, since Susan so obviously was not the kind of woman who needed a room for unrespectable reasons. Susan made a long explanation about not being well, being unable to shop without frequent rests for lying down. At last she was allowed to rent the room provided she paid a full night's price for it. She was taken up by the manageress and a maid, both concerned over the state of her health . . . which must be pretty bad if, living at Richmond (she had signed her name and address in the register), she needed a shelter at Victoria.

The room was ordinary and anonymous, and was just what Susan needed. She put a shilling in the gas fire, and sat, eyes shut, in a dingy armchair with her back to a dingy window. She was alone. She was alone. She was alone. She could feel pressures lifting off her. First the sounds of traffic came very loud; then they seemed to vanish; she might even have slept a little. A knock on the door: it was Miss Townsend, the manageress, bringing her a cup of tea with her own hands, so concerned was she over Susan's long silence and possible illness.

Miss Townsend was a lonely woman of fifty, running this hotel with all the rectitude expected of her, and she sensed in Susan the possibility of understanding companionship. She stayed to talk. Susan found herself in the middle of a fantastic story about her illness, which got more and more impossible as she tried to make it tally with the large house at Richmond, well-off husband, and four children. Suppose she said instead: Miss Townsend, I'm here in your hotel because I need to be alone for a few hours, above all *alone and with no one knowing where I am.* She said it mentally, and saw, mentally, the look that would inevitably come on Miss Townsend's elderly maiden's face. "Miss Townsend, my four children and my husband are driving me insane, do you understand that? Yes, I can see from the gleam of hysteria in your eyes that comes from loneliness controlled but only just contained that I've got everything in the world you've ever longed for. Well, Miss Townsend, I don't want any of it. You can have it, Miss Townsend. I wish I was absolutely alone in the world, like you. Miss Townsend, I'm besieged by seven devils, Miss Townsend, Miss Townsend, let me stay here in your hotel where the devils can't get me. . . ." Instead of saying all this, she described her anemia, agreed to try Miss Townsend's remedy for it, which was raw liver, minced, between whole-meal bread, and said yes, perhaps it would be better if she stayed at home and let a friend do shopping for her. She paid her bill and left the hotel, defeated.

At home Mrs. Parkes said she didn't really like it, no, not really, when Mrs. Rawlings was away from nine in the morning until five. The teacher had telephoned from school to say Joan's teeth were paining her, and she hadn't known what to say; and what was she to make for the children's tea, Mrs. Rawlings hadn't said.

All this was nonsense, of course. Mrs. Parkes's complaint was that Susan had withdrawn herself spiritually, leaving the burden of the big house on her.

Susan looked back at her day of "freedom" which had resulted in her becoming a friend of the lonely Miss Townsend, and in Mrs. Parkes's remonstrances. Yet she remembered the short blissful hour of being alone, really alone. She was determined to arrange her life, no matter what it cost, so that she could have that solitude more often. An absolute solitude, where no one knew her or cared about her.

But how? She thought of saying to her old employer: I want you to back me up in a story with Matthew that I am doing part-time work for you. The truth is that . . . But she would have to tell him a lie, too, and which lie? She could not say: I want to sit by myself three or four times a week in a rented room. And besides, he knew Matthew, and she could not really ask him to tell lies on her behalf, apart from being bound to think it meant a lover.

Suppose she really took a part-time job, which she could get through fast and efficiently, leaving time for herself. What job? Addressing envelopes? Canvassing?

And there was Mrs. Parkes, working widow, who knew exactly what she was prepared to give to the house, who knew by instinct when her mistress withdrew in spirit from her responsibilities. Mrs. Parkes was one of the servers of this world, but she needed someone to serve. She had to have Mrs. Rawlings, her madam, at the top of the house or in the garden, so that she could come and get support from her: "Yes, the bread's not what it was when I was a girl. . . . Yes, Harry's got a wonderful appetite, I wonder where he puts it all. . . . Yes, it's lucky the twins are so much of a size, they can wear each other's shoes, that's a saving in these hard times. . . . Yes, the cherry jam from Switzerland is not a patch on the jam from Poland, and three times the price. . . ." And so on. That sort of talk Mrs. Parkes must have, every day, or she would leave, not knowing herself why she left.

Susan Rawlings, thinking these thoughts, found that she was prowling through the great thicketed garden like a wild cat: she was walking up the stairs, down the stairs, through the rooms into the garden, along the brown running river, back, up through the house, down again. . . . It was a wonder Mrs. Parkes did not think it strange. But, on the contrary, Mrs. Rawlings could do what she liked, she could stand on her head if she wanted, provided she was *there.* Susan Rawlings prowled and muttered through her house, hating Mrs. Parkes, hating poor Miss Townsend, dreaming of her hour of solitude in the dingy respectability of Miss Townsend's hotel bedroom, and she knew quite well she was mad. Yes, she was mad.

She said to Matthew that she must have a holiday. Matthew agreed with her. This was not as things had been once—how they had talked in each other's arms in the marriage bed. He had, she knew, diagnosed her finally as *unreasonable.* She had become someone outside himself that he had to manage. They were living side by side in this house like two tolerably friendly strangers.

Having told Mrs. Parkes—or rather, asked for her permission—she went off on a walking holiday in Wales. She chose the remotest place she knew of. Every morning the children telephoned her before they went off to school, to encourage and support her, just as they had over Mother's Room. Every evening she telephoned them, spoke to each child in turn, and then to Matthew. Mrs. Parkes, given permission to telephone for instructions or advice, did so every day at lunchtime. When, as happened three times, Mrs. Rawlings was out on the mountainside, Mrs. Parkes asked that she should ring back at such-and-such a time, for she would not be happy in what she was doing without Mrs. Rawlings' blessing.

Susan prowled over wild country with the telephone wire holding her to her duty like a leash. The next time she must telephone, or wait to be telephoned, nailed her to her cross. The mountains themselves seemed trammeled by her unfreedom. Everywhere on the mountains, where she met no one at all, from breakfast time to dusk, excepting sheep, or a shepherd, she came face-to-face with her own craziness, which might attack her in the broadest valleys, so that they seemed too small, or on a mountaintop from which she could see a hundred other mountains and valleys, so that they seemed too low, too small, with the sky pressing down too close. She would stand gazing at a hillside brilliant with ferns and bracken, jeweled with running water, and see nothing but her devil, who lifted inhuman eyes at her from where he leaned negligently on a rock, switching at his ugly yellow boots with a leafy twig.

She returned to her home and family, with the Welsh emptiness at the back of her mind like a promise of freedom.

She told her husband she wanted to have an *au pair* girl.

They were in their bedroom, it was late at night, the children slept. He sat, shirted and slippered, in a chair by the window, looking out. She sat brushing her hair and watching him in the mirror. A time-hallowed scene in the connubial bedroom. He said nothing, while she heard the arguments coming into his mind, only to be rejected because every one was *reasonable.*

"It seems strange to get one now; after all, the children are in school most of the day. Surely the time for you to have help was when you were stuck with them day and night. Why don't you ask Mrs. Parkes to cook for you? She's even offered to—I can understand if you are tired of cooking for six people. But you know that an *au pair* girl means all kinds of problems; it's not like having an ordinary char in during the day. . . ."

Finally he said carefully: "Are you thinking of going back to work?"

"No," she said, "no, not really." She made herself sound vague, rather stupid. She went on brushing her black hair and peering at herself so as to be oblivious of the short uneasy glances her Matthew kept giving her. "Do you think we can't afford it?" she went on vaguely, not at all the old efficient Susan who knew exactly what they could afford.

"It's not that," he said, looking out of the window at dark trees, so as not to look at her. Meanwhile she examined a round, candid, pleasant face with clear dark brows and clear grey eyes. A sensible face. She brushed thick healthy black hair and thought: Yet that's the reflection of a madwoman. How very strange! Much more to the point if what looked back at me was the gingery green-eyed demon with his dry meager smile. . . . Why wasn't Matthew agreeing? After all, what else could he do? She was breaking her part of the bargain and there was no way of forcing her to keep it: that her spirit, her soul, should live in this house, so that the people in it could grow like plants in water, and Mrs. Parkes remain content in their service. In return for this, he would be a good loving husband, and responsible towards the children. Well, nothing like this had been true of either of them for a long time. He did his duty, perfunctorily; she did not even pretend to do hers. And he had become like other husbands, with his real life in his work and the people he met there, and very likely a serious affair. All this was her fault.

At last he drew heavy curtains, blotting out the trees, and turned to force her attention: "Susan, are you really sure we need a girl?" But she would not meet his appeal at all. She was running the brush over her hair again and again, lifting fine black clouds in a small hiss of electricity. She was peering in and smiling as if she were amused at the clinging hissing hair that followed the brush.

"Yes, I think it would be a good idea, on the whole," she said, with the cunning of a madwoman evading the real point.

In the mirror she could see her Matthew lying on his back, his hands behind his head, staring upwards, his face sad and hard. She felt her heart (the old heart of Susan Rawlings) soften and call out to him. But she set it to be indifferent.

He said: "Susan, the children?" It was an appeal that *almost* reached her. He opened his arms, lifting them palms up, empty. She had only to run across and fling herself into them, onto his hard, warm chest, and melt into herself, into Susan. But she could not. She would not see his lifted arms. She said vaguely: "Well, surely it'll be even better for them? We'll get a French or a German girl and they'll learn the language."

In the dark she lay beside him, feeling frozen, a stranger. She felt as if Susan had been spirited away. She disliked very much this woman who lay here, cold and indifferent beside a suffering man, but she could not change her.

Next morning she set about getting a girl, and very soon came Sophie Traub from Hamburg, a girl of twenty, laughing, healthy, blue-eyed, intending to learn English. Indeed, she already spoke a good deal. In return for a room—"Mother's Room"—and her food, she undertook to do some light cooking, and to be with the children when Mrs. Rawlings asked. She was an intelligent girl and understood perfectly what was needed. Susan said: "I go off sometimes, for the morning or for the day—well, sometimes the children run home from school, or they ring up, or a teacher rings up. I should be here, really. And there's the daily woman. . . ." And Sophie laughed her deep fruity fräulein's laugh, showed her fine white teeth and her dimples, and said: "You want some person to play mistress of the house sometimes, not so?"

"Yes, that is just so," said Susan, a bit dry, despite herself, thinking in secret fear how easy it was, how much nearer to the end she was than she thought. Healthy Fräulein Traub's instant understanding of their position proved this to be true.

The *au pair* girl, because of her own common sense, or (as Susan said to herself, with her new inward shudder) because she had been *chosen* so well by Susan, was a success with everyone, the children liking her, Mrs. Parkes forgetting almost at once that she was German, and Matthew finding her "nice to have around the house." For he was now taking things as they came, from the surface of life, withdrawn both as a husband and a father from the household.

One day Susan saw how Sophie and Mrs. Parkes were talking and laughing in the kitchen, and she announced that she would be away until teatime. She knew exactly where to go and what she must look for. She took the District Line to South Kensington, changed to the Circle, got off at Paddington, and walked around looking at the smaller hotels until she was satisfied with one which had FRED'S HOTEL painted on windowpanes that needed cleaning. The façade was a faded shiny yellow, like unhealthy skin. A door at the end of a passage said she must knock; she did, and Fred appeared. He was not at all attractive, not in any way, being fattish, and run-down, and wearing a tasteless striped suit. He had small sharp eyes in a white creased face, and was quite prepared to let Mrs. Jones (she chose the farcical name deliberately, staring him out) have a room three days a week from ten until six. Provided of course that she paid in advance each time she came? Susan produced fifteen shillings (no price had been set by him) and held it out, still fixing him with a bold unblinking challenge she had not known until then she could use at will. Looking at her still, he took up a ten-shilling note from her palm between thumb and forefinger, fingered it; then shuffled up two half-crowns, held out his own palm with these bits of money displayed thereon, and let his gaze lower broodingly at them. They were standing in the passage, a red-shaded light above, bare boards beneath, and a strong smell of floor polish rising about them. He shot his gaze up at her over the still-extended palm, and smiled as if to say: What do you take me for? "I shan't," said Susan, "be using this room for the purposes of making money." He still waited. She added another five shillings, at which he nodded and said: "You pay, and I ask no questions." "Good," said Susan. He now went past her to the stairs, and there waited a moment: the light from the street door being in her eyes, she lost sight of him momentarily. Then she saw a sober-suited, white-faced, white-balding little man trotting up the stairs like a waiter, and she went after him. They proceeded in utter silence up the stairs of this house where no questions were asked—Fred's Hotel, which could afford the freedom for its visitors that poor Miss Townsend's hotel could not. The room was hideous. It had a single window, with thin green brocade curtains, a three-quarter bed that had a cheap green satin bedspread on it, a fireplace with a gas fire and a shilling meter by it, a chest of drawers, and a green wicker armchair.

"Thank you," said Susan, knowing that Fred (if this was Fred, and not George, or Herbert or Charlie) was looking at her, not so much with curiosity, an emotion he would not own to, for professional reasons, but with a philosophical sense of what was appropriate. Having taken her money and shown her up and agreed to everything, he was clearly disapproving of her for coming here. She did not belong here at all, so his look said. (But she knew, already, how very much she did belong: the room had been waiting for her to join it.) "Would you have me called at five o'clock, please?" and he nodded and went downstairs.

It was twelve in the morning. She was free. She sat in the armchair, she simply sat, she closed her eyes and sat and let herself be alone. She was alone and no one knew where she was. When a knock came on the door she was annoyed, and prepared to show it: but it was Fred himself; it was five o'clock and he was calling her as ordered. He flicked his sharp little eyes over the room—bed, first. It was undisturbed. She might never have been in the room at all. She thanked him, said she would be returning the day after tomorrow, and left. She was back home in time to cook supper, to put the children to bed, to cook a second supper for her husband and herself later. And to welcome Sophie back from the pictures where she had gone with a friend. All these things she did cheerfully, willingly. But she was thinking all the time of the hotel room; she was longing for it with her whole being.

Three times a week. She arrived promptly at ten, looked Fred in the eyes, gave him twenty shillings, followed him up the stairs, went into the room, and shut the door on him with gentle firmness. For Fred, disapproving of her being here at all, was quite ready to let friendship, or at least acquaintanceship, follow his disapproval, if only she would let him. But he was content to go off on her dismissing nod, with the twenty shillings in his hand.

She sat in the armchair and shut her eyes.

What did she *do* in the room? Why, nothing at all. From the chair, when it had rested her, she went to the window, stretching her arms, smiling, treasuring her anonymity, to look out. She was no longer Susan Rawlings, mother of four, wife of Matthew, employer of Mrs. Parkes and of Sophie Traub, with these and those relations with friends, schoolteachers, tradesmen. She no longer was mistress of the big white house and garden, owning clothes suitable for this and that activity or occasion. She was Mrs. Jones, and she was alone, and she had no past and no future. Here I am, she thought, after all these years of being married and having children and playing those roles of responsibility—and I'm just the same. Yet there have been times I thought that nothing existed of me except the roles that went with being Mrs. Matthew Rawlings. Yes, here I am, and if I never saw any of my family again, here I would still be . . . how very strange that is! And she leaned on the sill, and looked into the street, loving the men and women who passed, because she did not know them. She looked at the downtrodden buildings over the street, and at the sky, wet and dingy, or sometimes blue, and she felt she had never seen buildings or sky before. And then she went back to the chair, empty, her mind a blank. Sometimes she talked aloud, saying nothing—an exclamation, meaningless, followed by a comment about the floral pattern on the thin rug, or a stain on the green satin coverlet. For the most part, she wool-gathered—what word is there for it?—brooded, wandered, simply went dark, feeling emptiness run deliciously through her veins like the movement of her blood.

This room had become more her own than the house she lived in. One morning she found Fred taking her a flight higher than usual. She stopped, refusing to go up, and demanded her usual room, Number 19. "Well, you'll have to wait half an hour, then," he said. Willingly she descended to the dark disinfectant-smelling hall, and sat waiting until the two, man and woman, came down the stairs, giving her swift indifferent glances before they hurried out into the street, separating at the door. She went up to the room, *her* room, which they had just vacated. It was no less hers, though the windows were set wide open, and a maid was straightening the bed as she came in.

After these days of solitude, it was both easy to play her part as mother and wife, and difficult—because it was so easy: she felt an impostor. She felt as if her shell moved here, with her family, answering to Mummy, Mother, Susan, Mrs. Rawlings. She was surprised no one saw through her, that she wasn't turned out of doors, as a fake. On the contrary, it seemed the children loved her more; Matthew and she "got on" pleasantly, and Mrs. Parkes was happy in her work under (for the most part, it must be confessed) Sophie Traub. At night she lay beside her husband, and they made love again, apparently just as they used to, when they were really married. But she, Susan, or the being who answered so readily and improbably to the name of Susan, was not there: she was in Fred's Hotel, in Paddington, waiting for the easing hours of solitude to begin.

Soon she made a new arrangement with Fred and with Sophie. It was for five days a week. As for the money, five pounds, she simply asked Matthew for it. She saw that she was not even frightened he might ask what for: he would give it to her, she knew that, and yet it was terrifying it could be so, for this close couple, these partners, had once known the destination of every shilling they must spend. He agreed to give her five pounds a week. She asked for just so much, not a penny more. He sounded indifferent about it. It was as if he were paying her, she thought: *paying her off*—yes, that was it. Terror came back for a moment when she understood this, but she stilled it: things had gone too far for that. Now, every week, on Sunday nights, he gave her five pounds, turning away from her before their eyes could meet on the transaction. As for Sophie Traub, she was to be somewhere in or near the house until six at night, after which she was free. She was not to cook, or to clean; she was simply to be there. So she gardened or sewed, and asked friends in, being a person who was bound to have a lot of friends. If the children were sick, she nursed them. If teachers telephoned, she answered them sensibly. For the five daytimes in the school week, she was altogether the mistress of the house.

One night in the bedroom, Matthew asked: "Susan, I don't want to interfere—don't think that, please—but are you sure you are well?"

She was brushing her hair at the mirror. She made two more strokes on either side of her head, before she replied: "Yes, dear, I am sure I am well."

He was again lying on his back, his blond head on his hands, his elbows angled up and part-concealing his face. He said: "Then Susan, I have to ask you this question, though you must understand, I'm not putting any sort of pressure on you." (Susan heard the word "pressure" with dismay, because this was inevitable; of course she could not go on like this.) "Are things going to go on like this?"

"Well," she said, going vague and bright and idiotic again, so as to escape: "Well, I don't see why not."

He was jerking his elbows up and down, in annoyance or in pain, and, looking at him, she saw he had got thin, even gaunt; and restless angry movements were not what she remembered of him. He said: "Do you want a divorce, is that it?"

At this, Susan only with the greatest difficulty stopped herself from laughing: she could hear the bright bubbling laughter she *would* have emitted, had she let herself. He could only mean one thing: she had a lover, and that was why she spent her days in London, as lost to him as if she had vanished to another continent.

Then the small panic set in again: she understood that he hoped she did have a lover, he was begging her to say so, because otherwise it would be too terrifying.

She thought this out as she brushed her hair, watching the fine black stuff fly up to make its little clouds of electricity, hiss, hiss, hiss. Behind her head, across the room, was a blue wall. She realized she was absorbed in watching the black hair making shapes against the blue. She should be answering him. "Do *you* want a divorce, Matthew?"

He said: "That surely isn't the point, is it?"

"You brought it up, I didn't," she said, brightly, suppressing meaningless tinkling laughter.

Next day she asked Fred: "Have inquiries been made for me?"

He hesitated, and she said: "I've been coming here a year now. I've made no trouble, and you've been paid every day. I have a right to be told."

"As a matter of fact, Mrs. Jones, a man did come asking."

"A man from a detective agency?"

"Well, he could have been, couldn't he?"

"I was asking you. . . . Well, what did you tell him?"

"I told him a Mrs. Jones came every weekday from ten until five or six and stayed in Number 19 by herself."

"Describing me?"

"Well, Mrs. Jones, I had no alternative. Put yourself in my place."

"By rights I should deduct what that man gave you for the information."

He raised shocked eyes: she was not the sort of person to make jokes like this! Then he chose to laugh: a pinkish wet slit appeared across his white crinkled face; his eyes positively begged her to laugh, otherwise he might lose some money. She remained grave, looking at him.

He stopped laughing and said: "You want to go up now?"—returning to the familiarity, the comradeship, of the country where no questions are asked, on which (and he knew it) she depended completely.

She went up to sit in her wicker chair. But it was not the same. Her husband had searched her out. (The world had searched her out.) The pressures were on her. She was here with his connivance. He might walk in at any moment, here, into Room 19. She imagined the report from the detective agency: "A woman calling herself Mrs. Jones, fitting the description of your wife (et cetera, et cetera, et cetera), stays alone all day in Room No. 19. She insists on this room, waits for it if it is engaged.

As far as the proprietor knows, she receives no visitors there, male or female." A report something on these lines Matthew must have received.

Well, of course he was right: things couldn't go on like this. He had put an end to it all simply by sending the detective after her.

She tried to shrink herself back into the shelter of the room, a snail pecked out of its shell and trying to squirm back. But the peace of the room had gone. She was trying consciously to revive it, trying to let go into the dark creative trance (or whatever it was) that she had found there. It was no use, yet she craved it, she was as ill as a suddenly deprived addict.

Several times she returned to the room, to look for herself there, but instead she found the unnamed spirit of restlessness, a pricking fevered hunger for movement, an irritable self-consciousness that made her brain feel as if it had colored lights going on and off inside it. Instead of the soft dark that had been the room's air, were now waiting for her demons that made her dash blindly about, muttering words of hate; she was impelling herself from point to point like a moth dashing itself against a windowpane, sliding to the bottom, fluttering off on broken wings, then crashing into the invisible barrier again. And again and again. Soon she was exhausted, and she told Fred that for a while she would not be needing the room, she was going on holiday. Home she went, to the big white house by the river. The middle of a weekday, and she felt guilty at returning to her own home when not expected. She stood unseen, looking in at the kitchen window. Mrs. Parkes, wearing a discarded floral overall of Susan's, was stooping to slide something into the oven. Sophie, arms folded, was leaning her back against a cupboard and laughing at some joke made by a girl not seen before by Susan—a dark foreign girl, Sophie's visitor. In an armchair Molly, one of the twins, lay curled, sucking her thumb and watching the grown-ups. She must have some sickness, to be kept from school. The child's listless face, the dark circles under her eyes, hurt Susan: Molly was looking at the three grown-ups working and talking in exactly the same way Susan looked at the four through the kitchen window: she was remote, shut off from them.

But then, just as Susan imagined herself going in, picking up the little girl, and sitting in an armchair with her, stroking her probably heated forehead, Sophie did just that: she had been standing on one leg, the other knee flexed, its foot set against the wall. Now she let her foot in its ribbon-tied red shoe slide down the wall, stood solid on two feet, clapping her hands before and behind her, and sang a couple of lines in German, so that the child lifted her heavy eyes at her and began to smile. Then she walked, or rather skipped, over to the child, swung her up, and let her fall into her lap at the same moment she sat herself. She said "Hopla! Hopla! Molly . . ." and began stroking the dark untidy young head that Molly laid on her shoulder for comfort.

*Well.* . . . Susan blinked the tears of farewell out of her eyes, and went quietly up through the house to her bedroom. There she sat looking at the river through the trees. She felt at peace, but in a way that was new to her. She had no desire to move, to talk, to do anything at all. The devils that had haunted the house, the garden, were not there; but she knew it was because her soul was in Room 19 in Fred's Hotel; she was not really here at all. It was a sensation that should have been frightening: to sit at her own bedroom window, listening to Sophie's rich young voice sing German nursery songs to her child, listening to Mrs. Parkes clatter and move below, and to know that all this had nothing to do with her: she was already out of it.

Later, she made herself go down and say she was home: it was unfair to be here unannounced. She took lunch with Mrs. Parkes, Sophie, Sophie's Italian friend Maria, and her daughter Molly, and felt like a visitor.

A few days later, at bedtime, Matthew said: "Here's your five pounds," and pushed them over at her. Yet he must have known she had not been leaving the house at all.

She shook her head, gave it back to him, and said, in explanation, not in accusation: "As soon as you knew where I was, there was no point."

He nodded, not looking at her. He was turned away from her: thinking, she knew, how best to handle this wife who terrified him.

He said: "I wasn't trying to . . . It's just that I was worried."

"Yes, I know."

"I must confess that I was beginning to wonder . . ."

"You thought I had a lover?"

"Yes, I am afraid I did."

She knew that he wished she had. She sat wondering how to say: "For a year now I've been spending all my days in a very sordid hotel room. It's the place where I'm happy. In fact, without it I don't exist." She heard herself saying this, and understood how terrified he was that she might. So instead she said: "Well, perhaps you're not far wrong."

Probably Matthew would think the hotel proprietor lied: he would want to think so.

"Well," he said, and she could hear his voice spring up, so to speak, with relief, "in that case I must confess I've got a bit of an affair on myself."

She said, detached and interested: "Really? Who is she?" and saw Matthew's startled look because of this reaction.

"It's Phil. Phil Hunt."

She had known Phil Hunt well in the old unmarried days. She was thinking: No, she won't do, she's too neurotic and difficult. She's never been happy yet. Sophie's much better. Well, Matthew will see that himself, as sensible as he is.

This line of thought went on in silence, while she said aloud: "It's no point telling you about mine, because you don't know him."

Quick, quick, invent, she thought. Remember how you invented all that nonsense for Miss Townsend.

She began slowly, careful not to contradict herself: "His name is Michael" (*Michael What?*)—"Michael Plant." (What a silly name!) "He's rather like you—in looks, I mean." And indeed, she could imagine herself being touched by no one but Matthew himself. "He's a publisher." (Really? Why?) "He's got a wife already and two children."

She brought out this fantasy, proud of herself.

Matthew said: "Are you two thinking of marrying?"

She said, before she could stop herself: "Good, God, *no!*"

She realized, if Matthew wanted to marry Phil Hunt, that this was too emphatic, but apparently it was all right, for his voice sounded relieved as he said: "It is a bit impossible to imagine oneself married to anyone else, isn't it?" With which he pulled her to him, so that her head lay on his shoulder. She turned her face into the dark of his flesh, and listened to the blood pounding through her ears saying: I am alone, I am alone, I am alone.

In the morning Susan lay in bed while he dressed.

He had been thinking things out in the night, because now he said: "Susan, why don't we make a foursome?"

Of course, she said to herself, of course he would be bound to say that. If one is sensible, if one is reasonable, if one never allows oneself a base thought or an envious emotion, naturally one says: Let's make a foursome!

"Why not?" she said.

"We could all meet for lunch. I mean, it's ridiculous, you sneaking off to filthy hotels, and me staying late at the office, and all the lies everyone has to tell."

What on earth did I say his name was?—she panicked, then said: "I think it's a good idea, but Michael is away at the moment. When he comes back, though—and I'm sure you two would like each other."

"He's away, is he? So that's why you've been . . ." Her husband put his hand to the knot of his tie in a gesture of male coquetry she would not before have associated with him; and he bent to kiss her cheek with the expression that goes with the words: Oh you naughty little puss! And she felt its answering look, naughty and coy, come onto her face.

Inside she was dissolving in horror at them both, at how far they had both sunk from honesty of emotion.

So now she was saddled with a lover, and he had a mistress! How ordinary, how reassuring, how jolly! And now they would make a foursome of it, and go about to theatres and restaurants. After all, the Rawlings could well afford that sort of thing, and presumably the publisher Michael Plant could afford to do himself and his mistress quite well. No, there was nothing to stop the four of them developing the most intricate relationship of civilized tolerance, all enveloped in a charming afterglow of autumnal passion. Perhaps they would all go off on holidays together? She had known people who did. Or perhaps Matthew would draw the line there? Why should he, though, if he was capable of talking about "foursomes" at all?

She lay in the empty bedroom, listening to the car drive off with Matthew in it, off to work. Then she heard the children clattering off to school to the accompaniment of Sophie's cheerfully ringing voice. She slid down into the hollow of the bed, for shelter against her own irrelevance. And she stretched out her hand to the hollow where her husband's body had lain, but found no comfort there: he was not her husband. She curled herself up in a small tight ball under the clothes: she could stay here all day, all week, indeed, all her life.

But in a few days she must produce Michael Plant, and—but how? She must presumably find some agreeable man prepared to impersonate a publisher called Michael Plant. And in return for which she would—what? Well, for one thing they would make love. The idea made her want to cry with sheer exhaustion. Oh, no, she had finished with all that—the proof of it was that the words "make love," or even imagining it, trying hard to revive no more than the pleasures of sensuality, let alone affection, or love, made her want to run away and hide from the sheer effort of the thing. . . . Good Lord, why make love at all? Why make love with anyone? Or if you are going to make love, what does it matter who with? Why shouldn't she simply walk into the street, pick up a man, and have a roaring sexual affair with him? Why not? Or even with Fred? What difference did it make?

But she had let herself in for it—an interminable stretch of time with a lover, called Michael, as part of a gallant civilized foursome. Well, she could not, and she would not.

She got up, dressed, went down to find Mrs. Parkes, and asked her for the loan of a pound, since Matthew, she said, had forgotten to leave her money. She exchanged with Mrs. Parkes variations on the theme that husbands are all the same, they don't think, and without saying a word to Sophie, whose voice could be heard upstairs from the telephone, walked to the underground, traveled to South Kensington, changed to the Inner Circle, got out at Paddington, and walked to Fred's Hotel. There she told Fred that she wasn't going on holiday after all, she needed the room. She would have to wait an hour, Fred said. She went to a busy tearoom-cum-restaurant around the corner, and sat watching the people flow in and out the door that kept swinging open and shut, watched them mingle and merge, and separate, felt her being flow into them, into their movement. When the hour was up, she left a half-crown for her pot of tea, and left the place without looking back at it, just as she had left her house, the big, beautiful white house, without another look, but silently dedicating it to Sophie. She returned to Fred, received the key of Number 19, now free, and ascended the grimy stairs slowly, letting floor after floor fall away below her, keeping her eyes lifted, so that floor after floor descended jerkily to her level of vision, and fell away out of sight.

Number 19 was the same. She saw everything with an acute, narrow, checking glance: the cheap shine of the satin spread, which had been replaced carelessly after the two bodies had finished their convulsions under it; a trace of powder on the glass that topped the chest of drawers; an intense green shade in a fold of the curtain. She stood at the window, looking down, watching people pass and pass and pass until her mind went dark from the constant movement. Then she sat in the wicker chair, letting herself go slack. But she had to be careful, because she did not want, today, to be surprised by Fred's knock at five o'clock.

The demons were not here. They had gone forever, because she was buying her freedom from them. She was slipping already into the dark fructifying dream that seemed to caress her inwardly, like the movement of her blood . . . but she had to think about Matthew first. Should she write a letter for the coroner? But what should she say? She would like to leave him with the look on his face she had seen this morning—banal, admittedly, but at least confidently healthy. Well, that was impossible, one did not look like that with a wife dead from suicide. But how to leave him believing she was dying because of a man—because of the fascinating publisher Michael Plant? Oh, how ridiculous! How absurd! How humiliating! But she decided not to trouble about it, simply not to think about the living. If he wanted to believe she had a lover, he would believe it. And he *did* want to believe it. Even when he had found out that there was no publisher in London called Michael Plant, he would think: Oh poor Susan, she was afraid to give me his real name.

And what did it matter whether he married Phil Hunt or Sophie? Though it ought to be Sophie, who was already the mother of those children . . . and what hypocrisy to sit here worrying about the children, when she was going to leave them because she had not got the energy to stay.

She had about four hours. She spent them delightfully, darkly, sweetly, letting herself slide gently, gently, to the edge of the river. Then, with hardly a break in her consciousness, she got up, pushed the thin rug against the door, made sure the windows were tight shut, put two shillings in the meter, and turned on the gas. For the first time since she had been in the room she lay on the hard bed that smelled stale, that smelled of sweat and sex.

She lay on her back on the green satin cover, but her legs were chilly. She got up, found a blanket folded in the bottom of the chest of drawers, and carefully covered her legs with it. She was quite content lying there, listening to the faint soft hiss of the gas that poured into the room, into her lungs, into her brain, as she drifted off into the dark river.

# The Words He Said

On the morning of the *braavleis,* Dad kept saying to Moira, as if he thought it was a joke, "Moy, it's going to rain." First she did not hear him, then she turned her head slowly and deliberately and looked at him so that he remembered what she had said the day before; and he got red in the face and went indoors, out of her way. The day before he had said to her, speaking to me, "What's Moy got into her head? Is the *braavleis* for her engagement or what?"

It was because Moira spent all morning cooking her lemon cake for the *braavleis,* and she went over to Sam the butcher's to order the best ribs of beef and best rump steak.

All the cold season she was not cooking, she was not helping Mom in the house at all, she was not taking an interest in life; and Dad was saying to Mom: "Oh, get the girl to town or something; don't let her moon about here. Who does she think she is?"

Mom just said, quiet and calm, the way she was with Dad when they did not agree: "Oh, let her alone, Dickson." When Mom and Dad were agreeing, they called each other Mom and Dad; when they were against each other, it was Marion and Dickson. And that is how it was for the whole of the dry season, and Moira was pale and moony and would not talk to me. It was no fun for me, I can tell you.

"What's this for?" Dad said once about halfway through the season, when Moira stayed in bed three days and Mom let her. "Has he said anything to her or hasn't he?"

Mom just said: "She's sick, Dickson."

But I could see what he said had gone into her, because I was in our bedroom when Mom came to Moira.

Mom sat down on the bed, but at the bottom of it, and she was worried. "Listen, girl," said Mom, "I don't want to interfere, I don't want to do that, but what did Greg say?" Moira was not properly in bed, but in her old pink dressing gown that used to be Mom's, and she was lying under the quilt. She lay there, not reading or anything, watching out of the window over at the big water tanks across the railway lines. Her face looked bad, and she said: "Oh, leave me alone, Mom."

Mom said: "Listen, dear, just let me say something. You don't have to follow what I say, do you?"

But Moira said nothing.

"Sometimes boys say a thing, and they don't mean it the way we think. They feel they have to say it. It's not they don't mean it, but they mean it different."

"He didn't say anything at all," said Moira. "Why should he?"

"Why don't you go into town and stay with Auntie Nora awhile? You can come back for the holidays when Greg comes back."

"Oh, let me alone," said Moira, and she began to cry. That was the first time she cried. At least, in front of Mom. I used to hear her cry at night when she thought I was asleep.

Mom's face was tight and patient, and she put her hand on Moira's shoulder, and she was worried I could see. I was sitting on my bed pretending to do my stamps, and she looked over at me and seemed to be thinking hard.

"He didn't say anything, Mom," I said. "But I know what happened."

Moira jerked her head up and she said: "Get that kid *away* from me."

They could not get me away from Moira because there were only two bedrooms, and I always slept with Moira. But she would not speak to me that night at all; and Mom said to me, "Little pitchers have big ears."

It was the last year's *braavleis* it happened. Moira was not keen on Greg then; I know for a fact because she was sweet on Jordan. Greg was mostly at the Cape in college; but he came back for the first time in a year, and I saw him looking at Moira. She was pretty then, because she had finished school and spent all her time making herself pretty. She was eighteen, and her hair was wavy because the rains had started. Greg was on the other side of the bonfire, and he came walking around it through the sparks and the white smoke, and up to Moira. Moira smiled out of politeness, because she wanted Jordan to sit by her, and she was afraid he wouldn't if he saw her occupied by Greg.

"Moira Hughes?" he said. Moira smiled, and he said: "I wouldn't have known you."

"Go on," I said, "you've known us always."

They did not hear me. They were just looking. It was peculiar. I knew it was one of the peculiar moments of life because my skin was tingling all over, and that is how I always know.

Because of how she was looking at him, I looked at him too, but I did not think he was handsome. The holidays before, when I was sweet on Greg Jackson, I naturally thought he was handsome, but now he was just ordinary. He was very thin, always, and his hair was ginger, and his freckles were thick, because naturally the sun is no good for people with white skin and freckles.

But he wasn't bad, particularly because he was in his sensible mood. Since he went to college he had two moods, one noisy and sarcastic; and then Moira used to say, all lofty and superior: "Medical students are always rowdy. It stands to reason because of the hard life they have afterwards." His other mood was when he was quiet and grown-up; and some of the gang didn't like it, because he was better than us—he was the only one of the gang to go to university at the Cape.

After they had finished looking, he just sat down in the grass in the place Moira was keeping for Jordan, and Moira did not once look around for Jordan. They did not say anything else, just went on sitting, and when the big dance began, with everyone holding hands around the bonfire, they stood at one side watching.

That was all that happened at the *braavleis,* and that was all the words he said. Next day Greg went on a shooting trip with his father, who was the man at the garage. They went right up the Zambezi valley, and Greg did not come back to our station during those holidays or the holidays after.

I knew Moira was thinking of a letter, because she bought some of Croxley's best blue at the store, and she always went herself to the post office on mail days. But there was no letter. But after that she said to Jordan, "No thanks, I don't feel like it," when he asked her to go into town to the pictures.

She did not take any notice of any of the gang after that, though before she was leader of the gang, even over the boys.

That was when she stopped being pretty again; she looked as she did before she left school and was working hard at her studies. She was too thin; the curl went out of her hair, and she didn't bother to curl it, either.

All that dry season she did nothing and hardly spoke and did not sing, and I knew it was because of that minute when Greg and she looked at each other—that was all; and when I thought of it, I could feel the cold-hot down my back.

Well, on the day before the *braavleis,* as I said, Moira was on the veranda, and she had on the dress she wore last year to the *braavleis*. Greg had come back for the holidays the night before; we knew he had, because his mother said so when Mom met her at the store. But he did not come to our house. I did not like to see Moira's face, but I had to keep on looking at it—it was so sad, and her eyes were sore. Mom kissed her, putting both her arms around her, but Moira gave a hitch of her shoulders like a horse with a fly bothering it.

Mom sighed, and then I saw Dad looking at her, and the look they gave each other was most peculiar; it made me feel very peculiar again. And then Moira started in on the lemon cake, and went to the butcher's, and that was when Dad said that about the *braavleis* being for the engagement. Moira looked at him, with her eyes all black and sad, and said: "Why have you got it in for me, Dad? What have *I* done?"

Dad said: "Greg's not going to marry you. Now he's got to college, and going to be a doctor, he won't be after you."

Moira was smiling, her lips small and angry.

Mom said: "Why, Dickson, Moira's got her diploma and she's educated. What's got into your head?"

Dad said: "I'm telling you, that's all."

Moira said, very grown-up and quiet: "Why are you trying to spoil it for me, Dad? I haven't said anything about marrying, have I? And what have I done to you, anyway?"

Dad didn't like that. He went red and he laughed, but he didn't like it. And he was quiet, for a bit at least.

After lunch, when she'd finished with the cakes, she was sitting on the veranda when Jordan went past across to the store, and she called out: "Hi, Jordan, come and talk to me."

Now I know for a fact that Jordan wasn't sweet on Moira any more. He was sweet on Beth from the store, because I know for a fact he kissed her at the last station dance; I saw him. And he shouted out, "Thanks, Moy, but I'm on my way."

"Oh, please yourself, then," said Moira, friendly and nice, but I knew she was cross, because she was set on it.

Anyway, he came in, and I've never seen Moira so nice to anyone, not even when she was sweet on him, and certainly never to Greg. Well, Jordan was embarrassed, because Moira was not pretty that season and all the station was saying she had gone off. She took Jordan into the kitchen to see the lemon cake and dough all folded, ready for the sausage rolls, and she said, slow and surprised, "But we haven't enough bread for the sandwiches, Mom. What are you thinking of?"

Mom said, quick and cross, because she was proud of her kitchen.

"What do you mean? No one's going to eat sandwiches with all that meat you've ordered. And it'll be stale by tomorrow."

"I think we need more bread," said Moira. And she said to me in the same voice, slow and lazy, "Just run over to the Jacksons' and see if they can let us have some bread."

At this I didn't say anything, and Mom did not say anything either, and it was lucky Dad didn't hear. I looked at Mom, and she made no sign; so I went out across the railway lines to the garage. At the back of the garage was the Jacksons' house, and there was Greg Jackson reading a book about the body because he was going to be a doctor.

"Mom says," I said, "can you let us have some bread for the *braavleis?*"

He put down the book and said, "Oh, hullo, Betty."

"Hullo," I said.

"But the store will be open tomorrow," he said. "Isn't the *braavleis* tomorrow?"

"It's Sunday tomorrow," I said.

"But the store's open now."

"We want some stale bread," I said. "Moy's making some stuffing for the chicken; our bread's all fresh."

"Mom's at the store," he said, "but help yourself."

So I went into the pantry and got half a stale loaf, and came out and said, "Thanks," and walked past him.

He said, "Don't mention it." Then, when I was nearly gone, he said, "And how's Moy?" And I said, "Fine, thanks, but I haven't seen much of her this vacation because she's busy with Jordan." And I went away, and I could feel my back tingling; and sure enough there he was coming up behind me. And then he was beside me, and my side was tingling.

"I'll drop over and say hello," said Greg; and I felt peculiar, I can tell you, because what I was thinking was: *Well!* If this is *love!*

When we got near our house, Moira and Jordan were side by side on the veranda wall, and Moy was laughing; and I knew she had seen Greg coming because of the way she laughed.

Dad was not on the veranda, so I could see Mom had got him to stay indoors.

"I've got you the bread, Moy," I said, and with this I went into the kitchen, and there was Mom, and she was looking more peculiar than I've ever seen her. I could have bet she wanted to laugh; but she was sighing all the time. Because of the sighing I knew she had quarreled with Dad. "Well, I don't know," she said, and she threw the bread I'd fetched into the waste bucket.

There sat Mom and I in the kitchen, smiling at each other off and on in a peculiar way, and Dad was rattling his paper in the bedroom where she had made him go. He was not at the station that day because the train had come at nine o'clock and there wasn't another one coming. When we looked out on the veranda in about half an hour Jordan was gone, and Greg and Moira were sitting on the veranda wall. And I can tell you she looked so pretty again—it was peculiar her getting pretty like that so suddenly.

That was about five, and Greg went back to supper at home. Moira did not eat anything; she was in our room curling her hair, because she and Greg were going for a walk.

"Don't go too far; it's going to rain," Mom said, but Moira said, sweet and dainty, "Don't worry, Mom, I can look after myself."

Mom and Dad said nothing to each other all the evening.

I went to bed early for a change, so I'd be there when Moy got in, although I was thirteen that season and now my bedtime was up to ten o'clock.

Mom and Dad went to bed, although I could see Mom was worried because there was a storm blowing up; the dry season was due to end, and the lightning kept spurting all over the sky.

I lay awake saying to myself, Sleep sleep, go away, come again another day. But I went to sleep, and when I woke up, the room was full of the smell of rain, of the earth wet with rain, and the light was on and Moira was in the room.

"Have the rains come?" I said, and then I woke right up and saw of course they hadn't, because the air was as dry as sand, and Moira said, "Oh, shut up and go to sleep."

She did not look pretty as much as being different from how I'd seen her; her face was soft and smiling, and her eyes were different. She had blue eyes most of the time, but now they seemed quite black. And now that her hair was all curled and brushed, it looked pretty, like golden syrup. And she even looked a bit fatter. Usually when she wasn't too thin, she was rather fat, and when she was one of the gang we used to call her Pudding. That is, until she passed her J.C., and then she fought everyone, and the boys, too, so that she could be called Moy. So no one had called her Pudding for years now except Dad, to make her cross. He used to say, "You're going to make a fine figure of a woman like your mother." That always made Moy cross, I can tell you, because Mom was very fat, and she wore proper corsets these days, except just before the rains when it was so hot. I remember the first time the corsets came from the store, and she put them on. Moy had to lace her in, and Mom laughed so much Moy couldn't do the laces; and anyway she was cross because Mom laughed, and she said to me afterwards, "It's disgusting, letting yourself *go*—I'm not going to let myself *go*."

So it would have been more than my life was worth to tell her she was looking a bit fatter already, or to tell her anything at all, because she sat smiling on the edge of her bed, and when I said, "What did he say, Moy?" she just turned her head and made her eyes thin and black at me, and I saw I'd better go to sleep. But I knew something she didn't know I knew, because she had some dead jacaranda flowers in her hair; that meant she and Greg had been at the water tanks. There were only two jacaranda trees at our station, and they were at the big water tanks for the engines; and if they were at the water tanks, they must have been kissing, because it was romantic at the tanks. It was the end of October, and the jacarandas were shedding, and the tanks looked as if they were standing in pools of blue water.

Well, next morning Moy was already up when I woke, and she was singing, and even before breakfast she began ironing her muslin dress that she had made for last Christmas.

Mom said nothing; Dad kept rustling his newspaper; and I wouldn't have dared open my mouth. Besides, I wanted to find out what Greg had said. After breakfast, we sat around, because of its being Sunday; Dad didn't have to be at the station office because there weren't any trains on Sundays. And Dad kept grinning at Moira and saying: "I think it's going to rain," and she pretended she didn't know what he meant, until at last she jumped when he said it and turned herself and looked at him just the way she had the day before. That was when he got red in the face and said: "Can't you take a joke these days?" and Moira looked away from him with her eyebrows up, and Mom sighed, and then he said, very cross, "I'll leave you all to it, just tell me when you're in a better temper," and with this he took the newspaper inside to the bedroom.

Anybody could see it wasn't going to rain properly that day, because the clouds weren't thunderheads, but great big white ones, all silver and hardly any black in them.

Moy didn't eat any dinner, but went on sitting on the veranda, wearing her muslin dress, white with red spots and big puffed sleeves and a red sash around her waist.

After dinner, time went very slowly, and it was a long time before Greg came down off the Jacksons' veranda and came walking slowly along the gum-tree avenue. I was watching Moy's face, and she couldn't keep the smile off it. She got paler and paler until he got underneath our veranda, and she was looking at him so that I had gooseflesh all over.

Then he gave a jump up our steps to the veranda and said, "Hoy, Moy, how's it?" I thought she was going to fall right off the veranda wall, and her face had gone all different again.

"How are you, Gregory?" said Moira, all calm and proud.

"Oh, skidding along," he said; and I could see he felt awkward, because he hadn't looked at her once, and his skin was all red around the freckles. She didn't say anything, and she was looking at him as if she couldn't believe it was him.

"I hope the rain will keep off for the *braavleis,*" said Mom, in her visiting voice; and she looked hard at me, and I had to get up and go inside with her. But I could see Greg didn't want us to go at all, and I could see Moy knew it; her eyes were blue again, a pale thin blue, and her mouth was small.

Well, Mom went into the kitchen to make the sausage rolls; and I went into our bedroom, because I could see what went on on the veranda from behind the curtains.

Greg sat on the veranda wall and whistled. He was whistling "I Love You, Yes I Do"; and Moira was gazing at him as if he were a Christmas beetle she had just noticed. And then he began whistling "Three Little Words"; and suddenly Moira got down off the wall and stretched herself like a cat when it's going to walk off somewhere, and Greg said, "Skinny!"

At this she made her eyebrows go up, and I've never seen such a look.

And he was getting redder in the face, and he said: "You'd better not wear that dress to the *braavleis;* it's going to rain."

Moira didn't say a word for what seemed about half an hour, and then she said, in that lazy sort of voice, "Well, Greg Jackson, if you've changed your mind, it's O.K. with me."

"Changed my mind?" he said, very quickly, and he looked scared; and she looked scared, and she asked: "What did you say all those things for last night?"

"Say what?" he asked, more scared than ever; and I could see he was trying to remember what he'd said.

Moira was just looking at him, and I wouldn't have liked to be Greg Jackson just then, I can tell you. Then she walked off the veranda, letting her skirt swish slowly, and through the kitchen, and into our room, and then she sat on the bed.

"I'm not going to the *braavleis,* Mom," she said, in that sweet, slow voice like Mom uses when she's got visitors and she wishes they'd go.

Mom just sighed and slapped the dough about on the kitchen table. Dad made the springs of the bed creak, and he said half aloud, "Oh, my God, preserve me!"

Mom left the pastry and glared through the door of their bedroom at Dad, and then came into our room. There was Moira sitting all lumped up on her bed as if she had a pain, and her face was like pastry dough. Mom said nothing to Moira, but went on to the veranda. Greg was still sitting there, looking sick.

"Well, son," Mom said, in her easy voice, the voice she has when she is tired of everything, but keeping up, "well, son, I think Moy's got a bit of a headache from the heat."

As I've said, I wasn't sweet on Greg that vacation; but if I was Moy I would have been, the way he looked just then—all sad, but grown-up, like a man—when he said: "Mrs. Hughes, I don't know what I've done." Mom just smiled and sighed. "I can't marry, Mrs. Hughes. I've got five years' training ahead of me."

Mom smiled and said, "Of course, son, of course."

I was lying on my bed with my stamps; and Moira was on her bed, listening, and the way she smiled gave me a bad shiver.

"Listen to him," she said, in a loud slow voice. "Marry? Why does everyone go on about marrying? They're nuts. I wouldn't marry Greg Jackson, anyway, if he were the last man on a desert island."

Outside, I could hear Mom sigh hard; then her voice, quick and low; and then the sound of Greg's feet crunching off over the cinders of the path.

Then Mom came back into our room, and Moira said, all despairing, "Mom, what made you say that about marrying?"

"He said it, my girl, I didn't."

"Marrying!" said Moira, laughing hard.

Mom said, "What did he say then—you talked about him saying something?"

"Oh, you all make me sick," said Moira, and she lay down on her bed, turned away from us. Mom hitched her head at me, and we went out. By then it was five in the afternoon and the cars would be leaving at six, so Mom finished the sausage rolls in the oven, and packed the food, and then she took off her apron and went across to Jordan's house. Moira did not see her go, because she was still lost to the world in her pillow.

Soon Mom came back and put the food into the car. Then Jordan came over with Beth from the store and said to me, "Betty, my mom says, will you and Moy come in our car to the *braavleis,* because your car's full of food?"

"I will," I said, "but Moira's got a headache."

But at this moment Moira called out from our room, "Thanks, Jordan, I'd like to come."

So Mom called to Pop, and they went off in our car together, and I could see she was talking to him all the time, and he was just pulling the gears about and looking resigned to life.

Moira and I went with Jordan and Beth in their car. I could see Jordan was cross because he wanted to be with Beth; and Beth kept smiling at Moira with her eyebrows up, to tell her she knew what was going on; and Moira smiled back and talked a lot in her visiting voice.

The *braavleis* was a high place at the end of a vlei, where it rose into a small hill full of big boulders. The grass had been cut that morning by natives of the farmer who always let us use his farm for the *braavleis*. It was pretty, with the hill behind and the moon coming up over it, and then the cleared space, and the vlei sweeping down to the river, and the trees on either side. The moon was just over the trees when we got there, so the trees looked black and big, and the boulders were big and looked as if they might topple over, and the grass was silvery; but the great bonfire was roaring up twenty feet, and in the space around the fire it was all hot and red. The trench of embers where the spits were for the meat was on one side, and as soon as she arrived Moira went there and helped with the cooking.

Greg was not there, and I thought he wouldn't come; but much later, when we were all eating the meat, and laughing because it burned our fingers it was so hot, I saw him on the other side of the fire talking to Mom. Moira saw him talking, and she didn't like it, but she pretended not to see.

By then we were seated in a half-circle on the side of the fire the wind was blowing, so that the red flames were sweeping off away from us. There were about fifty people from the station and some farmers from round about. Moira sat by me, quiet, eating grilled ribs and sausage rolls; and for once she was pleased I was there, so that she wouldn't seem to be by herself. She had changed her dress again, and it was the dress she had worn last year for the *braavleis;* it was blue with pleats, and it was the dress she had for best the last year at school, so it wasn't very modern any more. Across the fire, I could see Greg. He did not look at Moira, and she did not look at him. Except that this year Jordan did not want to sit by Moira but by Beth, I kept feeling peculiar, as if this year were really last year, and in a minute Greg would walk across past the fire, and say: "Moira Hughes? I wouldn't have known you."

But he stayed where he was. He was sitting on his legs, with his hands on his knees. I could see his legs and knees and his big hands all red from the fire and the yellow hair glinting in the firelight. His face was red, too, and wet with the heat.

Then everyone began singing. We were singing "Sarie Marais," and

"Sugar Bush," and "Henrietta's Wedding" and "We don't want to go home." Moira and Greg were both singing as hard as they could.

It was getting late. The natives were damping down the cooking trench with earth and looking for scraps of meat and bits of sausage roll, and the big fire was sinking down. It would be time in a minute for the big dance in a circle around the fire.

Moira was just sitting. Her legs were tucked under her sideways, and they had got scratched from the grass—I could see the white dry scratches across the sunburn—and I can tell you it was a good thing she hadn't worn her best muslin because there wouldn't have been much left of it. Her hair, that she had curled yesterday, was tied back in a ribbon, so that her face looked small and thin.

I said, "Here, Moy, don't look like your own funeral"; and she said, "I will if I like." Then she gave me a bit of a grin, and she said: "Let me give you a word of warning for when you're grown up: Don't believe a word men say, I'm telling you."

But I could see she was feeling better just then.

At that very moment the red light of the fire on the grass just in front of us went out and someone sat down. I hoped it was Greg, and it was. They were looking at each other again; but my skin didn't tingle at all, so I looked at his face and at her face, and they were both quiet and sensible.

Then Moira reached out for a piece of grass, pulled it clean and neat out of the socket, and began nibbling at the soft piece at the end; and it was just the way Mom reached out for her knitting when she was against Dad. But of course Greg did not know the resemblance.

"Moy," he said, "I want to talk to you."

"My name is Moira," said Moira, looking him in the eyes.

"Oh heck, Moira," he said, sounding exasperated, just like Dad.

I wriggled back away from the two of them into the crowd that was still singing softly "Sarie Marais" and looking at the way the fire was glowing low and soft, ebbing red and then dark as the wind came up from the river. The moon was half covered with the big, soft, silvery clouds, and the red light was strong on our faces.

I could just hear what they said. I wasn't going to move too far off, I can tell you.

"I don't know what I've said," said Greg.

"It doesn't matter in the slightest," said Moira.

"Moira, for crying out loud!"

"Why did you say that about marrying?" said Moira, and her voice was shaky. She was going to cry if she didn't watch out.

"I thought you thought I meant . . ."

"You think too much," said Moira, tossing her head carefully so that her long tail of hair should come forward and lie on her shoulder. She put up her hand and stroked the curls smooth.

"Moira, I've got another five years at university. I couldn't ask you to be engaged for five years."

"I never said you should," said Moira, calm and lofty, examining the scratches on her legs.

The way she was sitting, curled up sideways, with her hair lying forward like syrup on her shoulder—it was pretty, it was as pretty as I've ever seen, and I could see his face, sad and almost sick.

"You're so pretty, Moy," he said, jerking it out.

Moira seemed not to be able to move. Then she turned her head slowly and looked at him. I could see the beginning of something terrible on her face. The shiver had begun under my hair at the back of my neck and was slowly moving down to the small of my back.

"You're so beautiful," he said, sounding angry, leaning forward with his face almost against hers.

And now she looked the way she had last night, when I was not awake and asked was it raining outside.

"When you look like that," he said, quite desperate about everything, "it makes me feel . . ."

People were getting up now all around us. The fire had burned right down; it was a low wave of red heat coming out at us. The redness was on our shoulders and legs, but our faces were having a chance to cool off. The moon had come out again, full and bright, and the cloud had rolled on. It was funny the way the light was red to their shoulders, and the white of the moon on their faces, and their eyes glistening. I didn't like it; I was shivering; it was the most peculiar moment of all my life.

"Well," said Moira, and she sounded just too tired even to try to understand, "that's what you said last night, wasn't it?"

"Don't you see," he said, trying to explain, his tongue all mixed up, "I can't help—I love you, I don't know. . . ."

Now she smiled, and I knew the smile at once, it was the way Mom smiled at Dad when if he had any sense he'd shut up. It was sweet and loving, but it was sad, and as if she were saying, Lord, you're a fool, Dickson Hughes!

Moira went on smiling like that at Greg, and he was sick and angry and not understanding a thing.

"I love you," he said again.

"Well, I love you—and what of it?" said Moira.

"But it will be five years."

"And what has that got to do with anything?" At this she began to laugh.

"But Moy . . ."

"My name is Moira," she said, once and for all.

For a moment they were both white and angry, their eyes glimmering in the light of the big white moon over them.

There was a shout and a hustle; and suddenly all the people were in the big circle around the big low heap of fire; and they were whirling around and around, yelling and screaming. Greg and Moira stayed where they were, just outside the range of the feet, and they didn't hear a thing.

"You're so pretty," he was saying, in that rough, cross, helpless voice. "I love you, Moira. There couldn't ever be anyone but you."

She was smiling, and he went on saying: "I love you. I see your face all the time; I see your hair and your face and your eyes."

And I wished he'd go on, the poor sap, just saying it, for every minute it was more like last night when I woke up and I thought it had rained—the feeling of the dry earth with the rain just on it, that was how she was, and she looked as if she would sit there and listen and listen forever to the words he said, and she didn't want to hear him saying, "Why don't you say something, Moy? You don't say anything; you do understand, don't you?—It's not fair, it isn't right to bind you when we're so young." But he started saying it in just a minute, and then she smiled her visiting smile, and she said: "Gregory Jackson, you're a fool."

Then she got up off the grass and went across to Mom to help load the car, and she never once looked at Greg again, not for the rest of the holidays.

# A Letter from Home

. . . *Ja*, but that isn't why I'm writing this time. You asked about Dick. You're worrying about him?—man! But he's got a poetry scholarship from a Texas university and he's lecturing the Texans about letters and life too in Suid Afrika, South Africa to you (forgive the hostility), and his poems are read, so they tell me, wherever the English read poetry. He's fine, man, but I thought I'd tell you about Johannes Potgieter, remember him? Remember the young poet, The Young Poet? He was around that winter you were here. Don't tell me you've forgotten those big melting brown eyes and those dimples. About ten years ago (*ja,* times flies) he got a type of unofficial grace-gift of a job at St.—— University on the strength of those poems of his, and—God—they were good. Not that you or any other English-speaking *domkop* will ever know, because they don't translate out of Afrikaans. Remember me telling you and everyone else (give me credit for that at least; I give the devil his due, when he's a poet) what a poet he was, how blerry good he was—but several people tried to translate Hans's poems, including me, and failed. Right. *Goed.* Meanwhile a third of the world's population—or is it a fifth, or to put it another way, X5Y59 million people—speak English (and it's increasing by six births a minute) but one million people speak Afrikaans, and though I say it in a whisper, man, only a fraction of them can read it, I mean to read it. But Hans is still a great poet. Right.

He wasn't all that happy about being a sort of unofficial laureate at that university. It's no secret some poets don't make laureates. At the end of seven months he produced a book of poems which had the whole God-fearing place sweating and sniffing out heresy of all kinds, sin, sex, liberalism, brother love, and so forth and so on; but of course in a civilized country (I say this under my breath, or I'll get the sack from my university, and I've got four daughters these days, had you forgotten?) no one would see anything in them but good poetry. Which is how Hans saw them, poor innocent soul. He was surprised at what people saw in them, and he was all upset. He didn't like being called all those names, and the good country boys from their fine farms and the smart town boys from their big houses all started looking sideways, making remarks, and our Hans, he was reduced to pap, because he's not a fighter, Hans; he was never a taker of positions on the side of justice, freedom, and the rest, for tell you the truth, I don't think he ever got round to defining them. *Goed.* He resigned, in what might be called a dignified silence, but his friends knew it was just plain cowardice or, if you like, incomprehension about what the fuss was over, and he went to live in Blagspruit in the Orange Free, where his Tantie Gertrude had a house. He helped her in her store. *Ja,* that's what he did. What did we all say to this? Well, what do you think? The inner soul of the artist (et cetera) knows what is best, and he probably *needed* the Orange Free and his Auntie's store for his development. Well, something like that. To tell the truth, we didn't say much; he simply dropped out. And time passed. *Ja.* Then they made me editor of *Onwards,* and thinking about our indigenous poets, I remembered Johannes Potgieter, and wrote "What about a poem from you?"—feeling bad because when I counted up the years, it was eight since I'd even thought of him, even counting those times when one says drunk at dawn: Remember Hans? Now, there was a poet. . . .

No reply, so I let an editorial interval elapse and I wrote again, and I got a very correct letter back. Well phrased. Polite. But not just that, it took me an hour to work out the handwriting—it was in a sort of Gothic print, each letter a work of art, like a medieval manuscript. But all he said, in that beautiful black art-writing, was: he was very well, he hoped I was very well, the weather was good, except the rains were late, his Tantie Gertie was dead, and he was running the store. "*Jou vriend,* Johannes Potgieter."

Right. *Goed.* I was taking a trip up to Joburg, so I wrote and said I'd drop in at Blagspruit on my way back, and I got another manuscript, or missal, saying he hoped to see me, and he would prepare Esther for my coming. I thought, he's married, poor *kerel,* and it was the first time I'd thought of him as anything but a born bachelor, and I was right—because when I'd done with Joburg, not a moment too soon, and driven down to the Orange Free, and arrived on the doorstep, there was Hans, but not a sign of a wife, and Esther turned out to be—but first I take pleasure in telling you that the beautiful brown-eyed poet with his noble brow and pale dimpled skin was bald—he has a tonsure, I swear it—and he's fat, a sort of smooth pale fat. He's like a monk, lard-colored and fat and smooth. Esther is the cook, or rather, his jailer. She's a Zulu, a great fat woman, and I swear she put the fear of God into me before I even got into the house. Tantie Gertie's house is a square brick four-roomed shack, you know the kind, with an iron roof and verandas—well, what you'd expect in Blagspruit. And Esther stood about six feet high in a white apron and a white *doekie* and she held a lamp up in one great black fist and looked into my face and sighed and went off into her kitchen singing "Rock of Ages." *Ja,* I promise you. And I looked at Hans, and all he said was "It's O.K., man. She likes you. Come in."

She gave us a great supper of roast mutton and pumpkin fritters and samp, and then some preserved fruit. She stood over us, arms folded, as we ate, and when Johannes left some mutton fat, she said in her mellow hymn-singing voice: "Waste not, want not, Master Johannes." And he ate it all up. *Ja.* She told me I should have some more peaches for my health, but I defied her and I felt as guilty as a small kicker, and I could see Hans eyeing me down the table and wondering where I got the nerve. She lives in the *kia* at the back, one small room with four children by various fathers, but no man, because God is more than enough for her now, you can see, with all those kids and Hans to bring up the right way. Auntie's store is a Drapery and General Goods in the main street, called Gertie's Store, and Hans was running it with a colored man. But I heard Esther with my own ears at supper saying to his bowed bald shamed head: "Master Johannes, I heard from the cook at the predikant's house today that the dried peaches have got worms in them." And Hans said: "O.K., Esther, I'll send them up some of the new stock tomorrow."

Right. We spent all that evening talking, and he was the same old Hans. You remember how he used to sit, saying not a blerry word, smiling that sweet dimpled smile of his, listening, listening, and then he'd ask a question, remember? Well, *do* you? Because it's only just now *I'm* beginning to remember. People'd be talking about I don't know what—the Nats or the weather or the grape crop, anything—and just as you'd start to get nervous because he never said anything, he'd lean forward and start questioning, terribly serious, earnest, about some detail, something not quite central, if you know what I mean. He'd lean forward, smiling, smiling, and he'd say: "You really mean that? It rained all morning? It rained all *morning?* Is that the truth?" That's right, you'd say, a bit uneasy, and he'd say, shaking his head: "God, man, it rained all morning, you say. . . ." And then there'd be a considerable silence till things picked up again. And half an hour later he'd say: "You really mean it? The hanepoort grapes are good this year?"

Right. We drank a good bit of brandewyn that night, but in a civilized way—you know: "Would you like another little drop, Mr. Martin?" "*Ja,* just a small tot, Hans, thank you"—but we got pretty pickled, and when I woke Sunday morning, I felt like death, but Esther was setting down a tray of tea by my bed, all dressed up in her Sunday hat and her black silk, saying: "*Goeie môre,* Master du Preez, it's nearly time for church," and I nearly said: "I'm not a churchgoer, Esther," but I thought better of it, because it came to me, can it be possible, has our Hans turned a God-fearing man in Blagspruit? So I said, "*Goed,* Esther. Thanks for telling me, and now just get out of here so that I can get dressed." Otherwise she'd have dressed me, I swear it. And she gave me a majestic nod, knowing that God had spoken through her to send me to church, sinner that I was and stinking of cheap *dop* from the night before.

Right. Johannes and I went to *kerk,* he in a black Sunday suit, if you'd believe such a thing, and saying: "Good morning, Mr. Stein. *Goeie môre,* Mrs. Van Esslin," a solid and respected member of the congregation, and I thought, poor *kerel,* there but for the grace of God go I, if I had to live in this godforsaken dorp stuck in the middle of the Orange Free State. And he looked like death after the brandewyn, and so did I, and we sat there swaying and sweating in that blerry little church through a sermon an hour and a half long, while all the faithful gave us nasty curious looks. Then we had a cold lunch, Esther having been worshiping at the kaffir church down in the Location, and we slept it all off and woke covered with flies and sweating, and it was as hot as hell, which is what Blagspruit is, hell. And he'd been there ten years, man, ten years. . . .

Right. It is Esther's afternoon off, and Johannes says he will make us some tea, but I see he is quite lost without her, so I say: "Give me a glass of water, and let's get out from under this iron, that's all I ask." He looks surprised, because his hide is hardened to it, but off we go, through the dusty little garden full of marigolds and zinnias, you know those sun-baked gardens with the barbed-wire fences and the gates painted dried-blood color in those little dorps stuck in the middle of the veld, enough to make you get drunk even to think of them, but Johannes is sniffling at the marigolds, which stink like turps, and he sticks an orange zinnia in his lapel, and says: "Esther likes gardening." And there we go along the main street, saying good afternoon to the citizens, for half a mile, then we're out in the veld again, just the veld. And we wander about, kicking up the dust and watching the sun sink, because both of us have just one idea, which is: how soon can we decently start sundowning?

Then there was a nasty stink on the air, and it came from a small bird impaled on a thorn on a thorn tree, which was a butcherbird's cache, have you ever seen one? Every blerry thorn had a beetle or a worm or something stuck on it, and it made me feel pretty sick, coming on top of everything, and I was just picking up a stone to throw at the damned thorn tree, to spite the butcherbird, when I saw Hans staring at a lower part of this tree. On a long black thorn was a great big brown beetle, and it was waving all its six legs and its two feelers in rhythm, trying to claw the thorn out of its middle, or so it looked, and it was writhing and wriggling, so that at last it fell off the thorn, which was at right angles, so to speak, from the soil, and it landed on its back, still waving its legs, trying to up itself. At which Hans bent down to look at it for some time, his two monk's hands on his upper thighs, his bald head sweating and glowing red in the last sunlight. *Then he bent down, picked up the beetle and stuck it back on the thorn.* Carefully, you understand, so that the thorn went back into the hole it had already made. You could see he was trying not to hurt the beetle. I just stood and gaped, like a *domkop,* and for some reason I remembered how one used to feel when he leaned forward and said, all earnest and involved: "You say the oranges are no good this year? Honestly, is that really true?" Anyway, I said: "Hans, man, for God's sake!" And then he looked at me, and he said, reproachfully: "The ants would have killed it, just look!" Well, the ground was swarming with ants of one kind or another, so there was logic in it, but I said: "Hans, let's drink, man, let's drink."

Well, it was Sunday, and no bars open. I took a last look at the beetle, the black thorn through its oozing middle, waving its black legs at the setting sun, and I said: "Back home, Hans, and to hell with Esther. We're going to get drunk."

Esther was in the kitchen, putting out cold meat and tomatoes, and I said: "Esther, you can take the evening off."

She said: "Master Hans, I have had all the Sunday afternoon off talking to Sister Mary." Hans looked helpless at me, and I said: "Esther, I'm giving you the evening off. Good night."

And Hans said, stuttering and stammering: "That's right, Esther, I'll give you the evening off. Good night, Esther."

She looked at him. Then at me. Hey, what a woman. Hey, what a queen, man! She said, with dignity: "Good night, Mr. Johannes. Good night, Mr. du Preez." Then she wiped her hands free of evil on her white apron, and she strode off, singing "All Things Bright and Beautiful," and I tell you we felt as if we weren't good enough to wash Esther's *broekies,* and that's the truth.

*Goed.* We got out the brandy, never mind about the cold meat and the tomatoes, and about an hour later I reached my point at last, which was, what about the poems, and the reason I'd taken so long was I was scared he'd say: "Take a look at Blagspruit, man. Take a look. Is this the place for poems, Martin?" But when I asked, he leaned forward and stared at me, all earnest and intent, then he turned his head carefully to the right, to see if the door into the kitchen was shut, but it wasn't; and then left at the window, and that was open too, and then past me at the door to the veranda. Then he got up on tiptoes and very carefully shut all three, and then he drew the curtains. It gave me the *skriks,* man, I can tell you. Then he went to a great old black chest and took out a manuscript, because it was all in the beautiful black difficult writing, and gave it to me to read. And I sat and slowly worked it out, letter by letter, while he sat opposite, sweating and totting, and giving fearful looks over his shoulders.

What was it? Well, I was drunk, for one thing, and Hans sitting there all frightened scared me, but it was good, it was good, I promise you. A kind of chronicle of Blagspruit it was, the lives of the citizens—well, need I elaborate, since the lives of citizens are the same everywhere in the world, but worse in Suid Afrika, and worse a million times in Blagspruit. The manuscript gave off a stink of church and right-doing, with the sin and the evil underneath. It had a medieval stink to it, naturally enough, for what is worse than the *kerk* in this our land? But I'm saying this to you, remember, and I never said it, but what is worse than the stink of the *kerk* and the God-fearing in this our feudal land?

But the poem. As far as I can remember, because I was full as a tick, it was a sort of prose chronicle that led up to and worked into the poems: you couldn't tell where they began or ended. The prose was stiff and old-fashioned, and formal, monk's language, and the poems, too. But I knew when I read it it was the best I'd read in years—since I read those poems of his ten years before, man, not since then. And don't forget, God help me, I'm an editor now, and I read poems day and night, and when I come on something like Hans's poems that night I have nothing to say but—*Goed.*

Right. I was working away there an hour or more because of that damned black ornamented script. Then I put it down and I said: "Hans, can I ask you a question?" And he looked this way and that over his shoulder first, then leaned forward, the lamplight shining on his pate, and he asked in a low trembling sinner's voice: "What do you want to ask me, Martin?"

I said: "Why this complicated handwriting? What for? It's beautiful, but why this monkey's puzzle?"

And he lowered his voice and said: "It's so that Esther can't read it."

I said: "And what of it, Hans? Why not? Give me some more brandewyn and tell me."

He said: "She's a friend of the predikant's cook, and her sister Mary works in the Mayor's kitchen."

I saw it all. I was drunk, so I saw it. I got up, and I said: "Hans, you're right. You're right a thousand times. If you're going to write stuff like this, as true and as beautiful as God and all his angels, then Esther mustn't read it. But why don't you let me take this back with me and print it in *Onwards?*"

He went white and looked as if I might knife him there and then like a *totsti.* He grabbed the manuscript from me and held it against his fat chest, and he said: "They mustn't see it."

"You're right," I said, understanding him completely.

"It's dangerous keeping it here," he said, darting fearful looks all around.

"Yes, you're right," I said, and I sat down with a bump in my *rimpie* chair, and I said: "*Ja,* if they found that, Hans . . ."

"They'd kill me," he said.

I saw it, completely.

I was drunk. He was drunk. We put the manuscript *boekie* on the table and we put our arms around each other and we wept for the citizens of Blagspruit. Then we lit the hurricane lamp in the kitchen, and he took his *boekie* under his arm, and we tiptoed out into the moonlight that stank of marigolds, and out we went down the main street, all dark as the pit now because it was after twelve and the citizens were asleep, and we went staggering down the tarmacked street that shone in the moonlight between low dark houses, and out into the veld. There we looked sorrowfully at each other and wept some sad brandy tears, and right in front of us, the devil aiding us, was a thorn tree. All virgin it was, its big black spikes lifted up and shining in the devil's moon. And we wept a long time more, and we tore out the pages from his manuscript and we made them into little screws of paper and we stuck them all over the thorns, and when there were none left, we sat under the thorn tree in the moonlight, the black spiky thorns making thin purplish shadows all over us and over the white sand. Then we wept for the state of our country and the state of poetry. We drank a lot more brandy, and the ants came after it and us, so we staggered back down the gleaming sleeping main street of Blagspruit, and that's all I remember until Esther was standing over me with a tin tray that had a teapot, teacup, sugar and some condensed milk, and she was saying: "Master du Preez, where is Master Hans?"

I saw the seven o'clock sun outside the window, and I remembered everything, and I sat up and I said: "My God!"

And Esther said: "God has not been in this house since half past five on Saturday last." And went out.

Right. I got dressed, and went down the main street, drawing looks from the Monday-morning citizens, all of whom had probably been watching us staggering along last night from behind their black drawn curtains. I reached the veld and there was Hans. A wind had got up, a hot dust-devilish wind, and it blew about red dust and bits of grit, and leaves, and dead grass into the blue sky, and those pale dry bushes that leave their roots and go bouncing and twirling all over the empty sand, like dervishes, round and round, and then up and around, and there was Hans, letting out yelps and cries and shouts, and he was chasing about after screws of paper that were whirling around among all the dust and stuff.

I helped him. The thorn tree had three squirls of paper tugging and blowing from spikes of black thorn, so I collected those, and we ran after the blowing white bits that had the black beautiful script on them, and we got perhaps a third back. Then we sat under the thorn tree, the hard sharp black shadows over us and the sand, and we watched a dust devil whirling columns of yellow sand and his poems up and off into the sky.

I said: "But, Hans, you could write them down again, couldn't you? You couldn't have forgotten them, surely?"

And he said: "But, Martin, anyone can read them now. Don't you see that, man? Esther could come out here next afternoon off, and pick any one of those poems up off the earth and read it. Or suppose the predikant or the Mayor got their hands on them?"

Then I understood. I promise you, it had never crossed my *domkop* mind until that moment. I swear it. I simply sat there, sweating out guilt and brandy, and I looked at that poor madman, and then I remembered back ten years and I thought: You idiot. You fool.

Then at last I got intelligent and I said: "But, Hans, even if Esther and the predikant and the Mayor did come out here and pick up your poems, like leaves, off the bushes? They couldn't understand one word, because they are written in that *slim* black script you worked out for yourself."

I saw his poor crazy face get more happy, and he said: "You think so, Martin? Really? You really think so?"

I said: "*Ja,* it's the truth." And he got all happy and safe, while I thought of those poems whirling around forever, or until the next rainstorm, around the blue sky with the dust and the bits of shining grass.

And I said: "Anyway, at the best only perhaps a thousand, or perhaps two thousand, people would understand that beautiful *boekie*. Try to look at it that way, Hans, it might make you feel better."

By this time he looked fine; he was smiling and cheered up.

Right.

We got up and dusted each other off, and I took him home to Esther. I asked him to let me take the poems we'd rescued back to publish in *Onwards*, but he got desperate again and said: "No, no. Do you want to kill me? Do you want them to kill me? You're my friend, Martin, you can't do that."

So I told Esther that she had a great man in her charge, through whom Heaven Itself spoke, and she was right to take such care of him. But she merely nodded her queenly white-*doekied* head and said: "Goodbye, Master du Preez, and may God be with you."

So I came home to Kapstaad.

A week ago I got a letter from Hans, but I didn't see at once it was from him; it was in ordinary writing, like yours or mine, but rather unformed and wild, and it said: "I am leaving this place. They know me now. They look at me. I'm going north to the river. Don't tell Esther. *Jou vriend,* Johannes Potgieter."

Right.

*Jou vriend,*

Martin du Preez

# The Temptation of Jack Orkney

His father was dying. It was a telegram, saying also: *you unobtainable telephone.* He had been on the telephone since seven that morning. It was the housekeeper who had sent the telegram. Did Mrs. Markham not know that she could have asked the telephone authorities to interrupt his conversations for an urgent message? The irritation of the organizer who is manipulating intractable people and events now focused on Mrs. Markham, but he tried to alleviate it by reminding himself that Mrs. Markham was housekeeper not only to his father but to a dozen other old people.

It had been a long time since he had actually organized something political; others had been happy to organize *him*—his name, his presence, his approval. But an emotional telephone call from an old friend, Walter Kenting, before seven that morning, appealing that they "all" should make a demonstration of some sort about the refugees—the nine million refugees of Bangladesh, this time—and the information that he was the only person available to do the organizing, had returned him to a politically active past. Telephoning, he soon discovered that even the small demonstration they envisaged would be circumscribed, because people were saying they could see no point in a demonstration when television, the radio, and every newspaper did little else but tell the world about these millions of sufferers. What was the point of a dozen or twenty people "sitting down" or "marching" or even being hungry for twenty-four hours in some prominent place? Surely the point of these actions in the past had been to draw public attention to a wrong?

Now the strength of his reaction to Mrs. Markham's inadequacy made him understand that his enthusiastic response to Walter so early that morning had been mostly because of weeks, months, of inactivity. He could not be so exaggerating details if he were not underemployed.

He had been making occupation for himself, calling it stocktaking. He had been reading old diaries, articles of his own twenty or more years old, letters of people he had not seen, sometimes, for as long. Immersing himself in his own past had of course been uncomfortable; this is what it had been really like in Korea, Israel, Pretoria, during such-and-such an event: memory had falsified. One knew that it did, but he had believed himself exempt from this law. Every new day of this deliberate evocation of the past had made his own part in it seem less worthwhile, had diminished his purposes and strengths. It was not that he now lacked offers of work, but that he could not make himself respond with the enthusiastic willingness which he believed every job of work needed. Of his many possibilities the one that attracted him most was to teach journalism in a small college in Nigeria, but he could not make up his mind to accept: his wife didn't want to go. Did he want to leave her in England for two years? No; but at one time this certainly would not have been his reaction!

Nor did he want to write another adventure book; in such empty times in the past he had written, under *noms de plume,* novels whose attraction was the descriptions of the countries he had set them in. He had traveled a great deal in his life, often dangerously, in the course of this war or that, as a soldier and as a journalist.

He might also write a serious book of social or political analysis: he had several to his credit.

He could do television work, or return to active journalism.

The thing was that now the three children were through university he did not need to earn so much money.

"Leisure, leisure at last!" he had cried, as so many of his friends were doing, finding themselves similarly placed.

But half a morning's energetic organizing was enough to tell him—exactly as his mother had been used to tell him when he was adolescent: "Your trouble is, you haven't got enough to do!"

He sent a telegram to Mrs. Markham: *Arriving train early evening.* Flying would save him an hour; proper feeling would no doubt choose the air, but he needed the train's pace to adjust him for what was ahead. He rang Walter Kenting to say that with the organizing still undone, urgent family matters were claiming him. Walter was silent at this, so he said: "Actually, my old man is going to die in the next couple of days. It has been on the cards for some time."

"I am sorry," said Walter. "I'll try Bill or Mona. I've got to go to Dublin in fifteen minutes. Are you going to be back by Saturday—oh of course you don't know." Realizing that he was sounding careless or callous, he said: "I do hope things will be all right." This was worse and he gave up: "You think that a twenty-four-hour fast meets the bill better than the other possibilities? Is that what most people feel, do you think?"

"Yes. But I don't think they are as keen as usual."

"Well, of course not, there's too much of bloody everything, that's why. You could be demonstrating twenty-four hours a day. Anyway, I've got to get to my plane."

While Jack packed, which he knew so well how to do, in ten minutes, he remembered that he had a family. Should everyone be at the deathbed? Oh surely not! He looked for his wife; she was out. Of course! The children off her hands, she too had made many exclamations about the attractions of leisure, but almost at once she signed up for a psychology course as part of a plan to become a family counselor. She had left a note for him: "Darling, there's some cold lamb and salad." He now left a note for her: "Old man on his way out. See you whenever. Tell girls and Joseph. All my love. Jack."

On the train he thought of what he was in for. A family reunion, no less. His brother wasn't so bad, but the last time he had seen Ellen, she had called him a Boy Scout, and he had called her a Daughter of the British Empire. Considering it a compliment, she had been left with the advantage. A really dreadful woman, and as for her husband—surely he wouldn't be there too? He would have to be, as a man? Where would they all fit in? Certainly not in that tiny flat. He should have put in his note to Rosemary that she should telephone hotels in S——. Would the other grandchildren be there? Well, Cedric and Ellen would be certain to do the right thing, whatever that was: as for himself, he could telephone home when he had found what the protocol was. But good God, surely it was bad enough that three of them, grown-up and intelligent people —grown-up, anyway, were going to have to sit about waiting, in a deathbed scene, because of—superstition. Yes, that was what it was. Certainly no more than outdated social custom. And it all might go on for days. But perhaps the old man would be pleased? At the approach of a phrase similar to those suitable for deaths and funerals, he felt irritation again; this would lead, unless he watched himself, to self-mockery, the spirit of farce. Farce was implicit, anyway, in a situation which had himself, Ellen, and Cedric in one room.

Probably the old man wasn't even conscious. He should have telephoned Mrs. Markham before rushing off like—well, like a journalist, with two pairs of socks, a spare shirt, and a sweater. He should have bought a black tie? Would the old man have wished it? Jack noted the arrival of an indubitably "suitable" phrase, and feared worse for the immediate future.

The old man had not worn black or altered his cheerfulness when his wife died.

His wife, Jack's mother.

The depression that he had suspected was in wait for him now descended. He understood that he had been depressed for some time; this was like dark coming down into a fog. He had not admitted that he was depressed, but he ought to have known it by the fact that what he had woken up to each morning was not his own expectation of usefulness or accomplishment, but his wife's.

Now, if Rosemary died . . . but he would not think about that; it would be morbid.

When his mother died, his father had made the simplest of funerals for her—religious, of course. All the family, the grandchildren too, had stayed in the old house, together for the first time in years. The old man had behaved like a man who knew that his grief ought not to be inflicted on others. Jack had not been close to his mother; he had not liked her. He was close to no member of the family. He now knew that he loved his wife, but that had not been true until recently. There were his beautiful daughters. There was his son, Joseph, who was a chip off the old block—so everyone insisted on saying, though it infuriated Joseph. But they could not meet without quarreling. That was closeness of a kind?

He ought to have been more attentive, when the mother died, to the old man, who had probably been concealing a good deal behind his mild dignity. Of course! And, looking back ten years, Jack knew that he had known what his father was feeling, had been sympathetic, but had also been embarrassed and, unable to give anything of himself—out of fear that more would be asked?—had pretended obtuseness.

The old house was Church property, divided into units for old people who had been good parishioners. None had been friends before going to live there, but now it seemed that they were all close friends, or at least kept each other company in a variety of ways under the eyes of Mrs. Markham, who also lived there, looked after the house, after them. She put flowers in the church and mended surplices and garments of that sort—she was fifty, poor old thing. Jack now told himself that he was over fifty, although "the baby of the family," and that his sister Ellen, with whom he was to spend an unknown number of days, was fifty-five, while his boring brother Cedric was older still.

This train was not full and moved pleasantly through England's green and pleasant land. There were two other people in the compartment. Second-class. Jack traveled second-class when he could: this was one of the ways he used to check up on himself that he was not getting soft with success—if you could call what he had success. His brother and sister did, but that was the way they looked at life.

One fellow passenger was a middle-aged woman, and one a girl of about twenty-three or twenty-four who leaned an elbow on the window ledge and stared at Buckinghamshire, then Berkshire, then Wiltshire, all green and soft on this summery day. Her face was hidden behind glittering yellow hair. Jack classed her as a London secretary on her way home for a family visit, and as the kind of young person he would get on with—that is, like his daughters rather than his son.

He was finding the company of his girls all pleasure and healing. It seemed to him that everything he had looked for in women now flowed generously towards him from Carrie and Elizabeth. It was not that they always approved him, far from it; it was the quality of their beauty that caressed and dandled him. The silk of their hair flattered, their smiles, even when for somebody else, gave him answers to questions that he had been asking of women—so it seemed to him now—all his life.

Though of course he did not see much of them; while living in the same house, upstairs, they led their own lives.

The woman, whom he disliked because she was not young and beautiful—he was aware that he should be ashamed of this reaction, but put this shame onto an agenda for the future—got off the train, and now the girl at the window turned towards him and the rest of the journey was bound to be delightful. He had been right—of course, he was always right about people. She worked in an office in Great Portland Street, and she was going for a visit to her parents—no, she "got on" with them all right, but she was always pleased to be back in her flat with her friends. She was not a stranger to Jack's world; that is, she was familiar with the names of people whose lives expressed concern for public affairs, public wrong and suffering, and she used the names of his friends with a proprietary air—she had, as it were, eaten them up to form herself, as he, Jack, had in his time swallowed Keir Hardie, Marx, Freud, Morris, and the rest. She, those like her, now possessed "the Old Guard," their history, their opinions, their claims. To her, Walter Kenting, Bill, Mona, were like statues on plinths, each representing a degree of opinion. When the time came to give her his own name, he said it was Jack Sebastian, not Jack Orkney, for he knew he would join the pantheon of people who were her parents-in-opinion and, as he had understood, were to be criticized, like parents.

The last time he had been Jack Sebastian was to get him out of a tight spot in Ecuador, during a small revolution; he had escaped prison and possible death by this means.

If he told this girl about that, he knew that as he sat opposite her, she would gaze in judiciously measured admiration at a man retreating from her into history. He listened to her talk about herself, and knew that if things had been otherwise—he meant not his father's dying, but his recently good relations with his wife—he could easily have got off the train with the girl, and persuaded her to spend the rest of her holiday with him, having made excuses to her family. Or he could have met her in London. But all he wanted now was to hear her voice, and to let himself be stimulated by the light from her eyes and her hair.

She got off the train, with a small laughing look that made his heart beat, and she strode off across the platform with her banners of yellow hair streaming behind her, leaving him alone in the brown compartment full of brown air.

At the station he was looking for a taxi when he saw his brother Cedric. A brown suit that discreetly confined a small stomach came towards him. That suit could only clothe a member of the professional classes; it had to be taken into account before the face, which was, as it happened, a mild pale face that had a look on it of duty willingly performed.

Cedric said, in his way of dealing all at once with every possible contingency: "Mrs. Markham said it had to be this train. I came because Ellen has only just come herself; I arrived first."

He had a Rover, dark blue, not new. He and Jack, defined by this car and particularly accurately in this country town, drove through soothingly ancient streets.

The brothers drove more or less in silence to the church precincts. As they passed in under a thirteenth-century stone archway, Cedric said: "Ellen booked a room for you. It is the Royal Arms, and she and I are there too. It is only five minutes from Father."

They walked in silence over grass to the back door of this solid brick house which the Church devoted to the old. Not as a charity of course. These were the old whose own saved money or whose children could pay for their rooms and for Mrs. Markham. The poor old were elsewhere.

Mrs. Markham came forward from her sitting room and said: "How do you do, Mr. Orkney?" to Jack, smiling like a hostess at Cedric. "I am sure you would like some tea now," she directed. "I'll bring you some up." She was like the woman on the train. And like Ellen.

He followed his brother up old wooden stairs that gleamed, and smelled of lavender and wax polish. As always happened, the age of the town, and of the habits of the people who lived in it, the smell of tradition, enveloped Jack in well-being; he had to remind himself that he was here for an unpleasant occasion. At the top of the stairs various unmarked doors were the entrances to the lives of four old people. Cedric opened one without knocking, and Jack followed him into a room he had been in twice before on duty visits. It was a smallish but pleasant room with windows overlooking the lawns that surrounded the church.

Sister Ellen, in thick grey tweed, sat knitting. She said: "Oh Jack, there you are, we are all here at last."

Jack sat. Cedric sat. They had to arrange their feet so as not to entangle in the middle of the small floor. They all exchanged news. The main thing that had happened to the three of them was that the children had all grown up.

The grandchildren, eight of them, knew each other, and had complicated relationships: they were a family, unlike their parents.

Mrs. Markham brought tea, of the kind appropriate to this room, this town: scones, butter, jam, comb honey, fruit buns, cherry cake, fruit cake. Also cream. She left giving the three a glance that said: At last it is all as it should be.

Jack asked: "Have you seen him?"

"No," said Cedric, a fraction of a second before Ellen did. It was clear that here was competition for the perfect disposition of his death. Jack was remembering how these two had fought for domination over each other, and over, of course, himself.

"That is to say," said Ellen, "we have seen him, but he was not conscious."

"Another stroke?" asked Jack.

"He had another before Christmas," said Cedric, "but he didn't tell us, he didn't want to worry us."

"I heard about it through Jilly," said Ellen. Jilly was her daughter.

"And I through Ann," said Cedric. Ann was his.

Jack had now to remind himself that these names represented persons, not samples of pretty infancy.

"He is very close to Ann," said Cedric.

"He is fond of Jilly too," said Ellen.

"I suppose there is a nurse in there?" asked Jack. "Oh, of course, there must be."

"There is a day nurse and a night nurse, and they change places at dawn and dusk," said Ellen. "I must say I am glad of this tea. There was no restaurant on the train."

"I wonder if I could see him?" asked Jack, and then corrected it: "I shall go in to see him." He knew, as he spoke, that all the way on the train he had in fact been waiting for the moment when he could walk into the little bedroom, and his father would smile at him and say—he had not been able to imagine what, but it must be something that he had been waiting to hear from him, or from somebody, for years. This surely was the real purpose of coming here? That what he had in fact been expecting was something like a "deathbed scene," with vital advice and mutual comfort, embarrassed him, and he felt that he was stupid. Now he understood that embarrassment was the air of this room: the combat between elder brother and sister was nominal; they skirmished from habit to cover what they felt. Which was that they were in a position not allowed for by their habits of living. Jack had a vision of rapidly running trains—their lives; but they had had to stop the trains, had had to pull the emergency cords, and at great inconvenience to everyone, because of this ill-timed death. Death had to be ill-timed? It was its nature? Why was it felt to be? There was something ridiculous about this scene in which he was trapped: three middle-aged children sitting about in one room, idle, thinking of their real lives which stagnated, while in another room an old man lay dying, attended by a strange woman.

"I'm going in," he said, and this time got up, instinctively careful of his head: he was tall in this low-ceilinged room.

"Go in without knocking," said Ellen.

"Yes," Cedric confirmed.

Jack stooped under the doorframe. An inappropriate picture had come into his mind. It was of his sister, in a scarlet pinafore and bright blue checkered sleeves, tugging a wooden horse which was held by a pale plump boy. Jack had been scared that when Ellen got the horse a real fight would start. But Cedric held on, lips tight, being jerked by Ellen's tugs as a dog is tugged by the other dog who has fastened his teeth into the bit of meat or the stick. This scene had taken place in the old garden, for it had been enclosed by pink hydrangeas, while gravel had crunched underfoot. They must all have been very young, because Ellen had still been the classic golden-haired beauty; later she became large and ordinary.

What he was really seeing was his father sitting up against high pillows. A young woman in white sat with her hands folded watching the dying man. But he looked asleep. It was only when he saw the healthy young woman that Jack understood that his father had become a small old man: he had definitely shrunk. The room was dark, and it was not until Jack stood immediately above his father that he saw the mouth was open. But what was unexpected was that the eyelids had swelled and were blue, as if decomposition had set in there already. Those bruised lids affected Jack like something in bad taste, like a fart at a formal meal, or when making love of a romantic sort. He looked in appeal at the nurse who said in a normal voice, which she did not lower at all: "He did stir a moment ago, but he didn't really come to himself."

Jack nodded, not wanting to break the hush of time that surrounded the bed, and bent lower, trying not to see the dying lids, but remembering what he could of his father's cool, shrewd, judging look. It seemed to him as if the bruised puffs of flesh were trembling, might lift. But his stare did not have the power to rouse his father, and soon Jack straightened himself—cautiously. Where did the Church put its tall old people, he wondered, and backed out of the room, keeping his eyes on the small old man in his striped pajamas, which showed very clean under a dark grey cardigan that was fastened under the collar with a gold tiepin, giving him a formal, dressed-up look.

"How does he seem?" asked Ellen. She had resumed her knitting.

"Asleep."

"Unconscious," said Cedric.

Jack asserted himself—quite easily, he saw with relief. "He doesn't look unconscious to me. On the contrary, I thought he nearly woke up."

They knew the evening was wearing on: their watches told them so. It remained light; an interminable summer evening filled the sky above the church tower. A young woman came through the room, a coat over her white uniform, and in a moment the other nurse came past them, on her way out.

"I think we might as well have dinner," said Ellen, already folding her knitting.

"Should one of us stay perhaps?" corrected Cedric. He stayed, and Jack had hotel dinner and a bottle of wine with his sister; he didn't dislike being with her as much as he had expected. He was even remembering times when he had been fond of Ellen.

They returned to keep watch, while Cedric took his turn for dinner. At about eleven the doctor came in, disappeared for five minutes into the bedroom, and came out saying that he had given Mr. Orkney an injection. By the time they had thought to ask what the injection was, he had said that his advice was they should all get a good night's sleep, and had gone. Each hesitated before saying that they intended to take the doctor's advice: This situation, traditionally productive of guilt, was doing its work well.

Before they had reached the bottom of the stairs, the nurse came after them: "Mr. Orkney, Mr. Orkney . . ." Both men turned, but she said: "Jack? He was asking for Jack?"

Jack ran up the stairs, through one room, into the other. But it seemed as if the old man had not moved since he had last seen him. The nurse had drawn the curtains, shutting out the sky so full of light, of summer, and had arranged the lamp so that it made a bright space in the dark room. In this was a wooden chair with a green cushion on it, and on the cushion a magazine. The lit space was like the detail of a picture much magnified. The nurse said: "Really, with that injection, he ought not to wake now." She took her place again with the magazine on her lap, inside the circle of light.

Yet he had woken, he had asked for himself, Jack, and for nobody else. Jack was alert, vibrating with his nearness to what his father might say. But he stood helpless, trying to make out the bruises above the eyes, which the shadows were hiding. "I'll stay here the night," he declared, all energy, and strode out, only just remembering to lower his head in time, to tell his sister and his brother, who had come back up the stairs.

"The nurse thinks he is unlikely to wake, but I am sure it would be what he would wish if one of us were to stay."

That he had used another of the obligatory phrases struck Jack with more than amusement: now it was with relief as well. Now the fact that the prescribed phrases made their appearance one after the other was like a guarantee that he was behaving appropriately, that everything would go smoothly and without embarrassment, and that he could expect his father's eyes to appear from behind the corrupted lids—that he would speak the words Jack needed to hear. Cedric and Ellen quite understood, but demanded to be called at once if . . . They went off together across the bright grass towards the hotel.

Jack sat up all night, but there was no night, midsummer swallowed the dark; at midnight the church was still glimmering and people strolled, talking softly, over the lawns. He had skimmed through Trollope's *The Small House at Allington,* and had dipped into a book of his own called *With the Guerrillas in Guatemala*. The name on the spine was Jack Henge, and now he wondered if he had ever told his father that this was one of his *noms de plume,* and he thought that if so, it showed a touching interest on his father's part, but if not, that there must have been some special hidden sympathy shown in the choice or chance that led to its sitting here on the old man's shelves side by side with the complete works of Trollope and George Eliot and Walter Scott. But of course, it was unlikely now that he would ever know. . . . His father had not woken, had not stirred, all night. Once he had tiptoed in, and the nurse had lifted her head and smiled; clearly, though the old man had gone past the divisions of day and night, the living must still adhere to them, for the day nurse had spoken aloud, but now it was night, the nurse whispered: "The injection is working well. You try to rest, Mr. Orkney." Her solicitude for him, beaming out from the bright cave hollowed from the dark of the room, enclosed them together in the night's vigil, and when the day nurse came, and the night nurse went yawning, looking pale, and tucking dark strands of hair as if tidying up after a night's sleep, her smile at Jack was that of a comrade after a shared ordeal.

Almost at once the day nurse came back into the living room and said: "Is there someone called Ann?"

"Yes, a granddaughter; he was asking for her?"

"Yes. Now, he was awake for a moment."

Jack suppressed: "He didn't ask for me?"—and ran back into the bedroom, which was now filled with a stuffy light that presented the bruised lids to the nurse and to Jack.

"I'll tell my brother that Ann has been asked for."

Jack walked through fresh morning air that had already brought a few people onto the grass around the church, to the hotel, where he found Cedric and Ellen at breakfast.

He said that no, he had not been wanted, but that Ann was wanted now. Ellen and Cedric conferred and agreed that Ann "could reasonably be expected" never to forgive them if she was not called. Jack saw that these words soothed them both; they were comforting himself. He was now suddenly tired. He drank coffee, refused breakfast, and decided on an hour's sleep. Ellen went to telephone greetings and the news that nothing had changed to her family; Cedric to summon Ann, while Jack wondered if he should telephone Rosemary. But there was nothing to say. He fell on his bed and dreamed, woke, dreamed again, woke, forced himself back to sleep but was driven up out of it to stand in the middle of his hotel room, full of horror. His dreams had been landscapes of dark menacing shapes that were of man's making—metallic, like machines, steeped in a cold grey light, and scattered about on a plain where cold water lay spilled about, gleaming. This water reflected, he knew, death, or news, or information about death, but he stood too far away on the plain to see what pictures lay on its surfaces.

Now, Jack was one of those who do not dream. He prided himself on never dreaming. Of course he had read the "new" information that everyone dreamed every night, but he distrusted this information. For one thing, he shared in the general distrust of science, of its emphatic pronouncements; for another, traveling around the world as he had, he had long ago come to terms with the fact that certain cultures were close to aspects of life which he, Jack, had quite simply forbidden. He had locked a door on them. He knew that some people claimed to see ghosts, feared their dead ancestors, consulted witch doctors, dreamed dreams. How could he not know? He had lived with them. But he, Jack, was of that part of mankind delivered from all that; he, Jack, did not consult the bones or allow himself to be afraid of the dark. Or dream. He did not dream.

He felt groggy, more than tired: the cold of the dream was undermining him, making him shiver. He got back into bed, for he had slept only an hour, and continued with the same dream. Now he and Walter Kenting were interlopers on that death-filled plain, and they were to be shot, one bullet each, on account of nonspecified crimes. He woke again: it was ten minutes later. He decided to stay awake. He bathed, changed his shirt and his socks, washed the shirt and socks he had taken off, and hung them over the bath to drip. Restored by these small ritual acts which he had performed in so many hotel rooms and in so many countries, he ordered fresh coffee, drank it in the spirit of one drinking a tonic or prescribed medicine, and walked back across sunlit grass to the old people's house.

He entered on the scene he had left. Ellen and Cedric sat with their feet almost touching, one knitting and one reading the *Daily Telegraph*. Ellen said: "You haven't slept long." Cedric said: "He asked for you again."

*"What!"* While he had slept, his energies draining into that debilitating dream, he might have heard, at last, what his father wanted to say. "I think I'll sit with him a little."

"That might not be a bad idea," said his sister. Was she annoyed that she had not been "asked for"? If so, she showed no sign of it.

The little sitting room was full of light; sunshine lay on the old wood sills. But the bedroom was dark, warm, and smelled of many drugs.

The nurse had the only chair—today just a piece of furniture among many. He made her keep it, and sat down slowly on the bed, as if this slow subsidence could make his weight less.

He kept his eyes on his father's face. Since yesterday the bruises had spread beyond the lids: the flesh all around the eyes and as far down as the cheekbones was stained.

"He has been restless," said the nurse, "but the doctor should be here soon." She spoke as if the doctor could answer any question that could possibly ever be asked; and Jack, directed by her as he had been by his sister and his brother, now listened for the doctor's coming. The morning went past. His sister came to ask if he would go with her to luncheon. She was hungry, but Cedric was not. Jack said he would stay, and while she was gone the doctor came.

He sat on the bed—Jack had risen from it, retreating to the window. The doctor took the old man's wrist in his hand and seemed to commune with the darkened eyelids. "I rather think that perhaps . . ." He took out a plastic box from his case that held the ingredients of miracle-making: syringes, capsules, methylated spirits.

Jack asked: "What effect does that have?" He wanted to ask: Are you keeping him alive when he should be dead?

The doctor said: "Sedative and painkiller."

"A heart stimulant?"

Now the doctor said: "I have known your father for thirty years." He was saying: I have more right than you have to say what he would have wanted.

Jack had to agree; he had no idea if his father would want to be allowed to die, as nature directed, or whether he would like to be kept alive as long as possible.

The doctor administered an injection, as light and as swift as the strike of a snake, rubbed the puncture with one gentle finger, and said, "Your father looked after himself. He has plenty of life left in him yet."

He went out. Jack looked in protest at the nurse: what on earth had been meant? Was his father not dying? The nurse smiled, timidly, and from that smile Jack gathered that the words had been spoken for his father's sake, in case he was able to hear them, understand them, and be fortified by them.

He saw the nurse's face change; she bent over the old man, and Jack took a long step and was beside her. In the bruised flesh the eyes were open and stared straight up. This was not the human gaze he had been wanting to meet, but a dull glare from chinks in damaged flesh.

"Ann," said the old man. "Is Ann here?"

From the owner of those sullen eyes Jack might expect nothing; as an excuse to leave the room, he said to the nurse, "I'll tell Ann's father."

In the living room sunlight had left the sills. Cedric was not there. "It's Ann he wants," Jack said. "He has asked again."

"She is coming. She has to come from Edinburgh. She is with Maureen."

Ellen said this as if he was bound to know who Maureen was. She was probably one of Cedric's ghastly wife's ghastly relations. Thinking of the awfulness of Cedric's wife made him feel kindly towards Ellen. Ellen wasn't really so bad. There she sat, knitting, tired and sad but not showing it. When you came down to it she didn't look all that different from Rosemary—unbelievably also a middle-aged woman. But at this thought Jack's loyalty to the past rebelled. Rosemary, though a large, fresh-faced, greying woman, would never wear a suit which looked as if its edges might cut, or hair set in a helmet of ridges and frills. She wore soft pretty clothes, and her hair was combed straight and long, as she had always worn it: he had begged her to keep it like that. But if you came to think of it, probably the lives the two women led were similar. Probably they were all more alike than any one of them would care to admit. Including Cedric's awful wife.

He looked at Ellen's lids, lowered while she counted stitches. They were her father's eyes and lids. When she lay dying probably her lids would bruise and puff.

Cedric came in. He was very like the old man—more like him than any of them. He, Jack, was more like their mother, but when he was dying perhaps his own lids . . . Ellen looked up, smiled at Cedric, then at Jack. They were all smiling at each other. Ellen laid down her knitting, and lit herself a cigarette. The brothers could see that this was the point when she might cry. But Mrs. Markham came in, followed by a well-brushed man all white cuffs and collar and pink fresh skin.

"The Dean," she breathed, with the smile of a girl.

The Dean said: "No, don't get up. I dropped in. I am an old friend of your father's, you know. Many and many a game of chess have we played in this room . . ." and he had followed Mrs. Markham into the bedroom.

"He had Extreme Unction yesterday," said Ellen.

"Oh," said Jack. "I didn't realize that Extreme Unction was part of his . . ." He stopped, not wanting to hurt feelings. He believed both Ellen and Cedric to be religious.

"He got very High in the end," said Cedric.

Ellen giggled. Jack and Cedric looked inquiry. "It sounded funny," she said. "You know, the young ones talk about getting high."

Cedric's smile was wry; and Jack remembered there had been talk about his elder son, who had threatened to become addicted. What to? Jack could not remember; he would have to ask the girls.

"I suppose he wants a church service and to be buried?" asked Jack.

"Oh yes," said Cedric. "I have got his will."

"Of course, you would have."

"Well, we'll have to get through it all," said Ellen. It occurred to Jack that this was what she probably said, or thought, about her own life: Well, I've just got to get through it. The thought surprised him; Ellen was pleasantly surprising him. Now he heard her say: "Well, I suppose some people have to have religion."

And now Jack looked at her in disbelief.

"Yes," said Cedric, equally improbably, "it must be a comfort for them, one can see that." He laid small strong hands around his crossed knees and made the knuckles crack.

"Oh, Cedric," complained Ellen, as she had as a girl: this knuckle cracking had been Cedric's way of expressing tension since he had been a small boy.

"Sorry," said Cedric. He went on, letting his hands fall to his sides, and swing there, in a conscious effort towards relaxing himself. "From time to time I take my pulse—as it were. Now that I am getting on for sixty one can expect the symptoms. Am I getting God? Am I still myself? Yes, no, doubtful? But so far, I can report an even keel, I am happy to say."

"Oh one can understand it," said Ellen. "God knows, one can understand it only too well. But I really would be ashamed . . ."

Both Ellen and Cedric were looking to him, to add his agreement of which they were sure, of course. But he could not speak. He had made precisely the same joke a month ago, in a group of "the Old Guard," about taking his pulse to find out if he had caught religion. And everyone had confessed to the same practice. To get God, after a lifetime of enlightened rationalism, would be the most shameful of capitulations.

Now his feelings were the same as those of members of a particularly exclusive club on being forced to admit the lower classes; or the same as the Victorian bishop who, traveling to some cannibal land to baptize the converted, had been heard to say that he could wish that his Church admitted degrees of excellence in its material: he could not believe that his lifetime of impeccable service would weigh the same as those of these so recently benighted ones.

Besides, Jack was shocked: to hear these ideas from Ellen, looking as she did, leading the life she did—she had no right to them! She sounded vulgar.

She was saying: "Of course I do go to church sometimes to please Freddy." Her husband. "But he seems to be losing fervor rather than gaining it, I am glad to say."

"Yes," said Cedric. "I am afraid I have rather the same thing with Muriel. We have compromised on Christmas and Easter. She says it is bad for my image not to be a churchgoer. Petersbank is a small place, you know, and the good people do like their lawyers and doctors to be pillars of society. But I find that sort of trimming repulsive and I tell her so."

Again they waited for Jack; again he had to be silent. But surely by now they would take his opinions for granted? Why should they? If they could become atheist, then what might he not become? The next thing, they'll turn out to be socialists, he thought. Surely all this godlessness must be a new development? He could have sworn that Ellen had been devout and Cedric correct towards a Church which—as far as Jack had been concerned—had been irritation, humiliation, tedium, throughout his childhood. Even now he could not think of the meaningless services, the Sunday school, the fatuity of the parsons, the social conformity that was associated with the Church, without feeling as if he had escaped from a sticky trap.

Ellen was saying: "As for me, I am afraid I find it harder to believe as I get older. I mean, God, in this terrible world, with new horrors every minute. No, I am afraid it is all too much."

"I quite agree," said Cedric. "The devil's more like it."

"Yes," said Jack, able to speak at last. "Yes, that's about it, I'm afraid." It was the best he could do. The room was now full of good feeling, and they would have begun to talk about their childhood if the bedroom door had not opened, and the Dean come out. The smile he had shed on the nurse was still on his healthy lips, and he now let it benefit the three, while he raised his hand in what looked like a benediction. "No, don't get up!" He was almost at once out of the other door, followed close by Mrs. Markham.

The look the three now shared repudiated the Dean and all his works. Ellen smiled at her brother exactly as—he realized in capitulation to a totally unforeseen situation—his own wife would have done. Cedric nodded private comment on the stupidities of mankind.

Soon Cedric went to the bedroom, to return with the report that the old man looked pretty deep in. Then Ellen went and came back saying that she didn't know how the nurse could bear it in that dark room. But as she sat down, she said: "In the old days, one of us would have been in there all the time?"

"Yes," said Cedric. "All of us."

"Not just a nurse," said Ellen. "Not a stranger."

Jack was thinking that if he had stuck it out, then he would have been there when his father called for him, but he said: "I'm glad it is a nurse. I don't think there is very much left of *him*."

Ann arrived. What Jack saw first was a decided, neat little face, and that she wore a green jacket and trousers that were not jeans but "good," as her Aunt Ellen used the word. Ellen always had "good" clothes that lasted a long time. Ann's style was not, for instance, like Jack's daughters', who wore rags and rubbish and castoffs and who looked enchanting, like princesses in disguise. She kissed her father, because he was waiting for her to do this. She stood examining them with care. Her father could be seen in her during that leisurely, unembarrassed examination: it was both her right and her duty to do this. Now Jack saw that she was small, with a white skin that looked greenish where it was shaded, and hair as pale as her father's had been. Her eyes, like her father's, were green.

She said: "Is he still alive?"

The voice was her father's, and it took her aunt and her uncle back,

back—she did not know the reason for their strained, reluctant smiles as they gazed at her.

They were suffering that diminution, that assault on individuality which is the worst of families: some invisible dealer had shuffled noses, hands, shoulders, hair and reassembled them to make—little Ann, for instance. The dealer made out of parts a unit that the owner would feed, maintain, wash, medicate for a lifetime, thinking of it as "mine," except at moments like these, when knowledge was forced home that everyone was put together out of stock.

"Well," said Ann, "you all look dismal enough. Why do you?"

She went into the bedroom, leaving the door open. Jack understood that Ann had principles about attitudes towards death: like his own daughters.

The three crowded into the room.

Ann sat on the bed, high up near the pillow, in a way that hid the old man's face from them. She was leaning forward, the nurse—whom Ann had ignored—ready to intervene.

"Granddad!" she said. "Granddad! It's me!"

Silence. Then it came home to them that the improbable had happened, that she had called up Lazarus. They heard the old man's voice, quite as they remembered it: "It's you, is it? It is little Ann?"

"Yes, Granddad, it's Ann."

They crowded forward, to see over her shoulder. They saw their father, smiling normally. He looked like a tired old man, that was all. His eyes, surrounded by the puffy bruises, had light in them.

"Who are these people?" he asked. "Who are all these tall people?"

The three retreated, leaving the door open.

Silence from the bedroom, then singing. Ann was singing in a small clear voice: "All Things Bright and Beautiful."

Jack looked at Cedric, Ellen looked at Cedric. He deprecated: "Yes, I am afraid that she is. That's the bond, you see."

"Oh," said Ellen, "I see, that explains it."

The singing went on:

*All things bright and beautiful,*
*All creatures great and small,*
*All things wise and wonderful,*
*The Lord God made them all.*

The singing went on, verse after verse, like a lullaby.

"She came to stay with him," said Cedric. "At Easter, I think it was. She slept here, on the floor."

Jack said: "My girls are religious. But not my son of course."

They looked blankly sympathetic; it occurred to Jack that his son's fame was after all circumscribed to a pretty small circle.

"He takes after me," said Jack.

"Ah," said Cedric.

"A lot of them are religious," said Ellen, brisk.

"It's the *kind* of religion that sticks in one's craw," said Jack. "Simple faith and Celtic crosses."

"I agree," said Cedric. "Pretty low-level stuff."

"Does the level matter?" asked Ellen. "Surely *c'est le premier pas qui coûte?"*

At which Jack looked at his sister in a disbelief that was meant to be noticed. Cedric, however, did not seem surprised: of course, he saw Ellen more often. He said mildly: "I don't agree. One wouldn't mind if they went on to something a bit more elevated. It's this servants'-hall village-green mother's-meeting sort of thing. You spend a fortune trying to educate them decently and then it ends up in . . . My eldest was a Jesus freak for a few months, for example. After Winchester, Balliol, the lot."

"What is a Jesus freak?" inquired Ellen.

"What it sounds like."

Normally Jack would have cut out emotionally and mentally at the words "servants' hall," but he was still with them. He said: "What gets me is that they spout it all out, so pat and pretty, you know, and you get the feeling it might be anything, anything they had picked up or lay to hand—*pour épater le bourgeois,* you know." At this he had to think that the other two must be thinking, but were too polite to say, that his own socialism, a degree or two off full communism, when he was in his teens, had had no deeper cause. This unspoken comment brought the conversation to a stop.

The singing had stopped too. It was getting dark.

"Well," said Ellen, "I tell you what I am going to do, I am going to have a bath and then dinner and then a good night's sleep. I think Ann is meeting Father's requirements better than we could."

"Yes," said Cedric.

He went to the door, and communicated this news to his daughter, who said she would be fine, she would be super, she would stay with Granddad, and if she got tired she could sleep on the floor.

Over the dinner table at the hotel, it was a reunion of people who had not met for a long time. They drank some wine, and were sentimental.

But the little time of warmth died with the coffee, served in the hall, which let in drafts from the street every time somebody came in.

Jack said: "I'll turn in, I didn't sleep last night."

"Nor I."

"Nor I."

They nodded at each other; to kiss would have been exaggerated. Jack went upstairs, while Cedric and Ellen went to telephone their families.

In the bedroom he stood by the window and watched how the light filled the lime outside. Breaths of tree-air came to his face. He was full of variegated emotions, none, he was afraid, to do with his father: they were about his brother and his sister, his childhood, that past of his which everything that happened to him these days seemed to evoke, seemed to present to him, sharp, clear, and for the most part painful; he did not feel he could sleep, he was overstimulated. He would lie on his bed for a rest. Waking much later, to a silence that said the night had deepened all around him, with the heaviness of everybody's sleeping, he started up into a welter of feeling that he could not face, and so burrowed back into sleep again, there to be met by—but it was hard to say what.

Terror was not the word. Nor fear. Yet there were no other words that he knew for the state he found himself in. It was more like a state of acute attention, as if his whole being—memory, body, present and past chemistries—had been assaulted by a warning, so that he had to attend to it. He was standing, as it were, at the alert, listening to something which said: Time is passing, be quick, listen, attend.

It was the knowledge of passing time that was associated with the terror, so that he found himself standing upright in the dark room crying out: "Oh, no, no, I understand, I am sorry, I . . ." He was whimpering like a puppy. The dark was solid around him, and he didn't know where he was. He believed himself to be in a grave, and he rushed to the window, throwing it open as if he were heaving a weight off himself. The window was hard to open. At last he forced it, leaning out to let the tree-air come to his face, but it was not air that came in, but a stench, and this smell was confirmation of a failure which had taken place long ago, in some choice of his, that he had now forgotten. The feeling of urgency woke him: he was lying on his bed. Now he really did shoot into the center of the room, while the smell that had been the air of the dream was fading around him. He was terrified. But that was not the word. . . . He feared that the terror would fade, he would forget what he had dreamed; the knowledge that there was something that had to be done, done soon, would fade, and he would forget even that he had dreamed.

What *had* he dreamed? Something of immense importance.

But as he stood there, with the feeling of urgency draining away and his daytime self coming back, even while he knew, as powerfully as he had ever known anything, that the dream was the most important statement ever made to him, the other half of him was asserting old patterns of thought, which said that to dream was neurotic and to think of death morbid.

He turned on the light, out of habit, a child chasing away night-fears, and then at once switched it off again, since the light was doing its job too well: the dream was dwindling into a small feeling that remarked in a tiny nagging voice that he should be attending to something. And Jack was chasing after the dream: No, no, don't go. . . .

But the feeling of the dream had gone, and he was standing near the window, telling himself—but it was an intellectual statement now, without force—that he had had a warning. A warning? Was it that? By whom? To whom? He must do something . . . but what? *He had been terrified of dying:* he had been forced to be afraid of that. For the first time in his life he had been made to feel the fear of death. He knew that this is what he would feel when he was in his father's position, lying propped on pillows, with people around him waiting for him to die. (If the state of the world would allow his death such a degree of civilization!)

All his life he had said lightly: Oh, death, I'm not afraid of death; it will be like a candle going out, that's all. On these occasions when, just like his brother Cedric, he checked up on himself for internal weakness, he had said to himself: I shall die, just like a cat or a dog, and too bad, when I die, that's that. He had known the fear of fear of course: he had been a soldier in two wars. He had known what it was to rehearse in his mind all the possible deaths that were available to him, removing pain and horror by making them familiar, and choosing suitable ways of responding—words, postures, silences, stoicisms—that would be a credit to him, to humanity. He knew very well the thought that to be hit over the head like an ox, stunned before the throat was cut, was the highest that he could hope for: annihilation was what he had elected.

But his dream had been horror of annihilation, the threat of nothingness. . . . It already seemed far away. He stretched his arms up behind his head, feeling the strength of his body. *His* body, that was made of fragments of his mother and his father, and of their mothers and their fathers, and shared with little Ann, with his daughters, and of course with his son—exactly like him, his copy. Yes, his, his body, strong, and pulsing with energy—he pushed away the warning from the dream, and switched on the light again, feeling that *that* was over. It was one in the morning, hardly the hour, in an English country hotel, to ask for tea, for coffee. He knew he would not dare to lie again on that bed, so he went down to let himself out. He was going to his father.

Ann was wrapped in blankets, lying on the floor of the living room. He knelt by her and gazed at the young face, the perfect eyelids that sealed her eyes shut like a baby's, incisive but delicate, shining, whole.

He sat on his father's bed where Ann had sat, and saw that the old man was slipping away. Jack could not have said why he knew, but he did know the death would be this day: it occurred to him that if he had not had that dream, he would not have known; he would not have been equipped to know, without the dream.

He walked the rest of the night away, standing to watch the bulk of the old church dwindling down under a sky lightening with dawn. When the birds began, he returned to the hotel, bathed, and with confidence woke his sister and brother, saying that yes, they could have breakfast but should not take too much time over it.

At eight-thirty they arrived to find Ann again crouched up on the bed near the old man, crooning to him bits of hymn, old tunes, nursery rhymes. He died without opening his eyes again.

Cedric said he would deal with all the arrangements, and that he would notify them of the funeral, which would probably be on Monday. The three children of the old man separated in good feeling and with kisses, saying that they really ought to see more of each other. And Jack said to Ann that she must come and visit. She said yes, it would be super, she could see Elizabeth and Carrie again, how about next weekend? There was to be a pray-in for Bangladesh.

Jack returned to his home, or rather, to his wife. She was out. He suppressed grievance that there was no note from her; after all, he had not telephoned. She was at another class, he supposed.

He went to see if anybody was in the girls' flat. Carrie and Elizabeth had made rooms for themselves on the top floor, and paid rent for them. They both had good jobs. There was an attic room used occasionally by Joseph.

Hearing sounds, he knocked, with a sense of intruding, and was bidden to come in by Carrie, who seemed in conflict at the sight of him. This was because she, like the others, had been waiting for his coming, waiting for the news of the death. She had prepared the appropriate responses, but had just finished cooking a meal, and was putting dishes on the table. A young man whose face he did not know was coming towards the table, ready to eat.

Carrie was flushed, her long dark hair fell about, and she was wearing something like a white sack, bordered with deep white lace.

"My father died," he said.

"Oh poor you," said Carrie.

"I don't know," said Jack.

"This is Bob," said Carrie. "My father. Dad, would you like to eat with us? It is a business lunch, actually."

"No, no," said Jack. "I'll see you later." She called after him: "Dad, Dad, I'm sorry about Granddad."

"Oh, he was due to go," Jack called back.

He cut himself bread and cheese, and rang Walter's office. Walter was back from Dublin, but had to fly to Glasgow that afternoon: he was to appear on television in a debate on the Common Market. He would be back by midday Saturday: the Twenty-four-Hour Fast would start at two o'clock Saturday. Thirty people were expected to take part. It was a good thing Jack was back: he could take over again.

But what was there to be done?

Nothing much, really; he should keep a tag on the names; some might decide to drop out again. Considering the scale of the horror at that moment taking place in India, the mass misery, it would be a surprisingly small turnout—he was sorry, he had to leave, a car was waiting.

It is normal to feel, on returning to the place one lives in, after having been away, that one has not left at all: this is not what Jack was feeling now. Whether it was because he was so tired, or because he was more upset by his father's death than he knew, he felt at a distance from his commonplace self, and particularly at a distance from the Jack Orkney who knew so well how to organize a sit-down, or a march, or how to produce such occasions properly for the press or television.

Walter's contrasting the numbers of the people involved in the Bangladesh tragedy with the numbers who were prepared not to eat, publicly, for twenty-four hours in London, had struck him as bathos, as absurdity, but he knew that normally that was how he would be reacting himself.

Now he tried to restore himself by summoning well-tried thoughts. Every time the radio or television was turned on, every time you saw a newspaper, the figure *nine million* was used, with the information that these refugees had no future, or none of the normal kind. (India's short, sharp, efficient war that reprieved these same nine million was of course months in the future.) But there was nothing to be done; this catastrophe had the same feeling as the last, which had been Nigeria: a large number of people would die of starvation or would be murdered, but there was no power strong enough to stop this.

It was this feeling of helplessness that seemed to be the new factor; each time there was something of this kind, the numbers of people grew larger, and the general helplessness augmented. Yet all that had happened was that great catastrophes were being brought to general attention more forcefully than in the past. Not long ago, as recently as thirty years ago, it had been a commonplace for small paragraphs in newspapers to say that six, seven, eight million people had died, were dying of starvation, in China; communism had put an end to famine, or to the world's hearing about it. A very short time ago, a decade, several million might die in a bad season in India; the green revolution had (possibly temporarily) checked that. In Russia millions had died in the course of some great scheme or other: the collectivization of the peasants, for instance.

The most shocking thing that had happened to his generation was the event summed up by the phrase "six million Jews." Although so many millions of people had been killed or had died in that war, and in a thousand awful ways, it was that one thing, the *six million,* which seemed worst. Because, of course, as everyone knew, it had been willed and deliberate murder. . . . Was it really any more deliberate than the *nine million* of Stalin's forcible collectivization? And how about that *nine,* or *ninety million,* the figure for the deaths of black men in Africa caused by white men in the course of bringing civilization to that continent? (This figure, whatever it was, never could accumulate about it the quality of senseless horror that had the figure for the death camps and gas chambers under Hitler. Why not?) During the next twelve months, between *twelve* and *twenty-four million* would die of starvation in the world (the figure depended on the source of calculation). The twelve months after, this figure would double—by the end of a decade, the numbers of people expected to die annually of hunger was beyond calculation. . . . These figures, and many more, clicked through his well-stocked journalist's head, and against them he heard Walter's voice, rather tetchy, critical, saying that there would only be thirty people for the Twenty-four-Hour Fast.

Yes, of course it was ridiculous to think on these lines and particularly when you were tired; he had been thrown off balance worse than he knew. He would sleep for a little—no, no, better not, he would rather not; he would not go to bed unless Rosemary could be with him. Well, there were things that he ought to be doing, he was sure: for one thing, he had not read the newspapers for three days, nor listened to the news. He regarded it as his responsibility to read all the newspapers every day as if knowing what was bad could prevent worse. He did not want to read the papers; he wanted to sit down and wait quietly for his wife. This made him guilty, and he was associating his reluctance to plunge into the misery and threat of the newspapers with the brutalizing of everybody, everyone's acceptance of horror as normal—well, it was, when had storms of blood and destruction *not* swept continuously over the globe?

His will was being attacked: he had no will. This was why he needed to see Rosemary. This thought, he knew, had put a small whimsical grimace onto his face; the grimace was for the benefit of an observer. The observer was himself; it was there for the sake of his pride—a very odd thing had happened between him and his wife. For a long time, in fact for most of the marriage, they would have said that they were unhappily married. It had been a war marriage of course, like those of most of their contemporaries. It had begun in passion, separation, dislocation. They had felt, on beginning to live together for the first time, when they had been married for nearly six years, that their good times had been stolen from them. Then three children: they had turned Rosemary into an obsessed complaining woman; so he had seen her, and so she now saw herself during that period. He was most often out of England, and had many affairs, some of them serious. He knew she had been in love with someone else; she, like himself, had refused to consider a divorce because of the effect on the children. There was of course nothing remarkable in this history; but some of the men he knew had divorced, leaving first wives to bring up children. He knew that many of his friends' wives, like Rosemary, had been obsessed with grievance at their lot, yet had been dutiful mothers.

Various unhappy balances had been achieved by himself and Rosemary, always regarded as second best. Best was in fantasy, or what other people had. Then the children grew up, and were no longer there to be cooked for, worried about, shopped for, nursed—suddenly these two people who had been married thirty years discovered they were enjoying each other. They could not use the words "a second honeymoon" because they had never had a first. Jack remembered that at the other end of what now seemed like a long tunnel of responsibility, worry, guilt—relieved by frequent exile, whose enjoyability caused more guilt—had been a young woman with whom he had been more in love than anybody since. He relaxed into the pleasures of his home, pleasure with Rosemary, who, appreciated at last, took on energy and poise, lost her listlessness, her reproach, her patience under neglect.

It had been the completeness of her revival that was the only thing disturbing about their being in love again: Jack lived marveling that so little a thing as his own attention should be enough to nourish this creature, to burnish her with joy. He could not help being guilty anew that so little an effort towards self-discipline would have produced the kindness which could have made this woman's life happy, instead of a martyrdom. Yet he knew he had not been capable of even so small an effort: he had found her intolerable, and the marriage a burden, and that was the truth. But the thought he could not come to terms with was this: what sort of a creature was she, to be fed and made happy by the love of a creature like himself?

And Rosemary was not the only woman he observed enjoying a new lease on life. At parties of "the Old Guard" it was enough simply to look around at the wives of the same age as his own wife, the women recently released from nursery and kitchen, to see many in the same condition, without having to ask if a second honeymoon was in progress—and here was another source of unease. He was not able to ask, to discuss frankly, or even to raise the matter at all, and yet these were friends, he had been with them, worked with them, faced a hundred emergencies with them—but they did not have with each other the friendship of the kind that would enable them to talk about their relationships with each other, with their wives, their wives with them. Yet this was friendship, or at least it was as close to friendship as he was likely to get. Intimacy he had known, but with women with whom he was having affairs. Intimacy, frankness, trust, had, as it were, been carried inside him, to be bestowed on loved women, and withdrawn when that love had ended because he was married. So it was not that he had not known perfect intimacy; it was that he had known it with several people, one after another. What was left now of these relationships was a simplicity of understanding when he met these women again—those that he did meet, for after all, many of these affairs had taken place in other countries. But even now he had to admit that this state had never been achieved with his wife, as good as their relation now was; for what he could not share with her was a feeling he could not control that he had to value her less for being so satisfied—more, fulfilled—with so little. Himself.

Yet, for all these reservations, the last two years had been better than anything he had expected with a woman, except in the expectations of his dreams about marriage so long ago. They went for holidays together, for weekends to old friends, to the theatre, for special meals at restaurants, and for long walks. They made little treats for each other, gave each other presents, had developed the private language of lovers. And all the time her gaiety and energy grew, while she could not prevent herself watching him—not knowing that she did it, and this humbled him and made him wretched—for the return of the old tyrant, the boor. Always he was aware that their happiness lacked a foundation.

But what foundation ought there to be?

Now he wanted to tell his wife the dream he had had about death. This is why he had been longing to see her. But he had not allowed himself to understand the truth, which was that he couldn't tell her. She dreaded change in him; she would feel the dream as a threat. And it was. For another thing, this new easy affection they had would not admit the words he would have to use. What words? None he knew could convey the quality of the dream. The habits of their life together made it inevitable that if he said: Rosemary, I had a terrible dream; well, no, that was not it, its terribleness is not the point, wait, I must tell you—she would reply: Oh, Jack, you must have eaten something. Are you well?—And she would run off to get him a glass of medicine of some sort. Her smile at him, while she handed it to him, would say that she knew, they both knew, that he didn't really need it, but she enjoyed looking after him when at last he was enjoying being looked after.

Teatime came. Jack watched the young man from upstairs walk away under the summer's load of leaf. The telephone rang twice, both times for Rosemary. He took messages. He saw Elizabeth come up the path to the side door, nearly called to her, but decided not. He sat on into the summer afternoon, feeling that it was appropriate to be melancholy: it was what was expected of him. But that was not it! It was as if he had no substance at all, there was nothing to him, no purpose, no worth. . . . Something was draining quietly away from him, had been, for a long time.

Elizabeth came running in, saying: "Oh, Father, I am so sorry, you must be feeling low." Caroline came after her. Carrie was now dressed in a purple shawl over tight red cotton trousers. Elizabeth, still in what she had worn to work, had on a dark green trouser suit, but her own personality had been asserted since she came home: she had tied her hair back with an exotic-looking piece of red material, and it was making a froth of gold curls around her face. His cold heart began to stir and to warm, and they sat themselves down opposite ready to share his grief.

Rosemary now came in, a large, tall woman, smiling and shedding energy everywhere.

"Oh, darling," said she, "you didn't telephone. I am so sorry. You have had tea, I hope?"

"He's dead," said Elizabeth to her mother.

"He died this morning," said Jack, not believing that it had been that morning.

Rosemary slowed her movements about the room, and when she turned to him, her face, like the faces of her daughters, was not smiling.

"When is the funeral?"

"I don't know yet."

"I'll come with you," said Elizabeth.

"I won't," said Carrie. "I don't like funerals. Not our kind of funeral."

"And I won't either, if you don't mind," said Rosemary. "That is, not unless you want me there." A glass and decanter had appeared beside him, and Rosemary was causing whisky to descend into the glass in a gold stream.

The whisky was not the point, the women's serious faces not the point, the funeral and who was at it, not the point.

"There is no need for any of you to come," he said. And added, as he had been afraid he might: "It wouldn't be expected of you."

All three showed relief, even Elizabeth.

Rosemary hated funerals: they were morbid. Carrie, being sort of Buddhist, believed, apparently, in putting corpses out for the vultures. Elizabeth's Christianity, like Ann's, was without benefit of church services.

"Oh no, I want to come with you," said Elizabeth.

"Well, we'll see."

He told them about the death—a mild and well-ordered affair. He said that Ellen and Cedric had been there, and watched for his wife's humorous glance so that he could return it: she wanted to convey sympathy for having to be with his family even for two days. Then he began speaking about the Twenty-four-Hour Fast. He did not ask if they would join him, but he was hoping they would.

Now, while Rosemary had early on been inculcated with his left-wing opinions, during all the years of their unhappiness his activities had been seen by her as being in some subtle way directed against her, or, at any rate, as depriving her of something. But recently she had several times gone with him to a meeting or a demonstration. Looking guilty, she said that she couldn't join the fast, because she had a lecture on Saturday night on Stress in the Family. She made it sound funny, in her way of appearing like an intelligent child submitting to official pedantry; but there was no doubt she would be at the lecture. Carrie said nothing: she thought any kind of politics silly. Elizabeth said she would have joined the fast, but she had a demonstration of her own on Saturday.

Jack now remembered Ann's program, said that Ann was coming down at the weekend for a pray-in. It turned out that this was the same as Elizabeth's. Both girls were pleased that Ann was coming, and starting talking about her and her relations with her parents. These were not very good: Ann found them materialistic, conventional, bourgeois. Jack was not able to be much amused; he found himself in sympathy with Cedric, possibly even with his sister-in-law. Probably Elizabeth and Carrie said to their friends that their parents were materialistic and bourgeois. He knew that his son Joseph did.

The girls had been going out for the evening, but because of the death, and wanting to cheer their father up, they stayed in to supper. Rosemary's new practice, now that the decades of compulsive cooking, buying, fussing, were done with, was to keep food to its simplest. She offered them soup, toast, and fruit. The girls protested: the parents could see that this was because they needed to do something to show their sympathy. Rosemary and Jack sat hand in hand on the sofa, while the girls made a long and delicious meal for them all.

They went to bed early: it was still not quite dark outside. But he needed to make love with his wife, feeling that here at least the cold which threatened him would be held at bay.

But the shell of himself loved, the shell of himself held Rosemary while she fell asleep and turned away from him. He was awake, listening to the tides of blood moving in his body.

He crept downstairs again. He read the newspapers—making himself do so, like a penance for callousness. He listened to the radio, avoiding news bulletins. He did not go to bed again until it was fully light, and was woken an hour later by Cedric: practical reasons had set the funeral for tomorrow, Saturday, at eleven.

Friday he spent in the activities that the journalist was so good at. Saturday was not a good day for train and air services: to reach S—— in time for the funeral, and to be back by two, would need luck and ingenuity. He checked the weather forecast: rain and mist were expected. Having made the arrangements, he rang Mona, since Walter was still in Glasgow. Mona was not only a wife of an "Old Guard," but one in her own right. It had been agreed that he, Jack, would be on the steps of the church at ten, to welcome the fasters as they arrived, and to see that the posters proclaiming the event were in place. He now asked Mona to do all this, explaining why.

"Oh dear," she said, "I am so sorry about your father. Yes, luckily I can do it. Who is coming?—wait, I'll get a pencil."

He gave her the names over the telephone, while she wrote them down.

They were the names of people with whom he had been associated in a dozen different ways, ever since the war ended; it seemed now as if the war had been an instrument to shake out patterns of people who would work and act together—or against each other—for the rest of their lives. They had not known about this process while it was happening, but that was when "the Old Guard" had been formed. The phrase was a joke of course, and for family use: he certainly would never use it to Walter, Bill, Mona, and the rest—they would be hurt by it. Carrie had said one day, reporting a telephone call, "I didn't get his name, but it sounded like one of the Old Guard."

These names appeared constantly together on dozens, hundreds, of letterheads, appeals, protests, petitions; if you saw one name, you could assume the others. Yet their backgrounds had been very different, of all classes, countries, even races. Some had been communists, some had fought communism. They were Labour and Liberal, vegetarian and pacifist, feeders of orphaned children, builders of villages in Africa and India, rescuers of refugees and survivors of natural and man-made calamities. They were journalists and editors, actors and writers, filmmakers and trade unionists. They wrote books on subjects like Unemployment in the Highlands and The Future of Technology. They sat on councils and committees and the boards of semi-charitable organizations; they were Town Councillors, members of Parliament, creators of documentary film programs. They had taken the same stands on Korea and Kenya, on Cyprus and Suez, on Hungary and the Congo, on Nigeria, the Deep South, and Brazil, on South Africa and Rhodesia and Ireland and Vietnam and . . . and now they were sharing opinions and emotions on the nine million refugees from Bangladesh.

Once, when they had come together to express a view, it had been a minority view, and to get what they believed publicized had sometimes been difficult or impossible. Now something had happened which not all of them had understood: when they expressed themselves about this or that, it was happening more and more often that their views were identical with conventional views put forward freely by majorities everywhere. Once they had been armed with aggressive optimistic views about society, about how to change it; now they were on the defensive. Once they had forecast utopias; now they forecast calamity, failed to prevent calamity, and then worked to minimize calamity.

This view of the Old Guard had been presented to Jack by his son, the chip off the old block.

When Jack had finished the list of names, Mona said: "Surely we can do better than that?" and he said, apologetically (why, when it was not his fault?): "I think a lot of people are feeling that the media are doing it for us."

Then he decided to ring his son, who had not yet heard about his grandfather. To reach Joseph was not easy, since he worked for a variety of "underground" organizations, slept in many places, might even be out of the country.

At last Jack rang Elizabeth, who was already at her place of work, heard where Joseph was likely to be, and finally reached his son. On hearing that his grandfather was dead, Joseph said: "Oh that's bad, I am sorry." On being asked if he and his friends "with nothing better to do" would like to join the Twenty-four-Hour Fast, he said: "But haven't you been reading the newspapers?" Jack did not want to say that he had not read them enough to know what his son's program was likely to be, but it turned out that "all of us" were organizing a protest march for that Sunday.

In his son's briskness, modified because of the death, Jack heard his own youth speaking, and a sense of justice made him sound apologetic towards his son. He felt, too, the start of exhaustion. This was because his effort to be fair made it necessary to resurrect his own youth as he talked to Joseph, and it took the energy that in fantasy he would be using to bring Joseph around to see his point of view. He had recently been indulging fantasies of confronting Joseph with: Look, I have something of great importance to say, can you let me have an hour or two? He was on the point of saying this now, but Joseph said: "I have to rush off, I'm sorry, see you, give my love to everyone."

He knew exactly what he wanted to say, not only to his son—to his own youthful self—but to the entire generation, or rather, to that part of it which was political, the political youth. What he felt was, he knew, paradoxical: it was because his son was so much like him that he felt he had no son, no heir. What he wanted was for his son to carry on from himself, from where he, Jack, stood now: to be his continuation.

It was not that his youthful self had been, was, conceited, crude, inexperienced, intolerant: he knew very well that his own middle-aged capacities of tact and the rest were not much more than the oil these same qualities—not much changed—used to get their own way; he wasn't one to admire middle-aged blandness, expertise.

What he could not endure was that his son, all of them, would have to make the identical journey he and his contemporaries had made, to learn lessons exactly as if they had never been learned before.

Here, at precisely this point, was the famous "generation gap"; here it had always been. It was not that the young were unlike their parents, that they blazed new trails, thought new thoughts, displayed new forms of courage. On the contrary, they behaved exactly like their parents, thought as they had—and, exactly like their parents, could not listen to this simple message; that it had all been done before.

It was this that was so depressing, and which caused the dryness of only just achieved tolerance on the part of the middle-aged towards "the youth"—who, as they themselves had done, behaved as if youth and the freedom they had to "experiment" was the only good they had, or could expect in their lives.

But this time the "gap" was much worse because a new kind of despair had entered into the consciousness of mankind: things were too desperate, the future of humanity depended on humanity being able to achieve new forms of intelligence, of being able to learn from experience. That humanity was unable to learn from experience was written there for everyone to see, since the new generation of the intelligent and consciously active youth behaved identically with every generation before them.

This endless cycle, of young people able to come to maturity only in making themselves into a caste which had to despise and dismiss their parents, insisting pointlessly on making their own discoveries—it was, quite simply, uneconomic. The world could not afford it.

Every middle-aged person (exactly as his or her parents had done) swallowed the disappointment of looking at all the intelligence and bravery of his or her children being absorbed in—repetition, which would end inevitably in them turning into the Old Guard. Would, that is, if Calamity did not strike first. Which everybody knew now it was going to.

Watching his son and his friends was like watching laboratory animals unable to behave in any way other than that to which they had been trained—as he had done, as the Old Guard had done. . . . At this point in the fantasy, his son having accepted or at least listened to all this, Jack went on to what was really his main point. What was worst of all was that "the youth" had not learned, were repeating, the old story of socialist recrimination and division. Looking back over his time—and after all recently he had had plenty of time to do just this, and was not that important, that a man had reached quiet water after such a buffeting and a racing and could think and reflect?—he could see one main message. This was that the reason for the failure of socialism to achieve what it could was obvious: that some process, some mechanism was at work which made it inevitable that every political movement had to splinter and divide, then divide again and again, into smaller groups, sects, parties, each one dominated, at least temporarily, by some strong figure, some hero, or father, or guru figure, each abusing and insulting the others. If there had been a united socialist movement, not only in his time—which he saw as that since the Second World War—but in the time before that, and the epoch before that, and before that, there would have been a socialist Britain long ago.

But as night followed day, the same automatic process went on . . . but if it *was* automatic, he imagined his son saying, then why talk to me like this?—Ah, Jack would reply, but you have to be better, don't you see. You have to, otherwise it's all at an end, it's finished, can't you see that? Can't you see that this process where one generation springs, virginal and guiltless—or so it sees itself—out of its debased predecessors, with everything new to learn, makes it inevitable that there must soon be division, and self-righteousness and vituperation? Can't you see that that has happened to your lot? There are a dozen small newspapers, a dozen because of their differences. But suppose there had been one or two? There are a dozen little groups, each jealously defending their differences of dogma on policy, sex, history. Suppose there had been just one?

But of course there could not be only one; history showed there could not—history showed this, clearly, to those who were prepared to study history. But the young did not study history, because history began with them. Exactly as history had begun with Jack and his friends.

But the world could no longer afford this. . . . The fantasy did not culminate in satisfactory emotion, in an embrace, for instance, between father and son; it ended in a muddle of dull thoughts. Because the fantasy had become increasingly painful, Jack had recently developed it in a way which was less personal—less challenging, less real? He had been thinking that he could discuss all these thoughts with the Old Guard and afterwards there could perhaps be a conference? Yes, there might be a confrontation, or something of that kind, between the Old Guard and the New Young. Things could be said publicly which never seemed to get themselves said privately? It could all be thrashed out and then . . . Meanwhile there was the funeral to get through.

That night, Friday, the one before the funeral, no sooner had he gone to sleep than he dreamed. It was not the same dream, that of the night in the hotel room, but it came as it were out of the same area. A corridor, long, dark, narrow, led to the place of the first dream, but at its entrance stood a female figure which at first he believed was his mother as a young woman. He believed this because of what he felt, which was an angry shame and inadequacy: these emotions were associated for him with some childhood experience which he supposed he must have suppressed; sometimes he thought he was on the point of remembering it. The figure wore a straight white dress with loose lacy sleeves. It had been his mother's dress, but both Elizabeth and Carrie had worn it "for fun." This monitor was at the same time his mother and his daughters, and she was directing him forward into the darkness of the tunnel.

His wife was switching on lights and looking at him with concern. He soothed her back to sleep and, for the second night running, left his bed soon after he had got into it to read the night away and to listen to radio stations from all over the world.

Next morning, he traveled to the airport in light fog, to find the flight delayed. He had left himself half an hour's free play, and in half an hour the flight was called and he was airborne, floating west inside grey cloud that was his inner state. He who had flown unmoved through the skies of most countries of the world, and in every kind of weather, was feeling claustrophobic, and had to suppress wanting to batter his way out of the plane and run away across the mists and fogs of this upper country. He made himself think of something else: returned to the fantasy about the conference. He imagined the scene, the hall packed to the doors, the platform manned by the well known among the various generations of socialists. He saw himself there, with Walter on one side, and his son on the other. He imagined how he or Walter would speak, explaining to the young that the survival of the world depended on them, that they had the chance to break this cycle of having to repeat and repeat experience: they could be the first generation to consciously take a decision to look at history, to absorb it, and in one bound to transcend it. It would be like a willed mutation.

He imagined the enthusiasm of the conference—a sober and intelligent enthusiasm, of course. He imagined the ending of the conference when . . . and here his experience took hold of him, and told him what would happen. In the first place, only some of the various socialist groups would be at the conference. Rare people indeed would be prepared to give up the hegemony of their little groups to something designed to end little groups. The conference would throw up some strong personalities, who would energize and lead; but very soon these would disagree and become enemies and form rival movements. In no time at all, this movement to end schism would have added to it. As always happened. So, if this was what Jack knew was bound to happen, why did he . . . They were descending through heavy cloud. There was heavy rain in S——. The taxi crawled through slow traffic. By now he knew he would not be in time to reach the cemetery. If he had really wanted to make sure of being at the funeral, he would have come down last night. Why hadn't he? He might as well go back now for all the good he was doing; but he went on. At the cemetery the funeral was over. Two young men were shoveling earth into the hole at the bottom of which lay his father: like the men in the street who continually dig up and rebury drains and pipes and wires. He took the same taxi back to the house in the church precincts where he found Mrs. Markham tidying the rooms ready to hold the last years of another man or woman, and his brother Cedric sorting out the old man's papers. Cedric was crisp: he quite understood the delay; he too would have been late for the funeral if he had not taken the precaution of booking rooms in the Royal Arms.

But both he and Ellen had been there, with his wife and Ellen's husband. Also Ann. It would have been nice if Jack had been there, but it didn't matter.

It was now a warm day, all fog forgotten. Jack found a suitable flight back to London. High in sunlight, he wondered if his father had felt as if he had no heir? He had been a lawyer: Cedric had succeeded him. In his youth he had defended labor agitators, conscientious objectors, taken on that kind of case: from religious conviction, not from social feeling. Well, did it make any difference why a thing was done if it was done? This thought, seditious of everything Jack believed, lodged in his head—and did not show signs of leaving. It occurred to Jack that perhaps the old man had seen himself as his heir, and not Cedric, who had always been so cautious and respectable? Well, he would not now know what his father had thought; he had missed his chance to find out.

Perhaps he could talk to Ann and find out what the old man had been thinking? The feebleness of this deepened the inadequacy which was undermining him—an inadequacy which seemed to come from the dream of the female in a white dress? Why had that dream fitted his two lovely daughters into that stern unforgiving figure? He dozed, but kept waking himself for fear of dreaming. That he was now in brilliant sunshine over a floor of shining white cloud so soon after the flight through fog dislocated his sense of time, of continuity even more: it was four days ago that he had had that telegram from Mrs. Markham?

They ran into fog again above Heathrow, and had to crawl around in the air for half an hour before they could land. It was now four, and the Twenty-four-Hour Fast had begun at two. He decided he would not join them, but he would drop in and explain why not.

He took the underground to Trafalgar Square.

Twenty people, all well known to him and to the public, were grouped on the steps and porch of St. Martin's. Some sat on cushions, some on stools. A large professionally made banner said: THIS IS A TWENTY-FOUR-HOUR FAST FOR THE STARVING MILLIONS OF BANGLADESH. Each faster had flasks of water, blankets and coats for the night ahead. Meanwhile it was a warm misty afternoon. Walter had a thick black sweater tied around his neck by the sleeves. Walter was the center of the thing; the others related to him. Jack stood on the other side of the road thinking that his idea of talking with these his old friends about a joint conference with "the youth" was absurd, impractical; now that he was again in the atmosphere of ordinary partisan politics, he could see that it was.

He was longing to join them, but this was because he wanted to be enclosed in a group of like-minded people, to be supported by them, to be safe and shielded from doubts and fears. And dreams.

By Walter was his wife, Norah, a small pretty woman whom he had always thought of as Walter's doormat. He had done, that is, until he had understood how afraid Rosemary had been of himself. Norah had once said to him after a meeting: "If Walter had been an ordinary man, I might have resented giving up my career, but when you are married to someone like Walter, then of course you are glad to submerge yourself. I feel as if this has been my contribution to the Movement." Norah had been a journalist.

Walter's face, usually a fist of intention and power, was beaming, expansive: they all looked as if they were at a picnic, Jack thought. Smug, too. That he should think this astounded him, for he knew that he loved and admired them. Yet now, looking at Walter's handsome face, so well known to everyone from newspaper and television, it had over it a mask of vanity. This was so extraordinary a metamorphosis of Jack's view of his friend that he felt as if an alien was inhabiting him: a film had come over his eyes, distorting the faces of everyone he looked at. He was looking at masks of vanity, complacency, stupidity, or, in the case of Walter's Norah, a foolish admiration. Then Jack's sense of what was happening changed; it was not that he was looking through distorting film, but that a film had been stripped off what he looked at. He was staring at faces that horrified him because of their naked self-centeredness: he searched faces that must be like his own, for something he could admire, or need. And hastily he wiped his hand down over his own face, for he knew that on it was fastened a mask of vanity; he could feel it there. Under it, under an integument that was growing inwards into his flesh, he could feel something small, formless, blind—something pitiful and unborn.

Now, disgusted with his treachery, but still unable to take his hand down from his face, unable to prevent himself from trying to tug off that mask fastened there, he walked over to his friends who, seeing him come, smiled, and looked about them for a place where he could sit. He said: "I can't join you, I am afraid. Transport trouble," he added ridiculously, as first surprise, then incomprehension showed on their faces. Now he saw that Walter had already registered: *His father!* and saw that this born commander was framing the words he would use as soon as Jack turned his back: "His father has died, he has just come from the funeral." But this was no reason why he shouldn't be with them: he agreed, absolutely. Now he moved away, but glanced back with a wave and a smile; they were all gazing after the small drama embodied in: His father has just died. They looked as if they were hungry for the sensation of it—he was disliking himself for criticizing people whom he knew to be decent and courageous, who, ever since he had known them, had taken risks, given up opportunities, devoted themselves to what they believed to be right. To what *he* believed was right. . . . He was also a bit frightened. Thoughts that he would never have believed he was capable of accommodating were taking root in him; he felt as if armies of others waited to invade.

He decided to walk down to the river, perhaps even to take a trip to Greenwich, if he could get on a boat at all on a warm Saturday afternoon. He saw coming towards him a little procession under banners of: JESUS IS YOUR SAVIOUR and JESUS LIVES! All the faces under the banners were young; these young people were in no way distinguished by their clothes from the young ones he had watched marching, with whom he had marched, for the last fifteen years or more. Their clothes were gay and imaginative, their hair long, their faces all promise. He was smiling at Ann, who carried a square of cardboard that said: JESUS CARES ABOUT BANGLADESH. A voice said, "Hello, Dad!" and he saw his Elizabeth, her golden hair in heavy pigtails over either shoulder. Hands, Ann's and Elizabeth's, pulled him in beside them. In this way one of the most prominent members of the Old Guard found himself marching under a poster which said: CHRIST CAME TO FEED THE HUNGRY. REMEMBER BANGLADESH! Ann's little face beamed with happiness and the results of the exercise. "It was a nice funeral," she said. "I was telling Liz about it. It had a good feeling. Granddad liked it, I am sure."

To this Jack found himself unable to reply, but he smiled and, with a couple of hundred Jesus lovers, negotiated the square, aided by some indulgent policemen. In a few moments he would pass his friends on the steps of the church.

"I shouldn't be here," he said. "False pretenses."

"Oh why?" inquired his daughter, really disappointed in him. "I don't see that at all!"

Ann's look was affectionate and forgiving.

Around him they were singing "Onward, Christian Soldiers." They sang and marched or, rather, shuffled and ambled, and he modified his pace to theirs, and allowed his depression to think for him that whether the banners were secular and atheist on principle, or under the aegis of Jesus, twenty-four million people would die in the world this year of starvation, and that he would not give a new penny for the chances of anybody in this square living another ten years without encountering disaster.

He was now aware that Mona was staring at him: in her decisive face, in her unequivocal eyes, was not a trace of what he usually saw there—the reminder of their brief but pleasurable affair. She turned to tug at Walter's sleeve, in a way that betrayed panic—more than ordinary shock, anyway. Now they all turned to look at him; they were all blank, they could not take it in. He had a need to wave his arms and shout: Nonsense, can't you see that I am with my daughter and my niece? He felt he should apologize. He could not stand being condemned by them, his side, his family, but even as he nodded and smiled embarrassed greeting, he saw that Walter, whose mouth at first had really dropped open, had seen Elizabeth, whom of course he had known all her life. All was explainable! For the second time in half an hour Jack watched Walter framing words with which to exculpate him: Jack was with his daughter, that was it! After all, Jack was not the only one among them whose offspring had caught God in various extraordinary forms!

Jack entered the square with the children, was informed that they would come to visit him later, and he left them singing energetic hymns by a fountain.

He took a bus home. He was looking forward to letting the false positions of the day dissolve themselves into unimportance while he laughed over them with his wife; but now he remembered that she would not be there, nor expect him to be.

There was a note, not to him but to Carrie, saying: "Please feed the cat, shall be very late, might stay at Judy Miller's, please lock all doors much love."

It was seven: it seemed like midafternoon. He drew the curtains to make a night, and sat in it with a glass of whisky. Later Ann came in to tell him about the funeral, about Jesus. He moved his position in his chair so that he could look at her shining eyelids. Carrie came in, and he looked at her, but her eyes were a woman's. He knew about her love life, because she talked freely to her parents about it, but if she had never said a word he would have known from her knowledgeable breasts, from the way the flesh was molded to her eyeballs by kisses. She breathed tenderness, and care for him; he was happy she was there, but it was Ann he wanted to look at.

They discussed their respective faiths. Ann did not need to join a church because she had a direct relationship with Jesus, who loved her as she loved Him. Carrie defined her religion as "sort of Eastern, she supposed." No, she didn't think it was Buddhist so much as Hindu. She believed in reincarnation but could not see the point of cow worship, though anything that made people be nice to animals was worth it, she thought. Had Ann read the Upanishads? That was what she believed in. She was taking it for granted that her father had not, and would not. She would like to be a vegetarian, but after all she shared a kitchen with Elizabeth, who would object. . . . Here Elizabeth came in, having bathed and put on an ancient peacock-blue lace dinner dress that had holes in the sleeves; Jack remembered Rosemary in it, twenty years before. Elizabeth was indignant, and said she would not at all mind Carrie turning vegetarian, she was ready to be one herself. But what would they feed the cat on? Were human beings going to kill all the cats and dogs in the world because they weren't vegetarian? Carrie got angry at this, and said: There you are; I told you, I knew you didn't want to be vegetarian! Ann restored good feeling by laughing at them both.

They went on discussing the exact nuances of their beliefs, *I* believe that, no, I don't agree with that, no I think it is more that . . . surely not, oh no, how can you believe that? An hour or so went by. Jack lifted the drawn curtain: there was a heavy golden light everywhere, thunder in the evening sky, the trees had damp yellow aureoles. He dropped the curtain, and they were in a small low lamplight, and the three girls were discussing Women's Liberation. Jack hated women talking about this, not because he disagreed with any of it, but because he had never been able to cope with it; it was all too much for him. He felt increasingly that he had reason to feel guilty about practically every relationship he ever had with a woman except for two or three special love affairs, which were outside ordinary categorization, but did not know how to change himself—if, indeed, he wanted to. These three young women had different, but precisely defined, opinions about the roles of women, with Carrie representing an extreme of femininity, and Ann, surprisingly, militant. Elizabeth talked about the lot of working women and had no time for what she called "futile psychologizing." This phrase made them quarrel, and for the first time Jack saw Ann strident. The quarrel went on, and then they saw that Jack was silent, and they remembered that his father was just dead, and they cooked for him, handing him many dishes, each as if it were a poultice for some wound he had suffered. Then, with an effort towards being reasonable, they went on discussing their ideological positions about Women's Liberation. Jack was again in the condition he had been in in the square, when he had looked across traffic at his old friends. All he had been able to see there was a variety of discreditable emotions; all he could see in these charming faces was self-importance. What mattered to them was the moment when they said: I think so-and-so; no, I don't think that. He knew that what they believed was not as important to them as that they had come to an opinion and the reasons why they had reached that opinion. They possessed their beliefs or opinions; they owned them.

Now they were back to religion again: the other two attacked Ann for being Christian when Christianity's history in relation to women was so retrogressive. To which Ann said to Carrie: "You can talk, how about women in India?"

"Yes," said Carrie, "but then I don't believe in women being the same as men."

This started the quarrel again, and their voices rose.

He had to stop himself saying that they sounded like a Conference of World Churches debating doctrinal differences, because he knew that if it came to dogmas, and disagreements about historical personalities, then his faith, socialism, beat them all. He looked at, listened to, his daughters, his brother's daughter, and knew that in two, three, ten years (if they were all allowed to live so long) they would be laying claim, with exactly the same possessiveness, to other creeds, faiths, attitudes.

Again he felt like a threatened building, the demolition teams at work on its base. He was seeing, like a nightmare, the world like a little ball covered over with minuscule creatures all vociferously and viciously arguing and killing each other over beliefs which they had come to hold by accident of environment, of geography.

He told the girls he had not been sleeping well, must go to bed: he could no longer stand listening while they staked precise claims in fields of doctrine. They went off, kissing him fondly: he knew from the warmth of the kisses that they had talked about his reactions to Granddad's death; everything was bound to be much worse for him of course because he was an atheist and did not believe in survival after death.

They each had a different version of their futures. Ann for instance believed that she would sit up after her death, exactly as she was now, but better, and would recognize her friends and family, and Jesus would be there too.

Jack was thinking that his own attitude to life after death had been collected quite casually: when he was young and forming (or acquiring) his opinions, the people and writers he admired wore atheism like a robe of honor. Not to believe in an afterlife was like a certificate of bravery and, above all, clarity of thinking. If he had been young now, he might have collected, according to the chances of his experience, and just as lightly, any one of a variety of opinions. Reincarnation? Why not? After all, as Carrie said, it was an optimistic and forward-looking creed. But when he was young he couldn't have taken to a belief in reincarnation, if for no other reason than that he never met anyone who had it. He had known that a few cranks believed in it, and people in India, but that was about it.

Now he made a ritual of going to bed. The sky was still full of light, so he made the room black. He drank hot milk. He wooed sleep, which he had never done in his life, and soon lay awake, hands behind his head. But he could not spend a third night reading and listening to the radio. Then lights crashed on and his wife was in the room. She was apologetic, and quite understood that he hadn't felt like joining the fast. Her mind, he could see, was on her lecture and the friends she had met afterwards. He watched her dimming her vitality, damping her good mood, because she was afraid of it disturbing him. She lay in bed smiling, bright-eyed. She asked about the funeral, was sorry he had not reached it. Poor Jack! Smiling, she offered her arms, and grateful, he went into them. He would have gone on making love all night, but she went to sleep. In the close protective dark he lay beside his wife and in imagination saw the sky fill with dawn.

He fell asleep, he fell into a dream. In the dream he was thinking of what he had kept out of his consciousness all day, for to think of it was morbid. His father lay in a tight box under feet of wet soil. He, Jack, lay with him. He stifled and panicked, and the weight on him was as if he had been buried alive, in wet cement. He woke, and finding that although a cool damp light lay everywhere, and birds were at work on the lawn, it was only half past four; he went downstairs, turned on the radio, and made pictures in his head of the towns the stations were in, and lists of the people he had known in these towns, and then divided these into friends and enemies, and then, by a different classification, into the dead and the living, and so he returned in memory to the wars he had fought in or had reported, and relived, in a half-sleep, crisis points, moments of danger, when he might have been killed, that now made him sweat and tremble but which he had simply lived through. When it seemed to him as if hours of a new day had already passed, he went back upstairs and got into bed beside his wife.

But at breakfast she betrayed that she had known he had not been beside her: she started to talk about the job in Nigeria. He knew that she did not want to go away for two years, leaving all her new interests, new friends, new freedom. There she would be back inside duties she had escaped from. There would be much social life. Yet it sounded as if she was trying to bring herself to believe she wanted to go if he did: she was worried about him.

He said, instead of replying about Nigeria, that he would like to go to church, just to see what it was like these days. She took in a puzzled but patient breath, let it sigh out of her, and looked at him with loving and respectful eyes—just like, he thought, the way Norah looked at Walter. She said: "Oh, I can understand why. You mean, you missed the funeral service?"

Perhaps it was because he had missed the funeral service. He put on a suit and she a dress, and they went to church together, for the first time, except for weddings. Carrie and Elizabeth went with them, Carrie because God was everywhere, Elizabeth because He was particularly in churches. Ann would not come; she had Jesus by the hand as she sat on the floor reading the Sunday newspapers.

He sat through the service in a rage; perhaps it was a retrospective rage; certainly this was what he had felt throughout years of compulsory attendance at Evensong and Matins, and Services Early and Late, at his public school. He did not mind that it was mumbo jumbo: it was bound to be! What he minded was that people voluntarily submitted themselves to the ministry of men palpably no better than themselves, men whose characters were written on their faces. This was perhaps what had first directed him towards socialism? He had not been able to stand that people submitted to being lied to, cheated, dominated by their equals? He was again afflicted by yesterday's disability: a film had rolled away from what he looked at. That man, wearing black with white lace and embroidery, and dangling strips of this and that color—the sort of attractive nonsense that Carrie and Liz might wear—that man intoning and dancing and posturing through the service, had a face like Walter's. They were both public men, performers. Their features were permanently twisted by vanity and self-importance. Jack kept passing his hand across his own face, feeling the ugliness of the love of power on it. And Rosemary put her arm in his, asking if he felt well, if he had toothache? He replied with violence that he must have been mad to want to come; he apologized for inflicting it on her.

"Oh it doesn't matter for once," she said, with mildness, but glanced over her shoulder to see if Carrie and Elizabeth had heard: it was extraordinary how they all kowtowed to their children, as if they feared to offend them.

After the midday meal he felt as if he could sleep at last, and did so.

The dream pulled him down into itself as he rolled onto his bed in the sultry yellow afternoon light—and passed out. This time, as he sank down beside his father, who was very cold—he could feel the cold coming out and claiming him—the weight pressed them both down, right through the earth that was below the tight box. His father disappeared and he, Jack, quite alone, was rocking on a light blue sea. This too dissolved into air, but not before he had been pierced through and through with an extraordinary pain that was also a sweetness. He had not known anything like this before; in the dream he was saying to himself: That's a new thing, this sweetness. It was quickly gone, but astonishing, so that he woke up, pleased to wake up, as if out of a nightmare, yet what he had been happy to wake from was that high, piercing sweetness. Unhealthy, he judged it. It was not yet teatime; he had slept an hour and not been refreshed. He went down to be told as a joke by his wife that a journalist had rung that morning to find out his views on the Twenty-four-Hour Fast; did his not having been there mean that he was against it? Ann had answered, and had said that Mr. Orkney was at church. The journalist had seemed surprised, Ann said. She had had to repeat it more than once. Had she meant that Jack Orkney was at a wedding? At a christening? No, no, at church, at Sunday morning service.

Jack knew the journalist; they had been in several foreign fields together. Jack was now seriously worried, as a man is when faced with the loss of reputation. He said to himself: I was not worried what people thought of me when I was young. He was answered: You mean, you were not worried by what people said who were not *your side*. He said: Well, but now it is not a personal thing, criticism of me is a criticism of my side; surely it is right to worry about letting my own side down?

There was no answer to this, except a knowledge he was dishonest.

Rosemary suggested a long walk. He could see she had been thinking how to make him whole again—how to protect her own happiness, he could not prevent himself thinking. He was more than ready to walk as many miles away as they could before dark; when they had first met, before they married, one of their things had been to walk miles, sometimes for days on end. Now they walked until it was dark, at eleven o'clock; they worked out it was over fifteen miles, and were pleased that this was still so easy for them, at their age, and in the middle of their undemanding life. But the night now confronted Jack, a narrow tunnel at the end of which waited a white-robed figure, pointing him into annihilation. That night he did not sleep. The windows were open, the curtains drawn back, the room full of light from the sky. He pretended to sleep, so as to protect his wife from anxiety, but she lay alert beside him, also pretending sleep.

Next morning it was a week since Mrs. Markham's wire, and he became concerned for his health. He knew that not to sleep for night after night, as he was doing, was simply not possible. During the following days he went further into this heightened, oversensitized state, like a country of which he had heard rumors, but had not believed in. On its edges his wife and daughters smiled and were worried about him. He slept little, and when he did he was monitored by the female figure in white, now a composite of his mother, his wife, and his daughters, but quite impersonal; she used their features but was an impostor. This figure had become like an angel on a wedding cake, or on a tomb, full of false sentiment; its appearance was accompanied, like a strain of particularly nauseating and banal music, by the sweetly piercing emotion, only it was much worse now; it was the essence of banality, of mawkishness, like being rolled in powdered sugar and swallowed into an insipid smile. The horror of this clinging sickliness was worse even than the nightmare—he could no longer remember the quality of that, only that it had occurred—of the night in the hotel. His bed, the bedroom, soon the entire house, was tainted by this emotion, which was more a sensation, even like nausea, as if he could never rid himself of the taste of a concentration of saccharin which he had accidentally swallowed. He was all day in a state of astonishment, and self-distrust; he made excuses not to go to bed.

Walter came to see him. Unannounced. As soon as Jack saw him getting out of his car, he remembered something which told him why Walter had come. About four years before, Mona had reviewed a religious book, the memoirs of some sort of mystic, in a way which surprised them all. They would have expected a certain tone—light, carefully non-solemn, for it did not do to give importance to something which did not deserve it—not mocking, of course, which would have had the same result, but the tone you use to indicate to children that while you may be talking about, let's say, ghosts, or telling a story about a witch, the subject is not one to be taken seriously. But Mona had not used this subtly denigrating tone. Various of the Old Guard had commented on this. Then she had reviewed a book of religious poetry, which of course could not be dismissed in the light disinfecting tone, since poetry was obviously in a different category—but the point was that none of them would have reviewed it at all. For one thing no editor would think of asking them to. It was all very upsetting. There had been a party at Bill's house and Mona was not there. She had been discussed: she was at the age when women "get" religion. Jack, fond of Mona, offered to go and see her. His visit was to find out, as he put it to himself, if she was "still with us." He had found her amiable, and her usual self, helping to organize a conference for the coming week. He had probed—oh tactfully, of course. He mentioned an article in one of the Sundays about a certain well-known religious figure, and said he found the man a nauseating self-seeker. Mona had said that she was inclined to agree. He had said casually, "Of course I am only too ready to forgive somebody who can't face old age and all that without being cushioned by God." Mona had remarked that for her part she could not believe in personal survival after death. Well, of course not, but for years that she could not would have been taken for granted. He remembered feeling protective affection for her, as if he were helping to save her from a danger. Seeing Walter at a meeting to do with the Crisis in Our Communications a week later, he had said that he had made a point of visiting Mona and that she had seemed quite sound to him.

He knew now what to expect from Walter.

Walter was looking furtive. Of course Jack knew that this furtiveness was not anything he would have noticed normally: this state he was in exaggerated every emotion on other people's faces into caricatures. But Walter was playing a double part, almost that of a spy (as he had with Mona, of course, now he came to think of it), and Furtiveness was written large on him.

Walter mentioned the fast—a success—and then made a clumsy sort of transition which Jack missed, and was talking about Lourdes. Jack wondered why Lourdes? And then he laughed: it was a short laugh, of astonishment, and Walter did not notice it. Or rather, had not expected a laugh in this place, found it discordant, and therefore discounted it, as if it had not happened. Walter was trying to find out if Jack's religious conversion—the rumor had spread that he went to church on Sundays—included a belief in miracles, such as took place, they said, at Lourdes. Jack said he had been to Lourdes once for the *Daily* . . . over some so-called miracles some years ago. Walter nodded, as if to say: That's right. He was already feeling relieved, because Jack had used the right tone. But he was still showing the anxiety of a priest who knew his beliefs to be the correct ones and was afraid of a lamb straying from the flock. He mentioned that Mona was suspected of having become a Roman Catholic. "Good God, no," said Jack, "she can't have." He sounded shocked. This was because his reaction was that she had been deceiving him, had lied. He sat silent, trying to remember the exact tones of her voice, how she had looked. If she was a Catholic, could she have said she did not believe in a personal survival? But he knew nothing at all of what Catholics thought, except that they did not believe in birth control, but did believe in the Pope.

Remembering that Walter was still there, and silent, he looked up to see him smiling with relief. The smile seemed to him extraordinary in its vulgarity, yet he knew that what he was seeing was the pleasure of a good comrade: Walter was happy that nothing was going to spoil their long friendship. The spontaneity of his reply over Mona had reassured him; now, mission accomplished, Walter was already thinking about the various obligations he had to get back to. But he stayed a little, to discuss some committee on pollution he was helping to set up.

He talked: Jack listened, wondering if this was the right time to raise the question of "the young." Walter's two sons were both classic revolutionaries and they despised their father for his success, his position in the socialist world, for "his compromises with the ruling class." Jack was thinking that of all the people in the world it was Walter, so like himself in experience, position, and—he was afraid—character, with whom he should be able to talk about his preoccupation. But he was beginning to realize that there was a difference, and it was obviously an important one, between them. Jack was more on the outskirts of politics. He was more of a freelance, but Walter was always in the thick of every political struggle, always involved with the actual details of organization. He never did anything else. And this was why he was so far from Jack's present vision of things, which saw them all—the people like them—continually planning and arranging and organizing towards great goals, but fated to see these plans fail, or becoming so diluted by pressures of necessity that the results resembled nothing of what had been envisaged at the start. Sitting there, looking at his old friend's forceful and energetic face, it was in a double vision. On the one hand he thought that this was the one man he knew whom he would trust to see them all through any public or private tight spot; but at the same time he wanted to howl out, in a protest of agonized laughter, that if the skies fell (as they might very well do), if the seas rolled in, if all the water became undrinkable and the air poisoned and the food so short everyone was scratching for it in the dust like animals, Walter, Bill, Mona, himself, and all those like them, would be organizing Committees, Conferences, Sit-downs, Fasts, Marches, Protests, and Petitions, and writing to the authorities about the undemocratic behavior of the police.

Walter was talking about some negotiation with the Conservatives. Normally, Jack would be listening to an admirably concise and intelligent account of human beings in conflict. Now Jack could see only that on his friend's face was a look which said: *I am Power*. Jack suddenly got up, with a gesture of repulsion. Walter rose automatically, still talking, not noticing Jack's condition. Jack reminded himself that in criticizing Walter he had forgotten that he must be careful about himself: he had again, and suddenly, become conscious of the expressions that were fitting themselves down over his face, reflecting from Walter's, horrifying him in their complacency or their cruelty. And his limbs, his body, kept falling into postures of self-esteem and self-approval.

Walter was moving to the door, still talking. Jack, trying to keep his face blank, to prevent his limbs from expressing emotions which seemed to him appropriate for a monster, moved cautiously after him. Walter stood in the door—talking. Jack wanted him to go. It tired him, this self-observation he could not stop: there was his image at the door, oblivious to anything in the world but his own analysis of events. Yet at last, as Walter said goodbye and he saw Jack again—which he had not done for some minutes, being too self-absorbed—a worried look came into his face, and because of this look Jack knew that what Walter saw was a man standing in a rigid unnatural position who had his hands at his lower cheeks, fretfully fingering the jawbone, as if it were out of place.

Walter said, in a simple and awkward voice: "It's a bit of a shock when your old man goes. I know when mine died it took me quite a time to get back to normal."

He left, like a health visitor, and Jack thought that Walter had had to get back to normal when his father died. He was thinking, too, that the cure for his condition was activity. Walter was more sensible than himself: he filled every moment of his time.

He decided to go to the family doctor for sleeping pills. This was a house that self-consciously did not go in for pills of any kind. Or did not now: Rosemary, during what she now called "my silly time"—which after all had gone on for some years—had taken sleeping pills a lot. But that, even while she did it, had seemed to her a betrayal of her real nature. The girls went in for health in various ways—diets, yoga, homemade bread. His son was too strong—of course!—to need medicine. He smoked pot, Jack believed, and on principle—well, so would Jack have done at his age; the law on marijuana was absurd.

He told the doctor he was not sleeping well. The doctor asked for how long. He had to think. Well, for about a month, perhaps six weeks.

The doctor said: "That's not going to kill you, Jack!"

"All right, but before I get into the habit of not sleeping I'd like something—and *not* a placebo, please." The glance the doctor gave him at this told him that he had in fact been deciding to prescribe a placebo, but there had been something in Jack's voice to make him change his mind.

"Is there something else worrying you?"

"Nothing. Or everything."

"I see," said the doctor, and prescribed sleeping pills and antidepressants.

Jack had the prescriptions made up, then changed his mind; if he started taking these pills, it would be some sort of capitulation. To what, he did not know. Besides, he was thinking: Perhaps they might make it worse? "It" was not only the sweet mawkishness which threatened him at every turn, in a jingle of a tune for an advertisement on television, a shaft of light from behind a cloud at sunrise, a kitten playing in the next garden, but the feeling, getting worse, that he was transparent, an automaton of unlikable and predictable reactions. He was like a spy in his own home, noticing the slightest reactions of thought or emotion in his wife and daughters, seeing them as robots. If they knew how he was seeing them, how loathsome they were in their predictability, their banality, they would turn and kill him. And quite rightly. For he was not human. He was outside humanity. He even found himself walking abruptly out of rooms where he was sitting with Rosemary, or one or other of the girls; he could not stand his own horror and pity because of them, himself, everybody.

Yet they were treating him with perfect kindness. He knew that this was what it really was: even if he had to see it all as falsity, mere habits of kindness, sympathy, consideration, tact, which none of them really felt, wanting him to get back to normal, so that life could go on without stress. His wife particularly longed for this. While he took care that he did not betray the horror he was immersed in, she knew well enough their time was over—the gaiety and charm of it, the irresponsibility. Probably for good. Being what she was, thoughtful, considerate (taught by society to show thoughtfulness and sympathy when she wasn't really feeling it, he could not stop himself thinking), she was trying to decide what to do for the best. Sometimes she asked if he didn't think he should write another book—even if he would like to make a trip abroad without her; she talked about Nigeria. Each time Nigeria was mentioned his response to it was strong: it was the idea of forgetting himself entirely in an active and tightly planned life.

But he did not want to commit himself. He felt he would be losing an opportunity—but of what? And besides, how could he? He believed he was seriously ill, in some inconceivable, unprecedented way; how could he take a job when his energies had to go into presenting a bland and harmless surface to those around him, into preventing his hand rising furtively up to his face, to see if the masks of greed or power were fastened there, into watching the postures his body assumed, which must betray his vices to anyone looking his way—or would betray them, if everybody wasn't blind and deaf, absorbed in their kindness, their awful, automatic, meaningless "sympathy."

One night his son arrived upstairs. Joseph used sometimes to come, unannounced, and went up through the girls' room to the attic to sleep. He took food from his sisters' kitchen. Sometimes he brought friends.

About a year ago there had been a row over the friends. Feeling one evening as if the top part of his house had been invaded by a stealthy army, Jack had gone up and found a dozen or so young men, and a couple of girls, all lying about on sleeping bags and blankets under the rafters. They had moved in. A girl was cooking sausages in a frying pan that was on a camping stove; about a foot away was a drum that had written on it: PARAFFIN, INFLAMMABLE. The flame from the stove was turned too high, and showed around the edges of the frying pan. Jack jumped forward, turned it down, removed the pan, and stood up, facing them, the pan in his hand. His usual responses to his son—apology, or the exhaustion due to the effort to be fair, had been cut, and he asked: "What's the matter with you lot? What's wrong? You aren't stupid!"

Coming up the stairs he had been preparing a "humorous" remark—which he was afraid would sound pompous, to the effect: "How about introducing me to my guests?" Now he stared at them, and the young faces stared back. There was a half-scared smile on the face of the girl who had been cooking, but no one said anything. "I think you had better get out," said Jack at last, and went downstairs. Soon after he had watched the whole lot cross the garden like a tribe on the move, with their stove, their cartons, their paper carriers, their guitars, their sleeping bags.

Now he came to think of it, this incident had been the beginning of his inadmissible depression. He had spent days, weeks, months, thinking about it. He felt there was a contempt there, in the carelessness, that went beyond anything he knew how to cope with; he did not understand it, them—his son. Who, meanwhile, had resumed his habits, and continued to drop in for a night or two when he had nowhere better to sleep. So it was not, Jack reasoned, that Joseph despised a roof over his head, as such? They had all been so stoned they had not known what they were doing? No, it hadn't seemed like it. They had not bothered to look at the drum, had not known it was full? But that was scarcely an excuse—no, it was all too much, not understandable. . . . He had not talked to his son since, only seen him go past.

The telephone rang from upstairs: Carrie said that Joseph would be down to see him in a few moments, if Jack "had nothing better to do."

Instantly Jack was on the defensive: he knew that Joseph criticized him for having been away so much when the three children were growing up. This message was a reference to that—*again?* If it was simply careless, what had come into his head, then that made it even worse, in a way. . . . Joseph came running lightly down the stairs and into the living room. A muscular young man, he wore skin-tight blue jeans, a tight blue sweatshirt, and a small red scarf at his throat tied like a pirate's. The clothes were old, but as much care had gone into their choosing, preparation, and presentation as a model getting ready for a photograph. . . . While Jack knew he had already begun the process of comparison that always left him exhausted, he could not stop, and he was wondering: Was it that we were as obsessed with what we wore but I've forgotten it? No, it's not that: our convention was that it was bourgeois to spend time and money on clothes, that was it, but their convention is different; that's all it is and it is not important.

Joseph had a strong blue gaze, and a strong straight mouth. The mouth was hidden under a wiry golden beard. A mane of wiry yellow hair fell to his shoulders. Jack thought that the beard and the long hair were there because they were fashionable, and would be dropped the moment they were not. . . . *Well, why not? He wished very much he could have swaggered about in beard and mane—that was the truth.*

This aggressively vivid young man sat on a chair opposite Jack, put his palms down on his thighs with his fingers pointing towards each other, and the elbows out. In this considering, alert position he looked at his father.

Jack, a faded, larger, softer version of what he was seeing, waited.

Joseph said: "I hear you have got religion."

"The opium," said Jack, in a formal considering way, "of the people: Yes. If that's what it is, I have got it."

Jack felt particularly transparent, because of his son's forceful presence. He knew that his posture, the smile on his face, were expressing apology. He already knew the meeting was doomed to end unpleasantly. Yet he was looking for the words to appeal to his son, to begin the "real" talk that they should be having. Joseph said: "Well, that's your business." He sounded impatient; having raised the subject, or at least used it as an opener, now he was saying that his father's processes were of no interest or importance.

"You've been following the Robinson affair?"

Jack could not remember for a moment which affair that was, but did not like to say no.

"We have to pay the defense lawyer. And there's the bail. We need at least three thousand pounds."

Jack did not say anything. It was not from policy, but inadequacy, yet he saw his son beginning to make the irritable movements of power, of confidence, checked and thwarted. It crossed his mind that of course his son saw him as powerful and confident, and this it was that accounted for the aggression, the hostility, the callousness. Into Jack's mind now came sets of words framed rhetorically; since this was not how he was feeling, he was surprised. "Why does it have to be like this, that more hate is used on people of the same side, thus preventing us ever from uniting in a common front, preventing us from bringing down the enemy?" These were words from the imaginary conversation with Joseph that he so often indulged in: only now did it strike him that he never had fantasies of a personal relationship—of their going for a holiday together, for instance, or just spending an evening, or walking for an hour or so. "Can't you see?"—the inner rhetoric-maker was continuing, "that the vigor of your criticism, your iconoclasm, your need to condemn the past without learning from it, will take you relentlessly to stand exactly where your despised elders stand now?"

It suddenly occurred to Jack, and for the first time, that he had repudiated his past. This so frightened him, leaving him, as it must, by himself out in the air somewhere, without comrades and allies—*without a family*—that he almost forgot Joseph's presence. He was thinking: For weeks now, ever since the old man's death—before, even?—I've been thinking as if I have abandoned socialism.

Joseph was saying: "I don't have to tell you what the conditions are like in that prison, how they are being treated."

Jack saw that the "I don't have to tell you" was in fact an admission that in spite of everything he said, Joseph saw him as an ally. "You've come to me for money?" he asked, as if there could be another reason.

"Yeah. Yeah. That's about it, I suppose."

"Why do you have to be American?" Jack asked in sudden real irritation. "You're not American. Why do you all have to?"

Joseph said, with a conscious smile: "It's a mannerism, that's all." Then he looked stern again, in command.

Jack said: "I'm one of the old rich lefties you were publicly despising not long ago. You didn't want to have anything to do with us, you said."

Joseph frowned and made irritable movements which said that he felt that the sort of polemic which abused people not standing exactly where he stood was rather like breathing, a tradition, and he genuinely felt his father was being unreasonable in taking such remarks personally. Then he said, as if nothing better could be expected: "Then I take it it is no?"

"No," said Jack, "I am sorry."

Joseph got up; but he looked hesitant, and even now could sit down—if Jack said the right things. If he could push aside the rhetorical sentences that kept coming to his tongue: how should they not?—he had spent many hours of fantasy ensuring that they would!

Jack suddenly heard himself saying, in a low, shaking, emotional voice: "I am so sick of it all. It all just goes on and on. Over and over again."

"Well," said Joseph, "they say it is what always happens, so I suppose that ought to make us feel better." His smile was his own, not forced, or arranged.

Jack saw that Joseph had taken what he had said as an appeal for understanding between them personally: he had believed that his father was saying he was sick of their bad relations.

Had that been what he was saying? He had imagined he was talking about the political cycle. Jack now understood that if in fact he made enough effort, Joseph would respond, and then . . . He heard himself saying: "Like bloody automatons. Over and over again. Can't you see that it is going to take something like twenty years for you lot to become old rich lefties?"

"Or would if we aren't all dead first," said Joseph, ending the thing as Jack would, and with a calm, almost jolly smile. He left, saying: "The Robinson brothers are likely to get fifteen years if we don't do something."

Jack, as if a button had been pushed, was filled with guilt about the Robinson brothers and almost got up to write a check there and then. But he did not: it had been an entirely automatic reaction.

He spent a few days apparently in the state he had been in for weeks; but he knew himself to have reached the end of some long inner process that had proved too much for him. This interview with his son had been its end, as, very likely, the scene in the attic had been its beginning? Who knew? Who could know! Not Jack. He was worn out, as at the end of a long vigil. He found himself one morning standing in the middle of his living room saying over and over again: "I can't stand any more of this. I can't. I won't."

He found the pills and took them with the same miserable determination that he would have had to use to kill something that had to be killed. Almost at once he began to sleep, and the tension eased. He no longer felt as if he was carrying around, embodied in himself, a question as urgent as a wound that needed dressing, but that he had no idea what the language was in which he might find an answer. He ceased to experience the cloying sweetness that caused a mental nausea a hundred times worse than the physical. In a few days he had already stopped seeing his wife and daughters as great dolls who supplied warmth, charm, sympathy, when the buttons of duty or habit were pressed. Above all, he did not have to be on guard against his own abhorrence: his fingers did not explore masks on his face, nor was he always conscious of the statements made by his body and his limbs.

He was thinking that he was probably already known throughout the left as a renegade; yet, examining the furniture in his mind, he found it not much changed.

It occurred to him, and he went on to consider it in a brisk judicious way, that it was an extraordinary thing that whereas he could have sat for an examination at a moment's notice on the history, the ideas, and the contemporary situation of socialism, communism, and associated movements, with confidence that he would know the answers even to questions on the details of some unimportant sect in some remote country, he was so ignorant of religious history and thought that he could not have answered any questions at all. His condition in relation to religious questions was like that of a person hearing of socialism for the first time and saying: "Oh yes, I've often thought it wasn't fair that some people should have more than others. You agree, do you?"

He decided to go to the British Museum Reading Room. He had written many of his books there. His wife was delighted, knowing that this meant he was over the crisis.

He sent in his card for books on the history of the religions, on comparative religion, and on the relation of religion to anthropology.

For the first few days it seemed that he was still under the spell of his recent experience: he could not keep his attention from wandering from the page, and the men and women all around him bending over books seemed to him insane; this habit of solving all questions by imbibing information through the eyes off the printed page was a form of self-hypnotism. He was seeing them and himself as a species that could not function unless it took in information in this way.

But this soon passed and he was able to apply himself.

As he read, he conscientiously examined what he thought; was this changing at all? No, his distaste for the whole business could be summed up by an old idea of his, which was that if he had been bred, let us say, in Pakistan, that would have been enough for him to kill other people in the name of Mohammed, and if he had been born in India, to kill Moslems without a qualm. That had he been born in Italy, he would have been one brand of Christian, and if he had stuck with his family's faith, he would be bound to suspect Roman Catholicism. But above all what he felt was that this was an outdated situation. What was he doing sitting here surrounded by histories and concordances and expositions and exegetics? He would be better occupied doing almost anything else—a hundred years ago, yes, well, that had been different. The struggle for a Victorian inside the Church had meant something; for a man or a woman then to say: "If I had been born an Arab I would be praying five times a day looking at Mecca, but had I been a Tibetan I would have believed in the Dalai Lama"—that kind of statement had needed courage then, and the effort to make it had been worthwhile.

There were, of course, the mystics. But the word was associated for him with the tainted sweetness that had so recently afflicted him, with self-indulgence, and posturing, and exaggerated behavior. He read, however, Simone Weil and Teilhard de Chardin; these were the names he knew.

He sat, carefully checking his responses: he was more in sympathy with Simone Weil, because of her relations with the poor, less with Teilhard de Chardin, who seemed to him not very different from any sort of intellectual: he could have been a useful sort of politician, for instance? It occurred to him that he was in the process of choosing a degree or class of belief, like a pipe from a display of pipes, or a jacket in a shop, that would be on easy terms with the ideas he was already committed to and, above all, would not disturb his associates. He could imagine himself saying to Walter: "Well, yes, it is true that I am religious in a way—I can see the point of Simone Weil, she took poverty into account. She was a socialist of a kind, really."

He bought more books by both Simone Weil and Teilhard de Chardin, and took them home, but did not read them; he had lost interest, and besides an old mechanism had come into force. He realized that sitting in the Reading Room he had been thinking of writing a book describing, but entirely as a tourist, the varieties of religious behavior he had actually witnessed: a festival in Ceylon involving sacred elephants, for instance. The shape of this book was easy to find: he would describe what he had seen. The tone of it, the style—well, there might be a difficulty. There should not of course be the slightest tone of contempt; a light affectionate amusement would be appropriate. He found himself thinking that when the Old Guard read it they would be relieved as to the health of his state of mind.

Abandoning the Reading Room, he found that Carrie was becoming seriously interested in a young man met through her brother. He was one of the best of the new young revolutionaries, brave, forthright, everything a young revolutionary should be. Carrie was in the process of marrying her father? A difficulty was that this young man and Joseph had recently quarreled. They had disagreed so violently over some policy that Joseph had left his particular group, and had formed another. Rosemary thought the real reason for the quarrel was that Joseph resented his sister loving his friend but did not realize it. Jack took his wife to task over this, saying that to discredit socialist action because it had, or might have, psychological springs was one of the oldest of reaction's tricks. But, said Rosemary, every action had a psychological base, didn't it, so why shouldn't one describe what it was? Jack surprised himself by his vehemence in this discussion—it was, in fact, a quarrel. For he believed, with Rosemary, that probably Joseph was reacting emotionally: he had always been jealous of his sisters. Whatever the truth of it was, Carrie was certainly forgetting her "Eastern thing." She was already talking about it as of a youthful and outgrown phase.

Rosemary, in telling Jack this, kept glancing apologetically at him; the last thing she wanted to do, she said, was to disparage any experience which he might be going through himself. Or had gone through.

Had gone through.

There was a conference on the theme of Saving Earth from Man, and he had been afraid he wasn't going to be asked. He was, and Mona rang up to say she would like to go with him. She made some remarks that could be openings to his joining her in a position that combined belief in God with progressive action; he could see that she was willing to lay before him this position, which she had verbalized in detail. He closed that door, hoping it did not sound like a snub. He was again thinking of something called "religion" as an area colored pink or green on a map and in terms of belief in an afterlife like a sweetened dummy for adults. In addition to this, he had two sets of ideas, or feelings, in his mind: one, those he had always held, or held since his early maturity; the other, not so much a set of ideas as a feeling of unease, disquiet, guilt, which amounted to a recognition that he had missed an opportunity of some sort, but that the failure had taken place long before his recent experience. Which he now summarized to himself in Walter's words as: It's a shock when your old man dies. His life had been set in one current, long ago; a fresh current, or at least a different one, had run into it from another source; but, unlike the springs and rivers of myth and fairy tale, it had been muddied and unclear.

He could see that his old friends were particularly delighted to see him at the conference, ready to take an active part. He was on the platform, and he spoke several times, rather well. By the time the conference was over, there was no doubt he was again confirmed as one of the Old Guard, trusted and reliable.

Because of the attention the conference got, he was offered a good job on television, and he nearly took it. But what he needed was to get out of England for a bit. Again Rosemary mentioned Nigeria. Her case was a good one. He would enjoy it, it was work he would do well, he would be contributing valuably. She would enjoy it too, she added loyally. As of course she would, in many ways. After all, it was only for two years, and when she came back it would be easy for her to pick up what she had dropped. And family counselors would still be needed after all! Something that had seemed difficult now seemed easy, not much more than a long trip to Europe. They were making it easy, of course, because of that refusal to look at the consequences of a thing that comes from wanting to leave options open. Spending two years in Africa would change them both, and they did not want to admit that they had become reluctant to change.

On the night after he had formally agreed to go to Nigeria he had the dream again, the worst. If worst was the word?—in this region of himself different laws applied. He was dropping into nothingness, the void: he was fighting his way to a window and there he battered on panes to let in air, and as he hit with his fists and shouted for help the air around him thinned and became exhausted—and he ceased to exist.

He had forgotten how terrible—or how powerful—that dream had been.

He paced his house, wearing the night away. It was too late: he was going to Nigeria because he had not known what else it was he could do.

During that night he could feel his face falling into the lines and folds of his father's face—at the time, that is, when his father had been an elderly rather than an old man. His father's old-man's face had been open and sweet, but before achieving that goodness—like the inn at the end of a road which you have no alternative but to use?—he had had the face of a Roman, heavy-lidded, skeptical, obdurate, facing into the dark: the man whose pride and strength has to come from a conscious ability to suffer, in silence, the journey into negation.

During the days that followed, when the household was all plans and packing and arranging and people running in and out, Jack was thinking that there was only one difference between himself now and himself as he had been before "the bit of a shock." He had once been a man whose sleep had been—nothing, nonexistent, he had slept like a small child. Now, in spite of everything, although he knew that fear could lie in wait there, his sleep had become another country, lying just behind his daytime one. Into that country he went nightly, with an alert, even if ironical, interest—the irony was due to his habits of obedience to his past—for a gift had been made to him. Behind the face of the skeptical world was another, which no conscious decision of his could stop him exploring.

# FROM THE NOVELS

FROM

# *The Grass Is Singing*

MURDER MYSTERY

*By Special Correspondent*

Mary Turner, wife of Richard Turner, a farmer at Ngesi, was found murdered on the front veranda of their homestead yesterday morning. The houseboy, who has been arrested, has confessed to the crime. No motive has been discovered. It is thought he was in search of valuables.

The newspaper did not say much. People all over the country must have glanced at the paragraph with its sensational heading and felt a little spurt of anger mingled with what was almost satisfaction, as if some belief had been confirmed, as if something had happened which could only have been expected. When natives steal, murder, or rape, that is the feeling white people have.

And then they turned the page to something else.

But the people in "the district" who knew the Turners, either by sight, or from gossiping about them for so many years, did not turn the page so quickly. Many must have snipped out the paragraph, put it among old letters, or between the pages of a book, keeping it perhaps as an omen or a warning, glancing at the yellowing piece of paper with closed, secretive faces. For they did not discuss the murder; that was the most extraordinary thing about it. It was as if they had a sixth sense which told them everything there was to be known, although the three people in a position to explain the facts said nothing. The murder was simply not discussed. "A bad business," someone would remark; and the faces of the people round about would put on that reserved and guarded look. "A very bad business," came the reply—and that was the end of it. There was, it seemed, a tacit agreement that the Turner case should not be given undue publicity by gossip. Yet it was a farming district, where those isolated white families met only very occasionally, hungry for contact with their own kind, to talk and discuss and pull to pieces, all speaking at once, making the most of an hour or so's companionship before returning to their farms where they saw only their own faces and the faces of their black servants for weeks on end. Normally that murder would have been discussed for months; people would have been positively grateful for something to talk about.

To an outsider it would seem perhaps as if the energetic Charlie Slatter had traveled from farm to farm over the district telling people to keep quiet; but that was something that would never have occurred to him. The steps he took (and he made not one mistake) were taken apparently instinctively and without conscious planning. The most interesting thing about the whole affair was this silent, unconscious agreement. Everybody behaved like a flock of birds who communicate—or so it seems—by means of a kind of telepathy.

Long before the murder marked them out, people spoke of the Turners in the hard, careless voices reserved for misfits, outlaws, and the self-exiled. The Turners were disliked, though few of their neighbors had ever met them, or even seen them in the distance. Yet what was there to dislike? They simply "kept themselves to themselves"; that was all. They were never seen at district dances, or fetes, or gymkhanas. They must have had something to be ashamed of; that was the feeling. It was not right to seclude themselves like that; it was a slap in the face of everyone else; what had they got to be so stuck-up about? What, indeed! Living the way they did! That little box of a house—it was forgivable as a temporary dwelling, but not to live in permanently. Why, some natives (though not many, thank heavens) had houses as good; and it would give them a bad impression to see white people living in such a way.

And then it was that someone used the phrase "poor whites." It caused disquiet. There was no great money cleavage in those days (that was before the era of the tobacco barons), but there was certainly a race division. The small community of Afrikaners had their own lives, and the Britishers ignored them. "Poor whites" were Afrikaners, never British. But the person who said the Turners were poor whites stuck to it defiantly. What was the difference? What was a poor white? It was the way one lived, a question of standards. All the Turners needed were a drove of children to make them poor whites.

Though the arguments were unanswerable, people would still not think of them as poor whites. To do that would be letting the side down. The Turners were British, after all.

Thus the district handled the Turners—in accordance with that *esprit de corps* which is the first rule of South African society, but which the Turners themselves ignored. They apparently did not recognize the need for *esprit de corps;* that, really, was why they were hated.

The more one thinks about it, the more extraordinary the case becomes. Not the murder itself; but the way people felt about it, the way they pitied Dick Turner with a fine fierce indignation against Mary, as if she were something unpleasant and unclean, and it served her right to get murdered. But they did not ask questions.

For instance, they must have wondered who that "Special Correspondent" was. Someone in the district sent in the news, for the paragraph was not in newspaper language. But who? Marston, the assistant, left the district immediately after the murder. Denham, the policeman, might have written to the paper in a personal capacity, but it was not likely. There remained Charlie Slatter, who knew more about the Turners than anyone else, and was there on the day of the murder. One could say that he practically controlled the handling of the case, even taking precedence over the Sergeant himself. And people felt that to be quite right and proper. Whom should it concern, if not the white farmers, that a silly woman got herself murdered by a native for reasons people might think about, but never, never mentioned? It was their livelihood, their wives and families, their way of living, at stake.

But to the outsider it is strange that Slatter should have been allowed to take charge of the affair, to arrange that everything should pass over without more than a ripple of comment.

For there could have been no planning: there simply wasn't time. Why, for instance, when Dick Turner's farm boys came to him with the news, did he sit down to write a note to the Sergeant at the police camp? He did not use the telephone.

Everyone who has lived in the country knows what a branch telephone is like. You lift the receiver after you have turned the handle the required number of times, and then, click, click, click, you can hear the receivers coming off all over the district, and soft noises like breathing, a whisper, a subdued cough.

Slatter lived five miles from the Turners. The farm boys came to him first, when they discovered the body. And though it was an urgent matter, he ignored the telephone, but sent a personal letter by a native bearer on a bicycle to Denham at the police camp, twelve miles away. The Sergeant sent out half a dozen native policemen at once, to the Turners' farm, to see what they could find. He drove first to see Slatter, because the way that letter was worded roused his curiosity. That was why he arrived late on the scene of the murder. The native policemen did not have to search far for the murderer. After walking through the house, looking briefly at the body, and dispersing down the front of the little hill the house stood on, they saw Moses himself rise out of a tangled ant-heap in front of them. He walked up to them and said (or words to this effect): "Here I am." They snapped the handcuffs on him, and went back to the house to wait for the police cars to come. There they saw Dick Turner come out of the bush by the house with two whining dogs at his heels. He was off his head, talking crazily to himself, wandering in and out of the bush with his hands full of leaves and earth. They let him be, while keeping an eye on him, for he was a white man, though mad, and black men, even when policemen, do not lay hands on white flesh.

People did ask, cursorily, why the murderer had given himself up. There was not much chance of escape, but he did have a sporting chance. He could have run to the hills and hidden for a while. Or he could have slipped over the border to Portuguese territory. Then the District Native Commissioner, at a sundowner party, said that it was perfectly understandable. If one knew anything about the history of the country, or had read any of the memoirs or letters of the old missionaries and explorers, one would have come across accounts of the society Lobengula ruled. The laws were strict: everyone knew what they could or could not do. If someone did an unforgivable thing, like touching one of the King's women, he would submit fatalistically to punishment, which was likely to be impalement over an ant-heap on a stake, or something equally unpleasant. "I have done wrong, and I know it," he might say, "therefore let me be punished." Well, it was the tradition to face punishment, and really there was something rather fine about it. Remarks like these are forgiven from native commissioners, who have to study languages, customs, and so on; although it is not done to say things natives do are "fine." (Yet the fashion is changing: it is permissible to glorify the old ways sometimes, providing one says how depraved the natives have become since.)

So that aspect of the affair was dropped, yet it is not the least interesting, for Moses might not have been a Matabele at all. He was in Mashonaland; though of course natives do wander all over Africa. He might have come from anywhere: Portuguese territory, Nyasaland, the Union of South Africa. And it is a long time since the days of the great king Lobengula. But then native commissioners tend to think in terms of the past.

Well, having sent the letter to the police camp, Charlie Slatter went to the Turners' place, driving at a great speed over the bad farm roads in his fat American car.

Who *was* Charlie Slatter? It was he who, from the beginning of the tragedy to its end, personified Society for the Turners. He touches the story at half a dozen points; without him things would not have happened quite as they did, though sooner or later, in one way or another, the Turners were bound to come to grief.

Slatter had been a grocer's assistant in London. He was fond of telling his children that if it had not been for his energy and enterprise they would be running round the slums in rags. He was still a proper cockney, even after twenty years in Africa. He came with one idea: to make money. He made it. He made plenty. He was a crude, brutal, ruthless, yet kindhearted man, in his own way, and according to his own impulses, who could not help making money. He farmed as if he were turning the handle of a machine which would produce pound notes at the other end. He was hard with his wife, making her bear unnecessary hardships at the beginning; he was hard with his children, until he made money, when they got everything they wanted; and above all he was hard with his farm laborers. They, the geese that laid the golden eggs, were still in that state where they did not know there were other ways of living besides producing gold for other people.

They know better now, or are beginning to. But Slatter believed in farming with the sjambok. It hung over his front door, like a motto on a wall: "You shall not mind killing if it is necessary." He had once killed a native in a fit of temper. He was fined thirty pounds. Since then he had kept his temper. But sjamboks are all very well for the Slatters; not so good for people less sure of themselves. It was he who had told Dick Turner, long ago, when Dick first started farming, that one should buy a sjambok before a plow or a harrow, and that sjambok did not do the Turners any good, as we shall see.

Slatter was a shortish, broad, powerful man, with heavy shoulders and thick arms. His face was broad and bristled; shrewd, watchful, and a little cunning. He had a crop of fair hair that made him look like a convict; but he did not care for appearances. His small blue eyes were hardly visible, because of the way he screwed them up, after years and years of South African sunshine.

Bent over the steering wheel, almost hugging it in his determination to get to the Turners quickly, his eyes were little blue chinks in a set face. He was wondering why Marston, the assistant, who was after all his employee, had not come to him about the murder, or at least sent a note. Where was he? The hut he lived in was only a couple of hundred yards from the house itself. Perhaps he had got cold feet and run away.

Anything was possible, thought Charlie, from this particular type of young Englishman. He had a rooted contempt for soft-faced, soft-voiced Englishmen, combined with a fascination for their manner and breeding. His own sons, now grown up, were gentlemen. He had spent plenty of money to make them so; but he despised them for it. At the same time he was proud of them. This conflict showed itself in its attitude towards Marston: half hard and indifferent, half subtly deferential. At the moment he felt nothing but irritation.

Halfway he felt the car rock, and swearing, pulled it up. It was a puncture: no, two punctures. The red mud of the road held fragments of broken glass. His irritation expressed itself in the half-conscious thought, "Just like Turner to have glass on his roads!" But Turner was now necessarily an object of passionate, protective pity, and the irritation was focused on Marston, the assistant who, Slatter felt, should somehow have prevented this murder. What was he being paid for? What had he been engaged for? But Slatter was a fair man in his own way, and where his own race was concerned. He restrained himself, and got down to mending one puncture and changing a tire, working in the heavy red slush of the roads. This took him three-quarters of an hour, and by the time he was finished, and had picked the pieces of green glass from the mud and thrown them into the bush, the sweat was soaking his face and hair.

When he reached the house at last, he saw, as he approached through the bush, six glittering bicycles leaning against the walls. And in front of the house, under the trees, stood six native policemen, and among them the native Moses, his hands linked in front of him. The sun glinted on the handcuffs, on the bicycles, on the masses of heavy wet leaves. It was a wet, sultry morning. The sky was a tumult of discolored clouds: it looked full of billowing dirty washing. Puddles on the pale soil held a sheen of sky.

Charlie walked up to the policemen, who saluted him. They were in fezzes, and their rather fancy-dress uniform. This last thought did not occur to Charlie, who liked his natives either one way or the other: properly dressed according to their station, or in loincloths. He could not bear the half-civilized native. The policemen, picked for their physique, were a fine body of men, but they were put in the shade by Moses, who was a great powerful man, black as polished linoleum, and dressed in a singlet and shorts, which were damp and muddy. Charlie stood directly in front of the murderer and looked into his face. The man stared back, expressionless, indifferent. His own face was curious: it showed a kind of triumph, a guarded vindictiveness, and fear. Why fear? Of Moses, who was as good as hanged already? But he was uneasy, troubled. Then he seemed to shake himself into self-command, and turned and saw Dick Turner, standing a few paces away, covered with mud.

"Turner!" he said, peremptorily. He stopped, looking into the man's face. Dick appeared not to know him. Charlie took him by the arm and drew him towards his own car. He did not know he was incurably mad then; otherwise he might have been even more angry than he was. Having put Dick into the back seat of his car, he went into the house. In the front room stood Marston, his hands in his pockets, in a pose that seemed negligently calm. But his face was pale and strained.

"Where were you?" asked Charlie at once, accusingly.

"Normally Mr. Turner wakes me," said the youth calmly. "This morning I slept late. When I came into the house I found Mrs. Turner on the veranda. Then the policemen came. I was expecting you." But he was afraid: it was the fear of death that sounded in his voice, not the fear that was controlling Charlie's actions: he had not been long enough in the country to understand Charlie's special fear.

Charlie grunted: he never spoke unless necessary. He looked long and curiously at Marston, as if trying to make out why it was the farm natives had not called a man who lay asleep a few yards off, but had instinctively sent for himself. But it was not with dislike or contempt he looked at Marston now; it was more the look a man gives a prospective partner who has yet to prove himself.

He turned and went into the bedroom. Mary Turner was a stiff shape under a soiled white sheet. At one end of the sheet protruded a mass of pale strawish hair, and at the other a crinkled yellow foot. Now a curious thing happened. The hate and contempt that one would have expected to show on his face when he looked at the murderer, twisted his features now, as he stared at Mary. His brows knotted, and for a few seconds his lips curled back over his teeth in a vicious grimace. He had his back to Marston, who would have been astonished to see him. Then, with a hard, angry movement, Charlie turned and left the room, driving the young man before him.

Marston said: "She was lying on the veranda. I lifted her on the bed." He shuddered at the memory of the touch of the cold body. "I thought she shouldn't be left lying there." He hesitated and added, the muscles of his face contracting whitely: "The dogs were licking at her."

Charlie nodded, with a keen glance at him. He seemed indifferent as to where she might be lying. At the same time he approved the self-control of the assistant who had performed the unpleasant task.

"There was blood everywhere. I cleaned it up . . . I thought afterwards I should have left it for the police."

"It makes no odds," said Charlie absently. He sat down on one of the rough wood chairs in the front room, and remained in thought, whistling softly through his front teeth. Marston stood by the window, looking for the arrival of the police car. From time to time Charlie looked round the room alertly, flicking his tongue over his lips. Then he lapsed back into his soft whistling. It got on the young man's nerves.

At last, cautiously, almost warningly, Charlie said: "What do *you* know of this?"

Marston noted the emphasized *you*, and wondered what Slatter knew. He was well in control of himself, but as taut as wire. He said, "I don't know. Nothing really. It is all so difficult . . ." He hesitated, looking appealingly at Charlie.

That look of almost soft appeal irritated Charlie, coming from a man, but it pleased him too: he was pleased the youth deferred to him. He knew the type so well. So many of them came from England to learn farming. They were usually ex-public school, very English, but extremely adaptable. From Charlie's point of view, the adaptability redeemed them. It was strange to see how quickly they accustomed themselves. At first they were diffident, though proud and withdrawn; cautiously learning the new ways, with a fine sensitiveness, an alert self-consciousness.

When old settlers say "One had to understand the country," what they mean is, "You have to get used to our ideas about the native." They are saying, in effect, "Learn our ideas, or otherwise get out: we don't want you." Most of these young men were brought up with vague ideas about equality. They were shocked, for the first week or so, by the way natives were treated. They were revolted a hundred times a day by the casual way they were spoken of, as if they were so many cattle; or by a blow, or a look. They had been prepared to treat them as human beings. But they could not stand out against the society they were joining. It did not take them long to change. It was hard, of course, becoming as bad oneself. But it was not very long that they thought of it as "bad." And anyway, what had one's ideas amounted to? Abstract ideas about decency and goodwill, that was all: merely abstract ideas. When it came to the point, one never had contact with natives, except in the master-servant relationship. One never knew them in their own lives, as human beings. A few months, and these sensitive, decent young men had coarsened to suit the hard, arid, sun-drenched country they had come to; they had grown a new manner to match their thickened sunburned limbs and toughened bodies.

If Tony Marston had been even a few more months in the country it would have been easy. That was Charlie's feeling. That was why he looked at the young man with a speculative frowning look, not condemning him, only wary and on the alert.

He said: "What do you mean, it is all so difficult?"

Tony Marston appeared uncomfortable, as if he did not know his own mind. And for that matter he did not: the weeks in the Turners' household with its atmosphere of tragedy had not helped him to get his mind clear. The two standards—the one he had brought with him and the one he was adopting—conflicted still. And there was a roughness, a warning note, in Charlie's voice, that left him wondering. What was he being warned against? He was intelligent enough to know he was being warned. In this he was unlike Charlie, who was acting by instinct and did not know his voice was a threat. It was all so unusual. Where were the police? What right had Charlie, who was a neighbor, to be fetched before himself, who was practically a member of the household? Why was Charlie quietly taking command?

His ideas of right were upset. He was confused, but he had his own ideas about the murder, which could not be stated straight out, like that, in black and white. When he came to think of it, the murder was logical enough; looking back over the last few days he could see that something like this was bound to happen, he could almost say he had been expecting it, some kind of violence or ugliness. Anger, violence, death, seemed natural to this vast, harsh country . . . he had done a lot of thinking since he had strolled casually into the house that morning, wondering why everyone was so late, to find Mary Turner lying murdered on the veranda, and the police boys outside, guarding the houseboy; and Dick Turner muttering and stumbling through the puddles, mad, but apparently harmless. Things he had not understood, he understood now, and he was ready to talk about them. But he was in the dark as to Charlie's attitude. There was something here he could not get hold of.

"It's like this," he said, "when I first arrived I didn't know much about the country."

Charlie said, with a good-humored but brutal irony, "Thanks for the information." And then, "Have you any idea why this nigger murdered Mrs. Turner?"

"Well, I have a sort of idea, yes."

"We had better leave it to the Sergeant, when he comes then."

It was a snub; he had been shut up. Tony held his tongue, angry but bewildered.

When the Sergeant came, he went over to look at the murderer, glanced at Dick through the window of Slatter's car, and then came into the house.

"I went to your place, Slatter," he said, nodding at Tony, giving him a keen look. Then he went into the bedroom. And his reactions were as Charlie's had been: vindictiveness towards the murderer, emotional pity for Dick, and for Mary, a bitter contemptuous anger: Sergeant Denham had been in the country for a number of years. This time Tony saw the expression on the face, and it gave him a shock. The faces of the two men as they stood over the body, gazing down at it, made him feel uneasy, even afraid. He himself felt a little disgust, but not much; it was mainly pity that agitated him, knowing what he knew. It was the disgust that he would feel for any social irregularity, no more than the distaste that comes from failure of the imagination. This profound instinctive horror and fear astonished him.

The three of them went silently into the living room.

Charlie Slatter and Sergeant Denham stood side by side like two judges, as if they had purposely taken up this attitude. Opposite them was Tony. He stood his ground, but he felt an absurd guiltiness taking hold of him, simply because of their pose, standing like that, looking at him with subtle reserved faces that he could not read.

"Bad business," said Sergeant Denham briefly.

No one answered. He snapped open a notebook, adjusted elastic over a page, and poised a pencil.

"A few questions, if you don't mind," he said. Tony nodded.

"How long have you been here?"

"About three weeks."

"Living in this house?"

"No, in a hut down the path."

"You were going to run this place while they were away?"

"Yes, for six months."

"And then?"

"And then I intended to go on a tobacco farm."

"When did you know about this business?"

"They didn't call me. I woke and found Mrs. Turner."

Tony's voice showed he was now on the defensive. He felt wounded, even insulted that he had not been called: above all, that these two men seemed to think it right and natural that he should be bypassed in this fashion, as if his newness to the country unfitted him for any kind of responsibility. And he resented the way he was being questioned. They had no right to do it. He was beginning to simmer with rage, although he knew quite well that they themselves were quite unconscious of the patronage implicit in their manner, and that it would be better for him to try and understand the real meaning of this scene, rather than to stand on his dignity.

"You had your meals with the Turners?"

"Yes."

"Apart from that, were you ever here—socially, so to speak?"

"No, hardly at all. I have been busy learning the job."

"Get on well with Turner?"

"Yes, I think so. I mean, he was not easy to know. He was absorbed in his work. And he was obviously very unhappy at leaving the place."

"Yes, poor devil, he had a hard time of it." The voice was suddenly tender, almost maudlin, with pity, although the Sergeant snapped out the words, and then shut his mouth tight, as if to present a brave face to the world. Tony was disconcerted: the unexpectedness of these men's responses was taking him right out of his depth. He was feeling nothing that they were feeling: he was an outsider in this tragedy, although both the Sergeant and Charlie Slatter seemed to feel personally implicated, for they had unconsciously assumed poses of weary dignity, appearing bowed down with unutterable burdens, because of poor Dick Turner and his sufferings.

Yet it was Charlie who had literally turned Dick off his farm; and in previous interviews, at which Tony had been present, he had shown none of this sentimental pity.

There was a long pause. The Sergeant shut his notebook. But he had not yet finished. He was regarding Tony cautiously, wondering how to frame the next question. Or that was how it appeared to Tony, who could see that here was the moment that was the crux of the whole affair. Charlie's face: wary, a little cunning, a little afraid, proclaimed it.

"See anything out of the ordinary while you were here?" asked the Sergeant, apparently casual.

"Yes, I did," blurted Tony, suddenly determined not to be bullied. For he knew he was being bullied, though he was cut off from them both by a gulf in experience and belief. They looked up at him, frowning; glanced at each other swiftly—then away, as if afraid to acknowledge conspiracy.

"What did you see? I hope you realize the—unpleasantness—of this case?" The last question was a grudging appeal.

"Any murder is surely unpleasant," remarked Tony dryly.

"When you have been in the country long enough, you will understand that we don't like niggers murdering white women."

The phrase "When you have been in the country," stuck in Tony's gullet. He had heard it too often, and it had come to jar on him. At the same time it made him feel angry. Also callow. He would have liked to blurt out the truth in one overwhelming, incontrovertible statement; but the truth was not like that. It never was. The fact he knew, or guessed, about Mary, the fact these two men were conspiring to ignore, could be stated easily enough. But the important thing, the thing that really mattered, so it seemed to him, was to understand the background, the circumstances, the characters of Dick and Mary, the pattern of their lives. And it was not so easy to do. He had arrived at the truth circuitously: circuitously it would have to be explained. And his chief emotion, which was an impersonal pity for Mary and Dick and the native, a pity that was also rage against circumstances, made it difficult for him to know where to begin.

"Look," he said, "I'll tell you what I know from the beginning, only it will take some time, I am afraid. . . ."

"You mean you know why Mrs. Turner was murdered?" The question was a quick, shrewd parry.

"No, not just like that. Only I can form a theory." The choice of words was most unfortunate.

"We don't want theories. We want facts. And in any case, you should remember Dick Turner. This is all most unpleasant for him. You should remember him, poor devil."

Here it was again: the utterly illogical appeal, which to these two men was clearly not illogical at all. The whole thing was preposterous! Tony began to lose his temper.

"Do you or do you not want to hear what I have to say?" he asked, irritably.

"Go ahead. Only remember, I don't want to hear your fancies. I want to hear facts. Have you ever seen anything *definite* which would throw light on this murder. For instance, have you seen this boy attempting to get at her jewelry, or something like that. Anything that is definite. Not something in the air."

Tony laughed. The two men looked at him sharply.

"You know as well as I do this case is not something that can be explained straight off like that. You know that. It's not something that can be said in black and white, straight off."

It was pure deadlock; no one spoke. As if Sergeant Denham had not heard those last words, a heavy frown on his face, he said at last: "For instance, how did Mrs. Turner treat this boy? Did she treat her boys well?"

The angry Tony, fumbling for a foothold in this welter of emotion and half-understood loyalties, clutched at this for a beginning.

"Yes, she treated him badly, I thought. Though on the other hand . . ."

"Nagged at him, eh? Oh well, women are pretty bad that way, in this country, very often. Aren't they, Slatter?" The voice was easy, intimate, informal. "My old woman drives me mad—it's something about this country. They have no idea how to deal with niggers."

"Needs a man to deal with niggers," said Charlie. "Niggers don't understand women giving them orders. They keep their own women in their right place." He laughed. The Sergeant laughed. They turned towards each other, even including Tony, in an unmistakable relief. The tension had broken; the danger was over: once again, he had been bypassed, and the interview, it seemed, was over. He could hardly believe it.

"But look here," he said. Then he stopped. Both men turned to look at him, a steady, grave, irritated look on their faces. And the warning was unmistakable! It was the warning that might have been given to a greenhorn who was going to let *himself* down by saying too much. This realization was too much for Tony. He gave in; he washed his hands of it. He watched the other two in utter astonishment: they were together in mood and emotion, standing there in perfect understanding; the understanding was unrealized by themselves, the sympathy unacknowledged; their concerted handling of this affair had been instinctive: they were completely unaware of there being anything extraordinary, even anything illegal. And was there anything illegal, after all? This was a casual talk, on the face of it, nothing formal about it now that the notebook was shut—and it had been shut ever since they had reached the crisis of the scene.

Charlie said, turning towards the Sergeant, "Better get her out of here. It is too hot to wait."

"Yes," said the policeman, moving to give orders accordingly.

And that brutally matter-of-fact remark, Tony realized afterwards, was the only time poor Mary Turner was referred to directly. But why should she be?—except that this was really a friendly talk between the farmer who had been her next neighbor, the policeman who had been in her house on his rounds as a guest, and the assistant who had lived there for some weeks. It wasn't a formal occasion, this: Tony clung to the thought. There was a court case to come yet, which would be properly conducted.

"The case will be a matter of form, of course," said the Sergeant, as if thinking aloud, with a look at Tony. He was standing by the police car, watching the native policemen lift the body of Mary Turner, which was wrapped in a blanket, into the back seat. She was stiff; a rigid outstretched arm knocked horribly against the narrow door; it was difficult to get her in. At last it was done and the door shut. And then there was another problem: they could not put Moses the murderer into the same car with her; one could not put a black man close to a white woman, even though she were dead, and murdered by him. And there was only Charlie's car, and mad Dick Turner was in that, sitting staring in the back. There seemed to be a feeling that Moses, having committed a murder, deserved to be taken by car; but there was no help for it, he would have to walk, guarded by the policemen, wheeling their bicycles, to the camp.

All these arrangements completed, there was a pause.

They stood there beside the cars, in the moment of parting, looking at the red-brick house with its shimmering hot roof, and the thick encroaching bush, and the group of black men moving off under the trees on their long walk. Moses was quite impassive, allowing himself to be directed without any movement of his own. His face was blank. He seemed to be staring straight into the sun. Was he thinking he would not see it much longer? Impossible to say. Regret? Not a sign of it. Fear? It did not seem so. The three men looked at the murderer, thinking their own thoughts, speculative, frowning, but not as if he were important now. No, he was unimportant: he was the constant, the black man who will thieve, rape, murder, if given half a chance. Even for Tony he no longer mattered; and his knowledge of the native mind was too small to give him any basis for conjecture.

"And what about him?" asked Charlie, jerking his thumb at Dick Turner. He meant: where does he come in, as far as the court case is concerned?

"He looks to me as if he won't be good for much," said the Sergeant, who after all had plenty of experience of death, crime, and madness.

No, for them the important thing was Mary Turner, who had let the side down; but even she, since she was dead, was no longer a problem. The one fact that remained still to be dealt with was the necessity for preserving appearances. Sergeant Denham understood that: it was part of his job, though it would not appear in regulations, was rather implicit in the spirit of the country, the spirit in which he was soaked. Charlie Slatter understood it, none better. Still side by side, as if one impulse, one regret, one fear, moved them both, they stood together in that last moment before they left the place, giving their final silent warning to Tony, looking at him gravely.

And he was beginning to understand. He knew now, at least, that what had been fought out in the room they had just left was nothing to do with the murder as such. The murder, in itself, was nothing. The struggle that had been decided in a few brief words—or rather, in the silences between the words—had had nothing to do with the surface meaning of the scene. He would understand it all a good deal better in a few months, when he had "become used to the country." And then he would do his best to forget the knowledge, for to live with the color bar in all its nuances and implications means closing one's mind to many things, if one intends to remain an accepted member of society. But, in the interval, there would be a few brief moments when he would see the thing clearly, and understand that it was "white civilization" fighting to defend itself that had been implicit in the attitude of Charlie Slatter and the Sergeant, "white civilization" which will never, never admit that a white person, and most particularly a white woman, can have a human relationship, whether for good or for evil, with a black person. For once it admits that, it crashes, and nothing can save it. So, above all, it cannot afford failures, such as the Turners' failure.

For the sake of those few lucid moments, and his present half-confused knowledge, it can be said that Tony was the person present who had the greatest responsibility that day. For it would never have occurred to either Slatter or the Sergeant that they might be wrong: they were upheld, as in all their dealings with the black-white relationship, by a feeling of almost martyred responsibility. Yet Tony, too, wanted to be accepted by this new country. He would have to adapt himself, and if he did not conform, would be rejected: the issue was clear to him, he had heard the phrase "getting used to our ideas" too often to have any illusions on the point. And, if he had acted according to his by now muddled ideas of right and wrong, his feeling that a monstrous injustice was being done, what difference would it make to the only participant in the tragedy who was neither dead nor mad? For Moses would be hanged in any case; he had committed a murder, that fact remained. Did he intend to go on fighting in the dark for the sake of a principle? And if so, which principle?

If he had stepped forward then, as he nearly did, when Sergeant Denham climbed finally into the car, and had said: "Look here, I am just not going to shut up about this," what would have been gained? It is certain that the Sergeant would not have understood him. His face would have contracted, his brow gone dark with irritation, and, taking his foot off the clutch, he would have said, "Shut up about what? Who has asked you to shut up?" And then, if Tony had stammered out something about responsibility, he would have looked significantly at Charlie and shrugged. Tony might have continued, ignoring the shrug and its implication of his wrongmindedness: "If you must blame somebody, then blame Mrs. Turner. You can't have it both ways. Either the white people are responsible for their behavior, or they are not. It takes two to make a murder—a murder of this kind. Though, one can't really blame her either. She can't help being what she is. I've lived here, I tell you, which neither of you has done, and the whole thing is so difficult it is impossible to say who is to blame." And then the Sergeant would have said, "You can say what you think right in court." That is what he would have said, just as if the issue had not been decided—though ostensibly it had never been mentioned—less than ten minutes before. "It's not a question of blame," the Sergeant might have said. "Has anyone said anything about blame? But you can't get away from the fact that this nigger has murdered her, can you?"

So Tony said nothing, and the police car went off through the trees. Charlie Slatter followed in his car with Dick Turner. Tony was left in the empty clearing, with an empty house.

He went inside, slowly, obsessed with the one clear image that remained to him after the events of the morning, and which seemed to him the key to the whole thing: the look on the Sergeant's and Slatter's faces when they looked down at the body; that almost hysterical look of hate and fear.

He sat down, his hand to his head, which ached badly; then got up again and fetched from a dusty shelf in the kitchen a medicine bottle marked "Brandy." He drank it off. He felt shaky in the knees and in the thighs. He was weak, too, with repugnance against this ugly little house which seemed to hold within its walls, even in its very brick and cement, the fears and horror of the murder. He felt suddenly as if he could not bear to stay in it, not for another moment.

He looked up at the bare crackling tin of the roof, that was warped with the sun, at the faded gimcrack furniture, at the dusty brick floors covered with ragged animal skins, and wondered how those two, Mary and Dick Turner, could have borne to live in such a place, year in and year out, for so long. Why even the little thatched hut where he lived at the back was better than this! Why did they go on without even so much as putting in ceilings? It was enough to drive anyone mad, the heat in this place.

And then, feeling a little muddle headed (the heat made the brandy take effect at once), he wondered how all this had begun, where the tragedy had started. For he clung obstinately to the belief, in spite of Slatter and the Sergeant, that the causes of the murder must be looked for a long way back, and that it was they which were important. What sort of woman had Mary Turner been, before she came to this farm and had been driven slowly off balance by heat and loneliness and poverty? And Dick Turner himself—what had he been? And the native—but here his thoughts were stopped by lack of knowledge. He could not even begin to imagine the mind of a native.

Passing his hand over his forehead, he tried desperately, and for the last time, to achieve some sort of a vision that would lift the murder above the confusions and complexities of the morning, and make of it, perhaps, a symbol, or a warning. But he failed. It was too hot. He was still exasperated by the attitude of the two men. His head was reeling. It must be over a hundred in this room, he thought angrily, getting up from his chair, and finding that his legs were unsteady. And he had drunk, at the most, two tablespoons of brandy! This damned country, he thought, convulsed with anger. Why should this happen to me, getting involved with a damned twisted affair like this, when I have only just come; and I really can't be expected to act as judge and jury and compassionate God into the bargain!

He stumbled onto the veranda, where the murder had been committed the night before. There was a ruddy smear on the brick, and a puddle of rainwater was tinged pink. The same big shabby dogs were licking at the edges of the water, and cringed away when Tony shouted at them. He leaned against the wall and stared over the soaked greens and browns of the veld to the kopjes, which were sharp and blue after the rain; it had poured half the night. He realized, as the sound grew loud in his ears, that cicadas were shrilling all about him. He had been too absorbed to hear them. It was a steady, insistent screaming from every bush and tree. It wore on his nerves. "I am getting out of this place," he said suddenly. "I am getting out of it altogether. I am going to the other end of the country. I wash my hands of the thing. Let the Slatters and the Denhams do as they like. What has it got to do with me?"

That morning, he packed his things and walked over to the Slatters' to tell Charlie he would not stay. Charlie seemed indifferent, even relieved; he had been thinking there was no need for a manager now that Dick would not come back.

After that the Turners' farm was run as an overflow for Charlie's cattle. They grazed all over it, even up to the hill where the house stood. It was left empty: it soon fell down.

Tony went back into town, where he hung round the bars and hotels for a while, waiting to hear of some job that would suit him. But his early carefree adaptability was gone. He had grown difficult to please. He visited several farms, but each time went away: farming had lost its glitter for him. At the trial, which was, as Sergeant Denham had said it would be, a mere formality, he said what was expected of him. It was suggested that the native had murdered Mary Turner while drunk, in search of money and jewelry.

When the trial was over, Tony loafed about aimlessly until his money was finished. The murder, those few weeks with the Turners, had affected him more than he knew. But his money being gone, he had to do something in order to eat. He met a man from Northern Rhodesia, who told him about the copper mines and the wonderfully high salaries. They sounded fantastic to Tony. He took the next train to the copper belt, intending to save some money and start some business on his own account. But the salaries, once there, did not seem so good as they had from a distance. The cost of living was high, and then, everyone drank so much. . . . Soon he left underground work and was a kind of manager. So, in the end, he sat in an office and did paperwork, which was what he had come to Africa to avoid. But it wasn't so bad really. One should take things as they came. Life isn't as one expects it to be—and so on; these were the things he said to himself when depressed, and was measuring himself against his early ambitions.

For the people in "the district," who knew all about him by hearsay, he was the young man from England who hadn't the guts to stand more than a few weeks of farming. No guts, they said. He should have stuck it out.

FROM

# *Martha Quest*

Early in her sixteenth year, Martha was expected to pass the matric—it goes without saying, quite brilliantly. She did not even sit the examination; and it was not the first time she had withdrawn from a situation through circumstances which it occurred to no one, particularly Martha herself, to call anything but bad luck. At eleven, for instance, there had been just such a vital examination, and she had become ill the week before. She was supposed to be exceptionally musical, but by some fatality was always prevented from proving it by gaining the right number of marks. She was prepared for confirmation three times, and in the end the whole thing was allowed to drop, for it appeared that in the meantime she had become an agnostic. And now here was this important examination. For months Mrs. Quest was talking about university and scholarships, while Martha listened, sometimes eagerly, but more often writhing with embarrassment. A week before the vital date, Martha got pink eye, which happened to be raging through the school. Not a very serious affliction, but in this case it appeared Martha's eyes were weakened.

It was October, the month of heat and flowers, and dust and tension. October: the little town where Martha was at school was hung with flowers, as for a festival. Every street was banked with purple-blooming trees, the jacarandas held their airy clouds of blossom over every sidewalk and garden; and beneath them blew, like a descant, the pale pink-and-white bauhinias; and behind, like a deep note from the trumpet, the occasional splash of screaming magenta where a bougainvillea unloaded its weight of color down a wall. Color and light: the town was bombarded by light, the heat beat down from a whitish sky, beat up from the grey and glittering streets, hung over the roofs in shimmering waves. The greens of the foliage were deep and solid and shining, but filmed with dust, like neglected water where debris gathers. As one walked past a tree, the light shifted glittering from facet to facet of a branch or leaf. How terrible October is! Terrible because so beautiful, and the beauty springs from the loaded heat, the dust, the tension; for everyone watches the sky, and the heavy trees along the avenues, and the sullen clouds, while for weeks nothing happens; the wind lifts an eddy of dust at a street corner, and subsides, exhausted. One cannot remember the smell of the flowers without the smell of dust and petrol; one cannot remember that triumphant orchestra of color without the angry, white-hot sky. One cannot remember . . . Afterwards Martha remembered that her eyes had ached badly, then they closed and festered, and she lay in half-darkness making jokes about her condition because she was so afraid of going blind. She was even more afraid of her fear, because nothing could have been more absurd, since half the girls in the school were similarly afflicted. It was merely a question of waiting until her eyes grew better. She could not bear to lie in bed and wait, so she pestered the nurse until she could sit on a veranda, screened by a thick curtain of golden shower from the street, because she could assure herself she was not blind by looking through her glowing eyelids at the light from the sky. She sat there all day, and felt the waves of heat and perfume break across her in shock after shock of shuddering nostalgia. But nostalgia for what? She sat and sniffed painfully at the weighted air, as if it were dealing her blows like an invisible enemy. Also, there was the examination to be taken; she always relied on intensive study during the last fortnight before an examination, for she was the kind of person with a memory that holds anything, almost photographically, for about a month; afterwards what she had learned disappeared as if she had never known it. Therefore, if she took an examination, she would probably pass, but in a mediocre way.

Mrs. Quest was told that her daughter had pink eye. Then she got a letter from Martha, a very hysterical letter; then another, this time flat and laconic. Mrs. Quest went into town, and took her daughter to an oculist, who tested her and said there was nothing wrong with the eyes. Mrs. Quest was very angry, and took her to another oculist; the anger was the same as that she directed towards those doctors who did not immediately accept her diagnosis of her husband's condition. The second oculist was patient and ironical and agreed to everything Mrs. Quest said.

Curious that Mrs. Quest, whose will for years had been directed towards Martha distinguishing herself—curious that she should accept those damaged eyes so easily, even insist that they were permanently injured when Martha began to vacillate. For as soon as Mrs. Quest arrived in town and took the situation in hand, Martha found herself swept along in a way she had not foreseen. If one can use the word "see" in connection with anything so confused and contradictory. The end of it was that Martha went back to the farm—"to rest her eyes," as Mrs. Quest explained to the neighbors, with a queer pride in the thing which made Martha uneasy.

So here was Martha at home, "resting her eyes" but reading as much as ever. And how curious were the arguments between the two women over this illogical behavior. For Mrs. Quest did not say, "You are supposed to have strained your eyes, why are you reading?" She made remarks such as "You do it on purpose to upset me!" Or "Why do you have to read that kind of book?" Or "You are ruining your whole life, and you won't take my advice." Martha maintained a stubborn but ironical silence, and continued to read.

So here was Martha, at sixteen, idle and bored, and sometimes secretly wondering (though only for a moment, the thought always vanished at once) why she had not sat that examination, which she could have passed with such ease. For she had gone up the school head of her class, without even having to work. But these thoughts could not be clearly faced, so she shut them out. But why was she condemning herself to live on this farm, which more than anything in the world she wanted to leave? The matric was a simple passport to the outside world, while without it escape seemed so difficult she was having terrible nightmares of being tied hand and foot under the wheels of a locomotive, or struggling waist-deep in quicksands, or eternally climbing a staircase that moved backwards under her. She felt as if some kind of spell had been put on her.

Then Mrs. Quest began saying that Marnie had just passed the matric, and she said unpleasantly: Look, if she can pass it, why not you?

Martha did not want to see Marnie, and it was easy to avoid doing so, for the Van Rensbergs and the Quests were drifting apart. It was more than one of the inexplicable changes of feeling between neighbors; there was a good reason for it. Mr. Van Rensberg was becoming violently nationalist, and Mrs. Van Rensberg had an apologetic look on her face when she saw Mrs. Quest at the station. And so, by a natural reaction, the Quests began saying, "These damned Afrikaners," although the two families had been friends, shelving the question of nationality for so many years.

Martha did not want to think of these things, she was turned in on herself, in a heavy trancelike state. Afterwards she was to think of this time as the worst in her life. What was so frightening was this feeling of being dragged, being weighted. She did not understand why she was acting against her will, her intellect, everything she believed. It was as if her body and brain were numbed.

There was nothing to do. The farm lay about her like a loved country which refused her citizenship. She repeated the incantatory names of childhood like a spell which had lost its force. The Twenty Acres, the Big Tobacco Land, the Field on the Ridge, the Hundred Acres, the Kaffir Patch, the Bush by the Fence, the Pumpkin Patch—these words became words; and, walking by herself across the Twenty Acres, which was bounded on three sides by a straggle of gum trees (a memory of her father's afforestation phase), a patch of sloping land tinted pink and yellow, full of quartz reefs and loose white pebbles, she said to herself scornfully, Why Twenty Acres? It's about twelve acres. Why the Hundred Acres, when it is only seventy-six? Why has this family always given large-sounding names to things ordinary and even shabby? For everything had shrunk for her. The house showed as if an unkind light had been shone on it. It was not only shabby, it was sordid. Everything decayed and declined, and leaned inwards.

And, worse, far worse, she was watching her father with horror, for he was coming to have, for her, the fatal lethargy of a dream-locked figure. He had the look of a person half claimed by sleep. He was middle-aged, she told herself, neither young nor old; he was in the long middle period of life when people do not change, but his changelessness was imposed, not by a resisting vigor but by—what? He was rising late in the morning, he dreamed over breakfast, wandered off into the bedroom to test himself for his real disease and for various imaginary ones; returned early from the farmwork to lunch, slept after it, and for a longer time every day, and then sat immobile in his deck chair, waiting for the sunset. After it, supper—a calculatedly healthy meal—and an early bed. Sleep, sleep, the house was saturated by it; and Mrs. Quest's voice murmured like the spells of a witch, "You must be tired, darling; don't overtire yourself, dear." And when these remarks were directed at Martha, she felt herself claimed by the nightmare, as if she were standing beside her father; and, in fact, at the word "tired" she felt herself tired, and had to shake herself.

"I will *not* be tired," she snapped to her mother, "it's no good trying to make me tired": extraordinary words; and even more extraordinary that Mrs. Quest did not question them. Her face fell in patient and sorrowful lines, the eternal mother, holding sleep and death in her twin hands like a sweet and poisonous cloud of forgetfulness—that was how Martha saw her, like a baneful figure in the nightmare in which she herself was caught.

But sometimes their arguments were more sensible."You are terribly unfair to your father," Mrs. Quest complained. "He's ill, he's really ill."

"I know he's ill," said Martha, miserably, feeling guilty. Then she roused herself to say, "Look at Mr. Blank, he's got it, too, he's quite different." Mr. Blank, over the other side of the district, had the same disease, and much more seriously than Mr. Quest, and led an active life, as if this business of injecting oneself with substitute gland juices once a day was on the same level as cleaning one's teeth or making a point of eating fruit for breakfast. But Mr. Quest was completely absorbed in the ritual of being ill, he talked of nothing else—his illness and the war, the war and illness; it was as if a twin channel drove across his brain, and if his thoughts switched from one subject, they must enter the other, like a double track leading to the same destination.

It even seemed to Martha that her father was pleased that the Van Rensbergs no longer visited them, because with Mr. Van Rensberg he talked about the farm, while with Mr. McDougall, who took his place, he shared memories of the trenches.

Martha, coming down the veranda, a silent and critical figure, would see her father at one end, leaning back in his deck chair like a contemplative philosopher, and hear his voice: "We were out in no-man's-land, six of us, when the star shells went up, and we saw we weren't three paces from the Boche trenches and . . ."

At the other end of the veranda, Mrs. Quest was talking to Mrs. McDougall: "That's when we got the wounded in from Gallipoli and . . ."

Martha listened, absorbed in these twin litanies of suffering in spite of herself, for they had been murmuring down her childhood as far back as she could remember, and were twined with her deepest self. She was watching, fearfully, the effect on herself of the poetry of suffering; the words "no-man's-land," "star shells," "Boche," touched off in her images like those of poetry; no man's land was the black and wasted desert between the living forces; star shells exploded in colored lights, like fireworks, across her brain, drenched in reminiscence; Boche was fearful and gigantic, nothing human, a night figure; the tripping word "Gallipoli" was like a heroic dance. She was afraid because of the power of these words, which affected her so strongly, who had nothing to do with what they stood for.

On one such afternoon, when she was standing on the steps, listening, her father called out to her, "Matty, did I ever tell you about—" and she said ungraciously, but with discomfort, "Quite a thousand times, I should think."

He jerked up his head and stared at her, and onto his face came that look of baffled anger. "It's all very well for you," he said. "We came out of the trenches, and then suddenly the war was bad form. The Great Unmentionable, that's what you called it."

"*I* didn't call it anything," she remarked at last, sullenly humorous.

She moved away, but he called after her, "All you pacifists, there were pacifists before the last war, but when it started, you all fought. You'll fight, too, you'll see."

Martha had never thought of herself as a pacifist, but it seemed she was one; she played this part against her father's need, just as, for him, she was that group of people in the Twenties who refused to honor the war, although the Twenties were the first decade of her life, and she could hardly remember them. She was creating them, however, for herself, through reading, and because of this, the mere sound of the word "young," which had apparently been some sort of symbol or talisman during that decade, sprung in her a feeling of defiance and recklessness.

Similarly, when Mr. Quest comnlained about the international ring of Jews who controlled the world (which he had taken to doing lately, after reading some pamphlet sent to him through the post), Martha argued against him, in the most reasonable and logical manner; for one does not learn so young that against some things reason is powerless. And when Mrs. Quest said that all the kaffirs were dirty and lazy and inherently stupid, she defended them. And when both parents said that Hitler was no gentleman, an upstart without principles, Martha found herself defending Hitler too; it was this which made her think a little and question her feeling of being used, her conviction that when her parents raised their voices and argued at her, on a complaining and irritable note, insisting that there was going to be another war with Germany and Russia soon (this was at a time when everyone was saying another war was impossible, because whom would it benefit?), this new war was in some way necessary to punish her, Martha, who talked of the last one so critically.

Jonathan Quest, the younger brother, came home for the holidays from his expensive school, like a visitor from a more prosperous world. For the first time, Martha found herself consciously resenting him. Why, she asked herself, was it that he, with half her brains, should be sent to a "good school," why was it he should inevitably be given the advantages? There was something uneasy in this criticism, for she had been telling her mother fiercely that nothing would induce her to go to a snob school, even if her eyes did get better. She was becoming aware of several disconnected strands of her thinking. And this was brought to a climax by Jonathan himself. He was a simple, good-natured boy, very like his father to look at, who spent his holidays visiting the neighboring farmers, riding in to the station to visit Socrates the Greek, and the Cohen family at the little kaffir store. He was on the best of terms with everyone. But it struck Martha as unjust that this brother of hers who despised the Afrikaners (or rather, who took up the orthodox British attitude towards them, which was the same thing) should spend the day at the Van Rensbergs' house like a second son, and drop in for a chat with the Cohen brothers as if it was the most natural thing in the world.

Martha asked him sarcastically, "How do you reconcile the Jews ruining the world with going to see Solly and Joss?"

Jonathan looked uncomfortable and said, "But we've known them all our lives."

When she looked pointedly quizzical, he said, "But you never go and see them at all."

"That's not because I feel the way you do."

Jonathan was embarrassed, because he would not have said he felt any way rather than another; he merely repeated what his parents said, and what he had heard at school. "Well, if you think Hitler is all right, how do you reconcile that?"

"But I never said he was all right, all I said was—" She stopped and blushed; and it was his turn to look quizzical. It was true that all she had said was that Hitler's being an upstart was no criticism of his capabilities, but in this household it was as good as a defense.

She began a long rational argument; he refused to argue, merely teasing her, "Matty's lost her temper, Matty's lost her temper," singing it like a child.

"You're nothing but a baby," she concluded scornfully, which was how their arguments always ended, and she turned away. Now, that act of turning away implies something one turns towards—and she picked up a book, at random, from the bookcase. This was also a familiar act. How many times had she not simply reached for the nearest book, as if to remark, "I have authority for what I say"?

It occurred to her that the phrase "Martha is a great reader" was being used by herself exactly as her mother used it, and with as little reason. For what was she reading? She read the same books over and over again, in between intervals of distracted daydreaming, in a trance of recognition, and in always the same place, under the big tree that was her refuge, through which the heat pumped like a narcotic. She read poetry, not for the sense of the words, but for the melodies which confirmed the rhythm of the moving grasses and the swaying of the leaves over her head, or that ideal landscape of white cities and noble people which lay over the actual vistas of harsh grass and stunted trees like a golden mirage.

She went through the house searching for something different. It was full of books. Her own room had shelves packed with fairy stories from her childhood, and with poetry. In the living room, her parents' bookcases were filled with the classics, Dickens and Scott and Thackeray and the rest, inherited from prosperous Victorian households. These she had read years before, and she now read them again, and with a feeling of being starved. One might equate the small black child with Oliver Twist—but what then? There were also, lying everywhere, books on "politics" in her parents' sense of the word, such as the memoirs of Lloyd George, or histories of the Great War. None of these seemed to have any reference to the farm, to the gangs of native labor, to what was described in the newspapers, or even to *Mein Kampf,* which had started this restless condition of mind.

But one day, slipped behind the rows of dusty books, she found a volume of H. G. Wells, and, as she held it in her hand, was very conscious of a dull feeling of resistance, a disinclination. It was so strong that she nearly put it down and reached as usual for Shelley or for Whitman; then she became conscious of what she was doing, and stood wondering at herself. For she had felt this before. She looked at the book again. It was the *Concise History of the World,* and the name on the flyleaf was "Joshua Cohen." Now, she had dropped her childish friendship with the Cohen boys from the moment Marnie had said, "Joss Cohen is sweet on you." She missed them. And yet she could not face them. At first it was because the relief of escaping the barrage of criticism was so great: there was no longer any necessity to read their books, examine her own ideas. Recently it had been because of some obscure and unadmitted shame about her strained eyes. She took the book to her refuge, the tree, and read it through; and wondered why it was that she could read the most obscure and complicated poetry with ease, while she could not read the simplest sort of book on what she called "facts" without the greatest effort of concentration. She brought herself to decide she would make an effort to renew that friendship with the Cohens, for there was no one else who could help her. She wanted them to tell her what she must read. For there are two ways of reading: one of them deepens and intensifies what one already knows; from the other, one takes new facts, new views to weave into one's life. She was saturated with the first, and needed the second. All those books she had borrowed, two years before—she had read them, oh, yes; but she had not been ready to receive them.

And now what was she to do? For she had behaved very badly to the Cohen boys. She saw them at the station sometimes. Now, to avoid *seeing* people one has known for years is something of a feat, and

Martha achieved it by the simple device of saying to herself, They wouldn't think *that* of me—"*that*" being anti-Semitism—and smiling at them constrainedly, like an acquaintance. They nodded back, and left her alone, as she apparently desired.

The village held about fifty souls, and had sprung up untidily around the first store, owned by Socrates the Greek, who was known to the farmers as Sock. There was a garage, run by a Welshman; a farmers' hall; the station beside the railway, a long tin-roofed shack on wooden piles; a ganger's cottage; and a hotel, also owned by Socrates, in which there was a bar, which was the real social center of the district. These buildings were scattered over a few acres of red dust; and along the railway line was a stretch of brownish water, where ducks swam until Mrs. Socrates came out to catch one for the hotel dinner, and where the oxen from the farmers' wagons were unyoked while the wagons were loaded, and stood knee-deep in green scum, raising their eyes tranquilly as the train thundered past over their heads. There were two trains a week, and twenty miles away was the end of the line, for beyond was the long ascent to the great escarpment at the verge of the Zambezi valley. But there was a great deal of road traffic, and all day the cars stood in the dust outside the bar.

Years before, the Quests used to make the trip in to the station twice a week, for Mrs. Quest was sociable; but Mr. Quest disliked being disturbed so much that now they went once a month, and Mrs. Quest must begin fighting with her husband at least a week before.

"Alfred," she would say, with a sort of offhand defiance, "remember, we are going in to the station tomorrow."

He did not hear. Or rather, he raised vaguely irritable eyes towards her, and dropped them again, hunching his shoulders against her voice.

"Do listen, dear. I told you, we are out of flour, and the boys need new aprons, and the sugar's practically finished."

He kept his eyes lowered, and his face was stubborn.

"Alfred!" she shouted.

"What *is* it?" he demanded, and glared at her.

Startled by the glare, which nevertheless she had been provoking and facing with obdurate strength for years, she murmured, abashed but determined, "We must go to the station."

"We can send the wagon," he said hastily, getting up to escape.

"No, Alfred, you know you always say you can't spare the wagon, and it's silly to send the wagon for two sacks of . . ." He was at the door, on his way out; but she raised her voice after him: "Besides, I want to see if they've any nice materials, I'm really down to my last rag."

And now he stopped, and gave her another glare, in which there was guilt and reproach, for she was using the weapon he dreaded most: she was saying, The very least you can do is to let me have a little trip once a month, when you've made me live on this awful farm, and we're so poor, and my children have been dragged down to the level of the Van Rensbergs and . . .

"Oh, all right, all right, have it your own way," he said, and sat down, reached for the newspaper, and covered himself with it.

"Tomorrow," she said. "We will go in after lunch, and Martha can help me get ready."

Her husband's defiant eyes were hidden by the newspaper, which nevertheless gave a small protesting shake; but Martha's eyes were lifted towards her, with the sullen inquiry, "Why do we have to *get ready* for half an hour's trip?"

"Oh, well—you know—with everything . . ." Mrs. Quest lapsed into confusion.

"Good Lord," said Martha irritably, "to hear us talk, you'd think we were off to England or something."

This was a familiar joke, and allowed Mrs. Quest to give her girlish and rather charming laugh; though no one else laughed. "Well, with this family I've got, and no one lifts a finger but me . . ." This was not a grumble, but an appeal that please, please, for pity's sake, they should laugh, this irritable, resisting couple, and make things easier. She sighed, as Martha's face remained glum and the newspaper was held firmly upright against her.

Next morning at breakfast she said, "Don't forget we're going to the station."

Now he was resigned. "*Must* we?"

"Yes, we must. Besides, you know you'll enjoy it once we get there."

This was a mistake. "I do not enjoy it. I loathe it. Besides, we haven't any petrol."

"There's a spare tin in the storeroom," said Mrs. Quest firmly. And now there was no help for it; Mr. Quest groaned and accepted his fate; and as he went off to the garage he even looked interested; the cloud of introspection was lifting, and his eyes intently followed what his hands did. It always worried Martha, made her uneasy, to see how those brooding eyes must concentrate, force themselves outwards, watching his hands as if they were clumsy creatures that were separate from himself.

The garage was a roof of tin over two walls of plastered logs, open at each end; and he reversed the car slowly out into the bush, so that it bounced and jerked over the rough ground, and then forward into an empty space. Then he got out, and stood frowning at the car. It was a very old Ford; the paint had gone; there were no side curtains—they had been lost somewhere; one door was tied with rope; and a part of the canvas hood, which had decayed into holes, was thatched over. He had bought it for thirty pounds ten years before.

"The engine's as good as ever," he murmured proudly. And he called Martha to say, "It isn't the body of a car that matters. Only fools pay good money for paint and varnish. What matters is the engine." He liked to have Martha there when he attended to the car; he would even send the servant to fetch her. Now, Martha did not mind about how cars looked; but she was irritated because of this one's extreme slowness; so her face was as absent and dreamy as his own while he fetched water in a watering can, and fed the radiator, and took off the rope from the useless handle and retied it. Slowly, because he got no response to his remarks, he began glaring at her. "It's all very well," he would begin, "it's all very well for *you* . . ." More often than not, the sentence was never finished, for a humorous look would come over her face, and their eyes met.

"Oh, Daddy," she protested, grumbling, "why is it all very well, I haven't said a word!" Here she might begin edging away, with longing glances at the house. It was so hot; the heat and light glittered into her eyes from the battered old car.

"Where are you going?" he demanded, sounding offended; and she returned to sit on the running board, opening the book she had held in her hand. Now he was mollified, and he sounded cheerful, as he stroked the warm thatch on the roof, and said, "I always did like thatching, there's something about the look of a nice piece of thatch. I remember my cousin George—he was an expert thatcher, back Home. Of course, he knew his job, not like these damned niggers, they slam it on any old how. When you go back to England, Matty, the first thing you must do is go to Colchester and see if George's kids are half the man their father was—if so, you'll see a piece of thatching you'll find nowhere else in the world. *Matty!*" he shouted at her bent and absorbed head.

"*What?*" she asked, exasperated, lifting her eyes from the book.

"You're not listening."

"I am listening."

"It's all very well for *you*," came the grumbling voice.

When he had fiddled with the car for an hour or so, he came back to the house, followed by Martha, and demanded tea. He would not go down the farm that day. And then, about twelve o'clock, he began worrying that the lunch was late and they would never get off that afternoon.

"But Alfred," said poor Mrs. Quest, "first you won't go at all, and then you start fussing hours before—"

"It's all very well, you haven't got to nurse a twenty-year-old car over these roads."

Martha gritted her teeth in anger. Standing on the hill, one could see the other farmers' cars racing through the trees, like tiny black beetles, the red dust spurting up behind them. Other people made the journey to the station in a few minutes.

After lunch, the anxious Mr. Quest went to the car and again tested the radiator. It was likely to be empty; and then he would call for half a dozen eggs, and break them one after another into the cavity. The eggs would form a sticky sediment over the leaky bottom of the radiator. Once someone had suggested mealie meal, which he tried immediately, with all the cautious enthusiasm of a scientific experimenter. "There must be something in it," he murmured as he poured handfuls of the white floury stuff into the car. But halfway along the track, the cap shot off with an explosion, and lumps of porridge flew all over the windscreen, so that the car came to a blind and sliding stop against a large tree. "Well," said Mr. Quest thoughtfully, "that's interesting. Perhaps if one used a finer grain it might . . ."

On the whole, eggs were more predictable; though it was important not to drive too fast, and to stop frequently, so that the engine might cool, as otherwise the water might boil the clotted egg off the bottom of the radiator, and then . . .

After lunch Mr. Quest called peremptorily, "May! Matty! Come on, the engine's started, we must go." And Mrs. Quest, half laughing, half grumbling, ran to the car, adjusting her hat, while Martha followed unhurriedly, with a look of exhausted resignation.

The car was poised at the edge of a flattish space, on the brow of the hill. Mr. Quest sat urgently forward, clasping the brake with one hand, hugging the steering wheel with the other.

"Now!" he exclaimed, letting go the brake. Nothing happened. "Oh, damn it all," he groaned, as if this were the last straw. "Come on, then." And he and Mrs. Quest began swinging back and forth in their seats, so the car was joggled inch by inch over the edge, and slid precariously down the rutted pebbly road to the foot of the hill, where there was a great ditch. Into this it slid, and stopped. "Oh, damn it *all*," Mr. Quest said again, on a final note, and looked around at his women in an aggrieved way.

He tried the starter, without much hope. It worked at once, and the car flew up over the edge of the ditch in a screeching bounce, and down the track between the mealie fields. The maize stood now in its final coloring, a dead silvery gold, dry as paper, and its whispering against the wind was the sound of a myriad fluttering leaves. Below this Hundred

Acres Field lay the track, the old railroad track, and now Mr. Quest stopped the car, got out, took off the radiator cap, and peered in. There was a squelchy bubbling noise, and a faintly rotten smell. "It's all right so far," he said, with satisfaction, and off they went.

Halfway, they stopped again. "At three and a half miles, the petrol ought to show . . ." murmured Mr. Quest, looking at the petrol gauge. For it was seven miles to the station. Or rather, it was five and three-quarters; but just as it was seven miles to the Dumfries Hills (in fact, six) and seven to Jacob's Burg (at least nine), so the distance to the station must be seven miles, for to have a house in the dead center of a magically determined circle offers satisfaction beyond all riches, and even power. But a poetical seven miles is one thing, and to check one's petrol gauge by it another; and Mr. Quest frowned and said, "I'd better take the thing to the garage. I cannot understand—if these people can make an engine to last a lifetime, why is everything else so shoddy?"

At the station, Mrs. Quest descended at Socrates' with her shopping lists, and Mr. Quest drove off to the garage. Martha lagged on the veranda until her mother had forgotten her in her eager talk with the other women at the counter, and then walked quickly to the belt of trees which hid the kaffir store. It was a large square brick erection, with a simple pillared veranda. Martha went through the usual crowd of native women with their babies on their backs, pushed aside the colored bead curtain at the door, and was inside the store. It had a counter down the center, and on it were jars of bright sweets, and rolls of cotton goods. There were sacks of grain and sugar around the walls, bicycles, cans of paraffin, monkey nuts. Over the counter, cheap beads, strips of biltong, mouth organs, and glass bangles dangled and swung together. The smell was of sweat and cheap dyes and dust, and Martha sniffed it with pleasure.

Old Mr. Cohen nodded at her, with a distance in his manner, and, having asked politely after her parents, who owed him fifty pounds, waited for an order.

"Is Solly in?" she asked, rather too politely.

The old man allowed his eyebrows to lift, before replying, "He's in, for anyone who wants to see him."

"I would like to see him," she said, almost stammering.

"You used to know the way," he said laconically, and nodded at the closed flap of the counter, under which she had ducked as a child. She had expected him to lift it for her now; clumsily, she tried to move it, while he watched her. Then, taking his time, he lifted it, and moved aside so that she might go through.

She found herself saying, "You're mistaken, I didn't mean . . ."

His eyes snapped around at her, and he said sarcastically, "Didn't mean what?" He at once turned away to serve a native child, who was so red with dust from the road that his black skin had a rusty look, some acid-green sweets from a jar.

Martha walked into the back room, and found the Cohen boys reading, one in each of the two big easy chairs, which she privately thought in unpleasant taste, as was the whole room, which was very small, and crowded with glossy furniture and bright china ornaments; there was an effect of expensive ostentation, like the display window of a furniture store. And in this ugly and tasteless room sat Solly and Joss, the intellectuals, reading (as she took care to see) Plato and Balzac, in expensive editions.

After a startled look at her, they looked at each other, and after a long pause, Solly remarked, "Look who's here!" while Joss returned, "Well, well!" and they both waited, with blandly sarcastic faces, for her to speak.

She said, "I've brought back a book of yours," and held it out.

Solly said, "My grateful thanks," extended a hand, and took it.

Joss was pretending to read, and this annoyed her; for, as Mrs. Van Rensberg had suggested, he had once been her particular friend. But it was also a relief, and she said, rather flirtatiously, to Solly, "May I sit down?" and sat forthwith.

"She's got to be quite a smart girl, h'm?" said Solly to Joss, and the boys openly and rudely examined her.

As a result of her quarrels with Mrs. Quest, she was now making her own clothes. Also, she had starved herself into a fashionable thinness which, since she was plump by nature, was not to everyone's taste. Apparently not to the Cohen boys', for they continued, as if she were not present:

"Yellow suits her, doesn't it, Solly?"

"Yes, Joss, and that cute little slit down the front of the dress, too."

"But too thin, too thin, Solly, it comes of giving up that rich and unhealthy Jewish food."

"But better thin and pure, Joss, than fat and gross and contaminated by—"

"Oh, shut up," she said, in discomfort; and they raised their eyebrows and shook their heads and sighed. "I know you think . . ." she began, and once again found it hard to continue.

"Think *what?*" they demanded, almost together, and with precisely the keen, sarcastic intonation their father had used.

"It isn't so," she stammered, sincerely, looking at them in appeal; and for a moment thought she was forgiven, for Joss's tone was quite gentle as he began: "Poor Matty, did your mummy forbid you to come and see us, then?"

The shock of the words, after the deceptively gentle tone, which reached her nerves before the sense of them, caused her eyes to fill with tears. She said, "No, of course she didn't."

"Mystery," said Joss, beginning the game again, nodding at Solly; who sighed exaggeratedly and said, "We're not to know, dear, dear."

Suddenly Martha said, not at all as she had intended, but with a mixture of embarrassment and coyness, "Mrs. Van Rensberg was gossiping." She glanced at Joss, whose dark face slowly colored; and he looked at her with a dislike that cut her.

"Mrs. Van Rensberg was gossiping," said Solly to Joss; and before the exchange could continue, she cut in: "Yes, and I suppose it was silly, but I couldn't—take it." The defiant conclusion ended on a shortened breath; this interview was not as she had imagined.

"She couldn't take it," sighed Joss to Solly.

"She couldn't take it," Solly sighed back; and with the same movement, they picked up their books, and began to read.

She remained where she was, her eyes pleading with their averted faces, trying to subdue the flood of color she could feel tingling to the roots of her hair, and when, after a long silence, Solly remarked in a detached voice, "She couldn't take us, but she's still here," Martha got up, saying angrily, "I've apologized, you're making a mistake. Why do you have to be so thin-skinned?" She went to the door.

Behind her back, they began laughing, a loud and unpleasant laughter. "She's cut us dead for two years, and she says we're thin-skinned."

"I *didn't* cut you—why must you talk about me as if I weren't here?" she said, and stumbled out, past Mr. Cohen. She found the flap of the counter down, and had to wait, speechless, for him to lift it, for she was on the verge of crying.

He looked at her with what she thought was a tinge of kindliness; but he opened the flap, nodded quietly, and said, "Good afternoon, Miss Quest."

"Thank you," she said, with the effect of pleading; and walked back up the dusty path to the village, as the bead curtain swung and rattled into stillness behind her.

She walked over the railway tracks, which gleamed brightly in the hot sunlight, to the garage, where Mr. Quest was in absorbed conversation with Mr. Parry. He was repeating urgently, "Yes, there's going to be a war, it's all very well for you people . . ."

Mr. Parry was saying, "Yes, Captain Quest. No, Captain Quest." In the village, the war title was used, though Mr. Quest refused it, saying it was not fair to the regular soldier. Martha used to argue with him reasonably, thus: "Are you suggesting that it is only the peacetime soldier who deserves his title? Do you mean that if civilians get conscripted and killed it's on a different level from . . ." and so on and so on—ah, how exasperating are the rational adolescents! For Mr. Quest gave his irritable shrug of aversion and repeated, "I don't like being Captain, it's not fair when I haven't been in the Army for so long." What Martha thought privately was, How odd that man who thinks about nothing but war should dislike being Captain; and this point, the real one, was of course never mentioned during those *reasonable* discussions.

Mr. Parry was listening nervously to Mr. Quest, while his eyes anxiously followed his native assistant, who was dragging an inner tube through the hot dust. At last he could not bear it, and, saying, "Excusing me, but . . ." he darted forward and shouted at the native, "Look you, Gideon, how many times have I told you . . ." He grabbed the tire from the man's hand, and took it over to a tub of water. Gideon shrugged, and went off to the cool interior of the garage, where he sat on a heap of outer tires, and began making patterns on the dust with a twig. "Look you, Gideon. . . ." shouted Mr. Parry; but Gideon wrinkled his brows and pretended not to hear. Mr. Parry's Welsh speech had lost nothing of its lilt and charm; but the phrases had worn slack; his "Look you" sounded more like "Look ye"; and when he used the Welsh "whatever," it came haphazard in his speech, with a surprised, uncertain note.

Mr. Quest, disappointed of a listener, came to the car, climbed in, and said, "They don't listen. I was telling him the Russians are going to join with the Germans and attack us. I know they are. Just after the war—*my* war—I met a man in a train who said he had seen with his own eyes the way the Russians were kidnaping German scientists and forcing them to work in their factories so they could learn to make tanks to smash the British Empire. I said to Parry . . ."

Martha heard these words somewhere underneath her attention, which was given to her own problems. Mr. Quest looked over his shoulder at her, and said sarcastically, "But don't let me bore you with the Great Unmentionable. Your time'll come, and then I can say I told you so."

Martha turned her face away; her lids stung with tears; she felt the most rejected and desolate creature in the world. It occurred to her that the Cohen boys might have felt like this when she (or so it had appeared) rejected them; but she dismissed the thought at once. The possessors of this particular form of arrogance may know its underside is timidity; but they seldom go on to reflect that the timidity is based on the danger of thinking oneself important to others, which necessitates a return of feeling. She was saying to herself that she could not imagine the clever and self-sufficient Cohen brothers caring about her one way or the other. But we were friends all our childhood, a voice said inside her; and that other voice answered coldly, Friends are whom you choose, not the people forced on you by circumstances. And yet she was nearly crying with misery and humiliation and friendlessness, in the hot back seat of the car, while grains of sunlight danced through the fractured roof, and stung her flesh like needles. For the first time, she said to herself that the Cohens were almost completely isolated in the district. The farmers nodded to them, offered remarks about the weather, but never friendship. The Greek family maintained a complicated system of friendship with the other Greeks from stores all along the railway line. The Cohens had relations in the city, no one nearer.

At last Mr. Parry found a trail of bubbles sizzling up through the dirty water from the tube, and shouted to Gideon, "Come ye, now, you lazy black loafer, and do it quick whateffer you do, and listen well, now."

Gideon indolently lifted himself and went to mend the puncture, while Mr. Parry came back to the car in order to resume his conversation with Mr. Quest.

"Sorry, Captain, but if you want a good job, you do it yourself, whateffer else, it's no good trusting the blacks, they've no pride in their work."

"As I was saying, you people have your heads buried in the sand. Anyone can see war is coming. If it's not this year, it'll be the next, as soon as they're strong enough."

"You think the Jerries'll have another shot at us?" asked Mr. Parry, polite but doubtful, and turned so that he might keep an eye on Gideon.

Another native came loping across the railway tracks and stopped by the car. "Baas Quest?" he asked.

Mr. Quest, once again interrupted, turned his darkly irritable eyes on him. But Martha recognized him: he was the Cohens' cook; and she reached for the parcel he held.

"For me," she said, and asked the man to wait. He went off to help Gideon with the tire.

The parcel was a book from Joss, entitled *The Social Aspect of the Jewish Question,* and inside was a note: "Dear Matty Quest, This will be good for your soul, so do, *do* read it. Yours thin-skinnedly, Joss."

She was filled with outrageous delight. It was forgiveness. She interrupted her father once again to borrow a pencil, and wrote:

"Thanks for the book. As it happened, I borrowed it from you and of course agreed with it, three years ago. But I shall read it again and return it next time we come to the station." She was determined that would be very soon.

Next mail day she suggested that they should make the trip, but her father refused, with an air of being exploited.

"Why do you want to go?" asked Mrs. Quest curiously; and Martha said, "I want to see the Cohen boys."

"You're making friends with them?" demurred Mrs. Quest.

"I thought we always were friends with them," said Martha scornfully; and since this put the argument on that hypocritical level where it was maintained that of course the Quests did not think Jews, or even shopkeepers, beneath them, and the only reason they did not continually meet was an inconvenience of some sort, Mrs. Quest could not easily reply.

Martha telephoned the McDougalls to ask if they were going to the station. They were not. She asked the Van Rensbergs; Marnie said awkwardly that Pop didn't often go to the station these days. Finally she telephoned Mr. McFarline, the old miner from the small working in the Dumfries Hills; and he said yes, he was going to town tomorrow. She told her mother she would get a lift back (for "town" in this case meant the city, not the station, as it sometimes did), and added, with the apparently deliberate exaggeration which was so infuriating, "If I don't get a lift, I'll walk." Which of course was absurd, infringed one of the taboos—"a young white girl walking alone," etc.—and was calculated to provoke an argument. The argument immediately followed; and both women appealed to Mr. Quest.

"Why shouldn't she walk?" demanded Mr. Quest vaguely. "When I was a young man in England, I used to walk thirty miles an afternoon and think nothing of it."

"This isn't England," said Mrs. Quest tremulously, filled with horrid visions of what might happen to Martha if she encountered an evil native.

Martha came back with "I walk miles and miles all over the farm, but that doesn't matter, for some reason. How can you be so illogical?"

"Well, I don't like it, and you promised not to go more than half a mile from the house."

Martha laughed angrily, and chose this moment to say what until now she had been careful to keep dark: "Why, I often walk over to the Dumfries Hills, or even to Jacob's Burg, I've been doing it for years."

"Oh, my dear," said Mrs. Quest helplessly. She had known quite well that Martha was doing this, but to be told so now was another thing. "What would happen if a native attacked you?"

"I should scream for help," said Martha flippantly.

"Oh, my dear . . ."

"Oh, don't be ridiculous," said Martha angrily. "If a native raped me, then he'd be hung and I'd be a national heroine, so he wouldn't do it, even if he wanted to, and why should he?"

"My dear, read the newspapers, white girls are always being ra—attacked."

Now, Martha could not remember any case of this happening; it was one of the things people said. She remarked, "Last week a white man raped a black girl, and was fined five pounds."

Mrs. Quest said hastily, "That's not the point, the point is girls get raped."

"Then I expect they want to be," said Martha sullenly; and caught her breath, not because she did not believe the truth of what she said, but because of her parents' faces: she could not help being frightened. For they were united for once, in genuine emotion, and began lecturing her on the consequences of her attitude. It ended with "And so they'll drive us into the sea, and then the country will be ruined, what would these ignorant blacks do without us." And the usual inconsequent conclusion: "They have no sense of gratitude at all for what we do for them." It had all been said so often that it rang stale and false for both sides; and Martha remained silent in a way which they could take as an agreement, for comfort's sake.

Next morning she was waiting down on the track, by the signpost in the long grass, for Mr. McFarline; and they made the journey to the station in just over ten minutes.

Mr. McFarline was a charming and wicked old Scotsman who lived alone on his mine, which he worked in a way which cost him the very minimum in money, but a good deal in human life. There were always accidents on his mine. Also, his native compound was full of half-caste children, his own. He was extremely wealthy, and very popular. He gave generously to charity, and was about to stand for Parliament for one of the town constituencies. Because of the work in connection with getting himself elected, he often went into town.

As the car raced dangerously through the trees, he squeezed Martha's knee in an experimental way and tried to put his hand up her skirt. She held the skirt down, and moved coolly away to the other side of the car, as if she had not noticed the action. So he took his hand away, and concentrated on showing her how nearly it was possible to escape death, with perfect sang-froid, at every bend of the road. He took the paint off his back mudguard at the last raking turn; and they stopped before Sock's store in a billowing cloud of dust. Martha's heart was beating wildly for several reasons. No one had ever tried to put his hand up her skirt before, and she was petrified at the wild driving. She looked confused and alarmed; and the old Scotsman decided to see her as the little girl he had known for years. He took a ten-shilling note from his stuffed wallet, and gave it to her.

"For when you go back to school," he said bluffly.

Martha almost handed it back; but was unable to, partly because ten shillings was such a large sum for her, and partly because of a feeling which she described to herself as: If I refuse it, he will think it's because of the way he tried to touch me. She thanked him politely for the lift, and he roared away over the railway track on the road to the city, singing, "You're a bonny lassie . . ."

She had the book on the Jewish question (which she had not reread, thinking it unnecessary to gild the already sound coinage of her opinions) under her arm. She went over to the kaffir store. Mr. Cohen greeted her, and lifted the counter for her. He was a short, squat man; his hair was a close-growing, crinkling cap of black; his skin was pallid and unhealthy. He had, she thought secretly, the look of a toad, or something confined and light-shunning; and in fact he was hardly ever away from his counter; but the commercial look of the small shopkeeper was tempered in him by purpose and dignity, which was not only because of his ancient culture, but because this penniless immigrant from Central Europe had chosen such a barren place, such exile, for the sake of his brilliant sons. His eyes were black and wise and shrewd, and it was impossible not to like him. And yet Martha found him repulsive, and was guilty; it was strange that she could find the oily fatness of the Greek Socrates repulsive without any sense of guilt at all, but this question of anti-Semitism, this shrinking nerve, put her on guard against herself, so that her manner with Mr. Cohen was always strained.

In the back room Martha found Solly, alone; and was pleased that the brotherly solid act could not be repeated. Besides, there was something uneasy and false in it, for there was a strong current of antagonism between the two brothers, a temperamental difficulty which expressed itself politically—Solly being a Zionist, while Joss was a Socialist. Solly was a lanky, tall youth, with a big head on a long thin neck, and big bony hands at the end of long arms; he was altogether knobbly and unintegrated, and his enormous, somber black eyes brooded abstractedly on the world around him in a way that gave Martha a feeling of kinship to him; but this was perhaps not an altogether welcome relationship, reminding her, as it did, of her father. If she was to fight the morbid strain in herself, which was her father's gift, then how could she admire Solly wholeheartedly, as she wished to do? On the whole, she was easier with Joss, who was short and compact and robust, with humorous direct eyes and a sarcastic practicality, as if he were always saying, "Well, and what's the fuss about, it's all quite easy!"

Solly took the book, without any sign of the hostility of the previous meeting; and no sooner had she sat down than Mrs. Cohen came in with a tray. The older Cohens were strictly kosher, and the sons were lax. For years Mrs. Cohen had been scrupulously sorting her crockery and cutlery, washing them herself, forbidding the native servants even to touch them; but at the table, Joss and Solly, usually deep in bitter argument, would reach for the wrong knives, and stack the plates carelessly about them, while Mrs. Cohen scolded and pleaded. By now she had learned to say, "I'm too old to learn new ways," and with a sorrowful tolerance. She continued to wash and sort her things, but made no comment if her sons misused them. It was a compromise in which Martha could see no sense at all; if her own parents had been guilty of such *unreasonable* behavior, how irritably would she have argued with them! In Mrs. Cohen, however, it merely struck her as charming. The mere sight of the plump old Jewish woman, with her fine, dark, sad eyes, made her feel welcomed; and she at once accepted, enthusiastically, when she was bidden, "You'll stay eat with us?" In a few moments they were talking as if she had never absented herself from the family for two years.

Solly was leaving shortly to study medicine in Cape Town, and Mrs. Cohen was urging him to live with her cousin there. But Solly wanted independence, a life of his own; and since this vital point was never mentioned, the argument went on endlessly about buses and transport and inconvenience; and it reminded Martha of her own home, where this kind of surface bickering was equally futile.

Joss came in, gave Martha an ambiguous look, and forbore to comment, in a way which made her voice rise to a jaunty brightness. He was intending to study law, but was staying at home with his parents until they could move into town, which they planned to do. The store was to be sold. This solicitude for his father and mother only struck Martha as a kind of betrayal to the older generation; she found it extraordinary; even more strange that he sided with his parents against Solly's desire to fend for himself. He sounded more like an uncle than a brother.

They sat down to table, and Mrs. Cohen asked, "And when are you going back to your studies, Matty? Your mother must be worrying herself."

Martha replied awkwardly, "My eyes aren't better yet," and lowered them towards her plate. When she raised them, she found Joss critically studying her in the way she had feared.

"What's wrong with them?" he inquired bluntly. She gave an uncomfortable movement with her shoulders, as if to say, "Leave me alone." But in this family everything was discussed; and Joss said to Solly, "Her eyes are strained, well, well!"

Solly refused, this time, to make the alliance against her, and asked, "What's it got to do with you?"

Joss raised his brows, and said, "Me? Nothing. She used to be such a bright girl. Pity."

"Leave her alone," said Mr. Cohen unexpectedly, "she's all right." Martha felt a rush of warmth towards him, which as usual she could not express, but dropped her eyes, and even looked sullen.

"Of course she's all right," said Joss carelessly; but there was a note in his voice . . .

Martha looked quickly at him, and at once interpreted his agreement as a reference to her own appearance; and this she half resented, and half welcomed. Since her incarnation as a fairly successful imitation of a magazine beauty, the Cohen boys were the first males she had tried herself against. But she had never said to herself that her careful makeup and the new green linen had been put on to impress them, and therefore she felt it as a false note that either should mention or even react to her appearance—a confusion of feeling which left her silent, and rather sulky. After the meal, Mr. Cohen went back to the shop, and Mrs. Cohen to her kitchen, with the mishandled crockery; and the three young people were left together. Conversation was difficult, and soon Martha felt she should leave. But she lingered; and it was Solly who at last went out; and at once she and Joss were at ease, as she and Solly were, by themselves: it was three of them together that set up the jarring currents.

At once Joss inquired, "And now what's all this about not going to university?"

The direct question, which she had never put to herself, left her silent; but he persisted. "You can't hang about this dorp doing nothing."

She said, "But you are at home, too."

His look said that she must see this was no analogy; he tried not to sound bitter as he remarked, "My parents have no friends in the village. It'll be different when they're in town."

Again she was silent, feeling apologetic for herself and for her parents. She got up and went to the bookcase, to see what was new in it; but this represented the family: the Jewish classics, books on Palestine, on Poland and Russia; this was the source of the rapidly diverging streams which were Solly and Joss; and these new books would be in their shared bedroom. Into this room it was impossible to go, since she was now Miss Quest; and the glance she directed towards Joss was troubled.

He had been watching her, and, at the glance, he lifted from a table beside him a large pile of books and handed them to her. Again she felt that flush of delight; for he must have prepared them for her. He remarked calmly, "Take these, good for your soul."

She looked at the titles, and was at once indignant, as a child might be if a teacher urged her to study subjects she had mastered the year before.

"What's the matter?" he asked sardonically. "Not up your street?"

She said, "But I know all this." At once she wished the words unsaid, for they sounded conceited. What she meant was, "I agree with all the things these books represent."

He studied her, gave an incredulous grimace, and then fired the following questions at her, in the offhand indifferent manner of the initiate to a breed utterly without the law:

"You repudiate the color bar?"

"But of course."

"Of course," he said sardonically. And then: "You dislike racial prejudice in all its forms, including anti-Semitism?"

"Naturally"—this with a touch of impatience.

"You are an atheist?"

"You know quite well that I am."

"You believe in socialism?"

"That goes without saying," she concluded fervently; and suddenly began to laugh, from that sense of the absurd which it seemed must be her downfall as a serious person. For Joss was frowning at the laugh, and apparently could see nothing ridiculous in a nineteen-year-old Jewish boy, sprung from an orthodox Jewish family, and an adolescent British girl, if possible even more conventionally bred, agreeing to these simple axioms in the back room of a veld store in a village filled with people to whom every word of this conversation would have the force of dangerous heresy.

"You sound as if you were asking a catechism," she explained, giggling irrepressibly.

He frowned again; and at once she felt indignant that he might be surprised because she had made the same intellectual journey he had.

"So what are you going to do about it?" he demanded practically. Also, he sounded aggressive; she was beginning to feel childish and wrong for having laughed; she felt she had hurt him.

"I don't know," she said, and there was an appeal in it. She raised her eyes to his and waited. Because of the look on his face, she at once became conscious of the picture she presented, standing there in front of him, a young girl in a green linen frock that emphasized every line in her body.

"I suppose you are all right," he conceded slowly, looking at her with approval; and she felt the unfairness of it. This was an intellectual discussion, wasn't it? Why, then, that note in his voice?

Her look at him was now as aggressive as his had been. "It's all very well for you, you're a man," she said bitterly, and entirely without coquetry; but he said flippantly, even suggestively, "It will be all quite well for you too!"

He laughed, hoping she might laugh with him. But she stared at him in dismayed outrage, then muttered, "Oh, go to hell," and for the second time left that room, and went out into the glaring sunlight. No sooner had she gone than she understood she had been as touchy and thin-skinned as she had said he was, and almost went back. Pride forbade it; and she went on into the village.

The place had a deserted look. Four in the afternoon: the sky was huge and cloudless, the sun loomed swollen through a reddish haze, and the tin roofs reflected a dulled and somber light. It was likely to rain soon; but now the long brown pond had shrunk within lips of cracked mud to a narrow scummy puddle. Outside the bar stood half a dozen big cars, outside the station about twenty shabbier cars. Among them was the Van Rensbergs'; and they were packed with children of all ages.

What the British referred to as "the Afrikaans element" had come in for their mail.

Now, it is quite easy to remark the absurdities and contradictions of a country's social system from outside its borders, but very difficult if one has been brought up in it; and for Martha, who must have seen that very sight dozens of times before, it was a moment of illumination, perhaps because she was feeling sore and rejected under Joss's treatment of her; and there was something in the bearing and character of those people kin to what she felt.

On mail days there were cars of every degree of wealth, from the enormous American cars of the tobacco farmers down to eccentric creations like the Quests', but the owners of these cars met together without any consciousness of degree. English and Scotch, Welsh and Irish, rich and poor, it was all backslapping and Christian names, a happy family atmosphere which had a touch of hysterical necessity in it, since the mail days, gymkhanas and dances were false tokens of community—for what is a community if not people who share their experience? The fact was, this district was divided into several separate communities, who shared nothing but Christian names, cards at Christmas, and a member of Parliament. The eastern part of the district, all along the flanks and slopes of Jacob's Burg, was where the tobacco families lived, and here the common denominator was wealth; they were regarded by the rest with tolerance, for they went in for bottle parties, divorces, and modern restlessness. North and west of the Quests' farm Scots families were settled, mostly related, hard-working, modest, sociable people who visited a great deal among themselves. Half a dozen Irish inhabited the slopes of the Oxford Range; but this was not a group; one cannot think of the Irish except as picturesque individualists. Near them were five farms where lived a collection of the English eccentrics who reach their richest bloom only in the colonies. Colonel Castairs, for instance, who lived by himself in a ranging stone mansion, sleeping all day and reading all night, preparing himself to write that history of melancholia through the ages which he would one day begin; he was now over seventy. There was Lord Jamie, who walked naked around his farm, and ate only fruit and nuts; and quarreled bitterly with his wife because she clothed their children, for he held the view that even so much as a diaper on a baby was an insult to the God who created Adam and Eve. There was a story that once he had come raking into the village on a great black horse, quite naked, with his wild red beard and his mane of red hair sparking fire in the sunlight, a great rough-cast man, whose fiercely innocent blue eyes stared out from the waving locks of his hair like the eyes of an inquiring savage. He dismounted from his horse, and went into the store to buy a pound of tobacco, a bottle of whisky, and the weekly newspaper; and it seemed that everyone in the store greeted him as casually as if he were as decently covered as they. Then they began talking about the weather; and so it had never happened again; and the incident retreated into the fabulous past of kaffir wars, and pioneers, and violence. How exciting life must have been then, sighed the people in the district, remembering their distant origins—and yet the district had not been settled much more than thirty years. How wonderful if the wild man on the black horse appeared again in his scandalous glory! How wonderful if Commander Day walked into the store (as he had once, in the golden age) flanked by his two half-tamed leopards, with his three native concubines behind him—but alas, alas, he did not, they did not; the time for the creation of legends was past.

For many years, between this essential group of gentle maniacs and the Quests' farm there had been hundreds of acres of empty ground, considered too poor to farm. On its verge, sharing a boundary with the Quests, were the Van Rensbergs, like the solitary swallow which would one day make a summer; for five years before another Afrikaans family arrived, rocking along the track in a hooded wagon, a vehicle which had, to this district, only literary associations from the Great Trek. Soon there came another family, and then another . . . And now, inside this district whose pattern of living was a large farm and two or three children, with a governess and maybe an assistant, grew up a close-knit, isolated community of Dutch people, who worked fifty and a hundred acres where the British used thousands, and made their farming pay; who bred healthy children, eight and ten to a family; who built their own hall, and a thatched church where they worshiped their angry God. And their speech had the rich cadences of a living religion.

They came to fetch their mail on a day when the village would be empty. Their cars drew up together outside Socrates' store; moved away together to the garage across the railway track; returned together to the station building, one after another in a file, with the slow deliberation that suggested a team of covered wagons.

So it was today. There were eleven cars, standing behind each other; and from them had come enough people to populate a small village, men, women and children, talking, reading mail, playing in groups.

Martha stood on Socrates' veranda among the grain sacks and looked at them, and tried to find what it was which gave these people their look of cohesion. Physically they were strong and broadly built, with the blunt open features of their Dutch ancestry; but the word "Dutch" surely suggests a picture of fair skin and hair, blue eyes, an easy health? These people tended to be dark, as if the sun had fed a strain of resistance into defenseless light skin, and the light hair that becomes dry and limp in the south. The older women wore black—here the color of respectability, though in other cultures, other contexts, it may be the color of mourning or sophistication. The younger women wore print frocks that were pretty rather than smart; some of the children wore the flapping sunbonnets of the tradition; the men were in the male uniform of the country, khaki shorts and open-necked shirts. No, the clothing here expressed only a restlessness, a movement, even uncertainty; for if it was true that the pretty sunbonnets could have been seen nowhere else, the little girls' frocks were likely to have been made by a pattern from an English magazine; and if no one but a certain type of Dutchwoman would wear those black lace hats (so that, catching sight of one a hundred yards away, one might imagine the face under it, broad, practical, humorous, earthy), then the black dress she wore with it was probably mass-produced in America.

The closeness of this group expressed itself somewhere else, perhaps in the look of dogged self-sufficiency, the look of the inveterate colonizer; but in that case, they were colonizers in a country which considered itself past the colonizing stage. Not so easy to put flesh and blood on the bones of an intellectual conviction; Martha was remembering with shame the brash and easy way she had said to Joss that she repudiated race prejudice; for the fact was, she could not remember a time when she had not thought of people in terms of groups, nations, or color of skin first, and as people afterwards. She stood on the veranda of Socrates' store, and looked over the empty dusty space to the railway line, and thought of the different people who passed there: the natives, the nameless and swarming; the Afrikaans, whose very name held the racy, poetic quality of their vigorous origins; the British, with their innumerable subgroupings, held together only because they could say, "This is a British country"—held together by the knowledge of ownership. And each group, community, clan, color, strove and fought away from the other, in a sickness of dissolution; it was as if the principle of separateness was bred from the very soil, the sky, the driving sun; as if the inchoate vastness of the universe, always insistent in the enormous unshrouded skies, the enormous mountain-girt horizons, so that one might never, not for a moment, forget the inhuman, relentless struggle of soil and water and light, bred a fever of self-assertion in its children, like a band of explorers lost in a desert, quarreling in an ecstasy of fear over their direction, when nothing but a sober mutual trust could save them. Martha could feel the striving forces in her own substance; the effort of imagination needed to destroy the words "black," "white," "nation," "race," exhausted her, her head ached, and her flesh was heavy on her bones. She looked at the Van Rensbergs' car, and thought that she had known them for years, and yet she was reluctant even to cross the dust and greet them. She walked off the veranda and towards the car, smiling rather queerly, for when it was too late to retreat it occurred to her that they might not wish to have their friendship with the Quests so publicly emphasized.

She came to a standstill at the car door, and said good afternoon to Mr. Van Rensberg. He nodded at her, and went on reading the newspaper, having made a hunching movement with his shoulder towards the back of the car, where Marnie was sitting with two married sisters who held small babies. There was a young man beside Mr. Van

Rensberg, who greeted Martha, and she smiled at him hastily, thinking, This must be a cousin; for his face was the family face.

Marnie was smiling with constrained pleasure, and looked uncomfortably at her father's back; and this made Martha wish she had not come. Over his shoulder, she could see the name of the most rabid nationalist journal from the south; while she did not know the language, there was hardly any need to, for the words and phrases of nationalism are the same in any tongue, but the knowledge that the brain behind the close-cropped black head beside her was agreeing with what was bound to be a violent complaint about the very existence of the British made her drop her voice like a guilty person as she said to Marnie, "Why don't you come over and see me soon?"

"I'd like to, man, I'd like to," agreed Marnie, in the same low tone, and with another glance at her father. "Your dress is the tops, Martha," she added. "May I have the pattern?"

"Of course," said Martha, with an involuntary glance at Marnie's matronly body. "Come over for the day. . . ." She had lowered her voice almost to a whisper; the absurdity of it made her angry. She and Marnie quickly said goodbye, smiling at each other like conspirators; she dropped another smile in the direction of the attentive young man in the front seat, and hastily retreated back to the store.

She had no lift home. She would have liked to walk; she intended to, but . . . She imagined that eyes would follow her, queerly, as she set off, on foot, along a road where a dozen cars might be expected to pass that afternoon. *White girls do not* . . . As she was hesitating on the veranda, she saw Joss approaching, and smiled with what was, had she known it, a tenderly amused appreciation of the figure he cut. He wore a respectable dark suit, he carried books under his arm, he moved in a careful, constrained way, eyes watching the direction of his feet, his shoulders a little hunched. He seemed, in fact, already the sober professional man he intended to become; he was altogether out of place among these khaki-clad, open-air people; and knew it, and approved. For these farmers, these men of the soil: when they approached, one saw first the exposed developed limbs, the body; one marked the hard muscled forearm perhaps, or the bronze knotted pillar of the thigh, or the stride, or the swing of the arms; they moved magnificently, at ease, slowly, to match the space and emptiness of the country—no suggestion here of limbs grown cautious and self-contained, against possible undesired contact. Yes, here one stands at a distance from a man, a woman, and sees them whole. First the way of walking, the stance of the body. Then lift your eyes to the face, and the first impression is confirmed: what fine, exposed, frank faces, wholesomely weathered, unafraid, open to every glance. And then (but lastly) the eyes, look straight at the eyes—which of course meet yours with the completest frankness. Nothing to hide here, they say; everything aboveboard, take it or leave it. But always, behind the friendly brown eyes, the welcoming blue ones, is the uneasiness; something not easily defined, but expressed best, perhaps, in a moment of laughter. The man laughs, out loud, an infectious wholehearted laugh; but there is a faint sideways flickering movement of the eyes, the eyes are not altogether there, there is an absence, something blank and empty. Take, for instance, that contingent of fine young colonials marching down the Strand with their English cousins. What fine young men, what physique; a head taller than the rest, bronzed, muscled, strong as horses. Then look at the eyes. But the eyes seem to say, "What do you want with us? Aren't our bodies enough for you?" There is a pale and fretful look; the soft and luminous darkness that should lie behind the iris is simply not there. Something is missing.

And so it seems that one cannot have it both ways, one has to choose; and Joss chose, without any hesitation.

Martha, watching him approach, was conscious of the most perverse but definite feeling of pity. Why pity? She envied him almost to the point of bitterness, knowing exactly what he wanted, and how to get it. She saw how the compact, neat body, hidden under dark-grey flannel, moved carefully across the sunlit, filthy dust, as if every nerve and muscle were connected direct to his will; she saw how his eyes were focused, steady and direct, the whole of himself behind them, so that it was only when one looked into his eyes that one saw him; she saw the great difference there was between Joss and these farmers, and she half envied, half pitied him. Pity? What for? One does not pity a person who knows what it is he chooses, and why.

Martha was watching him in a way which would allow her to pretend, to herself at least, that she was not; she was afraid he might go past her with another of his formal nods. He came straight towards her, however, extended the books, and said brusquely, "I thought you'd like these."

"How did you know I was still here?"—with feminine obliquity.

"I can see the store through the trees."

For a moment Martha was irrationally angry, as if she had been spied upon; then he asked, "How are you getting home?" and she replied defiantly, "I'm walking." It seemed, however, that Joss could see no reason why she should not walk; and after a hesitation he merely said, "So long!" and walked back across the dust. Martha was disappointed—he might have asked her back to his home, she thought.

Then she understood that he was waiting for her to invite herself; and this confused her. She shrugged away the thought of Joss, who always made her feel deficient in proper feeling; and with the parcel of books under her arm, which gave her confidence, she walked away off Socrates' veranda, and along the road home.

She had never made this journey on foot; always by car, or, as a child, perched on top of the hot hairy grain sacks on the wagon. During the first mile she was remembering the creaking sway of the old wagon, which seemed always as if it might spring apart between the dragging weight of the sacks and the forward-heaving oxen; there was a place towards the front of the wagon where it seemed that the tension was localized, and here she had liked to sit, shuddering with excitement, because of the groaning timbers under her, which always were on the point of flying asunder, but never did, carrying their burden mile after slow and laboring mile. She was remembering the alarming way the sacks shifted under her; heavy sacks they were, but sliding and subsiding easily with the sway of the vehicle. She remembered the pleasurable warm smell of the cow droppings falling plop, plop into the red dust, and releasing, deliciously, the odors of fresh grass; so that, although the wagon wheels perpetually flung up rivers of red sand, and she traveled in a column of whirling ruddy dust, the sweet perfumes of newly cudded grass mingled with it, mile after mile, as if the four-divided stomachs of the great oxen were filled with nothing but concentrated memories of hours of grazing along the water-heavy vleis.

Later, she hesitated outside the McDougalls' farm; for if she went in she would be given a wonderful Scotch tea of bannocks and griddle cakes and newly churned butter. But she did not go in, for the McDougalls had not yet noticed that she was now Miss Quest; they still treated her like a child, and this she could not bear.

She walked more slowly now, not wanting the journey to end; she was savoring freedom: the station far behind, where she was convinced everyone remarked her, commented on her; the house not yet in sight, where the mere existence of her parents was like a reminder that she must be wary, ready to resist. Now there was no one to mark her, not a soul in sight; and she dawdled along the track, skipping from one rut to another, and pulling from their delicate green sheaths the long sweet-tasting grass stems that are as pleasant to chew along a dusty road as sticks of sugar cane. She was happy because she was, for the moment, quite free; she was sad because before long she would reach home; these two emotions deepened together, and it flashed across her mind that this intense, joyful melancholy was a state of mind she had known in the past and— But at once she dismissed the thought; it passed as lightly as the shadow of a wing of a bird, for she knew that the experience associated with that emotion was not to be courted. One did not lie in wait for it; it was a visitor who came without warning. On the other hand, even the fact that the delicious but fearful expectation had crossed her mind at all was enough to warn it away; the visitor liked darkness, this Martha knew, and she hastened to think of something else. At the same time, she was thinking that she had associated the experience with what she now, rather scornfully, called her "religious phase"; and becoming an atheist, which she had done from one day to the next, as easily as dropping a glove, had been painful only because she imagined she must pay the price for intellectual honesty by bidding farewell to this other emotion, this fabulous visitor. It seemed, then, that no such price had been asked of her, it seemed that—

Martha caught herself up, already bad-tempered and irritable: she must *not* analyze, she must not be conscious; and here she was, watching the movements of her own mind as if she were observing a machine. She noted, too, that she was walking very fast, quite blind to the beauties of the trees and grass. For it was evening, and very beautiful; a rich watery gold was lighting the dark greens of the foliage, the dark red of the soil, the pale blond of the grass, to the solemn intensity of the sunset hour. She noted a single white-stemmed tree with its light cloud of glinting leaf rising abruptly from the solid-packed red earth of an anthill, all bathed in a magical sky-reflecting light, and her heart moved painfully, in exquisite sadness. She consciously walked more slowly, consciously enjoyed the melancholy; and all at once found herself on a slight rise, where the trees opened across a wide reach of country; and the sight, a new one, caused her to forget everything else. She could see their house, crouched low on the green-shrouded hill, and between was an unbroken stretch of silver-gold mealies; it was perhaps five miles from where she stood to the Van Rensbergs' boundary, a dark belt of trees behind which solemn blue sky rose like a wall. The mealies swayed and whispered, and the light moved over them; a hawk lay motionless on a current of blue air; and the confused and painful delirium stirred in her again, and this time so powerfully she did not fear its passing. The bush lay quiet about her, a bare slope of sunset-tinted grass moving gently with a tiny rustling sound; an invisible violet tree shed gusts of perfume, like a benediction; and she stood quite still, waiting for the moment, which was now inevitable. There was a movement at the corner of her eye, and she turned her head, cautiously, so as not to disturb what was swelling along her nerves, and saw a small buck, which had come from the trees and stood quietly, flicking its tail, a few paces away. She hardly dared to blink. The buck gazed at her, and then turned its head to look into the bush, laying its ears forward. A second buck tripped out from the trees, and they both stood watching her; then they walked daintily across the ground, their hooves clicking sharp on the stones, the sun warm on their soft brown hides. They dropped their heads to graze, while their little tails shook from side to side impatiently, with flashes of white.

Suddenly the feeling in Martha deepened, and as it did so she knew she had forgotten, as always, that what she had been waiting for like a revelation was a pain, not a happiness; what she remembered, always, was the exultation and the achievement, what she forgot was this difficult birth into a state of mind which words like "ecstasy," "illumination," and so on could not describe, because they suggest joy. Her mind having been formed by poetic literature (and little else), she of course knew that such experiences were common among the religious. But the fact was, so different was "the moment" from what descriptions of other people's "moments" led her to believe was common, that it was not until she had come to accept the experience as ordinary and "incidental to the condition of adolescence" as she put it, sourly, and with positive resentment, that it occurred to her, Why, perhaps it is the same thing, after all? But if so, they were liars, liars one and all; and that she could understand, for was it not impossible for her to remember, in between, how terrible an illumination it was?

There was certainly a definite point at which the thing began. It was not; then it was suddenly inescapable, and nothing could have frightened it away. There was a slow integration, during which she, and the little animals, and the moving grasses, and the sun-warmed trees, and the slopes of shivering silvery mealies, and the great dome of blue light overhead, and the stones of earth under her feet, became one, shuddering together in a dissolution of dancing atoms. She felt the rivers under the ground forcing themselves painfully along her veins, swelling them out in an unbearable pressure; her flesh was the earth, and suffered growth like a ferment; and her eyes stared, fixed like the eye of the sun. Not for one second longer (if the terms for time apply) could she have borne it; but then, with a sudden movement forwards and out, the whole process stopped; and *that* was "the moment" which it was impossible to remember afterwards. For during that space of time (which was timeless) she understood quite finally her smallness, the unimportance of humanity. In her ears was an inchoate grinding, the great wheels of movement, and it was inhuman, like the blundering rocking movement of a bullock cart; and no part of that sound was Martha's voice. Yet she was part of it, reluctantly allowed to participate, though on terms—but what terms? For that moment, while space and time (but these are words, and if she understood anything it was that words, here, were like the sound of a baby crying in a whirlwind) kneaded her flesh, she knew futility; that is, what was futile was her own idea of herself and her place in the chaos of matter. What was demanded of her was that she should accept something quite different; it was as if something new was demanding conception, with her flesh as host; as if there were a necessity, which she must bring herself to accept, that she should allow herself to dissolve and be formed by that necessity. But it did not last; the force desisted, and left her standing on the road, already trying to reach out after "the moment" so that she might retain its message from the wasting and creating chaos of darkness. Already the thing was sliding backwards, becoming a whole in her mind, instead of a process; the memory was changing, so that it was with nostalgia that she longed "to try again."

There had been a challenge that she had refused. But the wave of nostalgia made her angry. She knew it to be a falsity; for it was a longing for something that had never existed, an "ecstasy," in short. There had been no ecstasy, only difficult knowledge. It was as if a beetle had sung. There should be a new word for "illumination."

She saw that she was standing off the road, in the grass, staring at the two little buck, who indifferently flicked their tails and grazed their way off into the bush. Martha thought that she had often shot these little creatures, and that she would never do so again, since they had shared the experience with her. And even as she made the decision, she was as helplessly irritable as if she had caught herself out in a lie which was pointless. She felt, above all, irritable; not sad, merely flat and stale; the more because not five minutes after "the moment" it had arranged itself in her mind as a blissful joy; it was necessary, apparently, to remember the thing as an extremity of happiness.

She walked slowly homewards, taking a shortcut along the fence through the mealies. The ground was hard and packed, cracked across with drought under her feet, which ached, for her sandals were meant for show and not use. She climbed the hill draggingly, and went to her room, so as to compose herself before meeting her parents, or rather, her mother, for to *meet* her father was rather like trying to attract the attention of an irritable specter.

Alas for visions and decisions. In her bedroom she felt nothing but angry resentment: against the people in the district, against Mr. McFarline, against Marnie, who would now "drop over" and borrow patterns.

Her mother entered with the oil lamp, for it was dusk, and

exclaimed, "My dear, I was worrying, and you don't even tell me you're home."

"Well, there's no harm done, safe and sound and still a virgin."

"My *dear—*" Mrs. Quest checked herself, and hung the lamp on the wall. The flame vibrated bluely, then sent a pleasant yellow glow over the uneven plaster, and up to the thatch, where a strand of tarnished silver glistened among shadow. "How did you get back?" asked Mrs. Quest cautiously.

"Walked," Martha said aggressively; and even felt disappointed because Mrs. Quest did not protest.

"Well, come on, we're going to have supper now."

Martha followed her mother obediently, and suddenly found herself saying, in a bright flippant voice, "That dirty old man, Mr. McFarline, he tried to make love to me." She looked at her father, but he was slowly crumbling his bread in time with his thoughts.

Mrs. Quest said hastily, "Nonsense, you're imagining it, he couldn't have done."

The suggestion that she was too young for such attentions made Martha say, "And then he had an attack of conscience, and offered me ten shillings." She giggled uncomfortably, with another glance at her abstracted father; and Mrs. Quest said, "He knows better, he's too nice."

"Nice," said Martha acidly, "with a compound full of his children."

Mrs. Quest said hastily, with a glance at the servant who was handing vegetables, "You shouldn't listen to gossip."

"Everybody knows it, and besides, I heard you saying so to Mrs. McDougall."

"Well, but that doesn't mean—I don't think . . ."

"Damned hypocrisy," said Martha, "all this color-bar nonsense, and Mr. McFarline can sleep with whoever he likes and—"

"My dear," said Mrs. Quest, with a desperate look towards the impassive servant, "do think of what you're saying."

"Yes, that's all you think of, provided all the lies and ugliness are covered up."

Mrs. Quest raised her voice in anger, and the battle was on; mother and daughter said the things both had said so often before; not even waiting for the other to finish a sentence, until the noise caused Mr. Quest to snap out, "Shut up, both of you."

They looked at him immediately, and with relief; one might have supposed this was the result they intended. But Mr. Quest said no more; after a baffled and exasperated glare, he dropped his eyes and continued to eat.

"You hear what your father says?" demanded Mrs. Quest unfairly.

Martha was filled with frightened pain, at this alliance against her; and she exclaimed loudly, "Anything for peace, you and your Christianity, and then what you do in practice . . ." But almost at once she became ashamed, because of the childishness of what she was saying. But the things we say are usually on a far lower level than what we think; it seemed to Martha that perhaps her chief grievance against her parents was this: that in her exchange with them she was held down at a level she had long since outgrown, even on this subject, which, to her parents, was the terrifyingly extreme outpost of her development.

But her remark at least had had the power to pierce her father's defenses, for he raised his head and said angrily, "Well, if we're so rotten, and you haven't any time for us, you can leave. Go on," he shouted, carried away by the emotions his words generated, "go on, then, get out and leave us in peace."

Martha caught her breath in horror; on the surface of her mind she was pointing out to herself that her own father was throwing her out of her home—she, a girl of seventeen. Deeper down, however, she recognized this for what it was, an emotional release, which she should ignore. "Very well," she said angrily, "I will leave." She and her father looked at each other across the breadth of the table—her mother sat in her usual place at the head; and those two pairs of dark and angry eyes stared each other out.

It was Mr. Quest who dropped his head and muttered, half guiltily, "I simply cannot stand this damned fight, fight, fight!" And he pettishly threw down his napkin. Immediately the servant bent and picked it up, and handed it to his master. "Thanks," said Mr. Quest automatically, arranging it again across his lap.

"My *dear*," said Mrs. Quest, in a small appealing voice to her husband.

He replied grumblingly, "Well, fight if you like, but not when I'm around, for God's sake."

Now they all remained silent; and immediately after the meal Martha went to her bedroom, saying to herself that she would leave home at once, imagining various delightful rescues. The parcel of books lay unopened on her bed. She cut the string and looked at the titles, and her feeling of being let down deepened. They were all on economics. She had wished for books which might explain this confusion of violent feeling she found herself in.

Next day she rose early, and went out with the gun and killed a duiker on the edge of the Big Tobacco Land (where her father had grown tobacco during his season's phase of believing in it). She called a passing native to carry the carcass home to the kitchen, which, as it happened, was already full of meat.

But put this way it implies too much purpose. Martha woke early, and could not sleep; she decided to go for a walk because the sunrise was spread so exquisitely across the sky; she took the gun because it was her habit to carry it, though she hardly ever used it; she shot at the buck almost halfheartedly, because it happened to present itself; she was surprised when it fell dead; and when it was dead, it was a pity to waste the meat. The incident was quite different from actually planning the thing, or so she felt; and she thought half guiltily, Oh, well, what does it matter, anyway?

After breakfast she again looked at Joss's books, skimming through them rapidly. They were written by clearly well-meaning people who disliked poverty. Her feeling was, I know this already; which did not only mean that she agreed with any conclusion which proved hopelessly unfair a system which condemned her, Martha Quest, to live on the farm, instead of in London with people she could talk to. She made this joke against herself rather irritably, for she knew it to be half true. What she felt was, Yes, of course poverty is stupid, so why say it again? How do you propose to alter all this? And "all this" meant the farm, the hordes of deprived natives who worked it, the people in the district, who assumed they had every right to live as they did and use the natives as they pleased. The reasonable persuasiveness of the books seemed merely absurd, when one thought of the violent passions ranged against them. She imagined the author of books like these as a clean, plump, suave gentleman, shut in a firelit study behind drawn curtains, with no sound in his ears but the movement of his own thoughts.

She kept the books a week, and then returned them on a mail day with the postboy. She also sent a note saying: "I wish you would let me have some books about the emancipation of women." It was only after the man had left that the request struck her as naïve, a hopeless self-exposure; and she could hardly bear to open the parcel which was sent to her. Inside was the note she expected: "I'm glad you have absorbed so much knowledge of economics in three days. What a clever girl you are. I enclose helpful handbook on sexual problems. I could ask Solly, who has a fine collection of psychology, etc., but alas, he has gone off to 'live his own life,' and our relations are not such that I could handle his books without asking him." The enclosed book was Engels's *Origin of the Family*. Martha read it, and agreed with every word of it—or rather, with what she gained from it, which was a confirmation of her belief that the marriages of the district were ridiculous and even sordid, and most of all old-fashioned.

She sat under her tree, hugging her sun-warmed arms, feeling the firm soft flesh with approval, and the sight of her long and shapely legs made her remember the swollen bodies of the pregnant women she had seen, with shuddering anger, as at the sight of a cage designed for herself. Never, never, never, she swore to herself, but with a creeping premonition; and she thought of Solly's books, now out of bounds, because he and Joss so unreasonably insisted on quarreling; and she thought of Joss, for whom she was feeling a most irrational dislike. At one moment she scorned him because he had dared to treat her like an attractive young female; and the next because he had taken her at her word, and simply offered books; and this confusion hardened into a nervous repulsion: Well, she could do without Joss!

She returned Engels, with such a formal note that no further word came from him, though she was waiting for one; and then melancholy settled over her, and she wandered around the farm like a girl under a spell of silence.

One morning she came on her father, seated on a log of wood at the edge of a field, watching the natives dig a furrow for storm water. Mr. Quest held his pipe between his teeth, and slowly rolled plugs of rich dark tobacco between his palms, while his eyes rested distantly on his laborers.

"Well, old son?" he inquired, as Martha sat beside him; for he might call either his male or his female child "old son."

Martha rested the rifle across her knees, pulled herself some chewing grass, and lapsed into his silence; for these two, away from Mrs. Quest, were quite easy together.

But she could not maintain it; she had to worry at him for his attention; and soon she began to complain about her mother, while Mr. Quest uneasily listened. "Yes, I daresay," he agreed, and "Yes, I suppose you are right"; and with every agreement his face expressed only the wish that she might remove this pressure on him to consider not only her position but his own. But Martha did not desist; and at last the usual irritability crept into his voice, and he said, "Your mother's a good woman," and he gave her a look which meant "Now, that's enough."

"Good?" said Martha, inviting him to define the word.

"That's all very well," he said, shifting himself slightly away.

"What do you mean by 'good'?" she persisted. "You know quite well she's— I mean, if goodness is just doing what you want to do, behaving in a conventional way, without thinking, then goodness is easy enough to come by!" Here she flung a stone crossly at the trunk of a tree.

"I don't see where you end, when you start like this," said Mr. Quest, complainingly. For this was by no means the first time this conversation had taken place, and he dreaded it. They were both remembering that first occasion, when he had demanded angrily, "Well, don't you love your mother, then?" and Martha had burst into peals of angry laughter, saying, "Love? What's love got to do with it? She does exactly as she wants, and says, 'Look how I sacrificed myself,' she never stops trying to get her own way, and then you talk about love."

After a long silence, during which Mr. Quest slowly slid away into his private thoughts, Martha said defiantly, "Well, I don't see it. You just use words and—it's got nothing to do with what actually goes on . . ." She stopped, confused; though what she felt was clear enough: not only that people's motives were not what they imagined them to be, but that they should be made to see the truth.

"Oh, Lord, Matty," said Mr. Quest, suddenly bursting into that helpless anger. "What do you want me to do? The last year has been hell on earth, you never stop bickering."

"So you want me to go away?" asked Martha pathetically; and her heart sang at the idea of it.

"I never said anything of the sort," said poor Mr. Quest, "you're always so extreme." Then, after a pause, hopefully: "It wouldn't be a bad idea, would it? You always say you've outgrown your mother, and I daresay you have."

Martha waited, and it was with the same hopeful inquiry she had felt with Joss: she was wanting someone to take the responsibility for her; she needed a rescue. Mr. Quest should have suggested some practical plan, and at once, very much to his surprise, he would have found an amenable and grateful daughter. Instead, the silence prolonged itself into minutes. He sighed with pleasure, as he looked over the sunlit field, the silent, heat-slowed bush; then he lowered his eyes to his feet, where there were some ants at work in an old piece of wood.

Suddenly he remarked, in a dreamy voice, "Makes you think, doesn't it, seeing these ants? I wonder how they see us, like God, I shouldn't be surprised? When that soil specialist was out last year, he said ants have a language, and a police force—that sort of thing."

There was no reply from Martha. At last he shot her an apprehensive glance sideways, and met eyes that were half angry, half amused, but with a persistent criticism that caused him to rise to his feet saying, "How about going up to the house and asking for some tea? Weather makes you thirsty."

And in silence the father and daughter returned to the house on the hill.

FROM

# *A Proper Marriage*

"Well, Matty, and now you'll be free to get on with your own work."

It was with these words that Douglas dropped his parting kiss on her cheek when he left for the office each morning, and with a look of pure satisfaction. The kindly, confident young man crossed the untidy bedroom towards the door, bouncing a little from the balls of his feet, smiling backwards at Martha, who was sitting in a tangle of crumpled and stained silk in a mess of bedclothes, and vanished whistling down the corridor. The gleam of proprietary satisfaction never failed to arouse in Martha a flush of strong resentment, which was as unfailingly quenched by a succeeding guilt. To account for the resentment, for above all it was essential to account for every contradictory emotion that assailed one, she had already formed a theory.

After Douglas had left, she kicked off the bedclothes, and allowed herself to fall backwards on the cooling sheets and pillows. She lay quiet. Opposite her, two neat squares of bright blue sky, in one of which was suspended the stilled black wheel of the fair; reflected sunlight quivered hot on the wall. From all around, from above, from below, the sound of voices, a broom swishing, a child crying. But here, in the heart of the building, two rooms, white, silent, empty. And, on the bed, Martha, uncomfortably fingering the silk of her nightdress, trying most conscientiously to relax into the knowledge of space and silence. At the same time she was thinking of Douglas, now already at his office; she could see the self-conscious look with which he allowed himself to be teased; every night he came back to share with her his pleasure in how the office had said this or that. And how she hated him for it! And it was her husband about whom she was feeling this resentment, this violent dislike.

Martha, ignoring the last few months in town before her marriage, because she could not bear to think about them, went back to that period when she was a girl on the farm. From this, several incidents had been selected by her need for a theory. There had been that young man who . . . and the other one . . . and that occasion when . . . After hours of determined concentration she would emerge with the phrase "Women hate men who take them for granted." It would have done for a story in a magazine. But that impersonal "woman" was a comfort—briefly, for no sooner had she reached it than she saw the image that the words conjured up: something sought, wooed, capricious, bestowing favors. No, there was something extremely distasteful about that capricious female; no sooner had Martha caught a glimpse of her than she must repudiate her entirely; she was certainly from the past! The suggestion of coyness was unbearable. Yet she and Douglas had achieved a brotherly friendliness almost immediately; and when he bounced cheerfully into bed, clutching her in a cheerful and companionable act of love that ignored the female which must be wooed, she undoubtedly loathed him from the bottom of her heart, an emotion which was as inevitably followed by a guilty affection. The situation was, as she jauntily and bleakly put it, unsatisfactory.

She therefore got out of bed and went into the living room, and knelt in front of the bookcase. Books. Words. There must surely be some pattern of words which would neatly and safely cage what she felt—isolate her emotions so that she could look at them from outside. For she was of that generation who, having found nothing in religion, had formed themselves by literature. And the books which spoke most directly were those which had come out of Western Europe during the past hundred years, and of those, the personal and self-confessing. And so she knelt in front of a bookcase, in driving need of the right arrangement of words; for it is a remarkable fact that she was left unmoved by criticisms of the sort of person she was by parents, relations, preachers, teachers, politicians, and the people who write for the newspapers; whereas an unsympathetic description of a character similar to her own in a novel would send her into a condition of anxious soul-searching for days. Which suggests that it is of no use for artists to insist, with such nervous disinclination for responsibility, that their productions are only "a divine play" or "a reflection from the creative fires of irony," etc., etc. while the Marthas of this world read and search with the craving thought, What does this say about my life? It will not do at all—but it must be admitted that there always came a point where Martha turned from the novelists and taletellers to that section of the bookcase which was full of books called *The Psychology of. . .*, *The*

*Behavior of. . . , A Guide to . . . ,* with the half-formulated thought that the novelists had not caught up with life; for there was no doubt that the sort of things she or Stella or Alice talked about found no reflection in literature—or rather, it was the attitudes of mind they took for granted that did not appear there, from which she deduced that women in literature were still what men, or the men-women, wished they were. In this other part of the bookcase, however, were no such omissions; she found what she was thinking and feeling described with an admirable lack of ambiguity. And yet, after hours of search among the complexities and subtleties of character, she was likely to return to her bedroom profoundly comforted, with some such resounding and original remark as "The young husband, therefore, must be careful to be specially understanding during the difficult weeks after marriage." For, since Douglas, the young husband in question, so logically insisted on relying upon the common sense *she* insisted on, she must with some part of herself take his place by being understanding, compassionate, etc. Martha was able to preserve an equilibrium because of an observing and satirical eye focused upon her own behavior from a superior vantage point that was of course in no way influenced by that behavior. She achieved quite extraordinary degrees of self-forbearance by this device.

In the bedroom the bedclothes were still lying dragged back, clothes lay everywhere; the morning was slipping past and she was not dressed. And now this question of work confronted her. She had understood she was not alone in her position of a woman who disdained both housework and a "job," but was vaguely expected by her husband—but only because of her own insistence on it—to be engaged in work of her own. Both Stella and Alice had claimed the state. Martha had heard their respective husbands speak to them in precisely the same tone of pride and satisfaction that Douglas used to her. Their wives were not as those of other men.

Feeling the distant pressure of this "work," Martha dutifully went to the bathroom to equip herself to face it.

The bathroom was modern. A high window showed yet another angle of clear blue sky, together with the tops of the trees in the park. A large white bath filled with heavy greenish water where spangles of light quivered, white cabinets, white shelves—it was all a gleam of white enamel. Martha took off her nightdress, and was alone with her body. But it was not that calm and obedient body which had been so pleasant a companion. White it was, and solid and unmarked—but heavy, unresponsive; her flesh was uncomfortable on her bones. It burned and unaccountably swelled; it seemed to be pursuing ideas of its own. Inside the firm thick flesh a branch of bones which presumably remained unchanged: the thought was comforting. Martha looked down at her shape of flesh with the anxious thought that it was upon this that the marriage depended; for this, in fact, they—she and Douglas—had been allowed by society to shut themselves away in two high rooms with a bathroom attached. It was almost with a feeling of a rider who was wondering whether his horse would make the course that she regarded this body of hers, which was not only divided from her brain by the necessity of keeping open that cold and dispassionate eye, but separated into compartments of its own. Martha had after all been provided with a map of her flesh by "the book," in which each area was marked by the name of a different physical sensation, so that her mind was anxiously aware, not only of a disconnected partner, a body, but of every part of it, which might or might not come up to scratch at any given occasion. There were moments when she felt she was strenuously held together by nothing more than an act of will. She was beginning to feel that this view of herself was an offense against what was deepest and most real in her. And again she thought of the simple women of the country, who might be women in peace, according to their instincts, without being made to think and disintegrate themselves into fragments. During those first few weeks of her marriage Martha was always accompanied by that other, black woman, like an invisible sister simpler and wiser than herself; for no matter how much she reminded herself of statistics and progress, she envied her from the bottom of her heart. Without, of course, having any intention of emulating her: loyalty to progress forbade it.

At that hour of the morning the sun fell in bright lances through the high window. Martha stood where they might fall on her flesh; her skin shone with a soft iridescence, the warmth kneaded together her unhappily disconnected selves, she began to dissolve into well-being. But first there was another ritual to be gone through. From the high cupboard she took down the cans and rubber tubes prescribed by Dr. Stern and washed away the sweats of love in the rocking green water. Then she refilled the bath for what she thought of as her own bath. In this she wallowed, while the sunlight moved up over the sides of the bath and into the water, and she was whole and at peace again, floating in sunlight and water like a fish. She might have stayed there all morning, if there wasn't this question of work; so she got out too soon, and thought with vague anxiety that those areas of tenderness on breasts and belly were no more than was to be expected after such an intensive love life. The thought of pregnancy crossed her mind; and was instantly dismissed. She felt that it was hard enough to keep Martha Quest, now Knowell, afloat on a sea of chaos and sensation without being pregnant as well—no, it was all too difficult. But her dress was tight; she might eat less, she told herself. Then she made tea and ate bread and butter with satisfaction at the thought that she was depriving herself of a meal.

And now it was ten in the morning, and her day was her own. Her work was free to start when it would. Martha went to the other room, and arranged herself comfortably on the divan. Or rather, it was with the intention of comfort, for the divan was a high, hard mattress on a native-made bed covered with loosely woven brown linen. Comfortable it was not; but it suitably supported the rest of the room, and Martha chose it because one might sit there without surrendering to the boundaries of a chair.

Into this little box of a room had flowed so many different items of furniture—and then out again. Now two small jolly chairs were set at neat angles on a clean green rug. A new table of light wood, surrounded by four chairs of the same, filled the opposite corner. The curtains, of that material known as folk-weave, whose rough grain held pockets of yellow light, were of the same brown she sat on. It was safe to say that the furniture that had flowed in and out of this room with the restless owners of it was indistinguishable from what filled it now. This thought gave Martha an undefined and craving hollowness, a sort of hunger. Yet everything was so practical and satisfactory! She looked at this room, from chair to window, from table to cupboard, and her eyes rested on nothing, but moved onwards hastily to the next article, as if *this* might provide that quality she was searching for.

It was not her flat; it belonged to that group of people who had seen her married. Almost at once her thoughts floated away from this place she sat in, these white boxes in the heart of the building, and slowly she tested various other shells for living in, offered to her in books. There were, after all, not so many of them; and each went with a kind of life she must dismiss instantly and instinctively. For instance, there was her father's childhood in the English country cottage, honest simplicity with the bones of the house showing through lathe and plaster. Outside, a green and lush country—but tame, tamed; it would not do at all. Or—and this was a dip into the other stream that fed her blood—a tall narrow Victorian house, crammed with heavy dark furniture, buttoned and puffed and stuffed and padded, an atmosphere of things unsaid. If that country cottage could be acknowledged with a self-conscious smile, like a charmingly naïve relation, this narrow dark house could not be admitted too close, it was too dangerous. And that house which was being built now everywhere, in every country of the world, the modern house, cosmopolitan, capable of being lifted up from one continent and dumped down in any other without exciting remark—no, certainly not, it was not to be thought of. So there remained the flat in which she was in fact now sitting? But she was not here at all; she did not live in it; she was waiting to be moved on somewhere . . .

At about eleven in the morning she roused herself. For she knew that since both Stella and Alice were as free for their own work as she was, either or both of them were likely to drop in. She therefore put the kettle on and made sandwiches, prepared to spend the rest of the morning gossiping or—as pleasantly—alone.

By now the stores would have delivered by native messenger the groceries, meat, and vegetables she had ordered by telephone; putting away these things interrupted work for a few minutes. Preparing a light lunch for Douglas could not take longer than half an hour. In the long interval before lunch, Martha drifted once more in front of her mirror, with her air of one prepared to be surprised by what she saw there. And from this, as a natural consequence of a long and dissatisfied examination of herself, she collected scissors and needle and material, and in a few moments she was at the table with the sewing machine. And now her look of vagueness had vanished; for the first time since she had risen that morning, she was centered behind what her hands did. She had the gift of running up sundowner frocks, dance dresses, out of a remnant from the sales, even discarded curtains or old-fashioned clothes that her mother had kept. She could transform them without effort—apart from the long, dreamy meditations which might fill half a week; for when a woman claims with disarming modesty that she has run up this dress for ten shillings, the long process of manipulating the material around her image of herself, those hours of creation, are not taken into account. Very few women's time is money, even now. But while the clothes she made for after dark were always a success, it seemed her sureness of touch must desert her for the daytime. Her friends might exclaim loyally that her morning clothes was absolutely wonderful, but it was only over the evening clothes that their voices held the authentic seal of envy. From which it follows?

The fact is that as soon as Douglas returned from the office for lunch, the day was already nearly at evening. For he returned finally at four; and after that, it was only a question of time before their eyes met on a query: at the Sports Club, everyone they knew would be delighted to see them, and afterwards there would be dancing there or at the hotels. It seemed as if the day was only a drab preliminary to the night, as if the pageant of sunset was meant only as a curtain raiser to that moment when the lights sprang up along the streets, and with them a feeling of vitality and excitement. For in the hotels, the clubs, and the halls, the orchestras struck up at eight, and from every point in the town dance music was flowing like water from a concealed reservoir of nostalgia hidden below it. These were the nights of African winter, sharp, clear, cold, a high and luminous starlit dark lifting away from the low, warm glitter of city lights. In the white courts of the hotels, braziers offered a little futile heat to the cold dry air, and groups of young people formed and dissolved around them: there was no room for everyone inside, there was no room for all the people who needed suddenly to dance.

Night after night, they moved from the Club to the Plaza and on to McGrath's; and the self-contained parties that began the evening expected to dissolve into a great whole as midnight approached. By midnight they were dancing as if they formed one soul; they danced and sang, mindless, in a half-light, they were swallowed up in the sharp, exquisite knowledge of loss and impending change that came over the seas and continents from Europe; and underneath it all, a rising tide of excitement that was like a poison. Uniforms were appearing here and there, and the wearers carried themselves with self-effacing modesty, as if on a secret mission, but conscious that all eyes in the room were fixed on them. The rumors were beginning. This regiment was going to be called up, they were going to conscript the whole population; but the question of conscription was surely an irrelevance when every young man in the town was thinking only of the moment when he could put on a uniform—and that before it was decided what the war was to be fought about. They were all longing to be swallowed up in something bigger than themselves; they were, in fact, already swallowed up. And since each war, before it starts, has the look of the last one, it did not matter how often stern and important young men assured hushed audiences that the world could not survive a month of modern warfare, they would all be bombed to pieces by new and secret weapons; it was necessary only for the orchestra to play "Tipperary" or "Keep the Home Fires Burning"—which they did on every conceivable occasion—for the entire gathering to become transformed into a congregation of self-dedicated worshipers of what their parents chose to remember of 1914.

In between dances, groups formed to discuss what was happening in Europe—or rather to exchange the phrases they had read that morning in the *Zambesia News*. The fact that this newspaper was contradicting itself with the calmest of assurance from day to day did not matter in the least; there was going to be a war, and night after night youth danced and sang itself into a condition of preparation for it. Their days and work, their loves and love making, were nothing but a preparation for that moment when hundreds of them stamped and shouted in great circles to the thudding drums, felt less as sound than as their own pulses; this was the culmination of the day, the real meaning of it, the moment of surrender.

Then the music stopped suddenly and disastrously, the managers came forward bowing with strained politeness, ignoring the pleas and imprecations about their hardheartedness—and the masses of young people streamed out into the still, frost-bound air, under the glitter of the Cross. It was at this point that Martha and Douglas were reminded that they were married; for "the gang"—those of them that remained unbound to the girls whose one preoccupation it was to get married to the doomed as quickly as possible—went off shouting and stamping to the fun fair, which they kept going until early morning. The young married couples departed to one of the flats; and it was then that it became apparent there was a certain difference of viewpoint between husbands and wives. Stella, Alice, Martha, might have been part of that single yearning heart only half an hour before, but now they tended to fall silent, and even exchanged tolerant glances as their respective young men held forth on their plans for joining up. For it is a strain on any marriage, which after all is likely to begin with the belief that it must provide satisfaction and happiness for at least a few years, when one of the partners show signs of such restlessness to "rush off to the wars"—as the girls acidly put it—the moment a war, any war, offers itself.

By the time Martha and Douglas reached home, reached the small, brightly lit, untidy bedroom, still littered with their day clothes and filled with the loud, sad, bitter music from the fun fair—for the wheel was still dragging its glittering load of cars in its circle—by this time, their elation was flagging, and there was a feeling of anticlimax. Now, drenched and submerged by the music, which it was impossible to keep out even with shut windows, Martha crept closer to Douglas and demanded the assurance that he did not really want to leave her; just as Stella and Alice were doing in their bedrooms. Douglas, manfully clasping Martha to him, murmured reassurances and looked over her head at the glitter of the wheel. He had not known how intolerably boring and empty his life was until there was a chance of escaping from it; and the more fiercely he determined not to be left out of things, the more tightly he held Martha and consoled her. He was holding a warm, confiding bundle of female flesh, he wished only to love her and be proud of her—for, above all, his pride was fed by her anxious demands for his love; but it was all no use. For, just as he was playing a role which was surely inconsistent with what he thought—the young hero off to the wars for adventure—so she began to speak in the ancient female voice which he found utterly irritating. After a long silence, during which he hoped she might have gone to sleep so that he might dream of adventure without a guilt, a small, obstinate, ugly voice remarked that there would be wars so long as men were such babies. At this point he would loosen his grip and lie stiff beside her, and begin to explain in an official tone that surely, Matty, she must see they must be prepared . . . But it was no use; that official tone carries no conviction any longer, not even to the people who use it. She sniggered derisively; and he felt foolish.

They rolled apart and lay without touching; even apologizing in an offhand, hasty way if they happened to touch by accident. Douglas soon fell asleep. Martha could not sleep while the wheel turned and churned out music. She was in a mood of angry self-contempt for being infected by that dangerous undertow of excitement. For she had caught herself daydreaming of being a nurse, and no less than a ministering angel. But, alas, alas, we know all about that ministering angel; we know what she comes to in the end; and Martha could only return to thoughts of her father. She considered the undoubted fact that while Mr. Quest might expatiate about the inefficiency and corruption of the leaders of his war, about the waste of life, the uselessness of the thing, while he might push into Martha's hands books like *All Quiet on the Western Front* with an irascible command that she should read it and understand that *that* was war, while he might talk of that war with the bitter, savage consciousness of betrayal, yet there was always an undercurrent of burning regret. Then he had been alive. "The comradeship," he would exclaim, "the comradeship! I've never experienced that since!" and then the terrible *"It was the only time in my life I was really happy."*

When the wheel stilled at last Martha was able to sleep; and in the morning she was a different creature, easily able to withstand the insinuations of the ministering angel in the white coif, and prepared to look soberly at the alternatives—or rather at a single alternative, for the possibility of in fact settling down to a life of tea parties, sundowners, and in due course, children, was out of the question. She was trying to form the confusion of feelings that afflicted her to fit the sharp, clear view of life held by Solly and Joss—that was how she saw it. What she actually wanted, of course, was for some man to arrive in her life, simply take her by the hand, and lead her off into this new world. But it seemed he did not exist. And so she read the newspapers, and enjoyed the cynicism they produced in her. There was the *Zambesia News,* for instance, at that period in a state of such uneasy uncertainty. On the one hand it was reminding its readers about the atrocious nature of Hitler's Germany; on the other it seemed to be suffering from a certain reluctance to do so. Hard to forget that these same atrocities, concentration camps and so on, had been ignored by the *Zambesia News,* as by its betters, until it was impossible to ignore them; while even now, like those great exemplars overseas, it showed real indignation only over Hitler's capacity for absorbing other countries. Nor was she able to feel any less derisive when she read the great exemplars themselves, the newspapers from Home. As for that other, deeper knowledge, the pulse that really moved her, gained from her almost religious feeling for literature, a knowledge that amounted to a vision of mankind as nobility bound and betrayed—this was vanishing entirely beneath the pressure of enjoyable cynicism which was being fed by everything about her, and particularly by her own behavior. For despite all her worried introspection, her determination to act rationally if only it was possible to find out what rational behavior should be, the fact was that her sluggish days were nothing but a preparation for the first drink at sundown, which led to that grand emotional culmination at midnight when she joined the swinging circle of intoxicated dancers controlled by the thudding of the drums.

It was about six weeks after her marriage that all this confusion was shaken into a single current by the fact that she was violently sick one morning. Lethargy caused her to murmur consolingly that it must be the result of not sleeping enough—probably nothing but a hangover. But she succeeded in forgetting it.

Two days later, in Stella's flat, after a dance, it happened that Maisie was there. She was wearing a dress of white tulle, frilled and flounced like a baby's bassinette, and from it her plump shoulders, her lazy pretty face, emerged with a placid enjoyment of life which apparently had not been disturbed by the fact that she had become engaged to one of the young men who was training to be a pilot. She came to sit by Martha, murmuring vaguely, "Well, Matty. . ." as if they saw each other every day. In fact they did, at dances, but from across the room. She bent down to rip off a strip of dirty white from the bottom of her dress where it had been trodden on, rolled it up, and tossed it into the corner of the room; and sat looking speculatively at Martha, her fair face flushed and beaded with the heat. "You look fine, you don't show yet," she remarked good-naturedly, looking frankly at Martha's stomach.

"What do you mean?" asked Martha.

Maisie was startled. "I'm sorry," she apologized hastily. "I thought . . ." Someone spoke to her, and she took the opportunity to get up and sit somewhere else. From time to time during the rest of the evening, she glanced towards Martha, but with the determination not to catch her eye. She left before Martha did, arm in arm with her pilot, including Martha with the rest of the room in a large, vague smile of farewell.

Afterwards Martha said indignantly to Douglas that it was the limit, people were saying she was pregnant. To which he replied a little awkwardly that some of the lads from the Club had suggested this was the case.

"Do you mean to say they think we got married because we *had* to?" she exclaimed, furious; for she felt this was an insult towards them as free beings able to do as they wished.

But he misunderstood her indignation, and said, laughing, "After all, Matty, since most of the people who get married get married because they have to . . ."

She laughed, but she was very uneasy.

Again she forgot about it, until there was a letter from her mother, which immediately caught her attention because of its casual tone. At the end of it was an inquiry as to how she felt. Again she burned with indignation—there was a conspiracy against her!

For some days, there was no reason to think of it; then she got a charming letter from Mrs. Talbot, which had the same hurried apologetic manner as her speech. She asked why dear Matty did not drop in to see her one morning, she would so like to have a proper talk.

The letters were always on thick white paper, in a fine-pointed black hand; they gave an impression of casual elegance which made Martha curious, for never had she known anyone whose letters were not utilitarian. The letters, like Mrs. Talbot herself, spoke of an existence altogether remote from this colonial town. But what was this life which Mrs. Talbot seemed so anxious Martha should share? And what was this proper talk?

"We have supper or spend the evening with them at least two or three times a week," Martha pointed out to Douglas, quite bewildered.

"Oh, go and see her, Matty, she'll be pleased."

Martha had discovered that Mrs. Talbot was not, as one might infer from her appearance, about thirty-five, but over sixty; she was very rich, but in a way that seemed to apologize for the unpleasant fact that there was such a thing as money in the world at all. During those evenings, she would take Douglas—apologizing first—into an inner room, and they would discuss investments and properties. "There are no flies on Mrs. Talbot," he said appreciatively. And then, always: "She's an absolute marvel, a wonder! Why, Matty, would you think she was a day over thirty. Isn't she terrific?"

"But Elaine. . ." pointed out Martha jealously.

"Oh, Elaine's all right, she's a nice kid," said Douglas, dismissing her.

That Elaine should be thought of as a nice kid made Martha laugh—

it was easier to tolerate the amazing Mrs. Talbot. For at the bottom of an uneasy disapproval of that lady was Martha's physical arrogance—the pride of the very young. *She* was young and whole and comely; secretly she felt a fierce, shuddering repulsion for the old and unsightly. For a brief ten years—she was convinced that thirty was the end of youth and good looks—she was allowed by nature to be young and attractive. For Mrs. Talbot to be beautiful at sixty was not fair.

"She *can't* be sixty," she had protested hopefully. But she was.

Martha told Douglas that she didn't want to have a proper talk with Mrs. Talbot; but on the morning after getting the letter she found herself disinclined for that "work," and set off on impulse for Mrs. Talbot's house. It was half past nine; the morning was well advanced for a society which began work at eight. Martha walked through the park and along the avenues: the house was one of the delightful houses of the older town. It was almost hidden from the street by trees and flowering bushes. The door opened immediately from the garden path, and not off a wide veranda. The house had an introspective, inward-turning look because of this discreet black door with its shining door knocker. Mrs. Talbot's house, like herself, could not help suggesting the England one knew from novels. The door might be flanked on either side by poinsettias, ragged pointed scraps of scarlet silk fluttering on naked, shining silken stems, but one felt they were there only to suggest an ironical contrast.

Martha rang, and was admitted by a native servant, and shown into a small side room kept for just this purpose. She summoned her memories of what she had read, and then saw, as she had expected, a tray on a stand, littered with visiting cards. At this it occurred to her that the phrase "dropping in" might have a different meaning to Mrs. Talbot than it had for herself and her friends. Before she could recover herself, Mr. Talbot came in. She had seen very little of him; he went to the Club in the evenings when his wife entertained. He was wearing a dark silk dressing gown, was tall and heavily built, with a dark, heavy face, and he came stooping forward with his hand outstretched, apologizing for his dressing gown. She was embarrassed because of her thoughts about him. She did not like him. She did not like the way he would come into his wife's drawing room, on his way out, a man paying forced tribute to women's amusements; besides, he suggested a spy—his look at Mrs. Talbot always made her uncomfortable. Finally, he was an old man, and distasteful because he had a sardonic, intimate manner with her that made it impossible to dismiss him so easily. He was forcing her now to think of him as a man, and she stammered a little as she said she had come to see Mrs. Talbot. He said very politely that he didn't think his wife was up yet, but that Martha might care to wait?

She said at once, no—of course not; she was only on a walk, and she would come up another time.

He held her eyes with his while he inquired if she would like to see Elaine.

Martha said yes, she would like to very much.

Mr. Talbot stood aside for her to precede him out of the door, and she felt uncomfortable as she passed him, as if he might suddenly put out his hands and grasp her. In the passage, he indicated the drawing-room door, and apologized again for his dressing gown. Then he opened another door; Martha caught a glimpse of a large brown leather chair, a pipe smoking on a small table, a litter of newspapers; he went inside, having held her eyes again in another direct glance.

She went into the drawing room, feeling its contrast with the brown masculine study he had gone into. It was large, low-ceilinged, rather dim. It was carpeted from wall to wall with a deep rosy, flowing softness that gave under her feet. It was full of furniture that Martha instinctively described as antiques. It was a charming room, it was like an Edwardian novel; and one could not be in it without thinking of the savage country outside. Martha kept looking out of the windows which were veiled in thin pale stuffs, as if to assure herself this was in fact Africa. It might have vanished, she felt, so strong was the power of this room to destroy other realities.

Elaine came forward, from a small sunny veranda enclosed by glass and filled with plants in such a way that it suggested a conservatory. Elaine was wearing a loose linen smock, and she was doing the flowers.

She asked Martha, with charming formality, if she would like to come to the sun porch, and Martha followed her. There was a small grass chair, and Martha sat on it and watched Elaine fitting pink and mauve sweet peas into narrow silver vases like small fluted trumpets.

Elaine said that her mother was never up before eleven, and accompanied this remark by a small smile which did not invite shared amusement, but rather expressed an anxious desire that no one should find it remarkable. Elaine, standing by her trestle, with her copper jugs for water, her shears, her rows of sweet peas and roses, her heavy gauntlets, had the air of a fragile but devoted handmaid to her mother's way of life. Martha watched her and found herself feeling protective. This girl should be spared any unpleasantness which might occur outside the shining glass walls of the sun porch. Her fragility, her air of fatigue, the blue shadows under her eyes, removed her completely from any possibility of being treated by Martha as an equal. Martha found herself censoring her speech; in a few minutes they were making conversation about gardening. Then a bell shrilled from close by, and Elaine hastily excused herself, laid down her flowers, and went to a door which led to Mrs. Talbot's bedroom.

In a few minutes she came back to say that her mother was awake and was delighted to hear that Martha had come to see her. If dear Matty did not mind being treated so informally—and here Elaine again offered a small anxious smile, as if acknowledging at least the possibility of amusement—would she like to come into the bedroom? Martha went to the door, expecting Elaine to come with her; but Elaine remained with her flowers, a pale effaced figure in her yellow smock, drenched in the sunlight that was concentrated through the blazing glass of the sun porch.

Martha's eyes were full of sunlight, and in this room it was nearly dark. She stood blinded just inside the door, and heard Mrs. Talbot murmuring affectionate greetings from the shadows. She stumbled forward, sat on a chair that was pushed under her, and then saw that Mrs. Talbot was up and in a dressing gown, a dim figure agitated by the delight this visit gave her, but even more agitated by apologies because she was not dressed.

"If I'd known you were coming, Matty darling . . . But I'm so terribly lazy, I simply can't get out of bed before twelve. It was so sweet of you to come so soon when I asked you—but we old women must be allowed our weaknesses. . . ."

Martha was astounded by that "old women"; but there was no suggestion of coyness in it. She tried to peer through the dark, for she was longing to see how Mrs. Talbot must look before she had created herself for her public. All she could see was a slender figure in an insinuating rustle of silks, perched on the bed. Mrs. Talbot lit a cigarette; almost at once the red spark was crushed out again; Martha saw that this flutter was due simply to a routine being upset.

"I rang up my hairdresser when I heard your voice, I told him not to come this morning. I'm sure it won't hurt me to show an inch or so of grey just for once. When you reach the age of going grey, Matty darling, don't be silly and dye your hair. It's an absolute martyrdom. If I had only known. . . ."

Martha was now able to see better. Mrs. Talbot's face came out of the shadow in a splash of white. It was some kind of a face mask. "Shall I go out till you are dressed?" she suggested awkwardly.

But Mrs. Talbot rose with a swirl of silk and said, "If you don't mind it all, Matty, I'd adore you to stay." There was a nervous gasp of laughter; she was peering forward to see Martha, to find out her reaction. It occurred to Martha that the apology, the deference, was quite sincere and not a pose, as she had assumed. Mrs. Talbot's nervousness was that of a duchess who had survived the French Revolution and timidly continued to wear powdered curls in the privacy of her bedroom because she did not feel herself in the new fashions.

Martha saw the slight figure rise, go to the window, and tug at a cord. At once the room was shot with hazy yellow light. Mrs. Talbot was wearing a shimmering grey garment with full flounced sleeves; she was covered in stark-white paste from collarbones to hairline, and from this mask her small eyes glimmered out through black holes. Her pale smooth hair was looped loosely on her neck; there was no sign of grey. She sat before a large dressing table and dabbed carefully at her face with tufts of cotton wool. The room was long, low, subdued, with shell-colored curtains, dove-grey carpet, and furniture of light, gleaming wood which looked as if it had been embroidered; it had a look of chaste withdrawal from the world; and Mrs. Talbot was a light, cool, uncommitted figure, even when she was poised thus on her stool, leaning forward into her mirror, her submissive charm momentarily lost in a focus of keen concentration. Her skin was emerging patchily from under the white paste, and she muttered, "In a minute, Matty."

Soon she rose and went to an old-fashioned washstand, where a graceful ewer stood in a shining rose-patterned basin. It was clear that taps running hot and cold would be too much of a modern note in this altar to the past. Mrs. Talbot splashed water vigorously over her face, while the air was pervaded by the odor of violets. In the meantime Martha, still examining every detail of the room, had noticed the bed. It was very big—too big, she thought involuntarily, for Mrs. Talbot. Then she saw it was a double bed, with two sets of pillows. She must readmit Mr. Talbot, whom she had again forgotten. This bed, untidy and sprawling, gave Martha the most uncomfortable feeling of something unseemly: it was, she saw, because a man's pajamas lay where they had been flung off, on the pillow. They were of maroon-striped silk, and strongly suggested the person of Mr. Talbot, as did a jar of pipes on the bed table. So uncomfortable did this make Martha that she turned away from the bed, feeling her face hot. Mrs. Talbot, however, returning from her ablutions, could not be aware of how Martha was feeling, for she carelessly rolled these pajamas together and tucked them under the pillow, observing, "Men are always so untidy." Then she sat herself on the edge of the bed, with the air of one prepared to devote any amount of time to friendship.

And now they must talk. There would follow the proper talk.

Martha saw the gleam of affection in Mrs. Talbot's eyes and was asking herself, Does she really like me? If so, why? But Mrs. Talbot was talking about Douglas: how he was such a dear boy, how he was always so clever and helpful, and with such a sense for these horrid, horrid financial things; and then—impulsively—how lovely it was that he had married such a sweet girl. At this Martha involuntarily laughed; and was sorry when she saw the look of surprise on this delightful lady's face. She rose from her chair and began walking about the room, touching the curtains, which slipped like thick silken skin through her fingers, laying a curious finger on the wood of the dressing table, which had such a gleaming softness that it was strange it should oppose her flesh with the hardness of real wood. Mrs. Talbot watched without moving. There was a small, shrewd smile on her lips.

"Are you shocked, Matty, at all this fuss?" she asked a little plaintively; and when Martha turned quickly to see what she could mean, she continued quickly, "I know it all looks so awful until it's tidied up; Elaine is so sweet, she comes in and tidies everything for me, and then this is a lovely room, but I know it must look horrid now, with face creams and cotton wool everywhere. The trouble is . . ." Here she tailed off, with a helpless shrug which suggested that there was nothing she would like better than to relapse into the comfortable condition of being an old woman, if only she knew how. Martha involuntarily glanced at Mr. Talbot's side of the bed and then blushed as she guiltily caught Mrs. Talbot's eyes. But it was clear that this was one thing she could not understand in Martha; she looked puzzled.

After a short pause she said, "I hope you'll be friends with Elaine, Matty. She's such a sweet thing, so sensitive, and she doesn't make friends easily. Sometimes I feel it is my fault—but we've always been so much together, and I don't know why it is, but . . ."

Now Martha's look was far more hostile than she had intended; and Mrs. Talbot's thick white skin colored evenly. She looked like an embarrassed young girl, in spite of the faint look of wear under her eyes. Martha could not imagine herself being friends with that gentle, flower-gathering maiden; she could not prevent a rather helpless but ironical smile, and she looked direct at Mrs. Talbot as if accusing her of being willfully obtuse.

Mrs. Talbot cried out, "But you're so artistic, Matty, and you would have so much in common."

Martha saw tears in her eyes. "But I'm not at all artistic," she observed obstinately—though of course with a hidden feeling that she might prove to be yet, if given the chance!

"But all those books you read, and then anyone can see . . ." Mrs.

Talbot was positively crying out against the fate that persisted in making Martha refuse to be artistic. "And Elaine is so sweet, no one knows as well as I do how sweet she is and—but sometimes I wonder if she's strong enough to *manage* things the way all you clever young things do. You are all so sure of yourselves!"

Here Martha could not help another rueful smile, which checked Mrs. Talbot. She was regarding Martha with extraordinary shrewdness. Martha, for her part, was waiting for the proper talk to begin; what was it that Mrs. Talbot wanted to say to her?

Mrs. Talbot sighed, gave the shadow of a shrug, and went back to her dressing table. Here she applied one cream after another, with steady method, and continued to talk, in between pauses for screwing up her mouth or stretching her eyelids smooth. "I would so much like Elaine to get married. If she could only get properly married, and I needn't worry any more . . . There is no greater happiness, Matty, none! She meets so few people, always my friends, and she is so shy. And you meet so many people, Matty, all you young people are so brave and enterprising."

For the life of her Martha could not see Elaine with the wolves of the Club, with the boys, the kids and the fellows. "I don't think Elaine would like the sort of men we meet," observed Martha; and she caught another shrewd glance. She felt there were things she ought to be understanding, but she was quite lost.

"There's your Douglas," said Mrs. Talbot, a trifle reproachfully. "He's such a nice boy."

Surely, wondered Martha, Mrs. Talbot could not have wanted Douglas for Elaine? The idea was preposterous—even brutal.

"So kind," murmured Mrs. Talbot, "so helpful, so clever with everything."

And now Martha was returned, simply by the incongruity of Douglas and Elaine, into her private nightmare. She could not meet a young man or woman without looking around anxiously for the father and mother; that was how they would end, there was no escape for them. She could not meet an elderly person without wondering what the unalterable influences had been that had created them just so. She could take no step, perform no action, no matter how apparently new and unforeseen, without the secret fear that in fact this new and arbitrary thing would turn out to be part of the inevitable process she was doomed to. She was, in short, in the grip of the great bourgeois monster, the nightmare *repetition*. It was like the obsession of the neurotic who must continuously be touching a certain object or muttering a certain formula of figures in order to be safe from the malevolent powers, like the person who cannot go to bed at night without returning a dozen times to see if the door is locked and the fire out. She was thinking now, But Mrs. Talbot married Mr. Talbot, then Elaine is bound to marry someone like Mr. Talbot, there is no escaping it; then what connection is there between Douglas and Mr. Talbot that I don't see?

But Mrs. Talbot was talking. "I'll show you something, Matty—I would like to show you, I don't everyone."

Mrs. Talbot was searching hurriedly through her drawers. She pulled out a large, leather-framed photograph. Martha came forward and took it, with a feeling that the nightmare was being confirmed. It was of a young man in uniform, a young man smiling direct out of the frame, with a young, sensitive, rueful look. "Hardly anybody knows," Mrs. Talbot cried agitatedly, "but we were engaged, he was killed in the war—the other war, you know—he was so sweet, you don't know. He was so nice." Her lips quivered. She turned away her face and held out her hand for the photograph.

Martha handed it back and returned to her chair. She was thinking, Well, then, so Elaine must get engaged to *that* young man; is it conceivable that Mrs. Talbot sees Douglas like that?

But more: her mother, Mrs. Quest, had been engaged to such another charming young man. This boy, weak-faced and engaging, smiled up still from a small framed photograph on her mother's dressing table, a persistent reminder of that love which Mr. Quest could scarcely resent, since the photograph was half submerged, in fact practically invisible, among a litter of things which referred to her life with him. Martha had even gone so far as to feel perturbed because this boy had not appeared in her own life; she had looked speculatively at Douglas with this thought—but no, weak and charming he was not, he could not take that role.

She sat silent in her chair, frowning; when Mrs. Talbot looked at her, it was to see an apparently angry young woman, and one very remote from her. She hesitated, came forward, and kissed Martha warmly on her cheek. "You must forgive me," she said. "We are a selfish lot, we old women—and you probably have troubles of your own. We forget . . ." Here she hesitated. Martha was looking through her, frowning. She continued guiltily: "And to have children—that's the best of all, I wish I had a dozen, instead of just one. But Mr. Talbot . . ." She glanced hastily at Martha and fell silent.

There was a very long silence. Martha was following the nightmare to its conclusion: Well then, so Elaine will find just such a charming young man, and there's a war conveniently at hand so that he can get killed, and then Elaine will marry another Mr. Talbot, and for the rest of her life, just like all these old women, she'll keep a photograph of her real and great love in a drawer with her handkerchiefs.

"There's nothing nicer than children, and you look very well, Matty," said Mrs. Talbot suddenly.

Martha emerged from her dream remarking absently, "I'm always well." Then she heard what Mrs. Talbot had said; it seemed to hang on the air waiting for her to hear it. She thought tolerantly, She's heard a rumor that I'm pregnant. She smiled at Mrs. Talbot and remarked, "I shan't have children for years yet—damn it, I'm only nineteen myself."

Mrs. Talbot suppressed an exclamation. She surveyed Martha up and down, a rapid, skilled glance, and then, coloring, said, "But, my dear, it's so nice to have your children when you're young. I wish I had. I was *old* when she was born. Of course, people say we are like sisters, but it makes a difference. Have them young, Matty—you won't regret it." She leaned forward with an urgent affectionate smile and continued, after the slightest hesitation, "You know, we old women get a sixth sense about these things. We know when a woman is pregnant, there's a look in the eyes." She put a cool hand to Martha's cheek and turned her face to the light. Narrowing her eyes so that for a moment her lids showed creases of tired flesh, she looked at Martha with a deep impersonal glance and nodded involuntarily, dropping her hand.

Martha was angry and uncomfortable; Mrs. Talbot at this moment seemed to her like an old woman: the utterly impersonal triumphant gleam of the aged female, the old witch, was coming from the ageless jeweled face.

"I can't be pregnant," she announced. "I don't want to have a baby yet."

Mrs. Talbot let out a small resigned sigh. She rose and said in a different voice, "I think I shall have my bath, dear."

"I'll go," said Martha quickly.

"You and Douggie'll be coming to dinner tomorrow?"

"We're looking forward to it very much."

Mrs. Talbot was again the easy hostess; she came forward in a wave of grey silk and kissed Martha. "You'll be so happy," she murmured gently. "So happy, I feel it."

Martha emitted a short ungracious laugh. "But, Mrs. Talbot!" she protested—then stopped. She wanted to put right what she felt to be an impossibly false position; honesty demanded it of her. She was not what Mrs. Talbot thought her; she had no intention of conforming to this perfumed silken bullying, as she most deeply felt it to be. But she could not go on. The appeal in the beautiful eyes silenced her. She was almost ready to aver that she wanted nothing more than to be happy with the dear boy Douglas, for Mrs. Talbot; to have a dozen children, for Mrs. Talbot; to take morning tea with Elaine every day, and see her married to just such another as Douglas.

Mrs. Talbot, arm lightly placed about her waist, gently pressed her to the door. She opened it with one hand, then gave Martha a small squeeze, and smiled straight into her eyes, with such knowledge, such ironical comprehension, that Martha could not bear it. She stiffened; and Mrs. Talbot dropped her arm at once.

"Elaine, dear," said Mrs. Talbot apologetically past Martha to the sun porch, "if you'd like to run my bath for me."

Elaine was now painting the row of pink and mauve sweet peas in the fluted silver vases. "Ah!" exclaimed Mrs. Talbot delightedly, moving forward quickly to look at the watercolor. She leaned over, kissing Elaine's hair. The girl moved slightly, then remained still under her mother's restraining arm. "Isn't this lovely, Matty, isn't she gifted?"

Martha looked at the pretty watercolor and said it was beautiful. Elaine's glance at her now held a real embarrassment; but she remained silent until her mother had gained her meed of admiration.

Then Mrs. Talbot waved goodbye and returned to her bedroom; and Elaine rose, and said, "Excuse me, Matty, I'll just do Mummy's bath—she likes me to do it, rather than the boy, you know." Martha looked to see if there was any consciousness here of being exploited, but no: there was nothing but charming deference.

They said goodbye, and Martha, as she turned away, saw Elaine knocking at the door that led into Mrs. Talbot's bedroom. "Can I come in, Mummy?"

Martha walked away down the street, thinking of that last deep glance into her eyes. Nonsense, she thought; it's nothing but old women's nonsense, old wives' superstition. There seemed nothing anomalous in referring to the youthful Mrs. Talbot thus at this moment. "How can there be a look in my eyes?"

When she reached home, it was nearly lunchtime. The butcher's boy had left a parcel of meat. For some reason she was unable to touch it. The soggy, bloody mass turned her stomach—she was very sick. But this was nonsense, she told herself sternly. She forced herself to untie the wet parcel, take out the meat, and cook it. She watched Douglas eating it, while she made a great joke of her weakness. Douglas remarked with jocularity that she must be pregnant. She flew into a temper.

"All the same, Matty, it wouldn't do any harm just to drop along to old Stern, would it? We don't want kids just when the war's starting, do we?"

That afternoon, since Stella was not there to gain priority for her, she sat out her time of waiting with the other women; and in due course found herself with Dr. Stern. He gave her instructions to undress. She undressed and waited. Dr. Stern, whose exquisite tact had earned him the right to have his waiting room perpetually filled with women who depended on him, explored the more intimate parts of Martha's body with rubber-clothed fingers, and at the same time made conversation about the international situation. Finally he informed Martha that he did not think she was pregnant; she might set her mind at rest.

He then made the mistake of complimenting her on her build, which was of the best kind for easy childbearing. Martha was stiff-lipped and resentful and did not respond. He quickly changed his tone, saying that she needn't think about such things yet; and suggested that there was no reason why she should be pregnant if she had been carrying out his instructions? The query dismayed Martha; but she had decided to remember that he had been definite about it.

When she had left, he remarked to his new nurse that it was just as well for the medical profession that laymen had such touching faith in them. The nurse laughed dutifully and summoned the next patient.

Martha walked home very quickly; she could not wait to tell Douglas that everything was all right.

FROM

# *A Ripple from the Storm*

Seven o'clock in Black Ally's; the smell of hot fat; the spitting and crackling of hot fat from the kitchen; the tables crammed as usual full of the Royal Air Force—unbuttoned, at ease, noisy, a thick mass of men under a grey haze of kitchen fumes and cigarette smoke. Anton sat in his usual corner, eating methodically, waiting for Martha. She came in brightly, smiling yet anxious, examining his face so as to match what she had learned of him during the last three weeks with how she had seen him before. He hastened to rise, draw back a chair, and settle her; this protective and almost fussy manner belonged to the man who had been a devoted nurse. She was thinking: He wouldn't have done that before. Is he doing it now because I've been sick or because I've become something different for him?

In a corner nearby the Royal Air Force group, Andrew, Jimmy, Murdoch, and Bill Bluett were steadily taking in eggs, bacon, and chips. Jimmy saw Martha, the color on his big cheekbones deepened, and he gave her a stiff nod. The three others greeted her with the jocular defensiveness they used for any woman, comrade or not, whom they met when they were in a group of the Royal Air Force. She saw them give Anton unfriendly looks, and remembered that while she had been away battles of principle had raged. Even Andrew, because he was with the others, allowed himself—while checking disparaging remarks about Anton in a brisk comradely voice—to ally himself with their hostility by smiling connivance. She looked at Anton to see how he felt, but he seemed unaware. She thought it impossible that he did not know they were hostile to him; therefore he must have decided it was unimportant. This made Martha feel better. Yet she asked, "Anton, why didn't you sit with them?"

"I was here first."

"You could have moved and sat with them?"

"I was waiting for you." There was an awkward gallantry in his manner which struck a note foreign to their relations before her illness, and discordant with the simple kindliness of his manner to her while she was ill.

She thought: I've become something else for him, and it made her uncomfortable and resentful. Again she felt caged and hemmed in: there was a new possessiveness in him, something dogged and cold.

I'm caught for life, she thought; but the words "for life" released her from anxiety. They all of them saw the future as something short and violent. Somewhere just before them was a dark gulf or chasm, into which they must all disappear. A Communist is a dead man on leave, she thought. That's what matters, and not how I feel about Anton. And, anyway, if Anton and I are unhappy it will be easy to separate.

These ideas flashed through her mind all at once, and she smiled at Anton and said, "Well, of course, I wanted to be with you too."

They continued their meal. Martha was conscious of the Air Force men in the corner, envying them because of the solidarity of their comradeship, even while she told herself it was sentimental to envy them: the comradeship was the uniform, that was all, and had nothing to do with them as individuals. All the same, she was possessed by an old feeling that she was being shut out of some warmth, some beautiful kind of friendship. She watched Anton eat, and told him about Maisie. She was wanting him to say that Maisie should have the baby and defy the world, but he broke a piece of bread carefully between long, thin fingers, and said, "There's nothing to an abortion if it's properly done."

At this moment the four Air Force men rose from their own table and came to stand by them. There were a few moments of banter, behind which Martha could feel a dislike of Anton which dismayed her. Was it simply because of the Royal Air Force solidarity? Because they had seen her choose Anton instead of one of themselves? Her instinct said no.

Andrew said bluffly, "What are you two lovebirds talking about?"

Martha grimaced at the "lovebirds" but, because she trusted Andrew, told him about Maisie: she wanted a more generous reaction than Anton's about the baby.

The three men with Andrew listened seriously, as Andrew did. She was grateful for it—because she was in trouble she became a comrade again, and one of them.

Jimmy said hotly, "It's a bleeding shame, that's what it is."

Bill Bluett said, "Serves her right for not bargaining over the wedding ring, poor bint."

Andrew said, "Never mind, we'll put it all right come the revolution."

"The revolution's not going to help her much," said Martha. "That is, unless we can make one in the next two or three days."

Anton said, "She should have thought of all that before, instead of getting pregnant and then feeling sorry for herself."

The atmosphere chilled. The four men stiffened inside their thick uniforms, and their eyes exchanged cold messages. Murdoch cried out in derision, "She should have thought of that before, should she?"

"That's the long and the short of it, mate," said Jimmy with solemnity—"look before you leap, a stitch in time saves nine, and if a girl gets caught out, that's her funeral."

Bill Bluett said to Martha, ignoring Anton, "See you upstairs." The other three men followed his jerk of his head towards the door.

Martha got up and said, "We'll be late."

Anton said, "There's five minutes." He lowered his chin obstinately, and hunched up his shoulders, sitting silent. Then he deliberately reached for the cheese plate and began to eat. Martha, sitting on the edge of her chair, watched him, thinking that the meeting was due to start now, that she had never known him be unpunctual before by so much as half a minute, and he had begun eating again in order to enforce himself against both her and the Royal Air Force men.

The fumes of hot wet cabbage and boiling fat filled her throat and she set herself not to feel sick. At the end of five minutes Anton rose and said, "Now it's time."

Upstairs there was a full complement of people. Anton went to sit by Jasmine, who was waiting for him with her papers spread ready. Martha sat beside Andrew McGrew, feeling a disloyal pleasure in the way the Royal Air Force opened their ranks to her, as if protecting her against Anton. She looked to see how Anton reacted: he had the appearance of someone on trial, and her instinct was confirmed by the expressions of satisfaction on the faces of the Royal Air Force men. Jimmy even whispered to her, "Don't you worry, lass, we'll fix everything."

At once her emotions swung over: it appeared that there had been some decision among the men to "fix" Anton. Well, they had no right to it; and no right to take her compliance for granted.

There was a crisis blowing up, and Anton was aware of it, and confident he could handle it.

He said, "Comrade Jasmine will now read the minutes of the last meeting."

Jasmine did so in her small voice, effacing herself as a good secretary should with such intensity that there was no need for Anton to sit as he did, gazing severely at the paper from which she read, in order to remind everyone that minutes were no mere formality, but something that needed everyone's attention.

Martha's mind wandered. She blamed herself for not concentrating. She had meant to listen behind the formal words for a sense of what really happened at the last meeting. She thought: Next week, the minutes will read: Minutes of the last meeting, that's all, just a formality, but actually something ugly is happening.

Martha, at the risk of earning Anton's disapproving stare, let her eyes move over the other faces. Elias Phiri, seated at the end of a bench, was staring at the floor. The smooth thick flesh of his forehead was puckering and smoothing and puckering again—like cat's paws of wind on warm smooth water. Martha thought: When illiterate natives—I mean, Africans, listen to something they don't understand, their foreheads pucker and smooth like that—but Elias isn't illiterate. That means he's worried about something. One of his feet shifted. It began to feel and move in rhythm. Listening for the rhythm, Martha heard a pulse of drumming from over the street: they were dancing at McGrath's. Elias swallowed a guilty yawn behind a large hand. Well, *he* wasn't listening either.

Marie and Piet sat side by side. She had her hand on his knee. They both stared before them. Impossible to tell whether they were listening or not.

Carrie Jones, seated beside Tommy, regarded her ten red fingernails, which were spread out on her knee. She wore a yellow linen dress as smooth as butter, and her face had the smooth prepared surface of a very pretty girl who feels men's eyes play over her like sunlight. Martha thought: She's what I used to be; she looks at herself in the looking glass, and she sees how her face and body form a sort of painted shell, and she adores herself, but she is waiting for a pair of eyes to melt the paint and shoot through into the dark inside—well, she'll have to wait! . . . Martha examined this idea, in a change of mood, and rejected it. She was again full of violent dissatisfaction. Half the things I think, she thought, are untrue and full of self-pity—I've only got to get tired or be sick, and I'm full of nostalgia again, but the Lord only knows for what!—full of self-pity, and my mind seems to breed dramatic and silly ideas on its own.

She yawned, still watching Carrie. Well, what *is* she doing here? She's such a pretty girl, she doesn't read, she isn't really political at all. There isn't a man in this room she could be interested in. And at this moment she's bored because she's sitting by Tommy—bored and ashamed of being bored.

Carrie, feeling Martha's eyes on her, offered her a companionable but rather tired smile. The tiredness in Carrie's smile restored Martha's mood of five minutes before. She thought: She's fed up with everything. She hates that painted shell of hers and she despises men for the look they get on their faces when they see her. She's become a Communist because she wants to be something different. She'll leave us soon—yes, of course. Because there isn't one man here who doesn't think, Carrie is such a pretty girl. They all have that defensive and rather shamefaced look, and their voices when they speak of her are different, simply because she's so pretty.

Here Jasmine's voice stopped and Bill Bluett leaned forward to speak. He had obviously been listening to every word of the minutes reading, for now he challenged three points in their wording. They were unimportant points. Jasmine submitted his order of words to the meeting, who accepted them without discussion. The minutes were changed. They all of them knew that Bill had done this, not because he cared about these details, but in order to challenge Anton: Anton knew it too. He initialed the altered minutes and said, "Anything else of importance, Comrade Bill?"

Bill shook his head, but remained leaning forward, on the alert. Martha looked at his hands, which lay loose on his knees. They were long, fine, white hands, but grimy with oil. He was a fitter. He even smelled of oil. Martha looked at the hands of the other Royal Air Force men and thought: Well, they don't have to have signatures of oil all over them. Bill does because he's middle-class. She had no time to pursue this thought, because Jimmy was speaking.

"Comrade Chairman, I want to put a resolution to this meeting."

"On what subject?" asked Anton. "This is item two on the agenda. Political instruction. Comrade Jasmine is to speak."

"I don't care about item two," said Jimmy. His face was flaming, his big mouth shoveled out the words. "I want something done. I want to do something instead of talk talk talk."

"Take it easy, mate," said Bill, in a low tone aside to Jimmy. Obviously something had been decided between the Royal Air Force men, and Jimmy had upset the plan by speaking now.

On the other side of Martha, Andrew shifted his body uncomfortably. He doesn't like all this, she thought, and looked inquiringly at him. He made a quick wry face, as if to say: I don't understand it either.

"I want to ask the meeting if I can put my resolution," said Jimmy, glaring around at them all, including his Royal Air Force comrades.

"Let's keep to the agenda," said Marie du Preez good-naturedly. "Otherwise we'll be yapping all night again."

Jimmy glowered at her. She smiled at him, maternal and quizzical. He blushed deeper and said, still angry but in a lower voice, "O.K., then. Only because the political education is the same thing. Then I demand my right to put a resolution. I demand it, see?"

Anton, ignoring Jimmy, said to Jasmine, "Comrade, will you now speak."

Jasmine spoke for fifteen minutes, her wristwatch propped in front of her, on racial and national hatreds. These, she said, together with any other forms of hostility between one group or subsection of humanity and another, were due to capitalism, and would vanish on the advent of socialism. When she had finished, Anton said, "We have ten minutes allowed for discussion. Who speaks first?"

"I want to put my resolution," said Jimmy.

"But this is the time for discussion."

"You can't just go upsetting the agenda like that," said Marjorie excitedly.

"I'm not upsetting anything," said Jimmy. "I want to put a resolution. It's a resolution about the things Jasmine has just said."

"I propose we set aside the agenda and let Comrade Jimmy put his resolution," said Andrew, in the humorous voice he used for difficult moments.

Martha glanced at Bill, who was grinning sardonically; apparently he was not unhappy about the way things were going.

"Agreed?" said Anton briefly.

"Agreed, yes, we agree," said various voices, some resigned, some amused, some impatient.

Jimmy took a piece of paper from his breast pocket, unfolded it, and held it before him. "I propose to put the following resolution to the meeting. One: all forms of racial prejudice are artificial, contrary to nature, and created by capitalists in order to divide and rule . . ."

Here Elias Phiri said, "Wait a minute, I want to ask a question."

"Comrade Elias," said Anton, turning to him.

"You are saying," said the African, looking to Jasmine, "that racial prejudice is created by capitalism. Is that what you are saying?"

There was a pause. Jasmine said precisely, but rather puzzled, "Yes, comrade, that was the subject of my talk."

"I see," said Elias. "I see." He looked back at the floor. His foot still tapped, tapped, stroked the floor, to the time of McGrath's hardly audible drums.

"What is Comrade Elias saying?" asked Marjorie. "I don't understand."

"I just wanted to be sure: the Communists say racial prejudice is created by capitalism—I wanted to know about that," Elias explained to Marjorie.

There was an even longer pause. He had said "the Communists," as if he wasn't one of them. And it had slipped out, which made it worse. They all felt uncomfortable.

"Can I go on?" asked Jimmy angrily.

"Go on," said Anton.

"Secondly, that anti-Semitism is just capitalist propaganda."

"Well, of course," said Marjorie at once.

"Thirdly, there's no such thing as national differences. It's all nonsense, talking about the British character, the German character, the Japanese character—we're all the same."

He now lowered his paper slightly and gazed about him aggressively, "We're all the same as each other," he said.

"Well, go on," said Anton calmly. Everyone looked puzzled.

"Well," said Jimmy, frowning at his piece of paper, momentarily at a loss, as if he had expected them to disagree. "That's not all. That's not all by a long chalk."

"But I don't see the point," said Marjorie. "I mean, we all know that, so what's the point of passing resolutions?"

"I'm just fed up with talking," said Jimmy. "I want something settled for once and for all."

Marjorie shrugged, and sat still.

"Fourthly," said Jimmy, "that all people are equal, and that everything is a question of education. And that's the most important thing of all—education."

"I don't understand," said Marie. "Of course everyone should have an equal education."

"It's more than saying of course. It seems that you're just paying lip service. Lenin said, every cook must govern the State. But when it comes down to it, you don't hold with it at all!"

"But why are you saying all this?" asked Marjorie. She was very excited and angry. Colin, phlegmatic and proprietary beside her, very much the new young husband, laid a large pale hand on her agitated arm. She almost shook it off, then remained still, sitting back, smiling crossly.

"There's no such thing as talent," said Jimmy. "It's all just a trick to scare the workers out of trying. Talent is education. Up to now, the educated people have had talent. They write books and that sort of thing. But it's because they have been educated."

Jasmine was observed to be looking at Anton, as if expecting him to call a halt. But he remained silent, drawing something on his agenda.

Marie said, in her direct honest way, "I don't understand what all this is in aid of, comrade. Are you saying everyone's exactly the same as everyone else?"

Here Piet let out a good-natured guffaw, and said, "If we are going to pass a resolution abolishing the little difference between men and women, then I'm going back to being a reactionary."

"*Oh!*" exclaimed his wife, with friendly exasperation. "Trust *him!*" They exchanged the rapid, understanding, cheerfully antagonistic glances of a well-matched couple. "Don't you take any notice of my old man. But, Jimmy, how can you say that? People are just born different."

Jimmy sat loosely on the bench inside the thick grey shell of uniform, like a heap of big bones roughly packaged up. His big face was scarlet, his eyes somberly unhappy. "There you are," he said. "I knew it would be like that!"

"But, Jimmy, you're saying there's no such thing as talent?"

Here Andrew came in again, with his "humorous" voice, saying, "I think Comrade Jimmy is framing his resolution carelessly. Why don't we put it like this, comrades: Fourthly, that unequal education has so far prevented the workers from making use of their talents."

"Very well," said Jimmy aggressively. "O.K. I'll accept that."

"But I don't see why we have to pass a resolution at all," said Marjorie. But again she made herself go quiet under the pressure of her husband's hand.

"I want it all clear," insisted Jimmy. "I want this meeting to pass this resolution."

"But we can't pass a resolution about this; it's simply what we all believe anyway," said Jasmine.

"But I don't believe it," said Tommy, writhing as usual because of the effort of speaking up in front of everyone. "I mean, it's not true. Take this book Jasmine made me read, *War and Peace*. Well, I can't see myself writing that in a thousand years, even if I was educated."

"Yes, you would," said Jimmy, glaring at him. He raised his voice and shouted, "There you are! They were all aristocrats! They were bourjoys. So why do you have to sit there and fall for it?"

"Well, I don't see what this is about," said Marjorie, "but if Jimmy wants the resolution passed, then I think we should pass it. And then we can get on with the agenda."

Jimmy said, "That's just contemptuous. You don't really think so at all, but you are saying, Let's pass the resolution, just to shut me up."

"I vote we pass the resolution," said Bill. As if Anton had been waiting for the sound of Bill's voice, he stopped doodling, and said, "Any further discussion? Who will second?"

Bill said, "I will."

The resolution was put and carried unanimously. They were all smiling awkwardly, feeling foolish.

But Jimmy was clearly almost in tears. He said, "But it hasn't been done right. I don't feel right about it all."

"Come off it," said Piet, brusque and rude. "Come off it now. You've got your resolution, now shut up and let us get on with the job."

Jimmy was looking so sad, so puzzled, that they all felt as if they had let him down.

Bill said to him in a low voice, leaning across Martha, "Come off it now, Jimmy boy. We're not going to end everything that's bad in the world by passing resolutions, are we now?"

Jimmy smiled back at him, but his eyes rejected him and everyone. They were turned inwards, on some sore miserable place which—they all felt—had been cruelly touched. They knew he was badly hurt. It was the first time it had occurred to any of them that perhaps he was not in his right mind, or that he was so ill he had become unbalanced.

Now they worked fast through the agenda. Clearly Anton was hurrying everything as much as he could. He was still afraid of some sort of showdown, that was obvious.

At five minutes to ten he said, "Any other business? We've got five minutes. I propose I formally close the meeting."

Martha felt Bill straighten and harden. Now, she thought, this is it.

Bill said, almost casually, "Comrade Chairman, this is the third time that we've scamped an item on the agenda after formally making a decision about it."

"We have taken a formal decision never to end a meeting later than ten," said Anton. "Your proposal, if you remember."

"We have also taken a formal decision to have self-criticism and criticism."

"We can't criticize fifteen people in five minutes."

"The camp bus is not leaving until eleven tonight."

"It seems that on certain occasions not only that the Royal Air Force comrades can all come to the meetings, but can also arrange for the bus to leave an hour later," said Anton.

Bill said unpleasantly, "Is that a formal criticism of the Royal Air

Force comrades? If so, will you bring it up in its correct place and in a form in which it can be answered seriously."

"You are suggesting that we should extend the meeting for an hour for the purpose of criticism? Anyone disagree?"

Marie du Preez grimaced at her husband; Colin attempted to exchange a rueful look with Marjorie; but she said reproachfully, "Of course we should have criticism. All serious Communist groups have criticism."

"Good," said Anton. "I suggest that the order in which the criticism should be conducted be as follows: First, self-criticism. Then, criticism of each other. Then criticism by individual comrades of the group work as a whole. Any objections?"

"Agreed," said Bill at once.

"I think it would be better to have criticism of each other first, then our self-criticism would be deeper," said Jasmine seriously.

"Agreed," said Anton, as impatiently as he ever allowed himself to sound. "Now, where do we start?"

There were two obvious people, sitting at the extreme ends of a rough semicircle: one was Jasmine and the other Jimmy. Various people said apprehensively, "Jasmine. Besides, she is the Secretary."

Jasmine stood up. She was self-possessed, but her hands were trembling. Martha, looking at the small slight girl in her tight flowered dress, her black hair in curls on her head, pale and rather stern in her effort to appear calm, felt protective. She looked around and saw that everyone felt the same. Piet appeared almost comically bewildered. Marie recovered herself first. She hissed at her husband, "Go on, you old ram, she's a human being as well, isn't she?"

No one said anything for a time.

"Well, comrades?" said Anton. "Criticism of Comrade Jasmine." He paused. "It is a well-known fact that in every person's character is a basic trend or type of weakness which, if he or she is not aware of it, so that it can be corrected, may destroy them as Communists and as persons."

Bill Bluett laughed out loud. They all laughed.

Andrew said to Anton, "I wish to pass a belated amendment to the previously passed resolution: namely, that national characteristics are of the utmost importance." It sounded affectionate. Anton glanced up, studied Andrew's face to see if he were being serious, and said, "You mean, I am a German? Well, comrades, in reply I would say that if I am pedantic, it is a useful and necessary counterbalance to your British frivolity."

"Oh, I say," said Colin, his spectacles flashing.

"Yes, yes, yes," said Anton. "If the fundamental fault of the German character is pedantry, then your fault is empiricism and a refusal to base your ideas upon serious analysis."

"And what happens to Jimmy's resolution?" asked Piet good-humoredly.

"I don't know what empiricism is," said Jimmy, in such a tone that they all sobered. The thin skin of his cheeks shone scarlet, and his eyes glittered.

Meanwhile, Jasmine stood upright behind the table, waiting. "It seems no one has any criticism of Comrade Jasmine," said Anton.

"I have," said Andrew. Jasmine turned to face him. He said gently, "Comrade Jasmine, you have a tendency to take on far too much work. I think you take jobs on and do them hurriedly instead of letting other people do them. It is the fault of the very efficient," he added, smiling at her.

"Yes, I know that is true," said Jasmine. She looked distressed, and they all felt embarrassed and wished she could sit down.

"Anything else?" said Anton. No one spoke, and he said, "All right, Comrade Jasmine. Sit down."

Murdoch said, "But that's not a fundamental fault, is it? And we've often told Jasmine that before, haven't we?" Jasmine involuntarily stood up again, facing Murdoch, who, as she did so, began the familiar half-humorous writhing that he used when he was the focus of attention.

"If there is any criticism of Comrade Jasmine you want to make, then make it," said Anton.

"But I didn't say there was," Murdoch cried out, and Jasmine sat down again.

Jimmy said fiercely, "I want to say something. But it's not just about Jasmine, it's about all the women comrades." He looked at Martha, then at Carrie Jones. She lifted her indolent dark eyes at him, and he shouted out, "All of you—lipstick and red nails and fashion magazines. That's not Communist. Women should be respected and not behave like . . . well, I can't bring myself to say like what."

Carrie, who had begun to frown, saw smiles on every face save Jimmy's, and smiled back, rather self-consciously. This self-conscious smile apparently drove Jimmy almost out of his senses, because he stood up and yelled, "There, you see? You think it's enough just to smile and put lipstick on. Well, I'll tell you something, I've got no time for any girl who messes herself up with paint and plaster."

"If that's the case," said Marjorie indignantly, "why do you take out that girl from McGrath's—she's got dyed hair."

Bill Bluett snorted with laughter. Now they all laughed, except Jimmy and Anton, who seemed angry.

"I would remind you," said Anton, "that this is a Communist group. Not a music hall. Comrade Jimmy, you can't bring up a big question like this casually. You are raising the whole question of the position of women. May I suggest that we appoint an evening for the discussion of the position of women?"

Martha watched in herself, and with surprise, because it was contrary to what her instincts told her about Anton, contrary to what she felt when she remembered the Austrian woman, the familiar feeling of trust and relief well up, as if Anton's words built a pillar on which she could support herself. Draping myself like a silly clinging vine on anything that sounds strong, she told herself disgustedly.

Andrew said, "Comrade Anton, you're behaving like a capitalist government asked an awkward question—they always appoint a select committee and hope everything will blow over before the report is published."

"But it *is* a question of the position of women," said Martha.

"*You* say that," said Jimmy, furious, direct to her, and it was at once obvious to everyone that his attack had from the first been directed to her. "You say that. You're worse than anyone."

Jasmine said, "I think Comrade Jimmy's attitude is very sectarian. I see no reason at all why women comrades should look ugly."

"I didn't say ugly," said Jimmy.

Jasmine said, with defiance, blushing, "If a majority vote decides that we should give up cosmetics, then I shall regard it as masculine domination—it's nine to five. I personally consider that all men, whether Communists or not, have remnants in them of middle-class ideas about women. Even Lenin. Even Lenin talked about greasy glasses."

"Hear hear," said Marjorie. "Men make me sick."

Martha said, "I quite agree." She laughed, however, and Jimmy turned on her and said, "And I want to criticize you, Comrade Matty. You're flippant. You aren't serious. Middle-class comrades are all the same."

"But Matty isn't being criticized," said Bill Bluett.

"Well, I'm criticizing her."

"I agree with Jimmy," said Tommy. He was perspiring, and his eyes begged apology from Martha, even while his whole body insisted on his right to say what was very important to him. "I've been thinking about it. Comrade Matty isn't serious. I mean, she acts seriously, but she doesn't talk seriously. Well, I've been reading this book—I've said about it before, this Count Tolstoy. Well, and I've discovered from that book that her manner is a middle-class manner. The middle class say things that are serious in an unserious way. Jasmine and Matty and Marjorie all do it, but Matty worse than anyone. It's contemptuous. They say something and you have to think, do they mean it or don't they."

"I protest," said Andrew. "I protest against two things: first, the working people are not grim as Tommy seems to think, he seems to suggest the middle class have a monopoly on humor . . ."

"Not being funny," said Tommy earnestly. "Not that. But saying things as if you're poking fun at yourself for saying them. It's snobbish."

". . . and secondly," continued Andrew, "Matty isn't under discussion at all at the moment. The next comrade on the list for criticism is Anton."

"That's right," said Bill. "And I'm surprised at our Chairman for not stopping the discussion before. So irregular too, and not a word out of Comrade Anton." To Martha he said, mock serious, "We'll deal with your flippant manner later."

"Comrade Anton," said Andrew. "Comrade Anton, kindly stand up for criticism."

Martha understood that both Bill and Andrew were protecting her. Also, that Andrew was about to protect Anton from Bill.

Anton slowly stood up. His hands, hanging down by his sides, were quite steady.

"And now I'm going to let you have it," said Andrew to Anton, in a gruff humorous voice. "You're an arrogant, stiff-necked, domineering bastard. You're a pedant and a hair-splitter . . ."

Anton was smiling slightly. He knew Andrew was protecting him from Bill, and resented it. The lines around his mouth quivered into life, giving his face a crumpled look, like a used table napkin.

"You're a bureaucrat, Comrade Anton. You're the image of a bureaucrat. I'd like to take you to a low pub every night for a week and see you drunk and making a fool of yourself. Then you might begin to be a good comrade. At the moment you're a pain in the neck."

Everyone was laughing. Elias Phiri was rolling on his bench with laughter. Anton, still smiling very slightly, nodded at Andrew.

"Anyone disagree with this criticism?" he inquired.

"No, we all agree," said Marie pleasantly. "You're just too good to be true, comrade. I wish you'd let up a little."

Elias Phiri, spluttering out laughter, said, "Ho, ho, ho," and tossed his feet up. Then, seeing that everyone was watching him, smiling, he stopped himself laughing and sat shaking his head, internal amusement shaking his whole frame, while his face remained grave.

"The point is," said Bill to Anton, "do *you* agree with these criticisms?"

Anton said stiffly, "Yes, comrade, I am well aware that I tend to be a bureaucrat . . ." It seemed he had been going to say something more, but he stopped.

"Right," said Andrew. "You may sit down, Comrade Anton. And mend your ways or we'll get another chairman."

Anton sat down. He glanced at Bill as he did so; Andrew also looked, with some apprehension, towards Bill. Bill was lolling back, arms folded. He said, "Comrade Andrew has taken the words out of my mouth. I'll bring up certain other criticisms later."

There was a pause. Then Carrie Jones stood up for criticism. But a note of frivolity had crept into the thing. She listened good-humoredly to criticisms of her "excessive attention to her personal appearance," and sat down, nodding. Before Tommy stood up, Anton warned them that this was a serious matter. But the rest of the criticism went fast, with plenty of laughter. Again, when they reached Martha, Anton insisted that they were being "fundamentally irresponsible," but it did no good: Martha, Andrew, Jimmy, and Murdoch were criticized fast, in a rapid crossfire of good-humored phrases from all over the room. Anton then said, "That's it, comrades. It's half past ten, and I suggest we leave the group criticism and self-criticism until next week."

Bill Bluett uncoiled his long thin body in one fast movement, sat forward and said, "Oh, no, oh, no you don't. Now we're going to be serious."

Anton laid down his pencil, and sat up, on the defensive. "I was under the impression we were being serious."

"You know perfectly well that this has been a farce. This is not how criticism is conducted in a serious Communist group."

"You're suggesting we should begin again?"

"No, since it is apparently impossible to conduct criticism properly in this group—at least, as presently constituted—then I propose we have general criticism."

Andrew said, slowly packing tobacco into his pipe, "Comrade Bill, haven't our criticisms been covered by the criticisms made of Comrade Anton?"

"*Your* criticisms," said Anton promptly, on the alert. He had been waiting for this, as they could all see. "Do I understand you to say that the Royal Air Force comrades are making a criticism, as a group, or the group as a whole?"

"Yes," said Andrew, "you're of course right if you are suggesting that is factionalism, but there are special circumstances here. Of course it is factionalism. And I would like to say in advance that I do not go all the way with the Royal Air Force comrades." He turned to Bill and urged, "Comrade, wouldn't you agree that what we intended to say has already been covered?"

"No, I would not."

"I'm not accepting the criticism of an inner group," said Anton. "That is contrary to every Party principle."

"If it makes you easy," said Bill, "I'll say I'm making criticisms for myself."

"I agree with Comrade Bill, though," said Murdoch excitedly.

"And so do I," said Jimmy.

"I will not, as Chairman, accept factionalism," insisted Anton.

"Oh, let up, Anton," said Marie, as she might have spoken to one of her children. "Let up, do."

Bill said, "I insist on saying this: the work of the whole group is a complete waste of time."

"Indeed?" said Anton. "You are proposing, I gather, that we need a fresh analysis of our work? In that case I shall put it on the agenda for next week. Make a note of it, Jasmine."

Bill said, "Oh, no you don't. Next week it would seem that we are discussing the position of women in capitalist society, in order that our lady comrades will know whether to use lipstick or not. Jesus!"

Anton said, "If you will kindly make detailed criticisms instead of broad generalizations, we can proceed to discuss what you have to say."

But before Bill could say anything, Murdoch shrilled out on the humorous defensive note he had been criticized for five minutes before, "Och, but it's a fact. And to my mind it's your doing, Comrade Anton. It's your attitude that does it."

"Comrade Anton has already been criticized and has accepted the criticism," said Andrew.

"Will you please be specific," said Anton. Now he was furious; his face quivered with anger.

"Hell, man—anyone can see it. O.K. then—take your attitude to Matty's friend who got herself in the family way. You're not human." He mimicked Anton's voice, " 'She should have thought of that before.' Hell, what sort of attitude is that for a Communist?"

Marie said, "What's all this, Matty? What's it about?"

Martha said, "A girl I know got herself pregnant. We were discussing it. That's all."

Anton said, "Am I to take it, comrades, that this group, a Communist group, now proposes to discuss seriously what to do about a girl who needs an abortion?"

"But she doesn't want to have an abortion," said Martha.

"This group is now going to accept the responsibility of finding abortionists or husbands for all the girls in the Colony who've got themselves pregnant?"

"There you are," cried out Jimmy. "That's what I mean. That's how you talk."

"You are criticizing me for a tone of voice?" inquired Anton.

Andrew said, "I agree with Anton that all this is quite irregular, but there's nothing wrong with us trying to help someone who's in trouble. I remember one of our lassies back home got herself in trouble and we fixed her up with a husband."

Anton said, "In that case, Comrade Andrew, since it seems that you are familiar with this type of important Party work, may we leave it that you will be responsible, with Comrade Matty, for the problems of this girl? And now, since that is dealt with, may we continue?"

Andrew said to Martha, "I'll be in town tomorrow for lunch. I'll have it with you and we'll talk it over."

"Thanks," said Martha gratefully, moving closer to him. He put his arm around her, and said, "Comrade Matty and I constitute ourselves a subcommittee for the solving of personal problems."

Anton had been watching them, in cold patience.

Bill said, "All of our energies go into the white minority in this country."

Anton allowed himself to appear ironically surprised.

"Again?" he said. "This has come up at every meeting we've had for the last six weeks. Every time it is the same thing. Do we really have to go through it again?"

Bill said, "Yes, we do."

Anton and Bill faced each other for the fight that both had been maneuvering for all evening, but Jimmy interposed. He said, "You say, we can't make contact with the Africans. But I have. While you town types sit on your arses and talk red revolution, and tell these white settlers about the glorious Red Army, I've been selling *The Watchdog* in the Location. Ask Elias if I haven't."

Elias moved unhappily on his bench. Again the soft brown skin above his brows was puckering. He said, sighing, "Yes, comrades, but it is not easy."

"It was a group decision that the Royal Air Force lads should not go into the Location," said Anton sharply. "And now I have come to my criticism of you—you have no discipline, you come to the meetings or not, as you feel inclined, you do Party work or not as the mood takes you, you are all absolutely unreliable."

"That's right," said Jimmy roughly. "And we break the sacred rules of the Colony by having Colored girls as friends."

Marie said impatiently, "We discussed all that last week. You know why we took the decision we did."

Here Tommy began to shift on his bench, grinning unhappily, in the way they all recognized and respected because of his desperate sincerity.

"I want to say something," he said. "It's this. There's something wrong. We say, we don't believe in inequality, we don't believe in the color bar and that. But when it gets down to it, we take a decision to behave like everyone else. We say, Don't let's upset people." He said apologetically to Elias, "I must say straight, comrade, that I don't think it's right for black and white to marry, but I know it's because I've been brought up here—I'm just trying to say what I think. . . ."

Elias nodded, his eyes lowered.

"But that's what we say we believe. Yet when Comrade Jimmy there falls in love . . ." He hesitated and changed it, ". . . likes a girl from the Colored Quarter, then we say no. Because it would make people say bad things about Communists. But it seems to me there is something wrong with it all."

"You're telling me," said Jimmy, direct to him.

"Comrades," said Anton, weary with exasperation. "If we all of us, at this moment, made ourselves red flags and walked out of this room and down into the Location, shouting, Arise ye starvelings from your slumbers—then what would happen? I would be put into the internment camp. Every Royal Air Force member would be posted. The two Government servants, Marjorie and Colin, would get the sack. Piet would be asked to resign from his job in the trade union. And anyone else would be deported. Is that what you want? Well, is it? Because that's the logical conclusion of what you're saying. And if you want this group to shout out about sexual equality, then it's the one way to get ourselves in trouble with everyone. Would it help matters if every single man here married an African or a Colored girl tomorrow—not that it would be possible. Or if we all took Colored mistresses? There's nothing new about white men sleeping with Colored and African girls. Is there? The basic problem is economic and not social. Use your heads, comrades."

"Why do you have to make every simple human problem into a big question of principle?" said Bill suddenly.

"Are we Communists, or aren't we?"

Jasmine said earnestly to Jimmy, "Your attitude is very bad, comrade. We explained everything last week and took decisions. But it makes no difference to you what decisions we take—you just go straight on doing what you like in any case. I don't see why you bother to come here at all—if you're a group member you have to accept discipline."

Jimmy stood up, straightening his tunic, tucking his cap over his heavy hair. "That's right," he said. "I don't know why I bother to come here either." Murdoch stood up beside him, grinning weakly, adjusting his cap. Bill Bluett rose and joined them.

Jimmy looked slowly around at them all, his fevered face and eyes burning. "You can count me out." He remarked to the wall above Martha's head, "I've got myself a real working girl, a girl like myself, and I've got myself comrades in the Colored Quarter and in the Location I can talk to as man to man. But I can't be a member any more of this talking shop."

He crashed out of the room; Murdoch went after him, saying "So long" in a hasty friendly way. Bill, nodding at them all around in an impartial manner, followed them.

Andrew stuffed his pipe away quickly, and said, "Well, comrades, I'm sorry about that, but I'll see what I can do about it." He, too, hurried out.

Elias, who had been looking under his eyebrows at them all, frowning, said, "And I must go too. I haven't got a pass to be out." He departed, while they said good night, good night, good night, after him.

"I suggest," said Anton, as if nothing in particular had happened, "that we now end this meeting."

"But aren't we going to do something?" asked Marjorie.

"Comrade Andrew will do what he can. If he can't then we shall work without the Royal Air Force comrades. Anything else? Then I declare the meeting closed." He slid his books and papers together, and went with the same abruptness as the others.

Jasmine was almost in tears. Marjorie seemed stunned. "But what's happened?" she said, appealing to everyone. "What's happened? I don't understand."

Colin patted her shoulder, and she irritably shrugged him away.

Carrie shrugged, slinging a soft white wool coat over her shoulders, as she went to the door. "Perhaps Communism isn't suited to this country?" she remarked. "Well, good night, I must get some beauty sleep." And she, too, departed.

The du Preez, standing side by side, gazed unhappily at the place where Anton had sat, as if he might rematerialize and solve all these problems. At last Marie sighed and said, "That boy, Jimmy, what he needs is a good doctor, if you ask me. He's dying on his feet of T.B.—anyone can see it by looking."

Piet said, grinning, "Women! We'd better make a rule that no one can come to group meetings unless their temperature is normal."

Tommy said, "But it wasn't Jimmy, it was Bill, wasn't it? I mean, Jimmy did the talking, but you could see it was Bill all the time."

Piet affectionately thumped the side of his fist against the boy's head and told him, "Now you shut up for tonight, and we'll give you a lift home. Who's for a lift?"

Down in the street the "town types" saw Jimmy under a lamp at a corner, surrounded by the three other Royal Air Force men. He was shouting and gesticulating; they were, apparently, trying to stop him from doing something.

They then saw Andrew, obviously in a bad temper, going off by himself away from the others. The three, Bill, Murdoch, and Jimmy, linked arms and strolled down the pavement, three abreast, so that the groups of townspeople coming the other way, out of the pictures, had to move off the pavement to make room for them.

"Bloody Raff," said Piet, angrily. "Time they all went home to where they belonged."

FROM

# *The Golden Notebook*

[The black notebook now fulfilled its original plan, for both sides had been written on. Under the left-side heading, *The Source,* was written:]

*11th November, 1955*

Today on the pavement a fat domestic London pigeon waddling among the boots and shoes of people hurrying for a bus. A man takes a kick at it, the pigeon lurches into the air, falls forward against a lamppost, lies with its neck stretched out, its beak open. The man stands, bewildered: he had expected the pigeon to fly off. He casts a furtive look around, so as to escape. It is too late, a red-faced virago is already approaching him. "You brute! Kicking a pigeon!" The man's face is by now also red. He grins from embarrassment and a comical amazement. "They always fly away," he observes, appealing for justice. The woman shouts: "You've killed it—kicking a poor little pigeon!" But the pigeon is not dead, it is stretching out its neck by the lamppost, trying to lift its head, and its wings strive and collapse, again and again. By now there is a small crowd including two boys of about fifteen. They have the sharp watchful faces of the freebooters of the streets, and stand watching, unmoved, chewing gum. Someone says: "Call the R.S.P.C.A." The woman shouts: "There'd be no need for that if this bully hadn't kicked the poor thing." The man hangs about, sheepish, a criminal hated by the crowd. The only people not emotionally involved are the two boys. One remarks to the air: "Prison's the place for criminals like 'im." "Yes, yes," shouts the woman. She is so busy hating the kicker she doesn't look at the pigeon. "Prison," says the second boy, "flogging, I'd say." The woman now sharply examines the boys, and realizes they are making fun of her. "Yes, and you too!" she gasps at them, her voice almost squeezed out of her by her anger. "Laughing while a poor little bird suffers." By now the two boys are in fact grinning, though not in the same shamefaced incredulous way as the villain of the occasion. "Laughing," she says. "Laughing. You *should* be flogged. Yes. It's true." Meanwhile an efficient frowning man bends over the pigeon, and examines it. He straightens himself and pronounces: "It's going to die." He is right: the bird's eyes are filming, and blood wells from its open beak. And now the woman, forgetting her three objects of hatred, leans forward to look at the bird. Her mouth is slightly open, she has a look of unpleasant curiosity as the bird gasps, writhes its head, then goes limp.

"It's dead," says the efficient man.

The villain, recovering himself, says apologetically, but clearly determined to have no nonsense: "I'm sorry, but it was an accident. I've never seen a pigeon before that didn't move out of the way."

We all look with disapproval at this hardened kicker of pigeons.

"An accident!" says the woman. "An accident!"

But now the crowd is dissolving. The efficient man picks up the dead bird, but that's a mistake, for now he doesn't know what to do with it. The kicker moves off, but the woman goes after him, saying: "What's your name and address, I'm going to have you prosecuted." The man says, annoyed: "Oh, don't make such a mountain out of a molehill." She says: "I suppose you call murdering a poor little bird a molehill." "Well, it isn't a mountain, murder isn't a mountain," observes one of the fifteen-year-olds, who stands grinning with his hands in his jacket pockets. His friend takes it up, sagaciously: "You're right. Molehills is murder, but mountains isn't." "That's right," says the first, "when's a pigeon a mountain? When it's a molehill." The woman turns on them, and the villain thankfully makes his escape, looking incredibly guilty, despite himself. The woman is trying to find the right words of abuse for the two boys, but now the efficient man stands holding the corpse, and looking helpless, and one of the boys asks derisively: "You going to make pigeon pie, mister?" "You cheek me and I'll call the police," the efficient one says promptly. The woman is delighted, and says: "That's right, that's right, they should have been called long ago." One of the boys lets out a long, incredulous, jeering, admiring whistle. "That's the ticket," he says, "call the coppers. They'll put you down for stealing a public pigeon, mister!" The two go off, rolling with laughter, but fast as they can without losing face, because the police have been mentioned.

The angry woman, the efficient man, the corpse, and a few bystanders remain. The man looks around, sees a rubbish receptacle on the lamppost, and moves forward to drop the dead bird into it. But the woman intercepts him, grasps the pigeon. "Give it to me," she says, her voice suffused with tenderness. "I'll bury the poor little bird in my window box." The efficient man thankfully hurries off. She is left, looking down with disgust at the thick blood dropping from the beak of the pigeon.

*12th November*

Last night I dreamed of the pigeon. It reminded me of something, I didn't know what. In my dream I was fighting to remember. Yet when I woke up I knew what it was—an incident from the Mashopi Hotel weekends. I haven't thought of it for years, yet now it is clear and detailed. I am again exasperated because my brain contains so much that is locked up and unreachable, unless, by a stroke of luck, there is an incident like yesterday's. It must have been one of the intermediate weekends, not the climacteric last weekend, for we were still on good terms with the Boothbys. I remember Mrs. Boothby coming into the dining room with a .22 rifle at breakfast and saying to our group: "Can any of you shoot?" Paul said, taking the rifle: "My expensive education has not failed to include the niceties of grouse and pheasant murder." "Oh, nothing so fancy like that," said Mrs. Boothby. "There are grouse and pheasant about, but not too many. Mr. Boothby mentioned he fancied a pigeon pie. He used to take out a gun now and then, but he's lost the figure for it, so I thought if you could oblige . . . ?"

Paul was handling the weapon quizzically. He finally said: "Well, I'd never thought of shooting birds with a rifle, but if Mr. Boothby can do it, so can I."

"It's not hard," said Mrs. Boothby, as usual letting herself be taken in by the polite surface of Paul's manner. "There's a small vlei down there between the kopjes that's full of pigeons. You let them settle and just pick them off."

"It's not sporting," said Jimmy, owlish.

"My God, it's not sporting!" cried Paul, playing up, clutching at his brow with one hand and holding the rifle away from him with the other.

Mrs. Boothby was not sure whether to take him seriously, but she explained: "It's fair enough. Don't shoot unless you're sure of killing, and then where's the harm?"

"She's right," said Jimmy to Paul.

"You're right," said Paul to Mrs. Boothby. "Dead right. We'll do it. How many pigeons for Host Boothby's pigeon pie?"

"There's not much use with less than six, but if you can get enough I can make pigeon pie for you as well. It'd make a change."

"True," said Paul. "It *would* make a change. Rely on us."

She thanked him, gravely, and left us with the rifle.

Breakfast was over, it was about ten in the morning, and we were glad to have something to fill our time until lunch. A short way past the hotel a track turned off the main road at right angles and wandered ruttily over the veld, following the line of an earlier African footpath. This track led to the Roman Catholic Mission about seven miles off in the wilderness. Sometimes the Mission car came in for supplies; sometimes farm laborers went by in groups to or from the Mission, which ran a large farm, but for the most part the track was empty. All that country was high-lying sandveld, undulating, broken sharply here and there by kopjes. When it rained the soil seemed to offer resistance, not welcome. The water danced and drummed in a fury of white drops to a height of two or three feet over the hard soil, but an hour after the storm, it was already dry again and the gullies and vleis were running high and noisy. It had rained the previous night so hard that the iron roof of the sleeping block had shaken and pounded over our heads, but now the sun was high, the sky unclouded, and we walked beside the tarmac over a fine crust of white sand which broke dryly under our shoes to show the dark wet underneath.

There were five of us that morning, I don't remember where the others were. Perhaps it was a weekend when only five of us had come down to the hotel. Paul carried the rifle, looking every inch a sportsman and smiling at himself in this role. Jimmy was beside him, clumsy, fattish, pale, his intelligent eyes returning always to Paul, humble with desire, ironical with pain at his situation. I, Willi, and Maryrose came along behind. Willi carried a book. Maryrose and I wore holiday clothes—colored dungarees and shirts. Maryrose wore blue dungarees and a rose-colored shirt. I wore rose dungarees and a white shirt.

As soon as we turned off the main road onto the sand track we had to walk slowly and carefully, because this morning after the heavy rain there was a festival of insects. Everything seemed to riot and crawl. Over the low grasses a million white butterflies with greenish-white wings hovered and lurched. They were all white, but of different sizes. That morning a single species had hatched or sprung or crawled from their chrysalises, and were celebrating their freedom. And on the grass itself, and all over the road were a certain species of brightly colored grasshopper, in couples. There were millions of them too.

"And one grasshopper jumped on the other grasshopper's back," observed Paul's light but grave voice, just ahead. He stopped. Jimmy, beside him, obediently stopped too. We came to a standstill behind them both. "Strange," said Paul, "but I've never understood the inner or concrete meaning of that song before." It was grotesque, and we were all not so much embarrassed as awed. We stood laughing, but our laughter was too loud. In every direction, all around us, were the insects, coupling. One insect, its legs firmly planted on the sand, stood still; while another, apparently identical, was clamped firmly on top of it, so that the one underneath could not move. Or an insect would be trying to climb on top of another, while the one underneath remained still, apparently trying to aid the climber whose earnest or frantic heaves threatened to jerk both over sideways. Or a couple, badly matched, would topple over, and the one that had been underneath would right itself and stand waiting while the other fought to resume its position, or another insect, apparently identical, ousted it. But the happy or well-mated insects stood all around us, one above the other, with their bright round idiotic black eyes staring. Jimmy went off into fits of laughter, and Paul thumped him on the back. "These extremely vulgar insects do not merit our attention," observed Paul. He was right. One of these insects, or half a dozen, or a hundred would have seemed attractive, with their bright paint-box colors, half submerged in thin emerald grasses. But in thousands, crude green and crude red, with the black blank eyes staring—they were absurd, obscene, and, above all, the very emblem of stupidity. "Much better watch the butterflies," said Maryrose, doing so. They were extraordinarily beautiful. As far as we could see, the blue air was graced with white wings. And looking down into a distant vlei, the butterflies were a white glittering haze over green grass.

"But my dear Maryrose," said Paul, "you are doubtless imagining in that pretty way of yours that these butterflies are celebrating the joy of life, or simply amusing themselves, but such is not the case. They are merely pursuing vile sex, just like these ever-so-vulgar grasshoppers."

"How do you know?" inquired Maryrose, in her small voice, very earnest; and Paul laughed his full-throated laugh which he knew was so attractive, and fell back and came beside her, leaving Jimmy alone in front. Willi, who had been squiring Maryrose, gave way to Paul and came to me, but I had already moved forward to Jimmy, who was forlorn.

"It really *is* grotesque," said Paul, sounding genuinely put-out. We looked where he was looking. Among the army of grasshoppers were two obtrusive couples. One was an enormous powerful-looking insect, like a piston with its great springlike legs, and on its back a tiny ineffectual mate, unable to climb high enough up. And next to it, the position reversed: a tiny bright pathetic grasshopper was straddled by, dwarfed, almost crushed by an enormous powerful driving insect. "I shall try a small scientific experiment," announced Paul. He stepped carefully among the insects to the grasses at the side of the road, laid down his rifle, and pulled a stem of grass. He went down on one knee in the sand, brushing insects aside with an efficient and indifferent hand. Neatly he levered the heavy-bodied insect off the small one. But it instantly sprang back to where it was, with a most surprisingly determined single leap. "We need two for this operation," announced Paul. Jimmy was at once tugging at a grass-stem, and took his place beside him, although his face was wrenched with loathing at having to bend down so close to the swarm. The two young men were now kneeling on the sandy road, operating their grass-stems. I and Willi and Maryrose stood and watched. Willi was frowning. "How frivolous," I remarked, ironical. Although, as usual, we were not on particularly good terms that morning, Willi allowed himself to smile at me and said with real amusement: "All the same, it is interesting." And we smiled at each other, with affection and with pain because these moments were so seldom. And across the kneeling boys Maryrose watched us, with envy and pain. She was seeing a happy couple and feeling shut out. I could not bear it, and I went to Maryrose, abandoning Willi. Maryrose and I bent over the backs of Paul and Jimmy and watched.

"Now," said Paul. Again he lifted his monster off the small insect. But Jimmy was clumsy and failed, and before he could try again Paul's big insect was back in position. "Oh, you idiot," said Paul, irritated. It was an irritation he usually suppressed, because he knew Jimmy adored him. Jimmy dropped the grass-stem and laughed painfully; tried to cover up his hurt—but by now Paul had grasped the two stems, had levered the two covering insects, large and small, off the two others, large and small, and now they were two well-matched couples, two big insects together and two small ones.

"There," said Paul. "That's the scientific approach. How neat. How easy. How satisfactory."

There we all stood, the five of us, surveying the triumph of common sense. And we all began to laugh again, helplessly, even Willi; because of the utter absurdity of it. Meanwhile all around us thousands and thousands of painted grasshoppers were getting on with the work of propagating their kind without any assistance from us. And even our small triumph was soon over, because the large insect that had been on top of the other large insect fell off, and immediately the one which had been underneath mounted him or her.

"Obscene," said Paul gravely.

"There is no evidence," said Jimmy, trying to match his friend's light grave tone, but failing, since his voice was always breathless, or shrill, or too facetious: "There is no evidence that in what we refer to as nature things are any better-ordered than they are with us. What evidence have we that all these—miniature troglodytes are nicely sorted out male above female? Or even—" he added daringly, on his fatally wrong note "—male with female at all? For all we know, this is a riot of debauchery, males with males, females with females . . ." He petered out in a gasp of laughter. And looking at his heated, embarrassed, intelligent face, we all knew that he was wondering why it was that nothing he ever said, or could say, sounded easy, as when Paul said it. For if Paul had made that speech, as he might very well have done, we would all have been laughing. Instead of which we were uncomfortable, and were conscious that we were hemmed in by these ugly scrambling insects.

Suddenly Paul sprang over and trod deliberately, first on the monster couple, whose mating he had organized, and then on the small couple.

"Paul," said Maryrose, shaken, looking at the crushed mess of colored wings, eyes, white smear.

"A typical response of a sentimentalist," said Paul, deliberately parodying Willi—who smiled, acknowledging that he knew he was being mocked. But now Paul said seriously: "Dear Maryrose, by tonight, or to stretch a point, by tomorrow night, nearly all these things will be dead—just like your butterflies."

"Oh no," said Maryrose, looking at the dancing clouds of butterflies with anguish, but ignoring the grasshoppers. "But why?"

"Because there are too many of them. What would happen if they all lived? It would be an invasion. The Mashopi Hotel would vanish under a crawling mass of grasshoppers, it would be crushed to the earth, while inconceivably ominous swarms of butterflies danced a victory dance over the deaths of Mr. and Mrs. Boothby and their marriageable daughter."

Maryrose, offended and pale, looked away from Paul. We all knew she was thinking about her dead brother. At such moments she wore a look of total isolation, so that we all longed to put our arms around her.

Yet Paul continued, and now he began by parodying Stalin: "It is self-evident, it goes without saying—and in fact there is no need at all to say it, so why should I go to the trouble?—However, whether there is any need to say a thing or not is clearly besides the point. As is well known, I say, nature is prodigal. Before many hours are out, these insects will have killed each other by fighting, biting, deliberate homicide, suicide, or by clumsy copulation. Or they will have been eaten by birds which even at this moment are waiting for us to remove ourselves so that they can begin their feast. When we return to this delightful pleasure resort next weekend, or, if our political duties forbid, the weekend after, we shall take our well-regulated walks along this road and see perhaps one or two of these delightful red and green insects at their sport in the grass, and think, how pretty they are! And little will we reck of the million corpses that even then will be sinking into their last resting place all about us. I do not even mention the butterflies who, being incomparably more beautiful, though probably not more useful, we will actively, even assiduously miss—if we are not more occupied with our more usual decadent diversions."

We were wondering why he was deliberately twisting the knife in the wound of Maryrose's brother's death. She was smiling painfully. And Jimmy, tormented continuously by fear that he would crash and be killed, had the same small wry smile as Maryrose.

"The point I am trying to make, comrades . . ."

"We know what point you are trying to make," said Willi, roughly and angrily. Perhaps it was for moments like these that he was the "father figure" of the group, as Paul said he was. "Enough," said Willi. "Let's go and get the pigeons."

"It goes without saying, it is self-evident," said Paul, returning to Stalin's favorite opening phrases just so as to hold his own against Willi, "that mine host Boothby's pigeon pie will never get made, if we go on in this irresponsible fashion."

We proceeded along the track, among the grasshoppers. About half a mile further on there was a small kopje, or tumbling heap of granite boulders; and beyond it, as if a line had been drawn, the grasshoppers ceased. They were simply not there, they did not exist, they were an extinct species. The butterflies, however, continued everywhere, like white petals dancing.

I think it must have been October or November. Not because of the insects, I'm too ignorant to date the time of the year from them, but because of the quality of the heat that day. It was a sucking, splendid, menacing heat. Late in a rainy season there would have been a champagne tang in the air, a warning of winter. But that day I remember the heat was striking our cheeks, our arms, our legs, even through our clothing. Yes, of course it must have been early in the season, the grass was short, tufts of clear sharp green in white sand. So that weekend was four or five months before the final one, which was just before Paul was killed. And the track we strolled along that morning was where Paul and I ran hand in hand that night months later through a fine seeping mist to fall together in the damp grass. Where? Perhaps near where we sat to shoot pigeons for the pie.

We left the small kopje behind, and now a big one rose ahead. The hollow between the two was the place Mrs. Boothby had said was visited by pigeons. We struck off the track to the foot of the big kopje, in silence. I remember us walking, silent, with the sun stinging our backs. I can *see* us, five small brightly colored young people, walking in the grassy vlei through reeling white butterflies under a splendid blue sky.

At the foot of the kopje stood a clump of large trees under which we arranged ourselves. Another clump stood about twenty yards away. A pigeon cooed somewhere from the leaves in this second clump. It stopped at the disturbance we made, decided we were harmless and cooed on. It was a soft, somnolent drugging sound, hypnotic, like the sound of cicadas, which—now that we were listening—we realized were shrilling everywhere about us. The noise of cicadas is like having malaria and being full of quinine, an insane incessant shrilling noise that seems to come out of the eardrums. Soon one doesn't hear it, as one ceases to hear the fevered shrilling of quinine in the blood.

"Only one pigeon," said Paul. "Mrs. Boothby has misled us."

He rested his rifle barrel on a rock, sighted the bird, tried without the support of the rock, and just when we thought he would shoot, laid the rifle aside.

We prepared for a lazy interval. The shade was thick, the grass soft and springy and the sun climbing towards midday position. The kopje behind us towered up into the sky, dominating, but not oppressive. The kopjes in this part of the country are deceptive. Often quite high, they scatter and diminish on approach, because they consist of groups or piles of rounded granite boulders; so that standing at the base of a kopje one might very well see clear through a crevice or small ravine to the vlei on the other side, with great, toppling glistening boulders soaring up like a giant's pile of pebbles. This kopje, as we knew, because we had explored it, was full of the earthworks and barricades built by the Mashona seventy, eighty years before as a defense against the raiding Matabele. It was also full of magnificent Bushmen paintings. At least, they had been magnificent until they had been defaced by guests from the hotel who had amused themselves throwing stones at them.

"Imagine," said Paul. "Here we are, a group of Mashona, besieged. The Matabele approach, in all their horrid finery. We are outnumbered. Besides, we are not, so I am told, a warlike folk, only simple people dedicated to the arts of peace, and the Matabele always win. We know, we men, that we will die a painful death in a few moments. You lucky women, however, Anna and Maryrose, will merely be dragged off by new masters in the superior tribe of the altogether more warlike and virile Matabele."

"They would kill themselves first," said Jimmy. "Wouldn't you, Anna? Wouldn't you, Maryrose?"

"Of course," said Maryrose, good-humored.

"Of course," I said.

The pigeon cooed on. It was visible, a small, shapely bird, dark against the sky. Paul took up the rifle, aimed and shot. The bird fell, turning over and over with loose wings, and hit earth with a thud we could hear from where we sat. "We need a dog," said Paul. He expected Jimmy to leap up and fetch it. Although we could see Jimmy struggling with himself, he in fact got up, walked across to the sister clump of trees, retrieved the now graceless corpse, flung it at Paul's feet, and sat down again. The small walk in the sun had flushed him, and caused great patches to appear on his shirt. He pulled it off. His torso, naked, was pale, fattish, almost childish. "That's better," he said, defiantly, knowing we were looking at him, and probably critically.

The trees were now silent. "One pigeon," said Paul. "A toothsome mouthful for our host."

From trees far away came the sound of pigeons cooing, a murmuring gentle sound. "Patience," said Paul. He rested his rifle again and smoked.

Meanwhile Willi was reading. Maryrose lay on her back, her soft gold head on a tuft of grass, her eyes closed. Jimmy had found a new amusement. Between isolated tufts of grass was a clear trickle of sand where water had coursed, probably last night in the storm. It was a miniature riverbed, about two feet wide, already bone dry from the morning's sun. And on the white sand were a dozen round shallow depressions, but irregularly spaced and of different sizes. Jimmy had a fine strong grass-stem, and, lying on his stomach, was wriggling the stem around the bottom of one of the larger depressions. The fine sand fell continuously in avalanches, and in a moment the exquisitely regular pit was ruined.

"You clumsy idiot," said Paul. He sounded, as always in these moments with Jimmy, pained and irritated. He really could not understand how anybody could be so awkward. He grabbed the stem from Jimmy, poked it delicately at the bottom of another sand pit, and in a second had fished out the insect which made it—a tiny anteater, but a big specimen of its kind, about the size of a large match-head. This insect, toppling off Paul's grass-stem onto a fresh patch of white sand, instantly jerked itself into frantic motion, and in a moment had vanished beneath the sand which heaved and sifted over it.

"There," said Paul roughly to Jimmy, handing back his stem. Paul looked embarrassed at his own crossness; Jimmy, silent and rather pale, said nothing. He took the stem and watched the heaving of the minute patch of sand.

Meanwhile we had been too absorbed to notice that two new pigeons had arrived in the trees opposite. They now began to coo, apparently without any intention of coordination, for the two streams of soft sound continued, sometimes together, sometimes not.

"They are very pretty," said Maryrose, protesting, her eyes still shut.

"Nevertheless, like your butterflies, they are doomed." And Paul raised his rifle and shot. A bird fell off a branch, this time like a stone. The other bird, startled, looked around, its sharp head turning this way and that, an eye cocked up skywards for a possible hawk that had swooped and taken off its comrade, then cocked earthwards where it apparently failed to identify the bloody object lying in the grass. For after a moment of intense waiting silence, during which the bolt of the rifle snapped, it began again to coo. And immediately Paul raised his gun and shot and it, too, fell straight to the ground. And now none of us looked at Jimmy, who had not glanced up from his observation of his insect. There was already a shallow, beautifully regular pit in the sand, at the bottom of which the invisible insect worked in tiny heaves. Apparently Jimmy had not noticed the shooting of the two pigeons. And Paul did not look at him. He merely waited, whistling very softly, frowning. And in a moment, without looking at us or at Paul, Jimmy began to flush, and then he clambered up, walked across to the trees, and came back with the two corpses.

"We don't need a dog after all," remarked Paul. It was said before Jimmy was halfway back across the grass, yet he heard it. I should imagine that Paul had not intended him to hear, yet did not particularly care that he had. Jimmy sat down again, and we could see the very white thick flesh of his shoulders had begun to flush scarlet from the two short journeys in the sun across the bright grass. Jimmy went back to watching his insect.

There was again an intense silence. No doves could be heard cooing anywhere. Three bleeding bodies lay tumbled in the sun by a small jutting rock. The grey rough granite was patched and jeweled with lichens, rust and green and purple; and on the grass lay thick glistening drops of scarlet.

There was a smell of blood.

"Those birds will go bad," remarked Willi, who had read steadily during all this.

"They are better slightly high," said Paul.

I could see Paul's eyes hover towards Jimmy, and see Jimmy struggling with himself again, so I quickly got up and threw the limp wing-dragging corpses into the shade.

By now there was a prickling tension between us all, and Paul said: "I want a drink."

"It's an hour before the pub opens," said Maryrose.

"Well, I can only hope that the requisite number of victims will soon offer themselves, because at the stroke of opening time I shall be off. I shall leave the slaughter to someone else."

"None of us can shoot as well as you," said Maryrose.

"As you know perfectly well," said Jimmy, suddenly spiteful.

He was observing the rivulet of sand. It was now hard to tell which antpit was the new one. Jimmy was staring at a largish pit, at the bottom of which was a minute hump—the body of the waiting monster; and a tiny black fragment of twig—the jaws of the monster. "All we need now is some ants," said Jimmy. "And some pigeons," said Paul. And, replying to Jimmy's criticism, he added: "Can I help my natural talents? The Lord gives. The Lord takes. In my case, he has given."

"Unfairly," I said. Paul gave me his charming wry appreciative smile. I smiled back. Without raising his eyes from his book, Willi cleared his throat. It was a comic sound, like bad theatre, and both I and Paul burst out into one of the wild helpless fits of laughing that often took members of the group, singly, in couples, or collectively. We laughed and laughed, and Willi sat reading. But I remember now the hunched enduring set of his shoulders, and the tight painful set of his lips. I did not choose to notice it at the time.

Suddenly there was a wild shrill silken cleaving of wings and a pigeon settled fast on a branch almost above our heads. It lifted its wings to leave again at the sight of us, folded them, turned round on its branch several times, with its head cocked sideways looking down at us. Its black bright open eyes were like the round eyes of the mating insects on the track. We could see the delicate pink of its claws gripping the twig, and the sheen of sun on its wings. Paul lifted the rifle—it was almost perpendicular—shot, and the bird fell among us. Blood spattered over Jimmy's forearm. He went pale again, wiped it off, but said nothing.

"This is getting disgusting," said Willi.

"It has been from the start," said Paul composedly.

He leaned over, picked the bird off the grass and examined it. It was still alive. It hung limp, but its black eyes watched us steadily. A film rolled up over them, then with a small perceptible shake of determination it pushed death away and struggled for a moment in Paul's hands. "What shall I do?" Paul said, suddenly shrill; then, instantly recovering himself with a joke: "Do you expect me to kill the thing in cold blood?"

"Yes," said Jimmy, facing Paul and challenging him. The clumsy blood was in his cheeks again, mottling and blotching them, but he stared Paul out.

"Very well," said Paul, contemptuous, tight-lipped. He held the pigeon tenderly, having no idea how to kill it. And Jimmy waited for Paul to prove himself. Meanwhile the bird sank in a glossy welter of feathers between Paul's hands, its head sinking on its neck, trembling upright again, sinking sideways, as the pretty eyes filmed over and it struggled again and again to defeat death.

Then, saving Paul the ordeal, it was suddenly dead, and Paul flung it onto the heap of corpses.

"You are always so damned lucky about everything," said Jimmy, in a trembling, angry voice. His full carved mouth, the lips he referred to with pride as "decadent" visibly shook.

"Yes, I know," said Paul. "I know it. The gods favor me. Because I'll admit to you, dear Jimmy, that I could not have brought myself to wring this pigeon's neck."

Jimmy turned away, suffering, to his observation of the anteaters' pits. While his attention had been with Paul, a very tiny ant, as light as a bit of fluff, had fallen over the edge of a pit and was at this moment bent double in the jaws of the monster. This drama of death was on such a small scale that the pit, the anteater, and the ant could have been accommodated comfortably on a small fingernail—Maryrose's pink little fingernail for instance.

The tiny ant vanished under a film of white sand, and in a moment the jaws appeared, clean and ready for further use.

Paul ejected the case from his rifle and inserted a bullet with a sharp snap of the bolt. "We have two more to get before we satisfy Ma Boothby's minimum needs," he remarked. But the trees were empty, standing full and silent in the hot sun, all their green boughs light and graceful, very slightly moving. The butterflies were now noticeably fewer; a few dozen only danced on in the sizzling heat. The heat waves rose like oil off the grass, the sand patches, and were strong and thick over the rocks that protruded from the grass.

"Nothing," said Paul. "Nothing happens. What tedium."

Time passed. We smoked. We waited. Maryrose lay flat, eyes closed, delectable as honey. Willi read, doggedly improving himself. He was reading *Stalin on the Colonial Question.*

"Here's another ant," said Jimmy, excited. A larger ant, almost the size of the anteater, was hurrying in irregular dashes this way and that between grass-stems. It moved in the irregular, apparently spasmodic way that a hunting dog does when scenting. It fell straight over the edge of the pit, and now we were in time to see the brown shining jaws reach up and snap the ant across the middle, almost breaking it in two. A struggle. White drifts of sand down the sides of the pit. Under the sand they fought. Then stillness.

"There is something about this country," said Paul, "that will have marked me for life. When you think of the sheltered upbringing nice boys like Jimmy and I have had—our nice homes and public school and Oxford—can we be other than grateful for this education into the realities of nature red in beak and claw?"

"I'm not grateful," said Jimmy. "I hate this country."

"I adore it. I owe it everything. Never again will I be able to mouth the liberal and high-minded platitudes of my democratic education. I know better now."

Jimmy said: "I may know better, but I shall continue to mouth high-minded platitudes. The very moment I get back to England. It can't be too soon for me. Our education has prepared us above all for the long littleness of life. What else has it prepared us for? Speaking for myself, I can't wait for the long littleness to begin. When I get back—if I ever do get back that is I shall . . ."

"Hallo," exclaimed Paul, "here comes another bird. No it doesn't." A pigeon cleaved towards us, saw us, and swerved off and away in midair, nearly settled on the other clump of trees, changed its mind and sped into the distance. A group of farm laborers were passing on the track a couple of hundred yards off. We watched them, in silence. They had been talking and laughing until they saw us, but now they, too, were silent, and went past with averted faces, as if in this way they might avert any possible evil that might come from us, the white people.

Paul said softly: "My God, my God, my God." Then his tone changed, and he said jauntily: "Looking at it objectively, with as little reference as we can manage to Comrade Willi and his ilk—Comrade Willi, I'm inviting you to consider something objectively." Willi laid down his book, prepared to show irony. "This country is larger than Spain. It contains one and a half million blacks, if one may mention them at all, and one hundred thousand whites. That, in itself, is a thought which demands two minutes silence. And what do we see? One might imagine—one would have every excuse for imagining, despite what you say, Comrade Willi, that this insignificant handful of sand on the beaches of time—not bad, that image?—unoriginal, but always apt—this million-and-a-little-over-a-half people exist in this pretty piece of God's earth solely in order to make each other miserable. . . ." Here Willi picked up his book again and applied his attention to it. "Comrade Willi, let your eyes follow the print but let the ears of your soul listen. For the *facts* are—the *facts*—that there's enough food here for everyone!—enough materials for houses for everyone!—enough talent though admittedly so well hidden under bushels at the moment that nothing but the most generous eye could perceive it—enough talent, I say, to create light where now darkness exists."

"From which you deduce?" said Willi.

"I deduce nothing. I am being struck by a new . . . it's a blinding light, nothing less . . ."

"But what you say is the truth about the whole world, not just this country," said Maryrose.

"Magnificent Maryrose! Yes. My eyes are being opened to—Comrade Willi, would you not say that there is some principle at work not yet admitted to your philosophy? Some principle of destruction?"

Willi said, in exactly the tone we had all expected: "There is no need to look any further than the philosophy of the class struggle," and as if he'd pressed a button, Jimmy, Paul, and I burst out into one of the fits of irrepressible laughter that Willi never joined.

"I'm delighted to see," he remarked, grim-mouthed, "that good socialists—at least two of you call yourselves socialists—should find that so very humorous."

"I don't find it humorous," said Maryrose.

"You never find anything humorous," said Paul. "Do you know that you never laugh, Maryrose? Never? Whereas I, whose view of life can only be described as morbid, and increasingly morbid with every passing minute, laugh continuously? How would you account for that?"

"I have no view of life," said Maryrose, lying flat, looking like a neat soft little doll in her bright bibbed trousers and shirt. "Anyway," she added, "you weren't laughing. I listen to you a lot—" (she said this as if she were not one of us, but an outsider) "—and I've noticed that you laugh most when you're saying something terrible. Well I don't call that laughing."

"When you were with your brother, did you laugh, Maryrose? And when you were with your lucky swain in the Cape?"

"Yes."

"Why?"

"Because we were happy," said Maryrose simply.

"Good God," said Paul in awe. "I couldn't say that. Jimmy, have you ever laughed because you were happy?"

"I've never been happy," said Jimmy.

"You, Anna?"

"Nor me."

"Willi?"

"Certainly," said Willi, stubborn, defending socialism, the happy philosophy.

"Maryrose," said Paul, "you were telling the truth. I don't believe Willi but I believe you. You are very enviable, Maryrose, in spite of everything. Do you know that?"

"Yes," said Maryrose. "Yes, I think I'm luckier than any of you. I don't see anything wrong with being happy. What's wrong with it?"

Silence. We looked at each other. Then Paul solemnly bowed towards Maryrose: "As usual," he said humbly, "we have nothing to say in reply."

Maryrose closed her eyes again. A pigeon alighted fast on a tree in the opposite clump. Paul shot and missed. "A failure," he exclaimed, mock tragic. The bird stayed where it was, surprised, looking about it, watching a leaf dislodged by Paul's bullet float down to the earth. Paul ejected his empty case, refilled at leisure, aimed, shot. The bird fell. Jimmy obstinately did not move. He did not move. And Paul, before the battle of wills could end in defeat for himself, gained victory by rising and remarking: "I shall be my own retriever." And he strolled off to fetch the pigeon; and we all saw that Jimmy had to fight with himself to prevent his limbs from jumping him up and over the grass after Paul. Who came back with the dead bird yawning, flinging it with the other dead birds.

"There's such a smell of blood I shall be sick," said Maryrose.

"Patience," said Paul. "Our quota is nearly reached."

"Six will be enough," said Jimmy. "Because none of us will eat this pie. Mr. Boothby can have the lot."

"I shall certainly eat of it," said Paul. "And so will you. Do you really imagine that when that toothsome pie, filled with gravy and brown savory meat, is set before you, that you will remember the tender songs of these birds so brutally cut short by the crack of doom?"

"Yes," said Maryrose.

"Yes," I said.

"Willi?" asked Paul, making an issue of it.

"Probably not," said Willi, reading.

"Women are tender," said Paul. "They will watch us eat, toying the while with Mrs. Boothby's good roast beef, making delicate little mouths of distaste, loving us all the more for our brutality."

"Like the Mashona women and the Matabele," said Jimmy.

"I like to think of those days," said Paul, settling down with his rifle at the ready, watching the trees. "So simple. Simple people killing each other for good reasons, land, women, food. Not like us. Not like us at all. As for us—do you know what is going to happen? I will tell you. As a result of the work of fine comrades like Willi, ever-ready to devote themselves to others, or people like me, concerned only with profits, I predict that in fifty years all this fine empty country we see stretching before us filled only with butterflies and grasshoppers will be covered by semidetached houses filled by well-clothed black workers."

"And what is the matter with that?" inquired Willi.

"It is progress," said Paul.

"Yes it is," said Willi.

"Why should they be semidetached houses?" inquired Jimmy, very seriously. He had moments of being serious about the socialist future. "Under a socialist government there'll be beautiful houses in their own gardens or big flats."

"My dear Jimmy!" said Paul. "What a pity you are so bored by economics. Socialist or capitalist—in either case, all this fine ground, suitable for development, will be developed at a rate possible for seriously undercapitalized countries—are you listening, Comrade Willi?"

"I am listening."

"And because a government faced with the necessity of housing a lot of unhoused people fast, whether socialist or capitalist, will choose the cheapest available houses, the best being the enemy of the better, this fair scene will be one of factories smoking into the fair blue sky, and masses of cheap identical housing. Am I right, Comrade Willi?"

"You are right."

"When then?"

"It's not the point."

"It's my point. That is why I dwell on the simple savagery of the Matabele and the Mashona. The other is simply too hideous to contemplate. It is the reality for our time, socialist or capitalist—well, Comrade Willi?"

Willi hesitated, then said: "There will be certain outward similarities but . . ." He was interrupted by Paul and myself, then Jimmy, in a fit of laughter.

Maryrose said to Willi: "They're not laughing at what you say, but because you always say what they expect."

"I am aware of that," said Willi.

"No," said Paul, "you are wrong, Maryrose. I'm also laughing at what he's saying. Because I'm horribly afraid it's not true. God forbid, I should be dogmatic about it, but I'm afraid that—as for myself, from time to time I shall fly out from England to inspect my overseas investments and peradventure I shall fly over this area, and I shall look down on smoking factories and housing estates and I shall remember these pleasant, peaceful pastoral days and . . ." A pigeon landed on the trees opposite. Another and another. Paul shot. A bird fell. He shot, the second fell. The third burst out of a bunch of leaves skywards as if it had been shot from a catapult. Jimmy got up, walked over, brought back two bloodied birds, flung them down with the others and said: "Seven. For God's sake, isn't it enough?"

"Yes," said Paul, laying aside his rifle. "And now let's make tracks fast for the pub. We shall just have time to wash the blood off before it opens."

"Look," said Jimmy. A small beetle, about twice the size of the largest anteater, was approaching through the towering grass-stems.

"No good," said Paul, "that is not a natural victim."

"Maybe not," said Jimmy. He twitched the beetle into the largest pit. There was a convulsion. The glossy brown jaws snapped on the beetle, the beetle jumped up, dragging the anteater halfway up the sides of the pit. The pit collapsed in a wave of white sand, and for a couple of inches all around the suffocating silent beetle, the sand heaved and eddied.

"If we had ears that could hear," said Paul, "the air would be full of screams, groans, grunts, and gasps. But as it is, there reigns over the sunbathed veld the silence of peace."

A cleaving of wings. A bird alighted.

"No, don't," said Maryrose in pain, opening her eyes and raising herself on her elbow. But it was too late. Paul had shot, the bird fell. Before it had even hit the ground another bird had touched down, swinging lightly on a twig at the very end of a branch. Paul shot, the bird fell; this time with a cry and a fluttering of helpless wings. Paul got up, raced across the grass, picked up the dead bird and the wounded one. We saw him give the wounded struggling bird a quick determined tight-mouthed look, and wring its neck.

He came back, flung down the two corpses and said: "Nine. And that's all." He looked white and sick, and yet in spite of it, managed to give Jimmy a triumphant amused smile.

"Let's go," said Willi, shutting his book.

"Wait," said Jimmy. The sand was now unmoving. He dug into it with a fine stem and dragged out, first the body of the tiny beetle, and then the body of the anteater. Now we saw the jaws of the anteater were embedded in the body of the beetle. The corpse of the anteater was headless.

"The moral is," said Paul, "that none but natural enemies should engage."

"But who should decide which are natural enemies and which are not?" said Jimmy.

"Not you," said Paul. "Look how you've upset the balance of

nature. There is one anteater the less. And probably hundreds of ants that should have filled its maw will now live. And there is a dead beetle, slaughtered to no purpose."

Jimmy stepped carefully over the shining round-pitted river of sand, so as not to disturb the remaining insects lying in wait at the bottom of their sand traps. He dragged on his shirt over his sweaty reddened flesh. Maryrose got up in the way she had—obedient, patient, long-suffering, as if she had no will of her own. We all stood on the edge of the patch of shade, reluctant to plunge into the now white-hot midday, made dizzy and giddy by the few remaining butterflies who reeled drunk in the heat. And as we stood there, the clump of trees we had lain under sang into life. The cicadas which inhabited this grove, patiently silent these two hours waiting for us to go, burst one after another into shrill sound. And in the sister clump of trees, unnoticed by us, had arrived two pigeons who sat there cooing. Paul contemplated them, his rifle swinging. "No," said Maryrose. "Please don't."

"Why not?"

"Please, Paul."

The heap of nine dead pigeons, tied together by their pink feet, dangled from Paul's free hand, dripping blood.

"It is a terrible sacrifice," said Paul gravely, "but for you, Maryrose, I will refrain."

She smiled at him, not in gratitude, but in the cool reproachful way she always used for him. And he smiled back, his delightful, brown, blue-eyed face all open for her inspection. They walked off together in front, the dead birds trailing their wings over jade-colored clumps of grass.

The three of us followed.

"What a pity," remarked Jimmy, "that Maryrose disapproves so much of Paul. Because there is no doubt they are what is known as a perfectly matched couple." He had tried the light ironic tone, and almost succeeded. Almost, not quite; his jealousy of Paul grated in his voice.

We looked: they were, those two, a perfect couple, both so light and graceful, the sun burnishing their bright hair, shining on their brown skins. And yet Maryrose strolled on without looking at Paul who gave her his whimsically appealing blue glances all in vain.

It was too hot to talk on the way back. Passing the small kopje on whose granite chunks the sun was beating, waves of dizzying heat struck at us so that we hurried past it. Everything was empty and silent, only the cicadas and a distant pigeon sang. And past the kopje we slowed and looked for the grasshoppers, and saw that the bright clamped couples had almost disappeared. A few remained, one above another, like painted clothes-pegs with painted round black eyes. A few. And the butterflies were almost gone. One or two floated by, tired, over the sun-beaten grass.

Our heads ached with the heat. We were slightly sick with the smell of blood.

At the hotel we separated with hardly a word.

FROM

# *The Golden Notebook*

*Whoever he be who looks in this*
*He shall be cursed,*
*That is my wish.*
*Saul Green,* his *book. (!!!)*

It is so dark in this flat, so dark, it is as if darkness were the shape of cold. I went through the flat turning on light everywhere, the dark retreated to outside the windows, a cold shape trying to press its way in. But when I turned on the light in my big room, I knew this was wrong, light was foreign to it, so I let the dark come back, controlled by the two paraffin heaters and the glow from the gas fire. I lay down, and thought of the little earth, half of it in cold dark, swinging in immense spaces of darkness. Soon after I lay down Saul came and lay beside me. "This is an extraordinary room," he said, "it's like a world." His arm under my neck was warm and strong, and we made love. He slept, and when he woke he was warm, not full of the deathly cold which frightens me. Then he remarked: "Well *now* perhaps I can work." The egoism was so direct, like mine when I need something, that I began to laugh. He laughed, and we couldn't stop. We rolled on the bed laughing and then on the floor. Then he jumped up off the floor, saying in a prissy English voice: "This won't do, it won't do at all," and went out, still laughing.

The devils had gone out of the flat. That is how I thought, sitting on my bed naked, warmed by the heat from the three fires. The devils. As if the fear, the terror, the anxiety were not inside me, inside Saul, but some force from outside which chose its moments to come and go. I thought like that, lying to myself; because I needed that moment of pure happiness—me, Anna, sitting naked on the bed, my breasts pressing between my naked arms, and the smell of sex and sweat. It seemed to me that the warm strength of my body's happiness was enough to drive away all the fear in the world. Then the feet began again upstairs, moving, driven, from place to place above my head, like armies moving. My stomach clenched. I watched my happiness leak away. I was all at once in a new state of being, one foreign to me. I realized my body was distasteful to me. This had never happened to me before; and I even said to myself: Hullo, this is new, this is something I have read about. I remembered Nelson telling me how sometimes he looked at his wife's body and hated it for its femaleness; he hated it because of the hair in the armpits and around the crotch. Sometimes, he said, he saw his wife as a sort of spider, all clutching arms and legs around a hairy central devouring mouth. I sat on my bed and I looked at my thin white legs and my thin white arms, and at my breasts. My wet sticky center seemed disgusting, and when I saw my breasts all I could think of was how they were when they were full of milk, and instead of this being pleasurable, it was revolting. This feeling of being alien to my own body caused my head to swim, until I anchored myself, clutching out for something, to the thought that what I was experiencing was not *my* thought at all. I was experiencing, imaginatively, for the first time, the emotions of a homosexual. For the first time the homosexual literature of disgust made sense to me. I realized how much homosexual feeling there is floating loose everywhere, and in people who would never recognize the word as theirs.

The sound of feet had stopped upstairs. I could not move, I was gripped by my disgust. Then I knew that Saul would come downstairs and say something that echoed what I was thinking; this knowledge was so clear that I simply sat and waited, in a fug of stale self-disgust, waiting to hear how this disgust would sound when said aloud in his voice, my voice. He came down and stood in the doorway, and he said: "Jesus, Anna, what are you doing there, sitting naked?" And I said, my voice detached and clinical: "Saul, do you realize we've got to the point where we influence each other's moods even when we are in different rooms?" It was too dark in my room to see his face, but the shape of his body, standing alert by the door, expressed a need to fly, to run from Anna sitting naked and repulsive on the bed. He said in the scandalized voice of a boy: "Put some clothes on." I said: "Did you hear what I said?" For he had not. He said: "Anna, I told you, don't sit there like that." I said: "What do you think this thing is that makes people like us have to experience everything? We're driven by something to be as many different things or people as possible." He heard this, and said: "I don't know. I don't have to try, it's what I am." I said: "I'm not trying. I'm being driven. Do you suppose that people who lived earlier were tormented by what they had not experienced? Or is it only us?" He said, sullen: "Lady, I don't know, and I don't care, I just wish I were delivered from it." Then he said, friendly, not out of disgust: "Anna, do you realize how damned cold it is? You'll be ill if you don't put on clothes. I'm going out." He went. As his feet went down the stairs, my mood of self-disgust went with him. I sat and luxuriated in my body. Even a small dry wrinkling of skin on the inside of my thigh, the beginning of being old, gave me pleasure. I was thinking: Yes, that's as it should be, I've been so happy in my life, I shan't care about being old. But even as I said it, the security leaked away again. I was back in disgust. I stood in the center of the big room, naked, letting the heat strike me from the three points of heat, and I knew, and it was an illumination—one of those things one has always known, but never really understood before—that all sanity depends on this: that it should be a delight to feel the roughness of a carpet under smooth soles, a delight to feel heat strike the skin, a delight to stand upright, knowing the bones are moving easily under flesh. If this goes, then the conviction of life goes too. But I could feel none of this. The texture of the carpet was abhorrent to me, a dead processed thing; my body was a thin, meager, spiky sort of vegetable, like an unsunned plant; and when I touched the hair on my head it was dead. I felt the floor bulge up under me. The walls were losing their density. I knew I was moving down into a new dimension, further away from sanity than I had ever been. I knew I had to get to the bed fast. I could not walk, so I let myself down on my hands and knees and crawled to the bed and lay on it, covering myself. But I was defenseless. Lying there I remembered the Anna who can dream at will, control time, move easily and is at home in the underworld of sleep. But I was not that Anna. The areas of light on the ceiling had become great watchful eyes, the eyes of an animal watching me. It was a tiger, lying sprawled over the ceiling, and I was a child *knowing* that there was a tiger in the room, even while my brain told me there was not. Beyond the triple-windowed wall a cold wind blew, striking the panes and making them shudder, and the winter's light thinned the curtains. They were not curtains, they were shreds of stinking sour flesh left by the animal. I realized I was inside a cage into which the animal could leap when it wished. I was ill with the smell of dead flesh, the reek of the tiger and with fear. And, while my stomach swayed, I fell asleep.

It was the kind of sleep I have known only when ill: very light, as if lying just under water, with real sleep in bottomless layers beneath me. And so all the time I was conscious of lying on the bed, and conscious of sleeping, and thinking extraordinarily clearly. Yet it was not the same as when I stood, in a dream, to one side and saw Anna sleeping, watching other personalities bend over to invade her. I was myself, yet knowing what I thought and dreamed, so there was a personality apart from the Anna who lay asleep; yet who that person is I do not know. It was a person concerned to prevent the disintegration of Anna.

As I lay on the surface of the dream-water, and began very slowly to submerge, this person said: "Anna, you are betraying everything you believe in; you are sunk in subjectivity, yourself, your own needs." But the Anna who wanted to slip under the dark water would not answer. The disinterested person said: "You've always thought of yourself as a strong person. Yet that man is a thousand times more courageous than you are—he has had to fight this for years, but after a few weeks of it, you are ready to give in altogether." But the sleeping Anna was already just under the surface of the water, rocking on it, wanting to go down into the black depths under her. The admonishing person said: "Fight. Fight. Fight." I lay rocking under the water, and the voice was silent, and then I knew the depths of water under me had become dangerous, full of monsters and crocodiles and things I could scarcely imagine, they were so old and so tyrannous. Yet their danger was what pulled me down, I wanted the danger. Then, through the deafening water, I heard the voice say: "Fight. Fight." I saw that the water was not deep at all, but only a thin sour layer of water at the bottom of a filthy cage. Above me, over the top of the cage, sprawled the tiger. The voice said: "Anna, you know how to fly. Fly." So I slowly crawled, like a drunk woman, to my knees in the filthy thin water, then stood up and tried to fly, treading down the stale air with my feet. It was so difficult that I almost fainted, the air was too thin, it wouldn't hold me. But I remembered how I had flown before, and so with a very great effort, fighting with every down-pushing step, I rose and clutched the top bars of the cage, over which the tiger lay sprawled. The smell of fetid breath suffocated me. But I pulled myself up through the bars and stood by the tiger. It lay still, blinking greenish eyes at me. Above me was still the roof of the building and I had to push down the air with my feet and tread up through it. Again I fought and struggled, and slowly I rose up and the roof vanished. The tiger lay sprawled at ease on a small ineffective cage, blinking its eyes, one paw stretched out and touching my foot. I knew I had nothing to fear from the tiger. It was a beautiful glossy animal lying stretched out in a warm moonlight. I said to the tiger: "That's your cage." It did not move, but yawned, showing white rows of teeth. Then there was a noise of men coming for the tiger. It was going to be caught and caged. I said: "Run, quickly." The tiger got up, stood lashing its tail, moving its head this way and that. It stank of fear now. Hearing the clamor of the men's voices and their running feet, it slashed with its paw at my forearm in a blind terror. I saw the blood running down my arm. The tiger leaped right down from the roof, alighting on the pavement, and it ran off into the shadows along the railings of the houses. I began to cry, filled with sorrow, because I knew the men would catch and cage the tiger. Then I saw my arm was not hurt at all, it had already healed. I wept with pity, saying: The tiger is Saul, I don't want him to be caught, I want him to be running wild through the world. Then the dream, or the sleep, became quite thin, close to waking, yet not quite waking. I said to myself: I must write a play about Anna and Saul and the tiger. The part of my mind concerned with this play went on working, thinking about it, like a child moving bricks about a floor—a child, moreover, who has been forbidden to play, because she knew it was an evasion, making patterns of Anna and Saul and the tiger was an excuse not to think; the patterns of what Anna and Saul would do and say were shapes of pain, the "story" of the play would be shaped by pain, and that was an evasion. Meanwhile, with the part of my mind which, I knew, was the disinterested personality who had saved me from disintegration, I began to control my sleep. This controlling person insisted that I must put aside the play about the tiger, must stop playing with the bricks. He said that instead of doing what I always do, making up stories about life, so as not to look at it straight, I should go back and look at scenes from my life. This looking back had a remarkable quality about it, like a shepherd counting sheep, or the rehearsal for a play, a quality of checking up, touching for reassurance. It was the same act as when I was a child and had bad nightmares every night: before I slept each night I lay awake, remembering everything in the day that had a quality of fear hidden in it; which might become part of a nightmare. I had to "name" the frightening things, over and over, in a terrible litany; like a sort of disinfection by the conscious mind before I slept. But now, asleep, it was not making past events harmless, by naming them, but *making sure they were still there.* Yet I know that having made sure they were still there, I would have to "name" them in a different way, and that was why the controlling personality was forcing me back. I revisited, first, the group under the eucalyptus trees at the Mashopi station in a wine-smelling moonlight, the patterns of leaves dark on white sand. But the terrible falsity of nostalgia had gone out of it; it was emotionless, and like a speeded-up film. Yet I had to watch George Hounslow come stooping his broad shoulders up from the black lorry standing by the glinting railway lines under the stars, to look with his fearful hunger at Maryrose and at me; and to hear Willi hum tunelessly in my ear the bars from Brecht's opera; and to see Paul bend slightly towards us with his mocking courtesy, before he smiled and went off up to the block of bedrooms near the tumbling granite boulders. And then, following him, we were walking along the sandy track. He was standing waiting for us, facing us, smiling with a cool triumph, looking not at us, the group sauntering towards him in hot sunlight, but past us, towards the Mashopi Hotel. One after another we, too, stopped and turned to look. The hotel building seemed to have exploded in a dancing whirling cloud of white petals or wings, millions of white butterflies had chosen the building to alight on. It looked like a white flower opening slowly, under the deep steamy blue sky. Then a feeling of menace came into us, and we knew we had suffered a trick of sight, had been deluded. We were looking at the explosion of a hydrogen bomb, and a white flower unfolded under the blue sky in such a perfection of puffs, folds, and eddying shapes that we could not move, although we knew we were menaced by it. It was unbelievably beautiful, the shape of death; and we stood watching in silence, until the silence was slowly invaded by a rustling, crawling, grating sound, and looking down we saw the grasshoppers, their gross tumbling fecundity inches deep, all around us. The invisible projectionist who was running this film now snapped the scene off, as if saying: "That's enough, you know it's still there." And immediately he began running a new part of the film. It was running slowly, because there was a technical hitch of some kind and several times he (the invisible projectionist) turned back the film so as to go through it again. The trouble was that the film was not clear, it had been shot badly. Two men, who were the same, yet separate, seemed to be fighting, in a silent duel of wills, to be in the film. One was Paul Tanner, the man from the working class, who had become a doctor, and whose quality of dry critical irony was what had sustained him in his struggle, the quality, however, which had fought with and slowly defeated the idealism in him. The other was Michael, the refugee from Europe. When these two figures finally merged, a new person was created. I could see the moment, it was as if the shape of a human being, a mold already created to contain the personality of Michael, or Paul Tanner, swelled out and altered, as if a sculptor working from inside his material was changing the shape of his statue by pressing his own shoulders, his own thighs, against the substance that had been Paul, been Michael. This new person was larger in build, with the heroic quality of a statue, but above all, I could feel his strength. Then he spoke, and I could hear the thin sound of the real voice before it was swallowed or absorbed by the new strong voice: "But my dear Anna, we are not the failures we think we are. We spend our lives fighting to get people very slightly less stupid than we are to accept truths that the great men have always known. They have always known, they have known for ten thousand years, that to lock a human being into solitary confinement can make a madman of him or an animal. They have always known that a poor man frightened of the police and his landlord is a slave. They have always known that frightened people are cruel. They have always known that violence breeds violence. And we know it. But do the great masses of the world know it? No. It is our job to tell them. Because the great men can't be bothered. Their imaginations are already occupied with how to colonize Venus; they are already creating in their minds visions of a society full of free and noble human beings. Meanwhile, human beings are ten thousand years behind them, imprisoned in fear. The great men can't be bothered. And they are right. Because they know we are here, the boulder-pushers. They know we will go on pushing the boulder up the lower slopes of an immensely high mountain, while they stand on the top of the mountain, already free. All our lives, you and I, we will use all our energies, all our talents, into pushing that boulder another inch up the mountain. And they rely on us and they are right; and that is why we are not useless after all." This voice faded; but already the film had changed. Now it was perfunctory. Scene after scene, flicked on, then off; I knew this brief "visiting" of the past was so that I should be reminded I had still to work on it. Paul Tanner and Ella, Michael and Anna, Julia and Ella, Molly and Anna, Mother Sugar, Tommy, Richard, Dr. West—these people appeared briefly, distorted with speed, and vanished again, and then the film broke off, or rather ran down, with a jarring dislocation. And the projectionist, in the silence that followed, remarked (and it was in a voice that struck me, because it was a new voice, rather jaunty, practical, jeering, a commonsensical voice): "And what makes you think that the emphasis you have put on it is the correct emphasis?" The word "correct" had an echoing parodic twang. It was a jeer at the Marxist jargon-word "correct." It also had a primness, like that of a schoolteacher. No sooner did I hear the word "correct," than I was attacked by a feeling of nausea, and I knew that feeling well—it was the nausea of being under strain, of trying to expand one's limits beyond what has been possible. Feeling sick, I listened to the voice saying: "And what makes you think that the emphasis you have put on it is correct?" while he, the projectionist, began running the film through again, or rather, the films, for there were several, and I was able, as they flicked past me on the screen, to isolate and "name" them. The Mashopi film; the film about Paul and Ella; the film about Michael and Anna; the film about Ella and Julia; the film about Anna and Molly. They were all, so I saw now, conventionally, well-made films, as if they had been done in a studio; then I saw the titles: these films, which were everything I hated most, had been directed by me. The projectionist kept running these films very fast, and then pausing on the credits, and I could hear his jeering laugh at *Directed by Anna Wulf*. Then he would run another few scenes, every scene glossy with untruth, false and stupid. I shouted at the projectionist: "But they aren't mine, I didn't make them." At which the projectionist, almost bored with confidence, let the scenes vanish, and he waited for me to prove him wrong. And now it was terrible, because I was faced with the burden of re-creating order out of the chaos that my life had become. Time had gone, and my memory did not exist, and I was unable to distinguish between what I had invented and what I had known, and I knew that what I had invented was all false. It was a whirl, an orderless dance, like the dance of the white butterflies in a shimmer of heat over the damp sandy vlei. The projectionist was still waiting, sardonic. What he was thinking got into my mind. He was thinking that the material had been ordered by me to fit what I knew, and that was why it was all false. Suddenly he said aloud: "How would June Boothby see that time? I bet you can't do June Boothby." At which my mind slipped into a gear foreign to me, and I began writing a story about June Boothby. I was unable to stop the flow of words, and I was in tears of frustration as I wrote in the style of the most insipid coy woman's magazine; but what was frightening was that the insipidity was due to a very slight alteration of my own style, a word here and there only: "June, a just-sixteen-year-old, lay on the chaise lounge of the veranda, looking past the luxuriant foliage of the golden shower to the road. She knew something was going to happen. When her mother came into the room behind her and said: June, come and help me with the hotel dinner—June did not move. And her mother, after a pause, went out of the room without speaking. June was convinced that her mother *knew*, too. She thought: Dear Mum, you know how I feel. Then it happened. A lorry drew up in front of the hotel beside the petrol pumps, and *he* got out. June, without hurrying, sighed and stood up. Then, as if impelled by an outer power, she left the house and walked, on the path which her mother had used a few moments before, towards the hotel. The young man standing beside the petrol pumps seemed to be conscious of her approach. He turned. Their eyes met . . ." I heard the projectionist laughing. He was delighted because I could not prevent these words emerging, he was sadistically delighted. "I told you," he said, his hand already lifted to start the film again. "I told you you couldn't do it." I woke into the stuffy dark of the room, illuminated in three places by glowing fire. I was exhausted by the dreaming. Instantly I knew I had woken because Saul was in the flat. I could hear no movement but I could feel his presence. I even knew just where he was, standing a little beyond the door on the landing. I could see him, in a tense indecisive pose, plucking at his lips, wondering whether to come in. I called: "Saul, I'm awake." He came in, and said in a jaunty false voice: "Hi, I thought you were asleep." I knew who had been the projectionist in my dream. I said: "Do you know, you've become a sort of inner conscience or critic. I've just dreamed of you like that." He gave me a long, cool, shrewd look, then said: "If I've become your conscience, then it's a joke, you're certainly mine." I said: "Saul, we're very bad for each other." He was on the point of saying: "I may be bad for you, but you're good for me—" because onto his face came the consciously whimsical but arrogant look that was the mask that went with those words. I stopped him by saying: "You're going to have to break it. I ought to, but I'm not strong enough. I realize you're much stronger than I am. I thought it was the other way around."

I watched anger, dislike, suspicion, move over his face. He was watching me sideways, eyes narrowed. I knew that now he was going to fight, out of the personality that would hate me for taking something away from him. I also knew that when he was "himself," he would think about what I had said, and being responsible, he would, in fact, do what I asked.

Meanwhile he said, sullen: "So you're kicking me out."

I said: "That's not what I said"—speaking to the responsible man.

He said: "I don't toe your particular line so you're going to kick me out."

Without knowing I was going to do it, I sat up and shrieked at him: "For Christ's sake, stop it, stop it, stop it, stop it." He ducked back, instinctively. I knew that for him a woman shrieking in hysteria meant that he would be hit. I thought how odd it was we two should be together at all, so close we should have become each other, for I had never hit anyone in my life. He even moved to the end of the bed, and sat ready to run off from a woman shrieking and hitting. I said, not shrieking, but crying: "Can't you see that this is a cycle, we go around and around?" His face was dark with hostility, I knew he was going to fight against going. I turned away from him, wrestled down the sickness in my stomach, and said: "Anyway, you'll go by yourself when Janet comes back."

I hadn't known I was going to say it, or that I thought it. I lay thinking about it. Of course it was true.

"What do you mean?" he asked, interested, not hostile.

"If I had had a son, you'd have stayed. You'd have identified with him. At least for a time, till you worked yourself through that. But since I've got a girl you'll go because you'll see us as two women, two enemies." He slowly nodded. I said: "How odd, I'm always afflicted by feelings of doom, fate, inevitability. But it was chance I had a girl and not a boy. Just pure chance. So it's chance you'll leave. My life will be changed, completely, because of it." I felt easier, less caged, holding on to chance. I said: "How strange, having a baby is where women feel they are entering into some sort of inevitable destiny. But right in the heart of where we feel most bound, is something that's just chance." He was watching me, sideways, unhostile, with affection. I said: "After all, no one in the world could make my having had a girl and not a boy into anything but chance. Imagine, Saul, if I'd had a boy, we'd have had what you Yanks call a relationship. A long relationship. It might have turned into anything, who knows?"

He said quietly: "Anna, do I really give you such a bad time?"

I said, with precisely his brand of sullenness—borrowed from him at a moment when he was not using it, so to speak, for now he was gentle and humorous: "I haven't done time with the witch doctors not to know that no one does anything to me, I do it to myself."

"Leaving the witch doctors out," he said, putting his hand on my shoulder. He was smiling, concerned for me. For that moment he was all there, the good person. Yet already I could see behind his face, the black power; it was coming back into his eyes. He was fighting with himself. I recognized that fight as the fight I had had while sleeping, to refuse entrance to alien personalities wanting to invade me. His fight got so bad he sat, eyes shut, sweat on his forehead. I took his hand, and he clutched at it, and he said: "O.K. Anna, O.K. O.K. Don't worry. Trust me." We sat on the bed, clutching at each other's hands. He wiped the sweat off his forehead, then kissed me, and said: "Put on some jazz."

I put on some early Armstrong. I sat on the floor. The great room was a world, with its glow of caged fire, and its shadows. Saul was lying on the bed, listening to the jazz, a look of pure contentment on his face.

Just then I couldn't "remember" sick Anna. I knew she was there in the wings, waiting to walk on, when some button was touched—but that was all. We were silent a long time. I wondered, when we began to talk, which two people would be talking. I was thinking that if there were a tape recorder of the hours and hours of talk in that room, the talk and the fighting and the arguing and the sickness, it would be a record of a hundred different people living now, in various parts of the world, talking and crying out and questioning. I sat and wondered what person would start crying out when I began talking, and I said:

"I've been thinking." This is already a joke when one of us says, "I've been thinking." He laughed and said: "So you've been thinking."

"If a person can be invaded by a personality who isn't theirs, why can't people—I mean people in the mass—be invaded by alien personalities."

He lay, popping his lips to the jazz, plucking at an imaginary guitar. He didn't reply, merely grimaced, saying: I am listening.

"The point is, comrade . . ." I stopped, hearing how I used the word, as we all do now, with an ironical nostalgia. I was thinking that it was first cousin to the jeering voice of the projectionist—it was an aspect of disbelief and destruction.

Saul said, laying aside his imaginary guitar: "Well, comrade, if you're saying that the masses are infected with emotions from outside, then I'm delighted, comrade, that you're holding fast to your socialist principles in spite of everything."

He had used the words "comrade" and "masses" ironically, but now his voice switched to bitterness: "So all we have to do, comrade, is to arrange that the masses are filled, like so many empty containers, with good useful pure kindly peaceful emotions, just the way we are." He spoke well beyond irony, not quite in the voice of the projectionist, but not far off it either.

I remarked: "That's the sort of thing I say, that kind of mocking, but you hardly ever do."

"As I crack up out of that one hundred percent revolutionary, I notice I crack up into aspects of everything I hate. That's because I've never lived with my eye on becoming what is known as mature. I've spent all my life, until recently, preparing myself for the moment when someone says: 'Pick up that rifle'; or, 'run that collective farm'; or, 'organize that picket line.' I always believed I'd be dead by the time I was thirty."

"All young men believe they are going to be dead by the time they're thirty. They can't stand the compromise of aging. And who am I to say they're not right?"

"I'm not *all* men. I'm Saul Green. No wonder I had to leave America. There's no one left who speaks my kind of language. What happened to them all—I used to know plenty once. We were all world-changers. Now I drive across my country, looking up my old friends, and they're all married or successful and having drunken private conversations with themselves because American *values* stink."

I laughed because of the sullen way he said married. He looked up to see why I laughed, and he said: "Oh yes, yes, I mean it. I'd walk into the fine new flat of an old friend, and I'd say: 'Hey, what the hell do you mean by doing this job, you know it stinks, you know you're destroying yourself?' And he'd say: 'But what about my wife and kids?' I'd say: 'Is it true what I heard—that you'd turned informer on your old friends?' And he'd swallow another quick drink and say: 'But Saul, there's my wife and kids.' Jesus, yes. And so I hate the wife and the kiddies, and I'm right to hate them. Yes, all right, laugh, what could be funnier than my kind of idealism—it's so old hat, it's so naïve! There's one thing you can't say to anyone any more, so it seems: You know in your heart of hearts you shouldn't be living like this. So, why do you? No, you can't say it, you're a prig . . . what's the use of saying it, some kind of guts have gone out of people. I should have gone to Cuba earlier this year and joined Castro, and been killed."

"Obviously not, since you didn't go."

"Determinism enters again, in spite of the chance you were saluting a moment ago."

"If you really want to be killed, there are a dozen revolutions around you can get killed in."

"I'm not fitted to live life as she is organized for us. Do you know what, Anna? I'd give anything to go back to when I was in the gang of idealist kids on the street corner, believing we could change everything. That's the only time in my life I've been happy. Yes, all right, I know what you're going to say."

So I said nothing. He lifted his head to look at me, and said: "But obviously I want you to say it."

So I said: "All American men look back and hanker after when they were in the group of young men before they had pressure on them to be successful or get married. Whenever I meet an American man, I wait for the moment when his face really lights up—it's when he's talking about the group of buddies."

"Thanks," he said, sullen. "That buttons up the strongest emotion I've ever felt and disposes of it."

"That's what's wrong with us all. All our strongest emotions are buttoned up, one after another. For some reason, they're irrelevant to the time we live in. What's my strongest need—being with one man, love, all that. I've a real talent for it." I heard my voice sullen, as his was, a moment before. I got up and went to the telephone.

"What are you doing?"

I rang Molly's number, and I said: "I'm ringing Molly. She'll say: How's your American? I'll say: I'm having an affair with him. An affair—that's the word. I always did love that word, so sophisticated and debonair! Well, and she'll say: That's not the most sensible thing you ever did in your life? I'll say no. That'll button this one up. I want to hear her say it." I stood listening to the telephone ring in Molly's flat. "I say now about five years of my life—that was when I loved a man who loved me. But of course I was very naïve in those days. Period. *That's* buttoned up. I say: Then I went through a time when I was looking for men who would hurt me. I needed it. Period. *That's* buttoned up." The telephone went on ringing. "I was a Communist for a time. On the whole, a mistake. A useful experience though, and one can never have too many of those. Period. That's buttoned up." There was no reply from Molly's house, so I put my receiver down. "So she'll have to say it another time," I said.

"But it won't be true," he said.

"Possibly not. But I'd like to hear it, all the same."

A pause. "What's going to happen to me, Anna?"

I said, listening to hear what I would say, to find out what I thought: "You're going to fight your way through what you are in now. You'll become a very gentle, wise, kind man who people will come to when they need to be told that—they're crazy in a good cause."

"Jesus, Anna!"

"You sound as if I'd insulted you!"

"Our old friend maturity again! Well, I'm not going to be bullied by *that* one."

"Oh, but ripeness is all, surely?"

"No, it is not!"

"But my poor Saul, there's no help for you, you're heading straight for it. What about all those marvelous people we know, aged about fifty or sixty. Well, there *are* a few of them . . . marvelous, mature, wise people. *Real* people, the phrase is, radiating serenity. And how did they get to be that way? Well, *we* know, don't we? Every bloody one of them's got a history of emotional crime, oh the sad bleeding corpses that litter the road to maturity of the wise serene man or woman of fifty-odd! You simply don't get to be wise, mature, et cetera, unless you've been a raving cannibal for thirty years or so."

"I'm going right on being a cannibal." He was laughing, but sullen.

"Oh no you're not. I can recognize a candidate for middle-aged serenity and ripeness a mile off. At thirty they are fighting mad, spitting fire and defiance and cutting sexual swathes in all directions. And I can see you now, Saul Green, living all strong and isolated from hand to mouth in some cold-water flat somewhere, sipping judiciously from time to time at some fine old Scotch. Yes, I can see you, you'll have filled yourself out to your proper shape again. You'll be one of those tough, square, solid middle-aged men, like a shabbying brown bear, your golden crew-cut greying judiciously at the temples. And you'll probably have taken to spectacles, too. And you'll have taken up silence, it might even come naturally by then. I can even see a neat blond temperately greying beard. They'll say: Know Saul Green? Now there's a man! What strength! What calm! What serenity! Mind you, from time to time one of the corpses will let out a small self-pitying bleat—*remember me?*"

"The corpses, I would have you know, are one and all on my side, and if you don't understand that, you understand nothing."

"Oh I understand it, but it doesn't make it less depressing, the way the victims are always so willing to contribute their flesh and blood."

"Depressing! I'm good for people, Anna. I wake them up and shake them and push them on their proper way."

"Nonsense. The people who are oh so willing to be victims are those who've given up being cannibals themselves, they're not tough or ruthless enough for the golden road to maturity and the ever-so-wise shrug. They know they've given up. What they are really saying is: *I've* given up, but I'll be happy to contribute my flesh and blood to you."

"Crunch, crunch, crunch," he said, his face clenched up so that his blond eyebrows met in a hard line across his brow, and his teeth showed, grinning angrily.

"Crunch, crunch, crunch," I said.

"You, I take it, not being a cannibal?"

"Oh yes indeed. But I've dished out aid and comfort too, from time to time. No, I'm not for sainthood, I'm going to be a boulder-pusher."

"What's that?"

"There's a great black mountain. It's human stupidity. There are a group of people who push a boulder up the mountain. When they've got a few feet up, there's a war, or the wrong sort of revolution, and the boulder rolls down—not to the bottom, it always manages to end a few inches higher than when it started. So the group of people put their shoulders to the boulder and start pushing again. Meanwhile, at the top of the mountain stand a few great men. Sometimes they look down and nod and say: Good, the boulder-pushers are still on duty. But meanwhile they are meditating about the nature of space, or what it will be like when the world is full of people who don't hate and fear and murder."

"Hmm. Well I want to be one of the great men on top of the mountain."

"Bad luck for both of us, we are both boulder-pushers."

And suddenly he leaped up and off the bed, like a black steel spring snapping, and stood, the hatred behind his eyes, as sudden as if switched on, and said: "Oh no, you don't, oh no, I'm not going to . . . I'm not . . . I, I, I." I thought, Well, so *he's* back is he. I went to the kitchen, got a bottle of Scotch, came back, lay on the floor, and drank the Scotch, while he talked. I lay on the floor, looking at the patterns of gold light on the ceiling, hearing the irregular pattering of big rain outside, and felt the tension lay hands on my stomach. Sick Anna was back. I, I, I, I, like a machine gun ejaculating regularly. I was listening and not listening, as if to a speech I had written someone else was delivering. Yes, that was me, that was everyone, the I. I. I. I am. I am. I am going to. I won't be. I shall. I want. I. He was walking around the room like an animal, a talking animal, his movements violent and charged with energy, a hard force that spat out I, Saul, Saul, I, I want. His green eyes were fixed, not seeing, his mouth, like a spoon or a spade or a machine gun, shot out, spewed out, hot aggressive language, words like bullets. "I'm not going to be destroyed by you. By anyone. I'm not going to be shut up, caged, tamed, told be quiet keep your place do as you're told I'm not . . . I'm saying what I think, I don't buy your world." I could feel the violence of his black power attack every nerve in me, I felt my stomach muscles churning, my back muscles tense as wires, I lay with the bottle of Scotch in my hand, sipping it steadily, feeling the drunkenness take hold, listening, listening . . . I realized I had been lying there a long time, hours perhaps, while Saul stalked and shouted. Once or twice I said something, threw words against his stream of talk, and it was if a machine, tuned or set by a mechanic to stop briefly at a sound from outside, stopped, checked itself mechanically, mouth or metal opening already in position to ejaculate the next stream of I I I I I I. I once got up, not really seen by him, for he was not seeing me, except as an enemy he had to shout down, and I put on Armstrong, partly for myself, clutching close as a comforter the pure genial music, and I said: "Listen Saul, listen." He frowned slightly, his brows twitching, and said mechanically: "Yeah? What?" Then I I I I I I, I'm going to show you all with your morality and your love and your laws, I I I I. So I took off the Armstrong, and put on his music, cool and cerebral, the detached music for men who refuse the madness and the passion, and for a moment he stopped, then sat, as if the muscles of his thighs had been cut, he sat, his head on his breast, eyes shut, listening to the soft machine-gun drumming of Hamilton, the drumming that filled the room as his words had, then he said, in his own voice: "My God, what we've lost, what we've lost, what we've lost, how can we ever get back to it, how can we get back to it again." And then, as if this had not happened, I could see how the muscles of his thighs tensed and jerked him up and I switched off the machine, since he was not listening, except to his own words, I I I, and lay down again and listened to the words spattering against the walls and ricocheting everywhere, I I I, the naked ego. I was so sick, I was clenched up into a ball of painful muscles, while the bullets flew and spattered, and for a moment I blacked out and revisited my nightmare where I knew, but really knew, how war waited, me running down the emptied street of white dirtied buildings in a silent city but filled with human beings silent with waiting, while somewhere close the small, ugly container of death exploded, soft, soft, it exploded into the waiting silence, spread death, crumbling the buildings, breaking the substance of life, disintegrating the structure of flesh, while I screamed, soundless, no one hearing, just as all the other human beings in the silent buildings screamed, no one hearing. When I came out of the blackout, Saul was standing against the wall, pressing against it with his back, the muscles of his thighs and back gripping the wall, looking at me. He had seen me. He was back again, for the first time in hours. His face was white, blood-drained, his eyes grey and strained and full of horror because I was lying there screwed up with pain. He said, in his own voice: "Anna, for God's sake, don't look like that," but then a hesitation, and back came the madman, for now it was not only I I I I, but I against women. Women the jailors, the consciences, the voice of society, and he was directing a pure stream of hatred against me, for being a woman. And now the whisky had weakened me and soddened me, and I felt in myself the weak soft sodden emotion, the woman betrayed. Oh boohoo, you don't love me, you don't love, men don't love women any more. Oh boohoo, and my dainty pink-tipped forefinger pointed at my white, pink-tipped betrayed bosom, and I began to weep weak, sodden whisky-diluted tears on behalf of womankind. As I wept I saw his prick stand up under his jeans, and I got wet, and I thought, derisive, oh so now he's going to love me, he's going to love poor betrayed Anna and her wounded white bosom. Then he said in the scandalized little voice of a schoolboy, a prig, "Anna, you're drunk, get off the floor." And I said, "I won't," weeping, luxuriating in the weakness. So he dragged me up, scandalized and lustful, and came into me, very big but like a schoolboy, making love to his first woman, too quick, full of shame and heat. And then I said, being unsatisfied: "Now be your age," using his language, and he said, scandalized: "Anna, you're drunk, now sleep it off." So he covered me and kissed me, went tiptoeing out, like a guilty schoolboy proud of his first lay, and I saw him, I saw Saul Green, the good American boy, sentimental and ashamed, having laid his first woman. And I lay and I laughed, and I laughed. Then I slept and woke laughing. I don't know what I had been dreaming, but I woke out of pure light heartedness, and then I saw he was beside me.

He was cold, so I held him in my arms, full of happiness. I knew, because of the quality of my happiness, that I must have been flying easily and joyfully in my sleep, and that meant I would not always be sick Anna. But when he woke he was exhausted from the hours of I I I I, and his face was yellow and agonized, and when we got out of bed we were both exhausted, and we drank coffee and read the newspapers silent, unable to say anything, in the big, brightly colored kitchen. He said: "I ought to work." But we knew we would not; and we went back to bed, too tired to move, and I even wished the Saul back from the night before, full of black murderous energy, it was so frightening to be so exhausted. Then he said: "I can't lie here." And I said: "No." But we didn't move. Then he got, or crawled, out of bed. And I thought: How is he going to get himself out of here, he's got to get steam up to do it. And though the tension in my stomach told me, I was even interested to see. He said, challenging: "I'm going for a walk." I said: "All right." He gave me a furtive look and went out to dress and then came back. He said: "Why don't you stop me?" And I said: "Because I don't want to." And he said: "If you knew where I was going, you'd stop me." And I said, hearing my voice harden: "Oh, I know you're going to a woman." And he said: "Well, you'll never know, will you?"

"No, and it doesn't matter."

He had been standing at the door, but now came into the room, hesitating. He had an air of being interested.

I remembered De Silva's: "I wanted to see what would happen."

Saul wanted to see what would happen. And so did I. I could feel in myself, stronger than anything else, a spiteful, positively joyous interest—as if he, Saul, and I, were two unknown quantities, two forces anonymous, without personality. It was as if the room held two totally malignant beings who, if the other suddenly fell dead or began screaming with pain, would say: "Well, so that's it, is it?"

"It doesn't matter," he said, now sullen, but in a kind of tentative sullenness, a rehearsal for sullenness, or a repetition of it too old for conviction. "It doesn't matter, you say, but you watch every movement I make like a spy."

I said, in a jaunty jolly voice, accompanying it with a laugh, like a weak ebbing gasp (a laugh I've heard from women under acute stress and which I was copying): "I'm a spy because you make me one." He stood silent, but looked as if he were listening, as if the words he must say next would be fed to him from a playback: "I'm not going to be corraled by any dame in the world, I've never been yet and I never shall."

The "I've never been yet and I never shall" came out in a hastening rush, as if a record had been speeded up.

And I said, in the same murderously jolly malicious voice: "If you mean by being corraled, that your woman should know every move you make, then you're corraled now."

And I heard myself letting out the expiring, weak, yet triumphant laugh.

"That's what you think," he said, malignant.

"That's what I know."

The dialogue had run itself out, and now we looked at each other, interested, and I said: "Well, we'll never have to say that again." And he said, interested: "I should hope not." With which he went out, in a rush, driven by the energy from this exchange.

I stood and thought: I can find out the truth by going upstairs and looking at his diary. But I knew I would not, and that I never would again. All that was finished. But I was very ill. I went to the kitchen for coffee, but measured myself a small measure of Scotch. I looked at the kitchen, very bright, very clean. Then vertigo attacked me. The colors were too bright, as if they were hot. And I became conscious of all the faults of the kitchen which usually gives me pleasure—a crack in glistening white enamel, dust on a rail, the paint beginning to discolor. I was overwhelmed with a feeling of cheapness and nastiness. The kitchen should all be painted again, but nothing would change the flat's being so old and the walls decaying in a decaying house. I switched off the lights in the kitchen and came back into this room. But soon it seemed as bad as the kitchen. The red curtains had an ominous yet tawdry gleam, and the white of the walls was tarnished. I found I was walking around and around the room, staring at the walls, curtains, the door, repelled by the physical substance of which the room was made, while colors attacked me by their hot unreality. I was looking at the room as I might look at the face of someone I know very well, for the marks of strain or tension. At my own, or Saul's for instance, knowing what is behind my neat, composed little face, what is behind Saul's broad, open, blond face, that looks ill, admittedly but who would guess, who had not experienced it, the explosion of possibilities that deploy through his mind? Or at the face of a woman on a train, when I can see from a tense brow or a knot of pain that a world of disorder lies hidden there and marvel at the power of human beings to hold themselves together under pressure. My big room, like the kitchen, had become, not the comfortable shell which held me, but an insistent attack on my attention from a hundred different points, as if a hundred enemies were waiting for my attention to be deflected so that they might creep up behind me and attack me. A doorknob that needed polishing, a trace of dust across white paint, a yellowish streak where the red of the curtains had faded, the table where my old notebooks lay concealed—these assaulted me, claimed me, with hot waves of rocking nausea. I knew I had to get to the bed, and again I had to crawl across the floor to reach it. I lay on the bed and I knew before I fell asleep that the projectionist was in wait for me.

I also knew what I was going to be told. Knowing was an "illumination." During the last weeks of craziness and timelessness I've had these moments of "knowing" one after the other, yet there is no way of putting this sort of knowledge into words. Yet these moments have been so powerful, like the rapid illuminations of a dream that remain with one waking, that what I have learned will be part of how I experience life until I die. Words. Words. I play with words, hoping that some combination, even a chance combination, will say what I want. Perhaps better with music? But music attacks my inner ear like an antagonist, it's not my world. The fact is, the real experience can't be described. I think, bitterly, that a row of asterisks, like an old-fashioned novel, might be better. Or a symbol of some kind, a circle perhaps, or a square. Anything at all, but not words. The people who have been there, in the place in themselves where words, patterns, order, dissolve, will know what I mean and the others won't. But once having been there, there's a terrible irony, a terrible shrug of the shoulders, and it's not a question of fighting it, or disowning it, or of right or wrong, but simply knowing it is there, always. It's a question of bowing to it, so to speak, with a kind of courtesy, as to an ancient enemy: All right, I know you are there, but we have to preserve the forms, don't we? And perhaps the condition of your existing at all is precisely that we preserve the forms, create the patterns—have you thought of that?

So all I can say is that before going to sleep I "understood" why I had to sleep, and what the projectionist would say, and what I would have to learn. Though I knew it already; so that the dreaming itself already had the quality of words spoken after the event, or a summing-up, for emphasis' sake, of something learned.

As soon as the dream came on, the projectionist said, in Saul's voice, very practical: "And now we'll just run through them again." I was embarrassed, because I was afraid I'd see the same set of films I had seen before—glossy and unreal. But this time, while they were the same films, they had another quality, which in the dream I named "realistic"; they had a rough, crude, rather jerky quality of an early Russian or German film. Patches of the film slowed down for long, long stretches while I watched, absorbed, details I had not had time to notice in life. The projectionist kept saying, when I had got some point he wanted me to get: "That's it lady, that's it." And because of his directing me, I watched even more closely. I realized that all the things to which I had given emphasis, or to which the pattern of my life had given emphasis, were now slipping past, fast and unimportant. The group under the gum trees, for instance, or Anna lying in the grass with Paul, or Ella writing novels, or Ella wanting death in the airplane, or the pigeons falling to Paul's rifle—all these had gone, been absorbed, had given place to what was really important. So that I watched, for an immense time, noting every movement, how Mrs. Boothby stood in the kitchen of the hotel at Mashopi, her stout buttocks projecting like a shelf under the pressure of her corsets, patches of sweat dark under her armpits, her face flushed with distress, while she cut cold meat off various joints of animal and fowl, and listened to the young cruel voices and crueler laughter through a thin wall. Or I heard Willi's humming, just behind my ear, the tuneless, desperately lonely humming; or watched him in slow motion, over and over again, so that I could never forget it, look long and hurt at me when I flirted with Paul. Or I saw Mr. Boothby, the portly man behind the bar, look at his daughter with her young man. I saw his envious, but unbitter gaze at this youth, before he turned away his eyes, and stretched out his hand to take an empty glass and fill it. And I saw Mr. Lattimer, drinking in the bar, carefully not-looking at Mr. Boothby, while he listened to his beautiful red-haired wife's laughter. I saw him, again and again, bend down, shaky with drunkenness, to stroke the feathery red dog, stroking it, stroking it. "Get it?" said the projectionist, and ran another scene. I saw Paul Tanner coming home in the early morning, brisk and efficient with guilt, saw him meet his wife's eyes, as she stood in front of him in a flowered apron, rather embarrassed and pleading, while the children ate their breakfast before going off to school. Then he turned, frowning, and went upstairs to lift a clean shirt down from a shelf. "Get it?" said the projectionist. Then the film went very fast, it flicked fast, like a dream, on faces I've seen once in the street, and have forgotten, on the slow movement of an arm, on the movement of a pair of eyes, all saying the same thing—the film was now beyond my experience, beyond Ella's, beyond the notebooks, because there was a fusion, and instead of seeing separate scenes, people, faces, movements, glances, they were all together, the film became immensely slow again, it became a series of moments where a peasant's hand bent to drop seed into earth, or a rock stood glistening while water slowly wore it down, or a man stood on a dry hillside in the moonlight, stood eternally, his rifle ready on his arm. Or a woman lay awake in darkness, saying No, I won't kill myself, I won't, I won't.

The projectionist now being silent, I called to him, It's enough, and he didn't answer, so I leaned out my own hand to switch off the machine. Still asleep, I read words off a page I had written: That was about courage, but not the sort of courage I have ever understood. It's a small painful sort of courage which is at the root of every life, because injustice and cruelty is at the root of life. And the reason why I have only given my attention to the heroic or the beautiful or the intelligent is because I won't accept that injustice and the cruelty, and so won't accept the small endurance that is bigger than anything.

I looked at these words which I had written, and of which I felt critical; and then I took them to Mother Sugar. I said to her: "We're back at the blade of grass again, that will press up through the bits of rusted steel a thousand years after the bombs have exploded and the world's crust has melted. Because the force of will in the blade of grass is the same as the small painful endurance. Is that it?" (I was smiling sardonically in my dream, wary of a trap.)

"And so?" she said.

"But the point is, I don't think I'm prepared to give all that much reverence to that damned blade of grass, even now."

At which she smiled, sitting in her chair foursquare and upright, rather bad-tempered because of my slowness, because I so invariably missed the point. Yes, she looked like an impatient housewife who has mislaid something or who is going to be out with her timetable.

Then I woke into a late afternoon, the room cold and dark, I was depressed; I was entirely the white female bosom shot full of cruel male arrows. I was aching with the need for Saul, and I wanted to abuse him and rail at him and call him names. Then of course he would say: Oh poor Anna, I'm sorry, then we would make love.

A short story: or a short novel: comic and ironic: A woman, appalled by her capacity for surrendering herself to a man, determines to free herself. She determinedly takes two lovers, sleeping with them on alternate nights—the moment of freedom being when she would be able to say to herself that she has enjoyed them both equally. The two men become instinctively aware of each other's existence; one, jealous, falls in love with her seriously; the other becomes cool and guarded. In spite of all her determination, she cannot prevent herself loving the man who has fallen in love with her; freezing up with the man who is guarded. Nevertheless, although she is in despair that she is as "unfree" as ever, she announces to both men that she has now become thoroughly emancipated, she has at last achieved the ideal of full sexual and emotional pleasure with two men at once. The cool and guarded man is interested to hear it, makes detached and intelligent remarks about female emancipation. The man she is in fact in love with, hurt and appalled, leaves her. She is left with the man she does not love and who does not love her, exchanging intelligent psychological conversation.

The idea for this story intrigued me, and I began thinking how it should be written. How, for instance, would it change if I used Ella instead of myself? I had not thought about Ella for some time, and I realized that of course she had changed in the interval; she would have become more defensive, for instance. I saw her with her hair altered—she would be tying it back again, looking severe; she would be wearing different clothes. I was watching Ella moving about my room; and then I began imagining how she would be with Saul—much more intelligent, I think, than I, cooler, for instance. After a while I realized I was doing what I had done before, creating "the third"—the woman altogether better than I was. For I could positively mark the point where Ella left reality, left how she would, in fact, behave because of her nature; and move into a large generosity of personality impossible to her. But I didn't dislike this new person I was creating; I was thinking that quite possibly these marvelous, generous things we walk side by side with in our imaginations could come in existence, simply because we need them, because we imagine them. Then I began to laugh because of the distance between what I was imagining and what in fact I was, let alone what Ella was.

I heard Saul's feet coming up the stairs, and I was interested to know who would come in. As soon as I saw him, although he looked ill and tired, I knew the devils would not be in my room that day; and perhaps never again, because I also knew what he planned to say.

He sat on the edge of my bed and said: "It's funny that you should have been laughing. I was thinking about you while I was walking around."

I saw how he had been walking through the streets, walking through the chaos of his imagination, clutching at ideas or sets of words to save him. I said: "Well, what were you thinking?"—waiting for the pedagogue to speak.

"Why are you laughing?"

"Because you've been rushing about a crazy city, making sets of moral axioms to save us both with, like mottoes out of Christmas crackers."

He said dryly: "It's a pity you know me so well, I thought I was going to astonish you with my self-control and brilliance. Yes, I suppose mottoes out of Christmas crackers is just."

"Well, let's have them."

"In the first place, you don't laugh enough, Anna. I've been thinking. Girls laugh. Old women laugh. Women of your age don't laugh, you're all too damned occupied with the serious business of living."

"But I was, in fact, laughing my head off—I was laughing about free women." I told him the plot of my short story, he sat listening, smiling wryly. Then he said: "That's not what I meant, I meant really laughing."

"I'll put it on my agenda."

"No, don't say it like that. Listen Anna, if we don't believe the things we put on our agendas will come true for us, then there's no hope for us. We're going to be saved by what we seriously put on our agendas."

"We've got to believe in our blueprints?"

"We've got to believe in our beautiful impossible blueprints."

"Right. What next?"

"Secondly, you can't go on like this, you've got to start writing again."

"Obviously if I could, I would."

"No, Anna, that's not good enough. Why don't you write that short story you've just told me about? No, I don't want all that hokum you usually give me—tell me, in one simple sentence, why not. You can call it Christmas-cracker mottoes if you like, but while I was walking about I was thinking that if you could simplify it in your mind, boil it all down to something, then you could take a good long look at it and beat it."

I began to laugh, but he said: "No, Anna, you're going to really crack up unless you do."

"Very well then. I can't write that short story or any other, because at that moment I sit down to write, someone comes into the room, looks over my shoulder, and stops me."

"Who? Do you know?"

"Of course I know. It could be a Chinese peasant. Or one of Castro's guerrilla fighters. Or an Algerian fighting in the F.L.N. Or Mr. Mathlong. They stand here in the room and they say, why aren't you doing something about us, instead of wasting your time scribbling?"

"You know very well that's not what any of them would say."

"No. But *you* know quite well what I mean. I know you do. It's the curse of all of us."

"Yes, I do know. But Anna, I'm going to force you into writing. Take up a piece of paper and a pencil."

I laid a sheet of clean paper on the table, picked up a pencil, and waited.

"It doesn't matter if you fail, why are you so arrogant? Just begin."

My mind went blank in a sort of panic, I laid down the pencil. I saw him staring at me, willing me, forcing me—I picked up the pencil again.

"I'm going to give you the first sentence then. There are the two women you are, Anna. Write down: 'The two women were alone in the London flat.' "

"You want me to begin a novel with 'The two women were alone in the London flat'?"

"Why say it like that? Write it, Anna."

I wrote it.

"You're going to write that book, you're going to write it, you're going to finish it."

I said: "Why is it so important to you that I should?"

"Ah," he said, in self-mocking despair. "A good question. Well, because if you can do it, then I can."

"You want me to give you the first sentence of your novel?"

"Let's hear it."

"On a dry hillside in Algeria, the soldier watched the moonlight glinting on his rifle."

He smiled. "I could write that, you couldn't."

"Then write it."

"On condition you give me your new notebook."

"Why?"

"I need it. That's all."

"All right."

"I'm going to have to leave, Anna, you know that?"

"Yes."

"Then cook for me. I never thought I'd say to a woman, cook for me. I regard the fact that I can say it at all as a small step towards what they refer to as being mature."

I cooked and we slept. This morning I woke first and his face, sleeping, was ill and thin. I thought it was impossible he should go, I couldn't let him, he was in no state to go.

He woke, and I was fighting the desire to say: You can't go. I must look after you. I'll do anything if only you'll say you'll stay with me.

I knew he was fighting his own weakness. I was wondering what would have happened if, all those weeks ago, he had not put up his arms around my neck, unconsciously, in his sleep. I wanted, then, for him to put his arms up around my neck. I lay, fighting not to touch him, as he was fighting not to appeal to me, and I was thinking how extraordinary, that an act of kindness, of pity, could be such a betrayal. My brain blacked out with exhaustion, and while it did, the pain of pity took me over and I cradled him in my arms, knowing it was a betrayal. He clung to me, immediately, for a second of genuine closeness. Then, at once, my falseness created his, for he murmured, in a child's voice: "Ise a good boy," not as he had ever whispered to his own mother, for those words could never have been his, they were out of literature. And he murmured them mawkishly, in parody. But not quite. Yet as I looked down at him, I saw his sharp ill face show first, the sentimental falseness that went with the words; then a grimace of pain; then, seeing me look down, in horror, his grey eyes narrowed into a pure hating challenge, and we looked at each other helpless with our mutual shame and humiliation. Then his face relaxed. For a few seconds he slept, blacked out, as I had blacked out the moment before, just before I had bent to put my arms around him. Then he jerked himself out of sleep, all tenseness and fight, jerked himself out of my arms, glancing alert and efficient around the room for enemies, then stood up; all in one moment, so fast did these reactions follow each other.

He said: "We can't either of us ever go lower than that."

I said: "No."

"Well *that's* played out," he said.

"Buttoned up and finished," I said.

He went up to pack his few things into his bag and cases.

He came down again soon and leaned against the door of my big room. He was Saul Green. I saw Saul Green, the man who had walked into my flat some weeks before. He was wearing the new close-fitting clothes that he had bought to clothe his thinness. He was a neat, smallish man with over-big shoulders and the bones of a too-thin face standing out, insisting that this was a stocky, strong-fleshed body, that this would again be a strong, broad-shouldered man when he had worked through his illness into health. I could see standing beside the small, thin, fair man, with his soft brush of blond hair, his sick yellow face, a strong sturdy brown-fleshed man, like a shadow that would absorb the body that cast it. Meanwhile he looked stripped for action, pared down, light on his feet, wary. He stood, thumbs hooked in his belt, fingers arrowing down (but now it was like a gallant parody of a rake's stance) and he was sardonically challenging, his cool grey eyes on guard, but friendly enough. I felt towards him as if he were my brother, as if, like a brother, it wouldn't matter how we strayed from each other, how far apart we were, we would always be flesh of one flesh, and think each other's thoughts.

He said: "Write the first sentence for me in the book."

"You want me to write it for you?"

"Yes, write it down."

"Why?"

"You're part of the team."

"I don't feel that, I hate teams."

"You think about it then. There are a few of us around in the world, we rely on each other even though we don't know each other's names. But we rely on each other all the time. We're a team, we're the ones who haven't given in, who'll go on fighting. I tell you, Anna, sometimes I pick up a book and I say: Well, so you've written it first, have you? Good for you. O.K., then I won't have to write it."

"All right, I'll write your first sentence for you."

"Good. Write it, and I'll come back and get the book and say goodbye and I'll be on my way."

"Where are you going?"

"You know quite well I don't know."

"Sometime you're going to have to know."

"All right, all right, but I'm not mature yet, have you forgotten?"

"Perhaps you'd better go back to America."

"Why not? Love's the same the world over."

I laughed, and I went to the pretty new notebook, while he went off downstairs, and I wrote: "On a dry hillside in Algeria, a soldier watched the moonlight glinting on his rifle."

Here Anna's handwriting ended, the golden notebook continued in Saul Green's handwriting, a short novel about the Algerian soldier. This soldier was a farmer who was aware that what he felt about life was not what he was expected to feel. By whom? By an invisible *they,* who might be God, or the State, or Law, or Order. He was captured, tortured by the French, escaped, rejoined the F.L.N., and found himself torturing, under orders to do so, French prisoners. He knew that he should feel something about this that he did not in fact feel. He discussed his state of mind late one night with one of the French prisoners whom he had tortured. The French prisoner was a young intellectual, a student of philosophy. This young man (the two men were talking secretly in the prisoner's cell) complained that he was in an intellectual prison-house. He recognized, had recognized for years, that he never had a thought, or an emotion, that didn't instantly fall into pigeonholes, one marked "Marx" and one marked "Freud." His thoughts and emotions were like marbles rolling into predetermined slots, he complained. The young Algerian soldier found this interesting, he didn't find that at all, he said, what troubled him—though of course it didn't really trouble him, and he felt it should—was that nothing he thought or felt was what was expected of him. The Algerian soldier said he envied the Frenchman—or rather, he felt he *ought* to be envying him. While the French student said he envied the Algerian from the bottom of his heart: he wished that just once, just once in his life, he felt or thought something that was his own, spontaneous, undirected, not willed on him by Grandfathers Freud and Marx. The voices of the two young men had risen more than was wise, particularly that of the French student, crying out against his situation. The Commanding Officer came in, found the Algerian talking, like a brother, with the prisoner he was supposed to be guarding. The Algerian soldier said: "Sir, I did what I was ordered: I tortured this man. You did not tell me I should not talk with him." The Commanding Officer decided that his man was some sort of a spy, probably recruited while he had been a prisoner. He ordered him to be shot. The Algerian soldier and the French student were shot together, on the hillside, with the rising sun in their faces, side by side, the next morning.

[This short novel was later published and did rather well.]

FROM

# The Four-Gated City

A bad time is announced by an event. A woman gasses herself because her will to survive is exhausted. This event is different in quality from previous events. It is surprising. But it should not have been surprising. It could have been foreseen. One's imagination had been working at half-pressure . . . Martha had been here before.

When a bad time starts, it is as if on a smooth green lawn a toad appears; as if a clear river suddenly floats down a corpse. Before the appearance of the toad, the corpse, one could not imagine the lawn as anything but delightful, the river as fresh. But lawns can always admit toads, and rivers corpses . . . Martha had been here before.

When Sally said she was going back to her flat for a day or so, leaving her little boy, that was so unlike her, so improbable, that if Martha had been alert, she would have—but what? Called the police? The doctors? There was no set of words which Martha could imagine herself using. "Sally, you're not thinking of . . . ? Oh, please don't!— You'll feel better in a few days . . . Lie down for a little and we'll get you a sedative. Sally, you're a coward! How *can* you think of . . . And what about your little boy, he won't be able to live without you . . ."

(People are infinitely expendable, feel themselves to be, or feel themselves to be *now*.)

*"Sally, we'll lock you up until you come to your senses!"*

Sally had gone back to her flat to become Sarah. What had she really felt when the family which had taken her in had done so only under the passport of Sally? "They've always called me Sally," she said, once, exchanging with Martha a look which the family itself could not be expected to understand. If she had refused to be Sally, had insisted on remaining Sarah, would she then have had to make the journey alone to her empty home where she could turn on the gas?

Before that double event, Colin's departure, Sally's death, the quality of life was different; seemed almost, looking back on it, as—no, not happiness. Happiness, unhappiness, these were not words that could be used anywhere near this family, every member of which held the potentiality for—disaster? But that had been true before the double event. How then had it been possible for Martha to feel that "the holding operation" could in fact hold off what had been so loudly heralded? Something had been bound to give. Yet to look back from the day after Sally's death, to even the day before it, it was as if a bomb had gone off.

So a war begins. Into a peacetime life comes an announcement, a threat. A bomb drops somewhere, potential traitors are whisked off quietly to prison. And for some time, days, months, a year perhaps, life has a peacetime quality, into which warlike events intrude. But when a war has been going on for a long time, life is all war, every event has the quality of war, nothing of peace remains. Events and the life in which they are embedded have the same quality. But since it is not possible that events are not part of the life they occur in—it is not possible that a bomb should explode into a texture of life foreign to it—all that means is that one has not understood, one has not been watching.

And, the bomb having exploded, the heralding (or so it seems) event having occurred, even then the mind tries to isolate, to make harmless. It was Martha's concern, and Mark's, to try and minimize the double event, as if they felt it to be an isolated thing, without results, as if it had had no causes. Or at least, that was what it seemed they felt; for with the little boy Paul playing upstairs, his mother dead, his father gone, they were discussing how to soften and make harmless. "How to break it"—as Mark put it.

Paul was going to be six next week. He had plans for his birthday. His mother had talked of a party. Some sort of a party there must be.

"Is my mother going to be here?" asked Paul.

"I expect so," said Mark, and turned away from the child's acutely fearful black eyes. Paul had never been separated from his mother, not even for one day. And now his uncle said: "I expect so." Paul became very gay, manic. He rushed all over the big house, bouncing on the beds, teasing the cat, standing to look out of all the windows, one after another. Through one of them, he would see his mother come. He turned, saw Mark and Martha watching him; and pulled the heavy curtains so that he was hidden from them. He took the black cat to bed with him, where he hugged and kissed the beast, which suffered it. But he did not like Martha touching him, nor Mark. Particularly not Mark. He was not used to contact with a man; his father having been kindly, but concerned (he had even said so) to make up for the emotionalism of the unfortunate Sally-Sarah by being cordial but restrained.

Mark and Martha were prisoners in the house, because the reporters patrolled outside. Paul asked to go for a walk. He did not say that he hoped to catch a glimpse of his mother in the streets. He was told that no one was going for walks. Through the windows he saw men trying to peer in; and asked who they were. He tried to slip out of the back door, but found a smiling man on the doorstep, who frightened him. He stood outside the study door, listening to Martha answering the telephone. No, Mr. Coldridge was not in; no, he could not come to the telephone; no, there was no comment about Mr. Coldridge's brother.

"Is Mr. Coldridge's brother my daddy?" he inquired.

The exchange was asked to alter the number. This was done; and for a couple of days there was peace. But then a reporter got the new number from Jimmy Wood at the factory. Jimmy Wood had been asked not to give it. In explanation he said that the man sounded "as if he really wanted it." The number was changed again. Jimmy was again asked not to give it. But he did: he thought, explained, that the man asking for it was an electronics expert. After all, he had said he was. Jimmy's part through the long siege was simply—not ever to understand it. Mark asked Jimmy to come to the house, so it could all be explained to him. He must be careful of the journalists, he was told. He arrived at the front door, and was enclosed by a group of news-hungry men. To them, smiling, he told everything he knew. Not much, not more than Mark knew; but affable and willing, he chatted, and entered the house, still smiling. But then, he always smiled. Sometime in his life he had decided that life must be faced with this smile, and he never switched it off. A defense? An explanation? Who knew? But this small, wispy man with his great head covered in baby hair—smiled, as if he could not help it. They said to him: Please be careful, please don't expose us, please don't talk to the press, and he smiled. Almost at once he began talking about affairs at the factory. It seemed he could not see the necessity for all this fuss.

But he agreed, not so much impatiently as with tolerance, not to give the telephone number to anyone at all.

For a while, then, it was quiet. But Margaret telephoned from her country home. She had not been near them since the election party. She was concerned about Francis. "You ought to get him back home," she said. "He must be having a dreadful time at that beastly school."

"But it would be worse here with the journalists."

"You think so? I don't know. Mark could get rid of them, easily, if he wanted to."

"Yes, but I don't think he'd want to do that."

"You ought to make him."

"Perhaps you'd like to talk to him?"

"No. No. I really haven't got any more patience with . . . Have you let the basement?"

"The basement!"

"Mrs. Ashe still wants it."

"But Margaret, for God's sake . . ."

Margaret had sounded embarrassed, about the basement. Now she hurried on: "But he always was so wrongheaded. Always."

"I think you ought to be discussing that with him."

"Well, yes, but—and don't forget about Mrs. Ashe, I must really ring off, I'm really very . . ." She rang off.

This was so odd, struck such a discordant note, that Martha was unable to think about it, forgot to tell Mark.

It was Mark who took the next call from his mother.

Margaret had telephoned Francis's school, and the headmaster said Francis was all right. As far as he knew the news had not reached the school. "But he's such a fool," Margaret said. "I asked him if he banned the newspapers there and he said, he was sure his boys understood the meaning of *esprit de corps.*"

"Perhaps you could take Francis for a week or two?"

"Oh, I don't know—anyway, I'm off to America next week."

"You could take him until then, couldn't you?"

"I don't really think . . ."

She then went on to talk about Mrs. Ashe.

Mark said he really hadn't time to worry about being a landlord, and rang off. It was so extraordinary of Margaret that Mark, like Martha, let it slide.

Paul had listened to this from outside the study door.

"Why should Francis go and live with his granny?" he asked.

"She's your granny too."

"No. She isn't. She doesn't like my mummy."

"Well, it would only be for a little time."

She tried to pick him up. He was a heap of heavy limbs. The black frightened eyes, already lit by cunning, held Martha's face, while he held himself rigid in her arms. She put him down.

"I don't want Francis's granny to come to my party."

"She's not coming."

His birthday was the day after the next.

"I want my party, I want my party," he sobbed, from the floor. He was saying, I want my mother.

Next morning, Martha put on a headscarf, and Mrs. Van's old coat, and got out of the house by eight in the morning, by the back door. Only two journalists had arrived, and they were at the front of the house. She went across London to Harrods, and bought a cake and presents for the party. When she arrived at the back door, it looked unoccupied. But before she could get in, a man ran up.

"Who are you?" he demanded.

"I work for Mr. Coldridge. I do the cleaning."

She had the key in the door, but she was gripped by her other arm which clutched parcels.

His face was alive with suspicion, but also with the delights of the chase.

"What's going on in there?"

"I don't know. I'm just the cleaner."

The clothes were right, but her voice was not. His face was hard, self-righteous. He was a man seeking to unmask evil. He took five pounds from his pocket. He hesitated. Five pounds was more than enough for a charwoman, but not for a friend or mistress or fellow conspirator of Mark Coldridge. Hesitating, he lost his force of purpose; Martha slipped her arm away, and shot indoors, scattering parcels onto the floor of the kitchen. Through the back window his face appeared, in an angry teeth-bared scowl. Framed thus, emphasized, it was almost—yes, funny. He looked like a bad actor in a melodrama: my prey has escaped.

One of the aspects of a bad time, before one has entered into its spirit, is that everything has a feel of parody, or burlesque. Martha stood in the kitchen, looking at the ugly, threatening face, and had to suppress laughter. Nervous laughter, certainly, and when he shook his fist at her, it was ugly and she was afraid. That evening, among the pile of newspapers that came from the newsagent, brought past the reporters by the newsagent's boy, was one which carried a story about a mysterious woman, who had entry to Mr. Coldridge's house, and who would not give her name.

Next day was the birthday. In the morning, Paul was given presents, which he opened, Mark and Martha watching. He tore through them, throwing them aside, one after another: he was looking for evidences of his mother. He had not mentioned his mother for some days. Clearly the birthday had become for him the talisman which could produce his mother. The presents had not, but there was still the party.

After breakfast he went to Mark's study and stood by the desk watching Mark pretending to work. By now they were waiting for him to ask: Where is my mother, so that they could tell him the truth. Which they should have done before. But the right time had gone past, and they did not know what to do. Everything was wrong, the "party" absurd, the presents a mistake.

But now they did not know how not to have the party.

Martha laid a party spread on the table in the dining room. But Paul demanded that it should be in the kitchen. Nothing came in the front door, only sheaves of newspapers, falling through the letter slot. But the back door could admit. It was through the back door that he expected his mother.

Martha spread out the cake, with its six candles, on the kitchen table, and some biscuits and little cakes. While Martha moved about in these pathetic preparations, Paul stood just inside the kitchen door, watching them. Mark, trying to engage Paul's attention, played with a wooden train on the floor. From time to time the two grown-up people exchanged glances of helplessness, and of shame, because things could have been allowed to reach this point.

There was a heavy knock on the back door; and the little boy, crying "There she is! There's my mummy!" rushed to open it. Two men stood there. One was the journalist of yesterday, looking angrily sullen. The other was a large smiling man.

"Where's my mummy?" shouted Paul.

The two looked at each other, then studied Martha, arranging cakes, and Mark, playing trains.

The large man said: "Take it easy, son, take it easy. Your mummy's not coming, you know."

"Why not, why not?" screamed Paul, and flung himself down. Lying face down, he banged his head hard on the floor while his face exploded tears.

"Is this Colin Coldridge's boy?" asked the sullen man, bending to examine him for describable details.

Mark now scrambled up off his knees, and advanced on the journalists. Yesterday's man was suspiciously angry. The large man was smiling, ingratiating. The child continued to bang his head, crying noisily. Mark, with his eyes wide, his mouth open, his face white, appeared comic.

"Take it easy," said the large man again, and backed away, in a parody of fear: he was making fun of Mark.

The self-righteous man was now making mental notes about the kitchen. Having done this, he returned his attention to Paul, who was writhing at his feet, and said accusingly: "Why didn't you tell the boy about his mother?"

At which Paul shot off the floor and grasped his uncle around the knees, so violently that Mark staggered and leaned sideways to catch hold of a chair back. "Tell me what?" screamed Paul. "Where's my mummy?"

"Your mummy's . . ." The journalist stopped, unable to say "dead" to the child's face.

With a mutter of inarticulate disgust, he backed out of the door. The goodfellow, smiling deprecatingly, said: "Here's my card." He laid a piece of card on the table by the cake. *Miles Tangin. The Daily* ——. "If you'd cooperate, Mr. Coldridge," he suggested, "then it would be better."

"I'll complain to your editor," said Mark over Paul's head. The child was sobbing noisily, and gripping Mark's knees, so that Mark had to hold himself upright with one hand on the chair back while with the other he tried to soothe Paul.

"You do that," said the first man, all contemptuous bitterness.

The two went out together.

Mark carried the sobbing child up to bed.

In bed he was quieter, whimpering a little, while he watched them both. He was waiting.

"Where is my mummy?" he asked at last.

Martha said: "She's dead, Paul."

Paul took it. It was a fact which marched with the events of the last week.

"And is my daddy dead too?"

"No," said Mark, with emphasis. But both he and Martha knew that of course he would not believe them. They had been lying to him: they were probably lying again.

"He's away," said Martha. "He'll come back."

Paul said nothing. He lay staring at them, with his black untrusting eyes. Then he turned his face to the wall, and shut them out. They stayed with him. Hour after hour passed. He was not asleep. He kept dropping off, but he whimpered in his sleep, and this woke him. It was nearly morning when at last he fell into a deep sleep.

Their days were now spent with Paul, the child who could not trust them. He had gone silent, evasive, listless. He spent hours curled in a chair in the kitchen, sucking his thumb. He usually did not answer when Martha or Mark spoke to him. This did not look as if he were trying to be a baby again, wanting to be fed; but as if he really could not take in the existence of food, of mealtimes. He would sit listening, or apparently listening, if they read to him or told him stories. He sat quietly for the children's programs on the radio. Put to bed, he slept. When he looked out of the back windows, the front windows, and saw the groups of reporters waiting there, he examined them, then looked at Mark or Martha for explanations. It seemed he was afraid to ask questions. But they wouldn't have known how to answer.

In the evenings the two sat in Mark's study. Mark's white face had acquired a staring masklike look, as if wide-eyed at the incredible, the impossible. He did not believe what was happening. This was because he was Mark Coldridge, to whom such things could not happen.

Yet he was also Mark Coldridge who had written that book about war which came from the heart of an understanding of how such things happened—must happen. Martha was waiting to talk to the man who had written that book: but he was not there.

Mark was saying things like: "We must get Paul to school so that he can get over it." Or: "When it's blown over, I'll take Francis and Paul for a holiday somewhere."

He was still talking in terms of a situation normal enough to blow over. He could not bear to see that a deep harm had been done; and that they, or at least he, must expect the results of it, and that the results were for life.

But how could Martha blame Mark when she caught herself thinking several times a day: Before Sally killed herself, before Colin went away—the double event which her nerves, geared to laziness, still felt as a watershed. And it was as much her fault as Mark's that Paul had not been told the truth (as much truth as could be told to a child of six) so that now he trusted no one; it was as much her fault that the affair had been handled so that the truth had come through journalists scavenging for news.

And what was the use of feeling guilt, blaming herself and Mark, when they still did not know how to act, still sat night after night in the quiet book-lined study, with a decanter of old brandy on the desk, and when they did act, absurdity or worse came of it. For they had lost a sense of the ordinary machinery of life.

One afternoon they had watched through the windows a couple of press men rummaging through their dustbins in search of incriminating documents.

One of them was Miles Tangin. Mark telephoned the editor to protest, could not get through, left a message that he would like to be rung back, was rung back by—Miles Tangin. The telephone number then had to be changed again.

Martha suggested that he should ask the police to guard front and back entrance, to keep the journalists off.

Mark was furious. "I'm not being guarded by police in my own house in my own country because of a lot of . . . I'll get Margaret to tell the editor what's going on. She must know him."

He rang his mother's home in the country. It was only when it had been ringing for some minutes that they realized it was after two in the morning. After a long wait, John came to the telephone. He was polite, of course. Mark spoke to the colorless husband of his mother, a man whom he despised, though of course, he had never been anything less than polite to him. Martha sat on an old brown sofa, feeling velvet rub soft under her fingers. She was watching Mark clutch the telephone as if the machine itself could come up with sense, or protection. In the last couple of weeks he had lost over a stone. His clothes were hanging on him. His fingers were stained with nicotine to the knuckles. He looked half crazy.

John said that Margaret was asleep after a hard day. The press had been out to the house, and the telephone was never silent.

"I want to speak to her," said Mark.

"I'll tell her in the morning that you rang."

"Then tell her to get hold of those editors and call off their dogs," said Mark.

A short affronted laugh.

"Perhaps if you were prepared to make some sort of announcement to the press?" suggested Margaret's husband.

"What announcement would you suggest?"

Another short laugh. "As things stand, your mother, my wife, is the mother of a man who has escaped behind the Iron Curtain, suspected of being a spy, and of another who refuses to disassociate himself from him."

"But he happens to be my brother," said Mark. Again, he sounded incredulous. It was precisely here: what he could not believe was happening, or could happen—to him.

"But what can they expect me to do?" he asked Martha again. And he listened with his wide fascinated look as if this time he might understand what previously he had failed to understand.

She said, again: "They expect you to make a public announcement that you repudiate your brother and all his works. And to make a public affirmation of loyalty to this country."

"But good God," he said softly, "I mean—but they can't—but this is *this* country, it's not . . . I mean, the Americans or the Russians or people like that, but not . . ."

He was looking at her with dislike.

"Don't tell me that's what you think I should do! He's my brother," he insisted. As if it were she who was his enemy.

"You keep asking me what they want."

His eyes were hot and dark with refusal. He sat locked in himself. Then he understood he was making an enemy of an ally, smiled, though stiffly, and poured her a brandy.

"I'm sorry," he said.

Next morning Margaret rang. It was very early. Mark was half asleep. He came up to Martha's room to say that he thought his mother had gone mad. She had telephoned about the basement and about Mrs. Ashe.

They could not understand it. Martha said that this was perhaps Margaret's way of preserving normality. She was probably right: to worry about letting basements was better than what they were all doing. It was even reassuring of her.

As they spoke, the telephone rang again. Mark went to it. Mark did not come back, so Martha went down to him. He was sitting, looking very white, by the telephone.

Margaret's second call was hysterical. She had shouted that Mark was ruining her life. The very least he could do was to have Mrs. Ashe. On being asked, please, to explain Mrs. Ashe, Margaret had muttered, after a silence, something about Hilary Marsh—restoring confidence in that quarter. And at last it had all become clear to Mark, but so suddenly that he had simply put down the receiver.

Hilary Marsh, the correct unnoticed gentleman from the election party, had been Margaret's friend for many years. He was in the Foreign Office. Weeks ago he had been to Margaret, to ask what she knew about her son Colin's connections. Margaret knew nothing. She had said that Mark did, but Mark would never talk to her, he was always so wrong-headed, always had been. Hilary Marsh had suggested that it might be a good idea if a very old friend of his, Mrs. Ashe, lived in the basement. She was a sensible sort of woman, and could keep an eye on Mark for both of them.

Mark having digested this, he rang back his mother to ask how she proposed to explain this attempt to spy on him. She said, cold: "You have no right to talk to me about spying!" Then, as he remained silent, she had screamed: "You've ruined my life. You've ruined John's career!" And had rung off.

It turned out that John Patten, in his capacity as representative of British Culture, had been going on a lecture tour to America. But the Americans had not been happy about this, since he was the husband of the woman who had given birth to Colin Coldridge. They had made unofficial and tactful representations to the body who employed John Coldridge. This body had been excessively apologetic and had quite understood America's feelings in the matter. After a long committee meeting, someone had suggested that it would be better if nothing were made public, but that the lecture tour on Contemporary British Literature might be postponed. Everyone agreed. The chairman telephoned John Patten while the meeting was still in progress. He asked them to wait while he thought it over—which would only take a few minutes. He asked Margaret what she thought. Margaret rang her old friend Hilary Marsh, who thought this procedure would be best for everyone concerned.

Mark offered these facts to Martha; sat waiting for her to explain them. He looked extremely ill. He was trembling. He kept dropping his cigarettes. The gap between what a Coldridge believed was possible and what was happening had widened to the point that he was in a kind of collapse. Martha suggested he should go back to bed and stay there that day. He went.

It was time to get Paul up. He was sitting cross-legged on his pillow, waiting for her. He said: "Am I going to live here now?"

"Yes, I think so."

"I don't want to."

"I'm afraid you'll have to, Paul." This was almost cool: her mind was with Mark, so near a breakdown. It was not a tone anyone had used with Paul before.

He gave her a very long thoughtful stare. Then he got out of bed. Sally's child had not been good at dressing himself. He dressed himself, slowly but competently, while she sat and watched.

"Now we'll have breakfast," she said. Obedient, he came down to the kitchen. He sat, obedient, while she cooked. He was looking at the window, which showed nothing. Martha went to see if the attendant journalists were there. But no, only a box of groceries left on the step by the delivery people.

She was about to open the door to fetch them in when Paul said: "I want to go for a walk."

"We can't go for walks yet," said Martha.

"You don't want them to tell me my daddy is dead," he said. Then he pushed the plate of eggs off the table, laughed as it crashed, and ran upstairs crying to his bedroom.

Martha opened the door to get in the groceries, and found Miles Tangin there.

"Good morning," he said affably.

She tried to shut the door, but his foot was in it.

"Nothing new to tell me?" he inquired.

"Nothing."

"May I ask who you are?"

"Certainly, I'm working for Mr. Coldridge."

"Living here?" he inquired. There were two expressions on his face, superimposed, as it were. At any rate, he managed to convey simultaneously a camaraderie of understanding for her situation—he was a man of the world, after all!—and the salaciousness with which he proposed to tell the story to the public.

"What's your name?"

"Find out. It'll give you something to do."

"Come, come," he said. "You're not in any position to use that tone, you know."

He was now propped against the doorframe, holding the door open. He was looking past her at the mess of broken eggs and bits of china on the floor.

"His wife's in a loony bin, I hear?"

She remembered that on the stove was the frying pan, with hot fat in it. She fetched the frying pan and stood facing him.

"In your face if you don't get out," she said.

"Temper, temper, temper!" he said softly. He was arranging on his face the smile that says: I admire a woman of spirit. Then, seeing she meant it, he looked ugly. She came nearer, with the pan poised.

"Tell me," she said, "while you've been chasing this juicy story, have you ever thought of that child?"

And now a great wash of sentiment: the blond goodfellow's face was all soft and sad. "But I'm only doing my job," he said. "But I can tell you, that poor little chap keeps me awake at nights."

"And I shall do mine if you don't get out."

He went, and she locked the door.

That evening the Coldridge story acquired a new element, in a piece by Miles Tangin. The previously mentioned sinister female figure now appeared as some sort of watchdog or guardian of Mark Coldridge. There were links, hinted at, with the Soviet embassy. She had a foreign accent. She was under orders of silence. For some days, the vigilance of the reporters was redoubled: it had shown signs of slacking off. Martha had to be careful to move around the house so that she could not be seen from the windows.

Upstairs in one room Paul lay on his bed, playing with the cat. She brought food to him there. And in another room, Mark lay in the dark, smoking and thinking. After a while he got up, went down to the study, and very carefully read all the newspapers from the start of the affair until the present time. There were several weeks of them; and they included the serious newspapers, the popular press, and the high-class magazines that were studying the subject of treason in depth, and in articles that had a very high intellectual tone.

When he had done this, Mark said that he had finally understood the meaning of the old saying that the last refuge of a scoundrel was patriotism.

He sounded rather cool about it. He was still ill though, or at least looked ill. But he was in possession of himself. And he had made a decision. He was going down to the country, to stay with his old nurse, who had looked after himself and Colin, and he would take Paul with him.

"And what about Francis, it's going to be holidays again in a month?"

"He can come to Nanny Butts too—it'll be quiet there. And perhaps things will have blown over."

When he and Paul were ready, suitcases packed, he said: "I'm afraid you'll have to be a decoy."

Martha put on a coat, made herself seem indifferent, and walked openly out of the front door. A group of men waiting there at first seemed stunned. At her impertinence, at daring them? At any rate, she had gone several yards before they chased after her. One of them offered her one hundred pounds for the story. She smiled. He put it up to two hundred pounds. She smiled again. She went around the corner and into a café. They all came in with her. She kept them there, discussing the possible sale of her revelations about the Coldridge household, until she judged Mark and Paul had got well away. Then she walked back to the front door. The car had gone. Mark Coldridge had gone. "Nice work," said one of them, laughing. But others, professionally hating, scowled and muttered, like parodies of journalists in a bad film, or in a comedy.

Inside the house was now only Martha. She went openly in and out, smiling politely at two hopeful journalists who remained. Then at one. But he went too. Then, peace, until Miles Tangin knocked at the front door and asked to be admitted. He had a proposition, he said. She was angry. He was affable. His manner was that of a wronged man concerned to give explanations. There was a genuine reproach for her lack of understanding. She should have retired to sharpen her anger, and set it on guard. But she let him in. Curiosity had a lot to do with it. Curious, she sat listening while he offered her one thousand pounds for the story of Mark's mistress. He accepted her refusal with the remark that everyone had their price, but that the story was not worth more. He seemed to expect that she would feel belittled by this; he even made a consoling remark: If Mark had a larger reputation, then more than one thousand pounds would have been forthcoming. Of course, if there were any justice, his reputation would be larger. It turned out that he admired Mark for having written the best novel for his money—Miles Tangin's—since *All Quiet on the Western Front.* If he, Miles Tangin, were a critic, that would be put right. But for his sins, he was a journalist. Only for the time being: he was writing a novel. He also admired Mark for (he hoped Martha would not take this amiss) his taste. The house must be empty, if Mark was away? He did not think Martha ought to take it like that, all was fair in love and war. Anyway, he'd be making the suggestion again later: she was his cup of tea, all right. Meanwhile he was busy, he was off to the country to find Mark Coldridge.

"There's a lot of Britain," said Martha.

"No, dear, there isn't. When one of these upper-class types goes to ground he's at an old teacher's, or nanny. I know how their minds work."

He left, affable.

She telephoned Mark, to warn him. But a journalist had already appeared at Nanny Butts's cottage. Mark was coming back to London.

He came that evening. He had been to his old school, explained the situation to the headmaster, and Paul was already installed.

And now, said Mark, they are welcome to me. He dictated a short piece for the press saying that he stood wholeheartedly behind his brother in whatever action he had seen fit to take. Asked if he was a Communist, he said he was, if that made him one.

And now, silence.

Mark was in his study. He stayed there. What sort of a state he was in, she did not know. His manner was cold, abrupt, but agitated.

She was in her room trying to see what was likely to happen next, trying not to be taken by surprise by events. The immediate facts were that Francis would be home soon, after what must be an awful time; Mark had been writing the usual weekly letters, but had not mentioned the sensational news which every paper had carried for weeks: Francis must surely have seen the newspapers. Paul, in a state of shock, had been dumped in a school which, "progressive" or not, was still a boarding school. Mark, as far as she could see, was in a state of shock. He certainly wasn't dealing with the problem, now pressing, of finance.

The bills for Lynda's hospital were unpaid. There was Francis's school—very expensive—and there would now be Paul's school. Ideally, Mark ought to find, in the next month, a couple of thousand pounds. He could not find so many shillings.

The factory? But she did not like to interfere with something she understood nothing about. Then Jimmy Wood arrived one afternoon to see Mark. Mark's door was locked. Martha therefore talked to Jimmy.

Or she tried to. They were in the kitchen, and they drank tea and ate cake—everything that was normal and reassuring. There he sat, smiling, as usual. And there she sat, opposite him, trying to understand him. She had seen that he was a human being constructed on a different model from most, but this did not help. Making contact with Jimmy, or trying to, one understood how one meshed with others. They were angry, they were pleased, they were sad, they were shocked. They might be several things in the course of an afternoon, but at any given moment one talked to an angry man, a frightened man, etc.; one contacted a state, an emotion. But Jimmy Wood? There he sat, smiling, while he heartily ate cake and asked for more, and even got up to refill the kettle and put it on the ring. All this went on, the activity of a man enjoying his tea. He had come to this house because he wanted to say something. Mark not being available he was saying it to Martha. But what? He was disturbed about something. His movements were those of an agitated man. His eyes were hidden behind the great spectacles and his mouth, a thin, pink, curved mouth, smiled.

He was upset by Mark calling himself a Communist? Martha tried this note—but no. There was no resonance. Yes, that was what was throwing her off balance: where other people resounded, he did not. He wanted to leave the factory and find work elsewhere. But he said this without emotion: it was a fact that emerged after an hour or so. Why? He talked about two contracts that had not been renewed. Did he know why? He thought it was because of the "fuss about Mark in the papers." But that was not his point. Did he think the factory was going to have to shut down? No, not necessarily. They could coast along for months, even a year or so. But there was a job that would suit him in a factory in Wales. Martha suggested that Mark would be upset if he, Jimmy, left. They had worked together for years. From what she could make out of the mask-face, this embarrassed Jimmy. She pressed on: "He's very fond of you." She was faced by the great baby-head and the round glinting spectacles, and the pink smiling mouth. She felt extremely uncomfortable. He poured himself more tea, and energetically dotted loose currants on the end of a wetted forefinger. Martha sat, going back in her mind over the various points that had come up. Not politics—no. To him, the greatest of irrelevancies. Not money—the business would survive temporary difficulties. At random she said: "I expect Mark will be back at work in a few days. Perhaps sooner." And now, just as if Jimmy had not said he would leave, he began talking about a machine he and Mark had planned to start making. It was as if she touched a switch, which had caused him to work again. From his remarks, all random, even disconnected, a picture emerged of Mark and him, spending days at a time in the office at the factory, with blueprints and scientific papers and their own imaginations—talking. Was it that, some sort of machine himself (or so she could not help feeling), he needed this, had been deprived of it, had felt deprived of something, but he did not know what—and now, knowing that this need to talk would at some time in the near future be met, was prepared to go on as before? At any rate, after three hours or so he left, smiling, with the remark that the foreman had said he'd like to see Mark sometime, to give him assurance that he and the men thought he had been shockingly treated: they were going to stand by him.

Martha wrote on a piece of paper: "I don't understand your Jimmy Wood. But he says the foreman wants to stand by you. I think Jimmy will leave if you don't go and talk to him soon." This she pushed under the door of the study.

The financial problems had not been solved.

One thing could be done at once: which was to let the basement.

Martha pushed another note under the door saying that Mark must at once write to Lynda's hospital asking for time to pay: the last account had been peremptory.

Mark telephoned. The doctor suggested that perhaps Mrs. Coldridge might come home for the weekend: she had a plan for her future which would involve Mark's cooperation, and which might help Mark financially. For his part, said Dr. Lamb, he was prepared to say Lynda was better. Not cured, but better.

Lynda came home for the weekend. She was like a guest. Mark came out of his study and was like a host. She said she wanted to leave the hospital, and live in the basement. No, she was not well enough to be by herself, but she could share it with a friend from the hospital. She said with a laugh that she did not think Mark would like her friend, who was called Dorothy. Sometimes she didn't like her either. But they got on.

Mark said he would of course do anything she wanted.

A moment later she took up her little box of pills and went up to bed.

Later, when Martha was ready for bed, her sense of things that were waiting to be said was strong enough to send her down to the kitchen. There sat Lynda in her dressing gown with a spread of cards in front of her.

"If I came to live here," said Lynda, continuing the conversation, "it wouldn't cost so much, would it? Oh—I don't mean, I want to be Mark's wife, I couldn't be that. But if I were here in the house, then it would be better, wouldn't it? Then they couldn't say you were taking him away from me."

"Why, are people saying that?"

"They are bound to be saying something, aren't they?"

"I suppose so. We've been too busy about this other thing."

"Oh, politics. Oh well, I don't care about that. That's just nothing at all. But Dorothy's got some money of her own. She could pay some rent. It would help, wouldn't it?"

She shuffled the cards, humming cheerfully for a time. "Of course, there's Francis. But he hasn't a mother anyway. I thought it would be better to have me in the house, than not at all—for what he has to say to his friends, I mean."

More shuffling of cards, more humming.

"And about clothes. I've all that money for clothes in my bank account. You must make him take it. That's what he wants, you see—that I shall be beautiful all the time."

"Yes, but I don't think he'd take it."

"I wouldn't mind if he divorced me. I know that would be best really. But he wouldn't ever divorce me, I know that."

"No, he wouldn't."

"I don't care about all that—all that's not what I care about."

And now she looked, very close, at Martha, studied her. She leaned forward, her chin in her hand, looking. As if she were trying to find out something? Was it that she wanted to know if Martha could guess what she did care about? She looked disappointed, she even sighed, and made a small pettish gesture of disappointment as she returned to the cards.

"You can go to bed, if you like," she said. "I'm all right by myself, you know."

That was on the Friday. Next morning early Paul's new headmaster telephoned to say that he would consider it a good thing if the child came home for the weekend: he and the staff thought it might help him.

His name was Edwards. He sounded very competent. He sounded in control. Martha felt that he and the staff would have every reason not to feel in control, with Paul in the state he was. She felt he might well have been entitled to say more than "Paul seems rather confused."

Paul was put on the train at the village station fifty miles away, and was met by Mark. When Paul got out of the car, a pale, spiky, black-eyed waif, he was already in the uniform of a progressive school—jeans and sweater. He came into the drawing room where Lynda sat, like a visitor in her pale fur coat, smoking and guarding her little box of pills.

She studied Paul, for a while, while he wriggled about in a chair opposite her. Then she smiled at him, her wide, beautiful smile. He, slowly, smiled back, a rather tentative offering. Slowly he approached Lynda, sidled around her, then tried to climb on her lap. But she held him off.

"I don't like being touched," she said. "But you can sit here." She indicated the patch of sofa beside her. He sat close, snuggling, as he would have done with his mother. But Lynda, at the touch, shrank from him. He felt it, and moved away, examining her face as a guide to how far he must go. Side by side they sat, a space between them.

Martha and Mark were busy with tea things. This ought probably not to happen at all. But then nothing of this ought to be happening.

"Why don't you like being touched?"

"Because I am ill."

"My mother liked it."

"But I'm not like your mother."

"She's dead."

"She killed herself," said Lynda.

"Why did she?"

"Some people don't like living."

"Didn't she like me?"

"Very much," said Lynda.

"I don't think she liked me. Or she wouldn't have killed herself."

"That doesn't follow."

"Yes it does."

Lynda had moved where she sat, so that she was looking at Paul with a direct, cool smile. And he was leaning forward, gazing up into her truth-telling face.

"Didn't my daddy like living?"

"You say that because you think he is dead."

"Yes, he's dead."

"No, I don't think he's dead."

"He is! He is! I know he is!"

Tears were imminent, but Lynda made no attempt to stop them.

"No. Perhaps he is, but we don't think so. And he may come back."

"He won't come back, because he doesn't like me."

"You are making yourself much too important," said the sick woman to the desperate child. "Your daddy had work to do. It was important. If he went away it wasn't because of you and your mother."

"Did my mother kill herself because he went away?"

"No. He went away and she killed herself—the two things at the same time."

"How did she kill herself."

"She made herself stop breathing."

"Could I?"

"Yes, if you wanted to."

"Do you want to?"

"Sometimes."

"Are you going to?"

"No."

"Why aren't you?"

"Because every time I think I will, then I decide to stay alive and see what happens next. It is interesting."

He gave a scared laugh, and snuggled closer. His hand, meeting hers, felt hers go away. He put his two hands carefully onto his knees.

"At the school, the other children have mothers and fathers for the holidays."

"Well, you haven't."

"Why haven't I?"

"I've told you."

They observed that his face had gone red, and his mouth was pinched up.

Lynda slapped him. "Stop it. You don't die by holding your breath."

"I shall if I want."

"Anyway, it's silly. You're unhappy now. But later you might be happy, who knows?"

"Am I unhappy?"

"Yes, you're very unhappy."

"I don't want to be."

"I dare say. But you are."

She smiled, and got up. At the tea tray she took up a cup of tea, and sugared it. She went towards the door, with the cup.

"Why are you going? Can I come too?"

"No. I can't be with people for long. I'm ill, you see."

"What sort of ill?"

And now a bad, twisted moment, a jar. "I have to be careful. I have to be on guard," she said, "so that's why I'm ill." He had rushed to her, stood near, looking up. She bent down and widened her eyes at him, smiling secretly, straight into his face: "I know things, you see. They don't like it."

He looked afraid, shrank. The small boy stood, pathetic, staring up at the tall woman. And she felt that she had made a mistake. Her smile faded. She looked sick and anxious.

But he needed her too badly to be afraid of her. Before she got out of the door, he was after her. Careful not to touch, he stood as close as he could get.

"Lynda. Lynda. Are you my mother now?"

"No. You have no mother."

"Are you Francis's mother?"

"Yes. No. I suppose so. Not really. I'm not much good at being that kind of person. Some people aren't."

He drooped away, his finger in his mouth.

"But Paul, I'm your friend. Do you want that?"

He nodded, merely, not looking at her. Then he gave her a scared glance, and saw her wonderful smile. He smiled, slowly.

She went to her room. Later that day, Paul went to her, was admitted. He was there for about half an hour. They did not know what was said, or felt; but Paul was cheerful through his supper, and he asked Mark to tell him a story. When that was over, he said he would like to go back to the school next morning.

Mark took him back in the car. When he arrived back at the house he found Lynda establishing herself in the basement.

He telephoned the hospital.

Mark said to her: "They say you've made a remarkable recovery."

He was watching Lynda and Martha arrange the bed for Lynda. What he was really saying was: You still might get quite better and be my wife again.

But Lynda smiled at him and said: "What awful fools they are. What fools! Well, thank God, they are." She laughed, was scornful. She continued to smile, scornfully, during the evening, but muttered once or twice: "But I must be careful though."

She did not feel able to stay alone in the basement. Martha moved down, and slept in the living room for a couple of nights. But then Dorothy, Lynda's friend, came to live with her. She was a Mrs. Quentin, but it seemed that her husband was living with another woman somewhere in Ireland. She was a large, dark, slow-moving woman, anxiously watchful of the impression she might be making, with a tendency to make jocular remarks. She had a large quantity of jackdaw possessions, which she set out all over the flat before even unpacking her clothes. She was not the person either Mark or Martha could associate easily with Lynda.

But Lynda was pleased to have her there, did not mind the embroidered velvet hearts, the magazine covers tacked to the walls, the dolls; did not mind her friend's possessiveness. It seemed that she liked Dorothy telling her to do this, and to do that; liked it when Dorothy said to Mark: "I think it's time Lynda went to bed now."

Mark did not like it. There was a moment when Lynda, being ordered to take her pills by Dorothy, looked across at Mark's hostile face and openly laughed. It was in a kind of triumph.

Lynda wanted Dorothy here as a protection against Mark, against having to be Mark's wife.

When Mark, or Martha, descended to the basement to offer help, or their company, the two women became a defensive unit, which excluded everybody. They exchanged private jokes, and made references to the hospital. There was something about them of two schoolgirls engaged in a world-hating friendship.

In short, having Lynda back in the basement, with a friend who had money and would pay some rent, would make a difference to the finances of the household; but not to much else.

FROM

# *Briefing for a Descent into Hell*

CENTRAL INTAKE HOSPITAL

*Friday 15th August 1969*

ADMITTANCE SHEET

NAME: *Unknown*

SEX: *Male*

AGE: *Unknown*

ADDRESS: *Unknown*

GENERAL REMARKS: *At midnight the police found Patient wandering on the Embankment near Waterloo Bridge. They took him into the station thinking he was drunk or drugged. They describe him as Rambling, Confused, and Amenable. Brought him to us at 3 a.m. by ambulance. During admittance Patient attempted several times to lie down on the desk. He seemed to think it was a boat or a raft. Police are checking ports, ships, etc. Patient was well dressed but had not changed his clothes for some time. He did not seem very hungry or thirsty. He was wearing trousers and a sweater, but he had no papers or wallet or money or marks of identity. Police think he was robbed. He is an educated man. He was given two Libriums but did not sleep. He was talking loudly. Patient was moved into the small observation ward as he was disturbing the other Patients.*

NIGHT NURSE. 6 A.M.

*Patient has been awake all day, rambling, hallucinated, animated. Two Librium three-hourly. Police no information. Clothes sent for tracing, but unlikely to yield results: Chain-store sweater and shirt and underclothes. Trousers Italian. Patient still under the impression he is on some sort of voyage. Police say possibly an amateur or a yachtsman.*

DOCTOR Y. 6 P.M.

I need a wind. A good strong wind. The air is stagnant. The current must be pounding along at a fair rate. Yes, but I can't feel it. Where's my compass? *That* went days ago, don't you remember? I need a wind, a good strong wind. I'll whistle for one. I would whistle for one if I had paid the piper. A wind from the East, hard onto my back, yes. Perhaps I am still too near the shore? After so many days at sea, too near the shore? But who knows, I might have drifted back again inshore. Oh no, no, I'll try rowing. The oars are gone, don't you remember, they went days ago. No, you must be nearer landfall than you think. The Cape Verde Islands were to starboard—when? Last week. Last *when*? That was no weak, that was my wife. The sea is saltier here than close inshore. A salt salt sea, the brine coming flecked off the horses' jaws to mine. On my face, thick crusts of salt. I can taste it. Tears, seawater. I can taste salt from the sea. From the desert. The deserted sea. Sea horses. Dunes. The wind flicks sand from the crest of dunes, spins off the curl of waves. Sand moves and sways and masses itself into waves, but slower. Slow. The eye that would measure the pace of sand horses, as I watch the rolling gallop of sea horses would be an eye indeed. Aye Aye. I. I could catch a horse, perhaps and ride it, but for me a sea horse, no horse of sand, since my time is man-time and it is God for deserts. Some ride dolphins. Plenty have testified. I may leave my sinking raft and cling to the neck of a sea horse, all the way to Jamaica and poor Charlie's Nancy, or, if the current swings me South at last, to the coast where the white bird is waiting.

Round and round and round I go, the Diamond Coast, the Canary Isles, a dip across the Tropic of Cancer and up and across with a shout at the West Indies to port, where Nancy waits for her poor Charlie, and around, giving the Sargasso Sea a miss to starboard, with Florida florissant to port, and around and around, in the swing of the Gulf Stream, and around, with the Azores just outside the turn of my elbow, and down, past the coasts of Portugal where my Conchita waits for me, passing Madeira, passing the Canaries, always *en passant,* to the Diamond Coast again, and so around, and so around again and again, for ever and ever unless the current swings me South. But that current could never take me South, no. A current is set in itself, inexorable as a bus route. The clockwise current of the Northern seas must carry me, carry me, unless . . . yes. They may divert me a little, yes they will, steering me with a small feather from their white wings, steadying me South, holding me safe across the cross not to say furious currents about the Equator but then, held safe and sound, I'd find the South Equatorial at last, at last, and safe from all the Sargassoes, the Scillas and the Charibs, I'd swoop beautifully and lightly, drifting with the sweet currents of the South down the edge of the Brazilian Highlands to the Waters of Peace. But I need a wind. The salt is seaming on the timbers and the old raft is wallowing in the swells and I am sick. I am sick enough to die. So heave ho my hearties, heave—no, they are all gone, dead and gone, they tied me to a mast and a great wave swept them from me, and I am alone, caught and tied to the North Equatorial Current with no landfall that I could ever long for anywhere in the searoads of all that rocking sea.

*Nothing from Police. No reports of any small boats yachts or swimmers unaccounted for. Patient continues talking aloud, singing, swinging back and forth in bed. He is excessively fatigued. Tomorrow: Sodium Amytal. I suggest a week's narcosis.*

DOCTOR Y. 17TH AUGUST.

*I disagree. Suggest shock therapy.*

DOCTOR X. 18TH AUGUST.

Very hot. The current is swinging and rocking. Very fast. It is so hot that the water is melting. The water is thinner than usual, therefore a thin fast rocking. Like heat waves. The shimmer is strong. Light. Different textures of light. There is the light we know. That is, the ordinary light let's say of a day with cloud. Then, sunlight, which is a yellow dance added to the first. Then the sparkling waves of heat, heat waves, making light when light makes them. Then, the inner light, the fast shimmer, like a suspended snow in the air. Shimmer even at night when no moon or sun and no light. The shimmer of the solar wind. Yes, that's it. Oh solar wind, blow blow blow my love to me. It is very hot. The salt has caked my face. If I rub, I'll scrub my face with pure sea salt. I'm becalmed, on a light, lit, rocking, deliriously delightful sea, for the water has gone thin and slippery in the heat, light water instead of heavy water. I need a wind. Oh solar wind, wind of the sun. Sun. At the end of Ghosts he said the Sun, the Sun, the Sun, the Sun, and at the end of

When We Dead Awaken, the Sun, into the arms of the Sun via the solar wind, around, around, around, around . . .

> *Patient very disturbed. Asked his name: Jason. He is on a raft in the Atlantic. Three caps. Sodium Amytal tonight. Will see him tomorrow.*
>
> DOCTOR Y.

DOCTOR Y: Did you sleep well?

PATIENT: I keep dropping off, but I mustn't, I must not.

DOCTOR Y: But why not? I want you to.

PATIENT: I'd slide off into the deep-sea swells.

DOCTOR Y: No you won't. That's a very comfortable bed, and you're in a nice quiet room.

PATIENT: Bed of the sea. Deep seabed.

DOCTOR Y: You aren't on a raft. You aren't on the sea. You aren't a sailor.

PATIENT: I'm not a sailor?

DOCTOR Y: You are in Central Intake Hospital, in bed, being looked after. You must rest. We want you to sleep.

PATIENT: If I sleep I'll die.

DOCTOR Y: What's your name? Will you tell me?

PATIENT: Jonah.

DOCTOR Y: Yesterday it was Jason. You can't be either, you know.

PATIENT: We are all sailors.

DOCTOR Y: I am not. I'm a doctor in this hospital.

PATIENT: If I'm not a sailor, then you aren't a doctor.

DOCTOR Y: Very well. But you are making yourself very tired, rocking about like that. Lie down. Take a rest. Try not to talk so much.

PATIENT: I'm not talking to you, am I? Around and around and around and around and around and around and around and around and around and around and around and around and . . .

* * *

NURSE: You must be feeling giddy. You've been going around and around and around for hours now, did you know that?

PATIENT: Hours?

NURSE: I've been on duty since eight, and every time I drop in to see you, you are going round and round.

PATIENT: The duty watch.
NURSE: Around and around what? Where? There now, turn over.
PATIENT: It's very hot. I'm not far away from the Equator.
NURSE: You're still on the raft then?
PATIENT: *You* aren't!
NURSE: I can't say that I am.
PATIENT: Then how can you be talking to me?
NURSE: Do try to lie easy. We don't want you to get so terribly tired. We're worried about you, do you know that?
PATIENT: Well, it is in your hands, isn't it?
NURSE: My hands? How is that?
PATIENT: *You.* You said *We.* I know that We. It is the categorical collective. It would be so easy for you to do it.
NURSE: But what do you want me to do?
PATIENT: *You* as *we.* Not you as *you.* Lift me, lift me, lift me. It must be easy enough for you. Obviously. Just use your—force, or whatever it is. Blast me there.
NURSE: Where to?
PATIENT: You know very well. Tip me South with your white wing.
NURSE: My white wing! I like the sound of that.
PATIENT: You can't be one of them. If you were, you'd know. You are tricking me.
NURSE: I'm sorry that you think that.
PATIENT: Or perhaps you're testing me. Yes, that's a possibility.
NURSE: Perhaps that is it.
PATIENT: It's just a question of getting out of the North Equatorial Current into the South Equatorial Current, from clockwise to anticlockwise. The wise anticlocks.
NURSE: I see.
PATIENT: Well, why don't you?
NURSE: I don't know how.
PATIENT: Is it a question of some sort of a password? Who was that man who was here yesterday?
NURSE: Do you mean Doctor Y? He was in to see you.
PATIENT: He's behind this. He knows. A very kindly contumacious man.
NURSE: He's kind. But I wouldn't say contumacious.
PATIENT: I say it, so why shouldn't you?
NURSE: And Doctor X was in the day before that.
PATIENT: I don't remember any Doctor X.
NURSE: Doctor X will be in later this afternoon.
PATIENT: In what?

NURSE: Do try and lie still. Try and sleep.

PATIENT: If I do, I'm dead and done for. Surely you must know that, or you aren't a maid mariner.

NURSE: I'm Alice Kincaid. I told you that before. Do you remember? The night you came in?

PATIENT: Whatever your name, if you sleep you die.

NURSE: Well, never mind, hush. There, poor thing, you are in a state. Just lie and—there, there. Shhhhh, hush. No, lie still. Shhh . . . there, that's it, that's it, sleep. Sleeeeeeeep. Sle-e-ep.

*Patient distressed, fatigued, anxious, deluded, hallucinated. Try Tofronil? Marplan? Tryptizol? Either that or Shock.*

DOCTOR X. 21ST AUGUST.

DOCTOR Y: Well now, Nurse tells me you are Sinbad today?

PATIENT: Sin bad. Sin bad. Bad sin.

DOCTOR Y: Tell me about it? What's it all about?

PATIENT: I'm not telling you.

DOCTOR Y: Why not?

PATIENT: You aren't one of Them.

DOCTOR Y: Who?

PATIENT: The Big Ones.

DOCTOR Y: No, I'm just an ordinary sort of size, I'm afraid.

PATIENT: Why are you afraid?

DOCTOR Y: Who are they, The Big Ones?

PATIENT: There were giants in those days.

DOCTOR Y: Would you tell them?

PATIENT: I wouldn't need to tell them.

DOCTOR Y: They know already?

PATIENT: Of course.

DOCTOR Y: I see. Well, would you tell Doctor X?

PATIENT: Who is Doctor X?

DOCTOR Y: He was in yesterday.

PATIENT: In and Out. In and Out. In and Out.

DOCTOR Y: We think it would help if you talked to someone. If I'm no use to you, there's Doctor X, if you like him better.

PATIENT: Like? Like what? I don't know him. I don't see him.

DOCTOR Y: Do you see me?

PATIENT: Of course. Because you are there.

DOCTOR Y: And Doctor X isn't here?

PATIENT: I keep telling you, I don't know who you mean.

DOCTOR Y: Very well then. How about Nurse? Would you like to talk to her? We think you should try and talk. You see, we must find out more about you. You could help if you talked. But try to talk more clearly and slowly, so that we can hear you properly.

PATIENT: Are you the secret police?

DOCTOR Y: No. I'm a doctor. This is the Central Intake Hospital. You have been here nearly a week. You can't tell us your name or where you live. We want to help you to remember.

PATIENT: There's no need. I don't need you. I need Them. When I meet Them they'll know my needs and there'll be no need to tell Them. You are not my need. I don't know who you are. A delusion, I expect. After so long on this raft and without real food and no sleep at all, I'm bound to be deluded. Voices. Visions.

DOCTOR Y: You feel that—there. That's my hand. Is that a delusion? It's a good solid hand.

PATIENT: Things aren't what they seem. Hands have come up from the dark before and slid away again. Why not yours?

DOCTOR Y: Now listen carefully. Nurse is going to sit here with you. She is going to stay with you. She is going to listen while you talk. And I want you to talk, tell her who you are and where you are and about the raft and the sea and about the giants. But you must talk more loudly and clearly. Because when you mutter like that, we can't hear you. And it is very important that we hear what you are saying.

PATIENT: Important to you.

DOCTOR Y: Will you try?

PATIENT: If I remember.

DOCTOR Y: Good. Now here is Nurse Kincaid.

PATIENT: Yes, I know. I know her well. She fills me full of dark. She darks me. She takes away my mind.

DOCTOR Y: Nonsense. I'm sure she doesn't. But if you don't want Nurse Kincaid either, we'll simply leave a tape recorder here. You know what a tape recorder is, don't you?

PATIENT: I did try and use one once but I found it inhibiting.

DOCTOR Y: You did? What for?

PATIENT: Oh some damned silly lecture or other.

DOCTOR Y: You give lectures do you? What sort of lectures? What do you lecture about?

PATIENT: Sinbad the sailor man. The blind leading the blind. Around and around and around and around and around and . . .

DOCTOR Y: Stop it! Please. Don't start that again. Please.

PATIENT: Around and around and around and around and . . .

DOCTOR Y: Around what? You are going around what? Where?

PATIENT: I'm not going. I'm being taken. The current. The North Equatorial, from the North African Coast, across, past the West Indies to the Florida Current, past Florida around the Sargasso Sea and into the Gulf Stream and around with the West Wind Drift to the Canaries and around past the Cape Verde Islands around and around and around and around . . .

DOCTOR Y: Very well then. But how are you going to get out?

PATIENT: They. They will.

DOCTOR Y: Go on now. Tell us about it. What happens when you meet them? Try and tell us.

*He gives lectures. Schools, universities, radio, television, politics? Societies to do with? Exploration, archeology, zoology? Sinbad. "Bad sin." Suggest as a wild hypothesis that just this once patient may have committed a crime and this not just routine guilt?*

DOCTOR Y.

*Accept hypothesis. What crime?*

DOCTOR X.

Setting off from the Diamond Coast, first there is the Southerly coastal current to get out of. Not once or twice or a dozen times, on leaving the Diamond Coast, the shore-hugging current has dragged us too far South and even within sight of that African curve which rounded would lead us in helpless to the Guinea Current to who knows what unwanted landfalls. But we have always managed just in time to turn the ship out and pointing West with Trinidad our next stop. That is, unless this time we encountered Them. Around and Around. It is not a cycle without ports we long to reach. Nancy waits for poor Charlie in Puerto Rico, George has his old friend John on Cape Canaveral, and I when the ship has swung far enough inshore wait to see Conchita sitting on her high black rock and to hear her sing her song for me. But when greetings and farewells have been made so many times, they as well as we want the end of it all. And when the songs have been heard so often, the singers no longer are Nancy, alone, poor Charlie alone, or any of us. The last few journeys past the garden where Nancy waits, she was joined by all the girls in her town, and they stood along the wall over the sea watching us sail past, and they sang together what had so often called poor Charlie and his crew in to them before.

Under my hand
flesh of flowers
Under my hand
warm landscape
You have given me back my world,
In you the earth breathes under my hand.

My arms were full of charred branches,
My arms were full of painful sand.
Now I sway in rank forests,
I dissolve in strong rivers,
I am the bone the flowers in flesh.

Oh now we reach it—
now, now!

The whistling hub of the world.
It's as if God had spun a whirlpool,

Flung up a new continent.

But we men stood in a line all along the deck and we sang to them:

If birds still cried on the shore,
If there were horses galloping all night,
Love, I could turn to you and say
Make up the bed,
Put fire to the lamp.
All night long we would lie and hear
The waves beat in, beat in,
If there were still birds on the dunes,
If horses still ran wild along the shore.

And then we would wave each other out of sight, our tears lessening with each circuit, for we were set for our first sight of Them, and they, the women, were waiting with us, for on us their release depended, since they were prisoners on that island.

On this voyage there were twelve men on board, with myself as Captain. Last time I played deckhand, and George was Captain. We were four days out from shore, the current swinging us along fair and easy, the wind coming from the North onto our right cheeks, when

Charles, who was lookout, called us forward and there it was. Or, there they were. Now if you ask how it is we knew, then you are without feeling for the sympathies of our imaginations in waiting for just this moment. And that must mean that you yourselves have not yet learned that in waiting for Them lies all your hope. No, it is not true that we had imagined it in just such a form. We had not said or thought, ever: They will be shaped like birds or be forms of light walking on the waves. But if you have ever known in your life a high expectation which is met at last, you will know that the expectation of a thing must meet with that thing—or, at least, that is, the form in which it must be seen by you. If you have shaped in your mind an eight-legged monster with saucer eyes then if there is such a creature in that sea you will not see anything less, or more—that is what you are set to see. Armies of angels could appear out of the waves, but if you are waiting for a one-eyed giant, you could sail right through them and not feel more than a freshening of the air. So while we had not determined a shape in our thoughts, we had not been waiting for evil or fright. Our expectations had been for aid, for explanation, for a heightening of our selves and of our thoughts. We had been set like barometers for Fair. We had known we would strike something that rang on a higher, keener note than ourselves, and that is why we knew at once that this was what we had been sailing to meet, around and around and around and around, for so many cycles that it might even be said that the waiting to meet up with Them had become a circuit in our minds as well as in the ocean.

We knew them first by the feeling in the air, a crystalline hush, and this was accompanied by a feeling of strain in ourselves, for we were not strung at the same pitch as that for which we had been waiting.

It was a smart choppy sea and the air was flying with spray. Hovering above these brisk waves, and a couple of hundred yards away, was a shining disc. It seemed as if it should have been transparent, since the eye took in first the shine, like that of glass, or crystal, but being led inwards, as with a glass full of water, to what was behind the glitter. But the shine was not a reflected one: the substance of the disc's walls was itself a kind of light. The day was racingly cloudy, the sky half cloud, half sun, and all the scene around us was this compound of tossing waves and foam, and flying spray, of moving light, everything changing as we watched. We were waiting for strangers to emerge from the disc and perhaps let down, using the ways of humanity, a dinghy or a boat of some kind so that we, standing along the deck's edge, grasping fast to ropes and spars, might watch Them approach and take their measure—and adjust our thoughts and manners for the time. But no one appeared. The disc came closer, though so unnoticeably, being part of the general restless movement of the blue and the white, that it was resting on the air just above the waves a few paces off before we understood by a sinking of our hearts that we were not to expect anything so comfortable as the opening of a door, the letting down of a ladder, a boat, and arms bending as oars swung. But we were still not expecting anything in particular when it was already on us. What? What we felt was a sensation first, all through our bodies. In a fever or a great strain of exhaustion, or in love, all the resources of the body stretch out and expand and vibrate higher than in ordinary life. Well, we were vibrating at a higher pitch, and this was accompanied by a high shrill note in the air, of the kind that can break glasses—or can probably break much more, if sustained. The disc that had been in our eyes' vision a few yards away, an object among others, though an object stronger than the others, more obliterating—seemed to come in and invade our eyes. I am describing the sensation, for I cannot say what was the fact. It was certain that this disc rose a little way up from the waves, so that it was level with our deck, and then passed over us, or through us. Yet when it was on us, it seemed no longer a disc, with a shape, but it was more a fast beating of the air, a vibration that was also a sound. It was intolerable while it lasted, as if two different substances were in conflict, with no doubt of the outcome—but it did not last more than a moment, and when my eyes had lost the feeling of being filled with a swift-beating light, or sound, and my whole body from having been stretched or expanded or invaded, as if light (or sound) had the capacity of passing through one's tissues, but in a shape as definite as one's own, then I looked to see if George, who stood nearest to me, was still alive. But he was gone, and when I turned in terror to see where he was, and where the others were, they weren't there. No one. Nothing. The disc, which had again become a crystal disc, hovering over the waves on the other side of the ship, was lifting into the sky. It had swept away or eaten up or absorbed my comrades and left me there alone. All the ship was empty. The decks were empty. I was in terror. And worse. For all these centuries I had been sailing around and around and around and around for no other reason than that one day I would meet Them, and now at last we had indeed inhabited the same space of air, but I had been left behind. I ran to the other rail of the ship and clung there and opened my mouth to shout. I might indeed have shouted a little, or made some feeble kind of sound, but to what or to whom was I shouting? A silvery shining disc that seemed, as it lifted up and away into the air, that it ought to be transparent but was not? It had no eyes to see me, no mouth to acknowledge my shouting with a sound of its own. Nothing. And inside were eleven men, my friends, who I knew better than I knew myself. Since we do know our friends better than we know ourselves. Then, as I stood there, gazing into the scene of blue and white and silver that tossed and sprayed and shook and danced and dazzled, sea and air all mixed together, I saw that I was looking at nothing. The disc had vanished, was no more than the shape of a cell on my retina. Nothing.

I was sickened with loss, with knowledge of an unforeseeable callousness on their part. To take them and to leave me? In all our voyagings we had never envisaged that we might simply be lifted up and taken away like a litter of puppies or kittens. We had wanted instructions, or aid, we need to be told how to get off this endless cycling and into the Southern Current. Now that this had not happened, and no instructions or information had been given, only a sort of kidnapping, then I wanted to scream against their coldness and cruelty, as one small kitten that has been hidden by a fold of a blanket in the bottom of a basket mews out in loneliness as it moves blindly about, feeling with its muzzle and its senses for its lost companions among the rapidly chilling folds of the blanket.

I stayed at the deck's edge. For while the ship needed steering and the sails setting, and for all I knew we had already swung about, I could not handle this ship by myself. I already knew that I must leave her, unless I was to choose to live on board her alone, on the small chance that the Disc would hover down again and discharge my companions in the same way it had taken them off. But I did not think this was likely to happen. And I was afraid to stay.

It was as if that Disc, or Crystal, in its swift passage across or through the ship, across or through me, had changed the atmosphere of the ship, changed me. I was shaking and shivering in a cold dread. I could hardly stand, but leaned clinging to a rope. When the shaking had seemed to stop, and I stood clenching my teeth and waiting for the puppy-warmth of life to come back, then the shaking began again, like a fit of malaria, though this was a sort of weakness, not a fever. Now everything in the ship was inimicable to me, as if the Disc's breath had started a rot in its substance. To say that I had been terrified and was still terrified would be too much of an everyday statement. No, I had been struck with foreignness, I had taken a deep breath of an insupportable air. I was not at all myself, and my new loathing that was so much more than a fear of the ship was in itself an illness. Meanwhile the sails shook and flapped and bellied or hung idle above my head. Meanwhile the ship shuddered and swung to every new shift in the fitfully changing wind. Meanwhile she was a creature that had been assaulted and left to die.

I began making a raft, using timber from the carpenter's store. I worked feverishly, wanting to get away. It never crossed my mind to stay on her, so strong was my fear. Yet I knew that to set off by myself on a raft was more dangerous than staying. On the ship was water, food, some shelter, until it foundered or crashed on a rock. Until then, it would be my safety. But I could not stay. It was as if my having been ignored, left behind, out of all my old comrades, was in itself a kind of curse. I had been branded with my ship.

I worked for many hours and when daylight went, I lashed a storm lantern to a spar and worked on through the night. I made a raft about twelve by twelve of balsa-wood poles. To this I lashed a locker full of rations, and a barrel of water. I fitted a sail on a mast in the middle of the raft. I took three pairs of oars, and lashed two spare pairs securely to the timbers of the raft. In the center of the raft I made a platform of planks about four feet across. And all this time I worked in a deadly terror, a cold sick fear, attacked intermittently by the fits of shaking so that I had to double up as if in cramp, and hold on to a support for fear I'd shake myself to pieces.

By the dawn my raft was done. The sky reddened in my face as I stood looking forward with the ship's movement, so I saw that the ship had already swung about and was heading back in the grip of the Guinea Current to the Cameroons or the Congo. I had to leave it as quickly as I could, and trust that I could still row myself out of this deadly shore-going current and back into the Equatorial stream once again. I put on all the clothes I could find. I let the raft fall into the sea, where it floated like a cork. And with all the sky aflame with sunrise like the inside of a ripening peach, I swarmed down a rope and swung myself onto the raft just as it was about to bob right out of my reach. I reached the raft still dry, though already beginning to be well damped by spray, and at once began rowing with my back to the sunrise. I rowed as if I were making towards safety and a good dry ship instead of away from one. By the time the sun stood up in a clear summer-hazy sky three or four handsbreadths from the horizon, our ship's sails were a low swarm of white, like a cluster of butterflies settled on the waves, and well behind me, and I was heading West on my real right course. And when I turned my head to look again, it was hard to tell whether I was looking at the white of the sails or at foam on a distant swell. For the sea had changed, to my advantage, and was rolling and rocking, and no longer chopping and changing. And so I rowed all that day, and most of that following night. I rowed and rowed and rowed, until my arms seemed separate from myself, they worked on without my knowing I was ordering them to. Then one day—I think it was three days after I last saw the sails of my ship vanishing East—there was a sudden squally afternoon and my clothes got soaked, and I lost my spare oars. And two days after that, a heavy sea dragged my last oars from me and since then I've been trusting myself to the current that curves West and North. And now I have all the time in the world to reflect that I am still engaged in the same journey in the same current, round and round and round, with the West Indies my next landfall, and poor Charlie's Nancy and her song, just as if I had stayed on the ship with my comrades. And after the women's song, just as before, around and around, past the Sargasso Sea, and around in the Gulf Stream, and around in the swing of the sea past the coasts of Portugal and Spain, and around and around. But now I am not in a tall ship with sails like white butterflies but on a small raft and alone, around and around. And everything is the same, around and around, with only a slight but worsening change in the shape of my hope: will They, or the Disc, or Crystal Thing, on its next descent, be able to see the speck of my raft on the sea? Will they see me and find the kindness to give me a hail or a shout in reply when I ask them, How may I leave this Current? Friends, set me fair for that other coast, I pray you.

Yes, I'll hail them, of course, though now a new coldness in my heart tells me of a fear I didn't have before. I had not thought once, not in all those cycles and circles and circuits, around and around, that they might simply not notice me, as a man might not notice a sleeping kitten or a blind puppy hidden under the fold of his smelly blanket. Why should they notice the speck of a raft on the wide sea? Yet there is nothing for it but to go on, oarless, rudderless, sleepless, exhausted. After all I know it would be a kindness to land on Nancy's coast and tell her that her Charlie has met up at last with—what? Them, I suppose, though that is all I can tell her, not even how he felt as he became absorbed into the substance of that shining Thing. Will she sing her song to me on my raft, drifting past, will the women line up along the walls of their summer gardens and sing, and shall I then sing back how the time is past for love? And then on I'll drift to George's friend and shout to him how George has—what? And where? And then on and on and on, until I see again my Conchita waiting, dressed in the habit of a nun, where all my wandering and sailing has put her.

Man like a great tree
Resents storms.
Arms, knees, hands,
Too stiff for love,
As a tree resists wind.
But slowly wakes,

And in the dark wood
Wind parts the leaves
And the black beast crashes from the cave.

My love, when you say:
"Here was the storm,
Here was she,
Here the fabulous beast,"
Will you say too
How first we kissed with shut lips, afraid,
And touched our hands, afraid,
As if a bird slept between them?
Will you say:
"It was the small white bird that snared me"?

And so she sings, each time I pass, around and around, and on and on.

DOCTOR X: Well, how are you this afternoon?
PATIENT: Around and around and around . . .
DOCTOR X: I'd like you to know that I believe you could snap out of this any time you want.
PATIENT: Around and around and around . . .
DOCTOR X: Doctor Y is not here this weekend. I'm going to give you a new drug. We'll see how that does.
PATIENT: In and out, out and in. In and out, out and in.
DOCTOR X: My name is Doctor X. What is your name?
PATIENT: Around and . . .

*I think he may very well have reverted to age eleven or twelve. That was the age I enjoyed sea stories. He is much worse in my opinion. The fact is, he never acknowledges my presence at all. Doctor Y claims he reacts to him.*

DOCTOR X. 24TH AUGUST.

DOCTOR Y: What is your name today?
PATIENT: It could be Odysseus?
DOCTOR Y: The Atlantic was surely not his sea?
PATIENT: But it could be now, surely, couldn't it?
DOCTOR Y: Well now, what's next?
PATIENT: Perhaps Jamaica. I'm a bit further South than usual.
DOCTOR Y: You've been talking practically nonstop for days. Did you know that?

PATIENT: You told me to talk. I don't mind thinking instead.

DOCTOR Y: Well, whatever you do, remember this: you aren't on a raft on the Atlantic. You did not lose your friends into the arms of a flying saucer. You were never a sailor.

PATIENT: Then why do I think I'm one?

DOCTOR Y: What's your real name?

PATIENT: Crafty.

DOCTOR Y: Where do you live?

PATIENT: Here.

DOCTOR Y: What's your wife's name?

PATIENT: Have I got a wife? What is she called?

DOCTOR Y: Tell me, why won't you ever talk to Doctor X? He's rather hurt about it. I would be too.

PATIENT: I've told you already, I can't see him.

DOCTOR Y: Well, we are getting rather worried. We don't know what to do. It's nearly two weeks since you came in. The police don't know who you are. There's only one thing we are fairly certain about: and that is that you aren't any sort of a sailor, professional or amateur. Tell me, did you read a lot of sailing stories as a boy?

PATIENT: Man and boy.

DOCTOR Y: What's George's surname? And Charlie's surname?

PATIENT: Funny, I can't think of them . . . yes of course, we all had the same name. The name of the ship.

DOCTOR Y: What was the name of the ship?

PATIENT: I can't remember. And she's foundered or wrecked long ago. And the raft never had a name. You don't call a raft as you call a person.

DOCTOR Y: Why shouldn't you name the raft? Give your raft a name now?

PATIENT: How can I name the raft when I don't know my own name. I'm called . . . what? Who calls me? What? Why? You are Doctor Why, and I am called Why—that's it, it was the good ship Why that foundered in the Guinea Current, leaving Who on the slippery raft and . . .

DOCTOR Y: Just a minute. I'll be away for four or five days. Doctor X will be looking after you till I get back. I'll be in to see you the moment I'm back again.

PATIENT: In and out, out and in, in and out . . .

*New treatment. Librium. 3 Tofronil 3 t.a.d.*

DOCTOR X. 29TH AUGUST.

The sea is rougher than it was. As the raft tilts up the side of a wave I see fishes curling above my head, and when the wave comes crashing over me fishes and weed slide slithering over my face, to rejoin the sea. As my raft climbs up up up to the crest the fishes look eye to eye with me out of the wall of water. There's that air creature, they think, just before they slop over my face and shoulders, while I think as they touch and slide, they are water creatures, they belong to wet. The wave curls and furls in its perfect whirls holding in it three deep sea fish that have come up to see the sky, a tiddler fit for ponds or jam jars, and the crispy sparkle of plankton, which is neither visible nor invisible, but a bright crunch in the imagination. If men are creatures of air, and fishes whether big or small creatures of sea, what then are the creatures of fire? Ah yes, I know, but you did not see me, you overlooked me, you snatched up my comrades and let me lie squeaking inside my fold of smelly blanket. Where are they, my friends? Administering justice, are they, from the folds of fire, looking at me eye to eye out of the silkily waving fronds of fire. Look, there's a man, that's an air creature, they think, breathing yellow flame as we breathe $H_2O$. There's something about that gasping gape, they think—George? poor Charlie?—that merits recognition. But they are beyond air now, and the inhabitants of it. They are flame throwers. They are fire storms. You think justice is a kindly commodity? No, it razes, it throws down, it cuts swathes. The waves are so steep, they crash so fast and furious I'm more under than up. They are teaching men—men are teaching men—to have fishes' lungs, men learn to breathe water. If I take a deep breath of water will my lungs' tissues adapt in the space of a wave's fall and shout: Yes, yes, you up there, you, sailor, breathe deep and we'll carry you on water as we carried you on air? After all *They* must have had to teach my friends George and Charles and James and the rest to take deep lungfuls of fire. You're not telling me that when the Crystal swirl enveloped me with the others it was ordinary air we breathed then, no, it was a cool fire, sun's breath, the solar wind, but there are lungs attached to men that lie as dormant as those of a babe in the womb, and they are waiting for the solar wind to fill them like sails. Air lungs for air, but organs made of crystal sound, of singing light, for the solar wind that will blow my love to me. Or me onwards to my love. Oh the waves rear so tall, they pitch and grow and soar, I'm more under than up, my raft is a little cork on the drafty sea and I'm sick, oh I'm so sick, pitch and toss, toss and pitch, my poor poor head and my lungs, if I stay on this thick heavy slimy barnacled raft which is shrieking and straining as the great seas crash then I'll puke my heart out and fall fainting away into the deep sea swells. I'll leave the raft, then.

Oh no, no, no, I've shed my ship, the good ship Why, and I've clung like limpets to my new hard bed the raft and now how can I leave, to go spinning down into the forests of the sea like a sick bird. But if I found a rock or an islet? Silly, there are no rocks or isles or islands or ports of call in the middle of the wide Atlantic sea here at forty-five degrees on the Equator. But the raft is breaking up. It breaks. There were only ordinary sea ropes to fasten the balsa poles side by side and across and through, and what ropes could I ever find that could hold this clumsy collection of cross rafters steady in this sea? It's a storm. It's a typhoon. The sky is thunder black and with a sick yellowish white at the cloud's edge and the waves are blue Stephen's black and higher than the church tower and all the world is wet and cold and my ears are singing like the ague. And there goes my raft, splitting apart under me like bits of straw in the eddy of a kitchen gutter. There it goes, and I'm afloat, reaching out for straws or even a fishbone. I'm all awash and drowning and I'm cold, oh I am so cold, I'm cold where all my own inside vital warmth should be held, there along my spine and in my belly but there it is cold cold as the moon. Down and down, but the corky sea upsends me to the light again, and there under my hand is rock, a port in the storm, a little peaking black rock that no main mariner has struck before me, nor map ever charted, just a single black basalt rock, which is the uppermost tip of a great mountain a mile or two high, whose lower slopes are all great swaying forests through which the sea buffalo herd and graze. And here I'll cling until the storm goes and the light comes clear again. Here at last I can stay still, the rock is still, having thrust up from the ocean floor a million years ago and quite used to staking its claim and holding fast in the Atlantic gales. Here is a long cleft in the rock, a hollow, and in here I'll fit myself till morning. Oh now I'm a land creature again, and entitled to a sleep steady and easy. I and the rock which is a mountain's tip are solid together and now it is the sea that moves and pours. Steady now. Still. The storm has gone and the sun is out on a flat calm solid sea with its surface gently rocking and not flying about all over the place as if the ocean wanted to dash itself to pieces. A hot singing salty sea, pouring Westwards past me to the Indies next stop, but pouring past me, fast on my rock. Fast asleep. Fast. Asleep.

NURSE: Wake up. Wake up there's a dear. Come on, *no* that's it. Sit up, all right I'm holding you.

PATIENT: Why? What for?

NURSE: You must have something to eat. All right you can go back to sleep in a minute. But you certainly can sleep, can't you?

PATIENT: Why make me sleep if you keep waking me up?

NURSE: You aren't really supposed to be sleeping quite so much. You are supposed to be relaxed and quiet, but you do sleep.

PATIENT: Who supposes? Who gave me the pills?

NURSE: Yes but—well never mind. Drink this.

PATIENT: That's foul.

NURSE: It's soup. Good hot soup.

PATIENT: Let me alone. You give me pills and then you keep waking me up.

NURSE: Keep waking you? I don't. It's like trying to wake a rock. Are you warm?

PATIENT: The sun's out, the sun . . .

Who has not lain hollowed in hot rock,
Leaned to the loose and lazy sound of water,
Sunk into sound as one who hears the boom
Of tides pouring in a shell, or blood
Along the inner caverns of the flesh,
Yet clinging like sinking man to sight of sun,
Clinging to distant sun or voices calling?

NURSE: A little more, please.

PATIENT: I'm not hungry. I've learned to breathe water. It's full of plankton you know. You can feed your lungs as you feed your stomach.

NURSE: It that so dear? Well, don't go too far with it, you'll have to breathe air again.

PATIENT: I'm breathing air *now*. I'm on the rock you see.

See him then as the bird might see
Who rocks like pinioned ship on warm rough air,
Coming from windspaced fields to ocean swells
That rearing fling gigantic mass on mass
Patient and slow against the stubborn land,
Striving to achieve what strange reversal
Of that monstrous birth when through long ages
Laboring, appeared a weed-stained limb,
A head, at last the body of the land,
Fretted and worn forever by a mothering sea
A jealous sea that loves her ancient pain.

NURSE: Why don't you go and sit for a bit in the day room? Aren't you tired of being in bed all the time?

PATIENT: A jealousy that loves. Her pain.

NURSE: Have you got a pain? Where?
PATIENT: Not me. You. Jealously loving and nursing pain.
NURSE: I haven't got a pain I assure you.
PATIENT: He floats on lazy wings down miles of foam,
And there, below, the small spread-eagled shape
Clinging to black rock like drowning man,
Who feels the great bird overhead and knows
That he may keep no voices, wings, or winds
Who follows hypnotized down glassy gulfs,
His roaring ears extinguished by the flood.

NURSE: Take these pills dear, that's it.

PATIENT: Who has not sunk as drowned man sinks,
Through sunshot layers where still the undercurve
Of lolling wave holds light like light in glass,
Where still a jeweled fish slides by like bird,
And then the middle depths where all is dim
Diffusing light like depths of forest floor.
He falls, he falls, past apprehensive arms
And spiny jaws and treacherous pools of death,
Till finally he rests on ocean bed.

Here rocks are tufted with lit fern, and fish
Swim shimmering phosphorescent through the weed,
And shoals of light float blinking past like eyes,
Here all the curious logic of the night.
Is this a sweet drowned woman floating in her hair?
The sea-lice hop on pale rock scalp like toads.
And this a gleam of opalescent flesh?
The great valves shut like white doors folding close.
Stretching and quavering like the face of one
Enhanced through chloroform, the smiling face
Of her long half-forgotten, her once loved,
Rises like thin moon through watery swathes,
And passes wall-eyed as the long dead moon.

He is armed with the indifference of deep-sea sleep
And floats immune through sea-roots fed with flesh,
Where skeletons are bunched against cave roofs
Like swarms of bleaching spiders quivering,
While crouching engines crusted with pale weed,
Their shafts and pistons rocking through the green . . .

NURSE: Now do come on dear. Oh dear, you are upset, aren't you? Everybody has bad times, everyone gets upset from time to time. I do myself. Think of it like that.

PATIENT: Not everyone has known these depths
The black uncalculated wells of sea,
Where any gleam of day dies far above,
And stagnant water slow and thick and foul . . .

NURSE: It's no good spitting your pills out.
PATIENT: Foul, fouled, fouling, all fouled up . . .
NURSE: One big swallow, that will do it, that's done it.
PATIENT: You wake me and you sleep me. You wake me and then you push me under. I'll wake up now. I want to wake.
NURSE: Sit up then.
PATIENT: But what is this stuff, what are these pills, how can I wake when you . . . who is that man who pushes me under, who makes me sink as drowned man sinks and . . .
NURSE: Doctor X thinks this treatment will do you good.
PATIENT: Where's the other, the fighting man?
NURSE: If you mean Doctor Y, he'll be back soon.
PATIENT: I must come up from the sea's floor. I must brave the surface of the sea, storms or no, because They will never find me down there. Bad enough to expect Them to come into our heavy air, all smoky and fouled as it is, but to expect them down at the bottom of the sea with all the drowned ships, no that's not reasonable. No I must come up and give them a chance to see me there, hollowed in hot rock.
NURSE: Yes, well, all right. But don't thrash about like that . . . for goodness' sake.
PATIENT: Goodness is another thing. I must wake up. I must. I must keep watch. Or I'll never get out and away.
NURSE: Well I don't know really. Perhaps that treatment isn't right for you? But you'd better lie down then. That's right. Turn over. Curl up. There. Hush. Hushhhhhhh. Shhhhhhhhhhhhhhhhhhhh.

PATIENT: Hushabye baby
lulled by the storm
if you don't harm her
she'll do you no harm

* * *

I've been robbed of sense. I've been made without resource. I have become inflexible in a flux. When I was on the Good Ship Lollipop, I was held there by wind and sea. When I was on the raft, there was nobody there but me. On this rock I'm fast. Held. I can't do more than hold on. And wait. Or plunge like a diver to the ocean floor where it is as dark as a fish's gut and there's nowhere to go but up. But I do have an alternative, yes. I can beg a lift can't I? cling on to the coattails of a bird or a fish. If dogs are the friends of man, what are a sailor's friends? Porpoises. They love us. Like to like they say, though when has a porpoise killed a man, and we have killed so many and for curiosity, not even for food's or killing's sake. A porpoise will take me to my love. A sleek-backed singing shiny black porpoise with loving eyes and a long whistler's beak. Hold on there porpoise, poor porpoise in your poisoned sea, filled with stinking effluent from the bowels of man, and waste from the murderous mind of man, don't die yet, hold on, hold me, and take me out of this frozen grinding Northern circuit down and across into the tender Southern-running current and the longed-for shores. There now. Undersea if you have to, I can breathe wet if I must, but above sea if you can, in case I may hail a passing friend who has taken the shape of a shaft of fire or a dapple of light. There, porpoise, am I true weight? A kind creature? Kith and Kind? Just take me South, lead me to the warmer current, oh now it is rough, we toss and heave as it was in the Great Storm, when my raft fell apart like straw, but I know now this is a good cross patch, it is creative, oh what a frightful stress, what a strain, and now out, yes out, we're well out, and still swimming West, but South West, but anticlock Wise, whereas before it was West with the clock and no destination but the West Indies and Florida and past the Sargasso Sea and the Gulf Stream and the West Wind Drift and the Canaries Current and around and around and around and around but now, oh porpoise, on this delicate soap bubble our earth, spinning all blue and green and iridescent, where Northwards air and water swirl in time's direction left to right, great spirals of breath and light and water, now oh porpoise, singing friend, we are on the other track, and I'll hold on, I'll clasp and clutch to the last breath of your patience, being patient, till you land me on that beach at last, for oh porpoise, you must be sure and take me there, you must land me fairly at last, you must not let me cycle South too far, dragging in the Brazil Current of my mind, no, but let me gently step off your slippery back onto the silver sand of the Brazilian coast where, lifting your eyes, rise the blue and green heights of the Brazilian Highlands. There, there, is my true destination and my love, so, purpose, be sure to hold your course.

There now, there's the shore. And now more than ever we must hold our course to true. There are no rocks, shoals, or reefs here, porpoise, which could stub your delicate nose or take strips of blubber off your sleek black back, but there is the shining coast and of all the dangers of the Southern Current this one is worst, that if we keep our eyes on that pretty shore wishing we were on it, then the current will sweep us on in our cycle of forgetting around and around and around and around again back to the coasts of Africa with hummocks of Southern ice for company, so hold on now porpoise and keep your mind on your work, which is me, my landfall, but never let yourself dream of that silver sand and the deep forests there for if you do, your strength will ebb and you'll slide away southwards like a dead or a dying fish.

There. Yes. Here we are, close in, and the thunder of the surf is in us. But close your ears, porpoise, don't listen or look, let your thoughts be all of a strong purposeful haul. In. And in. With the wash of the southdragging current cold on your left flank. In. Yes, and I'm not looking either dear porpoise, for if I did not reach that shore now and if we did have to slide away falling South and around again and again and again then I think I'd ask you porpoise to treat me as men treat porpoises and carve me up for your curiosity. But there, closer. Yes, closer. We are so close now that the trees of the beach and the lifting land beyond the beach are hanging over us as trees hang over a tame inland river. And we're in. But will you come with me, splitting your soft fat black shining tail to make legs to walk on, strolling up with me to the Highlands that are there? No, well then, goodbye porpoise, goodbye, slide back to your playful sea and be happy there, live, breathe, until the poison man makes for all living creatures finds you and kills you as you swim. And now I roll off your friendly back, thank you, thank you kind fish, and I find my feet steady under me on a crunching sand with the tide's fringe washing cool about my ankles.

And now leaving the sea where I have been around and around for so many centuries my mind is ringed with Time like the deposits on shells or the fall of years on tree trunks, I step up on the dry salty sand, with a shake of my whole body like a wet dog.

FROM

# *The Summer Before the Dark*

She got onto a bus and sat on it until she saw a gleam of water—a canal—and the word, scarlet on dead-white paint that shone in the heavy September sunlight, *Ristorante.* The rest of the street was all London, basic London, and she got off, and saw a noticeboard by a cigarette shop. As she approached it, she saw that the proprietor of the shop, a small old man wearing overalls, and a young man, were together putting up a new card on the board. The old man held up his thumb in that gesture which in some countries means: Good, that's fine, that's spot-on, but on its blade was a thumbtack, and this he applied hard to the center top of the white square. The young man had long Jesus-hair and his feet were bare. His face was sweet, childish, and open; and when the old man had gone back into the shop, he stood looking at the hundred or so bits of white card, among which his was now lost.

It said: Room in private flat to let until end of October five pounds a week share kitchen and bath.

Kate said to the young man, "Where is this room?"

"Around the corner."

"Is it yours?"

At this he grinned, politely, but with a small what-else-can-you-expect nod, which grin was making a statement she was meant to notice, for he followed it with, *"Mine?"*

It having thus been made clear that like all her generation she thought in terms of private property, while he, being of his age, was free, his grin became natural, and he followed it with, "Among others."

"If I took the room," said Kate, using the humorous adaptable tone that came easily after years of use with "the children," "would it be mine, or would I have to share it?"

At this he consented to laugh, and said, "Oh no, it would be yours. I'm going away for a bit, and most of us will be away."

"Then could you show it to me?"

He examined her. What he was seeing, of course, was an old woman. That she was ill, or had been, was being absorbed into "an old woman." Then he turned, to set himself beside her, thus indicating that she was possible, and they walked together along the pavement by the canal. He was giving her glances which she interpreted as: But we didn't want an old woman in the place.

She said, "I am clean, careful, house-trained."

He laughed, again in his way of making it clear that it was after careful consideration, and said, "I'm not hung up about that." Then, interpreting, "I don't mind what you do. But there's someone in the flat who . . ."

"I have to be approved, is that it?"

The flat was a basement flat, and rather dark, after the yellow September glare. The young man went ahead of her along a wide hall that was furnished with piles of cushions and some posters. There was the dry tang of marijuana. Kate followed him thinking she would be shown the room that was to let, but she was led into a large room that had French windows open onto a small patio, crammed with plants of all kinds. On a hard chair by the windows sat a girl in the sunlight. Her bare brown feet were planted side by side on rush matting. Quantities of thick yellow hair fell all around her face—fell forward over it, so that it was not until she lifted her head that Kate saw a brown healthy face in which were round blue candid eyes. She was doing nothing. She smoked.

She considered Kate, then looked at the young man.

He said to Kate, "I didn't ask your name?"

"Kate Brown."

"This is Kate," he said to the girl. To Kate he said, with the formality that must have come from his upbringing, which included a small stiff nod, like a curtailed bow, "This is Maureen." Turning back to the girl he said with the naïve awkwardness of his acquired manner, "I put up the card and she was there and said could she come along?"

"Oh," said Maureen. She pushed back hair, jumped up from her chair as if meaning to do something, but then sat down again, with the instant relaxation of a cat. She wore a very short brown skirt and a blue checked shirt, like the girl you see on a poster advertising milk or eggs.

At last she smiled and said, "Would you like to see it?"

"Yes," said Kate.

"You think she will be all right, do you?" said the young man to the girl—his girlfriend? This struck his upbringing as rude, and he even reddened a little, as he explained to Kate, "You see, I wanted to make sure that Maureen was all right before I took off."

Maureen's eyelids lowered abruptly; two white half-moons on brown cheeks. Kate thought that she stopped a smile.

"I'm fine, Jerry. I told you," said Maureen.

"Well in that case I'll just . . ."

"Yes, do."

Jerry nodded at Kate, gave Maureen a long steady look which was meant to impress something on her—but what, Kate could not decide—and went out of the room. And that was the last Kate saw of him.

Maureen considered. She was wondering if she should ask about Kate's qualifications to pay? All she said was, "It's the room at the end of the passage on the left. It's Jerry's but he's going to Turkey."

She did not come with Kate, but sat on, planted on her chair, in a cloud of blue smoke that smelled of other states and climates. The blue ripples and whorls and waves lay all about her as if she were sitting in sunny water.

The room was small, and had in it a narrow bed and a cupboard. It was many degrees colder than the front of the flat, which was on the south. This room had a chill on it that connected with the cold that lay permanently around Kate's stomach. But it would do.

She went back to the girl and said the room was all right, and that she would stay in it until the end of October—hearing herself say this, she realized she had made decisions her conscious self knew nothing about.

As Maureen said nothing about money, she put down five one-pound notes on a red cushion near the girl's feet.

At this Maureen allowed a smile to appear from behind her blind of yellow hair. "Thanks," she said. "But any time."

"The key?" prompted Kate.

"Oh yes. It's somewhere, I suppose. Yes, I remember." She jumped up, straightening herself into the perpendicular in a single movement, bent without bending her knees, in another sudden movement, and picked up cushions at random. Under one was a key. This she handed up to Kate—she had not straightened herself, and then, neatly folding her legs, jumped into a sitting position on the same cushion.

"You're a dancer?" said Kate.

"No, I'm not a dancer. I do dance." She was frowning—lost among the rigid categories of the old?

On the way out Kate stopped in front of a long old-fashioned swing mirror in the hall. She saw a thin monkey of a woman inside a "good" yellow dress, her hair tied into a lump behind her head. She pulled off the scarf and the hair stood there, stiff and thick. She noted that she was in the grip of a need to do something for herself—get her hair done, buy a dress that fitted; this was because of the girl with her healthy young flesh, and her fresh clothes. She noted, too, that this impulse had something to do with her own daughter: Maureen was about Eileen's age. She saw that the moment of returning to her own family was going to be a dramatic one, whether by that time she had pulled herself together—in other words, returned to their conception of her—or had decided not to . . . surely she couldn't stay as she was? Could she? What an interesting idea! But the family would, as it is said, have a fit. The idea was making her prickle pleasurably, with exactly the same sensation as if she had swallowed too large a mouthful of water ice, and her mouth and throat were being paralyzed by it—as she had felt yesterday, when Mary Finchley did not recognize her, and as she had felt while derisively watching Natalia Petrovna at her tricks of self-deceit.

This pleasurable sensation faded and left another, not nearly so agreeable. Now she was again in the grip of vanity. If she were to go home looking as she did now, all that her husband and four children would say was that she did not look herself—for they knew what she could look like. But Maureen, that girl sitting on her red cushion dreaming in the tangy blue-swirling clouds, had never seen her in any other guise but that of a sick monkey . . . there was no doubt at all that she was mad. What on earth did it matter to the girl, or to herself, what she looked like? Or, for that matter, what she was—if she, or if anyone, knew what that was. She, Kate, had hired a room from Maureen, that was all. It was a neat reversal of a recent situation for Kate, who, earlier that year, had let stay in her house a young girl who was the Belgian friend of James's best friend: the girl wanted to learn English. What Kate had cared about was that the girl should fit into the family atmosphere, adding to it because of her humorous friendly nature which was also a trifle pernickety and old-maidish—her upbringing had been conventional—but not disturbing it too much. This she could have done by falling in love with her own husband—not that Kate had thought her husband would have fallen in love with the girl . . . here Kate pulled herself up short and shouted to herself, Don't start that again, remember the *au pair* Monique, there was hell to pay because you thought Michael had fallen for her.

Kate finished the list of requirements she had had for the Belgian girl in the mode of the gloss: that she should not fall in love too much with any one of the three sons, unless the son in question fell equally in love with her. That she should not get pregnant, requiring her, Kate, to deal with the problem—like Monique, whose abortion had had to be paid for by the Browns, since the fetus's father, a young Frenchman met at a language class, had no money. That she should not take drugs like Rosalie, a former *au pair* from Frankfurt—that is, it would be all right if she smoked pot, but not anything stronger. That she should not play the hi-fi too loudly. That she should not . . . but in the tone of her present self, Kate summed it all up: that she should not do more than conform comfortably to her, Kate's, way of life because while it went without saying Kate would not claim any particular virtues for the way of life as such, she did not want to suffer the annoyance of it being disturbed.

Maureen had come into the hall, like a milkmaid in a nursery rhyme, on bare feet. Seeing Kate standing in front of the glass, in a semidark, she switched the light on, and walked in her springy energetic way quietly along the passage until she stood just behind Kate, reflected in the same glass.

Maureen pushed back her yellow hair and looked at herself and then at Kate. She frowned. The frown was the result of perplexity, the need to understand the situation?

Maureen smiled dazzlingly, all white teeth and red lips, and began dancing. It was an energetic hopping springing sort of dance, and she watched herself in the mirror as a child watches itself do something for the first time. She decided to be delighted with her dance, she smiled. Then, flinging back her head, flinging out her arm, she circled round and round, her feet pattering about under her as she got dizzy, when she slumped against a wall laughing.

All this had been self-absorbed, almost a private performance. But now she pushed herself up from the wall, using a heave of her shoulder, and came to stand by Kate. Kate caught the smile on her own face; it was a middle-aged smile, a bit sad, humorous, shrewd, patient. This smile was what had provoked that perky provocative dance?

Maureen leaned forward and looked at herself carefully past Kate's shoulder. She stuck out her tongue at Kate. This was out of resentment, of self-assertion. Then, equally disliking, she stuck it out again, but at herself. Then with a false jolly smile at Kate, she returned rapidly to her sunny room.

Kate felt assaulted. No matter how her mind said that it had been friendly, a sharing—the girl had come to share her moment at the glass—she felt it as aggression, and this was because, quite simply, of the marvelous assurance of the girl's youth. Of her courage in doing what she felt like doing. Yes, that was it, that was what she, Kate, had lost.

But it was no good standing on and on here, in this large hall full of cushions—which were all tumbled and disarranged, as if they had been slept on the night before—simply because she did not want to go out into the street, to expose her weakness. And she had to rest soon. She should start eating.

She went out again into the sunlight, up cement steps. She stood under the heavy trees that lined the canal and was two steps from the *Ristorante*. She had decided that she ought to be hungry, or at least, that the demands of the coming weeks meant she must be fed—but why, with nothing to do, with no claims on her, did she think of demands, claims, strain? She would go and eat well, keep the meal down, enjoy it if possible . . . She went towards the *Ristorante* that had little bay trees on either side of the entrance. Through the glass of the frontage she could see a waiter bending attentively over a woman of about her own age, who was absorbing his flattering deference and smiling—like a silly old fool, Kate thought. At the door she was thinking that before her flight into the international elite, she would have gone into such a restaurant on special occasions; that she would as automatically have passed this place and looked for a cheaper one as now she singled this one out as being the only possible one in this road. Now, as she turned herself away from it, it was with a feeling of real deprivation. A hundred yards on she went into a restaurant of the kind that occurs in every street in London at intervals of a few yards. It was nearly empty. The lunchtime rush had not started. She sat by herself and waited for service. In front of her stood the unvarying British menu. At the other end of the room, a waitress was talking to a customer, an elderly man. She was in no hurry to come over.

When she did come, she did not look at Kate, but scribbled the order down hastily on a small pad, and went back to talk to the customer, before shouting the order through a hatch into the kitchen. It seemed a long time before the food came. Kate sat on, invisible, apparently, to the waitress and to the other customers: the place was filling now. She was shaking with impatient hunger, the need to cry. The feeling that no one could see her made her want to shout, "Look, I'm here, can't you see me?" She was not far off that state which in a small child is called a tantrum. It was checked by the arrival of a plate of liver and chips and watery cabbage, which was set in front of her by the waitress who still had not looked at her. Kate could not eat the food. She felt like a small child who has been told to sit in a corner and eat its food because it has been naughty, and then is forgotten. She was raging with emotions which stopped any sensible thought. Saying to herself that she had been ill, and was not to blame, she knocked over a glass of water. She expected the waitress to come over, even to be angry with her, but she did not notice. Kate got up herself, crossed the room to the waitress, who was now chatting with another customer, and said, "I'm sorry, but I've spilt my glass of water." Her voice was tremulous.

The waitress now looked at her—only long enough to see that here was a woman being difficult. She said, "I'll come in just a tick, love," and went off to lay a table. When she did come, she gave the sodden patch on the cloth an indifferent look, and said, "If you can manage, I'll change the cloth when you are finished."

And off she went.

What could be more sensible? thought the housewife in Kate—a wet patch on the cloth would not hurt her. But after a minute she called for the bill, and noted that as she left the restaurant, it was with a little flounce of her skirt that she could swear she had never used in her life before: it was like the sniff of a woman who means to convey: Well, I don't care! Why should you think that I care one way or the other?

Midday in the Edgware Road. The liveliest of scenes, particularly on a summer's day, particularly with everyone dropping in and out of cafés and sandwich bars where they were well known, for lunch, for a cup of tea, for a sit-down. Kate walked slowly across to the *Ristorante,* and looked through the thin muslin into the interior. If she had been inside there, with that attentive young man bent over her, she would not have wished to weep, to make pettish gestures—she would not have spilt her glass of water!

Well, being so long in that hotel, being looked after by Silva, by Marie, had done her no good at all. She had been returned to childishness, she needed to have someone's flattering attention all the time.

She descended from the bright leafy day into the shade of the flat. On the floor of the hall, sprawled over cushions, lay a young man, face down, his arms spread. He was asleep. Maureen did not seem to be about.

Kate went to her room, saw there were no sheets on the bed, found a cupboard in the hall that had in it sheets and towels, took out what she needed without disturbing the youth, who hadn't slept for some time to judge by the depth of his sleep now, and put herself to bed. There she did something she usually did not allow herself to do. She wept, long and deliberately. A safety valve? That, too; but it was more an acknowledgment that there was something to cry about. She was being assailed on all sides, and from within, too, by loneliness. So a small child weeps on learning that he is to be sent away to boarding school, or that his parents are going off on a long voyage and leaving him with strangers.

But while her body heaved and manufactured tears, she was thinking, quite coolly, that coming here, coming to the hired room where no one knew her, was the first time in her life that she had been alone and outside a cocoon of comfort and protection, the support of other people's recognition of what she had chosen to present. But here no one expected anything, knew anything about her supports, her cocoon. Now she was looking back with pleasure at the little scene in the hall when Maureen came to the mirror: Maureen had been responding directly to Kate, to what Kate was, to what Maureen saw of Kate—which was a dry, wry, cautious smile.

She finished crying, went to sleep, woke in a strange room that was chilly but had in it a long ray of sunlight: since that morning the sun had moved from one side of the flat to the other.

She had to buy food. Now the cushions in the hall were empty; and she did not see the young man again.

In the kitchen Maureen was sitting by herself, eating baby food with a teaspoon. Apricot and prune pudding. There was a stack of baby food tins on a shelf, all desserts.

Maureen wore a scarlet frilled mother hubbard, and her hair was in a pony tail. She looked ten years old.

She said, "You'll find everything you want somewhere, I think," and jumped up, still licking the spoon. She flung the empty jar into the rubbish bin and the spoon into the sink, where it landed with a tinkle. She danced out.

Kate pulled towards her a shopping basket on wheels and a roomy grass basket, and was at the door before remembering she was not shopping for anything between six and sixteen people, but for herself. She went back up into the sunlight, with a plastic carrier bag. It was late afternoon, and the shops were about to close. There were a lot of shops which were the counterparts of the restaurant in which she had eaten, or rather, not eaten her lunch. They were all small, and crammed with tinned and frozen foods. There were no shops in this road like the ones she used in middle-class Blackheath. Block towers of flats were all about, and in between old houses whose inhabitants had lived there all their lives: these were the people who used the shops, which sold nothing which Kate would normally dream of buying. Inside one she bought a loaf of dead, white bread, half a pound of butter that had been dyed yellow, a packet of processed cheese, and a pot of strawberry jam of a kind which she would at home consider herself criminal for even considering. She noted that her emotions over buying these second-rate goods were very strong indeed. What she was feeling would be appropriate to hearing that she was about to be put into prison for a year: for all her married life a good part of her energies had gone into such classifications of excellence. She was thinking, too, that the people in the village in Spain had probably never seen such bad dead food, though they were poorer than anyone who ever came into this shop, which was full of what is known as ordinary people, that is to say, the British working people, who used the awful restaurants, these awful shops . . . *and so what,* what was wrong with her, what did it matter, she was on the point of bursting into tears, she could easily stamp her foot and rage and scream—why? Meanwhile millions of people were dying all over the poor parts of the world because they got nothing to eat, millions of children would never be normal because such food as she had put in her pretty plastic bag that had a design of orange and pink daisies on it did not come their way at all . . . At the cash desk, she was in a rage of childish resentment, and tears stood behind her eyes. Why? The man had not looked at her, had not smiled and said, Oh Mrs. Brown, oh Kate, oh Catherine, how nice to see you—that was all. His manner, she was feeling, was cold. She was insane, there was no doubt of it—so spoke her intelligence, while her emotions were those of a small child.

She walked in the direction of Marble Arch. There was a street market, ready to close. Then it must be Saturday?—there had never been a time in her life when Kate had not known the hour of the day, let alone the day of the week.

In front of her was a wooden platform on which rolled some tomatoes among flattening lettuce, the ravaged remains of that morning's display of fresh growth. In front of her descended a wooden flap. Like a door shutting—a panic of deprivation made her run around the side of the stall and almost shout—but she was smiling; she could feel the desperate grimace stretching her lips, "Can I have some tomatoes, a pound of tomatoes?"

The man said, showing dislike, "I'm shutting. It's past my time."

"Oh, please," she gasped, and heard her own voice making it a life-and-death matter.

The man now deliberately looked her up and down. Then he as deliberately turned and looked along a stretch of stalls open, still showing a scattering of fruit and vegetables. He then turned his back on her, and pulled down the side flap of the stall. To the air he delivered the verdict she deserved, as formalized as the rituals of a law court: "Some mothers do have 'em."

She went to a near stall, queued, and listened to the woman in front of her—a woman like the normal Kate, or rather, the normal Kate of the past, with a shopping basket on wheels and carriers and net bags, buying a large family's supply for the week.

She moved away, bowed down, weighed down, a slave, her shoulders saying how satisfying it was to bear burdens for others. Since Kate had her attention on this woman, she missed her place in the queue, and that complex of emotion was set going that is part of the queue rituals. The woman who had taken Kate's place was aggressive, and kept an adamant self-righteous cheek towards Kate, while she said to the woman on the other side, "I haven't got time to stand here all day if she has."

Kate bought, from a man who didn't look at her, two lemons and a green pepper, having suppressed the reflex to buy a dozen lemons and two pounds of green peppers.

She returned to the flat, knowing that she had not begun to understand what she had to face. She had not had an inkling of it before today. If she had not been low in vitality, if she had not been ill, she would not have had these excessively strong reactions—of course not. But how glad she ought to be that this was happening—otherwise, each one of these violent emotions would have been small impulses, minor spurts of pettiness. She might easily have not known what they were, might have been able to pretend she did not feel them.

But what was she going to do about this monster inside whom she was trapped, a monstrous baby, who had to be soothed and smiled at and given attention on demand: the woman who for years has been saying, implicitly, of course, *Have you forgotten who I am, my position in this house?* Natalia Petrovna came straight out with it; the fact that Kate Brown would be ashamed to say it aloud showed there had been some progress?

Outside the flat, on a low wall, sat a languid young lady with a large yellow chignon, eyes limned with blue paint, a bright pink doll's mouth. She was wearing an ancient black dinner dress in lace and satin.

The young lady's haughty face vanished in a wide smile, and Maureen said, "Why are you so thin?"

"Because I have lost a lot of weight."

"Makes sense."

"Not to me—yet," said Kate, and descended into the flat.

And now, like someone trying to deal with a faulty machine, an engine needing oil perhaps, she set about the business of making herself a meal she could eat. She had to eat. She needed the energy. She had to build up energy in order to defeat the monster which had swallowed her whole.

She made toast out of the awful bread, buttered and cheesed it, and sat herself down at the kitchen table to eat it. But each mouthful became an unswallowable mass. Maureen strode in, her lace dress flapping about naked ankles and feet.

"Have you been ill?" she demanded.

"A little."

Maureen pulled down off the stack a jar of baby food called Plum and Semolina and, hitching up her lace, sat on the end of the table and began to eat. Seeing Kate chewing, she waved her hand at the baby food and said, "Try that instead? I never eat anything else."

"You'll get a vitamin deficiency," said Kate, automatically, and sat fighting tears as Maureen rocked with derisive laughter.

Maureen handed her a jar of apple purée, and Kate was able to swallow the stuff.

"I like being ill," said Maureen. "It's better than hash."

"Hash didn't do anything for me when I tried it."

"You didn't persevere with it, did you?" stated Maureen.

There now entered a young man with a King Charles haircut, jeans, and a frilly silk shirt. He nodded at Kate, went past her to Maureen, lifted her off the table, and said, "We must move. It starts in five minutes."

Maureen pulled on a pair of white kid lace-up boots, and arranged a rather beautiful Spanish shawl, which was full of moth holes, over her bare shoulders.

The two left, nodding at Kate, who felt a wash of violent anguish appropriate to saying goodbye to loved ones departing for several years. She was full of loss because this delightful, ruthless inconsequence had been taken from her, even for an evening. Her children were much more solemn, not nearly so casual. It was her fault this was so? She ought to have . . .

She checked herself, as it were pleading with guilt, and with sorrow, to stay away till she had strength to withstand them.

Kate piled blankets on her bed and dived into them. She slept. She was searching for the dream of the seal but could not find it. Other dreams captured her, kept her prisoner, dreams smaller and less important; in her sleep she felt like someone a couple of yards from the center of the maze, but no matter how she turned and tried, she could not reach it. The seal was there; it was being carried north by Kate whose business it was to do this, but this was going on in a part of Kate that was obscured from her by dreams like so many parcels that she had to balance and secure.

She woke. Air was flowing, carrying a multicolored music. It was heavy air, damp, but reminiscent of irresponsibility, of gaiety, of people mixing and moving: this summer air, a summer Saturday night's current tingled across Kate's face in a thin dark that had leaf shadows printed on it from the window: there was a streetlight on the pavement outside. One of the patterns of music came from inside the flat.

Kate thought she was much better: the violences of the day seemed gone. It was because she had eaten something at last—she would go and eat again. It pleased her that she would probably run into Maureen. She put on a yellow beach robe, and went out into the hall. It was empty. She saw herself in the long mirror: there was nothing for it but to laugh at what she saw. It didn't matter, it would only be Maureen. The kitchen door was shut. She opened it with a smile, onto a scene that confused her, like an undeserved assault.

Five young people sat around the kitchen table, which had plates of food, and glasses of wine. A dark girl played a guitar. Kate realized that the smile that she wore was a habit of that other house, her own home: walking into a room there that had in it her children, their friends, it would be with this smile that expected a welcome, even if the welcome had to be inside the family convention of teasing, the "love talk."

"Ohhhh, look who has come in!"

"I suppose you are going to tell us to come and eat."

"That's my mother, that is! I told you, she's not too bad, I suppose."

That was from earlier, from the mid-teens, a raucous jeering that was quite friendly really, was full of need, which knew that she, mother, would be there, would come in always with that smile, would say not more than, "Thanks for the compliment. Yes, supper's ready."

Now it was adult politeness, much harder to take:

"Come in mother. This is my friend from Scotland/Penzance/Spain/The States. Can he/she stay here a bit? I've bought a new sleeping bag. There's no need to bother about a lot of extra cooking, please."

It seemed to her now that the five faces, one of them Maureen's, were turning towards her in the same slow movement set to seem indifferent, which indifference was of course an affectation, but necessary to them, as protection against—what?

Five faces stared at a skeleton in a shocking-yellow robe, her hair in a dry mass around a worried face.

She fled from what seemed to her like a glare of hostility, muttering, "I'm so sorry. . . ."

In her room she knew that her feeling of total rejection was outside the range of anything rational; she could only observe it. She hurried herself into one of summer's beautiful dresses, bones inside a tent, tried to push her hair closer to her head, and gave up, then went out into the street. Under the street lamps, groups of young men hung about, hoping that something would happen: the pubs must just have closed.

She thought, *I can't, I can't go past them:* for each group of men, even a couple of young boys standing by themselves, seemed threatening. But she forced herself, a self-prescribed corrective to a need to dive back down into the flat, pull blankets over her head, and stay there. The street seemed wide, endless, each object in it embodied danger; she seemed to herself all vulnerable surfaces. She walked, with her eyes straight ahead, as she would in Italy or Spain, where women are made to feel over-exposed, roped off like municipal grass: *Keep Off.*

No one took any notice. She received indifferent glances, which turned off her at once, in search of stimulus.

Again, she might have been invisible.

Her whole surface, the shields of her blank staring eyes, her body, even her trimly set feet, had been set to receive notice, like an adolescent girl who has spent three hours making up and who has staked everything on what will happen when she presents herself to batteries of search-lighting eyes. Kate felt light, floating, without ballast; her head was chaotic, her feelings numbed with confusion, she was suppressing impulses so far from anything she had ever had, or could have imagined as hers, that she was shocked by them as if reading about them in a newspaper: she knew that if she were not careful she would march up to one of these groups of lolling men and lift up her skirts to expose herself: *There,* look at that, I'm here, can't you see? Why don't you look at me?

A small café, serving exactly the same food as the one she had been into for lunch, was still open. But beside this menu was a slighter, almost apologetic card that indicated the Greek parentage of the place. They offered the skeleton of the Greek menu abroad: hummus, taramasalata, shish kebab. It was full of young people from the tall council flats, who did not want to go to bed now the pictures were finished, the pubs closed. No one took any notice of her, though she had stiffened herself to take criticism. She knew now, she had to know at last, that all her life she had been held upright by an invisible fluid, the notice of other people. But the fluid had been drained away. She swayed, had to sit down quickly at a table which had a young married couple and another girl—the sister, apparently, of the wife. The sister was sulking about something, but enjoyably: she was acting out being huffed and indifferent; the young wife was nagging to get back to her baby, because the neighbor who was looking after it would want to get to bed; the young man was looking around the restaurant and contrasting present bondage with past freedom.

The Greek who served the shish kebab was trying to make the sixteen-year-old look at him; and so Kate did not ask why they had not seasoned the food at all, did not say that not all English palates were bland; did not suggest that they might cook for her as they would for themselves. *Especially for me* were the words she found on her tongue.

She ate fast, and left the noisy friendly scene which seemed, as closing hour came near, to be swelling up like a boiling liquid which would overflow everywhere into the street.

Kate was congratulating herself that she had *not,* when she paid the bill, attracted attention by presenting an emphatic smile, sending out the signal: I am accustomed to being noticed.

In the flat, the door to the kitchen was now open, and Maureen stood against the wall near it, beside a young man Kate had not seen before. They held hands. Maureen saw Kate and said, "Why didn't you come into the kitchen before? You must, any time. You mustn't mind what we do." Before the girl had even finished, Kate's emotional self was weak with grateful emotion.

"This is Philip," said Maureen, and, removing her hand and giving the young man a small push towards Kate, "this is Kate. She's a friend."

Philip obeyed Maureen with a small smiling bow at Kate, and then went off down the hall to the door, remarking, "Right then, tomorrow." There was something admonishing about it, like an ultimatum. Maureen was reacting with a shrug, and a look of strain.

"All right," she said. "I promise. But I *do* think about it. But you come on so strong about everything."

"Of course I do. *I* know what I want," said Philip, and without looking around, went out into the night.

Maureen sighed noisily, wanting it to be seen that a weight had been taken off her, and went into the kitchen. In the half an hour since Kate had looked in on it, the scene had quite changed. The young people had vanished, the tables were cleared of plates, glasses, food. Only the guitar player was still there, her hair and her hands sweeping the strings. She took no notice of Kate.

Maureen was looking frankly and critically at Kate. She examined the mass of crinkling hair, with its wide grey band down the middle. She looked at Kate's dress, walking, or stepping, carefully around Kate to do so. Then she said, "Wait" and went off for a minute. She came back with some dresses, and held them up one by one, frowning, in front of Kate. The two women began to laugh: the laugh built up so that the guitar player glanced up to see what was so funny. At a skinny frilled dress stretched against Kate's bones, she smiled briefly, and retired back into her music.

One of the dresses was a straight dark-green shift, and Kate unwrapped herself from the one she wore and put it on.

It delighted Maureen that it fitted.

"You'd better keep that. No, use it till you get fatter again. No, really, you look such a sad sack of a thing in those awful couture-ish clothes of yours. You must be rich, I suppose."

Great waves of self-pity washed over Kate: never had she foreseen that she could be called a sad sack. But it was the girl's kindness that was forcing tears. To hide them, she made tea, her back turned, and when she turned to the table, with her cup, the guitar player wandered off, and could be heard from another room, and Maureen, spreading her black lace flounces, setting the heels of her white laced boots apart, had sat down and was frowning at Kate.

"You wear a wedding ring?"

"Yes."

"Are you divorced?"

"No."

Kate was afraid to use these monosyllables, in case the girl might withdraw her friendship, but after a while Maureen inquired, "Are you sorry you married?"

At this Kate first let out the small sort of laughter that announces it has been prompted by an indiscreet question; and then surprised herself by sitting down and laughing. Uncontrollably. She had to stop, for she was starting to cry. During this Maureen leaned her chin on her two forearms, that were on the back of a chair which she was using like a gate into a field on which she was leaning to watch horses, or at any rate, some kind of animal, and stared at Kate with a steady, stubborn blue gaze.

This she kept up when Kate had stopped laughing, so that Kate had to explain: "It is funny to be asked that, don't you see? I mean, after having been married ever since you were a girl."

"I don't see why it is funny," said Maureen.

"But I have children. Four. The youngest is nineteen."

Maureen changed neither her pose nor her steady gaze for some moments after that. Then she got up, and dismissed what she obviously felt as a disappointment by shrugging, and then rolling herself a cigarette, in which were carefully shredded some strands of the acrid weed. She went striding off after the music, not saying goodbye or good night.

Kate went to bed. It was midday when she woke. She lay looking through the window at the white wall that had plants in pots against it, and beyond the wall at trees, foliage, everything in heavy sunlight. There was not a sound in the flat. Without running into anyone she bathed, and went into the kitchen. No one had been in there since the night before. The telephone began ringing in the hall. Maureen answered it, and then came to stand in the doorway. Where Kate had stood last night, looking in at the five faces all turned to stare at her, now Maureen stood, looking at Kate. She wore white beach pajamas, and her hair was in two pigtails over either shoulder, tied with white ribbons.

She came in, cut herself bread off Kate's loaf, spread jam over it, and sat down to eat.

"Are you going to dye your hair again?"

"I don't know yet. I've got nearly six weeks before I have to decide."

"What color was it when you were young?"

"This color." Kate saw an end of brassy red on her right shoulder, and said, "No, it was dark red."

"You must have been pretty," said Maureen.

"Thank you."

"If I went away and left you in the flat would you look after it? I mean, there wouldn't be all these people floating in and out, just you."

At this reversal to her life's condition, or life style, Kate could not help laughing.

"You wouldn't want to then?"

"No." With an effort, Kate stopped herself from saying, "But if you want me to, *of course* I will." She said, "You see, it's not often that I get the chance to be absolutely free, and not to have to do things, look after things. I don't know when I shall have it again."

"How long?"

"What?"

"Since you had it, since you were free."

"This is the first time in my whole life that I've had it." Kate could hear the irritable despair in her voice, the statement: It's not possible, I can't believe it myself.

Maureen shot her a look that seemed unfriendly; then Kate saw it was because she was scared. Maureen got up, lit a cigarette—an ordinary one—and walked or stepped lightly around the room, on an invisible pattern that she was making as she went.

"Never?" she asked at last.

"Never."

"You married young?"

"Yes."

Another long, indrawn breath, of fright, of apprehension: the girl halted her stepping dance, that was like a bird's on a shore, and demanded, "But *are* you sorry? Are you? Are you?"

"How can I answer that? Don't you see that I can't?"

"No. Why can't you?"

"Are you thinking of marrying?"

"I might."

She went on with her dance—it was like the private dance-walk a little girl who has been brought up too strictly makes for herself: she was stepping over invisible bars, barriers, lines on the floor. Then she saw that her careful avoidance of these lines was making another pattern. She frowned, irritable, discouraged. At the other end of the room sunlight lay in a yellow square. She began walking around the square of sunlight, on tiptoe, like a soldier, one, two, one, two.

"If I left I'd go and meet Jerry in Turkey."

"To marry him?"

"No. He doesn't want to marry me. But Philip does."

"You mean, you want to run away to Jerry for fear of marrying Philip?"

At this Maureen laughed, but went on with her fast tiptoe walk around the square.

"And if I don't watch it, I'll start feeling guilty for refusing to be a housekeeper in the flat, thus forcing you into marrying Philip."

Maureen laughed again, and sat down suddenly at the table.

"Have you daughters?"

"One."

"Is she married?"

"No."

"Does she want to?"

"Sometimes yes and sometimes no."

"What do you want for her?"

"Can't you see that I can't answer that?"

"No." She shouted it. "No, no, no, no. I don't see why. Why can't you?" And she ran out of the kitchen, her pigtails flying.

FROM

# *The Memoirs of a Survivor*

The child was left with me in this way. I was in the kitchen, and, hearing a sound, went into the living room, and saw a man and a half-grown girl standing there. I did not know either of them, and advanced with the intention of clearing up a mistake. The thought in my mind was that I must have left my front door open. They turned to face me. I remember how I was even then, and at once, struck by the bright, hard, nervous smile on the girl's face. The man—middle-aged, ordinarily dressed, quite unremarkable in every way—said, "This is the child." He was already on the way out. He had laid his hand on her shoulder, had smiled and nodded to her, was turning away.

I said, "But surely . . ."

"No, there's no mistake. She's your responsibility."

He was at the door.

"But wait a minute. . . ."

"She is Emily Cartright. Look after her." And he had gone.

We stood there, the child and I, looking at each other. I remember the room had a wash of sun: it was still morning. I was wondering how the two had got in, but this already seemed irrelevant, since the man had gone. I now ran to the window: a street with a few trees along the pavement; a bus stop with its familiar queue of people waiting; and on the wide pavement opposite, underneath the trees there, some children from the Mehtas' flat upstairs playing with a ball—dark-skinned boys and girls, all dazzling white shirts, crisp pink and blue dresses, white teeth, gleaming hair. But the man I was looking for—not a sign.

I turned back to the child; but now I took my time over it, and was wondering what to say, how to present myself, how to handle her—all the pathetic little techniques and tricks of our self-definition. She was watching me, carefully, closely: the thought came into my mind that this was the expert assessment of possibilities by a prisoner observing a new jailer. Already my heart was heavy: anxiety! My intelligence was not yet making much of what was happening.

"Emily?" I said tentatively, hoping that she would choose to answer the questions in my mind.

"Emily Mary Cartright," she said, in a manner that matched her bright impervious voice and smile. Pert? At any rate a hard, an enameled presence. I was trying to get past or around it; I was conscious that I was desperately making signals—my smile, gestures—which might perhaps reach something softer and warmer that must be there behind that cold defense of hers.

"Well, will you sit down? Or can I make you something to eat? Some tea? I do have some real tea, but of course . . ."

"I'd like to see my room, please," she said. And now her eyes were, quite without her knowing it, an appeal. She needed, she needed very much, to know what walls, what shelter she was going to be able to pull around her, like a blanket, for comfort.

"Well," I said, "I haven't thought yet . . . I don't quite . . . I must . . ." Her face seemed to shrivel. But she preserved her bright desperation. "You see," I went on, "I wasn't expecting . . . Let's see, now." She waited. Stubbornly, she waited. She knew that she was to live with me. She knew that her shelter, her four walls, her den, the little space that was hers and which she could creep into, was here somewhere. "There's the spare room," I said. "I call it that. But it isn't very . . ." But I went, and I remember how helplessly and unhappily I did, into the little front lobby, and through it to the spare room.

The flat was on the front of the building, the south side. The living room took up most of the space: its size was why I had taken the flat. At the end away from the entrance lobby, so that you had to walk through the living room to get to it, was the kitchen, on the corner of the building. This was quite large, with cupboards and storage space, and was used for eating as well. From the entrance lobby went two doors, one to the living room, one to the room I called a spare room. This room was connected with the bathroom. My bedroom was on the front of the building, reached from the living room. The bathroom, lobby, spare room took up the same space as my bedroom, which was not large. It will be seen that the spare room was very small. It had a small high window. It was stuffy. There was no way of making it attractive. I never used it except for keeping things in or, with apologies, for a friend staying the night.

"I'm sorry that it is so small and dark. . . . Perhaps we should . . ."

"No, no, I don't mind," she said, in the cool jaunty way which was so much hers; but she was looking at the bed with longing, and I knew she had found her refuge, hers; here it was at last. "It's lovely," she said. "Oh, yes, you don't believe me—you don't know what . . ." But she left the possibility of an explanation of what she had been experiencing, and waited, her whole body expressing how she wanted me to leave.

"And we'll have to share the bathroom," I said.

"Oh, I'll be ever so tidy," she assured me. "I'm really very good, you know, I won't make a mess, I never do."

I knew that if I were not in this flat, if she did not feel she must behave well, she would be between the blankets, she would already be far away from the world.

"I won't be a tick," she assured me. "I must get tidy. I'll be as quick as I can."

I left her and waited for her in the living room, first standing by the window looking out, wondering perhaps if fresh surprises were on the way. Then I sat down—rather, I imagine, in the attitude of *The Thinker,* or some such concentrated pose.

Yes, it was extraordinary. Yes, it was all impossible. But, after all, I had accepted the "impossible." I lived with it. I had abandoned all expectations of the ordinary for my inner world, my real life in that place. And as for the public, the outer world, it had been a long time since that offered the normal. Could one perhaps describe that period as "the ordinariness of the extraordinary"? Well, the reader should have no difficulty here: these words are a description of the times we have lived through. (A description of all life?—probably, but it is not much help to think so.)

But these words convey perfectly the atmosphere of what was happening when Emily was brought to me. While everything, all forms of social organization, broke up, we lived on, adjusting our lives as if nothing fundamental was happening. It was amazing how determined, how stubborn, how self-renewing were the attempts to lead an ordinary life. When nothing, or very little, was left of what we had been used to, had taken for granted even ten years before, we went on talking and behaving as if those old forms were still ours. And indeed, order of the old kind—food, amenities, even luxuries—*did* exist at higher levels; we all knew that, though of course those who enjoyed these things did not draw attention to themselves. Order could also exist in pockets, of space, of time—through periods of weeks and months or in a particular district. Inside them, people would live and talk and even think as if nothing had changed. When something really bad happened, as when an area got devastated, people might move out for days, or weeks, to stay with relatives or friends, and then move back, perhaps to a looted house, to take up their jobs, their housekeeping—their order. We can get used to anything at all; this is a commonplace, of course, but perhaps you have to live through such a time to see how horribly true it is. There is nothing that people won't try to accommodate into "ordinary life." It was precisely this which gave that time its peculiar flavor; the combination of the bizarre, the hectic, the frightening, the threatening—an atmosphere of siege or war—with what was customary, ordinary, even decent.

For instance, on the newscasts and in the papers they would pursue for days the story of a single kidnapped child, taken from its pram perhaps by some poor unhappy woman. The police would be combing the suburbs and the countryside in hundreds, looking for the child, and for the woman, to punish her. But the next news flash would be about the mass deaths of hundreds, thousands, or even millions of people. We still believed, wanted to believe, that the first—the concern about the single child, the need to punish the individual criminal, even if it took days and weeks and hundreds of our hard-worked police force to do it—was what really represented us; the second, about the catastrophe, was, as such items of news had always been for people not actually in the threatened area, an unfortunate and minor—or at least not crucial—accident, which interrupted the even flow, the development, of civilization.

This is the sort of thing we accepted as normal. Yet for all of us there were moments when *the game we were all agreeing to play* simply could not stand up to events: we would be gripped by feelings of unreality, like nausea. Perhaps this feeling, that the ground was dissolving under our feet, was the real enemy . . . or we believed it to be so. Perhaps our tacit agreement that nothing *much*—or at least nothing irrecoverable—was happening was because for us the enemy was Reality, was to allow ourselves to know what was happening. Perhaps our pretenses, everyone's pretenses, which in the moments when we felt naked, defenseless, seemed like playacting and absurd, should be regarded as admirable? Or perhaps they were necessary, like the games of children who can make playacting a way of keeping reality a long way from their weaknesses? But increasingly, all the time, one had to defeat the need simply to laugh: oh, not a good laughter—far from it. Rather, bellows and yells of derision.

For instance again: in the same week that a horde of two hundred or so hooligans had surged through our neighborhood—leaving a corpse on the pavement across the street from my windows, leaving smashed windows, looted shops, the remains of bonfires—a group of middle-aged women, self-appointed vigilantes, were making formal protests to the police about an amateur-theatricals group some youngsters had set up. This group had written and put on a play describing the tensions within an ordinary family living in a block of flats like ours, a family which had taken in half a dozen refugees from the eastern counties. (As long as travelers were with the migrating gangs, they were "hooligans," but when they hived off to find shelter with some family or household, they were "refugees.") A household that had held five people suddenly held twelve, and the resulting frictions led to adultery and an incident where "a young girl seduced a man old enough to be her grandfather," as the good women indignantly described it. They managed to organize a not very well attended meeting about the "decay of family life," about "immorality," about "sexual indulgence." This was comic, of course. Unless it was sad. Unless—as I've suggested—it was admirable; a sign of the vitality of the said "ordinary life" which would in the end defeat chaos, disorder, the malevolence of events.

Or what can one say about the innumerable citizens' groups that came into existence right up to the end, for any ethical or social purpose you could think of: to improve old-age pensions, at a time when money was giving way to barter; to supply vitamin tablets to schoolchildren; to provide a visiting service for housebound invalids; to arrange formal legal adoption for abandoned children; to forbid the news of any violent or "unpleasant" event, so as not to "put ideas into young people's heads"; to reason with the gangs of hooligans as they came through the streets, or alternatively to birch them; to go around and about the streets, exhorting people to "restore a sense of decency to their sexual practices"; to agree not to eat the meat of cats and dogs; and so on, and on, and on—there was really no end to it. Farce. Spitting into a hurricane; standing in front of a mirror to touch up one's face or straighten a tie as the house crashes around one; extending the relaxed accommodating hand of the royal handshake to a barbarian who will certainly bend and take a good bite out of it—such similes come to mind. Such analogies were being made then, of course, in the conversations that were our meat and drink, and by the professional comedians.

In such an atmosphere, in a time of such happenings, that an unknown man should arrive in my home with a child, saying she was my responsibility, and then leave without further remark was not as strange as all that.

When Emily at last came out of her bedroom, having changed her dress and washed from her face what looked like an assault of miserable tears, she said, "The room will be a bit small for Hugo and me, but it doesn't matter a bit."

I saw that she had beside her a dog—no, a cat. What was it? An animal, at any rate. It was the size of a bulldog, and shaped more like a dog than a cat, but its face was that of a cat.

It was yellow. Its hide was harsh and rough. It had a cat's eyes and whiskers. It had a long whiplike tail. An ugly beast. Hugo. She sat herself down carefully in my deep old sofa opposite the fireplace, and the beast got up beside her and sat there, as close as he could get, and she put her arm about him. She looked at me from beside the animal's cat face. They both looked at me, Hugo with his green eyes, and Emily with her defensive shrewd hazel eyes.

She was a large child, of about twelve. Not a child, really; but in that halfway place where soon she would be a girl. She would be pretty, at least good-looking. Well-made: she had small hands and feet, and good limbs that were brown with health and sun. Her hair was dark and straight, parted on one side, held with a clip.

We talked. Or, rather, we offered each other little remarks, both waiting for that switch to be turned somewhere which would make our being together easier. While she sat there silent, her brooding dark gaze, her mouth with its definite possibilities of humor, her air of patient thoughtful attention made her seem someone I could like very much. But then, just as I was sure she was about to respond in kind to my attempts, my feeling of pleasure in her potentialities, there would come to life in her the vivacious self-presenting little *madam*—the old-fashioned word was right for her: there was something old-fashioned in her image of herself. Or perhaps it was someone else's idea of her?

She chattered: "I'm awfully hungry, and so is Hugo. Poor Hugo. He hasn't eaten today. And neither have I, if the truth must be told."

I made my apologies and hastened out to the shops to buy whatever cat or dog foods I could find for Hugo. It took some time to find a shop which still stocked such things. I was an object of interest to the shop assistant, an animal lover, who applauded my intention to stand up for my rights to keep "pets" in these days. I also interested one or two of the other customers, and I was careful not to say where I lived, when one asked me, and went home by a misleading route, and made sure I was not being followed. On the way I visited several other shops, looking for things I usually did not bother with, they were so hard to track down, so expensive. But at last I did find some biscuits and sweets of a quite decent quality—whatever I thought might appeal to a child. I had plenty of dried apples and pears, and stocks of basic foodstuffs. When at last I got back home, she was asleep on the sofa, and Hugo was asleep beside her. His yellow face was on her shoulder, her arm was around his neck. On the floor beside her was her little suitcase, as flimsy as a small child's weekend case. It had in it some neatly folded dresses and a jersey and a pair of jeans. These seemed to be all she owned in the way of clothes. I would not have been surprised to see a teddy or a doll. Instead there was a Bible, a book of photographs of animals, some science-fiction paperbacks.

I made as welcoming a meal as I could for both her and Hugo. I woke them with difficulty: they were in the exhausted state that follows relief after long tension. When they had eaten, they wanted to go off to bed, though it was still midafternoon.

And that was how Emily was left with me.

In those first few days, she slept and she slept. Because of this, and because of her invincible obedience, I was unconsciously thinking of her as younger than she was. I sat waiting quietly in my living room, knowing that she was asleep, exactly as one does with a small child. I did a little mending for her, washed and ironed her clothes. But mostly I sat and looked at that wall and waited. I could not help thinking that to have a child with me, just as the wall was beginning to open itself up, would be a nuisance, and in fact she and her animal were very much in the way. This made me feel guilty. All kinds of emotions I had not felt for a long time came to life in me again, and I longed simply to walk through the wall and never come back. But this would be irresponsible; it would mean turning my back on my responsibilities.

It was a day or two after Emily came: I was beyond the wall, and I kept opening doors or turning the corners of long passages to find another room or suite of rooms. Empty. That is, I did not see anyone, although the feeling of someone's presence was so strong I even kept turning my head quickly, as if this person could be expected to step out from behind a wall in the few seconds my back had been turned. Empty but inhabited. Empty but furnished . . . Wandering there, between tall white walls, from room to room, I saw that the place was filled with furniture. I knew these sofas, these chairs. But why? From what time in my life did they date? They were not my taste. Yet it seemed that they had been mine, or an intimate friend's.

The drawing room had pale pink silk curtains, a grey carpet with delicate pink and green flowers laid on it, many small tables and cabinets. The sofas and chairs were covered in tapestry, had pastel cushions placed exactly here and there. It was a room too formal and too self-sufficient ever to have been mine. Yet I knew everything in it. I walked there, slowly filling with irritated despair. Everything I looked at would have to be replaced or mended or cleaned, for nothing was whole or fresh. Each chair would have to be re-covered, for the material was frayed. The sofas were grimy. The curtains had little rents and the roughened patches moths leave, each with its minuscule holes. The carpet showed its threads. And so with all the many rooms of this place, which was giving me a feeling of things slipping away from me through clumsy and stiff fingers. The whole place should be cleared out, I kept saying to myself. It should be emptied, and what was in it now should be burned or thrown away. Bare rooms would be better than this infinitely genteel shabbiness, the gimcrackery. Room after room after room—there was no end to them, or to the work I had to do. Now I kept looking for the empty room that had in it a painter's ladder and a half-glimpsed figure in overalls: if I could see this, it would mean a start had been made. But there were no empty rooms, every one was crammed with objects, all needing attention.

It must not be thought that all my energy was going into this hidden place. For days at a time I did not think of it. The knowledge of its being there, in whatever shape it was using for the moment, came to me in flashes during my ordinary life more and more often. But I would forget it, too, for days. When I was actually through that wall, nothing else seemed real; and even the new and serious preoccupations of my life—Emily and her attendant animal—slid away, were far off, were part of another distant life which did not concern me. And this is my difficulty in describing that time: looking back now, it is as if two ways of life, two lives, two worlds, lay side by side and closely connected. But then, one life excluded the other, and I did not expect the two worlds ever to link up. I had not thought at all of their being able to do so, and I would have said this was not possible. Particularly now, when Emily was there; particularly when I had so many problems that centered on her being with me.

The main problem was, and remained for some time, that she was so infinitely obliging and obedient. When I got up in the morning, she was already up, dressed in one of her neat little dresses, the clothes of a good child whose mother needs her children to be well-dressed, even remarkably so. Her hair was brushed. Her teeth were cleaned. She was waiting for me in the living room, with her Hugo, and instantly she began chattering, offering this or that to me, how she had slept marvelously, or how she had dreamed, or how she had had this amusing or foolish or valuable thought—and all in a rushing, almost frantic way of forestalling some demand or criticism from me. And then she began about breakfast, how she would "adore" to cook it—oh, she would simply love to, please, for really she was ever so handy and capable. And so she and I would go into the kitchen, the beast padding behind us, and Hugo and I sat watching her preparations. And she was, indeed, competent and nifty. And then we ate whatever it was, Hugo's head at her waist-level, his eyes calmly watching her, me, our hands, our faces, and when he was offered a bit of food he took it delicately, like a cat. Then she would offer to wash up. "No, no, I love washing-up, incredible as it might seem, but I really do!" And she washed up and made the kitchen neat. Her bedroom had been tidied already, but not her bed, which was always a nest or womb of coiled blankets and pillows. I never reproved her for this; on the contrary, I was delighted that there was one place she felt was her own, that she could make her refuge, where she could hide away from this really awful need always to be so bright and good. Sometimes, unpredictably, during the day, she went to her room—abruptly, as if *something* had been too much. She shut the door and, I knew, crawled into the heap of disorder, and there she lay and recovered—but from what? In the living room she sat on my old sofa, her legs curled up, in a pose which was as much an offering to what might be expected of her as was her manner, her obedience. She watched me, as if anticipating commands or needs, or she might read. Her taste in reading was adult: seeing her there, with what she had chosen, made her bright child's manner even more impossible, almost as if she were deliberately insulting me. Or she would sit with her arm around the yellow beast, and he licked her hand, and put his cat's face on her arm and purred, a sound which rumbled through the rooms of my flat.

Had she been some kind of a prisoner?

I did not ask. I never asked her this question. And she did not volunteer information. Meanwhile my heart ached for her, recognizing her manner for what it was; and at the same time, while I was really quite soft and ridiculous with pity for her, I was in a frenzy of irritation because of my inability ever, even for a moment, to get behind the guard she had set up. There she was, the solemn, serious little girl, in her good little girl's dress, showing every mark of the solitary child, all self-consciousness and observation, and then off she'd go, chattering and rattling, being "amusing," offering me little skills and capacities as a return for—but what? I did not feel myself to be so formidable. I almost felt myself not to exist, in my own right. I was a continuation, for her, of parents, or a parent, a guardian, foster parents. And when we left here, presumably I would hand her over to someone else? The man who had given her into my care would come to take her back? Her parents would arrive? Otherwise, what was I going to do with her? When I started my travels north or west, joining the general movement of the population away from the southern and eastern parts of the country, what would I be moving into? What sort of life? I did not know. But I had not envisaged a child, never a responsibility of such a total sort . . . and besides, even in the few days she had been here, she had changed. Her breasts were shaping, pushing out the child's bodice. Her round face with its attractive dark eyes needed very little to shape it into a young girl's face. A "little girl" was one thing, and bad enough—"child with her pet"—but the "young girl" would be quite another, and particularly in these times.

It will sound contradictory when I say that another thing that bothered me was her indolence. Of course there wasn't very much to do in my flat. She sat for hours at my window and watched, absorbed in everything that went on. She entertained me with comment: this was a deliberate and measured offering; she had been known, it was clear, for her "amusing" comments. Here again I did not know quite what it was I had to reckon with, for these were certainly not a little girl's perceptions. Or perhaps I was out-of-date, and this was what one had to expect in this time, for what strains and stresses did children now not have to accept and make part of themselves?

Professor White would come out of the lobby and down the steps, and then stop, looking up and down the street, almost in a military way: *Who goes there!* Then, reassured, he stood for a moment: almost he could be imagined pulling on a pair of gloves, adjusting a hat. He was a slight man, young for a professor, still in his thirties; a precise, an ashy man, with everything in his life in its proper place. Onto Emily's face would come a smile as she watched him, a sour little smile, as if she was thinking, I've got *you,* you can't escape me! And over her attendant animal's pricked yellow ears she would say, "He looks as if he were pulling on a pair of gloves!" (Yes, this was her observation.) And then: "He must have a terrible temper!" "But why? Why do you think so?" "Why? Well of course, all that control, everything so neat and clean, he must burst out somewhere." And, once, "If he has a mistress"—the use of the old-fashioned word was deliberate, part of the act—"then she would have to be someone with a bad reputation, someone rather awful, or *he* would have to think she was, or other people would have to think so even if he didn't. Because he would have to feel wicked, don't you see?" Well, of course she was right.

I found myself making excuses to sit there, to hear what she would come out with. But I was reluctant, too, watching the knife being slipped in so neatly, so precisely, and again and again.

Of Janet White, a girl of about her age: "She'll spend her life looking for someone like Daddy, but where will she find him. I mean *now*—he won't exist." She meant, of course, the general breakup of things, times which were not conducive to the production of professors with very clean white shirts and a secret passion for the unrespectable—since respectability itself was sentenced to death, and with it the distinctions his secret needs must feed on. The Professor she called the White Rabbit.

His daughter she called Daddy's Girl, making the point that in doing so she was of course describing herself: "What else, after all?" When I suggested that she might enjoy making a friend of Janet, she said, "What, me and her?"

Most of the day she lolled in a large chair that she pulled up for the purpose: a child, presenting herself as one. One could almost see the white socks on her plump well-turned legs, the bow in her hair. But what one really did see was different. She wore jeans and a shirt she had ironed that morning whose top two buttons were undone. Her hair was now parted in the middle, and at a stroke she was turned into a young beauty: yes, already, there she was.

And, as if in acknowledgment of this step forward into vulnerability, now her worst, or best, comments were for the boys who went past: this one's way of walking, which she knew represented an uncertainty about himself; that one's flashy way of dressing; the other one's bad skin, or unkempt hair. These unattractive grubs represented a force, an imperative, which there was no way of evading, and like a girl on a too high swing she was shrieking in thrilled terror.

She was dreadful in her accuracy. She depressed me—oh, for many reasons; my own past being one of them. Yet she did not suspect this, she really did believe—so the bright manner, her confident glances at me said—that she was, as usual, "paying her way"; and this time by her perspicacity. She simply could not let anyone pass without swallowing them, and regurgitating them covered in her slime: the clever child, the one who could not be deceived, who could not have anything put over on her—who had been applauded for being like this, had been taught it.

And yet I came into the room once and saw her talking through the window with Janet White: she was earnest, warm, apparently sincere. If she did not like Janet White, she intended Janet White to like her. Infinite promises were made by both girls on the line of joint forays into the markets, visits, a walk. And when Janet went off, smiling because of the warmth she had absorbed from Emily, Emily said, "She's heard her parents talking about me, and now she'll report back." True enough, of course.

The point was that there wasn't anybody who came near her, into her line of sight, who was not experienced by her as a threat. This *was* how her experience, whatever that had been, had "set" her. I found I was trying to put myself in her place, tried to be her, to understand how it was that people must pass and repass sharply outlined by her need to criticize—to defend; and found I was thinking that this was only what everyone did, what I did, but there was something in her which enlarged the tendency, had set it forth, exaggerated. For of course, when someone new approaches us, we are all caution; we take that person's measure. A thousand incredibly rapid measurements and assessments go on, putting him, her, in an exact place, to end in the silent judgment: yes, this one's for me; no, we have nothing in common; no, he, she, is a threat. . . . Watch out! Danger! And so on. But it was not until Emily heightened it all for me that I realized what a prison we were all in, how impossible it was for any one of us to let a man or a woman or a child come near without the defensive inspection, the rapid, sharp, cold analysis. But the reaction was so fast, such a habit—probably the first ever taught us by our parents—that we did not realize how much we were in its grip.

"Look how she walks," Emily would say; "look at that fat old woman." (The woman, of course, was about forty-five or fifty; she might even be thirty!) "When she was young, people said she had a sexy walk—'Oh, what a sexy little wriggle you have there; ooh, you sexy thing, you!' " And her parody was horrible because of its accuracy: the woman, the wife of a former stockbroker who had become a junk dealer, and who lived on the floor above, was given to a hundred little winsome tricks of mouth and eyes and hips. This is what Emily saw of her: it was what everybody must see first of her; and on these tricks she was likely to be judged by most people. It was impossible not to hear Emily without feeling one's whole being, one's sense of oneself, lowered, drained. It was an assault on one's vitality: listening to her was to acknowledge the limits we all live inside.

I suggested she might like to go to school—"for something to do," I added hastily as I saw her quizzical look. This look was not measured: it was her genuine reaction. So I was catching a glimpse of what I had needed for some time: to know what she thought of me, made of me—it was tolerance.

She said, "But what's the point?"

What was the point? Most schools had given up the attempt of teaching; they had become—for the poorer people, at least—extensions of the Army, of the apparatus for keeping the population under control. There were still schools for the children of the privileged class, the administrators and overseers. Janet White went to one of them. But I thought too much of Emily to offer to send her to one, even if I was able to get a place for her. It was not that the education there was bad. It was irrelevant. It merited—a quizzical look.

"Not much point, I agree. And I suppose we won't be here long, anyway."

"Where do you think you'll go, then?"

This broke my heart: her forlorn isolation had never shown itself so sharply: she had spoken tentatively, even delicately, as if she had no right to ask, as if she had no right to my care, my protection—no share in my future.

Because of my emotion, I was more definite about my plans than I felt. I had, in fact, often wondered if a certain family I had known in north Wales would shelter me. They were good farming folk—yes, that is exactly the measure of my fantasies about them. "Good farming folk" was how safety, refuge, peace—utopia—shaped itself in very many people's minds in those days. But I did know Mary and George Dolgelly, had been familiar with their farm, had visited their guesthouse, open through the summers. If I made my way there, I might perhaps live there for a while? I was handy, liked to live simply, was as much at home out of cities as in them. . . . Of course, these qualifications belonged these days to large numbers of people, particularly the young, who could increasingly turn their hands to any job that needed doing. I did not imagine the Dolgellys would find me a prize. But at least they would not, I believed, find me a burden. And a child? Or, rather, a young girl? An attractive, challenging girl? Well, they had children of their own. . . . You can see that my thoughts had been pretty conventional, not very inventive. I talked to Emily, on these lines, while she listened, her sour little smile slowly giving way to amusement. But amusement concealed from politeness: I could not yet bring myself to believe that it was affection. She knew this fantasy for what it was; yet she enjoyed it, as I did. She asked me to describe the farm: I had once spent a week there, camping on a moor, with silvery water in little channels on a purple hillside. I took a can to Mary and George every morning for new milk, buying at the same time a loaf of their homemade bread. An idyll. I developed it, let it gather detail. We would take rooms in the guesthouse, and Emily would "help with the chickens"—a storybook touch, that. We would eat at the guesthouse table, a long wooden table. There was an old-fashioned stove in a recess. Stews and soups would simmer there, real food, and we would eat as much as we liked—no, that was not realistic, but as much as we needed—of real bread, real cheese, fresh vegetables, perhaps even, sometimes, a little good meat. There would be the smell of herbs from the bunches hanging to dry. The girl listened to all this, and I could not keep my eyes off her face, where the knowing sharp little smile alternated with her need to shield *me* from my inexperience, my sheltered condition! Stronger than anything else was something she was quite unconscious of, would certainly destroy all evidence of, if she knew she was betraying weakness. Stronger than the tricks, the need to please and to buy, the painful obedience, was this: a hunger, a need, a pure thing, which made her face lose its hard brightness, her eyes their defensiveness. She was a passion of longing. For what? Well, that is not so easy; it never is! But I recognized it, knew it, and talk of the farm in the Welsh hills did as well as anything to bring it out, to make it shine there: good bread, uncontaminated water from a deep well, fresh vegetables; love, kindness, the deep shelter of a family. And so we talked about the farm, our future, hers and mine, like a fable where we would walk hand in hand together. And then "life" would begin, life as it ought to be, as it had been promised—by whom? When? Where?—to everybody on this earth.

FROM

# *Shikasta*

## *History of Shikasta,* VOL. 3012, *The Century of Destruction*

### EXCERPT FROM SUMMARY CHAPTER

During the previous two centuries, the narrow fringes on the northwest of the main landmass of Shikasta achieved technical superiority over the rest of the globe, and, because of this, conquered physically or dominated by other means large numbers of cultures and civilizations. The Northwest fringe people were characterized by a peculiar insensitivity to the merits of other cultures, an insensitivity quite unparalleled in previous history. An unfortunate combination of circumstances was responsible. (1) These fringe peoples had only recently themselves emerged from barbarism. (2) The upper classes enjoyed wealth, but had never developed any degree of responsibility for the lower classes, so the whole area, while immeasurably more wealthy than most of the rest of the globe, was distinguished by contrasts between extremes of wealth and poverty. This was not true for a brief period between Phases II and III of the Twentieth Century War. [SEE VOL. 3009, *Economies of Affluence.*] (3) The local religion was materialistic. This was again due to an unfortunate combination of circumstances: one was geographical, another the fact that it had been a tool of the wealthy classes for most of its history, another that it retained even less than most religions of what its founder had been teaching. [SEE VOLS. 998 and 2041, *Religions as Tools of Ruling Castes.*] For these and other causes, its practitioners did little to mitigate the cruelties, the ignorance, the stupidity, of the Northwest fringers. On the contrary, they were often the worst offenders. For a couple of centuries at least, then, a dominant feature of the Shikastan scene was that a particularly arrogant and self-satisfied breed, a minority of the minority white race, dominated most of Shikasta, a multitude of different races, cultures, and religions which, on the whole, were superior to that of the oppressors. These white Northwest fringers were like most conquerors of history in denuding what they had overrun but they were better able than any other in their ability to persuade themselves that what they did was "for the good" of the conquered: and it is here that the above-mentioned religion is mostly answerable.

World War I—to use Shikastan nomenclature (otherwise the First Intensive Phase of the Twentieth Century War)—began as a quarrel between the Northwest fringers over colonial spoils. It was distinguished by a savagery that could not be matched by the most backward of barbarians. Also by stupidity: the waste of human life and of the earth's products was, to us onlookers, simply unbelievable, even judged by Shikastan standards. Also by the total inability of the population masses to understand what was going on: propaganda on this scale was tried for the first time, using methods of indoctrination based on the new technologies, and was successful. What the unfortunates were told who had to give up life and property—or at the best, health—for this war, bore no relation at any time to the real facts of the matter; and while of course any local group or culture engaged in war persuades itself according to the exigencies of self-interest, never in Shikastan history, or for that matter on any planet—except for the planets of the Puttioran group—has deception been used on this scale.

This war lasted for nearly five of their years. It ended in a disease that carried off six times as many people as those killed in the actual fighting. This war slaughtered, particularly in the Northwest fringes, a generation of their best young males. But—potentially the worst result—it strengthened the position of the armament industries (mechanical, chemical, and psychological) to a point where from now on it had to be said that these industries dominated the economies and therefore the governments of all the participating nations. Above all, this war barbarized and lowered the already very low level of accepted conduct in what they referred to as "the civilized world"—by which they meant, mostly, the Northwest fringes.

This war, or phase of the Twentieth Century War, laid the bases for the next.

Several areas, because of the suffering caused by the war, exploded into revolution, including a very large area, stretching from the Northwest fringes thousands of miles to the eastern ocean. This period saw the beginning of a way of looking at governments, judged "good" and "bad" not by performance, but by label, by name. The main reason was the deterioration caused by war: one cannot spend years sunk inside false and lying propaganda without one's mental faculties becoming impaired. (This is a fact that is attested to by every one of our emissaries to Shikasta!)

Their mental processes, for reasons not their fault never very impressive, were being rapidly perverted by their own usages of them.

The period between the end of World War I and the beginning of the Second Intensive Phase contained many small wars, some of them for the purpose of testing out the weapons shortly to be employed on a massive scale. As a result of the punitive suffering inflicted on one of the defeated contestants of World War I by the victors, a Dictatorship arose there—a result that might easily have been foreseen. The Isolated Northern Continent, conquered only recently by emigrants from the Northwest fringes, and conquered with the usual disgusting brutality, was on its way to becoming a major power, while the various national areas of the Northwest fringes, weakened by war, fell behind. Frenzied exploitation of the colonized areas, chiefly of Southern Continent I, was intensified to make up for the damages sustained because of the war. As a result, native populations, exploited and oppressed beyond endurance, formed resistance movements of all kinds.

The two great Dictatorships established themselves with total ruthlessness. Both spread ideologies based on the suppression and oppression of whole populations of differing sects, opinions, religions, local cultures. Both used torture on a mass scale. Both had followings all over the world, and these Dictatorships, and their followers, saw each other as enemies, as totally different, as wicked and contemptible—while they behaved in exactly the same way.

The time gap between the end of World War I and the beginning of World War II was twenty years.

Here we must emphasize that most of the inhabitants of Shikasta were not aware that they were living through what would be seen as a hundred years' war, the century that would bring their planet to almost total destruction. We make a point of this, because it is nearly impossible for people with whole minds—those who have had the good fortune to live (and we must never forget that it is a question of our good fortune) within the full benefits of the substance-of-we-feeling—it is nearly impossible, we stress, to understand the mentation of Shikastans. With the world's cultures being ravaged and destroyed, from end to end, by viciously inappropriate technologies, with wars raging everywhere, with whole populations being wiped out, and deliberately, for the benefit of ruling castes, with the wealth of every nation being used almost entirely for war, for preparations for war, propaganda for war, research for war; with the general levels of decency and honesty visibly vanishing, with corruption everywhere—with all this, living in a nightmare of dissolution, was it really possible, it may be asked, for these poor creatures to believe that "on the whole" all was well?

The reply is—yes. Particularly, of course, for those already possessed of wealth or comfort—a minority; but even those millions, those billions, the ever-increasing hungry and cold and unbefriended, for these, too, it was possible to live from meal to scant meal, from one moment of warmth to the next.

Those who were stirred to "do something about it" were nearly all in the toils of one of the ideologies which were the same in performance, but so different in self-description. These, the active, scurried about like my unfortunate friend Taufiq, making speeches, talking, engaged in interminable processes that involved groups sitting around exchanging information and making statements of good intent, and always in the name of the masses, those desperate, frightened, bemused populations who knew that everything was wrong but believed that somehow, somewhere, things would come right.

It is not too much to say that in a country devastated by war, lying in ruins, poisoned, in a landscape blackened and charred under skies low with smoke, a Shikastan was capable of making a shelter out of broken bricks and fragments of metal, cooking himself a rat and drinking water from a puddle that of course tasted of oil and thinking, "Well, this isn't too bad after all. . . ."

World War II lasted five years, and was incomparably worse in every way than the first. All the features of the first were present in the second, developed. The waste of human life now extended to mass extermination of civilian populations. Cities were totally destroyed. Agriculture was ruined over enormous areas. Again the armament industries flourished, and this finally established them as the real rulers of every geographical area. Above all, the worst wounds were inflicted in the very substance, the deepest minds, of the people themselves. Propaganda in every area, by every group, was totally unscrupulous, vicious, lying—and self-defeating—because in the long run, people could not believe the truth when it came their way. Under the Dictatorships, lies and propaganda *were* the government. The maintenance of the dominance of the colonized parts was by lies and propaganda—these more effective and important than physical force; and the retaliation of the subjugated took the form, first of all and most importantly in influence, of lies and propaganda: this is what they had been taught by their conquerors. This war covered and involved the whole globe—the first war, or phase of the war, involved only part of it: there was no part of Shikasta by the end of World War II left unsubjected to untruth, lies, propaganda.

This war saw, too, the use of weapons that could cause total global destruction: it should go without saying, to the accompaniment of words like democracy, freedom, economic progress.

The degeneration of the already degenerate was accelerated.

By the end of World War II, one of the great Dictatorships was defeated—the same land area as saw the worst defeat in the first war. The Dictatorship which covered so much of the central landmass had been weakened, almost to the point of defeat, but survived, and made a slow, staggering recovery. Another vast area of the central landmass, to the east of this Dictatorship, ended half a century of local wars, civil wars, suffering, and over a century of exploitation and invasion by the Northwest fringes by turning to Dictatorship. The Isolated Northern Continent had been strengthened by the war and was now the major world power. The Northwest fringes on the whole had been severely weakened. They had to let go their grip of their colonies. Impoverished, brutalized—while being, formally, victors—they were no longer world powers. Retreating from these colonies they left behind technology, an idea of society based entirely on physical well-being, physical satisfaction, material accumulation—to cultures who, before encounter with these all-ravaging Northwest fringers, had been infinitely more closely attuned with Canopus than the fringers had ever been.

This period can be—is by some of our scholars—designated *The Age of Ideology*. [For this viewpoint SEE VOL. 3011, SUMMARY CHAPTER.]

The political groupings were all entrenched in bitterly defended ideologies.

The local religions continued, infinitely divided and subdivided, each entrenched in their ideologies.

Science was the most recent ideology. War had immeasurably strengthened it. Its ways of thought, in its beginnings flexible and open, had hardened, as everything must on Shikasta, and scientists, as a whole—we exclude individuals in this area as in all others—were as impervious to real experience as the religionists had ever been. Science, its basic sets of mind, its prejudices, gripped the whole globe and there was no appeal. Just as individuals of our tendencies of mind, our inclinations towards the truth, our "citizens" had had to live under the power and the threat of religions who would use any brutalities to defend their dogmas, so now individuals, with differing inclinations and needs from those tolerated by science had to lead silent or prudent lives, careful of offending the bigotries of the scientific global governing class: in the service of national governments and therefore of war—an invisible global ruling caste, obedient to the warmakers. The industries that made weapons, the armies, the scientists who served them—these could not be easily attacked, since the formal picture of how the globe was run did not include this, the real picture. Never has there been such a totalitarian, all-pervasive, all-powerful governing caste anywhere: and yet the citizens of Shikasta were hardly aware of it, as they mouthed slogans and waited for the deaths by holocaust. They remained unaware of what "their" governments were doing, right up to the end. Each national grouping developed industries, weapons, horrors of all kinds, that the people knew nothing about. If glimpses were caught of these weapons, then government would deny they existed. [SEE *History of Shikasta,* VOLS. 3013, 3014, and CHAPTER 9 this volume, "Use of Moon as Military Base."] There were space probes, space weapons, explorations of planets, use of planets, rivalries over their moon, about which the populations were not told.

And here is the place to say that the mass of the populations, the average individual, were, was, infinitely better, more sane, than those who ruled them: most would have been appalled at what was being done by "their" representatives. It is safe to say that if even a part of what was being kept from them had come to their notice, there would have been mass risings across the globe, massacres of the rulers, riots . . . unfortunately, when peoples are helpless, betrayed, lied to, they possess no weapons but the (useless) ones of rioting, looting, mass murder, invective.

During the years following the end of World War II, there were many "small" wars, some as vicious and extensive as wars in the recent past described as major. The needs of the armament industries, as much as ideology, dictated the form and intensities of these wars. During this period savage exterminations of previously autonomous "primitive" peoples took place, mostly in the Isolated Southern Continent (otherwise known as Southern Continent II). During this period colonial risings were used by all the major powers for their own purposes. During this period psychological methods of warfare and control of civilian populations developed to an extent previously undreamed of.

Here we must attempt to underline another point which it is almost impossible for those with our set of mind to appreciate.

When a war was over, or a phase of war, with its submersion in the barbarous, the savage, the degrading, Shikastans were nearly all able to perform some sort of mental realignment that caused them to "forget." This did not mean that wars were not idols, subjects for pious mental exercises of all sorts. Heroisms and escapes and braveries of local and limited kinds were raised into national preoccupations, which were in fact forms of religion. But this not only did not assist, but prevented, an understanding of how the fabric of cultures had been attacked and destroyed. After each war, a renewed descent into barbarism was sharply visible—but apparently cause and effect were not connected, in the minds of Shikastans.

After World War II, in the Northwest fringes and in the Isolated Northern Continent, corruption, the low level of public life, was obvious. The two "minor" wars conducted by the Isolated Northern Continent reduced its governmental agencies, even those visible and presented to the public inspection, to public scandal. Leaders of the nation were murdered. Bribery, looting, theft, from the top of the pyramids of power to the bottom, were the norm. People were taught to live for their own advancement and the acquisition of goods. Consumption of food, drink, every possible commodity was built into the economic structure of every society. [VOL. 3009, *Economies of Affluence.*] And yet these repulsive symptoms of decay were not seen as direct consequences of the wars that ruled their lives.

During the whole of the Century of Destruction, there were sudden reversals: treaties between nations which had been at war, so that these turned their hostilities on nations only recently allies; secret treaties between nations actually at war; enemies and allies constantly changing positions, proving that the governing factor was in the need for war, as such. During this period every major city in the northern hemisphere lived inside a ring of terror: each had anything up to thirty weapons aimed at it, every one of which could reduce it and its inhabitants to ash in seconds—pointed from artificial satellites in the skies, directed from underwater ships that ceaselessly patrolled the seas, directed from land bases perhaps halfway across the globe. These were controlled by machines which everyone knew were not infallible—and everybody knew that more than once the destruction of cities and areas had been avoided by a "miracle." But the populations were never told how often these "miracles" had taken place—near-lethal accidents between machines in the skies, collisions between machines under the oceans, weapons only *just* not unleashed from the power bases. Looking from outside at this planet it was as if at a totally crazed species.

In large parts of the northern hemisphere was a standard of living that had recently belonged only to emperors and their courts. Particularly in the Isolated Northern Continent, the wealth was a scandal, even to many of their own citizens. Poor people lived there as the rich have done in previous epochs. The continent was heaped with waste, with wreckage, with the spoils of the rest of the world. Around every city, town, even a minor settlement in a desert, rose middens full of discarded goods and food that in other less favored parts of the globe would mean the difference between life and death to millions. Visitors to this continent marveled—but at what people could be taught to believe was their due, and their right.

This dominant culture set the tone and standard for most of Shikasta. For regardless of the ideological label attaching to each national area, they all had in common that technology was the key to all good, and that good was always material increase, gain, comfort, pleasure. The real purposes of life—so long ago perverted, kept alive with such difficulty by us, maintained at such a cost—had been forgotten, were ridiculed by those who had ever heard of them, for distorted inklings of the truth remained in the religions. And all this time the earth was being despoiled. The minerals were being ripped out, the fuels wasted, the soils depleted by an improvident and shortsighted agriculture, the animals and plants slaughtered and destroyed, the seas being filled with filth and poison, the atmosphere was corrupted—and always, all the time, the propaganda machines thumped out: more, more, more, drink more, eat more, consume more, discard more—in a frenzy, a mania. These were maddened creatures, and the small voices that rose in protest were not enough to halt the processes that had been set in motion and were sustained by greed. By the lack of substance-of-we-feeling.

But the extreme riches of the northern hemisphere were not distributed evenly among their own populations, and the less favored classes were increasingly in rebellion. The Isolated Northern Continent and the Northwest fringe areas also included large numbers of dark-skinned people brought in originally as cheap labor to do jobs disdained by the whites—and while these did gain, to an extent, some of the general affluence, it could be said that looking at Shikasta as a whole, it was the white-skinned that did well, the dark-skinned poorly.

And this *was* said, of course, more and more loudly by the dark-skinned, who hated the white-skinned exploiters as perhaps conquerors have never before been hated.

Inside each national area everywhere, north and south, east and west, discontent grew. This was not only because of the gap between the well-off and the poor, but because their way of life, where augmenting consumption was the only criterion, increasingly saddened and depressed their real selves, their hidden selves, which were unfed, were ignored, were starved, were lied to, by almost every agency around them, by every authority they had been taught to, but could not, respect.

Increasingly the two main southern continents were torn by wars and disorders of every kind—sometimes civil wars between blacks, sometimes between blacks and remnants of the old white oppression, and between rival sects and juntas and power groups. Local dictators abounded. Vast territories were denuded of forests, species of animals destroyed, tribes murdered or dispersed. . . .

War. Civil War. Murder. Torture. Exploitation. Oppression and suppression. And always lies, lies, lies. Always in the name of progress, and equality and development and democracy.

The main ideology all over Shikasta was now variations on this theme of economic development, justice, equality, democracy.

Not for the first time in the miserable story of this terrible century, this particular ideology—economic justice, equality, democracy, and the rest—took power at a time when the economy of an area was at its most disrupted: the Northwest fringes became dominated by governments "of the left," which presided over a descent into chaos and misery.

The formerly exploited areas of the world delighted in this fall of their former persecutors, their tormentors—the race that had enslaved them, enserfed them, stolen from them, above all, despised them because of their skin color and destroyed their indigenous cultures now at last beginning to be understood and valued . . . but too late, for they had been destroyed by the white race and its technologies.

There was no one to rescue the Northwest fringes, in the grip of grindingly repetitive, dogmatic Dictatorships, all unable to solve the problems they had inherited—the worst and chief one being that the empires that had brought wealth had not only collapsed, leaving them in a vacuum, but had left behind false and unreal ideas of what they were, their importance in the global scale. Revenge played its part, not an inconsiderable part, in what was happening.

Chaos ruled. Chaos economic, mental, spiritual—I use this word in its exact, Canopean sense—ruled while the propaganda roared and blared from loudspeaker, radio, television.

The time of the epidemics and diseases, the time of famine and mass deaths had come.

On the main landmass two great Powers were in mortal combat. The Dictatorship that had come into being at the end of World War I, in the center, and the Dictatorship that had taken hold of the eastern areas now drew into their conflict most of Shikasta, directly or indirectly. The younger Dictatorship was stronger. The older one was already in decline, its empire fraying away, its populations more and more in revolt or sullen, its ruling class increasingly remote from its people—processes of growth and decay that had in the past taken a couple of centuries now were accomplished in a few decades. This Dictatorship was not able to withstand the advance of the eastern Dictatorship whose populations were bursting its boundaries. These masses overran a good part of the older Dictatorship, and then overran, too, the Northwest fringes, in the name of a superior ideology—though in fact this was but a version of the predominating ideology of the Northwest fringes. The new masters were clever, adroit, intelligent; they foresaw for themselves the dominance of all the main landmass of Shikasta, and the continuance of that dominance.

But meanwhile the armaments piled up, up, up. . . .

The war began in error. A mechanism went wrong, and major cities were blasted into death-giving dusts. That something of this kind was bound to happen had been plentifully forecast by technicians of all countries . . . but the Shammat influences were too strong.

In a short time, nearly the whole of the northern hemisphere was in ruins. Very different, these, from the ruins of the second war, cities which were rapidly rebuilt. No, these ruins were uninhabitable, the earth around them poisoned.

Weapons that had been kept secret now filled the skies, and the dying survivors, staggering and weeping and vomiting in their ruins, lifted their eyes to watch titanic battles being fought, and with their last breaths muttered of "Gods" and "Devils" and "Angels" and "Hell."

Underground were shelters, sealed against radiation, poisons, chemical influences, deadly sound impulses, death rays. They had been built for the ruling classes. In these a few did survive.

In remote areas, islands, places sheltered by chance, a few people survived.

The populations of all the southern continents and islands were also affected by pestilence, by radiations, by soil and water contamination, and were much reduced.

Within a couple of decades, of the billions upon billions of Shikasta perhaps one percent remained. The substance-of-we-feeling, previously shared among these multitudes, was now enough to sustain, and keep them all sweet, and whole, and healthy.

The inhabitants of Shikasta, restored to themselves, looked about, could not believe what they saw—and wondered *why* they had been mad.

FROM

# *Shikasta*

### INDIVIDUAL FIVE *(Terrorist Type 12)*

X was the son of rich parents, business people who had made a fortune through armaments and industries associated with war: World War I provided the basis of this fortune. His parents had both been married several times, he had known no family life, had been emotionally self-sufficient since a small child. He spoke many languages, could claim citizenship from several countries. Was he Italian, German, Jewish, Armenian, Egyptian? He was any one of these, at his convenience.

A man of talent and resources, he could have become an efficient part of the machinery of death that was his inheritance, but he would not, could not, be any man's heir.

He was fifteen when he brought off several coups of blackmail—emotional legerdemain—among the ramifications of his several families' businesses. These showed the capacity to analyze; a cold farsightedness, an indifference to personal feelings. He was one of those unable to separate an individual from her, his circumstances. The man who was his real father (though he did not think of him as such, claimed a man met half a dozen times almost casually, whose conversation had illuminated his life, as "father"), this ordinary, harassed, anxious man, who died in middle age of a heart attack, one of the richest men in the world, was seen by him as a monster, because of the circumstances he had been born into. X had never questioned this attitude: could not. For him, a man or a woman *was* his, her circumstances, actions. Thus guilt was ruled out for him; it was a word he could not understand, not even by the processes of imaginative effort. He had never made the attempt to understand the people of his upbringing: they were all rotten, evil. His own milieu, the "network," was his family.

Meeting The Brand was important to him. He was twelve years younger than she was. He studied her adventures with the total absorption others might bring to "God," or some absolute.

First there had been that casually met man whose ruthless utterances seemed to him the essence of wisdom. Then there was The Brand.

When they had sexual relations—almost at once, since for her sex was an appetite to be fed, and no more—he felt confirmed in his deepest sense of himself: the cold efficiency of the business, never far from perversity, seemed to him a statement of what life was.

He had never felt warmth for any human being, only admiration, a determination to understand excellence, as he defined it.

He did not want, or claim, attention from the public or the press or any propaganda instrument: the world was contemptible to him. But when he had pulled off, with or without the "network" (he often worked alone, or with The Brand), a coup that was always inside the empire of one of his families, he would leave his mark, so that they should know whom they had to thank: an X, like that of an illiterate.

In bed with The Brand, he would trace an X over the raised pattern of the concentration camp number on her forearm, particularly in orgiastic moments.

He was never caught. Later, he joined one of the international police forces that helped to govern Shikasta in its last days.

### INDIVIDUAL SIX *(Terrorist Type 8)*

The parents of this individual were in camps of various kinds throughout World War II. The father was Jewish. That they survived at all was "impossible." There are thousands of documents testifying to these "impossible" survivals, each one a history of dedication to survival, inner strength, cunning, courage—and luck. These two did not leave the domain of the camps—they were in a forced labor camp in the eastern part of the Northwest fringes for the last part of the war—until nearly five years after the war ended. There was no place for them. By then the individual who concerns us here had been born, into conditions of near starvation, and cold: *impossible* conditions. He was puny, damaged, but was able to function. There were no siblings: the parents' vitality had been exhausted by the business of setting themselves up, with the aid of official charitable organizations, as a family unit in a small town where the father became an industrial worker. They were frugal, careful, wary, husbanding every resource: people such as these understand, above all, what things cost, what life costs. Their love for the child was gratitude for continued existence: nothing unthinking, animal, instinctive, about this love. He was to them something that had been rescued—impossibly—from disaster.

The parents did not make friends easily: their existence had cut them off from the people around them, all of whom had been reduced to the edge of extinction by the war—but few had been in the camps. The parents did not often speak about their years in the camps, but when they did, what they said took hold of the child with the strength of an alternative vision. What did these two rooms they lived in, poor, but warm and safe, have to do with that nightmare his parents spoke of? Sometimes at this time of life, youngsters in the grip of glandular upheaval crystallize in opposition to their parents with a vigor that preserves opposition for the rest of their lives.

This boy looked at his parents, and was appalled. *How was it possible?* was his thought.

I digress here to the incredulity referred to in my report on Individual Three, who spent years examining the deprivations of the people around him with: *How is it possible? I simply don't believe it!* Meaning partly: Why do they put up with it? Meaning, too: That human beings should treat each other like this? I don't believe it!

In Individual Six this incredulity was wider by far than that of Individual Three, who saw the streets around him, then a town, and could only with difficulty envisage the Northwest fringes, let alone the central landmass, the world: it took years of experience in the war to enlarge his boundaries.

But Individual Six felt *himself* to be the war, and the war had been a global event: had printed his vision of life as a system of interlocking, interacting processes.

From the time he first began to think for himself, he was unable to see the developments of events as the generation before his had done. There was no such thing as a "guilty nation," any more than there could be defeated or victorious nations. A single nation could not be solely responsible for what it did, since groups of nations were a whole, interacting as a whole. The geographical area called "Germany"—it had become another name for wickedness—could not be responsible entirely for the mass murders and brutalities it had perpetrated: how could it be, when one day with the facts in a library was enough to show that "World War II" was multicaused, an expression of the whole of the Northwest fringes, a development of "World War I." *How was it possible* that these old people saw things in this isolated piecemeal way, like children, or like idiots! They were simple-minded. They were stupid!

Above all, *they did not seem to have any idea at all of what they were like.*

A boy of fifteen imposed on himself a regime completely distressing to his parents. He did not have a room of his own, but there was a folding bed in the kitchen, and this he covered with what they had been given in the camps: a single, thin, dirty blanket. He shaved his head, and kept it shaved. On one day a week he ate only the diet provided in the camp during the final days of the war: hot greasy water, potato peelings, scraps from rubbish bins. He was careful, not to say obsessed, in getting his "food" for himself, and put the filthy stuff on the table at mealtimes, eating reverently—a sacrament. Meanwhile, his parents ate their frugal meals; their damaged stomachs could not absorb normal amounts of food. He read to them passages from biographies, accounts of conditions in camps, the negotiations or lack of them that led to "World War II"—always stressing multicause and effect; if that nation had done that, then this would not have happened. If such and such warnings had been heeded . . . that step taken . . . that statesman listened to . . .

For these poor people it was as if a nightmare they had escaped from only by a miracle had returned and was taking over their lives. They had made for themselves a little sheltered place, where they could believe themselves kept safe, because evil was the property of that other place, or that other nation; wickedness was contained in the past, in history—terror might come again, but thank God, that would be the future, and by then with luck, they would be dead and safe . . . and now their refuge was being broken open, not by "history" or "the future," but by this precious child of theirs, who was all they had been able to bring out from the holocaust.

The father begged him to take his truths elsewhere.

"Are they true or not?" the youngster challenged.

"Yes . . . no . . . I don't care, for *God's* sake . . ."

"You don't care!"

"Your mother . . . you don't know what she had to put up with, go easy on her!"

The boy added to his discipline by wearing, on certain days of the week, dirty rags and tatters. All over the walls of the kitchen, which after all was the only room he had, and he was entitled to consider them his, were a thousand pictures of the concentration camps, but not only those of the Northwest fringes: soon the pictured record of the atrocious treatment of man by man covered the walls.

He sat quiet at the table, his father and mother hastily eating their meal in a silence that was a prayer he would not "begin again"—and then he *would* begin again, reciting facts, figures, litanies of destruction, deaths by ill treatment and torture in communist countries, non-communist countries, any country anywhere.

[SEE *History of Shikasta,* VOL. 3011, *The Age of Ideology,* "Self-Portraits of Nations." Geographical areas, or temporary associations of peoples for the purposes of defense or aggression. Such an entity capable of believing itself different, better, more "civilized" than another, when in fact to an outside view there is nothing to choose between them. And VOL. 3010, *Psychology of the Masses,* "Self-Protective Mechanisms."]

Through a series of chances, it had become impossible for this youngster to identify himself with national myths and self-flatteries. He literally could not understand how others did. He believed that they must be pretending, or were being willfully cowardly. He was of that generation—part of a generation—who could not see a newspaper except as a screen for lies, automatically translated any television newscast or documentary into what the truth *probably* was, reminded himself all the time, as a religious person might remind himself of the wiles of the devil, that what was being fed to the world or nation about any event was by definition bound to be only a small part of real information, knew that at no time, anywhere, was the population of a country told the truth: facts about events trickled into general consciousness much later, if ever.

All this was good, was a step towards freedom from the miasmas of Shikasta.

But it was useless to him, for he had no kindness.

He was intolerable to his parents. The mother, still only a middle-aged woman by ordinary reckoning, seemed old to herself, became ill, had a heart attack. The father remonstrated, pleaded, even used words like: Spare her, spare us.

The stern avenging angel of righteousness remained in the meager rooms that held the family, his eyes fixed in unbelieving dislike on his parents: How is it possible that you are like this!

At last his father said to him that if he could not treat his mother—"Yes, and me too! I admit it!"—more gently, then he must leave home.

The boy was sixteen. They are throwing me out! he exulted, for everything he knew was being confirmed.

He found himself a room in the home of a school friend, and thereafter did not see his parents.

At school he set himself to be an unsettling presence. It was an ordinary small-town school, providing nothing remarkable for its pupils in the way of teachers and teachings. He sat at the back of a class and emanated a punishing dislike, arms folded, legs stretched to one side, maintaining a steady unblinking stare first at one target, and then at another. He would rise to his feet, first having most correctly held his hand up to ask permission: "Is it not a fact that . . . ? Are you perhaps unaware . . . ? You are of course familiar with Government Report No. XYZ . . . ? I take it that such and such a book will be part of the curriculum for this subject? No? But how can that be possible?"

He was feared by the staff, and by most of the pupils, but some of these admired him. At this time, when every kind of extreme political group tormented the authorities, and "the youth" was by definition a threat, he had not reached his seventeenth year when his name was known to the police, for the headmaster had mentioned him to them with the air of one covering himself against future probabilities.

He drifted towards various groups, first right-wing and unaffiliated to a political party, then fell in with a left-wing revolutionary group. But this had very specific allegiances: this country was good, that bad, this creed abhorrent, this one "correct." Again he was saying: "But surely you must be aware . . . ? Have you not read . . . ? Don't you know that . . . ?" It was clear that he would have to form his own group, but he was in no hurry. To keep himself he pilfered, and took part in various petty crimes. He was indifferent about how he came by a couple of months in a flat somewhere, or free meals for a week, or a girlfriend. He was completely, even amiably, amoral. Accused of some lie or theft he might allow himself a smile that commented unfavorably on everything around him. His reputation among the political groups was still unformed, but on the whole he was seen as clever, as skillful at surviving in ways respected by them, but careless.

When his group of a dozen young men and women crystallized out finally it was not on the basis of any particular political creed. Everyone had been formed by experiences of emotional or physical deprivation, had been directly affected by war. None could do anything but fix the world with a cold, hating eye: *This is what you are like.* They did not dream of utopias in the future: their imaginations were not tuned to the future at all, unlike those of previous revolutionaries or religionists: it was not that "next year, or in the next decade, or next century, we create paradise on earth . . . ," only, "*This* is what you are like." When this hypocritical, lying, miserably stupid system was done away with, then everyone would be able to see. . . .

It was their task to expose the system for what it was.

But they had a faith, and no program. They had the truth—but what to do with it? They had a vocabulary, but no language.

They watched the exploits of guerrilla groups, the deeds of the terrorists.

They saw that what was needed was to highlight situations, events.

They staged the kidnapping of a certain politician who had been involved in some transaction they disapproved of, demanding the release of a man in prison who seemed to them innocent. They detailed the reasons why this imprisoned man was innocent, and when he was not released, shot their hostage and left him in the town square. *This is what you are like* was what they felt, as they murdered him, meaning, the world.

The murder had not been planned. The details of the kidnapping had been adequately worked out, but they had not expected they would kill the politician, had half believed that the authorities would hand over their "innocent." There was something careless, unthought-out about the thing, and several of the members of the group demanded a more "serious" approach, analyses, reconsideration.

Our Individual Six listened to them, with his characteristic careless smile, but his black eyes deadly. "Of course, what else can be expected from people like you?" he was communicating.

Two of the protesting individuals met with "accidents" in the next few days, and he now commanded a group that did not think of him as "careless"—or not as they had done previously.

There were nine of them, three women.

One of the women thought of herself as "his," but he refused to accept this view of the situation. They had group sex, in every sort of combination. It was violent, ingenious, employing drugs and weapons of various kinds. Sticks of gelignite, for instance. Four of the group blew themselves up in an orgy. He did not recruit others.

It was observed by the four remaining that he had enjoyed the publicity. He insisted on staging a "funeral service" which, although police did not know which group had been responsible for this minor massacre, was asking for notice and arrest. Elegies for the dead, poems, drawings of a heroic nature were left in the warehouse where the "socialist requiem" was held.

By then it had occurred to them that he was mad, but it was too late for any of them to leave the group.

They staged another kidnapping. The carelessness of it amounted to contempt, and they were caught and put on trial. It was a trial that undermined the country, because of their contempt for the law, for legal processes.

At that time, throughout the Northwest fringes, almost every person regarded the processes of the law as a frail—the frailest possible—barrier between themselves and a total brutal anarchy.

Everyone knew that "civilization" depended on the most fragile supports. The view of the older people of what was happening in the world was no less fearful, in its way, than that of the young ones like Individual Six and his group, or of the other terrorists, but it was opposite in effect. They knew that the slightest pressure, even an accident or something unintended, could bring down the entire fabric . . . and here were these madmen, these young idiots, prepared to risk everything—more, *intending* to bring it down, *wanting* to destroy and waste. If people like Individual Six "could not believe it," then ordinary citizens "could not believe it" either: they never did understand each other.

When the five were brought to trial and stood in the dock loaded with chains, and behind barriers of extra bars, they reached their fulfillment, the apex of achievement.

"This is what you are like," they were saying to the world. "These brutal chains, these bars, the fact that you will give us sentences that will keep us behind bars for the rest of our lives—this is what *you* are like! Regard your mirror, in us!"

In prison, and in court, they were elated, victorious, singing and laughing, as if at a festival.

About a year after sentence, Individual Six and two others escaped. They went their separate ways. Individual Six got fat, wore a wig, and acquired a correct clerkly appearance. He did not contact either the escaped members of his group or those in prison. He hardly thought of them: that was the past!

He deliberately courted danger. He would stand chatting to policemen on the street. He went into police stations to report minor crimes, such as the theft of a bicycle. He was arrested for speeding. He actually appeared in court on one charge. All this with a secret glowing contempt: this is what you are like, stupid, incompetent . . .

He went back to the town he had grown up in, and got an undemanding job, and made a life for himself that lacked any concealment except for the change of name and appearance. People recognized him, and he was talked about. Knowing this gave him pleasure.

His father was now in an institution for the elderly and incapacitated, his mother having died, and, hearing his son was in town, he took to hanging about the streets in the hope of seeing him. He did, but Individual Six waved his hand in a jolly, friendly, don't-bother-me-now gesture, and walked on.

He was expecting from his inevitable rearrest a trial of the same degree of publicity as his first. He wanted that moment when he would stand, chained, like a dog, behind double bars. But when he was arrested, he was sent back to jail to serve his sentence.

An elation, a lunacy—which had been carrying him up, up, up, from the moment of truth when he had first seen what the world was like, had "had his eyes opened"—suddenly dissolved, and he committed suicide.

### INDIVIDUAL SEVEN (*Terrorist Type 5*)

This was a child of rich parents, manufacturers of an internationally known household commodity of no use whatsoever, contributing nothing except to the economic imperative: thou shalt consume.

She had a brother, but as they were at different schools and it was not thought important that they should meet, she had little physical or emotional contact with him after early childhood.

She was unhappy, unnurtured, without knowing what was wrong with her. When she reached adolescence she saw there was no central place in the family, no place where responsibility was taken: no father, or mother, or brother—who never had any other destiny but to be his father's heir—imposed themselves on circumstances. They were passive in the face of events, ideas, fashions, expected conduct. When she had understood it—and she could not believe how she had taken so long—she saw that she was the only one of her family who thought like this. It occurred to none that it was ever possible to say "no." She saw them and herself as bits of paper or refuse blown along streets.

She did not hate them. She did not despise them. She found them irrelevant.

She went to university for three years. There she enjoyed the double life of such young people: democratic and frugal in the university, and the luxuriousness of an indulged minority to whom everything was possible at home.

She was not interested in what she was taught, only in whom she met. She drifted in and out of political sects, all on the left. She used in them the cult vocabulary obligatory in those circles, the same in all of them—and they might very well be enemies at various times.

What they all had in common was that "the system" was doomed. And would be replaced by people like themselves, who were different.

These groups, and there were hundreds of them in the Northwest fringes—we are not now considering other parts of the world—were free to make up their own programs, frameworks of ideas, exactly as they liked, without reference to objective reality. (This girl never saw for instance that during her years among the groups she was as passively accepting as she had ever been in her family.) [SEE *History of Shikasta,* VOL. 3011, *The Age of Ideology,* "Pathology of Political Groups."]

From the time the dominant religions lost their grip not only in the Northwest fringes, but everywhere throughout Shikasta, there was a recurrent phenomenon among young people: as they came to young adulthood and saw their immediate predecessors with the cold unliking eye that was the result of the breakdown of the culture into barbarism, groups of them would suddenly, struck for the first time by "truth," reject everything around them and seek in political ideology (emotionally this was of course identical to the reaction of groups that continuously formed and re-formed under the religious tyrannies) solutions to their situation, always seen as new-minted with themselves. Such a group would come into existence overnight, struck by a vision of the world believed by them to be entirely original, and within days they would have framed a philosophy, a code of conduct, lists of enemies and allies, personal, intergroup, national, and international. Inside a cocoon of righteousness, for the essence of it was that they were in the right, these young people would live for weeks, months, even years. And then the group would subdivide. Exactly as a stem branches, lightning branches, cells divide. But their emotional identification with the group was such that it prohibited any examination of the dynamics which must operate in groups. While studies by psychologists, researchers of all kinds, the examiners of the mechanics of society, became every day more intelligent, comprehensive, accurate, these conclusions were never applied to political groups—any more than it had ever been possible to apply a rational eye to religious behavior while the religions maintained tyrannies, or for religious groups to apply such ideas to themselves. Politics had joined the realm of the sacred—the tabooed. The slightest examination of history showed that every group without exception was bound to divide and subdivide like amoeba, and could not help doing this, but when it happened it was always to the accompaniment of cries of "traitor," "treachery," "sedition," and similar mindless noises. For the member of any such group to suggest that the laws known (in other areas) must be operating here, was treachery; and such a person would be instantly flung out, exactly as had happened inside religions and religious groups, with curses and violent denunciations and emotionalism—not to mention physical torture or even death. Thus it came about that in this infinitely subdivided society, where different sets of ideas could exist side by side without their affecting each other—or at least not for long periods—the mechanisms like parliaments, councils, political parties, groups championing minority ideas, could remain unexamined, tabooed from examination of a cool rational sort, while in another area of the society, psychologists and sociologists could be receiving awards and recognition for work, which were it to be applied, would destroy this structure entirely.

When Individual Seven left university, nothing she had learned there seemed of any relevance to her. Her family expected her to marry a man like her father or her brother, or to take a job of an unchallenging kind. It seemed to her, suddenly, that she was nothing at all, and nothing of interest lay ahead of her.

This was a time when "demonstrations" took place continually. The populace was always taking to the streets to shout out the demands of the hour.

She had taken part in demonstrations at university, and, looking back on them, it seemed to her that during the hours of running and chanting, of shouting and singing, in great crowds, she had been more alive and feeling than ever in her entire life.

She took to slipping away from home when there were demonstrations, for a few hours of intoxication. It did not matter what the occasion was, or the cause. Then, by chance, she found herself at the front of a crowd fighting the police, and soon she was engaged in a hand-to-hand struggle with a policeman, a young man who grabbed her, called her insulting names, and tossed her like a bundle of rags into the arms of another, who threw her back. She screamed and struggled, and she was dragged away from the police like a trophy and found herself with a young man whose name she knew as "a leader."

He was a common type of that time: narrow-minded, ill-informed, dogmatic, humorless—a fanatic who could exist only in a group. She admired him completely and without reservation, and had sex with him that night before returning home. He was indifferent to her, but made a favor of it.

She now set herself to win this youth. She wanted to be "his woman." He was flattered when it became known that this girl was the daughter of one of the city's—no, the Northwest fringes'—rich families. But he was stern, even brutal with her, making it a test of her devotion to the cause (and himself, for he saw these as the same) that she should engage herself more and more in dangerous activity. This was not the serious, well-planned type of feat, or coup planned by terrorists type 12, or 3. He demanded of her that she should be with him in the forefront of demonstrations, and fling herself at lines of police, that she should shout and scream louder than the other girls, that she should struggle in the hands of the police, who in fact enjoyed these hysterical women. He was demanding of her, in fact, an ever-increasing degree of voluntary degradation.

She enjoyed it. More and more her life was spent dealing with the police. He was always being arrested, and she was in and out of police stations standing bail, or going with him in police wagons, or handing out leaflets about him and associates. These activities came to the notice of her parents, but after consultation with other parents, they consoled themselves with the formula: young people will be young people. She was furious at their attitude: she was not being taken seriously. Her lover took her seriously. So did the police. She allowed herself to be arrested and spent some days in jail. Once—twice—three times. And then her parents insisted on bailing her out and so she was always leaving "her man" and her comrades in police cells while she was being driven home behind a chauffeur in one of the family cars.

She changed her name, and left home, insisting that she should live with her man. Which meant, a group of twelve or so young people. She accepted everything, living in a filthy hovel that had been condemned years before. She exulted in the discomfort, the dirt. She found herself cooking and cleaning and waiting on her man and his friends. They took a certain pleasure in this, because of her background, but she felt she was taken seriously, even that she was being forgiven.

Her parents found her, came after her, and she sent them away. They insisted on opening bank accounts for her, dispatching messengers with cash, food, artifacts of all kinds, clothes. They were giving her what they had always given her—*things*.

Her lover would sit, legs astraddle on a hard chair, arms folded on the back of it, watching her with a cold sarcastic smile, waiting to see what she would do.

She did not value what she knew had cost her parents nothing enough to return them: but dedicated all these things, and the money, to "the cause."

Her lover was indifferent. That they eat anything pleasant, wear anything attractive, care about being warm or comfortable, seemed to him contemptible. He and his cronies discussed her, her class position, her economic position, her psychology, at length, shuffling and reshuffling the jargon of the left-wing phrase books. She listened feeling unworthy, but taken seriously.

He demanded of her that at the next "demo" she should seriously assault a policeman. She did it without question: never had she felt so fulfilled. She was three months in prison, where her lover visited her once. He visited others more often. Why? she humbly wondered. Not all of them were of the poor and the ignorant; one of his associates was in fact quite well-off, and educated. But she was very rich, yes, that must be it. They were all more worthy than she was. In prison, among the other prisoners, most of them unpolitical, she radiated a smiling unalterable conviction which manifested itself as humility. She was always doing things no one else would do. Dirty tasks and punishment were food and drink to her. The prisoners christened her, disgusted, the Saint; but she took it as a compliment. "I am trying to be worthy to become a real member of—" and she supplied the name of her political group. "To become a real socialist one has to suffer and aspire."

When she came out, her man was living with another woman. She accepted it: of course it was because she was not good enough. She served them. She waited on them. She crouched on the floor outside the room her lover and the woman were wrapped together in, comparing herself to a dog, glorying in her abasement, and she muttered, like the phrases of a rosary, I will be worthy, I will overcome, I will show them, I will . . . and so on.

She took a kitchen knife to the next "demo" and did not even look to see if it was sharpened: the gesture of carrying it was enough. Intoxicated, lifted above herself, she fought and struggled, a Valkyrie with flying dirty blond hair, reddened blue eyes, a fixed, ugly smile. (In her family she had been noticed for her "sweet gentle look.") She attacked policemen with her fists, and then took out the—as it happened—blunt knife, and hacked about her with it. But she was not being arrested. Others were. There was such a disproportion between the atmosphere, and even the purpose, of this demonstration, and her appearance and her frenzy, that the police were puzzled by her. A senior official sent word around that she was not to be arrested: she was clearly unbalanced. Ecstatic with renewed effort, she yelled and waved the knife about, but perceived that the demonstration was ending and people streaming home. *She was not being taken seriously.* She was standing watching the arrested being piled into the police vans like a child turned away from a party, the knife held in her hand as if she were intending to chop meat or vegetables with it.

A group of people had been watching her: not only this day, but at previous demonstrations.

A girl standing like a heroic statue on the edge of the pavement with the knife at the ready in her hand, hair falling bedraggled round a swollen and reddened face, weeping tears of angry disappointment, saw in front of her a man waiting for her to notice him. He had a smile which she thought *kind.* His eyes were "stern" and "penetrating": he understood her emotional type very well.

"I think you should come with me," he suggested.

"Why?" said she, all belligerence, which nevertheless suggested a readiness to obey.

"You can be of use."

She automatically took a step towards him, but stopped herself, confused.

"What to?"

"You can be of use to socialism."

Briefly onto her face flitted the expression that means: You can't get me as easily as that! while phrases from the *vocabulary* whirled through her brain.

"Your particular capacities and qualities are just what are needed," he said.

She went with him.

This group was in a large shabby flat on the outskirts of the city, a workman's home, one of the refuges of these twelve young women and men whose leader had accosted her. While the circumstances—poverty made worse, and emphasized—of her previous living place had been of emotional necessity to the work of self-definition of her previous group, these people were indifferent to how they lived, and moved from opulence, to discomfort, to middle-class comfort in the space of a day, as necessary, without making anything of what they were surrounded by. The girl adapted herself at once. Although she had been lying, exulting in her misery, outside the door of her lover and his new woman, for days, now she hardly thought of that life—*where she had not been appreciated.* She did not immediately see what was to be asked of her, but was patient, obedient, gentle, doing any task that suggested itself.

These new comrades were engaged in planning some coup, but she was not told what. Soon she was taken to yet another flat, where she had not been before, and told that she was to strip and examine a young woman brought in for "questioning." This girl was in fact an accomplice, but just before the "examination" began, Individual Seven was told that "this one was a particularly hard case" and that "there was no point in using kid gloves on her."

Alone with her victim, who seemed dazed and demoralized, the girl felt herself uplifted by the same familiar and longed-for elation of her combats with the police, the atmosphere of danger. She "examined" the captive, who, it seemed to her, had every mark of disgusting stupidity and corruption. It was not far off torture, and she enjoyed it.

She was complimented on the job she had done by this group of severe, serious, responsible young revolutionaries. Thus they described themselves. But she had not yet heard them define their particular creed or commitment. And in fact she was never to hear it.

She was told not to go out, to keep herself hidden: she was too valuable to risk. When the group moved, she was always blindfolded. She accepted this with a humble joy: it must be necessary.

This group added to the kidnapping of rich or well-known individuals a refinement, which was the kidnapping and torture, or threat of torture, of their relatives—mistresses, sisters, wives, daughters. Always women. The girl was given the task of torturing, first in minor ways, and then comprehensively, one young woman after another.

She looked forward to it. She had accepted her situation. Moments of disquiet were silenced with: They have more experience than I have, they are better than I am, and it must be necessary.

Reflecting that she did not know their allegiances, she was comforted by the phrases she was familiar with, and had been ever since—as she put it—she had become politically mature.

At moments when sharp pleasure held her in its power either because of some encounter just over or one promised her, she wondered if perhaps she had been physically drugged: whether these new friends of hers were feeding her stimulants, so alive did she feel, so vital and full of energy.

This group lasted three years before it was taken by the police, and the girl committed suicide when it was evident she could not avoid arrest. The impulse behind this act was a continuation of their dictate that she must not ever be visible—go out, be seen, or even know where she was. She felt that under torture—she now lived in her mind in a world where torture was not merely possible but inevitable—she would "betray them." Her suicide was, therefore, in her own eyes, an act of heroism and self-sacrifice in the service of socialism.

It will have been noted that none of the individuals categorized here was among those identified with a particular injustice, such as suffering under an arbitrary or tyrannous power, or being deprived of a country, or persecuted for being one of a despised or subjugated race, or kept in poverty by the thoughtless, the careless, or the cruel.

I could not contact the next individual through the Giants, or anything like them. I had been looking for someone suitable, and during my trips in and out of Shikasta, I had seen an old friend, Ranee, waiting on the margins of Zone Six at that place where the lines form for their chance of re-entry. I had told her that I needed very soon to spend time with her, and why. Now, searching up and down the lines I could not see her, and saw, too, that they were shorter and more sparse. I heard that there were rumors of an emergency, of frightful danger, in Zone Six, and all those able to understand had left to help people escape. The souls remaining in the lines were too fixed on their hope of an early re-entry, crowding forward each time the gates opened, jostling each other, their eyes only for the gates, and I could not get anything more out of them.

I walked on past them into the scrub and thin grasses of the high plateau, quite alone, as evening came on. I felt uneasy, and thought first this was because I had been told there was danger, but soon the sense of threat was so strong that I left the scrublands and climbed a small ridge, scrambling from rock to rock upwards, in the dark. I set my back to a small cliff, and my face to where I could expect the dawn. It was silent. But not completely silent. I could hear a soft whispering, like a sea . . . a sea where no sea was, or could be. The stars were crowding bright and thick, and their dim light showed low bushes and outcrops of stone. Nothing to account for this sound, which I could not remember ever hearing before. Yet it whispered danger, danger, and I stayed where I was, turning myself about and sensing and peering, like an animal alerted to some menace it cannot understand. When the light came into the sky and the stars went, the sound was there, and stronger. I descended from the ridge, and walked on, soon coming to the desert's edge, where I could hear the steady sibilant hissing. Yet there was no wind to blow the sand. Everything was quite still, and there was a small sweetness of dew rising from around my feet as I set them down on a crunchy surface. I walked on, every step slower, for all my senses shouted warnings at me. I kept close to my right the low ridge I had used for shelter the night before. It ran on in front of me until it joined black jagged peaks far ahead that were somber and even sinister in the cool grey dawn. The rustling voice of the sands grew louder . . . not far from me I saw wisps of sand in the air, which vanished: yet there was no wind! The lower clouds hung dark and motionless, and the higher clouds, all tinted with the dawn, were in packed unmoving masses. A windless landscape and a still sky: and yet the whispering came from everywhere. A small smudge in the air far in front of me enlarged, and close to me the sands seemed to shiver. I left them and again climbed on the ridge, where I turned to look back at where I had been standing. At first, nothing; and then, almost exactly where I had been, I saw the sands shake. They lay still again. But I had not imagined it. At various places now over the plain of sands that lay on the left of the ridge I saw smudges of sand hanging. To the right of the ridge I had not yet looked, not daring to take my eyes away from the place I had been in, for it seemed essential to watch, as if something might pounce out like an animal, if I once removed my gaze. There was no reason in it, but I had to stand fixed there, staring . . . the place where the sands had moved quaked again. They moved, definitely, and stopped. As if an enormous invisible stick had given half a stir . . . the soft whistling filled my ears and I could hear nothing else. I waited. An area I could span with my arms stretched wide was stirred again by the invisible stick: there was the slow, halting movement of a whirlpool, which stopped. Half a mile ahead I believed I could see a spinning underneath one of the air smudges. But I kept my eyes on the birth—for now I knew that this was what I was watching—of the sand whirlpool near to me. Slowly, creakingly, with halts, and new beginnings, the vortex formed, and then at various distances around it, the sand shivered, and lay still, and began again. . . . Then the central place was in a slow regular spin, and grains of sand flung up and off to one side glittered as they fell. So the sun was up, was it? I looked, and saw all the sky in front a wild enraged red, shedding a ruddy glow down onto the gleam of the sands.

The whirlpool was now established, and steadily encompassing more and more of the sands around it, and the places near it where I had noted small movements, each were beginning to circle and subside, then start again as the new subsidiary pools formed. I saw that all the plain was covered with these spots of movement, and the air above them each showed a small cloud that hung there, enlarging but not drifting, because of the lack of wind. And now, with difficulty, I made myself look away from this dreadfully treacherous plain, and I gazed out to my right. Desert again, stretching interminably, and I could see no movement here. The wastes lay quiet and still, inflamed by the wild scarlet of the skies, but then a desert fox came towards me, its soft yellow all aglow, and it trotted into the ridge of rocks and disappeared. Another came. Suddenly I saw that there were many animals in flight from some danger behind them. Far behind them: for I could see no movement in the sands on this side of the ridge, though on the other side all the plain was shaking and quivering between the whirlpools of sand. Far over this solid and ordinary plain, I could see that the sky, now fully light in a clear morning where the reds and pinks rapidly faded, was hung with a low haze, which I now understood.

I had taken in what was happening, was going to happen, and I ran clumsily forward along the rocky ridge, which I believed, or hoped, would not succumb to the movement of the sands, was solidly rooted.

I was looking for refugees from these terrible whirlpools who might have climbed to the safety of the rocks, but believed they were more likely to be on the mountains that still seemed to be such a distance from me. And then I did see a party of five approach, a woman, a man, and two half-grown children, and these were dazed and silly with the dangers they had survived, and could not see me. They were accompanied by someone whose face I knew from the lines at the frontier, and I stopped her and asked what was happening. "Be quick," she said, "there are still people on the sands. But you must be quick"—and she went on along the ridge, calling to her charges to hurry. They were standing with their mouths hanging open, eyes fixed on the shivering and swirling sands of the plain to my left, their right, and seemed unable to hear me. She had to hustle them on, pushing them into movement. Again I ran onwards, clumsily, scrambling and falling over the rocks, and several times passed little groups, each shepherded by a person from the lines. The rescued ones shook and trembled, and stared at the liquid-seeming desert, and had to be continually reminded to move on, and to keep their eyes in front of them.

When at last I reached the beginnings of the mountain peaks, which rose straight up out of the sands, it was not too soon, for I had seen that if the great sands on my right were to dissolve into movement as they had on the other side, the ridge could not stand for long, but must be engulfed. I turned to look back from the mountain and saw that on the one side of the ridge there were no unmoving places left: all that desert was shivering, swirling, dissolving. On the other side, still, things seemed safe, yet, looking over those reaches of sands as far as I could, it was possible to see crowds of hopping, running, flying animals and birds. None looked back, none was panicky or stricken or had lost their senses, but purposefully and carefully picked their way through the dunes and hollows of the sands to the ridge, where they must all be working their way back through the rocks to the plateau I had come from. But from a certain point on that plain of sand, there was no movement of animals at all: I was seeing the last exodus of the refugees, and behind them the sands lay quiet. On the horizons, the dust clouds had risen higher into the cobalt blue of the morning sky.

I was not certain what I should do next. I had not met groups of refugees for some time now. Perhaps everyone had been rescued, there were none left? I went forward up the stony, cracked sides of the mountain, towards the right, and when I reached a small outcrop of young, harsh cracked rocks and dry bushes, I was able to see straight down into the plain where, ahead, suddenly, there were the beginnings of movement, the birth of sand whirlpools. And, at the same time, I saw down there a little bunching of black rocks, and on them two people. They had their backs to me, and they stood staring away across the plain. I seemed to know them. I ran down again towards them, with many thoughts in my mind. One, that a symptom of the shock suffered by these victims was that they were stricken into a condition where they could do nothing but stare, hypnotized, unable to move. Another, that I *could* get to them in time, but whether I could lead them out again was another matter . . . and I was thinking, too, that these were my old friend Ben and my old friend Rilla, together, and at least safe, if marooned.

As I reached the plain of the desert and ran forward I could feel the sands trembling under me. I staggered on, shouting and calling to them, but they did not hear me, or if they did, could not move. When I came up to their little outcrop, a whirlpool had formed not far away, and I jumped up onto the rock they stood on, and shouted, Rilla! Ben! They stood shivering like dogs that have got wet and cold and did not look at me, but stared at the liquefying whirling desert. I shouted, and then they turned vague eyes on me but could not recognize me. I grabbed them and shook them, and they did not resist. I slapped their cheeks and shouted, and their eyes, turned towards me, seemed to have in them the shadow of an indignant, What are you doing that for? But already they had turned to stare, transfixed.

I climbed around so that I stood immediately in front of them. "This is Johor," I said, "Johor, your friend." Ben seemed to come slightly to himself, but already he was trying to peer around me, so as to watch the sand. Rilla, it seemed, had not seen me. I took out the Signature and held it up in front of their staring eyes. Both sets of eyes followed the Signature as I stepped downwards, and they followed. They followed!—but like sleepwalkers. Holding up the Signature and walking backwards in front of them, I reached the desert floor, which was quivering everywhere now, with a singing hiss of sound, and I shouted, "Now follow me! Follow me!" continuously moving the Signature so that it flashed and gleamed. I walked as fast I could, first backwards, and then, because I could see the terrible danger we were in, with the beginnings of vortexes everywhere around us, I turned myself half sideways and so led them forward. They stumbled and they fell, and seemed all the time drawn by a need to look back, but I pulled them forward with the power of the Signature, and at last we stood on the firm slopes of the mountain. There they at once turned and stood staring, clutching each other. And I stood with them, for I was affected, too, by that hypnotizing dreadfulness. Where we had come stumbling to safety was already now all movement and shifting subsidence: as far as we could see, the golden sands were moving. And we stood there, we stood there, for I was lost as they, and we were staring at a vast whirlpool, all the plain had become one swirling centrifuge, spinning, spinning, with its center deep, and deeper and then out of sight. Some appalling necessity was dragging and sucking at this place, feeding on the energies, the released powers, and I could not pull my eyes away, it seemed as if my eyes themselves were being sucked out, my mind was going away, draining into the spin—and then from the sky swooped down a black screaming eagle, and it was warning us: "Go . . o . . o . . . Go . . o . . o . . . Go . . o . . o . . . and the clattering rush of its wings above my head brought me back into myself. I had even dropped the Signature, and I had to scramble and search for it, and there was its gleam under some rocks. I had to shake and slap and wake Ben and Rilla, and again move the Signature back and forth in front of their eyes to charm them away from their contemplation of the sands. Above, the eagle that had saved us swung in a wide circle, peering to see if we were indeed safely awake, and then, when it knew we were watching, turned its glide so that it was off towards the east, where the ground climbed from the level of the sands, up into scrubland, grasses, low rocks, safe from the deadly plain which it was essential for us to get away from as soon as we could. Ben and Rilla were passive, almost imbecile, as I shepherded them on, the eagle showing the way. I did not try to talk to them, only wondered what to do, for we were walking in the opposite direction from the borders of Zone Six with Shikasta, which was where we all had to go. But I followed the eagle, I had to. If he had known enough to rescue me from my trance, then I must trust him . . . and after hours of stumbling heavy walk, beside my two dazed companions, the great bird screamed to attract my attention, and swung away leftwards in a deep and wide arc, and I knew that that was where we must make our way. And we traveled on all that day, until evening, trusting in the bird, for I did not know where we were. Rilla and Ben were talking a little now, but only clumsy half-phrases and random words. At night we found a sheltered place, and I made them sit quietly beside me and rest. They slept at last, and I got up and climbed to a high place where I could look back over the scrub of the plateau to the desert. Under the starlight I saw a single great vortex, which filled the whole expanse: the spine of the rocky ridge had been sucked down and had gone entirely. Nothing remained but the horizons-wide swirl, and the sound of it now was a roar, which made the earth I stood on shake. I crept back again through the dark to my friends and sat by them until the dawn, when the eagle, which was sitting on a high peak of rock, screamed a greeting to me. There was an urgency in it, and I knew we must move on. I roused Ben and Rilla, and all that day we followed the bird, through the higher lands that surrounded the sand plains, which we were working our way around. We could not see them, but we could hear, always, the roaring of the enraged and compelled earth. Towards evening I recognized where we were. And now I was thinking that I was late with my tasks on Shikasta, and that it was most urgent and necessary for me to get back to them. But I could not trust Ben and Rilla yet, to be alone. As they walked they kept turning their heads to listen to that distant roaring like a sea that keeps crashing itself again and again on shores that shake and tremble, and I knew that left alone they would drift back to the sands. I could not leave them the Signature: they were not reliable. After all, I had nearly lost it, and compared to them, my senses had been my own. I called up to the eagle that I needed its help, and as it circled above us, asked it to shepherd Ben and Rilla onwards. I held the Signature in front of them again, and said that the bird was the servant of the Signature, and they must do exactly what it told them. I said I would see them again on the borders of Shikasta, and they must not give up. Thus exhorting and pleading, I impressed on them everything I could, and then went on by myself alone, fast. I looked back later and saw them stumbling slowly forward, their eyes raised to the glide and the swerve and the balance of the eagle, who moved on, on, on, in front.

I found Ranee with a group she had saved from the whirlpools not far from the frontier. I asked if I might travel with her, so that I could make contact as I had to, and she agreed. So I went on with her. Her charges were as stunned, as lost to their selves, as poor Ben and Rilla. But they did seem slowly to improve, while Ranee talked to them in a low steady compelling voice, as a mother talks a child up out of a nightmare, soothing, and explaining.

FROM

# The Marriages Between Zones Three, Four, and Five

Rumors are the begetters of gossip. Even more are they the begetters of song. We, the Chroniclers and song-makers of our Zone, aver that before the partners in this exemplary marriage were awake to what the new directives meant for both of them, the songs were with us, and were being amplified and developed from one end of Zone Three to the other. And of course this was so in Zone Four.

*Great to Small*
*High to Low*
*Four into Three*
*Cannot go.*

This was a children's counting game. I was watching them at it from my windows the day after I heard the news. And one of them rushed up to me in the street with a "riddle" he had heard from his parents: If you mate a swan and a gander, who will ride?

What was being said and sung in the camps and barracks of Zone Four we do not choose to record. It is not that we are mealymouthed. Rather that every chronicle has its appropriate tone.

I am saying that each despised the other? No, we are not permitted actively to criticize the dispensations of the Providers, but let us say that we in Zone Three did not forget—as the doggerel chanted during those days insisted:

*Three comes before Four.*
*Our ways are peace and plenty.*
*Their ways—war!*

It was days before anything happened.

While this famous marriage was being celebrated in the imaginations of both realms, the two most concerned remained where they were. They did not know what was wanted of them.

No one had expected the marriage. It had not reached even popular speculation. Zones Three and Four were doing very well, with Al•Ith for us, Ben Ata for them. Or so we thought.

Quite apart from the marriage, there were plenty of secondary questions. What could it mean that our Al•Ith was ordered to travel to the territory of Ben Ata, so that the wedding could be accomplished on his land? This was one of the things we asked ourselves.

What, in this context, was a wedding?

What, even, a marriage?

When Al•Ith first heard of the Order, she believed it to be a joke. She and her sister laughed. All of Zone Three heard how they laughed. Then arrived a message that could only be regarded as a rebuke, and people came together in conferences and councils all over the Zone. They sent for us—the Chroniclers and the poets and the song-makers and the Memories. For weeks nothing was talked of but weddings and marriages, and every old tale and ballad that could be dug up was examined for information.

Messengers were even sent to Zone Five, where we believed weddings of a primitive kind did take place. But there was war all along their frontiers with Zone Four and it was not possible to get in.

We wondered, if this marriage was intended to follow ancient patterns, whether Zones Three and Four should join in a festival? But the Zones could not mingle, were inimical by nature. We were not even sure where the frontier was. Our side was not guarded. The inhabitants of Zone Three, straying near the frontier, or approaching it from curiosity as children or young people sometimes did, found themselves afflicted with repugnance, or at the least by an antipathy to foreign airs and atmospheres that showed itself in a cold lethargy, like boredom. It cannot be said that Zone Four had for us the secret attractions and fascinations of the forbidden: the most accurate thing I can say is that we forgot about it.

Ought there perhaps to be two festivals, simultaneously, and each would celebrate that our two lands, so different, could nevertheless mirror something, at least in this way? But what would be the point of that? After all, festivals and celebrations were not exactly pleasures we had to do without.

Should there then be small wedding parties among us, to mark the occasion?

New clothes? Decorations in our public places? Gifts and presents? All these were sanctioned by the old songs and stories.

More time passed. We knew that Al•Ith was low in spirits, and was keeping to her quarters. She had never done this before, had always been available and open to us. The women everywhere were out of temper and despondent.

The children began to suffer.

Then came the first visible and evident manifestation of the new time. Ben Ata sent a message that his men would come to escort her to him. This curtness was exactly what we expected from his Zone. A realm at war did not need the courtesies. Here was proof of the rightness of our reluctance to be brought low by Zone Four.

Al•Ith was resentful, rebellious. She would not go, she announced.

Again there was an Order, and it said, simply, that she must go.

Al•Ith put on her dark blue mourning clothes, since this was the only expression of her inner feelings she felt she still had the latitude to use. She gave out no instructions for a Grief, but that was what was being felt by us all.

Felt confusingly and—we suspected—wrongly. Emotions of this kind are not valued by us. Have not been for so long we have no records of anything different. As individuals we do not expect—it is not expected of us—to weep, wail, suffer. What can happen to any one of us that does not happen at some time to everyone? Sorrow at bereavement, at personal loss, has become formalized, ritualized, in public occasions seen by us all as channels and vehicles for our little personal feelings. It is not that we don't feel!—but that feelings are meant always to be directed outwards and used to strengthen a general conception of ourselves and our realm. But with this new dispensation of Al•Ith the opposite seemed to be happening.

Never had our Zone known so many tears, accusations, irrational ill feelings.

Al•Ith had all her children brought to her and when they wept she did not check them.

She insisted that this much must be allowed her without it being considered active rebellion.

There were those—many of us—who were perturbed; many who began to be critical of her.

We could not remember anything like this; and soon we were talking of how long it had been since there had been any kind of Order from the Providers. Of how previous changes of the Need—always referred to by us simply, and without further definition, in this one word—had been received by us. Of why, now, there should be such a reversal. We asked ourselves if we had grown into the habit of seeing ourselves falsely. But how could it be wrong to approve our own harmonies, the wealths and pleasantness of our land? We believed our Zone to be the equal at least of any other for prosperity and absence of discord. Had it then been a fault to be proud of it?

And we saw how long it had been since we had thought at all of what lay beyond our borders. That Zone Three was only one of the realms administered generally from Above, we knew. We did think, when we thought on these lines at all, of ourselves in interaction with these other realms, but it was in an abstract way. We had perhaps grown insular? Self-sufficing?

Al•Ith sat in her rooms and waited.

And then they appeared, a troop of twenty horsemen, in light armor. They carried shields that protected them against our higher finer air which would otherwise have made them ill, and these they had to have. But why head protection, and the famous reflecting singlets of Zone Four that could repel any weapon? Those of us who were near the route chosen by our unwelcome guests stood sullen and critical. We were determined not to give any indications of pleasure. Nor did the horsemen greet us. In silence the troops made their way to the palace, and came to a standstill outside Al•Ith's windows. They had with them a saddled and bridled horse without a rider. Al•Ith saw them from her windows. There was a long wait. Then she emerged on the long flight of white steps, a somber figure in her dark robes. She stood silent, observing the soldiers whose appearance in this manner, in her country, could only have the effect of a capture. She allowed plenty of time for them to observe her, her beauty, her strength, the self-sufficiency of her bearing. She then descended the steps slowly, and alone. She went straight to the horse that had been brought for her, looked into his eyes, and put her hand on his cheek. This horse was Yori, who became celebrated from this moment. He was a black horse, and a fine one, but perhaps no more remarkable than the others the soldiers were riding. Having greeted him, she lifted off the heavy saddle. She stood with this in her arms, looking into the faces of the men one after another until at last a soldier saw what it was she wanted. She threw the saddle to him, and his horse shifted its legs to adjust the weight as he caught it. He gave a comical little grimace, glancing at his fellows, while she stood, arms folded, watching them. It was the grimace one offers to a clever child trying something beyond its powers, yet succeeding. This was of course not lost on Al•Ith, and she now showed they had missed her real point, by the slow deliberation with which she removed the bridle and tossed that, too, to a soldier.

Then she shook back her head, so that the black hair that was bound lightly around it cascaded down her back. Our women wear their hair in many ways, but if it is up, in braids or in another fashion, and a woman shakes her hair loose, in a particular manner, then this means grief. But the soldiers had not understood, and were admiring her foolishly; perhaps the gesture had been meant for the onlookers who were by now crowding the little square. Al•Ith's lips were curling in contempt of the soldiers, and with impatience. I must record here that this kind of arrogance—yes, I have to call it that—was not something we expected from her. When we talked over the incident, it was agreed that Al•Ith's bitterness over the marriage was perhaps doing her harm.

Standing with loosened hair and burning eyes, she slowly wound a fine black veil around her head and shoulders. Mourning—again. Through the transparent black glowed her eyes. A soldier was fumbling to get down off his horse to lift her onto hers, but she had leapt up before he could reach the ground. She then wheeled and galloped off through the gardens in an easterly direction, towards the borders with Zone Four. The soldiers followed. To those of us watching, it looked as if they were in pursuit.

Outside our city she pulled in her horse and walked it. They followed. The people along the roads greeted her, and stared at the soldiers, and it did not look like a pursuit now, because the soldiers were embarrassed and smiling foolishly, and she was the Al•Ith they had always known.

There is a descent off the high plateau of our central land through passes and gorges, and it was not possible to ride fast, apart from the fact that Al•Ith stopped whenever someone wanted to talk to her. For when she observed this was so, she always pulled up her horse and waited for them to approach her.

Now the grimaces among the soldiers were of a different kind, and they were grumbling, for they had expected to be across their own frontier by nightfall. At last, as another group of her people waved and called to her, and she heard the voices of the soldiers rising behind her, she turned her horse and rode back to them, stopping a few paces before the front line of horsemen, so that they had to rein in quickly.

"What is your trouble?" she inquired. "Would it not be better if you told me openly, instead of complaining to each other like small children?"

They did not like this, and a small storm of anger rose, which their commander quelled.

"We have our orders," he said.

"While I am in our country," said she, "I will behave according to custom."

She saw they did not understand, and she had to explain. "I am in the position I hold because of the will of the people. It is not for me to ride past arrogantly, if they indicate they want to say something."

Again they looked at each other. The commander's face showed open impatience.

"You cannot expect me to overturn our customs for yours in this way," she said.

"We have emergency rations for one light meal," he said.

She gave a little incredulous shake of her head, as if she could not believe what she was hearing.

She had not meant it as contempt, but this was what transmitted itself to them. The commander of the horsemen reddened, and blurted out: "Any one of us is capable of fasting on a campaign for days at a time if necessary."

"I hadn't asked as much," she said gravely, and this time, what they heard was humor. They gratefully laughed, and she was able to give a brief smile, then sighed, and said, "I know that you are not here by your own will, but because of the Providers."

But this, inexplicably to her, they felt as insult and challenge, and their horses shifted and sidled as the emotions of their riders came into them.

She gave a little shrug, and turned and went to the group of young men who stood waiting for her at the road's edge. Below them now lay a wide plain, behind them were the mountains. The plains still lay yellowed by the evening sun, and the high peaks of the mountains sun-glittered, but where they were it was cold and in dusk. The young men crowded around her horse as they talked, showing no fear or awe, and the watching horsemen's faces showed a crude disbelief. When a youth put up his hand to pat the horse's cheek briefly, the men let out, all together, a long breath of condemnation. But they were in doubt, and in conflict. It was not possible for them to despise this great kingdom or the rulers of it: they knew better. Yet what they saw at every moment contradicted their own ideas of what was right.

She held up her hand in farewell to the young men, and the men behind her put their horses forward at this signal which had not been to them. She rode on, before them, until they were all on the level of the plain, and then turned again.

"I suggest that you make a camp here, with the mountains at your back."

"In the first place," said the commander, very curt—because he had been annoyed his soldiers had instinctively answered her gesture by starting again, instead of waiting for him—"in the first place, I had not thought of stopping at all till we reached the frontier. And in the second . . ." But his anger silenced him.

"I am only making the suggestion," she said. "It will take nine or ten hours to reach the frontier."

"At this pace it will."

"At any pace. Most nights a strong wind blows over the plain from the east."

"Madam! What do you take these men for? What do you take us for?"

"I see that you are soldiers," said she. "But I was thinking of the beasts. They are tired."

"They will do as they are ordered. As we do."

Our Chroniclers and artists have made a great thing of this exchange between Al•Ith and the soldiers. Some of the tales begin at this point. She is erect before them, on her horse, who hangs his head, because of the long difficult ride. She is soothing it with her white hand, which glitters with jewels . . . but Al•Ith was known for her simple dress, her absence of jewels and splendor! They show her long black hair streaming, the veil streaming with it and held on her forehead with a brilliant clasp. They show the angry commander, his face distorted, and the jeering soldiers. The bitter wind is indicated by flying tinted clouds, and the grasses of the plain lie almost flat under it.

All kinds of little animals have crept into this picture. Birds hover around her head. A small deer, a great favorite with our children, has stepped onto the dust of the road, and is holding up its nose to the drooping nose of Al•Ith's horse, to comfort it, or to give it messages from other animals. Often these pictures are titled "Al•Ith's Animals." Some tales tell how the soldiers try to catch the birds and the deer, and are rebuked by Al•Ith.

I take the liberty of doubting whether the actual occasion impressed itself so dramatically on the soldiers, or even on Al•Ith. The soldiers wanted to ride on, and get away from this land they did not understand, and which continually discomfited them. The commander did not want to be put into the position of taking her advice, but nor did he want to ride for hours into a cold wind.

Which in fact was already making itself felt.

Al•Ith was more herself now than she had been for many weeks. She was seeing that while she mourned in her rooms, there had been other things she should have done! Duties had been neglected. She remembered that messages had come in to her from all over the country, which she had been too absorbed in her fierce thoughts to respond to.

She was seeing in herself disobedience, and the results of it. This made her, now, more gentle with this troop of barbarians, and its small-boy commander.

"You did not tell me your name," she asked.

He hesitated. Then: "It is Jarnti."

"You command the king's horses?"

"I am commander of all his forces. Under the king."

"My apologies." She sighed, and they all heard it. They thought it weakness. Throughout these experiences with her, they could not help feeling in themselves the triumph that barbarian natures show when faced with weakness; and the need to cringe and crowd together when facing strength.

"I want to leave you for some hours," she said.

At this they all, on a single impulse, and without any indication from their leader, crowded around her. She was inside a ring of captors.

"I cannot allow it," said Jarnti.

"What were your orders from the king?" she inquired. She was quiet and patient but they heard subservience.

And a great roar of laughter went up from them all. Long tension exploded in them. They laughed and shouted, and the crags behind them echoed. Birds that had already settled themselves for the night wheeled up into the skies. From the long grasses by the road, animals that had been lying hidden broke away noisily.

What Ben Ata had finally shouted at his commander of all the forces, was: "Go and get that ——— ——— ——— and bring her here. I'm for it if I don't ——— ———" For while Al•Ith had been weeping and rebellious in her quarters, he had been raging and cursing up and down the camps of his armies. There was not a soldier who had not heard what his king thought of this enforced marriage, while the camps commiserated with him, drinking, laughing, making up ribald toasts which were repeated from one end of Zone Four to the other.

This scene is another favorite of our storytellers and artists. Al•Ith, on her tired horse, is ringed by the brutal laughing men. The cold wind of the plains is pressing her robe close around her. The commander is leaning over her, his face all animal. She is in danger.

And it is true that she was. Perhaps for the only time.

Now night had fallen. Only in the skies behind them was there any light. The sunset sent up flares high towards the crown of the heavens, and made the snow peaks shine. In front of them lay the now black plain, and scattered over it at vast distances were the lights of villages and settlements. On the plateau behind them that they had traveled over, our villages and towns were crowded: it was a populous and busy land.

But now they seemed to stand on the verge of nothingness, the dark. The soldiers' own country was low and mostly flat, and their towns were never built on hills and ridges. They did not like heights. More: as we shall see, they had been taught to fear them. They had been longing for the moment when they could get off that appalling plateau lifted so high among its towering peaks. They had descended from it and, associating flat lands with habitation, saw only emptiness. Their laughter had panic in it. Terror. It seemed they could not stop themselves laughing. And among them was the small silent figure of Al•Ith, who sat quietly, while they rolled about in their saddles, making sounds, as she thought, like frightened animals.

Their laughing had to stop at some point. And when it did nothing had changed. She was still there. They had not impressed her with their noise. The illimitable blackness lay ahead.

"What was Ben Ata's order?" she asked again.

An explosion of sniggers, but the commander directed a glance of reproof towards the offenders, although he had been laughing as hard as any of them.

"His orders?" she insisted.

A silence.

"That you should bring me to him, that was it, I think."

A silence.

"You will bring me to him no later than tomorrow."

She remained where she was. The wind was now howling across the plains so that the horses could hardly keep their footing.

The commander gave a brief order which sounded shamefaced. The posse broke up, riding about on the edge of the plain, to find a camping place. She and the commander sat on their tired horses, watching. But normally he would have been with his men who, used to orders and direction, were at a loss. At length he called out that such a place would do, and they all leapt off their horses.

The beasts, used to the low relaxed air of Zone Four, were exhausted from the high altitudes of this place, and were trembling as they stood.

"There is water around that spur," said Al•Ith. He did not argue, but shouted to the soldiers to lead the horses around the spur to drink. He got off his horse, and so did she. A soldier came to lead both animals with the others to the water. A fire was blazing in a glade between deep rocks. Saddles lay about on the grass at intervals: they would be the men's pillows.

Jarnti was still beside Al•Ith. He did not know what to do with her.

The men were already pulling out their rations from their packs, and eating. The sour powdery smell of dried meat. The reek of spirits.

Jarnti said, with a resentful laugh, "Madam, our soldiers seem very interesting to you! Are they so different from your own?"

"We have no soldiers," she said.

This scene, too, is much celebrated among us. The soldiers, illuminated by a blazing fire, are seated on their saddles among the grasses, eating their dried meat and drinking from their flasks. Others are leading back the horses, who have drunk at a stream out of sight behind rocks. Al•Ith stands by Jarnti at the entrance to this little natural fortress. They are watching the horses being closed into a corral that is formed by high rocks. They are hungry, and there is no food for them that night. Al•Ith is gazing at them with pity. Jarnti, towering over the small indomitable figure of our queen, is swaggering and full of bravado.

"No soldiers?" said Jarnti, disbelieving. Though of course there had always been rumors to this effect.

"We have no enemies," she remarked. And then added, smiling straight at him, "Have you?"

This dumbfounded him.

He could not believe the thoughts her question aroused.

While she was still smiling at him, a soldier came out from the entrance of the little camp and stood at ease close to them.

"What is he standing there for?"

"Have you never heard of a sentry?" he inquired, full of sarcasm.

"Yes. But no one is going to attack you."

"We always post sentries," he said.

She shrugged.

Some soldiers were already asleep. The horses drooped and rested behind their rocky barriers.

"Jarnti, I am going to leave you for some hours," she said.

"I cannot allow you."

"If you forbid me, you would be going beyond your orders."

He was silent.

Here again, a favorite scene. The fire roaring up, showing the sleeping soldiers, the poor horses, and Jarnti, tugging at his beard with both hands in frustrated amazement at Al•Ith, who is smiling at him.

"Besides," he added, "you have not eaten."

She inquired good-humoredly: "Do your orders include your forcing me to eat?"

And now he said, confronting her, all trouble and dogged insistence, because of the way he was being turned inside out and upside down by her, and by the situation, "Yes, the way I see it, by implication my orders say I should make you eat. And perhaps even sleep, if it comes to that.

"Look, Jarnti," said she, and went to a low bush that grew not ten paces away. She took some of its fruit. They were lumpy fruits sheathed in papery leaves. She pulled off the leaves. In each were four segments of a white substance. She ate several. The tightness of her mouth showed she was not enjoying them.

"Don't eat them unless you want to stay awake," she said, but of course he could not resist. He blundered off to the bush, and gathered some for himself, and his mouth twisted up as he tasted the tart crumbly stuff.

"Jarnti," she said, "you cannot leave this camp, since you are the commander. Am I correct?"

"Correct," he said, in a clumsy familiarity, which was the only way he knew how to match her friendliness.

"Well, I am going to walk some miles from here. Since in any case you intend to keep that poor man awake all night for nothing, I suggest you send him with me to make sure I will come back again."

Jarnti was already feeling the effects of the fruit. He was alert and knew he could not fall off to sleep now.

"I will leave him on guard and come with you myself," he said.

And went to give orders accordingly.

While he did this, Al•Ith walked past the sleeping soldiers to the horses, and gave each of them, from her palm, a few of the acrid fruits from the bush. Before she had left their little prison they were lifting their heads and their eyes had brightened.

She and Jarnti set off across the blackness of the plain towards the first of the glittering lights.

This scene is always depicted thus: there is a star-crowded sky, a slice of bright moon, and the soldier striding forward made visible and prominent because his chest armor and headpiece and his shield are shining. Beside him Al•Ith is visible only as a dark shadow, but her eyes gleam softly out from her veil.

It could not have been anything like this. The wind was straight in their faces, strong and cold. She wrapped her head completely in her veil, and he had his cloak tight about him and over the lower part of his face; and the shield was held to protect them both from the wind. He had chosen to accompany this queen on no pleasant excursion, and he must have regretted it.

It took three hours to reach the settlement. It was of tents and huts: the herdsmen's headquarters. They walked through many hundreds of beasts who lifted their heads as they went past, but did not come nearer or move away. The wind was quite enough for them to withstand, and left them no energy for anything else. But as the two came to within calling distance of the first tents, where there was shelter from low scrubby trees, some beasts came nosing towards Al•Ith in the dark, and she spoke to them and held out her hands for them to smell, in greeting.

There were men and women sitting around a small fire outside a tent.

They had lifted their heads, too, sensing the approach of strangers, and Al•Ith called out to them, "It is Al•Ith," and they called back to her to approach.

All this was astonishing to Jarnti, who went with Al•Ith into the firelight, but several paces behind.

At the sight of him, the faces of the fire-watchers showed wonderment.

"This is Jarnti, from Zone Four," said Al•Ith, as if what she was saying was an ordinary thing. "He has come to take me to their king."

Now there was not a soul in our land who did not know how she felt about this marriage, and there were many curious glances into her face and eyes. But she was showing them that this was not her concern now. She stood waiting while rugs were brought from a tent, and when they were spread, she sat down on one and indicated to Jarnti that he should do the same. She told them that Jarnti had not eaten, and he was brought bread and porridge. She indicated that she did not want food. But she accepted a cup of wine, and Jarnti drank off jugs of the stuff. It was mild in taste, but potent. He was showing signs of discomfort if not of illness: the altitude of our plateau had affected him, he had taken too many of the stimulant berries, and he had not eaten. He was cut through and through by the winds that swept over their heads where they all leaned low over their little fire.

This scene, too, is one much depicted.

It always shows Al•Ith, alert and smiling, surrounded by the men and women of the settlement, with her cup of wine in her hand, and beside her Jarnti, drowsy and drugged. Above them the wind has scoured the sky clean and glittering. The little trees are leaning almost to the ground. The herds surround the fireside scene, looking in and wondering, waiting for a glance from their queen.

She said at once: "As I rode out from the capital today, and down through the passes, I was stopped by many of you. What is this that they are saying about the animals?"

The spokesman was an old man.

"What have they told you, Al•Ith?"

"That there is something wrong."

"Al•Ith, we have ourselves sent in messengers to the capital, with information."

Al•Ith was silent, and then said, "I'm very much to blame. Messages came, and I was too much preoccupied with my own trouble to attend."

Jarnti was sitting with a bent head, half asleep, but at this his head jerked up, and he let out a gruff triumphant laugh, and muttered, "Punish her, beat her, you hear? She admits it!" before his head dropped again. His mouth hung open, and the cup was loose in his hand. One of the girls took it from him gently. He snatched at it, thrust forward his bottom lip and lifted his chin belligerently at her, saw she was pretty, and a female—and would have put his arm around her, but she swiftly moved back as he submerged again in drunkenness.

Al•Ith's eyes were full of tears. The women first, then the men, seeing this oaf and his ways, saw too what was in store for her—and they were about to raise their voices in lament, keening, but she lifted her hand and stopped them.

"There is no help for it," she said, in a low voice, her lips trembling. "We have our orders. And it is clear down in Zone Four they don't like it any more than we do."

They looked inquiringly at her and she nodded. "Yes. Ben Ata is very angry. So I understand today from something that was said."

"Ben Ata . . . Ben Ata . . ." muttered the soldier, his head rolling. "He will have the clothes off you before you can get at him with your magic berries and your tricks."

At this, one of the men rose to his feet and would have dragged Jarnti off, with two hands under his armpits, but Al•Ith raised her hand to stop him.

"I am more concerned with the animals," she said. "What was in the messages you sent me?"

"Nothing definite, Al•Ith. It is only that our animals are disturbed in their minds. They are sorrowful."

"This is true everywhere on the plains?"

"It is true everywhere in our Zone, or so we hear. Were you not told of it up on the plateau?"

"I have already said that I am much to blame. I was not attending to my duties."

A silence. The wind was shrieking over them, but not as loud.

Jarnti was slumped, his cup leaning in his hand, blinking at the fire. Really he was listening, since the berries have the effect of preserving attention even while the muscles are slack and disobedient. This conversation was to be retold everywhere through the camps of Zone Four, and not inaccurately, though to them the emphasis must be that the queen of all the land was sitting "like a serf" by the fire. And, of course, that "up there" they spoke of animals as if they were people.

Al•Ith said to the old man, "You have asked the animals?"

"I have been among the herds since it was noticed. Day after day I have been with them. Not one says anything different. They do not know why, but they are sad enough to die. They have lost the zeal for living, Al•Ith."

"They are conceiving? Giving birth?"

"They are still giving birth. But you are right to ask if they are conceiving . . ."

At this Jarnti let out a muttering. "They tell their queen she is right! They dare! Drag them off! Beat them. . . ."

They ignored him. With compassion now. He was sitting loose and rolling there, his face aflame, and they saw him as worse than their beasts. More than one of the women was weeping, silently, at the fate of their sister, as they watched him.

"We believe they are not conceiving."

A silence. The wind was not shrieking now. It was a low wail. The animals that were making a circle all around lifted their muzzles to sniff the air: soon the wind would be gone, and their nightly ordeal over.

"And you, the people?"

They all nodded, slowly. "We believe that we are the same."

"You mean, that you begin to feel in yourselves what the animals feel?"

"Yes, Al•Ith."

And now they sat quiet for a long time. They looked into each other's faces, questioning, confirming, allowing their eyes to meet, and to part, letting what each felt pass from one to another, until they all were feeling and understanding as one.

While this went on, the soldier was motionless. Later, in the camps, he was to say that "up there" they had vicious drugs and used them unscrupulously.

The wind had dropped. It was silent. In a swept sky the stars glittered cold. But wisps of cloud were forming in the east, over the borders with Zone Four.

One of the girls spoke up at last. "Al•Ith, some of us have been wondering if this new Order from the Providers has something to do with this sadness of ours."

Al•Ith nodded.

"None of us remembers anything like it," said the old man.

Al•Ith said, "The Memories speak of such a time. But it was so long ago the historians knew nothing about it."

"And what happened?" asked Jarnti, suddenly finding his tongue.

"We were invaded," said Al•Ith. "By Zone Four. Is there nothing in your history? Your tales?"

At this Jarnti wagged his pointed beard at them, grinning—triumphant.

"Is there nothing you can tell us?" asked Al•Ith.

He smirked at the women, one after another, and then his head fell forward.

"Al•Ith," said a girl who had been sitting, letting her tears run, "Al•Ith, what are you going to do with such men?"

"Perhaps Ben Ata won't be so bad," said another.

"This man is the commander of all the armies," said Al•Ith, and could not prevent herself shuddering.

"*This* man? *This?*"

Their horror and shock made itself felt in Jarnti, and he would have punished them if he could. He did manage to raise his head and glare, but he was shaking and weak.

"He is going to have to get back to the camp at the foothills," said Al•Ith.

Two of the young men glanced at each other, and then rose. They grasped Jarnti under the armpits, hauled him to his feet, and began walking him up and down. He staggered and protested, but complied, in the end, for his brain, clear all this time, told him it was necessary.

This scene is known as "Jarnti's Walk," and gives much opportunity for humor to our artists and tellers.

"I don't see that there is anything we can do?" asked Al•Ith of the others. "If this is an old disease, nothing is known of it in our medicine. If it is a new disease, our doctors will shortly come to terms with it. But if it is a malady of the heart, then the Providers will know what to do."

A silence.

"Have already known what to do," she said, smiling, though not pleasantly. "Please tell everyone on the plain that I came here tonight and we talked, and what we thought together."

We will, they said. Then they all rose to their feet, and went with her through the herds. A young girl called three horses, who came and stood willingly, waiting, while the young man put Jarnti on one, and Al•Ith mounted another, and the girl herself got on a third. The animals crowded around Al•Ith on her horse, and called to her as the three rode past.

Out on the plain, headed back towards the camp, the grasses were now standing up grey in a dim light, and the eastern sky was aflame.

Jarnti had come awake, and was sitting straight and soldierly on his horse.

"Madam," he asked, "how do you people talk to your animals?"

"Do you not talk to yours?"

"No."

"You stay with them. You watch them. You put your hands on them and feel how they feel. You look into their eyes. You listen to the tones of their cries and their calling to each other. You make sure that when they begin to understand that you understand them, you do not miss the first tones of what they say to you. For if you do not hear, then they will not trouble to try again. Soon you will feel what they are feeling, and you will know what they are thinking, even if they do not tell you themselves."

Jarnti said nothing for a while. They had now left the herds behind.

"Of course we watch them and take notice of how they look, if they are ill or something like that."

"There are none among you who know how to feel with your animals?"

"Some of us are good with animals, yes."

Al•Ith did not seem inclined to say any more.

"Perhaps we are too impatient," said Jarnti.

Neither Al•Ith nor the girl said anything to this. They trotted on towards the foothills. Now the great peaks of the high lands were pink and shining from the wild morning sky.

"Madam," he said, blustering, because he did not know how to be on an equality with her, or with anyone, "when you are with us, can you teach some of the soldiers who are in charge of the horses this way of yours?"

She was silent. Then: "Do you know that I am never called anything but Al•Ith? Do you understand that I have never been called Madam, or anything like it before?"

Now he was silent.

"Well, will you?" he asked gruffly.

"I will if I can," she said at last.

He was struggling with himself to express gratitude, pleasure. Nothing came out.

They were more than halfway between the herds and the camp.

Jarnti put his heels into his horse suddenly, and it neighed and bucked. Then it stood still.

The two women stopped too.

"Did you want to go on ahead?" asked the girl.

He was sullen.

"He won't carry you now," she said, and slid off her horse. Jarnti got down from his. "Now get on mine." He did so. She soothed the bewildered animal he had kicked, and mounted it.

"*Think* that you want to go on in front of us," said the girl.

He had an ashamed, embarrassed look. He went red.

"I'm afraid you will have to put up with us," said Al•Ith at last.

When they were in sight of the camp, she jumped down from her horse. It at once turned and began cantering back towards the herds. Jarnti got off his. And this one too cantered back. He was standing looking in admiration at the lovely girl on her horse, who was turning around to go.

"If you ever come to Zone Four," he shouted at her, "let me know."

She gave a long look of commiseration at Al•Ith, and remarked, "Luckily for me I am not a queen." And she sped off across the plain with the two other horses neighing and tossing up their heels on either side of her.

Al•Ith and Jarnti walked towards the camp with the sunrise at their backs.

Long before they reached the camp, the smell of burning meat was strong on the air.

Al•Ith did not say anything, but her face spoke.

"Do you not kill animals?" he asked, unwillingly but forced to by his curiosity.

"Only if it is essential. There are plenty of other foods."

"Like those horrible berries of yours," he said, trying to be good-humored.

In the camp they had killed a deer. Jarnti did not eat any of it.

As soon as the meal was over, the horses were saddled, all but Al•Ith's. She stood watching the beasts adjust their mouths and their teeth uncomfortably as the bit went in.

She vaulted onto her horse, and whispered to it. Jarnti watched her, uneasy.

"What did you say to it?" he asked.

"That I am his friend."

And again she led the way forward, into the east, back across the plain.

They rode to one side of the herds they had been with in the night, but far enough off to see them as a darkness on the plain.

Jarnti was riding just behind Al•Ith.

Now he was remembering the conversation around the fire last night, the tone of it, the ease of it. He yearned for it—or something in it, for he had never known that quality of easy intimacy. Except, he was saying to himself, with a girl, sometimes, after a good screw.

He said, almost wistfully, to Al•Ith, "Can you feel that the animals out there are sad?" For she was looking continually towards them, and her face was concerned.

"Can't you?" she asked.

He saw she was weeping, steadily, as she rode.

He was furious. He was irritated. He felt altogether excluded from something he had a right to.

Behind them clattered the company of soldiers.

A long way in front was the frontier. Suddenly she leaned down to whisper to the horse and it sped forward. Jarnti and the company broke into speed after her. They were shouting at her. She did not have the shield that would protect her from the—to her—deadly atmosphere of Zone Four. She rode like the wild winds that scoured the plains every night until early dawn, and her long hair swept out behind her, and tears ran steadily down her face.

It was not for miles that Jarnti came up with her—one of the soldiers had thrown the shield to him, and he had caught it, and was now riding almost neck and neck with her.

"Al•Ith," he was shouting, "you must have this." And held up the shield. It was a long time before she heard him. At last she turned her face towards him, not halting her mad pace in the slightest, and he wilted at the sight of her blanched, agonized face. He held up the shield. She raised her hand to catch it. He hesitated, because it was not a light thing. He remembered how she had thrown the heavy saddle the day before, and he heaved the shield towards her. She caught it with one hand and did not abate her pace at all. They were approaching the frontier. They watched her to see how she would be affected by the sudden change in the density of the air, for they had all been ill to some extent, the day before. She went through the invisible barrier without faltering, though she was pale, and did not seem well. Inside the frontier line were the observation towers, rising up at half-mile distances from each other, bristling with soldiers and armaments. She did not stop. Jarnti and the others fled after her, shouting to the soldiers in the towers not to shoot. She went between the towers without looking at them.

Again they were on the edge of a descent through hills and rocks above a wide plain. When she reached the edge of this escarpment she at last stopped.

They all came to a standstill behind her. She was looking down into a land crowded with forts and encampments.

She jumped down from her horse. Soldiers were running to them from the forts, holding the bridles of fresh horses. The jaded horses of the company were being herded off to recover. But Al•Ith's did not want to leave her. He shivered and whinnied and wheeled all about Al•Ith, and when the soldiers came to catch him, would not go.

"Would you like him as a present, Al•Ith?" asked Jarnti, and she was pleased and smiled a little, which was all she could manage.

Again she removed the saddle from this fresh horse, and the bridle, and tossed them to the amazed soldiers. And she rode forward and down into Zone Four, with Yori trotting beside her and continually putting up his nose to nuzzle her as they went.

And so Al•Ith made the passage into the Zone we had all heard so much of, speculated about, and had never been in.

Not even with the shield could she feel anything like herself. The air was flat, dispiriting. The landscape seemed to confine and oppress. Everywhere you look, in our own realm, a wild vigor is expressed in the contours of uplands, mountains, a variegated ruggedness. The central plateau where so many of our towns are situated is by no means regular, but is ringed by mountains and broken by ravines and deep river channels. With us the eye is enticed into continual movement, and then is drawn back always to the great snowy peaks that are shaped by the winds and the colors of our skies. And the air tingles in the blood, cold and sharp. But here she looked down into a uniform dull flat, cut by canals and tamed streams that were marked by lines of straight pollarded trees, and dotted regularly by the ordered camps of the military way of life. Towns and villages did not seem any larger than these camps. The sky was a greyish blue and there was a dull shine from the lines of water. A wide low hill near the center of the scene where there seemed to be something like a park or gardens was all the consolation she could find.

Meanwhile, they were still descending the escarpment.

A turn in the road showed an enormous circular building of grey stone, squatting heavily between canals. It seemed recent, for rocks and earth near it were raw, broken. Her dismay that this might be where she was bound for brought her horse to a faltering stop. The company halted behind her, and she looked back to see a furtive triumph on every face. Jarnti was suppressing a smile as a leader does when he wishes to indicate he would like to join with his juniors in a show of emotion. Then as they remained there, with no sound but the horses shifting their hooves for relief, on the stony road, she saw that she had been mistaken: what she feared was not matched by the particular variety of triumph these captors of hers were showing.

"When may we expect to reach the king?" she asked, and Jarnti at once interpreted this as a reminder from her of higher authority. He rebuked his company with a strong look and adjusted his own face to obedience.

All this she watched, understood—and it came to her what a barbarous land this was.

They had imagined she had been intimidated by the sight of the rumored "round fortress of the deadly rays" as one of our songs described it.

She told herself, not for the first time, or the tenth, that she was not likely to adjust herself quickly to these people with their slavish minds, and to make a test of them, moved her horse on and towards the road that led to the building. At once Jarnti was beside her, and his hand was reaching out for her horse's head. She stopped. "I would like to see into one of the famed round fortresses of your Zone," she said.

"Oh, no, no, you must not, it is forbidden," said he, still full of importance.

"But why? Your weapons are not directed against us, surely?"

"It is dangerous . . ." but at this moment, around the side of the building came some children running, and in scattering for some game, two of them darted into an open doorway.

"So I see," she said, and rode on, without looking again at Jarnti or at the soldiers.

When nearly at the level of the plain, there were grazing cattle near the road, and a half-grown boy attending them.

Jarnti shouted at the boy to come forward, and the boy was already running towards them, before Jarnti said, "You could teach him your ways with the animals," and as the boy arrived at the roadside, pale and startled, Jarnti was shouting, "Down on your face! Can't you see who this is we are taking to the king?"

The lad was face down, full length on the grass, and this was no more than a half-minute since he had first been hailed.

Jarnti was giving her half-pleading, half-commanding looks, and his horse was dancing under him, because of his master's eagerness to learn her lore.

"Well," she said, "I don't think we are likely to learn or teach anything in this way."

But he had seen himself that he had mishandled the occasion and because of it was red and angry. He shouted, "The lady here would like to know if your beasts are well."

No reply, then a whimper which sounded like, "Very well, yes, well, sir."

Al Ith slid down from her horse, walked over to the boy, and said, "Stand up." She made her voice a command, since commands were what he understood. He slowly shivered his way to his feet, and stood, almost collapsing, before her. She waited until she knew he had seen, from his furtive glances, that she was not so frightening, and said, "I am from Zone Three. Our animals have not been well. Can you say if you have noticed anything unusual with yours?"

His hands were clenched at his chest, and he was breathing as if he had run several miles. Finally he brought out: "Yes, yes, that is, I think so."

From behind them Jarnti's voice, jocular and loud: "Are they having sorrowful thoughts?" And the entire company sniggered.

She saw there was nothing that could be done, and said to the boy, "Don't be frightened. Go back to your beasts." She waited until he sped off, and she returned to her horse. Again, Jarnti knew he had behaved clumsily, and yet it had been necessary to him, for the sight of her, small, unarmed, standing rather below them near the defenseless and frightened boy, had roused in him a need to show strength, dominance.

She swung herself onto her horse and at once rode on, not looking at them. She felt very low, our poor Al•Ith. This was the worst time of all. Everything in her was hurt by the way the poor boy had been treated: yet these were the ways of this land, and she could not believe then, in that bad hour, that there could be any way of communicating with these louts. And of course she was thinking of what she was going to find when she was led to Ben Ata.

They rode on, through the middle of the day, across the plain, with the ditches and the lines of dull bunchy trees accompanying them all the way. She went first. Yori, the riderless horse, was just behind, with Jarnti, and behind them the company. They were all silent. She had not said anything about the incident of the boy, but they were thinking now that she would be soon with the king, and were not expecting she would give a good report of them. So they were sullen, sulky. There were few people on the roadside, or in the flat boats of the canals, but those who saw the little company go past reported that there was not a smile to be seen: this wedding party was fit for a funeral. And the riderless horse caused rumors to spread that Al•Ith had fallen and was dead, for the slight figure on the leading horse that they did see, had nothing about her to command their attention. She seemed to them a serving woman, or an attendant, in her plain dark blue, with her head in its black veils.

There was a ballad about how the horse of the dead Al•Ith had gone with the troop of soldiers to the king to tell him that there could be no marriage. The horse stood on the threshold of the wedding chamber and neighed three times, Ben Ata, Ben Ata, Ben Ata—and when he came out, said to him:

*Cold and dark your wedding bed,*
*O King, your willing bride is dead.*
*The realm she rules is cold and dark.*

And this was popular, and sung when everyone knew that Al•Ith was not dead, and that the marriage was a fact. That it was not the smoothest of marriages was of course known from the beginning. How? But how do these things get themselves known? The song was always being added to. Here is a verse that came from the married quarters of the army camps:

*Brave King, your realm is strong and fine.*
*Where beasts may mate, then women pine.*
*I will be your slave, brave King.*

Not anywhere with us, or at any time, have such verses as these been possible, though there were plenty of compassionate and tender ballads made up about Al•Ith. There are some who say that where there is rulership, there has to be criticism of this ribald kind, because no matter the level of the ruler, it is in the nature of the ruled to crave identification of the lowest sort. We say this is not so, and Zone Three proves it. To recognize and celebrate the ordinary, the day-to-day levels of an authority, is not to denigrate it.

Such Zone Four ballads, traveling upwards to us, found themselves transformed as they crossed the frontier. For one thing, there was no need of the inversions, the ambiguities, that are always bred by fear of an arbitrary authority.

We may almost say that a certain type of ballad is impossible with us: the kind that has as its ground or base lamentation, the celebration of loss.

In their Zone the riderless horse gave birth to songs of death and sorrow; in ours to songs about loving friendship.

The road, which cut straight across the plain, and was intersected at about the middle by one running equally straight, began to lift a little to reach the small hill that Al•Ith had seen with relief from the top of the escarpment. The canals were left behind, with their weight of dead water. There were a few ordinary trees, which had not been hacked into lumps and wands. At the top of the hill were gardens, and here the water had been forced into movement, for they rode now beside channels where it ran swiftly, fell from several levels to others, and broke into fountains. The air was lively and cool, and when she saw ahead of her a light pavilion, with colored springing pillars and arches, she was encouraged. But there was no one to be seen. She was contrasting this empty garden and the apparently deserted pavilion with the friendly amplitude of her own courts, when Jarnti called an order, and the whole company came to a stop. The soldiers jumped off their horses, and surrounded Al•Ith, who, when she got down from her horse, found herself being marched forward in their midst, like a captive of war—and she saw that this was not the first time they had done this, from the ease of their arrangements.

But as they had enclosed her, Jarnti in front, she put out her hand to hold the horse she had been given, Yori, by the neck.

And this was how she arrived at the steps of the pavilion, when Ben Ata came out to stand in the doorway, arms folded, legs apart, bearded soldier, dressed in no way different from Jarnti or the others. He was large, blond, muscular from continual campaigning, and burned a ruddy brown on the face and arms. His eyes were grey. He was not looking at Al•Ith but at the horse, for his first thought too was that his bride had been killed.

Al•Ith went quickly through the soldiers, suspecting that there were precedents here she might not want followed, and arrived in front of him, still holding the horse.

And now he looked at her, startled and frowning.

"I am Al•Ith," said she, "and this horse has been kindly given to me by Jarnti. Please, will you give orders for him to be well treated?"

He found himself speechless. He nodded. Jarnti then grasped the horse's neck and attempted to lead him away. But he reared and tried to free himself. Before he would allow himself to be taken away, Al•Ith had to comfort him and promise she would visit him very soon. "Today, I swear it." And, turning to Jarnti, "So you must not take him too far away. And please see he is well fed and looked after."

Jarnti was sheepish, the soldiers grinning, only just hiding it, because Ben Ata's face gave them no guidance. Normally, on such occasions, the girl would have been bundled across a threshold, or pushed forward roughly, according to the convention, but now no one knew how to behave.

Al•Ith said, "Ben Ata, I take it you have some sort of place I can retire to for a time? I have been riding all day."

Ben Ata was recovering. His face was hard, and even bitter. He had not known what to expect, and was prepared to be flexible, but he was repelled by this woman in her somber clothes. She had not taken off her veil, and he could not see much of her except that she had dark hair. He preferred fair women.

He shrugged, gave a look at Jarnti, and disappeared into the room behind him. It was Jarnti then who led her into another room, which was part of a set of rooms, and saw that she had what she needed. She refused food and drink, and announced that she would be ready to join the king in a few minutes.

And she did join him, emerging unceremoniously from the retiring rooms just as she had arrived, in her dark dress. But she had removed her veil, and her hair was braided and hanging down her back.

Ben Ata was lounging on a low divan or settee, in a large light airy room that had nothing very much in it. She saw that this was a bridal room, and planned for the occasion. Her bridegroom, however, sprawling on one edge of the divan, his chin on his hand, his elbow on his knee, did not move as she came in. And there was nowhere else to sit, so she sat down on the edge of the divan, at a distance from him, resting her weight on her hand in the position of one who has alighted somewhere for just a moment and has every intention of leaving again. She looked at him, without smiling. He looked at her, very far from smiling.

"Well, how do you like this place?" he asked, roughly. It was clear he had no idea of what to say or do.

"It has been built specially then?"

"Yes. Orders. Built to specification. Exactly. It was finished only this morning."

"It is certainly very elegant and pleasant," she said. "Quite different from anything else I've seen on my way here."

"Certainly not my style," he said. "But if it is yours, then that's the main thing."

This had a sort of sulky gallantry, but he was restless, and sighing continually, and it was evident all he wanted to do was to make his escape.

"I suppose the intention was that it should be suited to us both?" she remarked.

"I don't care," said he violently and roughly, his inner emotions breaking out of him. "And obviously you don't either."

"We're going to have to make the best of it," she said, intending consolation, but it was wild and bitter.

They looked at each other with a frank exchange of complicity: two prisoners who had nothing in common but their incarceration.

This first, and frail, moment of tolerance did not last.

He had flung himself back on this marriage couch of theirs, arms behind his head, his sandaled feet dusty on the covers, which were of fine wool, dyed in soft colors, and embroidered. Nowhere could he have seemed more out of place. She was able to construct his usual surroundings by how he slouched there, gazing at the ceiling as if she did not exist.

She examined the place. This was a very large room, opening out on two sides into gardens through a series of rounded arches. The other two sides had unobtrusive doors leading—on one—to the rooms for her use where she had already been, and on the other, presumably, to his. The ceiling was rounded and high, fluted at the edges. The whole room was painted a softly shining ivory, but there were patterns of gold, soft red, and blue, and beside each archway embroidered curtains were caught back with jeweled clasps. The fountains could be heard, and the running of the waters. This was not far from the gaiety and freshness of the public buildings of Andaroun, our capital, though her own quarters were plainer than these.

The great room was not all one empty sweep of space. A column sprung up from its center, and curved out, and divided into several, all fluted and defined in the same gold, sky blue, and red. The floors were of sweetly smelling wood. Apart from the great low couch, there was a small table near one of the arches, with two graceful chairs on either side of it.

A horse whinnied. A moment later, Yori appeared outside one of the arches, and would have come in if she had not run across and stopped him. It was easy to guess what had happened. He had been confined somewhere, and had jumped free, and the soldiers set to guard him did not dare to follow into these private gardens with the pavilion all the country had been talking of for weeks. She put her hands up to his cheeks, pulled down his head, whispered into first one ear, and then the other, and the horse swung around and went out of sight, back to its guard.

When she turned, Ben Ata was standing just behind her, glaring.

"I can see that it is true, what we have heard here. You are all witches in your country."

"It is a witchcraft easy to learn," she said, but as he continued to glare, her humor went, and now she crossed swiftly to the bed and, throwing down one of the big cushions, sat on it cross-legged. She had not thought that now he must do the same, or remain above her on the bed, but he was uncertain, seemed to feel challenged by her, and in his turn pulled a cushion off the bed, pushed it against a wall, and sat.

They sat opposite each other, on their two cushions.

She was at home, since this was how she usually seated herself, but he was uncomfortable, and seemed afraid to make any movement, in case the cushion slid about the polished floor.

"Do you always wear clothes like that?"

"I put this on especially for you," she countered, and he reddened again: since her arrival she had seen more angry, embarrassed men than ever in her life, and she was on the point of wondering if they had some disorder of the blood or the skin.

"If I had known you were going to arrive like this I would have ordered dresses for you. How was I to know you'd turn up like a servant?"

"Ben Ata, I never wear elaborate clothes."

He was eyeing the plain looseness of her robe with annoyance and exasperation.

"I thought you were supposed to be the queen."

"You cannot be distinguished from one of your own soldiers."

Suddenly he bared his teeth in a grin, and muttered something that she understood meant: "Take the thing off, and I'll show you."

She knew he was angry, but not how much. On their campaigns, when the army reached new territory, into his tent would be thrust some girl, or she was thrown down at his feet. She would nearly always be crying. Or she might be hissing and spitting. She might bite and scratch as he entered her. She could weep throughout and not cease weeping. A few gritted their teeth, and their loathing of him did not abate. He was not a man who enjoyed inflicting suffering, so these he would order to be returned to their homes. But those who wept or who struggled in a way he recognized he did enjoy, and would tame them, slowly. These were the conventions. These he obeyed. He had penetrated, and often impregnated, women all over his realm. But he had not married, he did not plan to marry, for the present arrangement did not come within his notions of marriage, about which he had the sentimental and high-flown ideas of a man ignorant of women. This woman with whom he was to be afflicted almost indefinitely, at least at intervals, was something outside his experience.

Everything about her disturbed him. She was not unbeautiful, with her dark eyes, dark hair, and the rest of the usual appurtenances, but there was nothing in her that set out to challenge him physically, and so he was cold.

"How long am I supposed to stay with you?" she inquired next, in exactly the cut-and-dried way he now—dismally—expected of her.

"They said, a few days."

There was a long silence. The great pleasant room was full of water sounds, and watery reflections from the pools and fountains.

"How do you do it in your country?" he inquired, knowing this was clumsy but not able to think of anything else.

"Do *what?*"

"Well, we hear you have a lot of children, for a start."

"I have five of my own. But I am the mother of many. More than fifty."

She could see that everything she said put greater distance between them.

"It is our custom, if a child is left an orphan, that I should become its mother."

"Adopt it."

"It is not one of our words. I become its mother."

"I suppose you feel about them exactly as you do about your own," he said, and this was a mimicry. But of something she had not said.

"No, I did not say that. Besides, fifty children are rather more than one can keep very close to."

"Then how are they your children?"

"They all have the same rights. And I spend the same time with each of them, as I am able."

"It's not my idea of a mother for *my* children."

"Is that what is expected of us, you think?"

This infuriated him! He had not *thought* very much at all about this appalling, affronting imposition, he had been too emotional. But at the least he had supposed that there would be children "to cement the alliance"—or something of that sort.

"Well, what else? What did you have in mind? Amorous dalliance once every few weeks? *You!*" And he snorted out his disgust with her.

She was trying not to look at him too closely. She had seen that a close steady look—which was her way—discomfited him. And besides, he appealed to her less than she did to him. She found this great soldier gross, with his heavy overheated flesh, his hot, resentful eyes, his rough sun-bleached hair which reminded her of the fleeces of a much prized breed of sheep that flourished on a certain mountain.

"There's more to mating than children," she observed.

And the commonsensicalness of this caused him to groan out loud and strike his fists hard on the floor beside him.

"Well, if so, one wouldn't think you knew much about *that*."

"Indeed," she retorted. "But in fact it is one of the skills of our Zone."

"Oh, no," he said. "Oh, no, no, no, no." And he sprang up and went striding about the room, beating the delicate walls with his fists.

She, still cross-legged on her cushion, watched him, interested, as she would have done some strange new species.

He stopped. He seemed to make an effort. Then he turned, teeth gritted, strode across to her, picked her up, and threw her on the couch. He put his hand across her mouth in the approved way, twitched up her dress, fingered himself to see if he was up to it, thrust himself into her, and accomplished his task in half a dozen swift movements.

He then straightened himself, for he had not removed his feet from the floor during this process and, already embarrassed, showed his feeling that all was not right by a gesture of concern most unusual in him: he twitched her dress down again and removed his hand from her mouth quite gently.

She was lying there looking up at him quite blank. Amazed. She was not weeping. Nor scratching. Nor calling him names. Nor showing the cold relentless repulsion that he dreaded to see in his women. Nothing. It occurred to him that she was *interested* in a totally unsuspected phenomenon.

"Oh, you," he groaned out, between his teeth, "how did I get saddled with you."

At which she suddenly let out a snort of something that was unmistakably amusement. She sat up. She swung her legs down over the couch, then she all at once burst into swift tears that shook her shoulders quite soundlessly, and then, just as suddenly, she stopped crying, and crept to her cushion, where she sat with her back to the wall, staring at him.

He noted that she was afraid of him, but not in a way that could appeal to him.

"Well," he said, "that's that." He gave her uneasy sideways glances, as if waiting for a comment.

"Is that really what you do?" she inquired. "Or is it because you don't like me?"

At this he gave her a look which was all appeal, and he sat on the bottom of the bed, and pounded it hard, with his fists.

She saw, at last, that he was a boy, he was not much more than a small boy. She saw him as one of her own half-grown sons, and for the first time, her heart softened.

Looking at him with the tears still full in her great eyes, she said, "You know, I think there might be something you could learn from us."

He gave a sort of shake of his great shaggy head, as if too much was reaching his ears all at once. But he remained leaning forward, not looking at her, but listening.

"For one thing, have you never heard that one may choose the times to conceive children?"

He winced. But only because again she talked of children. He pounded the bed with one fist, and stopped.

"You did not know that the nature of a child may be made by its conception?"

He shook his head and hung it. He sighed.

"If I am pregnant now, as I could be, then this child will have nothing to thank us for."

He suddenly flung himself down on the bed, prone, and lay there, arms outstretched.

Again, a long silence. The smell of their coupling was a small rank reminder of lust, and he looked up at her. She sat leaning against the wall, very pale, tired, and there was a bruise by her mouth, where his thumb had pressed.

He let out a groan. "It seems there is something I can learn from you," he said, and it was not in a child's voice.

She nodded. Looking at each other, they saw only that they were unhappy, and did not know what to expect from the other.

She it was who got up, sat by him on the couch, and laid her small hands on both sides of his great neck as he still lay prone, chin on his fist.

He turned over. It was an effort for him to face her.

He took her hands, and lay there on his back, she sitting quietly close to him. She tried to smile, but her lips trembled, and tears rolled down her face. He gave an exclamation, and pulled her down beside him. He was astounded that his own eyes had tears in them.

He tried to comfort this strange woman. He felt her small hands on his shoulders, in a pressure of consolation and pity.

Thus they fell asleep together, worn out by it all.

This was the first lovemaking of these two, the event which was fusing the imaginations of two realms.

FROM

# The Making of the Representative for Planet 8

You ask how the Canopean Agents seemed to us in the times of The Ice.

It was usually Johor who came, but whichever one of them it was, he arrived without prior warning and apparently casually, stayed for a short or a long time, and during these agreeable visits—for we always looked forward to them—gave us advice, showed us how we could more effectively use the resources of our planet, suggested devices, methods, techniques. And then left without saying when we might expect to see Canopus again.

The Canopean Agents were not much unlike each other. I and the few others who had been taken to other Colonized Planets for instruction or training of various kinds knew that the officials of the Canopean Colonial Service were to be recognized by an authority they all had. But this was an expression of inner qualities, and not of a position in a hierarchy. On these other planets the Canopeans were always distinguishable from the natives, once we had learned what to look for. And this made us more aware of what it was they brought to our own Planet 8.

Everything on Planet 8 that had been planned, built, made—everything that was not natural—was according to their specifications. The presence of our kind on the planet was because of them: because of Canopus. They had brought us here, a species created by them from stock originating on several planets.

Therefore it is not accurate to talk of obedience: does one talk of *obeying* when it is a question of one's origin, and existence?

Or talk of rebellion . . .

There was once a near rebellion.

It was when Johor said we should circle our little globe with a tall thick wall, and brought instructions in how to make building substances not then known by us. We had to mix chemicals in certain proportions with our own crushed local stones. To make this wall would take all our strength, all our effort, and all our resources for a long time.

We pointed this out: as if it were likely Canopus did not already know it! This was our protest, for we called it that, among ourselves. And it was the limit of our "rebellion." Johor's smiling silence told us that a wall would have to be built.

What for?

We would find out, was the reply.

By the time the wall was completed, those who had been infants when it was started were old—I was one of them; and their children's children saw the ceremony when the last slab of shining black was swung into place on top of a construction fifty times as high as our tallest building, and with a breadth to match.

It was a marvel, this wall.

The black *thing* that circled our globe—though not at its widest part, not at its middle, a fact that made us question and doubt even more—drew us to it, attracted our minds and imaginations, absorbed us. Always were to be seen knots and groups and crowds of us, standing along its top; or on the observation platforms that had been placed all along it, for this purpose; or on high ground that overlooked it—high ground at a distance, for nothing near could give us an ample enough view. We were there in the early mornings when our sun flashed out over it, or at midday, when the glistening black flashed back light and color to the sky, and at night, when the brilliant clustering stars of Planet 8 seemed to shine forth from within it as from dark water. Our planet did not have moons.

This wall had become our achievement, our progress, our summing-up and definition: we were no longer developing in other ways, our wealth did not increase. We no longer expected, as we had in the past, always to be augmenting our resources: always to be making more subtle and fine and inventive our ways of living.

A wall. A great black shining wall. A *useless* wall.

Johor, the others who came, said: Wait, you will see, you will find out, you must trust us.

Their visits became more frequent, and their instructions were not always to do with the wall, and the nature and purposes of what we had to do were not easy to understand.

We knew that we had ceased to understand. We *had* understood—or believed we had—what Canopus wanted for us, and from us: we had been taking part, under their provision, in a long, slow progress upwards in civilization.

During this period of change, while our expectations for ourselves and our children were being tempered, our world continued mild in climate, and agreeable, and very beautiful. As always, we continued to grow more crops and beasts than we needed, and exchanged these with other near planets for their surpluses. Our population remained at the exact level required of us by Canopus. Our wealth was not increasing but we were not poor. We had never suffered harshness or threat.

We were a favored planet, climatically, physically. Other planets suffered extremes of climate, knew heat that flayed and withered, and cold that kept great parts of them uninhabitable. Planet 8's position from its sun was such that along a narrow central zone there was heat, and sometimes discomfort. Temperate zones spread on either side. At the poles were frigid regions: but these were very small. The planet did not incline on its axis, or only so little that it made no difference. We did not have seasons as we knew other planets did.

In the regions where we all lived, there was never snow or ice.

We would tell our children: "If you travel as far as you can that way, as far as you can that way, you will come to places that lie more distant from our sun than we do. You will find thick water, not light and quick-moving as it is with us. The water is slow with cold, and on its surface it wrinkles as it moves, or even, sometimes, makes plates or flakes that are solid. This is ice."

When, rarely, storms brought lumps of ice from the sky, a great thing was made of it; we called our children; we said: "Look, this is ice! At the poles of our world the cold slow water sometimes makes this substance, you might walk half a day and see no water that was not in this form: white, solid, glistening."

And, when they were older: "On some other planets as much of their surface is ice as on our planet is vegetation and fruitfulness."

We would say to them: "On our planet, in those regions lying back from the sun, sometimes from the sky fall small white flakes so light and so delicate you can blow them about and around with a breath. This is snow, this is how the water that is always in the air, though invisible to us, changes in those parts when it is frozen by the cold."

And the children would of course marvel and wonder and wish they might see snow, and the gelid wrinkling waters, and the ice that sometimes made crusts or even plates and sheets.

And then, snow fell.

Across light blue sunlit skies drove thick grey that came swarming down around us in a white fall, and everywhere we stood about, gazing up, gazing down, holding out our hands where the faint white flakes of the tales we told our children lay for an instant before they sank into blobs and smears of water.

It was not a prolonged fall, but it was heavy. One instant our world was as always, green and brown, and colored with the shine and glisten of moving water, and the easy movement of light clouds. And the next it was a white world. Everywhere, white, and the black jut of the wall rising from it, and on the top of the black, a white crest.

Very often, looking back, we say that we did not understand clearly what was happening, the importance of an event. But I can say that this fall of white from our capacious and mild skies was something that struck into us, into our minds and our understandings. Oh yes, we knew, we understood. And, looking into each other's faces for confirmation of what we felt, it was there—the future.

That scene is as clear in my memory as any. We were all out of our dwellings, we had run together everywhere and were in groups and little crowds, and we were gazing into more than this cold white that had so suddenly enveloped us.

We were a tall lithe people, lightly but strongly built, and our color was brown, and our eyes were black, and we had long straight black hair. We loved strong and vibrant colors in clothes and in the decoration of our houses: these were what we saw when we looked out at our world—the many blues of the sky, the infinite greens of the foliage, the reds and browns of our earth, mountains shining with pyrites and quartz, the dazzle of water and of sun.

We had not thought, ever, to wonder about our congruity with our surroundings, but on that day we did. We have never seemed to ourselves anything but comely, but against the white glisten that now covered everything we seemed to ourselves dingy and shrunken. Our skins were yellow, and our eyes puckered and strained because of the cold glare we could not escape except by shutting them. The strong colors of our clothes were harsh. We stood there shivering with the suddenness of the drop in temperature, and everywhere could be seen the same involuntary movement: of people looking at each other, finding what they saw ugly, and then, as they remembered that this was how they must be striking others, their eyes turning away, while they hugged themselves in their own arms not only because of the cold, but in a way that suggested a need for comfort, consolation.

Canopus arrived while the snow still lay, unmelted.

There were five of them, not the usual one, or two; and this alone was enough to impress us. They were among us while the snow melted so that our world returned to its warmth and the comfortable colors of growth—and while the snow again fell, and this time stayed for longer.

Nor did they leave when this second affliction of white shrank and went. It was never the way of Canopus to demand, announce, threaten—or even to stand high on the crest of our wall, as we sometimes did on civic occasions, to address large crowds. No, they moved quietly among us, staying for a while in one dwelling, and then moving on to another, and while nothing dramatic or painful was ever said, before long we had all gathered from them what was needed.

The snow would come again, and more often; slowly the balance of warmth and cold on our planet would change, and there would be more snow and ice for us than there would be green and growth. And this and this and this was what we must do to prepare ourselves . . .

We were learning how those on harsher planets matched themselves against cold. We were hearing of houses built thick and strong to withstand weights of snow and the pressures of winds we had never known. We were told of clothing, and footwear, and how to wrap a head in thick cloth so that only the eyes would be exposed—this last impressed us fearfully, for the falls of snow we had seen had not done more than make us shiver and pull our light clothes more tightly around us.

While we were deciding how to make sure those settlements and towns nearest the poles would be protected first, we were told by Canopus that they should be abandoned altogether. All day and night, along that great black wall of ours, pressed crowds of people. We stood on it, we massed beside it. We laid our hands on the cold hard shine of it. We looked at the vast weight and thickness of it. We crowded close under it and looked up at how it towered and we felt it as a safety and guarantee. The wall—our wall—our great black useless monument, that had swallowed all our wealth and our labor and our thoughts and our capacities . . . it was going to save us all.

We were all now to live on one side of it, leaving the smaller part of our globe empty, for it would soon be uninhabitable. We traveled, many of us, all over those mild and agreeable lands where the crops were still in the fields, the vegetation many-colored and warm. We were moving there, we knew, because of our need to comprehend. For we did not. One may be told something, act on it, trust in it—but that is not the same as *feeling* it, as a truth. We—those of us entrusted with the task of moving the populations out of their threatened homes—were always at work, in our imaginations, on the task of *really* knowing that shortly ice and snow would rule here. And those who had to submit to the move were not taking it in either.

Soon there were new towns and manufactories everywhere on the side of the wall that we believed would remain more or less as it had been . . . with perhaps snow and even storms, but not so very different from what we had known.

And now, when we stood gathered on the summit of that barrier wall that was going to have to hold the pressures of massing and thrusting ice, and gazed over a still fertile landscape where the future was not visible, except in the skies that had a pallid and pinched look, we felt grief, we were struck and slowed with grief, for at last we had become enabled to feel, really feel, in our substance, in our deepest selves, that our world, our way of living, everything we had been—was done, was over. Finished.

How dark it was, in our minds and our hopes, during that time of preparation, while we busied ourselves with resettling so many people in their new homes, while we took in what we could from Johor and the other emissaries they sent us.

And then we waited. Massing there—for we were now overcrowded and uncomfortable—on the inhabited part of our world, we came to think in this way: that at least the wall, that always visible reminder of our situation, was a proof that we had a future. Our planet had a future.

The time that passed then seemed long to us, and it was; but it was slowed, as well, by the events and thoughts that packed it. Our lives, from being easy, had become hard, the ideas that had inhabited our minds without being questioned were each one tested and—so far had everything changed for us—for the most part set aside.

The crops we had grown and that we were known for in all the near planets no longer thrived. The beasts we had understood and who understood us dwindled and went, and we had new strains of animal who, because their habits were to withstand hardship and threat, did not respond to us lovingly. We had not known how much of the happiness of our lives had been because, as we went among the fields and into the wilder places, we had always been greeted by affectionate creatures. I remember how I and some other representatives of cantons and provinces went out from a town we had used as a meeting place, into a valley we were accustomed to walk in for relaxation after our discussions; and where there had been a fresh bright green, and running streams, and light, quick, playful animals, there were hillsides covered with short, rough greyish plants and rocks growing new species of lichen, grey and thick, like fur—and there was a herd of heavy-shouldered, heavy-jawed cattle, all facing us, their horns lowered, great hooves planted solidly. And, as we stood, trying not to be dismayed, because we had learned to fear our grief, the greyish-brown of their shaggy hides lightened to silvery grey. The air was shedding greyish crumbs. We put out our hands and saw them fill with this rough grey substance. A grey sky seemed to lower itself, pulled down by the weight of itself. We stood there, shivering, pulling close the new clothes Canopus had told us to use, thick and warm and not easy to move about in, and we were there a long time, despite the cold, knowing that we needed such moments of sharp revelation so that we might change inwardly, to match our outward changes.

That part of our world beyond the wall was now grey and gelid and slow and cold, and filled with the creatures of the cold. First it was all bitter frosts, and flaking and then splitting stones, so that whole mountains changed their aspect, becoming littered and loose; and lowered and sullen skies, where clouds had become thick and dark—and then the snows came, showers and squalls of snow, and after that storms that raged a day, and then days at a time. Everything beyond our wall was white, and the new animals came crowding down towards us, their coats dragging with snow, their eyes looking sullenly out from the snow on their faces. But the snows melted, leaving the greys and the browns, and then came again—and again; and did not melt so quickly, and then did not melt at all.

Canopus said to us that we, the Representatives, should walk around our planet on the top of the wall. About fifty of us, then, set out; and Canopus came with us. The task took us almost a year. We walked into, not with, the revolving of the planet so that the sun always rose ahead of us, and we had to turn ourselves around when we wanted to see how the shadows gathered at nightfall. Because the top of the wall for the greater part of its way was so narrow, we walked no more than two or three abreast, and those at the back of this company had it brought into us how small and few we were under skies that on our right were packed with snow clouds. On the other side of the wall, but far down towards the pole, the skies were often still blue, and sometimes even warm, and down there were the greens and browns of a summery land, and the streams were quick and lively. To our right the grey and dour landscape was obscured again and again by snow. We could see that the whiteness of cold had claimed the far mountains on our right, and was covering the foothills and spreading out down the valleys. And the winds that come pouring down from there hurt our lungs and made our eyes sting, so that we turned our heads away and looked down over the part of our world that still said to us, Welcome, here nature is as warm and as comfortable as your flesh. But Canopus kept directing us—gently, but making sure we did it—to look as much as we could into the world of cold.

And so we went, day after day, and it was as if we walked into a spreading blight, for soon, even on the left side of the wall we saw how grasses shrank and dimmed and vegetation lost its luster, and the skies lowered themselves with a white glare somewhere behind the blue. And on the right the snows were reaching down, down, towards us, and our familiar landscapes were hard to recognize.

There was a day that we stood all together on our barrier wall, looking up into the freezing immensities, with Canopus among us, and we saw that the enormous heavy animals that Canopus had brought us from another of their planets were crowding close into the wall. They massed there, in vast herds, with the snow driving down behind them, and they were lifting their great heads and wild trapped eyes at the wall, which they could not cross. A short way ahead of us was a narrow gap which we had closed with a sliding door half the wall's height.

Canopus did not have to tell us what we must do. Some of us went down the side of the wall onto the rough soil, where the grasses had long since gone, leaving a thin crust of lichens, and pulled back the gates. The herds lifted their heads and swung their horns and trampled their feet in indecision, and then saw that this was their deliverance—and first one beast and then another charged through the gap, and soon from all over the frozen lands came charging and thundering herds of animals, and they all, one after another, went through the gap. What heavy clumsy beasts they were! We could never become accustomed to their mass and weight and ponderousness. On their heads were horns which at their base were thicker than our thighs, and sometimes they had four and even six horns. Their hooves left behind prints that would make small ponds. Their shoulders, to support these crests and clubs of bone, were like the slopes of hills. Their eyes were red and wild and suspicious, as if their fate was to query forever what had ordained them to carry such weights of bone and horn and meat and hair, for their coats hung down around them like tents.

These herds passed through the gap in our wall, taking twenty of our days to do it, and soon there were none of these beasts of the cold in that part of our world that was doomed to be swallowed by the cold. They were all in the more favored parts—and we knew, without Canopus having to say anything to us, what it meant.

Had we really imagined that our guardian wall would contain all of the snow and ice and storm on one side of it, leaving everything on the other side warm and sweet? No, we had not; but we had not, either, really taken into our understandings that the threat would strike so hard into where we now all lived . . . into where we were crowding, massed, jostling together, with so much less of food and pleasantness that our former selves, our previous conditions, seemed like a dream of some distant and favored planet that we only imagined we had known.

We stood there, looking into hills and valleys where grass still grew, though more thinly, and where the movement of water was still quick and free; we saw how the herds of the animals of the cold spread everywhere, making our ears ring and hurt with their savage exulting bellowing because they had found some grass. We were a company of thin yellow light-boned birdlike creatures, engulfed in the thick pelts of the herds, wildly gazing at a landscape that no longer matched us. And, as we had taken to doing more and more, we gazed up, our eyes kept returning to the skies, where the birds moved easily. No, they were not the small and pretty birds of the warm times, flocks and groups and assemblies darting and swirling and swooping as one, moving as fast as water does when its molecules are dancing. They were the birds of this chilly time, individual, eagles and hawks and buzzards, moving slowly on wings that did not beat, but balanced. They too had heavy shoulders and their eyes glared from thick feathers, and they circled and swept about the skies on the breath of freezing winds that had killed our familiar flocks sometimes as they flew; so that, seeing the little brightly colored bodies drop from the air, we had looked up and imagined we could see, too, the freezing blast that had struck them down out of the sky. But they were birds, these great savage creatures; they could move; they could sweep from one end of a valley to the other in the time we could hold a breath. We had once been as they were, we told ourselves, as we stood there on the wall slowed and clumsy in our thick skins—the wall which, on the side towards the ice, was dimmed and clouded, no longer a brilliant shining black, but shades of grey. Frosted grey.

Now that the herds had all gone through the wall, we filled the gap by pushing across the gate. But Canopus said that as soon as we got back to our homes, work parties must be sent out, and this gap, and the others that had been left, must be built up as strongly and thickly as all the rest of the wall. For the openings that had been ordered to be left in the wall long before there had been cold, or even the first signs of cold, to save animals that had not even been brought to our planet, had fulfilled their purpose. We no longer needed them. The wall must be perfect and whole and without a weak place.

We walked on for some days after that before there was a blizzard of an intensity we had not even been able to imagine. We huddled on the safe side of the wall, while the winds screamed over us and sometimes came sucking and driving down where we were, and we shivered and we shrank, and knew that we had not begun to imagine what we had, all of us, to face. And when the screaming and scouring stopped and we climbed up the little projecting steps to the top, carefully because of the glaze of ice on them, we saw that on the cold side snow had fallen so heavily that all the hollows and the heights of the landscape were filled in with billowy white, and the wall was only half its previous height.

By then we were not far from our starting place, and we all longed to be back in our homes, our new thick-walled solid houses with roofs that had been pitched to throw off any snowfall—so we had thought. But now wondered. Were we going to have to live under snow as some creatures lived under water? Were we going to have to make little tunnels and caves for ourselves under a world of snow?

But still, on our side of the wall, where our towns and cities and farms spread, there was some green, there was the shine of moving water. And knowing of our hunger and our desperation and our longing, Canopus did not now make us turn our faces from this livingness, but allowed us to stumble on, looking warmthwards, trying to ignore the snowy wilderness that was crowding down on us.

And it was during these days that Johor fell back with me, and talked to me, alone. I listened to him and I had my eyes on my fellows in front, the Representatives, and when I knew that what I was being told was for me, and not for them—not yet, at least, because they could not yet face it—there came into me an even deeper sense of what was in store. But what worse could there possibly be?

Ahead of us this great wall of ours stood high and black above marshes where the snows of the blizzard had partly melted, leaving streaks and blobs of thin white on dark water. We stood there, Johor and I, and watched our companions walk away, and become no more than a moving blur on the crest of the wall where it rose to cross a ridge and then disappeared from our view. It climbed again, and we saw it, still mighty and tall though so far away, showing exactly what its nature was, for on one side the snows piled, and on the other the beasts fed on wintry grass and on low grey bushes.

Johor touched my arm, and we walked forward to stand where the marshes lay on either side. On the right the dark white-streaked waters seemed channels to the world of snow and ice. But on the other side the marshes were an estuary which led to the ocean. We called it that, though it was really a large lake, enclosed by land. We had been told of, and some of us had seen, planets that were more water than land—where lumps and pieces and even large areas of land were in watery immensities. It is hard to believe in something very far from experience. With us everything was the other way about. Our "ocean" was always a marvel to us. Was precious. Our lives depended on it, we knew that, for it helped us to make our atmosphere. It seemed to us to represent distant and rare truths, was a symbol to us of what was hard to attain and must be guarded and sheltered. Those of you who live on planets where liquids are as common as earth and rocks and sand will find it as hard to imagine our cherishing of this "ocean" of ours as we found it to visualize planets where water masses bathed the whole globe in a continuous living movement, speaking always of wholeness, oneness, interaction, of rapid and easy interchange. For the basis of our lives, the substance which bound us in continuity, was earth. Oh yes, we knew that this soil and rock that made our planet, with water held so shallowly in it, and only in one place, except for the streams and rivers that fed it, was something that moved, just as water moved—we knew rock had its currents, like water. We knew it because Canopus had taught us to think like this. Solidity, immobility, permanence—this was only how we with our Planet 8 eyes had to see things. Nowhere, said Canopus, was permanence, was immutability—not anywhere in the galaxy, or the universe. There was nothing that did not move and change. When we looked at a stone, we must think of it as a dance and a flow. And at a hillside. Or a mountain.

I was standing there with my back to the icy winds, face towards our precious lake that was out of sight beyond tall plumy reeds, and I was thinking: And ice?—we must see this new enemy of ours as something all fluidity and movement? And it was at that moment that it came into me for the first time that our ocean might freeze. Even though it was on the "safe" side of our barrier wall. The thought came like a blast of cold. I knew it would be so, and I already felt something of what Canopus was going to tell me. I did not want to turn and face Johor—face what I had to.

I felt his touch on my elbow again and I did turn.

I saw him as he saw me, fragile and vulnerable inside thick pelts, hands hidden inside sleeves, eyes peering out from deep shaggy hoods.

It is a hard thing, to lose the sense of physical appropriateness—and again my eyes went skywards where an eagle lay poised on air just above us.

"Representative," said Johor gently, and I made my gaze return downwards, to what I could see of his yellow face.

"Your ocean will freeze," he said.

I could feel my bones huddle and tremble inside my thin flesh.

I tried to joke: "Canopus can bring us new beasts with heavy bones for the cold—but what can you do for our bones? Or shall we all die out as our other animals did, to make way for new species—new races?"

"You will not die out," he said, and his strong brown eyes—inflamed though, and strained—were forcing me to look at him.

Another new thought came into me, and I asked: "You were not born on Canopus, so you said. What kind of planet did you come from?"

"I was given existence on a warm and easy planet."

"As Planet 8 was, once."

"As the planet is that you will all be going to."

At this I was silent for a very long time. There were too many adjustments to make in my thoughts—which whirled about and did not settle into patterns that could frame useful questions.

When I was slightly recovered, I still was facing Johor, who stood with his back to a wind that came pouring down from the snow fields.

"You are always traveling," I said. "You are seldom on your own planet—do you miss it?"

He did not answer. He was waiting.

"If we are all to be space-lifted away from our home, then why the wall? Why were we not taken away when the snows first began to fall?"

"The hardest thing for any one of us to realize—every one of us, no matter how high in the levels of functioning—is that we are all subject to an overall plan. A general Necessity."

"It was not convenient?" And my voice was bitter.

"When we took you for training to the other planets, did you ever hear of the planet Rohanda?"

I had, and my curiosity was already expectation—and even a warm and friendly expectation.

"Yes, it is a beautiful planet. And quite one of our most successful attempts. . . ." He smiled, though I could not see his smile, only the change in the shape of his eyes, for his mouth was covered: and I smiled too—ruefully, of course. For it is not easy to accept oneself as an item among many.

"Our poor planet is not a successful attempt!"

"It is not anyone's fault," he said. "The Alignments have changed . . . unexpectedly. We believed that Planet 8 was destined for stability and slow growth. As things have not turned out that way, we mean to take you to Rohanda. But first another phase of development there must be concluded. It is a question of raising a certain species there to a level where, when your kind are brought in, you will make a harmonious whole. That is not yet. Meanwhile you, on this planet, must be sheltered from the worst of what will happen."

"The wall, then, is something to hold off the worst of the snow?"

"The worst of the ice that will come pressing down in great sheets and plates and will rise against the wall. Down there, where we look now"—and he turned me about to face away from the cold towards the warm pole—"it will be bad enough. You may have a hard time of it, surviving. And this wall will hold, so we believe, the force of the ice. For long enough."

"And you do not want us all to know that we must leave our Home Planet for Rohanda?"

"It is enough that one of you knows."

It took time to digest this. Time and observation. For without my ever telling anyone at all, not even the other Representatives, it became known that we would all be space-lifted to another beautiful warm planet, where our lives would become again as they had once been—in a past that seemed so far from us. Though it was not far, only on the other side of the physical change in our lives that had been so sharp and sudden that we could hardly believe what we had been.

Johor and the other Canopeans left us, having made sure that all the gaps in our wall were well and strongly filled. And that no living thing was left on the cold side of the wall. It seemed a dead place, where now the blizzards raged almost continuously, the winds howled and shrieked, and the snows heaped themselves up and up so that even the mountains seemed likely to become buried. And then, standing on our wall to gaze there, our gloved hands held to shield our streaming eyes, we saw that the mountains had a glassy look, and that between the foothills crept tongues of ice. A few of us did wrap ourselves, and made little carts that could slide on runners, and we ventured up into that frigid and horrible land to find out what we could. It was like a journey into another part of ourselves, so slowed and difficult were our movements, so painful the breaths we had to take. All we could see was that the snows piled up, up, into the skies, and the packs of ice crept down. And, this expedition over, we stood huddled on our wall, looking at where we had been, and saw how the snow came smoking off fields of white and eddied up into skies that were a hard cold blue.

We had a great deal to do, all of us, and most particularly we Representatives. The physical problems, bad enough, were the least of it. Now that it had spread from mind to mind that we had a home waiting for us, in a favored part of the galaxy, where we could again be congruous with our surroundings, a quick-moving, shining-brown-skinned, healthy race under blue skies—now that this dream had taken hold of us, our present realities seemed to numb us even more. And when we looked up and saw how the snows had massed themselves into packs of gleaming ice with great cracks that could run from one horizon to another—this present horror came to seem less real to us than Rohanda, where we were bound. When? We were coming to yearn, to long, for our deliverance, and against this I and the others had to fight. For if we allowed ourselves to lapse into daydreams and longings, then none of us would be alive to make that final journey to the lovely planet.

One of our difficulties was that when our peoples had been moved away from the cold, everything that had been built to shelter them and their beasts faced away from the blizzards. Standing on the wall, what had to strike us first was how villages and towns huddled and crept and hid away, and there seemed no windows or openings, for these were on the other side. Before, our towns had been spread about and seemed haphazard, as towns do, when built to catch the advantages of an amenable slope, or of a fertile wind. Now, as we looked down, a town might seem like a single building, in which one might walk from room to room through a valley. So vulnerable they looked, our new homes, so easily crushed, as we stood high there, feeling the winds tear and buffet us, knowing the strength of what was to come—and yet, down again at earth level, inside a town, it was easy to forget what threatened. It was sheltered, for the winds streamed above. All the apertures showed hills still green, and mountains green for a good part of the way up to their summits, and there was the glint and shine of water, and patches of misty blue appeared among the thick grey of the cloud. Down there was fertility and warmth and pleasantness. . . . At the margins of the eye's reach was our heart's desire.

FROM

# The Making of the Representative for Planet 8

We were watching not only the dreary spaces of moor and tundra around the column but, more than these, each other. Increasingly, our eyes were on each other, searchingly, patiently—as if we did not know every one of us, as in fact we did; so very well that we could at any moment take on each other's work and—in a sense—become each other. We gazed close into eyes and faces as if there was very much more to be learned there than we had ever believed. And, soon, we were all in a rough circle, looking in and not out at the little spaces of our "summer." We faced inwards, as if the truth available to us was there, between us . . . in us . . . among us. In our being there together, in that way, in our extremity.

And so, later, were we found by Alsi and Johor, who came out of the white wilderness towards us, showing by the way they stumbled and slid over the roughnesses of the ground how exhausted they were. And they flung themselves down among us, and lay there, eyes closed. And we saw how the yellow skin stretched over the bones of their faces.

We waited until Alsi opened her eyes and sat up, and Johor did the same.

I said to her, "And how was it with you, as Doeg?" She said, smiling, "Doeg, it seemed to me that as I spoke, everything that had happened to me, all my thoughts and my feelings, everything that I believed I had to be, was being put together in words, words, words—parceled up, packaged up, and sent away . . . yes Doeg, I-Doeg—saw Alsi doing this and that, feeling thus or thinking so—and who was Alsi? I watched her, saw myself moving there among all the others . . . and now, I look back at myself as Doeg sitting in the shed with Johor, I see myself there, and see Johor, two people sitting together talking. And who was Doeg? Who, Doeg, is Doeg? And where now are Alsi or Doeg—for what is left of us all now? And to whom will you or I or any one of us be telling our little tales, singing our little songs?" And she looked, smiling, at me, and then at Johor who was listening as he lay propped on his elbow, and then at all the others. Slowly she looked at one after another, and we all looked back at her. When Alsi came back to us, with Johor, our small assembly of people had been made even more sharply aware of ourselves, our situation. We *felt* ourselves, as sharply as we saw—on a cold hillside, under a low cold hurrying sky, half a hundred individuals sitting together, fifty heaps of dirty shaggy animal skin and inside each a shivering parcel of bones and flesh, and thoughts and feelings too (but where were they, what were they?). We huddled there, listening to how the blizzards on the horizon squealed and raged and threatened this brief summer of ours which was no more than a small space or time at the very extremity of our planet, for the frosts of the approaching winter were beginning to show themselves. White on black, small white particles on black soil, crumbs and crystals of white scattered on the rocks and the grey-green grasses and on the wiry little plants—and in the air around us white flakes, only a few still, drifting, catching the weak sunlight, floating and sinking to settle with the frost on the earth. High above us, under heavy white clouds that had black crevasses, circled the great birds of the snow, white on white.

"If you are no longer Alsi," I said to her, "that means the snow animals are dead?"

"The pens are empty now, all of them."

We all looked, and then understood that this was what we were doing, at her hands: those knots of thin bones that had once been so large and so capable, tending so well the small, the weak, the vulnerable.

And she was looking at Johor. And that was a look not so easily described. For one thing, there was nothing in it of suppliance. Or even of need. What was there, and most strongly, was the recognition of him, of Canopus.

"I am no longer Alsi," she said to him. "Not in any way, or in any capacity." This sounded almost like a question; and in a moment she answered it. "Somewhere else there is Alsi—another place, another time. Alsi cannot disappear since Alsi is and must be continually re-created." Again she seemed to wait for him to speak, but he only smiled. "Though we cannot see them, since it is day now, and the sunlight up there obscures this truth, our sky is full of stars and planets and on them there is Alsi, Alsi—there I am, since it must be so."

"Since it must be so," voices echoed her from our group.

"So, since this is not Alsi, who am I, Johor, *and what is my name?*"

I said to him: "Doeg tells tales and sings songs in all times and all places, everywhere people use sounds to communicate, so if I am no longer Doeg, then Doeg still is, and perhaps as the dark comes down . . ."—and it was coming down, as we talked, and small distant stars appeared—". . . we are looking as we raise our eyes at worlds where Doeg is at work, for Doeg has to be. But who am I, Johor, and what is my name?"

And then Klin, the Fruit Maker, the Guardian of the Orchards: "There is not one orchard or fruit tree or fruit anywhere in this world of ours, nothing is left of all that beauty and richness—and so Klin I am not, since Klin was what I did—Klin is at work somewhere else, there Klin grafts shoots to shoots, Klin buds and blends and makes, and causes branches to lie heavy with blossom and then with fruit. But not here, not anywhere here, and so I am no longer Klin. And what is my name?"

And Bratch: "The skill in my mind and in my hands is at work now, at work everywhere there are creatures of flesh and sinew, and blood and bone—Bratch is needed, and so Bratch must be, though it is not here, for here there is nothing left to do, since all over this world of ours our populations lie dying in their icy homes. Bratch I am not, since Bratch is what I did—and what is my name, Johor, what is my name?"

And Pedug: "Where species reproduce themselves, where the young are born continually to replace those that have to die, there Pedug is, since Pedug has to be. Pedug is re-created always and everywhere, in every time and place, where Pedug is needed. So Pedug is not lost and gone because Pedug no longer exists on our planet. But I am not Pedug, Johor, and—what is my name?"

So it went, with every one of us, and the dark was heavy around us, and the chant, or song, or plaint, continued through the night, one after another of us, asking Johor, asking him, saying where and how and why, but answering ourselves, answering all we wanted to know ourselves, but ending always with that question we could not answer, since it was beyond us—what am I, who am I, and what is my name? Or, *what was our name?*—we, the Representatives, who represented now no skills, or abilities, or working functions, but who still sat there, cold and small and so very few, on that hillside, through the night, all through the night—and then the weak sun was shining dimly, a greyish gleam from greyish skies, and there was no color left anywhere, for snow had fallen gently and silently, and the tall column Canopus had set there rose up out of fresh soft white, through which pushed the tips of low plants and the stiff dead grasses.

"There is one of us who still has a name," said Alsi, as we became silent, since everyone had spoken.

"But Marl is not here," one said. "The Keepers of the Herds are not here."

"And the herds are not here either, yet there is nowhere else for them to be."

We sat on there, that day, as the snow fell quietly around us, for Johor said nothing, and we did not know what it was we ought to be doing.

And, as the light went, for another night, three figures came staggering towards us out of the gloom, and fell among us, breathing deep and painfully, and slept for a time, while we waited. These were Marl, and until they spoke, we could not feel that this particular stage of our being together was concluded.

It was in the night that they came up out of their exhaustion, and told us the tale of the herds—yes, it was Doeg we listened to for a while, Marl as Doeg, and this was what we were told.

That multitude of great hungry beasts found themselves crowding closer together every day, as the snows spread down and around them, making a natural corral of snowbanks, a barrier that the beasts showed no disposition to cross, since all the food that remained to them on the entire planet was in this small area around the tall black column. The hay masses from the last summer did not provision them for long, and then they browsed on the wiry plants and the bitter grasses, and then on the soil that is half vegetable. And still the snow crept in around them, and soon they stood together body to body, many thousands of them, a multitude, and there was nothing to eat. Many died, and those that were alive were spurred by their situation into an intelligence no one could have believed possible to them—they pushed the corpses out of the mass of the living with those horns of theirs that were so heavy and, we had thought when we first saw the beasts, so useless: What could they possibly be used for? Yet these horns had turned over the soil, when it became necessary to eat it, had dug roots out of the earth, had overturned boulders in the desperate search for food, had been used, finally, to push their dead out of what remained of the useable space.

And then, for a time, they stood, facing out into the world of snow, all of them, their tails into the center. And then Marl, watching from the hillsides, anguished at their inability to aid these poor beasts, saw that from every part of the multitude, small groups of them, and then larger and larger numbers, were breaking away. For days Marl watched how the mass that remained at the pole thinned, and still thinned, as the beasts left. But where were they going? There was nowhere for them to go! Yet they went. Lowing and lumbering, pawing the earth as they went, and scarring it with sweeps and scythings of their horns, as if wishing to damage and wound what would no longer supply them with sustenance; screaming out their rage and despair, their eyes red and wild and furious—these herds thundered up and away in every direction from their last grazing grounds, and then their going, which had shaken the earth, was silent, for the deep snows quieted the battering of those multitudes of hooves. The watchers on the hillsides had heard the wild lamenting bellowing of the herds as they rushed up and into the blizzards—and soon none was left around the pole, there was only the black earth that had been horned up, and fouled with masses of droppings, and eaten quite bare. And not one beast, not one. Marl, then, separating, followed the herds up into the thick blizzards, though following them was not easy, since there was no spoor in those heavy snows. But at last, each one of these Representatives reached the populated area, and thought that perhaps the beasts had believed that here there might be food for them, or at least the companionship of people: who could say what there might be in the minds of these doomed animals, or what degrees of hope or intelligence were being forced out of them by their situation? But no, the herds had thundered up to the old towns and villages, empty now, and gone through them, not pausing for anything, except when some beast needed to punish and scar as had been done in the southlands, their old feeding grounds, and had raked horns into soil—so they directed the thrust of their horns along the sides of buildings and sheds and pens, and trampled down what they could, till the settlements looked as if we had destroyed them as we left. And then the herds had gone on—with nowhere to go. Where the wall had collapsed, making passes into the terrible lands of the perpetual blizzards, the herds had climbed up, and then stood waiting on the other side, white beasts now, their coats heavy with snow, their breath white on white air, till all of their particular group had joined them. Having assembled, as if this had been some plan worked out by them, they all charged up into the north, all togther, bellowing and lamenting, to their certain deaths.

Marl, at various places along the wall, where it had fallen forward under the glaciers, saw this, saw the herds go off to seek death. And having seen it and understood, met together again, and then, knowing that there was no point at all in following the beasts, for they would have been swallowed up by the blizzards, traveled slowly down to where they knew we all would be. We, the Representatives, sitting on our snowy hillside, waiting. Waiting, as it turned out, for them, for Marl, who was no longer Marl, since there were no beasts left alive on our planet anywhere, not one, and so—elsewhere Marl worked, had to work; in other times and places Marl was and had to be, Marl used the skills of matching and mating and making and feeding and breeding and caring. Marl could not cease to be, since Marl was needed. But here, with us, on our cold planet, Marl was not. "And so, Johor, since we are no longer Marl, what is our name? For while I know I am not what I was, am not Marl, since I was what I did—well, now I do nothing, but here I am, am something, I sit here, among the falling snow, with us all, I look at you, Johor, you look at us, at me—and I feel myself to be here, here; I have thoughts and I have feelings—but where are they, what are they, these thoughts, these feelings, in these packages of frozen bones and chilly flesh? So I am not nothing, Johor, yet what am I? If I have a name, then what is it?"

And so it was with all of us, Johor with the Representatives, sitting there on our cold hillside, while the snow fell, it fell, it fell, so that we sat to our waists in light loose snow, and then the white pall was up to our shoulders—and first one, then another, rose slowly up out of the white as if out of water, shaking flakes and crumbs and clots of snow everywhere, and soon we were all standing, with the white drift up to our mid-thighs, and still the snow fell, it was falling with no signs of any end to it at all. We stood facing in to each other, looking into each other's eyes. There was not one word of Canopus, or of rescues—all that way of thinking seemed to us to belong to some distant childishness; and we could hardly remember, between the lot of us, how we had been in those days of our juvenescence, and now our thoughts were of a very different necessity. Then we turned ourselves so that we all, every one, faced away from the southern extremity of our planet, marked by the slim black shining column which, however, was beginning now to grey over with frost, so that soon it would hardly be visible where it stood amid the heaping drifts and flying clouds of snow. Our faces were to the north, and we began to move in unison, as if there was no other thing that could be done, as if what we had to do was ordained for us, and inevitable—we, like the empty and starving herds before us, were heading up into the realms of the winter; but it was a winter that would soon have covered everything, claimed everything, and our little planet would be swinging there in space, all white and glittering while the sun and the stars shone on it, and then, being all frozen over, with nothing left on it that had been living—what new processes would begin, once the processes of freezing had been accomplished? For nothing can be static and steady and permanent, it could not possibly be that our little world would spin there in space, unaltering, a planet of snow and ice: no, it would go on, gathering more to itself as a snowball does when traveling, or change into something else entirely, become a world we could not begin to imagine, with our senses tuned as they were to Planet 8—and not even this Planet 8, the freezing one, but the old and delightful world of the time before The Ice . . . no, changes we could not begin to imagine would—must—come to this home of ours, but they would be of no concern to us, for we would not be here.

We moved on, slowly, with our faces to the freezing winds that came down on us, came pitilessly, not ceasing at all, day or night; we went on cold, empty, as insubstantial inside our thick coats as if we were already bones and bits of dried tendon and skin. And Johor was with us, one of us, and his eyes looked back at us, from between the shaggy fringes of his hood, with the same hollow and painful and peering way we all had to use—for the snow glare was in our eyes, and in our minds, and there was no way of shutting it out and finding a soft and companionable darkness where we could rest; for even when the dark did come down, there was so much of the snow-light in us we could not shut our lids, they would not stay shut, but flew open, as if we had the snow and ice inside us as well as out, and our eyes were windows that looked both ways onto landscapes of white, white, a flat hard white.

Half blinded, deaf with the perpetually screaming winds, numbed, dying, we stumbled past the snow huts and sheds we had built for the populations to take refuge in from the advancing glaciers—and did not look inside, for we knew what we would find. As we went through this zone, it was evident that soon the little excrescences of snow and ice, small rounds and bumps among the drifts, would have gone under the white, for already some were gone, quite covered over. And, looking back from the mountain passes that led up into the parts of the planet that had been so thronged with people, we could not see now where these ice settlements were—or had been, for the storms were so thick between us and them. We went on, the few of us, looking out as we went for our old towns, but the glaciers had come down over them, we could not see any sign of settlements or cities, though once we did go struggling past a room sticking up out of the snow, that had square apertures all around, and, in it, some sticks and bits that had been furniture but had been pulverized by the cold. This room was the very top of a tall building, and we were advancing past it at a level where once only the great solitary birds of the age of the cold had swung and circled. And, when we looked ahead of us something like an escarpment or a cliff, there was nothing at all: the ice pushing down from above the wall had brought it all crashing and crumbling down, and in any case it was now a long way beneath where we traveled over the crests and billows of the snow. So we crossed over that famous wall of ours, the impregnable, the unbreachable, the impervious: the wall that would stand there forever between us and disaster, until Canopus would come with her shining fleets. We crossed it without knowing when we did, and were in a landscape where there were no mountains or hills, unless they were of ice or piled snow, for all the natural unevennesses of the terrain had been buried.

It is not true to say that we traveled easily, for we labored and stumbled and dragged ourselves forward—but this was not because we contended with inclines and descents of mountains and valleys. Yet it was such long hard dragging work. There was nothing left of us! We were as empty as if scoured inside with wind as well as out. We were truly nothing but skin and bone and our poor hearts thumped sluggishly and irregularly, trying to move the thick blood through our drying veins and arteries. We were half dead, and how hard it was, to shift forward these desiccating carcasses even a few steps at a time.

How heavy we were—how very very heavy . . . The drag on every particle of our bodies of the gravity of the spin of the planet was as if we were being held fast by it, and not merely by the thicknesses of the snow. Heavy, heavy, heavy—was the pull of our mortality; even though we were all as transparent as shadows and the flesh on our bones had long since dwindled down and gone. Heavy, the shuffling steps we took, one after another, making ourselves, forcing ourselves to move, our wills hammering there in the painful efforts of our hearts: *Move . . . move . . . move . . . yes, that's it . . . take one more step—yes, that's it . . . and now another . . . yes, and now just one more . . . move . . . and keep moving* . . . and so it was with every one of us, dragging ourselves there, among the clouds of snow that hung so low over the snowdrifts it was hard to tell what was air and what had already fallen from the air. We were half ghosts, half gone, and yet so heavy we could feel the weight of us depending on the substance of our wills, hanging there, dragging—and what was this thing, *will,* that kept us moving up and on, into the high passes of snow, towards the other pole, the far extremity of our planet? In and through and among these bundles of bones and skin and already desiccated tissues, burned something else, *will*—and where was it, that pulse or pull in the vast spaces that lie between the minute pull or pulses that make up the atom?

Heavy, heavy, oh so heavy, we dragged and pushed ourselves; we waded and seemed to swim, up and up and through, and at nights we rested together, poor wraiths, while the winds shrieked or the stars talked overhead. When we reached where we knew must be the gorge where Nonni had slipped, there was a clear fresh sweep of white, and the caves we had sheltered in were buried and gone; and when we came to the high valley between the ringing peaks where we had crouched to stare at the glitter of the stars and heard them rustle and sing, what we saw were the little tips of the mountains, hillocks merely, and if we had not known mountains were there, could not have guessed that they stood so tall and sharp. We made a stop there, as dark fell, in a hollow at the top of one of the small hills; and the winds rose screaming and we felt the snow thud and push and whirl all around us—and in the morning there was the most marvelous sight. For we were huddled between rocks on the summit of a great mountain—the winds had in the night cleared the valley of loose snow, so that we saw it as we had on our previous visit here, emptied. The winds had a pattern and a movement that filled this valley to the top, and then swept it: all over the planet the snow masses were moved about, piled high and then blasted away again, heaped up and then whisked off by gales to be dumped somewhere else. We looked down at a glassy glittering icy place many days walking across and very deep, between enormous icy black peaks. All we looked at had a glassy awfulness that hurt into our dying eyes; and as we peered down over the edge of the miniature valley we were stranded in at the top of the mountain peak, we knew we would never leave it. How could we, weak as we were, descend the ghastly precipices of that peak? And so, for the last time with our old eyes, we sat close and looked into each other's faces, until, one after another, our faces shuttered themselves in death, and our bundles of bones settled inside the heaps of our shag-skin coats, so that, as we slid away from that scene, and saw it with eyes we had not known we possessed, all we could see was what looked like a herd of beasts crouched in sleep or in death high up there on a mountaintop.

We went on together, light now, so buoyant and easy in moving that it was with disbelief and with horror we thought back to our so recent dreadful heaviness, the old weight of us, each step or lurch forward against the pull and the drag that held every tiniest atom in a lock. Our new eyes had no steady perspective. We went floating onwards, free and light, and when we looked back for orientation at the carcasses we had inhabited, we saw only that we were among throngs of the most marvelous intricate structures and shapes: glittering crystals surrounded us, all different, each a marvel of subtlety and balance, each a thing we could have stayed to contemplate and wonder over . . . yet there were myriads of them, they came floating and drifting all about us, and, as our eyes kept changing their capacity, sometimes these crystals seemed enormous, as large as we were, and sometimes small. It was not at once that we understood that these multitudes of infinitely various shapes were snowflakes; that were, or had recently been, our enemy: it was by the agency of such loveliness that our little planet had slowly been done to death. But we had not suspected it, had not known when we stretched out a hand to let a white flake settle there, so that we might show it to our children: "See? That is snow! That is the water vapor that is always in the air around us in a new shape"—had never thought that this little crumb, or froth of white, might be seen thus, as a conglomeration of structures so remarkable that one might examine them with admiration that could never wear out. Floating through them, feeling ourselves to change shape and size constantly, we tried to stay our movement, so that we could take our fill of gazing at these miracles; but that scene dissolved and went, the crystal structures vanished, for they belonged to some sphere or realm that we had passed through. Now, when we looked back to that huddle of bodies under their piles of dirty skins, to see how far we had traveled from that mountain peak, we saw them as webs and veils of light, saw the frail lattice of the atomic structure, saw the vast spaces that had been what in fact we mostly were—though we had not had eyes to comprehend that, even if our minds knew the truth. But the little dazzle or dance we looked at, the fabric of the atomic structure, dissolved as we watched: yes, we saw how those old bodies of ours inside their loads of hide were losing their shapes, how the atoms and the molecules were losing their associations with each other, and were melding with the substance of the mountain. Yes, what we were seeing now with our new eyes was that all the planet had become a fine frail web or lattice, with the spaces held there between the patterns of the atoms. But what new eyes were these that could see our old home thus, as interlocking structures of atoms, and where were we, the Representatives?—*what* were we, and how did we seem to those who could watch us, with their keener finer sight? For, certainly, as we changed eyes and ways of seeing so that every moment it seemed that we inhabited a different world, or zone, or reality, it must be that others could watch us, see us—but see what? If we had lost our old shapes, which had already disintegrated and gone into the substance of mountain and snow and wind and rock, lost those faint webs or veils or templates that had been more space than substance—if we had lost what we had been, then we were still something, and moved on together, a group of individuals, yet a unity, and had to be, *must* be, patterns of matter, matter of a kind, since everything is—webs of matter or substance or something tangible, though sliding and intermingling and always becoming smaller and smaller—matter, a substance, for we were recognizing ourselves as existent; we were feelings, and thought, and will. These were the web and the woof and the warp of our new being, though in our old being there had seemed no home or place for them, and we had imagined how love and hate and the rest had howled and swept and pulsed about in the vast spaces that lie between the core of an atom (if anything that dissolves as you think of it may be termed a core) and the particles that surround it (if a vibration and a flow may be called a particle)—and these feelings and thoughts made up our new selves, or self, and our minds were telling us that we were still a tenuous though strict dance, just as our old minds had told us what we were, though we had not had eyes to see what we were. Once, before we became dead beasts lying frozen on a mountaintop, these layers or veils fitted into each other, had been a whole, had functioned together—but now one pattern had already sunk back into the physical substance of Planet 8, and another went forward, our eyes changing with every moment so that we were continually part of a new scene, or time. Nor were we something already fixed, with an entity that could not be changed, for we came upon a ghost or a feeling or a flavor that we named *Nonni*: a faintly glittering creature or shape or dance that had been, we knew, Nonni, the dead boy, Alsi's companion, and this entity or being came to us, and married with us, with our new substance, and we all went on as one, but separate, in our journey towards the pole.

Who went? And what was our name?

The teacher of children was there; and the guardian of the waters; the maker and creator of grains and fruits and plants; the keeper and breeder of animals; the storyteller who continually makes and remakes the memories of populations; the tender of the very small and vulnerable; the healer—the discoverer of medicines and remedies; the traveler who visits planets so that knowledge may not be imprisoned and unshared—all these were there, among us and of us; all our functions and the capacities of our work were in the substance of these new beings, this Being, we now were—Johor with and of us, Johor mingled with us, the Representative of Canopus part of the Representative of Planet 8, the destroyed one—destroyed at least for our purposes—for who could say how this lump of ice spinning in the spaces of the heavens would modify itself, becoming gas perhaps, on its way back to soil and a shape and substance that would be recognizable to the eyes we once had owned.

The Representative swept on and up, like a shoal of fishes or a flock of birds; one, but a conglomerate of individuals—each with its little thoughts and feelings, but these shared with the others, tides of thought, of feeling, moving in and out and around, making the several one.

What were we seeing there, feeling there—and where? In what place or time were we, then: what were we, and when? We did not see wastes of snow or ice, no, but a perpetual shifting and changing—we were seeing our planet in myriad guises, or possibilities. We saw it in a flash or a glimpse as it had been, our warm and lovely place where everything had blessed us, and beside this brief vision, a thousand variations of the same, each slightly different, so that each one, had we seen it by itself, could have been judged by us as a stage in the development of our planet—but seen thus, merging so fast, and so subtly different, we knew that what we saw were *possibilities*, what could have been, but had not been, not in our space and time. But had been elsewhere? Yes, that was it, we were observing how, behind or beside or beyond—at any rate, some *where* or *when*—the various stages of development of our planet, had been so many others, the possibilities that had not been given actuality in the level of existence we had known, had experienced; but hovered just behind the veil, potentials, what might have been or could have been . . . Myriads there were, the unachieved possibilities; but each real and functioning on its own level—*where* and *when* and *how?*—each world every bit as valid and valuable as what we had known as real. Just as once, I, Doeg, had stood in front of mirrors in my old self and seen stretching out in an interminable line of possibilities, all the variations in the genetic storehouse made visible—sometimes so similar to what I was that I could hardly tell the difference, but then more and more of me, each a variation, and a variation further away from what "I" was—each one the possible and potential housing of this feeling of me, Doeg, some easily recognizable to my fellows as I, Doeg, and others so wildly distant that only a turn of the head or the slightest familiarity in a slide of the eyes or a set of the shoulders could say, "Yes, this, too, is of the family of Doeg, is Doeg's potential that did not step forward into this dimension or place"—so now we could see all the worlds that were not our planet, but lay there, lapping and touching it, each an absolute and a reality in its place and time.

Oh who then were Doeg and Alsi—were Klin and Nonni and Marl and the rest of us? What was our planet, which was one of so many? And, as we swept on there, ghosts among the ghostly worlds, we felt beside us, and in us, and with us, the frozen and dead populations that lay buried under the snows. Inside caves and huts and mounds of ice and snow the peoples of our old world lay frozen—the carcasses of these were held there for as long as the ice stayed, before it changed, as everything must, to something else—a swirl of gases perhaps, or seas of leaping soil, or fire that had to burn until it, too, changed . . . *must* change . . . *must* become something else. But what these had been, our peoples, our *selves*—were with us then, *were* us, had become us—could not be anything but us, their representatives—and we, together, the Representative, at last found the pole that was the extremity of our old planet, the dark cold pole that had been built, once, to guide in the spacefleets of Canopus, when they visited us. There we left that planet, and came to where we are now. We, the Representative, many and one, came here, where Canopus tends and guards and instructs.

You ask us how the Canopean Agents seemed to us in the days of The Ice.

This tale is our answer.

FROM

# The Diaries of Jane Somers

Maudie's day.

She wakes inside a black smothering weight, she can't breathe, can't move. They've buried me alive, she thinks, and struggles. The weight shifts. Oh, it's the cat, it's my pretty, she thinks, and heaves. The weight lifts, and she hears a thud as the cat arrives on the floor. Petty? she asks, for she is not sure, it is so dark and her limbs are so stiff. She hears the cat moving about and knows she is alive. And warm . . . and in bed . . . Oh, oh, she says aloud, I must get to the toilet or I'll wet the bed again. Panic! Have I wet the bed already? Her hand explores the bed. She mutters, Dreadful, dreadful, dreadful, dreadful, thinking how, a few days ago, she had wet the bed, and the trouble and difficulty of getting everything dry.

But it is as if her hand has disappeared, she can't feel it. She clenches and unclenches her left hand, to know she *has* hands, and waits for the tingling to begin in her right. It takes a long time, and then she pulls out the half-numb right hand from under the clothes and uses the left to massage it awake. She still does not know if she has wet the bed. Almost she sinks back into the black bed, black sleep, but her bowels are moving and she smells a bad smell. Oh no, no, no, she whimpers, sitting there in the dark. No, dreadful, for she believes she might have shat in the bed. At last, with such effort and trouble, she climbs out of the bed, and stands beside it, feeling in it to see what is there. She can't be sure. She turns, carefully, tries to find the light switch. She has a torch by the bed, but the batteries ran low, she meant to ask Janna to get new ones, and forgot. She thinks, surely Janna would think to look for herself, she knows how I need the torch! She finds the switch, and there is light . . . and anxiously she inspects the bed, which is dry. But she has to get to the toilet. She never uses the commode for more than a pee. She must get herself to the outside toilet. But there is a hot wet thrusting in her bowels and she gets herself to the commode, just in time. She sits there, rocking herself, keening. Dreadful, dreadful, for now she will have to take the pot out, and she feels so low and bad.

She sits there a long time, too tired to get up. She even sleeps a little. Her bottom is numb. She pulls herself up, looks for the paper. No lav paper, because she doesn't use it here. She cannot find anything to use . . . At last she struggles to the cupboard, her bottom all wet and loathsome, finds an old petticoat, rips off a piece, uses it to clean herself, and shuts down the lid on the smell—and worse, for while she does allow herself a fearful peep, she refuses to let her mind acknowledge that there is something wrong with her stool. Dreadful, she mutters, meaning the stuff her bowels seem to produce these days, and shoves the curtains back off the windows.

It is light outside. But it is summer, it could be the middle of the night still. She cannot bear to think of the difficulties of getting back into bed, and then out of it again. Her little clock has its face turned away from her, she doesn't want to cross the room to it. She pulls around herself an old shawl, and huddles in the chair by the dead fire. No birds yet, she thinks: has the dawn chorus been and gone or am I waiting for it? She thinks of how, a child, she lay with her sisters in the bed in the cottage of the old woman in the summers, and woke to the shrill violence of the dawn chorus and slept again, thinking of the lovely hot day ahead, a day that had no end to it, all play and pleasure and plentiful tasty meals.

And so Maudie drifts off to sleep, but wakes, and sleeps and wakes for some hours, each time remembering to move her hands so that they don't stiffen up too much. At last she wakes to the cat rubbing and purring around her legs. Which are stiff. She tests her hands. The right one gone again. With the left she caresses the cat, Pretty, petty, pretty pet, and with the right she tries to flex and unflex fingers until she is whole again.

Morning . . . oh, the difficulties of morning, of facing the day . . . each task such a weight to it . . . She sits there, thinking, I have to feed the cat, I have to . . . I have to . . . At last, she drags herself up, anxious, because her bowels are threatening again, and, holding on to door handles, chair backs, she gets herself into the kitchen. There is a tin of cat food, half empty. She tries to turn it onto a saucer, it won't come out. It means she has to get a spoon. A long way off, in the sink, are her spoons and forks, she hasn't washed up for days. She winkles out the cat food with her forefinger, her face wrinkled up—is it smelling perhaps? She lets the saucer fall from a small height onto the floor, for bending forward makes her faint. The cat sniffs at it and walks away, with a small miaow. Maudie sees that under the table are saucers, bone dry and empty. The cat needs milk, she needs water. Slowly, slowly, Maudie gets herself to the sink, pulls out of it a dirty saucer which she has not got the energy to wash, runs water into it. Finds a half bottle of milk. Has it gone off? She sniffs. No. She somehow gets the saucer onto the floor, holding on to the table and nearly falling. The cat drinks all the milk, and Maudie knows she is hungry.

Under the table not only the saucers, one, two, three, four, five, but a cat mess. This reminds Maudie she has to let the cat out. She toils to the door, lets out the cat, and stands with her back to the door, thinking. A general planning a campaign could not use more cleverness than Maudie does, as she outwits her weakness and her terrible tiredness. She is already at the back door: the toilet is five steps away; if she goes now it will save a journey later . . . Maudie gets herself to the toilet, uses it, remembers there is the commode full of dirt and smell in her room, somehow gets herself along the passage to her room, somehow gets the pot out from under the round top, somehow gets herself and the pot to the toilet. She splashes a bit as she empties it, and, looking, smelling, her mind has to acknowledge that there is something very wrong. But she thinks, as long as *she* (meaning Janna) does not see what I am making, no one will know. *And they won't put me away . . .*

When all that is done it seems to her that a long time has passed, yet she knows that it is still early, for she cannot hear those noisy Irish brats. She needs a cup of tea very badly, all her energy has gone into the cat.

She stands by her kitchen table, holding on to it, thinking of how she will carry the cup of hot reviving tea next door. But hot tea makes you run, no, better cold milk. She gets the cold milk into the glass. That is the end of the milk. She needs: milk, toilet paper, cat food, matches, tea, and probably a lot else, if she could think of it.

Perhaps Janna will come soon and . . .

She looks sternly at the cat mess, which seems to her a long way down, measuring it in her mind with the need to stoop, and thinks, Janna will . . .

She gets herself and the milk next door. Sits down. But she is cold now, summer or not. She sits in that old chair of hers, by the cold grate, and feels the heat leaking out of her. She has to get the fire made. Should she plug in the heater? But it takes so much electricity, she is only *just* balancing her needs with her pension. She at last struggles up and plugs it in. The room has the warm red glow of the heater, her legs seem to loosen and become themselves. She sits there, sipping her milk, and muttering, Dreadful, dreadful, dreadful.

Then she drifts off into a dream that Janna has taken her into her own home and is looking after her. She is fiercely possessive of this dream, and cuddles and cossets it, taking it out and adding to it whenever she sits there by herself, but she knows it will not happen. *Cannot* happen. But why not? It was impossible that Janna should fly into her life the way she did, who would ever have thought of it? And then how she comes in and out, with her jokes and her flowers and cakes and stuff, all her stories about her office, she is probably making it up, after all, how can she, a poor old woman, know better, if Janna chooses to embellish it all a little? So why, then, should not another impossible thing happen, that she should be taken into a lovely warm flat and there she would be looked after, things done for her . . .

Or Janna would come and live here. There is that room next door . . . That is what Maudie really wants. She does not want to leave here. Get yourself your own place and never let go of it: Maudie repeats this whenever she is tempted—as now—to leave here and go and live with Janna. No, no, she mutters, she will have to come here. And she sits there, sometimes dozing, thinking of how Janna is living there, looking after her, and of how, when she wakes in the night, alone and frightened that she is in the grave, she can call out, and hear Janna's reply.

But soon her bowels force her to get up. Although she emptied the pot she did not wash it out, and it is disgusting to her. So she goes outside to the toilet, letting in the cat, who is waiting and who goes to the saucer with the smelly food in it, and disdains it, and patiently comes into the room with Maudie. Who, now she is up, decides to make a fire. It takes her over an hour, the crawling along the corridor to get the coal, the crawling back, the raking of the ashes, the lighting of the fire. She blows at it in small shallow puffs, because she gets dizzy, so it takes a long time to get going. Then she sits again, longing for a cup of tea, but refusing herself, because above all else she dreads the demands of her bladder, her bowels. She thinks, the Meals on Wheels will be here soon . . . it is only eleven, though. Perhaps they will be early today? She is hungry, she is so hungry she cannot now distinguish between her hunger pangs and the possibility that she must go again to the toilet. Before the cheerful young Meals on Wheels woman, who has a key, slams in and out, calling, Hello, Mrs. Fowler, you all right—she has had to go out to the lavatory again.

It is early. Only half past twelve. Maudie at once takes the two small foil containers to the table and, hardly looking at what is in them, eats everything. She feels much better. She thinks, oh, if Janna would come now, and if she said, Come to the park, I'd not growl and grumble at her, I'd love to go. But she sees out of the window that it is raining. What a summer, she mutters. The cat is on the table sniffing at the empty containers, and Maudie is distressed at her greed, for she knows the cat is hungry and she should have shared.

Out she goes to the cold smelling kitchen and reaches about—yes, oh joy, there is a full unopened tin. So happy is Maudie that she even does a little dance there, clutching the tin to her chest. Oh, petty, petty, she cries, I can feed you. At last the tin is opened, though Maudie cuts her forefinger on the tin opener. The cat eats every bit. Maudie thinks, and now she should go out, to save me letting her out later . . . but the cat won't go out, she takes herself back into the room with the fire, sinks to sleep on Maudie's bed. Which has not been made. Maudie should make up her bed—she thinks, it's not nice for Janna. She does not, but sits in the chair by the fire, and leans forward to stack it up with coal, and then sleeps like the dead for three hours. Though she does not know what time it is, five in the afternoon, when she wakes, for her clock has stopped.

The cat is still asleep, the fire is out . . . she builds it up again. She could do with something. She *has* to have a cup of tea. She makes herself a full pot, brings the biscuits, and has a little feast at her table. She feels so much better for the tea that it is easy to disregard how she has to go out to the toilet once more, twice, three times. Her bowels are like an angry enemy down there, churning and demanding. What's wrong with you then? she cries, rubbing her hand round and round on the little mound of her belly. Why won't you leave me alone?

She ought to have a wash . . . she ought . . . she ought . . . but Janna will come, Janna will . . .

But Maudie sits there, waiting, and Janna does not come, and Maudie gets up to let out the insistent cat, and Maudie fetches the coal, and Maudie attends to the fire, and Maudie searches about to see if there is a little brandy, for suddenly she feels bad, she feels trembly, she could fall to the ground and lie there, she is so empty and tired . . . No brandy. Nothing.

She can go out to the off-license? No, no, she could not possibly get herself up the steps. Janna has not come and it is getting dark. That means it must be getting on for ten. Janna is not coming . . . and there is no milk, no tea, no food for poor petty, nothing.

And Maudie sits by her roaring furious fire thinking bitterly of Janna, who does not care, wicked unkind cruel Janna . . . In the middle of all this, loud knocks at the door, and Maudie's relief explodes into a raucous shout: Oh, all right, I'm *coming*. And scrambles along the passage, crabwise, to the door, afraid Janna might fly off before she gets there. Terrible, terrible, she mutters, and her face, as she opens the door, is fierce and accusing.

"Oh my God, Maudie," cries Janna, "let me in, I'm dead. What a day."

Oh then, if she's tired I can't ask her . . . thinks Maudie, and stands aside as Janna comes crashing in, all energy and smiles.

In the room, Maudie see Janna smile as she sees the wonderful fire, and sees, too, a wrinkling of her nose, which is at once suppressed.

Janna says, "I said to the Indian man, Don't close, because he was closing, wait, I must get Mrs. Fowler some things."

"Oh, I don't need anything," says Maudie, at once reacting to the news that she has to be beholden to the Indian man, with whom she quarrels nearly every time she goes in . . . he overcharges, he is cheating her over her change . . .

Janna, thank goodness, has taken no notice, but is whirling around in the kitchen, to see what is missing, and out she rushes with a basket, before poor Maudie can remember the batteries. In such a hurry, she always is! And they are all like that, rushing in, rushing out, before I have time to turn myself round.

In no time Janna comes crashing back, slam the outside door, slam-bang this door, with a basket full of stuff which Maudie checks, with such relief and thankfulness. Everything is here, nice fresh fish for the cat and a tin of Ovaltine. Janna has thought of everything.

Has she noticed the cat mess, the unwashed stuff in the sink . . . ?

Maudie goes quietly to sit by the fire, on a smile from Janna which says, It is all right. Janna cleans up the cat mess, does the washing-up, puts away the crockery, and does not think, because she is young and so healthy, to leave out on the kitchen table some saucers and a spoon and the tin opener so that Maudie won't have to bend and peer and rummage about.

Maudie sits listening to Janna working away, *looking after me*—and thinks, oh, if she doesn't remember about the commode . . .

But when Janna comes in, she brings a small bottle of brandy and two glasses, and, having handed Maudie her brandy, she says, "I'll just . . ." and whisks out the dirty pot and takes it away.

I hope there is nothing left in it for her to notice, Maudie worries, but when Janna brings back the scoured pot, smelling nicely of pine forests, she says nothing.

Janna lets herself crash down into the chair near the fire, smiles at Maudie, picks up her glass of brandy, swallows it in a mouthful, says: "Oh, Maudie, what a day, let me tell you . . ." And she sighs, yawns—and is asleep. Maudie sees it, can't believe it, knows it is so, and is in a rage, in a fury. For she has been waiting to talk, to listen, to have a friend and some ordinary decent communication, perhaps a cup of tea in a minute, never mind about her bowels, and her bladder . . . And here is Janna, fast asleep.

It is so dark outside. Maudie pulls the curtains over. Maudie goes out to the back door and sees that all the dirty saucers are gone from under the table, and the cat mess gone, and there is a smell of disinfectant. She lets in the cat, and takes the opportunity for a quick visit to the lavatory. She comes back, and pokes up the fire, and sits down opposite Janna, who is sleeping like . . . the dead.

Maudie has not had this opportunity before, of being able to stare and look and examine openly, to pore over the evidence, and she sits leaning forward, looking as long as she needs into the face of Janna, which is so nicely available there.

It's an agreeable face, thinks Maudie, but there's something . . . Well, of course, she's young, that's the trouble, she doesn't understand yet. But look at her neck there, folded up, you can see the age there, and her hands, for all they are so clean and painted, they aren't young hands.

Her clothes, oh her lovely clothes, look at that silk there, peeping out, that's real silk, oh *I* know what it's worth, what it is. And her pretty shoes . . . No rubbish on her, ever. And she didn't get any change out of what she paid for that hat of hers! Look at it, she flings it down on the bed, that lovely hat, the cat is nearly on top of it.

Look at those little white quills there . . . the Rolovskys used to say that they never had anyone to touch me for making those little quills. I could do them now, it is all here still, the skill of it in my fingers . . . I wonder if . . .

Maudie carefully gets up, goes to the bed, picks up the lovely hat, goes back to her chair with it. She looks at the satin that lines the hat, the way the lining is stitched in—blown in, rather; oh yes, the one who did this hat knew her work all right! And the little white quills . . .

Maudie dozes off, and wakes. It is because the fridge upstairs is rumbling and crashing. But almost at once it stops—that means it has been on for a long time, because it runs for an hour or more. Janna is still asleep. She hasn't moved. She is breathing so lightly that Maudie is afraid, and peers to make sure . . .

Janna is smiling in her sleep? Or is it the way she is lying? Oh, she's going to have a stiff neck all right . . . is she going to stay here all night then? Well, what am *I* expected to do? Sit up here while the night goes? That's just like them, they think of nobody but themselves, they don't think of me . . .

Rage boils in Maudie Fowler, as she sits caressing the lovely hat, looking at sleeping Janna.

Maudie sees Janna's eyes are open. She thinks, oh my *Gawd*, has she died? No, she is blinking. She hasn't moved anything else, but she is lying there in the chair, eyes open, looking past Maudie at the window that has hours ago shut out the wet and blowy night with old greasy yellow curtains.

Maudie thinks, she is taking a long time to come to herself, surely? And then Janna's eyes move to her face, Maudie's: Janna looks, suddenly, terrified, as if she will get up and run—and for a moment all her limbs gather together in a spring, as if she will be off. And then the horrible moment is past, and Janna says, "Oh, Maudie, I have been asleep, why didn't you wake me?"

"I have been looking at this gorgeous hat," says Maudie, stroking it delicately with her thick clumsy fingers.

Janna laughs.

Maudie says, "You could stay the night next door, if you like."

Janna says, "But I have to be home to let in a man to do the electricity."

Maudie knows this is a lie, but does not care.

She thinks, Janna has been asleep here half the night, as if this is her place!

She says, "I have been thinking, this is the best time of my life."

Janna sits straight up in her chair, because, being young, her limbs don't stiffen up, and she leans forward and looks into Maudie's face, serious, even shocked.

"Maudie," she says, "you can't say that!"

"But it's true," says Maudie. "I mean, I'm not talking about the short joyful days, like carrying my Johnnie, or a picnic here and a picnic there, but now, I know you will always come and we can be together."

Janna has tears filling up her eyes, and she blinks them back and says, "For all that, Maudie . . ."

"Will you remember to bring me in some batteries for my torch?" says Maudie, in the humble but aggressive way she makes requests.

Janna says, "I tell you what, I'll bring in my torch from the car, and you can have that."

She goes out, in her usual striding way, but then comes back to say, "Maudie, it's morning, the sky is alight."

The two women stand in Maudie's entrance and see the grey light in the streets.

Maudie does not like to say that now she will probably lie on her bed, with the curtains drawn, and stay there for some hours. She suspects Janna of intending not to sleep again that night. Well, she's young, she can do it. She would so much like to have Janna's torch, because after all Janna might not come tomorrow—no, today.

But Janna kisses her, laughs, and goes rushing off down the dingy wet pavements. She has forgotten her hat.

Janna's day.

The alarm makes me sit up in bed. Sometimes I switch it off, sink back, today not: I sit in the already bright morning, five o'clock, and look through the day ahead: I cannot believe that by the time I end it I shall have done so much. I make myself jump out of bed, I make myself coffee, I am at my typewriter ten minutes after I am awake. I should have put in: I emptied my bladder, but I am still "young" and do not count that among the things that have to be done! But today I shall write down the visits to the loo, otherwise how can I compare my day with Maudie's? The articles I wrote, so tentatively, and without confidence, last year, have become a book. It is nearly finished. I said it would be done by the end of this month. It will be. *Because I said it would be.* That I do what I say gives me such strength! And then, there is a project no one knows about: a historical novel. It was Maudie gave me the idea. I think of that time as quite recent, my grandmother's; but Vera Rogers speaks of it as I might speak of, I don't know, let's say Waterloo. I plan a historical novel, conceived and written as one, about a milliner in London. I long to begin it.

I work hard until eight. Then I drink coffee and eat an apple, shower, am into my clothes, am off, in half an hour. I like to be there by nine, and I always am. Today, Phyllis was late. No Joyce. I collected mail for the three of us and called the secretary and it was done and out of the way by ten and the Conference. Phyllis most apologetic: she is like me, never late, never away, never ill. The Conference is as usual, lively and *wonderful.* It was Joyce who said it would be like a Think Tank. Everyone, from the PRs and the photographers' assistants to Editorial, encouraged to have ideas, no matter how wild, how crazy, because you never know. As usual, Phyllis writes it all down. It was she who volunteered to do it, and both Joyce and I knew, when she did, that she was thinking, it is a key position. Phyllis does not let these ideas disappear, she lists them, she has them duplicated on all our desks through all the departments. An idea that drops out of sight might emerge again a year later. Today somebody revived one, that the "uniforms for women" series should include the types of clothes worn, for instance, by female television announcers or women going out to dinners with their husbands for career reasons. That is, a certain kind of dinner gown, or style, as uniform . . . that makes my style a uniform! But I knew that! I wear it all the time. Even, said Freddie, in bed. I never wear anything but real silk, fine cotton, lawn, in bed . . . he used to joke that if I were to wear a nylon nightie, it would be the same for me as if I committed a crime.

Thinking about Freddie in the office, I surprised myself in tears, and was glad that I had said I would interview Martina, and got to Brown's Hotel just in time. I am *never* late. She easy to interview, professional, competent, no time wasted, full marks. I got back at twelve-thirty, asked Phyllis if she would do the Eminent Women Luncheon. She said firmly no, she could not, I must. I am a stand-in for Joyce, who is the eminent woman, but she is ill, and Phyllis is of course right, was right to look surprised: for it would not be appropriate for Phyllis to do it. Once I would not have made such a slip, but the truth is, my mind is more and more on my two books, the one nearly finished, my lovely historical novel soon to be started.

I look at myself in the washroom. I forgot this morning about the Luncheon, no marks for that, I am slipping! A button hanging on its thread, and my nails were not perfect. I did my nails in the taxi. The Luncheon agreeable, I made a speech on behalf of Joyce.

On the way back from the Luncheon I go into Debenham's and up to the top floor, and there I look for Maudie's kind of vests, real wool, modest high petticoats, and long close-fitting knickers. I buy ten knickers, and three vests, three petticoats—because she wets her knickers now, and sometimes worse. Rush, rush, rush, but I'm back by three-thirty. I phone to make an appointment with the hairdresser, another for the car. Phyllis said she felt awful. She looked it. So apologetic, such a criminal! For God's sake, go to bed, I said, and swept all her work from her desk to mine. I did the recipes, summer food, I did Young Fashion, went off with the photographers to Kenwood for a session, came back and worked by myself in the office, no one else there, until nine. I love being by myself, no telephones, nothing, only the watchman. He went out for Indian take-away, I asked him to join me, we had a quick supper on the corner of my desk. He's nice, George, I encouraged him to talk about his problems, won't go into that, but we can help, he needs a loan.

I was tired by then and suddenly longing for bed. I did some more work, rang Joyce in Wales, heard from her voice that she was better, but she was noncommittal. I don't give a damn, she said, when I asked if she were going to the States. She is saying, too, I don't give a damn about you either. This made me think about the condition of not giving a damn. On my desk, in the "Too difficult" basket, an article about stress, how enough stress can cause indifference. It is seen in war, in hard times. Suffer, suffer, emote, emote, and then suddenly, you don't care. I wanted this published. Joyce said, No, not enough people would recognize it. Irony!

I said good night to George at nine-thirty, and got a taxi to where I leave my car, and drove up towards home, thinking, no, no, I can't go in to Maudie, I simply cannot. When I banged, I was irritable, I was tired, I was thinking, I hope she is in the lavatory and doesn't hear. But when she opened, I could see by her face . . . I switched on everything I have, and made myself crash in, all gaiety and liveliness, because I am afraid of her black moods, for once she starts I can't shift her out of them. That is why I arrived, female Father Christmas, HM the Queen Mum, all radiant, I have to stop her muttering and raging.

When I reach her back room, it is hot and smelly, the smell hits me, but I make myself smile at the fire. I see from her face what is needful, and I go into the kitchen. I was nearly sick. I whirl around the kitchen, because I know the Indian grocer is about to close, and I run across the road, saying, "Please, just another minute, I need stuff for Mrs. Fowler." He is patient and kind, but he is a grey-violet color from tiredness. Sometimes he is in here from eight until eleven at night. Often by himself. He is educating three sons and two daughters . . . He asks, "How is she?" I say, "I think she isn't well." He says, as always, "It is time her people looked after her."

When I get back, I cut up fish for the cat. It is no good, I cannot make myself appreciate cats, though that makes me an insensitive boor. I clean up the cat's mess, I get the brandy and glasses. I realize I have forgotten the vests and knickers in the office. Well, tomorrow will do. I take out her commode, because she is *not* looking at it, with a trembling pride on her face I know only too well by now. As I wash it, I think, here's something very wrong. I shall have to tell Vera Rogers. I rinse the inside of the commode carefully and use a lot of disinfectant.

When I sit down opposite her, with brandy for her and me, I fully mean to tell her about the Luncheon, with all the famous women, she'd like that, but—that was the last I remember, until I came to myself, out of such a deep sleep I could not find myself when I woke. I was looking at a yellow little witch in a smelly hot cave, by her roaring fire, her yellow shanks showing, for she had no knickers on and her legs were apart, and on her lap she held my hat, and she was using it for some bad purpose . . . I was terrified, and then suddenly I remembered, I am Jane Somers, I am here, in Maudie's back room, and I fell asleep.

She did not want me to go. She made an excuse about batteries for her torch. I went to the door into the street, and it was morning. We stood there, looking up—oh, England, dismal and drear, a grey wet dawn. It was four-thirty when I got home. I had a long, long proper bath, and then to my book again.

But I cannot concentrate on it. I am thinking about Maudie's "This is the best time of my life." What I cannot stand is that I believe she means it. My running in at the end of the day, an hour, two hours, so little, is enough to make her say that. I want to howl when I think of it. And too, I feel so trapped. She might live for years and years, people live to be a hundred these days, and I am a prisoner of her "This is the best time of my life," lovely gracious Janna, running in and out, with smiles and prezzies.

I wrote Maudie's day because I want to understand. I *do* understand a lot more about her, but is it true? I can only write what I have experienced myself, heard her say, observed . . . I sometimes wake with one hand quite numb . . . But what else is there I cannot know about? I think that just as I could never have imagined she would say, "This is the best time of my life," and the deprivation and loneliness behind it, so I cannot know what is behind her muttered "It is dreadful, dreadful," and the rages that make her blue eyes blaze and glitter.

And I see that I did *not* write down, in Janna's day, about going to the loo, a quick pee here, a quick shit, washing one's hands . . . All day this animal has to empty itself, you have to brush your hair, wash your hands, bathe. I dash a cup under a tap and rinse out a pair of panties, it all takes a few minutes . . . But that is because I am "young," only forty-nine.

What makes poor Maudie labor and groan all through her day, the drudge and drag of *maintenance*. I was going to say, For me it is nothing; but the fact is, once I did have my real proper baths every night, once every Sunday night I maintained and polished my beautiful perfect clothes, maintained and polished *me,* and now I don't, I can't. It is too much for me.

# NON-FICTION

FROM

# *Going Home*

Salisbury was a wide scatter of light over spaces of dark. To fly over it is to see how fast it is growing—not vertically, save for a few tall buildings in its center, but outwards, in a dozen sprawling suburbs.

I was reminded of the first time I saw Johannesburg from above by night. A few years ago one could not, even at one's most optimistic, compare Salisbury with Johannesburg: it was only a small patterning of lit streets in a great hollow of darkness. Now the regular arrangements of street lighting—all these cities are laid out on the American plan, with streets regularly bisecting each other—confine the veld in sparkling nets of light.

The darkness of the earth at night is never complete in Africa, because even the darkest night sky has a glow of light behind it. And so these cities dissolve after sundown, as if points of strong, firm light were strewn wide over a luminous, dark sea.

To drive from the airport to the house I was staying in on the outskirts of the town took seven minutes. I knew that my sense of space, adjusted to sprawling London, was going to take a shock; but I was more confused than I had thought possible. If you live in a small town, you live in all of it, every street, house, garden is palpable all the time, part of your experience. But a big city is a center and a series of isolated lit points on the darkness of your ignorance. That is why a big city is so restful to live in; it does not press in on you, demanding to be recognized. You can choose what you know.

But it was right; and the town at night was always to me a different place than the candid daytime town. Now the car swept up along avenues of subdued light; for the moon was full and hard, the stars vivid; the trees rippled off light; and the buildings were luminous, their walls thin shells over an inner glow, and the roofs plates of shining substance.

The garden of the house was full of roses, pale in the moonlight, and black shadow lay under the bougainvillea bush.

I stepped from the garden into the creeper-hung veranda and at once into the living room. It was strange to be in a house again that was pressed close to the earth, with only a thin roof between me and the sky. In London buildings are so heavy and tall and ponderous they are a climate of their own; pavements, streets, walls—even parks and gardens—are an urban shell.

But in Africa the wildness of the country is still much stronger than the towns.

But even so, this house was wrong; it was not this that I had come home to find. For me all houses will always be wrong: all bungalows, cottages, mansions, and villas will be uncomfortable and incongruous and confining. I only like blocks of flats, the most direct expression of crammed town living. I did not understand why this should be so for a long time, until I took to dreaming nightly of the house I was brought up in; and then at last I submitted myself to the knowledge that I am the victim of a private mania that I must humor. I worked out recently that I have lived in over sixty different houses, flats and rented rooms during the last twenty years and not in one of them have I felt at home. In order to find a place I live in tolerable, I have not to see it. Or rather, I work on it until it takes on the coloring suggested by its shape, and then forget it. If, in an unguarded moment, I actually see it, all of it, what it is, then a terrible feeling of insecurity and improbability comes over me. The fact is, I don't live anywhere; I never have since I left that first house on the kopje. I suspect more people are in this predicament than they know.

But that first house crumbled long ago, returned to the soil, was swallowed by the bush; and so I was glad after we had had dinner to go out again in the car, ostensibly to look for someone whose address we did not know, but hoped we might find by chance; in fact to get out of the town into the bush.

In five minutes we were there.

And now for the first time I was really home. The night was magnificent; the Southern Cross on a slant overhead; the moon a clear, small pewter; the stars all recognizable and close. The long grass stood all around, tall and giving off its dry, sweetish smell, and full of talking crickets. The flattened trees of the highveld were low above the grass, low and a dull silver-green.

It was the small intimate talking of the crickets which received me and made me part of that nightscape.

Before I left home seven years ago I used to walk endlessly at night along the streets, tormented because there was a barrier between me and the steady solemn magnificence of those skies whose brilliance beat the thin little town into the soil. I saw them, but I was alien to them. This barrier is the urgent necessity of doing the next thing, of getting on with the business of living; whatever it is that drives us on. But on that first night there was no barrier, nothing; and I was effortlessly and at once in immediate intimacy with the soil and its creatures.

It was only so the first night, for at once habit took over and erected its barriers; and if I had had to fly back to England the next day, I would have been given what I had gone home for.

For to stand there with the soft dust of the track under my shoes, the crickets talking in my ear, the moon cold over the bush, meant I was able to return to that other house.

There are two sorts of habitation in Africa. One is of brick, cement, plaster, tile, and tin—the substance of the country processed and shaped; the other sort is made direct of the stuff of soil and grass and tree. This second kind is what most of the natives of the country live in; and what I, as a child, lived in. The house was not a hut, but a long cigar-shaped dwelling sliced several times across with walls to make rooms.

To make such a house you choose a flat place, clear it of long grass and trees, and dig a trench two feet deep in the shape you want the house to be. You cut trees from the bush and lop them to a size and insert them side by side in the trench, as close as they will go. From the trunks of living trees in the bush fiber is torn; for under the thick rough bark of a certain variety of tree is a thick layer of smooth flesh. It is colored yellow and pink; and when it is still alive, newly torn from the tree, it is wet and slippery to the touch. It dries quickly; so it is necessary to have several laborers stripping the fiber, with others ready immediately to use it for tying the trees of the walls into place. At this stage the house will look like a small space enclosed by a palisade—tall, uneven logs of wood, greyish-brown in color, laced tightly with yellow and rose-colored strips. The palisade will have spaces in it for doors and windows.

On this frame is set the skeleton of the roof. More trees have been cut, slimmer ones, and laid slantwise from the tops of the wall poles to a ridge in the center. They are tied with strips of the fiber to this center pole, which is an immensely long gum tree or thorn tree made smooth and slim, lying parallel to the ground.

Now the house will look like an immense birdcage, set in the middle of the bush. For the trees have not been cut back around it yet; and the grass is still standing high all around, long swatches of grass, a browny-gold in color. One cannot build this sort of house save when the grass is dry, at the season for thatching.

Standing inside the cage of rough poles, the sun comes through in heavy bars of yellow. Strips of fading fiber lie everywhere in tangles; chips of wood send off a warm, spicy smell.

Now it is time to make the walls.

From an ant-heap nearby earth is cut in spadefuls and laid in a heap. Ant-heap earth is best, because it has already been blended by the jaws of myriad workers.

It is not always easy to find the right ant-heap, even in ant-heap country; for even ants cannot make suitable wall-earth where the ingredients are not right at the start. And, having found a properly composed heap, there may be snags. For instance, when we were building our house, the ant-heap we were working had three skeletons laid side by side, in such a way that showed these were the bones of chiefs of a tribe. Earthen cooking pots buried beside the skeletons still showed traces of white meal mingled with the earth.

Our laborers would not go near this ant-heap again, for they feared the spirits of their ancestors. So we had to choose another. But meanwhile, some of the earth had already been pounded into mud for the walls; and so the walls of our house had in them the flesh and the blood of the people of the country.

To make mud for walls, a great heap of ant-worked earth is built up and wetted. Then the feet of the builders squelch it into the right consistency. Also, in this case, the feet of my brother and myself, who were small children.

To lay the mud on the poles it is carried in petrol tins from the men who are softening it to the men who are plastering; great handfuls are taken up quickly from the tins, before it can dry out, and slapped on to the poles. Sometimes there are gaps between the poles too wide to hold the mud; and then handfuls of grass are caught up and inserted and worked in with the mud. The smell of this mud is fresh and sweet, if the water used is good, clean water.

Soon all the walls are covered with a thick, dark mud-skin; and this is quickly smoothed over with trowels or flat bits of tin. Now the house is a house and not a frame of tree-poles; for the walls cannot be seen through.

Next, the long, pale grass is cut from those parts of the farm where it grows best and tallest, and is laid in piles ready for the thatchers. It is laid swathe over swathe beginning from ridgepole and working downwards, and each swathe is tied into place with the bush-fiber. The grass is laid thick, eighteen inches deep; and finally the loose, long tips that draggle almost to the ground are cut off straight and clean with long, sharpened bits of metal.

And now the roof of the house is a gleaning golden color, laced with rose-pink and yellow; and so it stays until the rains of the first wet season dim the colors.

Meanwhile, the doors have been hung and the windows fitted; and this is not easy when the poles of the walls are likely to be uneven. Nor are those doors and windows ever likely truly to fit; for the wood of lintels and frames swells and contracts with the wetness and the dryness of the time of the year.

The floor is done last. More ant-heap earth is piled, and on it fresh cow dung; and it is wetted with the fresh blood of an ox and with water, and is stamped free of lumps. This mixture is laid all over the earth inside the house and smoothed down. It has a good, warm, sweet smell, even when it dries, which takes about a week.

Now the house is finished and can be lived in. The mud-skin of the walls has dried a pleasant light-grey, or a yellowish-grey. Or it can be color-washed. The mud of the floor is dark and smooth and glossy. It can be left bare, or protected with linoleum, for after a time this kind of floor tends to scuff into holes and turns dusty, so linoleum is useful, though not as pleasant to look at as the bare, hard, shining earth floor.

A pole-and-dagga house is built to stand for two, three, four years at most; but the circumstances and character of our family kept ours standing for nearly two decades. It did very well, for it had been built with affection. But under the storms and the beating rains of the wet seasons, the grass of the roof flattened like old flesh into the hollows and bumps of the poles under it; and sometimes the mud-skin fell off in patches and had to be replaced; and sometimes parts of the roof received a new layer of grass. A house like this is a living thing, responsive to every mood of the weather; and during the time I was growing up it had already begun to sink back into the forms of the bush. I remember it as a rather old, shaggy animal standing still among the trees, lifting its head to look out over the vleis and valleys to the mountains.

I wrote a poem once about a group of suburban town houses; which I could not have written had I not been brought up in such a house as I have described:

*THE HOUSE AT NIGHT*

*That the house grew there, self-compact;*
*And with what long hopeless love*
*I walked about, about—*
*To make the creature out.*

*First with fingers: grainy brick*
*That took its texture from the earth;*
*The roof, membranous sheath*
*On rafters stretched beneath.*

*Yet, though I held the thing as close*
*As child's toy gathered in my hand—*
*Could shatter it or not;*
*No nearer truth I got.*

*Eluded by so frail a thing?*
*But if touch fails then sight succeeds.*
*But windows shadowed in*
*My face that peered within.*

*And through my shadowing face I saw*
*A room where someone lived, and there*
*The glow of hidden fire;*
*A secret, guarded fire.*

*Should I fail by closeness? Then*
*Move back and see the house from far,*
*Gathered among its kind,*
*No unit hard-defined.*

*And there a herd of houses! Each*
*Brooding darkly on its own,*
*Settled in the shade*
*That each small shape had made.*

*Till suddenly a mocking light*
*Flashed on from that one house I'd searched,*
*As if a beast had raised*
*His head from where he grazed.*

*And brilliant to my blinded face*
*As if with laughter openly,*
*These dazzling panes comprise*
*All dazzling gold eyes.*

The house was built high, on a kopje that rose from a lower system of vleis and ridges. Looking from the windows you seemed on a level with the circling mountains, on a level with the hawks which wheeled over the fields.

My room was the third down from the top or end of the house; and it was very big and very light, for it had a large, low window, and a door which I kept propped open with a stone. The stones on the kopje were not of the quartz which cropped up all over the farm, but tended to be flattened and layered, and were brown, a light, bright brown, and when they were wet with rain, yellowish. To the touch they were smooth and velvety, because of the dust surface. Such a stone I used to prop my door open, so that I could look down on the hawks that hung over the fields, and watch them turn and slide down the currents of air with their stretched wings motionless. The great mountain ten miles off was the chrome mountain, scarred all over with workings; and it was part of the chain of hills and peaks over which the sun rose. The big field below the house was a mealie field. Newly plowed it was rich reddish-brown, a sea of great, tumbling clods. From the path which ran along its edge the field showed a pattern of clods that had fallen over from the plowshares one after another, so that walking slowly beside it avenues opened and shut, lanes of sunlight and shadow. And each clod was like a rock, for the interest of its shape and color: the plowshare cutting smooth through the hard soil left a clean, shining surface, iridescent, as if it had been oiled with dark oil.

And sometimes, from the height of the house, looking down, these clean, shared surfaces caught the sun all over the field at the same moment so that a hundred acres of clods glittered darkly together, flashing off a sullen light; and at such times the hawks swerved off, high and away, frightened.

Then the harrows drove over the field, side by side, the heavy, shining oxen plunging and scrambling over the great earth boulders; they drove over it again and again, till the beasts walked easily, setting their feet down in soft tilthed soil; and the field was flat, without shadows, an even reddish-brown. And so it stood a while, waiting for the rains. During this time the air was full of dust, for the wind-devils danced and played continuously over the field; and sometimes columns of whirling, fiery red dust mingled with fragments of last year's mealie-stalks that glittered gold and silver, stood in the air higher than eye level from the house; and the hawks were gone out of the dusty air into the clean air currents over the far bush. Through the dust that shone a soft red at sunset and sunrise, the great soft-stepping oxen moved, two by two, in front of the planters; Afrikander oxen with their long, snaky horns; and behind the planting machines the small, white, flat seeds popped into the earth and were covered. The flocks of guinea fowl moved down out of the bush at dawn and at sunset after those precious mealie-grains, flocks of sometimes fifty, a hundred, two hundred birds; and my brother and I, waiting in the bush with our rifles, saw them as industrious as farmyard birds over the hidden mealie-seeds.

Now the long tension of the dry season had built up into a crescendo of bad temper and irritability and anxiety that means the rains will come soon; and at night, lying in bed, I saw the lightning dance and quiver over the mountains while the thunder growled. The long stretches of bush and field were dark; this was the only time of the year the fields were dark; for all the light had gone into the electricity that darted along the edges of the cloud masses.

And then, one night, I would wake and hear a rushing and a pouring and a rustling all around; the rains had come. Over my head the old thatch was soaking and swelling, and in the weak places the wet seeped through, so that from half a dozen patches of floor over my room came a soft dulcet pattering. I crept out from under the mosquito net to set basins and jugs to catch the drops; and looking out from the door into the wet darkness a battering of rain ricocheting up from the earth came as high as my waist so that I had to step back fast into dryness. But until the lightning drove down through the wet and broken cloud masses it was dark; when the light came, it drove down the shining rods of white rain, and showed the trees crouching under the downpour and a thick dance of white raindrops like hailstones a foot deep all over the earth.

So I would go back to sleep, lulled by the roar of the rain outside and splash of the roof leaks into the basins. In the morning I was woken not by the warmth of the sun on my bed but by a new intenser glare of light on my eyelids: the air had been washed clean of smoke from the veld fires and of dust, and the skies had lifted high and bright, and the trees were green and clean. The sun had come close again, shining free and yellow direct onto the big field, which was now a dark, rich, sodden red, a clear, red space among rich, sodden foliage. The thatch was still dropping long stalactites of shining water, and it was as if the house was enclosed by a light waterfall.

By midday the wetness had been whirled up into the air in clouds of steam; the big field steamed and smoked; and it was as if one could feel the growth being sucked up out of the mealie-grains by the heat and the wet.

During the first days of the wet season the storms and the showers advanced and retreated, and we watched the drama from the kopje-top; the now rich green bush stretching all around for miles would be blotted out suddenly in one place by a grey curtain, or the clouds would open violently overhead, enclosing us in a grey, steaming downpour. Below, the field was already showing a sheen of green. From the path beside the field, walking, the field was again opening and shutting, but now in avenues of green. Each plant was an inch high, a minute, green, divided spear, as crisp as fresh lettuce, and in the heart of each a big, round, shining globule of water.

Now the farmer would be pleased if the rain stopped for a week or ten days, so as to drive the roots down into the earth and strengthen the plants. Sometimes he was obliged; and the field of mealies stood faintly wilting, limp with thirst. But however the rain fell, the green film over the dark earth thickened, so that soon there were a hundred acres of smooth, clear apple-green that shimmered and rippled under the hot sun.

In the moonlight, looking down, it was a dim green sea, moving with light.

Soon the plants put out their frothy white crests; in the moonlight there was foam on the sea; and in the daytime, when the winds were strong, the whole field swayed and moved like a tide coming in. At this time the hawks hung low over the field with bunched, ready claws, working hard, so that from the house you looked down on their wide, stiff wings.

The rainy season passed; and the brilliant green of the field dimmed, and the sound of the wind in it was no longer a wet, thick rustle, but more like the sound of an army of tiny spears. Soon all the field was a tarnished silvery-gold, and each mealie-plant was like a ragged, skeleton scarecrow, and the noise of the wind was an incessant metallic whispering.

From the house now the field could be seen populated with black, small figures, moving between the rows and laying them flat. Soon the dark, dry earth was bared again, patterned with mealie-stooks, each a small, shining pyramid; and all over the soil a scattered litter of soft, glinting, dead leaf and stalk. Then came the heavy wagons, behind sixteen oxen led by the little black boy who pulled six inches in front of the tossing, curving, wicked horns; with the driver walking behind, yelling and flickering his long whiplash in the air over their backs.

The field was bare completely, the stooks stripped of maize cobs, the stooks themselves carried off to make manure in the cattle kraals. It was all rough, dark-red earth, softly glinting with mealie-trash. In came the plows, and again the earth fell apart into the great shining clods.

This cycle I watched from my bedroom door, when I was not absorbed by what went on in the room itself. For after a decade or so of weathering, the house had become the home of a dozen kinds of creatures not human, who lived for the most part in the thatch of the roof.

Rats, mice, lizards, spiders and beetles, and once or twice snakes, moved through the thatch and behind the walls; and sometimes, when the oil lamp was flickering low, which it did in a steady, leaping rhythm till it flared up and out—in a way which I am reminded of by the pedestrian-crossing lights in the street outside my window, flickering all night on my wall in London—sometimes, as the yellow glow sank, a pair of red eyes could be seen moving along the top of the wall under the thatch. A mouse? A snake perhaps? For some reason they seldom came down to the floor. Once I saw a pair of eyes shining in the light coming through the window from the moon, and called for my parents to kill what I was convinced was a snake, but it was a frog. In the wet season, the frogs from the vlei two miles away were so loud they drowned the perpetual singing of the night crickets; and the irregular pattering of frogs on the floor of my room was something I learned to take no more notice of than the pattering of rain from leaks in the roof. It must not be imagined that I am a lover of wildlife. I am frightened of all these creatures—or rather, of touching them by accident in the dark, or putting my foot on one; but if you live in a house which is full of them, then your area of safety contracts within it to the bed. I never went to bed without taking it completely apart to make sure nothing had got into the bedclothes; and once safely in, with the mosquito net tucked down, I knew that nothing could fall on me from the roof or crawl over me in the dark.

The family attitude towards the role of mosquito nets is illustrated by a dialogue I overheard between my parents in the next room.

It was the first rains of the season; and the roof had begun to leak in a dozen places. I had already lit my candle and set out the pails and basins; and I knew that my father was awake because I could see the fluctuating glow of his cigarette on the wall through the crack of the door which did not close properly.

I knew that he was waiting for my mother to wake up. At last I heard him say in a sort of hushed shout: "Maud, Maud wake up!" Nothing happened and the rain roared on.

"*Maud!*"

She woke with a crash of the bedsprings. "What's the matter?"

"It's raining."

"I can hear that it's raining."

"The roof's really bad this year," he said. "Like a sieve."

"When the grass swells, it won't be so bad."

"It's worse than it was last year."

"We'll get the thatching boy up in the morning," she said sleepily, and turned over.

"But it's raining," he said desperately.

"Go to sleep."

"But it's raining on *me*."

"You've got your mosquito net down, haven't you?"

"A mosquito net has holes in it."

"A mosquito net will absorb a lot of water before it starts to leak."

"It has already started to absorb the water."

"What if I slung another mosquito net over the first?"

"Wouldn't it be easier to move the bed?"

"Oh. Yes. I suppose so."

My father spent a large part of his nights sitting up in his bed smoking and thinking. Sometimes, if I lit my candle for something, he would say cautiously: "Is that *you?*"

"Yes, it's me, I'm only just . . . ."

"Well then, go to sleep."

"But I'm only just . . ."

"You're not to read at this time of night." And then, after a moment, "Are you asleep?"

"No."

"Hear that owl? It must be in the tree right outside."

"It sounds to me in the bush at the bottom of the kopje."

"Do you think so? You know, I've been sitting here thinking. Supposing we caught an owl and crossed it with one of your mother's Rhode Island Reds. What do you think would happen?"

"Almost anything, I should think."

"I was being serious," he said reprovingly from the dark room next door. "I don't suppose *they* have thought of that, do you? An owl and a chicken. They could graft the seed somehow if they wouldn't do it naturally. A rat-eating chicken. Or a chicken-eating chicken."

A stir in my mother's bed.

"Shhhhh," my father would say hastily. "Go to sleep at once."

Or: "Are you asleep?"

"No."

"I've been thinking."

"What about?"

"You know the center of the earth is all molten, so they say?"

"Well?"

"Suppose they sank down a borehole and tapped it. Power. Much more effective than all these dams and things. Do you think *they* have thought of that yet?"

"Bound to."

"You're not much good, are you? No imagination. Not a scrap of imagination between the lot of you, that's your trouble."

# *My Father*

We use our parents like recurring dreams, to be entered into when needed; they are always there for love or for hate; but it occurs to me that I was not always there for my father. I've written about him before, but novels, stories, don't have to be "true." Writing this article is difficult because it has to be "true." I knew him when his best years were over.

There are photographs of him. The largest is of an officer in the 1914–18 war. A new uniform—buttoned, badged, strapped, tabbed—confines a handsome, dark young man who holds himself stiffly to confront what he certainly thought of as his duty. His eyes are steady, serious, and responsible, and show no signs of what he became later. A photograph at sixteen is of a dark, introspective youth with the same intent eyes. But it is his mouth you notice—a heavily jutting upper lip contradicts the rest of a regular face. His mustache was to hide it: "Had to do something—a damned fleshy mouth. Always made me uncomfortable, that mouth of mine."

Earlier a baby (eyes already alert) appears in a lace waterfall that cascades from the pillowy bosom of a fat, plain woman to her feet. It is the face of a head cook. "Lord, but my mother was a practical female—almost as bad as you!" as he used to say, or throw at my mother in moments of exasperation. Beside her stands, or droops, arms dangling, his father, the source of the dark, arresting eyes, but otherwise masked by a long beard.

The birth certificate says: Born 3rd August, 1886, Walton Villa, Creffield Road, S. Mary at the Wall, R.S.D. Name, Alfred Cook. Name and surname of Father: Alfred Cook Tayler. Name and maiden name of Mother: Caroline May Batley. Rank or Profession: Bank Clerk. Colchester, Essex.

They were very poor. Clothes and boots were a problem. They "made their own amusements." Books were mostly the Bible and *The Pilgrim's Progress*. Every Saturday night they bathed in a hip-bath in front of the kitchen fire. No servants. Church three times on Sundays. "Lord, when I think of those Sundays! I dreaded them all week, like a nightmare coming at you full tilt and no escape." But he rabbited with ferrets along the lanes and fields, bird-nested, stole fruit, picked nuts and mushrooms, paid visits to the blacksmith and the mill and rode a farmer's carthorse.

They ate economically, but when he got diabetes in his forties and subsisted on lean meat and lettuce leaves, he remembered suet puddings, treacle puddings, raisin and currant puddings, steak and kidney puddings, bread and butter pudding, "batter cooked in the gravy with the meat," potato cake, plum cake, butter cake, porridge with treacle, fruit tarts and pies, brawn, pig's trotters and pig's cheek and home-smoked ham and sausages. And "lashings of fresh butter and cream and eggs." He wondered if this diet had produced the diabetes, but said it was worth it.

There was an elder brother described by my father as: "Too damned clever by half. One of those quick, clever brains. Now I've always had a slow brain, but I get there in the end, damn it!"

The brothers went to a local school and the elder did well, but my father was beaten for being slow. They both became bank clerks in, I think, the Westminster Bank, and one must have found it congenial, for he became a manager, the "rich brother," who had cars and even a yacht. But my father did not like it, though he was conscientious. For instance, he changed his writing, letter by letter, because a senior criticized it. I never saw his unregenerate hand, but the one he created was elegant, spiky, careful. Did this mean he created a new personality for himself, hiding one he did not like, as he hid his "damned fleshy mouth"? I don't know.

Nor do I know when he left home to live in Luton or why. He found family life too narrow? A safe guess—he found everything too narrow. His mother was too down-to-earth? He had to get away from his clever elder brother?

Being a young man in Luton was the best part of his life. It ended in 1914, so he had a decade of happiness. His reminiscences of it were all of pleasure, the delight of physical movement, of dancing in particular. All his girls were "a beautiful dancer, light as a feather." He played billiards and Ping-Pong (both for his county); he swam, boated, played cricket and football, went to picnics and horse races, sang at musical evenings. One family of a mother and two daughters treated him "like a son only better. I didn't know whether I was in love with the mother or the daughters, but oh I did love going there; we had such good times." He was engaged to one daughter, then, for a time, to the other. An engagement was broken off because she was rude to a waiter. "I could not marry a woman who allowed herself to insult someone who was defenseless." He used to say to my wryly smiling mother: "Just as well I didn't marry either of *them;* they would never have stuck it out the way you have, old girl."

Just before he died he told me he had dreamed he was standing in a kitchen on a very high mountain holding X in his arms. "Ah, yes, that's what I've missed in my life. Now don't you let yourself be cheated out of life by the old dears. They take all the color out of everything if you let them."

But in that decade—"I'd walk ten, fifteen miles to a dance two or three times a week and think nothing of it. Then I'd dance every dance and walk home again over the fields. Sometimes it was moonlight, but I liked the snow best, all crisp and fresh. I loved walking back and getting into my digs just as the sun was rising. My little dog was so happy to see me, and I'd feed her, and make myself porridge and tea, then I'd wash and shave and go off to work."

The boy who was beaten at school, who went too much to church, who carried the fear of poverty all his life, but who nevertheless was filled with the memories of country pleasures; the young bank clerk who worked such long hours for so little money, but who danced, sang, played, flirted—this naturally vigorous, sensuous being was killed in 1914, 1915, 1916. I think the best of my father died in that war, that his spirit was crippled by it. The people I've met, particularly the women, who knew him young, speak of his high spirits, his energy, his enjoyment of life. Also of his kindness, his compassion and—a word that keeps recurring—his wisdom. "Even when he was just a boy he understood things that you'd think even an old man would find it easy to condemn." I do not think these people would have easily recognized the ill, irritable, abstracted, hypochondriac man I knew.

He "joined up" as an ordinary soldier out of a characteristically quirky scruple: it wasn't right to enjoy officers' privileges when the Tommies had such a bad time. But he could not stick the communal latrines, the obligatory drinking, the collective visits to brothels, the jokes about girls. So next time he was offered a commission he took it.

His childhood and young man's memories, kept fluid, were added to, grew, as living memories do. But his war memories were congealed in stories that he told again and again, with the same words and gestures, in stereotyped phrases. They were anonymous, general, as if they had come out of a communal war memoir. He met a German in no-man's-land, but both slowly lowered their rifles and smiled and walked away. The Tommies were the salt of the earth, the British fighting men the best in the world. He had never known such comradeship. A certain brutal officer was shot in a sortie by his men, but the other officers, recognizing rough justice, said nothing. He had known men intimately who saw the Angels at Mons. He wished he could force all the generals on both sides into the trenches for just one day, to see what the common soldiers endured—*that* would have ended the war at once.

There was an undercurrent of memories, dreams, and emotions much deeper, more personal. This dark region in him, fate-ruled, where nothing was true but horror, was expressed inarticulately, in brief, bitter exclamations or phrases of rage, incredulity, betrayal. The men who went to fight in that war believed it when they said it was to end war. My father believed it. And he was never able to reconcile his belief in his country with his anger at the cynicism of its leaders. And the anger, the sense of betrayal, strengthened as he grew old and ill.

But in 1914 he was naïve, the German atrocities in Belgium inflamed him, and he enlisted out of idealism, although he knew he would have a hard time. He knew because a fortuneteller told him. (He could be described as uncritically superstitious or as psychically gifted.) He would be in great danger twice, yet not die—he was being protected by a famous soldier who was his ancestor. "And sure enough, later I heard from the Little Aunties that the church records showed we were descended the backstairs way from the Duke of Wellington, or was it Marlborough? Damn it, I forget. But one of them would be beside me all through the war, she said." (He was romantic, not only about this solicitous ghost, but also about being a descendant of the Huguenots, on the strength of the "e" in Tayler; and about "the wild blood" in his veins from a great-uncle who, sent unjustly to prison for smuggling, came out of a ten-year sentence and earned it, very efficiently, along the coasts of Cornwall until he died.)

The luckiest thing that ever happened to my father, he said, was getting his leg shattered by shrapnel ten days before Passchendaele. His whole company was killed. He knew he was going to be wounded because of the fortuneteller, who had said he would know. "I did not understand what she meant, but both times in the trenches, first when my appendix burst and I nearly died, and then just before Passchendaele, I felt for some days as if a thick, black velvet pall was settled over me. I can't tell you what it was like. Oh, it was awful, awful, and the second time it was so bad I wrote to the old people and told them I was going to be killed."

His leg was cut off at mid-thigh, he was shell-shocked, he was very ill for many months, with a prolonged depression afterwards. "You should always remember that sometimes people are all seething underneath. You don't know what terrible things people have to fight against. You should look at a person's eyes, that's how you tell. . . . When I was like that, after I lost my leg, I went to a nice doctor man and said I was going mad, but he said, don't worry, everyone locks up things like that. You don't know—horrible, horrible, awful things. I was afraid of myself, of what I used to dream. I wasn't myself at all."

In the Royal Free Hospital was my mother, Sister McVeagh. He married his nurse which, as they both said often enough (though in different tones of voice), was just as well. That was 1919. He could not face being a bank clerk in England, he said, not after the trenches. Besides, England was too narrow and conventional. Besides, the civilians did not know what the soldiers had suffered, they didn't want to know, and now it wasn't done even to remember "The Great Unmentionable." He went off to the Imperial Bank of Persia, in which country I was born.

The house was beautiful, with great stone-floored high-ceilinged rooms whose windows showed ranges of snow-streaked mountains. The gardens were full of roses, jasmine, pomegranates, walnuts. Kermanshah he spoke of with liking, but soon they went to Teheran, populous with "Embassy people," and my gregarious mother created a lively social life about which he was irritable even in recollection.

Irritableness—that note was first struck here, about Persia. He did not like, he said, "the graft and the corruption." But here it is time to try and describe something difficult—how a man's good qualities can also be his bad ones, or if not bad, a danger to him.

My father was honorable—he always knew exactly what that word meant. He had integrity. His "one does not do that sort of thing," his "no, it is *not* right," sounded throughout my childhood and were final for all of us. I am sure it was true he wanted to leave Persia because of "the corruption." But it was also because he was already unconsciously longing for something freer, because as a bank official he could not let go into the dream-logged personality that was waiting for him. And later in Rhodesia, too, what was best in him was also what prevented him from shaking away the shadows: it was always in the name of honesty or decency that he refused to take this step or that out of the slow decay of the family's fortunes.

In 1925 there was leave from Persia. That year in London there was an Empire Exhibition, and on the Southern Rhodesian stand some very fine maize cobs and a poster saying that fortunes could be made on maize at twenty-five shillings a bag. So on an impulse, turning his back forever on England, washing his hands of the corruption of the East, my father collected all his capital, eight hundred pounds, I think, while my mother packed curtains from Liberty's, clothes from Harrods, visiting cards, a piano, Persian rugs, a governess, and two small children.

Soon, there was my father in a cigar-shaped house of thatch and mud on the top of a kopje that overlooked in all directions a great system of mountains, rivers, valleys, while overhead the sky arched from horizon to empty horizon. This was a couple of hundred miles south from the Zambezi, a hundred or so west from Mozambique, in the district of Banket, so called because certain of its reefs were of the same formation as those called "banket" on the Rand. Lomagundi—gold country, tobacco country, maize country—wild, almost empty. (The Africans had been turned off it into reserves.) Our neighbors were four, five, seven miles off. In front of the house . . . no neighbors, nothing; no farms; just wild bush with two rivers but no fences to the mountains seven miles away. And beyond these mountains and bush again to the Portuguese border, over which "our boys" used to escape when wanted by the police for pass or other offenses.

And then? There was bad luck. For instance, the price of maize dropped from twenty-five to nine shillings a bag. The seasons were bad, prices bad, crops failed. This was the sort of thing that made it impossible for him ever to "get off the farm," which, he agreed with my mother, was what he most wanted to do.

It was an absurd country, he said. A man could "own" a farm for years that was totally mortgaged to the Government and run from the Land Bank, meanwhile employing half-a-hundred Africans at twelve shillings a month and none of them knew how to do a day's work. Why, two farm laborers from Europe could do in a day what twenty of these ignorant black savages would take a week to do. (Yet he was proud that he had a name as a just employer, that he gave "a square deal.") Things got worse. A fortuneteller had told him that her heart ached when she saw the misery ahead for my father: this was the misery.

But it was my mother who suffered. After a period of neurotic illness, which was a protest against her situation, she became brave and resourceful. But she never saw that her husband was not living in a real world, that he had made a captive of her common sense. We were always about to "get off the farm." A miracle would do it—a sweep-stake, a gold mine, a legacy. And then? What a question! We would go to England where life would be normal with people coming in for musical evenings and nice supper parties at the Trocadero after a show. Poor woman, for the twenty years we were on the farm, she waited for when life would begin for her and for her children, for she never understood that what was a calamity for her was for them a blessing.

Meanwhile my father sank towards his death (at sixty-one). Everything changed in him. He had been a dandy and fastidious, now he hated to change out of shabby khaki. He had been sociable, now he was misanthropic. His body's disorders—soon diabetes and all kinds of stomach ailments—dominated him. He was brave about his wooden leg, and even went down mine shafts and climbed trees with it, but he walked clumsily and it irked him badly. He greyed fast, and slept more in the day, but would be awake half the night pondering about . . .

It could be gold divining. For ten years he experimented on private theories to do with the attractions and repulsions of metals. His whole soul went into it but his theories were wrong or he was *unlucky*—after all, if he had found a mine he would have had to leave the farm. It could be the relation between the minerals of the earth and of the moon; his decision to make infusions of all the plants on the farm and drink them himself in the interests of science; the criminal folly of the British Government in not realizing that the Germans and the Russians were conspiring as Anti-Christ to . . . the inevitability of war because no one would listen to Churchill, but it would be all right because God (by then he was a British Israelite) had destined Britain to rule the world; a prophecy said ten million dead would surround Jerusalem—how would the corpses be cleared away?; people who wished to abolish flogging should be flogged; the natives understood nothing but a good beating; hanging must not be abolished because the Old Testament said "an eye for an eye and a tooth for a tooth. . . ."

Yet, as this side of him darkened, so that it seemed all his thoughts were of violence, illness, war, still no one dared to make an unkind comment in his presence or to gossip. Criticism of people, particularly of women, made him more and more uncomfortable till at last he burst out with: "It's all very well, but no one has the right to say that about another person."

In Africa, when the sun goes down, the stars spring up, all of them in their expected places, glittering and moving. In the rainy season, the sky flashed and thundered. In the dry season, the great dark hollow of night was lit by veld fires: the mountains burned through September and October in chains of red fire. Every night my father took out his chair to watch the sky and the mountains, smoking, silent, a thin shabby flyaway figure under the stars. "Makes you think—there are so many worlds up there, wouldn't really matter if we blow ourselves up—plenty more where we came from."

The Second World War, so long foreseen by him, was a bad time. His son was in the Navy and in danger, and his daughter a sorrow to him. He became very ill. More and more often it was necessary to drive him into Salisbury with him in a coma, or in danger of one, on the back seat. My mother moved him into a pretty little suburban house in town near the hospitals, where he took to his bed and a couple of years later died. For the most part he was unconscious under drugs. When awake he talked obsessively (a tongue licking a nagging sore place) about "the old war." Or he remembered his youth. "I've been dreaming—Lord, to see those horses come lickety-split down the course with their necks stretched out and the sun on their coats and everyone shouting. . . . I've been dreaming how I walked along the river in the mist as the sun was rising. . . . Lord, lord, lord, what a time that was, what good times we all had then, before the old war."

AFTERWORD TO

# *The Story of an African Farm*

## *by Olive Schreiner*

A new novel, *The Story of an African Farm,* was being discussed around London in 1883. The writer, a Mr. Ralph Iron, was unknown. South Africa was still a long way off, a land of native risings, kaffir wars, wild animals. Missionaries and explorers went there, and young men looking for adventure. Africa, large parts of it still unmapped, was the setting for tales of danger—and imagination. In his preface Ralph Iron wrote: "It has been suggested by a kind critic that he would better have liked the little book if it had been a history of wild adventure; of cattle driven into inaccessible *kranzes* by Bushmen; 'of encounters with ravening lions, and hair-breadth escapes.' This could not be. Such works are best written in Piccadilly or in the Strand. . . ." Also, and gently enough, he asked for a broader sympathy from a habit of criticism whose weakness was—and still is—a partiality for "the charm that hangs about the ideal representation of familiar things." One may profitably think about the nature of the society, safe, ordered, stable—or believed to be so by that part of it who so experience it; but more profitably about the writer who understood the readers, and the critics, he hoped to engage, so well that he could choose such apposite words, and who, in rejecting stronger ones, was already showing such strength and maturity.

The novel had had a hard birth, refused by one publisher after another. Not only was it about an Africa unfamiliar to England, but it had an unmarried mother whom the author refused to provide with a wedding ring. Then Chapman and Hall took it on the advice of George Meredith. Cuts and changes were suggested, and some made: it is said with resentment.

Soon it leaked out that Ralph Iron was a woman, and a young one: she was not yet thirty. She had been a governess in the Cape. She was lodging in London. She was very pretty and vivacious. Attractive female authors were then a rarity. She was around and about in London society for a while. It was not only Meredith who recognized the novel. An extraordinary assortment of the remarkable people of her time praised it. It was one of the best novels in the English language. It was greater than *The Pilgrim's Progress*. It had genius. It had splendor. For the rest of her life she was the famous author of this novel that she had written in her early twenties. And, until she died, people from every part of the world would come up to her and say that it had changed their lives. Some claim that it would have made no difference if she had never written another word. This is true, from the point of view of literature; but there were other sides to her.

Now I must write personally; but I would not, if I didn't know that nothing we can say about ourselves is personal. I read the novel when I was fourteen or so; understanding very well the isolation described in it; responding to her sense of Africa the magnificent—mine, and everyone's who knows Africa; realizing that this was one of the few rare books. For it is in that small number of novels, with *Moby Dick, Jude the Obscure, Wuthering Heights,* perhaps one or two others, which is on a frontier of the human mind. Also, this was the first "real" book I'd met with that had Africa for a setting. Here was the substance of truth, and not from England or Russia or France or America, necessitating all kinds of mental translations, switches, correspondences, but reflecting what I knew and could see. And the book became part of me, as the few rare books do. A decade or so later, meeting people who talked of books, they talked of this one, mentioning this or that character, or scene; and I discovered that while I held the strongest sense of the novel, I couldn't remember anything about it. Yet I had only to hear the title, or "Olive Schreiner," and my deepest self was touched.

I read it again, for the first time as an experienced reader, able to judge and compare—and criticize. The first shock was that Olive Schreiner, who had always felt so close, like a sister, could have been my grandmother. The second was that, if I used the rules that turn out a thousand good forgettable novels a year, let the book spread out from the capsuled essence of it I had held, so that it became a matter of characters and a plot, it was not a good novel. But, then, of course, neither is *Wuthering Heights*. Well, then, what are these rules? Faced with one of the rare books, one has to ask such questions, to discover, again, that there aren't any. Nor can there be; the novel being that hybrid, the mixture of journalism and the *Zeitgeist* and autobiography that comes out of a part of the human consciousness which is always trying to understand itself, to come into the light. Not on the level where poetry works, or music, or mathematics, the high arts; no, but on the rawest and most workaday level, like earthworms making new soil where things can grow. True lovers of the novel must love it as the wise man in the fable did the crippled beauty whose complaint against fate was that she was beautiful—for what use was her beauty? She was always trying for humanity and failing. And he replied that it was because of the trying that he loved her.

The true novel wrestles on the edge of understanding, lying about on all sides desperately, for every sort of experience, pressing into use every flash of intuition or correspondence, trying to fuse together the crudest of materials, and the humblest, which the higher arts can't include. But it is precisely here, where the writer fights with the raw, the intractable, that poetry is born. Poetry, that is, of the novel: appropriate to it. *The Story of an African Farm* is a poetic novel; and when one has done with the "plot" and the characters, that is what remains: an endeavor, a kind of hunger, that passionate desire for growth and understanding, which is the deepest pulse of human beings.

There was nothing unconscious about Olive Schreiner's method, as this letter to Havelock Ellis shows. The book she discusses is her *From Man to Man*.

> One thing I am glad of is that it becomes less and less what you call "art" as it goes along. My first crude conceptions are always what you call "art." As they become more and more *living* and real, they become what I call higher art, but what you call no "art" at all. I quite understand what you meant, but I cannot think that your use of the word in that sense is right, i.e., not misleading, and therefore *untrue*. If I understand what you mean, *Wilhelm Meister* is not art, one of Balzac's novels is. *Wilhelm Meister* is one of the most immortal deathless productions of the greatest of the world's artists, the result of twenty years labor, worth any six of Balzac's novels, great and glorious as Balzac is. Yet if you were writing it, you would, ridiculous as it would seem, be *obliged* to call it "not art." You seem to say "I will call 'art' only that artistic creation in which I can clearly *see* the artist manufacturing the parts and piecing them together; when I cannot see that, though the thing be organic, true, inevitable, like a work of God's, I will not call it art; I must see the will shaping it (of course there always has been a will shaping it, whether it is visible or not) or I will not call it art." This of course is not in justification of my method but touches what seems to me a weakness and shallowness in your mode of criticism. It *is* very valuable that the two kinds of art should be distinguished, but

> not that the one should be called art and the other not art. It would be better to call the one artificial and the other real art. But that wouldn't be just. I should rather call the one organic, and the other inorganic.

And in reply to his answer: "No, I deny that you can see how *Wilhelm Meister* was made; you can see how it *grew,* not how it was *made. . . .* It came like that, like a tree, not like a Greek temple. You never know where you are going to turn next in *Wilhelm Meister.* No more did Goethe—yet all was of necessity, nothing of chance."

The "plot." On a Karroo farm in the second part of last century lived a widowed Dutchwoman, Tant' Sannie. There is a daughter, Em, who will inherit the farm, and a niece, Lyndall. Em is sweet, gentle, humble, "womanly." Lyndall is all beauty, fire, and intelligence. She is an orphan. Lyndall dreams of an education: knowledge frees. She will make the Dutchwoman send her to school. The saintly German overseer has a son, Waldo. He and Lyndall love each other as prisoners may do. To the farm comes a mountebank, Bonaparte Blenkins, who tricks the rich Dutchwoman into wanting to marry him. While under his spell she treats Waldo and his father abominably: he wants to get rid of them. Also, he enjoys cruelty. He is afraid of Lyndall, who sees through him. Discovered by Tant' Sannie making love to her much richer niece, he leaves in disgrace. Time passes. The girls are grown to marriageable age: Em is a "yellow-haired little woman of sixteen." A new arrival, Gregory Rose, who has hired part of the farm, is in love with her. But Em tells him that when Lyndall arrives back from her boarding school he will see a really beautiful woman, a princess, and change his mind. This happens. Lyndall despises the womanish Gregory, and spends her time with the "low, coarse" fellow Waldo. He listens, she talks, mostly about the humiliating position of woman in her time. "A little bitterness, a little longing when we are young, a little futile striving for work, a little passionate striving for room for the exercise of her powers—and then we go with the drove. A woman must march with her regiment. In the end she must be trodden down or go with it." In her girls' school she had not learned what she had expected. "I have discovered that of all cursed places under the sun, where the hungriest soul can hardly pick up a few grains of knowledge, a girls' boarding school is the worst. They are called finishing schools and the name tells accurately what they are. . . ." Olive Schreiner has been described as "a suffragette before there were any."

Waldo and Lyndall drive together over the veld. They sit on a kopje and talk. He takes her to a Boer dance. Then she goes away. Gregory

Rose feels the first real emotion of his life: he goes in search of her, wants nothing but to serve her. Waldo leaves in search of wider experience. Em stays and suffers. Lyndall has become pregnant by a "stranger, his tall slight figure reposing in the broken armchair, his keen blue eyes studying the fire from beneath delicately penciled drooping eyelids. One white hand plays with a heavy flaxen mustache." This figure, or a similar one, appears and reappears through Olive Schreiner's work. He is charged with the high tension of conflict, a man found overwhelmingly sexually attractive, but contemptibly wanting by a woman who demands moral and intellectual companionship, as well as physical, from her lover. The stranger wants to marry Lyndall. She will not: it will put her in his power, and he only decided to marry her when he realized that she might not want to. But she agrees to stay with him, unmarried, for the sake of the child. They travel around the Cape, but some quarrel occurs. She is left alone and ill. Gregory Rose tracks her down to a country hotel. She needs a nurse. He dresses himself in women's clothes and looks after her. The baby dies soon after it is born. She dies too. Waldo returns to the farm, after eighteen months of every sort of degrading labor. He has learned that: "You may work and work and work until you are only a body and not a soul." Gregory returns with the news of Lyndall's death. He will marry Em because Lyndall has told him to. Em says: "Why is it always so, Waldo, always so? We long for things and long for them and pray for them. Then at last, too late, when we don't want them any more, when all the sweetness is taken out of them, then they come."

Waldo goes off to sit in the sunshine—and dies.

Lyndall is dead. Waldo is dead. The saintly old man is dead.

Gregory Rose lives to carry on the farm with gentle uncomplaining Em who, Lyndall says, "is so much better than me that there is more goodness in her little finger than in my whole body." Tant' Sannie, remarried, flourishes with her new husband.

Well, that's the story. Parts are well done by the conventional yardstick: the scenes of rural Boer life; the dance, the scene where the young man comes in "his hopeless resignation" to court Tant' Sannie; Tant' Sannie coming to visit with her new baby; Tant' Sannie on the joys of marriage; Tant' Sannie on progress: "Not that I believe in this new plan of putting soda into the pot. If the dear Father had meant soda to be put into soap, what would He have made milkbushes for, and stuck them all over the veld, as thick as lambs in lambing season." This woman, as near animal as they come, is written with love and with humor—a triumph. Em, too, the maiden dreaming of motherhood: "I always come to watch the milking. That red cow with the short horns is bringing up the calf of the white cow that died. She loves it so—just as if it were her own. It is so nice to see her lick its little ears. Just look!" Now, these are characters that could have appeared in any good novel called *Scenes from the Karroo, 18——*. It did not take Olive Schreiner to create them. The novel's greatness lies precisely in where it breaks from "lifelike" characters, and an easily recognizable probability.

There is the question of Bonaparte Blenkins, the charlatan. Later Olive said she was sorry that she had given him no real humanity, made him two-dimensional. But her first instinct was right. Evil is not personified in this book—neither is goodness. Human beings are small things in the grip of gigantic forces. They cry out and fight and struggle to understand the incomprehensible, which is beyond good and evil. Had Bonaparte been given depth and weight, we would have had to ask questions about the saintliness of the old German, Bonaparte's counterweight, whom he has to destroy. He is saintly: but very silly. And Bonaparte is wicked—and silly. Not damaging? Indeed, yes: his persecution of the old German, his treatment of Waldo, the brutal beating he gave him, scarred Waldo, and taught him his helplessness; taught Lyndall her helplessness, and enforced her determination to free herself. But he was stupid, undid himself—and ran away. Wickedness is arbitrary, almost grotesque. And innocent childlike goodness is impotent. But—does it matter all that much? The sun burns down over the Karroo; the pitilessly indifferent stars wheel and deploy; and two young creatures look up at the skies where they see their unimportance written, and ask questions, can find no answers—and suffer most frightfully.

Lyndall and Waldo: Olive said that in these two she had put herself. They share a soul; and when Lyndall dies, Waldo has to die. But it is Waldo who is the heart of the book, a ragged, sullen, clumsy farm boy, all inarticulate hunger—not for education, like Lyndall, but for the unknown. And it is to Waldo that Olive gave the chapter that is the core, not only of this novel, but of all her work. It is called "Waldo's Stranger," and in it a man traveling through the Cape stops to rest on the farm for an hour. Waldo has carved a piece of wood. "It was by no means lovely. The men and birds were almost grotesque in their labored resemblance to nature, and bore signs of patient thought. The stranger turns the thing over on his knee . . ." and offers to buy it for five pounds. Waldo, whom he sees as "a hind," says no: it is for his father's grave. The visitor is touched, presses the boy to talk, and finally, understanding his need, puts what Waldo has carved on the stick into a story. This is the legend of The Hunter. A version, or germ, of this tale appears in Attar's *Parliament of the Birds*. "An astonishing thing! The first manifestation of the Simurgh" (God or what you will) "took place in China in the middle of the night. One of his feathers fell on China and his reputation filled the world. Everyone made a picture of this feather, and from it formed his own system of ideas, and so fell into a turmoil. This feature is still in the picture gallery of that country: hence the saying: 'Seek knowledge, even as far as China.' But for his manifestation there would not have been so much noise in the world concerning this mysterious Being. This sign of his existence is a token of his glory. All souls carry an impression of the image of his feather. Since the description of it has neither head nor tail, beginning nor end, it is not necessary to say more about it. Now, any of you who are for this road, prepare yourself and put your feet on the Way." The Hunter of the stranger's tale has tried all his life to climb the mountains whose summits hold the Truth, cutting steps in the rock so that he, and others after him, can climb. He lies dying, alone. Long ago he has shed the childish arrogance that let him believe he could find Truth: what matters is that he has spent his life trying. Then: "Slowly from the white sky above, through the still air, came something falling, falling, falling. Softly it fluttered down and dropped on to the breast of the dying man. He felt it with his hands. It was a feather. He died holding it." What Olive makes of this tale is both all her own, and from that region of the human mind called Anon.

Lyndall, too, is visited by a stranger, who gave her, at just the time she needed that book, a book. In Olive's own life it was Spencer's *First Principles,* and she read it, sleepless, for the three days she was able to keep it. To us, the battle for education having been won, at least for this time and for the fortunate of the world, knowledge as it emerges filtered through school and university is perhaps not as covetable as what Olive Schreiner was able to make of books, by herself, using her own instinct to find what she needed. But Lyndall's passion for an education would be understood now by an African boy (or girl) who wants an education so badly that he will walk or bicycle ten, fifteen miles, from a mud hut, or a bunk in a shed in a shantytown shared with half a dozen others, to a day's hard labor; walk or cycle back; and then walk, bicycle, as many miles in another direction to sit up till midnight in an ill-equipped classroom run by a half-equipped teacher, so as to learn to read, write, and do arithmetic. For which "education" he will pay, or his parents will, money he needs for food and clothes. There are millions of them in Africa. To such people books, learning, are a key to freedom—as they are to Lyndall, who, when she got them, discovered their limits.

But Waldo wanted a different kind of knowledge, and that is what he was given by his stranger, to whom he says: "All my life I have longed to see you." He was thinking: Ah, that man who believed nothing, hoped nothing, felt nothing: *how he loved him.* And, when the stranger was gone, he stooped and kissed passionately a hoof-mark in the sand.

Lyndall has given her name to dozens of little South African girls: the beautiful young woman who chooses to die alone rather than marry a man she cannot respect. Lyndall is that projection of a novelist created as a means of psychic self-preservation. Olive, at that time, was very much alone. If not estranged from her family, she could not get from it the moral support she so badly needed. She was very young. She was ill: was to be ill all her life. She had been through violent religious conflicts that had left her drained, exhausted. She had been in love with, possibly jilted by, a man who found her socially inadequate, and morally and mentally his superior—or so the evidence suggests. That Olive should have needed Lyndall is not surprising: she had to love Lyndall, and stand by her, and protect her—and explain her; for Lyndall was the first of her kind in fiction. Of her we can say: that kind of embattled woman was the product of that kind of society, where women had a hard time of it. But Waldo is the truth of Lyndall, and he is timeless.

Women novelists' men . . . Male novelists' women can be as instructive, particularly in their archetypal state, like Haggard's *She*—as the psychologists have pointed out. This "she" is best studied in bad novels, for in good novels she is a human being. And so with women writers' men; the most useful exemplars we have being Rochester and Heathcliff. They are the unregenerate strong man, the unfulfilled hero. In the psyche of men, is the goddess, "she." In women, the hero; but it is as if women, looking for strength, the hero, the strong wise man who embodies humanity's struggle upwards, and not finding him, may take instead his failed brother, who at least has had potentiality; rather than a nothing-man who has never aimed at anything. Lyndall's lover, with his flaxen mustache and his heavy eyelids; the rest of the attractive men who capture Olive Schreiner's heroines against their will—they are nothing-men, put there to be despised. But the hero, the strong man who challenges destiny: well, his place is of course with "she"—in legend, myth, and magic. He cannot exist, in his pure form, in the novel, that struggling and impure art. He is out of place there, as "she" is. You find her, him, only in romantic or second-rate novels. But Waldo is the first appearance in women's writing of the true hero, in a form appropriate to the novel; here a kind of Caliban who mysteriously embodies Prospero's spirit, or Faust's.

Waldo is the son of the old German, Otto, who is a portrait of Olive's father.

To the creation of a woman novelist seem to go certain psychological ingredients; at least, often enough to make it interesting. One of them, a balance between father and mother where the practicality, the ordinary sense, cleverness, and worldly ambition is on the side of the mother; and the father's life is so weighted with dreams and ideas and imaginings that their joint life gets lost in what looks like a hopeless muddle and failure, but which holds a potentiality for something that must be recognized as better, on a different level, than what ordinary sense or cleverness can begin to conceive.

Olive's mother was the daughter of a minister of religion destined for a good middle-class marriage. She met Gottlob Schreiner at a missionary meeting. He was a student, the son of a German shoemaker, in a family of peasants and preachers. At the wedding the minister tore the trimmings off Rebecca's hat, as unsuitable for the wife of a missionary. They went off together to the Cape, in a mood of high evangelical fervor, to convert the heathen. Gottlob never lost his sense of mission, but his wife later declared it was all "claptrap and nonsense." She tried to preserve some intellectual life, and the respectable standards of her upbringing, in isolation and in poverty, while he loved and idealized her as a being quite above him. She was educated, beautiful, clever—and frustrated. Olive, the sixth child, experienced her as cold and unloving. "My mother has never been a mother to me. I have had no mother. She is a brilliant, wonderful little woman, all intellect and genius. The relation between us is a very curious one . . . she seems to me like a favorite brilliant child of mine." Olive was solitary, "queer," and fanciful in a way all the family found uncomfortable. She grew up on poor mission stations, in close relationship with the wild untenanted landscape of the Cape. This saved her: according to modern ideas, she was brutally treated; but she escaped to the rocks, the bushes, the sun, the stars. *Undine* describes her childhood. From the time she was a baby playing with dolls, she was tormented by God, by hell, by redemption—she was reading the Bible before she read anything—and by her own passionate uncompromising temperament, and the conscience that was the product of her Lutheran, Wesleyan heritage. In crises of misery over God, there could be no comfort in her family: she was locked up, punished. She was beaten: her worst was from her mother, who gave her fifty strokes on her bare body with a bunch of quince rods. This was for using a crude Dutch expression: she said "Ach!" Rebecca and her fight for respectability emerges, in this incident, as if into a spotlight. Olive was never able to forget this experience. To read *Undine* is painful even now, not so much for the punishings and the beating, but because of her hunger for love, for understanding, and the mental anguish that she suffered for years. Lying awake at night she listened to the clock tick: every tick meant souls were being sent to hell by an unforgiving God. She cried out to be given some burden or sacrifice so that even one soul might be spared because of her. She staged sacrifices like Abraham, putting a mutton chop saved from dinner onto a rock in the midday sun, and waiting for the fire to come from heaven—for she had as much faith as Abraham. But nothing happened, God was indifferent to her. She got up at night to read the Bible by moonlight, to find some words that might comfort her, and found: "Strive to enter in at the strait gate, for many, I say unto you, shall seek to enter in and shall not be able." She flung the Bible across the room and wept, and stared at the stars out of the window, and was tormented by eternity and the littleness of human beings on their earth. She lost her faith, and knew that she was wicked, and was damned, but preferred the expectation of hell and rejection by God than to accept God's injustice, which made some souls elect from the beginning of time, and others inevitably damned. Many Victorians, fighting a narrow and bigoted religion, lost their reputations, their jobs, sometimes their reason: their conflicts are described in plentiful memoirs from that time. But this frightful battle was fought out in a small girl, who had no one to help her. When still a girl she became "a freethinker" and remained one, always contemptuous of conventional religion. Asked for help, much later, by a parson threatened with loss of faith, she wrote: "If I must put it into words, I would say, the Universe is One, and It lives; or, if you would put it into older phraseology, There is NOTHING but God." Sympathetic but not very insightful contemporaries defended her by saying she was a religious woman who did not believe in God. She said of herself that she had that deep faith that took the form of a lifelong battle with God, and which took for granted she would be forgiven: which is not the same thing at all. But to her, our almost casual rejection of God, an indifferent irreligiousness, would have been impossible. The Victorians who fought that battle carried their freethinking, their agnosticism, their atheism, like flags of faith in the free spirit of man. The question she makes us ask, as do all the great ones of the past, is: If she were alive now, what battle would she be fighting? The freedoms she fought for, we take for granted. Because of people like her. We tend to forget that. She never did; was searching literature and history for allies even as a child; and before she was twenty had read Darwin and Spencer, Montaigne, Goethe, Carlyle, Gibbon, Locke, and Lecky; J. S. Mill, Shakespeare, Ruskin, and Schiller. And had made amateur attempts, her mother aiding, at medicine and biology and anatomy. For poor Rebecca had once dreamed of studying medicine.

The family disintegrated in poverty, Gottlob was irremediably incompetent, and gave away what he possessed, often to rogues. He died, and the mother, extraordinarily, became a Roman Catholic, though according to the chapel creed, "one of the three grand crimes was to believe in the possible salvation of a Roman Catholic." Some of the children found it a crime; but not Olive, who continued to love her mother with that kind of love that is all a hopeful need. It was rewarded. As a woman she wrote, with deep emotion, how one night she woke to find her mother crying by her bed. Rebecca had read something Olive had written and was saying: "Oh, my child, my wonderful beautiful child. Am I really your mother? Have I really given birth to a human being who could write like that? You could never have written this if you had not been thinking of your own childhood. Forgive me, please."

At nineteen Olive became a governess, and taught for seven years in the families of Boer farmers. Here she learned "to love and admire the Boer." In one of her places her room was mud-floored, and when it rained she had to put up an umbrella, because the roof leaked. The furniture was a bed and a box for her clothes. There was no looking glass, not even a basin: she washed in the stream that ran past her door. But she was content here, moved for health reasons: her asthma began at this time. In these years she wrote drafts of *Undine, From Man to Man,* and completed *The Story of an African Farm.* Because of "the autobiographical element" she had affection for *Undine*, but she asked for it to be destroyed. She was right: it is an undigested, mental book, in parts not far away from the pathetic Victorian novel at its worst. Other people knew better, and it was published. *From Man to Man* she cared for, and worked on it all her life. But while it is full of plums, that fusing that makes a work of art never took place. What, then, fused the *Farm?* Possibly the unhappy love affair. We do not know. She did not care for these emotions to be made public, and we should respect that. Though certainly they scarred her, and she said so; but for her, pain was a teacher, and painful experience necessary for growth.

After she became a literary figure in London, it is harder to see her clearly. She appears in the reminiscences of other people, as in a series of posed photographs. "Distinctly pretty with large dark eyes and black hair and the little square, strong figure." That was Frank Harris. And Havelock Ellis on their first meeting: ". . . the short sturdy, vigorous body in loose shapeless clothes, sitting on the couch, with the hands spread on her thighs and, above, the beautiful head with the large dark eyes, at once so expressive and so observant."

Her first desire to meet people was soon swallowed in the necessity for privacy: she found she had no time to write or to study. She seems always to be in flight—away from people, and towards some place where at last she could feel well. There are letters; but letters, as I think biographers tend to forget, are written to people, and reflect those people, or the phase of a relationship, as much as they do the writer.

Letters to Havelock Ellis are best: she called him her other self, her brother; and over the decades they were in correspondence there is maintained the steady note of intellectual sympathy, even when in emotional stress with each other. They might have married. He was more explicit about his side than she about hers: she did not love him enough, he said. But both were contradictory about each other, as they were bound to be in a friendship that lasted till she died and survived their marriages to other people. Her letters describe her conflicts over marriage. "I can't marry, Henry, I can't. And some awful power seems to be drawing me on. I think I shall go mad. I couldn't. I *must* be free you know, I *must* be free. . . ." "Oh Henry, when passion enters a relationship it does spoil the holy sweetness. But perhaps those people are right who say no such thing as friendship is possible between man and woman, though I can't bear to think so." "The lesson of the last 5 years has been that there is no such thing as friendship, just as the lesson of the two before was that there is no such thing as sex-love, only sex-selfishness." "Please love me. I wish I could believe anything was real. . . ." "Life would be so perfect, so beautiful, so divine, but I think I'm reaching a kind of Nirvana. I can't feel much personally, nor desire much for myself. . . . *Self* seems to be dead in me. Other people want to kill self, but I want so to wake mine to life again, but it won't wake. You know I didn't kill myself two years ago, but I really died then. . . ." "Sweet brother soul, don't feel far from me. I too am going through a very dark and bitter moment of my life. . . ." ". . . for so many years I have longed to meet a mind that should understand me, that should take away from the loneliness of my life. Now I have found it. . . ." "In that you are myself, I love you, and am near to you, but in that you are a man I am afraid of you, I shrink from you."

I think all this is simpler than it sounds. The "anguish and ecstasy" of her childhood had burned her out emotionally before childhood had properly ended. She was tranquil—but dead. She was writing about such states before she was out of her teens, a kind of dark night of the emotions where she felt neither love, nor hate, nor hope, and would have welcomed even pain. Then she fell in love, came to life in hopes for the marriage that did not happen, and was again in the cold hell of no-feeling. Havelock Ellis could not free her from it, but later her husband did. Her letters to Ellis show the evasiveness of a woman who is fond of a man she does not find sexually compelling. She needed him, loved him; but could not respond as he wanted—and as she wanted.

She was in Europe, mostly England, for almost a decade. Through a fog of illness: asthma, heart trouble, neuralgia, which she knew to be what we call psychosomatic, though knowing it did not help her;

through the confusion of her emotional conflicts; we can watch the growth of another side of Olive Schreiner. The social reformer was becoming a socialist. She met, became friends with, the socialists: Eleanor Marx was an intimate. And the feminist learned that what had been, in her girlhood, a solitary personal conviction, considered eccentric, was what the best men and women of her time were studying. It was called The Woman Question. Always practical, always at the roots of any problem, she was helping poor women, prostitutes, women in every kind of trouble. She started work on a "big scientific work" on sex, which she discussed with Havelock Ellis. It never saw the light; was destroyed in the Boer War. A pity; no one else could have written it so well, and no one can write it now. For sex changes, like everything else, must be part of a climate. Between that time, such a short time ago, and ourselves is such a gulf of experience that it is hard to imagine ourselves in an air where so much was twisted, dark, murky. For instance, part of her suffering was due to celibacy: she said it herself. But: "I would so much like to have a child, but I couldn't bear to be married; neither could I bear any relationship that was not absolutely open to the world—so I could never have one." This was written at a time she was being asked to leave lodgings by landladies who considered her immoral because she had single men and "unrespectable" women visiting her. She continued to act as she believed she had the right to act; yet she was a woman so sensitive to notice she hated even to eat in public. There is one large lesson we can still learn from the battle over "the woman question." It is that a change in physical relations and conditions changes mental and emotional states beyond what even the most revolutionary of reformers can begin to foresee. Even Olive, considered wildly visionary about the future of women, was far from seeing how much that was considered innate, inherent, could disappear and how fast. None of them ever seemed far from a microclimate of semi-invalidism. Take what used to be called "the change of life," which even our mothers faced and suffered like a dreaded illness. For most women now it doesn't exist, and for many it happens without the aid of drugs. Less than a hundred years has done it. How? Why? The book that was destroyed could have helped with these and with other questions that ought to be asked. But there is a generation of girls enjoying liberties won for them by women like Olive Schreiner and looking back with what seems to be patronage, amusement. It is really a shudder of terror at what they've escaped from—and it stops them thinking.

It was mostly South Africa's sun, which might help her health, that took her back there in 1889. She was now a public figure; and she took a stand on "The Native Question" and on Rhodes's acquisition of what became Southern Rhodesia. At first she admired Rhodes, who always admired her. She became his enemy over his double-dealing in the Jameson Raid; and wrote a novel called *Trooper Peter Halkett of Mashonaland,* which was good enough for its purpose: an effort to arouse public indignation. It did. But it didn't stop Rhodes from annexing Mashonaland. She continued to protest and to warn while the bases of modern South Africa and Rhodesia were being well and truly laid. If Africans were not admitted now, she said, into the fellowship of civilization, it would soon be too late; and the future would be all bloodshed and misery. She was prophetic about this, as about so much else; and emotionally clear in a way that she must have found hard to achieve. It is difficult enough now for a white person brought up in white-dominated Africa to free himself, herself, from a prejudice that starts when, from the moment you see anything, you see Africans as inferiors. The child Olive was taught to despise "kaffirs" and "niggers." Parts of *Undine* show an ignorance and prejudice that is now shocking. She was also taught to despise the Dutch. When she was four, a small Boer girl gave her some sugar. She accepted, "not liking to refuse," but dropped it afterwards, for one did not eat anything that had been held in the hand of a Boer child. She also had conventionally prejudiced ideas about Jews, though there is a possibility she was part Jewish. All this she had to fight in herself, to change, in order to become the champion of racial tolerance. Nor was she that kind of liberal that South Africa still produces, the paternalist who believes that the kindly-master-to-grateful-servant relationship is the only one possible, since it is the only one he has ever seen. Olive, a real revolutionary, knew that the dispossessed must always work for, and win, their own rights, their own freedom; because it is in the fighting, the working, that they grow and develop and learn their measure. She expressed this idea particularly well in her writing about women.

When she was nearly forty, this woman who said she could not marry married a South African farmer, rather younger than herself. There were times of great happiness, though the marriage was difficult, as it was bound to be. The much-longed-for child died, and particularly cruelly; it choked in its sleep the night after it was born. Her grief turned her again towards the dark, weakened her, and, it seems, the marriage, which, however, continued to be buoyed by their common love for South Africa and by their sympathy over political questions. In the Boer War she championed the Boers against her own countrymen, by whom she was reviled. She loved England. She loved the Boers. She suffered acutely, but she kept her good judgment, as her book *An English South African's View of the Situation* shows. It throws light even now, for the violent emotionalism of the time did not prevent her from holding on to the essentials: that it was the black people who would shape the future; and that in South Africa any conflicts were (and are) bound to be over who owns the gold, the diamonds, the minerals. In the bitter aftermath of the war she worked for an alliance between British and Dutch that would include the black people. These views were as unpopular then as they are now: but now she would be in exile or in prison. Her husband always supported her, though some sympathies were wearing thin. He had made sacrifices for the marriage. The farm he loved (so did she) was given up: her health was bad there. He had made another profession for himself, but there were money shortages; and he complained that he had counted on her earning money through books that in fact she did not get written. Above all, her health grew worse. She spent nights without sleep, walking around the house, talking to herself, fighting for breath. The drugs she took affected her badly. Her behavior, always "free," was increasingly unconventional, and Cronwright was upset by it. She had never cared about her dress. At this time she is described as dowdy, unimpressive, with none of her old fire and brilliance—until she stands up to address a meeting, when she is electrifying. She is described as the sort of woman who in an older society would have been made the prophetess of a tribe. In short, being married to her must have been extremely uncomfortable; and the older she grew, the less important became the small everyday things where a marriage has to live. She suffered, increasingly, from the states of mind we label, in one of our sterilizing, nullifying words, "depressions." She also had deeper, more frequent glimpses into states of insight and ecstatic oneness that were for her the meaning of life.

In some ways, she narrowed; was finding far too many things, and people, and kinds of writing "coarse" or "crude." She sounded, sometimes, like a prissy maiden aunt. Women as they get older seem prone to this: witness Virginia Woolf on James Joyce. I think it is because women find it hard to be public. If it is not against our deepest nature, for what our deepest nature is seems a matter of doubt, when things change so fast, it is certain that public women attract a certain kind of spite, a bitchiness, from both men and women. Learning not to care about this can create a reactive overemphasis: "You say I am unfeminine: look at my traditional female moral attitudes!" Olive earned her share of spite; and she continued oversensitive, an unfortunate trait for someone always in the public eye and always fighting on the unpopular side. She never grew a most essential protective skin: somewhere in her was the young woman who, like Charlotte Brontë, had chosen to be a young man, "Ralph Iron," rather than expose herself to criticism, and this at a time when she was known as a feminist. But these are small faults in a big woman, whose essential self was generous and wide, whose scope was always enlarging, and who continued to work for women. Cronwright does not seem to have been as sympathetic over this as over her other crusades. At least, there is a note of tetchiness here. But he did support and help her; and in 1911 she published *Woman and Labour,* which had an immediate and extraordinary influence, became a kind of bible for the feminists. But, like all her social writing, it goes much deeper than the temporary conditions it describes.

The First World War interrupted the suffragettes' and Olive's work for women; Olive's work for South Africa—and for peace. She was a pacifist. She was in England during the war. Her husband stayed in South Africa. These years must have been bad ones for her. Most of the socialists and suffragettes who were her natural allies had swung into support of the war. Many of her oldest friends found her position unsympathetic. She hated all wars, for any reason, and this one seemed to her particularly wrong. The jingoist nationalism of the time was loathsome to her. She remained for the most part quiet and alone—when she was not being turned out of lodgings and reported to the police because of her German name. In 1917 she saluted the birth of communist Russia among a most remarkable assortment of people, in The 1917 Club: Ramsay MacDonald, Oswald Mosley, Bertrand Russell, E. M. Forster, H. W. Nevinson. But she had said for years that the future lay with Russia and with America: a view that seemed absurd. When the war ended, her husband did not recognize the old woman who answered the door to him. She asked him to go back to the Cape with her. But she sailed alone, seen off by him and by Havelock Ellis. She was very ill. Soon afterwards she died alone in a hotel at the Cape.

What is left of this wonderful woman is *The Story of an African Farm.* The great influence she had is hidden from us in the events she helped to shape. It is the right time for this book to be republished. There is an atmosphere that is sympathetic to it, particularly among young people. It makes me very happy to introduce Olive Schreiner to a fresh generation of readers because:

> "It seems to me more and more that the only thing that really matters in life is not wealth or poverty, pleasure or hardship, but the nature of the human beings with whom one is thrown into contact, and one's relation with them."

PREFACE TO

THE FRENCH EDITION OF

# *Seekers After Truth*

It is safe to say that until twenty years ago few people in the West had heard of Sufis or Sufism. Now everyone has, but probably the associations are with gurus, weird cults, whirling dervishes, certainly Islam. And people calling themselves Sufis abound.

Twenty years ago *The Sufis* appeared, by Idries Shah, a book which drew the attention of very diverse kinds of people, from literati to scientists. It made an astonishing impact, considering that the atmosphere in Europe then was one of reckless confidence in the ability of Western civilization to provide ever-expanding material paradises, and, considering, too, the subject was one which on the face of it was exotic. But those who commended the book all described the feeling of recognition: *This is for me.* As Robert Graves, who wrote the preface, put it: "This book is not addressed to the intellectuals or other orthodox thinkers or to anyone who will fail to recognize it at once as addressed to himself."

It is necessary to mention *The Sufis,* because it is this book that heralded the arrival of a genuine Sufi teaching in the West. It is a complex book, many-layered, offering information about the great Sufi teachers and exemplars who have had such an influence on Eastern history and culture that everyone from North Africa to Indonesia, from Turkestan to the Sudan, recognizes Sufis and Sufism as cornerstones of their different cultures; telling us, too, of how very much these ways of thinking have influenced the West, our own cultures, and many of our prominent men and women. Sufis have been a powerful influence on Europe and, through Europe, on the Americas—everywhere, in fact, that Western culture has spread.

When asking why this has been so ignored in scholarship, it is necessary to make a difficult effort of the imagination: the centuries-long wars with the Saracen, when everything of the East was the enemy, and the subsequent, now over, era of Western imperialism, when Eastern cultures were despised by us, have caused a block in European thinking, making it hard for us to acknowledge what we all owe to the East. Two great religions have influenced Europe, we say: Christianity and Judaism, but we scarcely mention Islam, which has been the third. We are the heirs, we claim proudly, of Greece and Rome, but seldom think of the Arabs, the Persians, the Moors, who, through Spain, fed culture into a Europe that was considered a poor and backward place, with a culture far below the dazzling civilizations of the cities of North Africa, Spain, the Middle East, India. It is being recognized that these blocks have caused a pitiful imbalance in our view of ourselves as Europeans. We Europeans are Euro-centered. We know it; we say so; but are only beginning to understand how much we are, and to what an extent it has impoverished us.

The Sufi way of thinking is a treasure-house of ways in which we can deprovincialize ourselves. When *The Sufis* appeared a few orientalists objected; but when Idries Shah pointed out that all he had done in collating parts of the book dealing with the West was to use Western scholarship, scattered about in a hundred libraries and not fitted together in this way before, scholars looked again at the sources he pointed out to them.

Thus, in two decades, *The Sufis*, and the books by Idries Shah that followed it, have influenced a dozen disciplines, from the study of history and art, to new ways of thinking in the "hard" and the "soft" sciences.

But the main aim of Sufis is the development and transformation of people. There is some quality—a vitality, a yeast—in Sufi work that affects us in ways not easily explained. *The Sufis* nowhere said that a Sufi "school" was being prepared; but people from all over the world who read it approached Shah to become pupils. I was one of them. Rather, perhaps, to my own surprise and—as I have discovered since from the conversations with many others who work with Shah—quite typically, I had become interested, but in an ineffective and undirected way in "mysticism." Even the word had unpleasant associations which, when analyzed, amounted to ignorance. My problem was that I didn't know where to look.

People in the West in this condition—there are more of them every day—soon find what serious lacks there are in our culture—gaps in information. It is easy to find out about the Christian mystics. If you turn to the libraries, you soon find yourself in a maze of quite extraordinarily contradictory books about Buddhism and Yoga, Hinduism and Zen, and a thousand cults and sects, many with magical connotations. If Sufism is mentioned, it is likely to be called "an Islamic sect."

Those who, like myself, are unable to admire Christianity, who want to find a discipline that is not cultish or sectarian, and which is rooted in ordinary life, discover many difficulties in their way. But it was something I had to do, for I had come to the end of a stage in my life. In parenthesis, I think many people do this, but often fail to recognize that this is what has happened to them. In my case, it was the processes of my own work that changed me: writing *The Golden Notebook,* I wrote myself out of my previous mental "set." My mind had been formed by the current dogmas of the West, the education of our time, a package consisting of membership of one of the churches of that great religion socialism, or sympathy with it; atheism held as a rigid article of faith; a dose of Marxism; a tincture of Freud; and materialism in both the philosophic sense and the practical one: like everyone else in the West I saw material progress as the sum of all human good. My mind had been set—though it took me years to see how rigidly—by Christianity with its rewards and its punishments and its threats, its heaven and hell and paradise; a structure which underlies European thinking and which is repeated in the beliefs of socialism. I was the child of a priest-culture: for two thousand years we Europeans have had to do what the priests told us, and when the Protestants threw off the dictatorship of Rome, so deep was the pattern embedded in them they retained priests; and when Christianity was dethroned we chose to be dominated by political leaders, the priests' successors.

I was the child of the oldest, longest-lasting tyranny the world has ever known, which forbade any ways of thinking but its own, punished with torture and death any divagation from narrow and intolerant creeds. And, when I believed I had turned my back on all that, I had spent years of my life in the company of Christianity's successors, the politicos with their leaders and their bosses, their heresies, their creeds to which one has to conform, their dogmas and rigidities.

This, then, was my background. It is, of course, a typical one. It was a handicap to me when I approached the Sufis asking to be a pupil.

People who want to follow the Sufi Way now, with Idries Shah as a guide, have to be prepared to examine, and then shed, the ideas that are the result of patterns laid down in us by our European history. The "guru phenomenon," for instance, is considered by Sufis an aberration: in the West the need for a guru is seen as a symptom of an unacknowledged desire for a leader, a priest. I have heard Idries Shah say that one of his greatest difficulties as a teacher is that we have flattering ideas about ourselves: we see ourselves as free, democratic, individual, and able to exercise free choice. But, in fact, we are conditioned to want authority and authority figures, we want to be members of groups and packs and herds: our education does not teach us that this is what we are like. Since the Sufis aim to teach and not to condition, he has to find methods of imparting Sufi knowledge that bypass our conditioning. The Sufi Guide, or Teacher, or Exemplar, operates in ways unfamiliar to our culture, imparts information and knowledge on a different principle, aims to produce, as soon as possible, an individual who is able to "see himself as others see him," a person able to teach himself or herself.

This is easy enough to say; but it may take years for a pupil to understand the Sufi way of teaching. "The Teacher, the Teaching, and the Taught are a single phenomenon." "The Teaching is like a yeast or a food." "The Teacher is in a sense in the deepest part of the pupil." "If you want to fill a pot with clean water, then the pot has first of all to be emptied." As you study the Sufi Way remarks like these slowly become clearer. You begin to understand what is meant by "Learning How to Learn"—which is the title of one of the Shah's books. You learn how far a Sufi teacher is from the father figure (the priest) of tradition. You are able to distinguish the genuine Sufi teacher from the many imitators who offer bizarre practices, insist on a narrow range of ideas, are authoritarian, are often deluded or cynical. In short, it is not too much to say that if you want to study Sufism, then what a Teacher is *not*, is what you first of all have to study. It is easy enough to say on some early impulse, an inkling, as a result of, let's say, reading a book like this one, "I can see that my ideas have been too narrow," but it is hard indeed to allow oneself to change.

The Sufis say that in the West the greatest of all barriers to our learning is our having a consuming society, where we are all taught that we are entitled to everything we want, when we want it. We are the products of the advertising industry. . . . We transfer these attitudes to mysticism, to Sufism. We hear of mysticism, learn perhaps for the first time that such and such a way of thinking, previously unsuspected by us, is available, and the reaction is, because of our education: "I want it—*now*."

There is a true story about a certain unscrupulous guru in India who capitalizes on this Western tendency. His ashram is besieged by Western "seekers." On the morning after their arrival there is a ceremony, during which they are presented with an impressive testimonial: "This is to certify that you are now fully Enlightened." The genuine Sufi, on the contrary, will insist that you are not entitled to anything you have not earned, that it is hard work, that it is only people who are prepared to give time and trouble to this study who may become students, and that ultimately our aim should be to learn how to serve society, and not to take and consume.

These attitudes are of course no different from those of any genuine mystical tradition. There is nothing new in what Idries Shah and his associates offer: but he insists that an authentic "Path" or "Way" or "School" has always to be freshly introduced, fashioned to suit the time, the place, the culture: a genuine version of the Sufic Way can never be a rehash of past formulas which were, and had to be, for their time, their place, their cultural context. Sufism is not peculiar to Islam, or the property of Islam, though for historic reasons it developed—in the public form—within the Islamic context. The great Sufi teachers in Islam all had innumerable Christian and Jewish pupils. Sufism predated Islam by thousands of years, under many different names, in a hundred different guises.

This way of thinking—this "yeast," or "wine," "food," "water," "tree," or "vine"—there are a hundred ways of saying it—is an ancient tradition which has been kept alive and viable by skilled experts, has always been in operation in every country, sometimes openly, more often not, and its function is to develop humanity in every age according to the possibilities of that age. But there can be no discord, says Shah, say the Sufis, between any of the genuine paths to God: in their outward regions it may seem as if there is discord, but in their inwardness that would be impossible, for that is where all the Paths, the Ways, the religions, the disciplines, meet. Disagreement is usually a question of argument over terms, over the outward manifestations.

It seems to me that most of the difficulty experienced by people approaching Sufis for the first time is in this area: terminology, an unwillingness or inability to let go familiar and comforting concepts or sets of words, even temporarily, even as an experiment.

I have a friend who, on her insistence, I gave *The Sufis*. But she said she was put off by all those Eastern saints and savants. "Even when they have so strongly influenced Europe?" I asked; for she is a scholar. "Perhaps I am too old to change my ideas. I am a Westerner, after all." So I offered her the books which Shah has written in modern terminology, within the ways of thinking of Europe: *Learning How to Learn, The Perfumed Scorpion, Seeker After Truth, Reflections*. She read half of one and said that Idries Shah sounded like an anthropologist or a psychologist; she had believed that these books were about mysticism? I said that Sufism, when it is being freshly introduced for a new time and place, is always put—or partly put—into the current "language." Psychology and anthropology are two of our "dialects." In the end she directed herself to Christianity because she said she was used to the idea of it. But she is an atheist. . . .

Sufis do not at all mind being approached by atheists and freethinkers. Atheism, they say, is a religion too, a system of passionately defended belief. "The Sufi current is to be found in the fierce repressed energy of the scoffer of Sufism as much as in the devout believer, or a scientist studying the stars." *Belief* is not something the Sufis admire or wish to develop. Belief and disbelief are stages of immaturity through which the seeker will pass on the way to Knowledge.

But many people who turned their backs on religion are now interested in getting towards "what really is in Christianity." It is not Christianity (or any other religion) which is responsible for indoctrinating people to believe in a narrow system which traps them. It is, rather, that large areas of all religions are captured, as a matter of history, by cultists who oversimplify and then use the result to trap people with. So it is a certain type of mind which is responsible. Dogmas and liturgy, and so on, are not found in the initial stages of a religion in such oversimplified forms. The successors or adopters of the original workers in the field are the ones who distort the religion into a sociopsychological straitjacket. Then, after that, reformers try to adjust things, and in turn slip into mechanicality. This process can be seen if one looks.

Meanwhile, the inner aspect (the Path within each religion) is obscured. Most Christians would admit that no Church today looks anything like what Jesus' school looked like. From that realization it is easy to see what has happened and why. The why is the (deliberate or unconscious) need to control the adherents. "Mysticism" is given a bad name because "mystics" in all societies usually oppose, ignore, evade the narrow dogmas. And they do this because they are engaged in reclaiming the life beneath the straitjacket.

Since the problem which current religion poses us is not a religious one as such, but a problem of analyzing the nonreligious social coercion which overlays it, it is natural that what Idries Shah does is to point to what look like temporary social or psychological problems. These are the current terms for a process which has been going on from remote times. Shah is doing what Sufis in the past have done: freeing the inner core of religion from dogma. When the irrelevant fossilization has been dealt with, the spiritual activity may begin.

What has happened over and over again in the past is that spiritual "schools" have been turned into secondary and derivative forms, called religions, which have changed the genuine spiritual core into social behavior and practice. This is due to an unacknowledged "conspiracy" between those who want to control and those who not only want to be controlled but who want a quiet life. It is easier to accept that religion means emotional and intellectual activity and outward action and show, than to look for the more subtle, the spiritual, ingredient.

Shah has written about these problems in various ways. One book is

*The Elephant in the Dark*, which is a discussion of the common ground shared by Christianity and Islam, now and historically.

It will be seen that it is not possible to write about *Seeker After Truth* without emphasizing that it is part of an assembly of books carefully chosen by Idries Shah to present Sufism now, and to us. Thus, he is doing what every new Sufi exemplar does: the "bequest" of Sufi material has to be pruned of what was for past time and has become redundant, useless. What is useful for now is re-presented; new material is written.

*Seeker After Truth* has to be considered as a facet of the whole. The books that Shah has published himself, through the Octagon Press, or has had published with the aid of friendly conventional publishers, make up a pattern, a matrix, on which a different, more flexible and open way of thinking can be built. People are asked to "familiarize" themselves with these books, and that means not using the academic mode of thinking, which is what we are taught through our education: to look for ideas which we can match or compare with ideas we already have and consider respectable, ignoring the others. Reading in this new way means to learn a different mode of the mind, one little used in the West, and is in itself an exercise in Sufic thinking: something more passive, open, ready to examine unfamiliar ideas or influences—watchful in an attempt to be more sensitive to unfamiliar impacts and currents that normally we might overlook. But of course there are people who read Shah's books in many countries and languages who are not students of Sufism. They are attracted by this lively, iconoclastic original way of thinking. It is a body of literature unique in our time for the wide uses to which it is put, and by the wide range of people it reaches.

These include people who perhaps read very little at all: young people whose habit it is to listen rather than to read, or who perhaps read only space fiction; intellectuals and scientists who find the material full of new ideas for their particular disciplines; and artists of all kinds. And there are people who feel themselves to be students of Shah who have never met him: they use this material for self-development.

It is a many-sided literature: the Sufic use of literature has aspects which are unfamiliar to us. It was they who developed, they claim, the Teaching Story, an artifact created specifically for influencing the deepest and most hidden part of a human being—a part not accessible to any other approach. There are twelve of these teaching tales in this book. They are reminiscent of our European fairy tales, which are to be found all over the world, in different versions. Did you know that Cinderella is to be found in over three hundred fifty variations, in many different countries?

The teaching story is not to be considered as a parable, which the

Sufis use too; for the parable has a more limited aim, such as the inculcation of a moral, or ethics, or to transmit information. The Sufis teach through jokes, tales thousands of years old, anecdotes taken from that day's newspaper, stories of an exemplary or warning kind deliberately constructed to highlight a point. They cite recent scientific discovery which confirms traditional Sufi practice, claiming that in their tradition can be found, from the early Middle Ages, references to the atom, evolution, the circulation of the blood, the projection of pictures from a distance, like television. Jung's "the collective unconscious" was taken from the East, as he acknowledged, and is to be found in the works of Ibn el Arabi and El Ghazzali, both of whom in their time were known and reverenced in the West, El Arabi as Doctor Maximus.

The many-sidedness, the richness, the unexpectedness of this Sufi "bequest" can be glimpsed from this book, which I am sure will turn out to be for many people, as *The Sufis* was for me twenty years ago, a door into a new astonishing world.

PERMISSIONS ACKNOWLEDGMENTS

Grateful acknowledgment is made to the following for permission to reprint previously published material:

JONATHAN CLOWES LIMITED: "My Father" by Doris Lessing, Copyright © 1963 by Doris Lessing; the "Afterword" by Doris Lessing to *The Story of an African Farm* by Olive Schreiner, Copyright © 1968 by Doris Lessing; and an excerpt from *The Summer Before the Dark* by Doris Lessing, Copyright © 1973 by Doris Lessing. Reprinted by permission of Jonathan Clowes Limited on behalf of The Doris Lessing Trust. The "Preface" by Doris Lessing to *Chercheur de la Verité* by Idries Shah, published by Albin Michel, Copyright © 1984 by Doris Lessing. Reprinted by permission of Jonathan Clowes on behalf of Doris Lessing.

HARPER & ROW, PUBLISHERS, INC.: Excerpt from *The Grass Is Singing* by Doris Lessing, Copyright 1950, 1978 by Doris Lessing; "The Eye of God in Paradise," "The Habit of Loving," and "The Words He Said" from *The Habit of Loving* by Doris Lessing, Copyright © 1957 by Doris Lessing. Reprinted by permission of Harper & Row, Publishers, Inc.

ALFRED A. KNOPF, INC.: Excerpt from *Briefing for a Descent into Hell* by Doris Lessing, Copyright © 1971 by Doris Lessing; excerpt from *The Diaries of Jane Somers* by Doris Lessing, Copyright © 1983 by Jane Somers; excerpt from *The Four-Gated City* by Doris Lessing, Copyright © 1969 by Doris Lessing Productions, Ltd.; excerpt from *The Making of the Representative for Planet 8* by Doris Lessing, Copyright © 1982 by Doris Lessing; excerpt from *The Marriages Between Zones Three, Four, and Five* by Doris Lessing, Copyright © 1980 by Doris Lessing; excerpt from *The Memoirs of a Survivor* by Doris Lessing, Copyright © 1974 by The Octagon Press; excerpt from *Re: Colonised Planet 5, Shikasta* by Doris Lessing, Copyright © 1979 by Doris Lessing; and "The Temptation of Jack Orkney" from *The Temptation of Jack Orkney and Other Stories* by Doris Lessing, Copyright © 1963 by Doris Lessing. Reprinted by permission of Alfred A. Knopf, Inc.

WARNER BOOKS, INC.: Chapter II from *Going Home* by Doris Lessing. Reprinted by permission of Popular Library, a division of Warner Books/New York.

SIMON & SCHUSTER, INC.: "The Old Chief Mshlanga" and "A Sunrise on the Veld" from *African Stories* by Doris Lessing, Copyright 1951, 1953, 1954, © 1957, 1958, 1962, 1963, 1964, 1965 by Doris Lessing; "How I Finally Lost My Heart," "England V. England," "Outside the Ministry," "One off the Short List," "Homage for Isaac Babel," "Between Men," and "A Letter from Home" from *A Man and Two Women* by Doris Lessing, Copyright © 1958, 1962, 1963 by Doris Lessing; excerpt from *Martha Quest* by Doris Lessing, Copyright 1952 by Doris Lessing; excerpt from *A Proper Marriage* by Doris Lessing, Copyright 1954 by Doris Lessing; excerpt from *A Ripple from the Storm* by Doris Lessing, Copyright © 1958 by Doris Lessing; and an excerpt from *The Golden Notebook* by Doris Lessing, Copyright © 1962 by Doris Lessing. Reprinted by permission of Simon & Schuster, Inc.

## A NOTE ON THE TYPE

*The text of this book was set in Sabon, a type face designed by Jan Tschichold (1902–1974), the well-known German typographer. Because it was designed in Frankfurt, Sabon was named for the famous Frankfurt type founder Jacques Sabon, who died in 1580 while manager of the Egenolff foundry. Based loosely on the original designs of Claude Garamond (c. 1480–1561), Sabon is unique in that it was explicitly designed for hot-metal composition on both the Monotype and Linotype machines as well as for film composition.*

*Composed by American–Stratford Graphic Services, Inc.,*
*Brattleboro, Vermont*
*Printed and bound by The Murray Printing Company,*
*Westford, Massachusetts*
*Typography and binding design by*
*Dorothy Schmiderer Baker*